Computer Organization and Assembly Language Programming

For IBM PCs and Compatibles

Computer Organization and Assembly Language Programming

For IBM PCs and Compatibles

SECOND EDITION

Michael Thorne
Sunderland Polytechnic

THE BENJAMIN/CUMMINGS PUBLISHING COMPANY, INC.

Menlo Park, California • Reading, Massachusetts • New York
Harlow, England • Don Mills, Ontario • Amsterdam • Bonn
Sydney • Singapore • Tokyo • Madrid • San Juan • Milan
Mexico City • Seoul • Taipei

Cover designed by Hybert Design and Type, Maidenhead.
Disk conversion by Columns Typesetters of Reading.

Printed and Bound in Canada

First edition published 1986. Reprinted 1987, 1988, 1989 and 1990.
Second edition printed 1990. Reprinted 1991, 1992, 1993, 1994 (twice), 1996 and 1998 (twice).

British Library Cataloguing in Publication Data
Thorne, Michael
Computer organization and assembly language programming for IBM PCs and compatibles.–2nd ed.
1. Computer systems. Assembly languages
I. Title II. Thorne, Michael: Programming the 8086/8088 for the IBM. PC compatibles
005.136

ISBN 0–8053–6879–5

Library of Congress Cataloguing in Publication Data
Thorne, Michael
Computer organization and assembly language programming for IBM PCs and compatibles/Michael Thorne.–2nd ed.
p. cm.
Rev. ed. of: Programming the 8086/8088 for the IBM PC and compatibles. c1986.
Includes index.
ISBN 0–8053–6879–5
1. Intel 8086 (Microprocessor)–Programming. 2. Intel 8088 (Microprocessor)–Programming. 3. Assembler language (Computer program language) 4. IBM Personal Computer–Programming.
I. Thorne, Michael. Programming the 8086/8088 for the IBM PC and compatibles. II. Title.
QA76.8.I292T458 1990
005.265–dc20 90–14391
CIP

Preface

Aims

At the heart of every microcomputer there is a microprocessor which can be programmed using assembly language. The object of this book is to provide an introduction to programming the 8086 family of microprocessors at the assembly language level.

In the real computing world it is modern practice to avoid programming in assembly language whenever possible, since it takes so much longer than using a high-level language and the result, being much more complex, is considerably less trustworthy. Unfortunately, the microcomputer industry has clouded an otherwise clear-cut distinction between tasks best solved using high-level languages and those for which assembly language has, unfortunately, to be used, simply because of inadequate memory resources or machine efficiency considerations.

But the philosophy of this book is that undergraduates should learn about assembly language programming, not just in its own right but, more importantly, for the insight this can give into the code generation phase of a compiler, and into the relationship between the (instruction-set) architecture of a microprocessor and the implementations of high-level languages using that architecture. To summarize, the aims are:

(1) Introduce the reader to assembly language programming.

(2) Introduce the reader to the 8086-family microprocessor architecture.

(3) Introduce the reader to the organization of computers based on an 8086-family microprocessor.

(4) Reinforce and supplement the reader's Pascal (or other, similar, high-level language) programming experience.

(5) Further the reader's progress in understanding and employing more advanced data structuring and data typing facilities.

(6) Introduce the reader to the relationship between high-level language and machine language from the compiler writer's point of view.

Audience

This book is suitable for undergraduates majoring in Computer Science, Electrical Engineering and related disciplines – though computer hobbyists may also find the contents of interest. The reader is assumed to have a fairly good knowledge of a high-level language such as Pascal. By means of carefully chosen examples, he or she is acquainted with the whole 8086-family instruction set. Each chapter has a plentiful supply of exercises which form an integral part of the text: assembly language programming is far too complicated to learn without actually writing and debugging some programs.

About the book

The first chapter explains what assembly language is and its relationship to higher level languages such as Pascal, and discusses when and when not to use it. There is a summary of the background knowledge concerning binary and hexadecimal arithmetic which is assumed in this book, and a description of the various ways of representing numeric and text data in binary form. The final sections begin an examination of 8086-family assembly language instructions. By the end of this chapter the reader should be able to write some very simple programs in 8086-family assembly language and know how to use the technique of tracing to follow the effect of a small program.

Chapter 2 focuses on the organization of computers based on a member of the 8086 family of microprocessors. It begins with a building-block view of the architecture of such a computer and then studies memory and input/output organization in a little more detail, including segmented memory. Then follows an outline description of the bus interface unit which to a large extent controls communication between the microprocessor and memory. The diagrammatic view of computer organization is then related to the actual electrical connections which must be made to an 8086 microprocessor (the 8086 pin-out). This leads to a description of the functions of the main chips used to build a microcomputer based on an 8086 microprocessor. A similar but even briefer look is taken at the 80286 and 80386 pin-out and support chips. Finally, some of the properties of the different members of the 8086 family are summarized.

The main focus of Chapter 3 is on the storage and retrieval of data items in memory. It begins by examining just three of the 8086 family's rich supply of jump instructions. These are the mechanism by which loops can be created in assembly language programs – just as **for**, **repeat** and **while** make this possible in Pascal. It ends by describing the layout for assembly language programs which is adopted throughout the book, except where it is necessary to depart from it in order to describe particular features of 8086-family assembly language.

Chapter 4 deals with how to have programs assembled and executed. The process is illustrated by means of an example program. This chapter also examines some of the DOS operating system functions, a set of ready-made routines which will carry out jobs such as displaying characters on the screen automatically – provided we bring them into action in the appropriate way. One of these will even display a complete message at one go, so long as the message has first been stored in memory. Consequently, the chapter begins by explaining how storage is assigned to fixed items of data (such as a message which is to be displayed repeatedly during the execution of a program) in an assembly language program.

It is indeed rare that an assembly language program will assemble and eventually run as predicted at the first attempt. Typically, several approximations to the truth will have to be made before a final working program is produced. Chapter 5 describes how to locate errors in an 8086-family assembly language program, using either DEBUG, among the simplest of the tools for locating errors in machine code programs, or the more recent Code View debugger, which has many more comprehensive and sophisticated features and allows sight of the original assembly language program during debugging.

Chapter 6 begins by showing how the flags can be used to monitor the outcome of arithmetic operations and describes the 8086-family instructions for the addition, subtraction, multiplication and division of signed and unsigned numbers.

Normally, assembly language instructions are executed in the order in which they are given to the microprocessor (or, what often amounts to the same thing, in the order that they occur in the program). The programmer can use jump instructions to alter this mechanism. Conditional jump instructions cause execution to continue not from the next instruction in sequence, but from some remote instruction *provided some condition is satisfied*, and these are described in Chapter 7. It also covers the most important ways in which conditional jumps can be used to change the flow of control in a program, namely, by the implementation of loops similar to **for**, **repeat** and **while** loops in Pascal and by taking decisions.

Chapter 8 describes the recommended method for developing programs. It helps to contain the occurrence of errors by mimicking some of the facilities of a structured programming language like Pascal. It also relies on the use of subroutines wherever sensible. Subroutines are assembly language's version of Pascal's procedures, and make it possible for a large program to be built up out of smaller components which are already known to be working. These subroutines are set to work by passing them any necessary parameters. The chapter ends with a description of two of the most important subroutine parameter-passing mechanisms.

Microprocessors are not just used as the foundation stone of microcomputer architecture. They are also used to make control devices for a range of equipment including large-scale manufacturing production machinery on the one hand, and traffic light controllers on the other. All of these require the ability to manipulate individual bits since, for example, a given bit can be set to

1 to turn a traffic light on, or to 0 to turn it off. Consequently, the designer of a microprocessor must include in its instruction set an appropriate repertoire for these types of microprocessor applications. Chapter 9 discusses a key subset of those available for this purpose from 8086-family microprocessors.

Chapter 10 illustrates the use of the program development methodology outlined in Chapter 8 to produce a substantial machine code program which simulates the operation of a simple four-function electronic calculator.

The vast majority of commercial computer use involves non-arithmetic work such as word processing, searching files for invoices and sorting payments received into customer file order. Consequently, the 8086 family is well endowed with instructions for handling text or, more precisely, strings. Chapter 11 describes each of the 8086-family string manipulation instructions in detail. The 8086 family of microprocessors also have special table manipulation instructions and these are featured in the later sections of this chapter in complete example programs.

Chapter 12 describes the construction of a simple text editor program featuring the string manipulation instructions introduced in Chapter 11, and using the program development methodology of Chapter 8.

Chapter 13 studies 8086-family addressing modes in relation to the problem of implementing the machine code generation phase of a compiler for a high-level language such as Pascal. The 8086-family machine code instruction formats are highly dependent on these addressing modes, and so in turn is the way in which 8086-family assembly language instructions are encoded into binary. Consequently, this chapter concludes with a description of the encoding process itself.

Perhaps the most important tool for constructing large assembly language programs efficiently is modular programming. Chapter 14 describes how to construct a large program by combining smaller ones called modules. These modules are then linked together by the linker to form the final executable program. Consequently, the linker and the pseudo-ops used to control its operation are examined in detail. Before this, the chapter considers the operation of an 8086-family assembler itself as an essential step in understanding certain assembly language instructions, as well as in appreciating the role of the linker sufficiently to comprehend its role in achieving modular programming.

By representing numbers in Binary Coded Decimal (BCD) form we can avoid having to convert decimal numbers into binary on input and can easily represent numbers of arbitrary precision. It is also useful when dealing with decimal numbers which must have many digits before the decimal point and a few after the decimal point. Chapter 15 begins by examining the different ways of representing numbers in BCD form. Then separate sections cover how to write programs for performing the four basic arithmetic operations between BCD numbers. The penultimate section gives a complete example program using BCD arithmetic and the chapter concludes with programs which illustrate how to convert between BCD and binary numbers and vice versa.

Chapter 16 then turns to a presentation of some of the more advanced

MASM program development tools: nearly all of them aimed at saving programmer effort. Thus, some features save the programmer the bother of working out the length of a declared data structure, others allow us to specify a formula to be used in an instruction and leave MASM to work out the actual corresponding value. Further, there are features which allow redefinition of data items in different ways to suit different purposes.

Pascal offers the convenience of records to programmers because these aid efficient program development. The 8086-family assembly language is also a programming language in its own right, so its designers decided to include several means of structuring data equivalent to Pascal's records and sets, so that similar efficiency gains could be made. Chapter 17 looks at two of these: structure variables and record variables. Structure variables correspond to Pascal's records and enable several groups of bytes to be considered as a single data item. Record variables correspond to Pascal's sets and allow us to refer to groups of bits as a single unit.

Chapter 18 also concerns two important features of assembly language which aid programmer productivity: macros and conditional assembly. Macros allow the programmer to name a group of statements and have them placed in the assembly language program automatically whenever that name is invoked, so that they are assembled in place. Conditional assembly allows groups of assembly language statements in a program to be included or excluded from the assembly process, depending on the values of certain parameters. One assembly language program could therefore contain all the code for two versions: one for an IBM-PC with basic 640K memory, and one for a machine with, perhaps, a megabyte of expanded memory. This is more organizationally convenient (less house-keeping) than having two distinct versions of the same program, and generally produces a smaller object program than if the production version contained code for both possibilities.

DOS allows the programmer to handle disk storage via operating system function calls. Chapter 19 studies the use of DOS disk-handling facilities in detail, and constructs four complete example programs. This chapter also shows how DOS functions allow us to regard the standard input and output devices such as the keyboard, display and printer as files, and describes the COM file format.

The theme of the next three chapters is how to use assembly language programs to drive some of the I/O devices connected to a microcomputer, namely: a printer, the keyboard, and the display. There will be a chapter which discusses driving each of these three devices. But also, each chapter will have as an equally important theme one of the three main ways in which it is possible to drive hardware devices: through I/O ports; using (hardware) interrupts; and direct memory access.

The final chapter introduces some of the instructions available only with the more advanced members of the 8086 family of microprocessors. The main aim is to survey the general-purpose (32-bit) instructions which only the higher members of the 8086 family can execute. From the applications programmer's point of view, these may be viewed as extensions of the instructions with which we are already familiar. The chapter concludes with a brief overview of the instructions possessed by the 80286 microprocessor and higher members of the 8086 family which were provided by their designers to facilitate the development of sophisticated operating systems, such as those which allow multitasking and the use of virtual memory.

A note to instructors

The programs in this book are available on disk from the publisher, as is an *Instructor's Manual.* Instructors should contact their nearest Addison-Wesley or Benjamin/Cummings representative for details.

Acknowledgements

This book grew out of the many, many courses I have given on assembly language programming to industrialists, undergraduates, adult education classes and to groups of teachers over the past decade. For their lively and uncompromising feedback all of those students must be thanked. Addison-Wesley must also be thanked for the total professionalism with which they address the whole business of publishing. Their thoroughness has substantially improved this book as did the comments of Jerrold Siegel, Robert Sterling and other anonymous reviewers and large numbers of readers of the first edition. Acknowledgement must also be made of the continued patience of my long-suffering family, larger now thanks to William and more sophisticated thanks to Jonathan's taste in music. But most of all I must express my debt of gratitude to my wife Valerie who, while I wrote this book, thankfully made sure that I didn't miss the children growing up.

Michael Thorne
Sunderland Polytechnic
England
January 1991

Brief Contents

Contents

1 Assembly Language

Contents

At the heart of every microcomputer there is a microprocessor which can be programmed using assembly language. This book describes the assembly language of a family of microprocessors, the 8086 family, one of which – the 8088 microprocessor – is found inside the IBM-PC, and the necessary internal computer organization when a microcomputer is built around one of the microprocessors in this family.

This chapter explains what assembly language is, its relationship to higher level languages such as Pascal, and discusses when and when not to use it. We also summarize the background knowledge concerning binary and hexadecimal arithmetic which is assumed in this book, and describe the various ways of representing numeric and text data in binary form. In the final sections we begin our examination of 8086-family assembly language instructions, including a description of the four general-purpose registers AX, BX, CX and DX, the eight general-purpose 8-bit registers which pairwise make up AX, BX, CX and DX, and the flags register.

By the end of this chapter the reader should be able to write some very simple programs in 8086-family assembly language and know how to use the technique of tracing to follow the effect of a small program. Details of how to have these programs executed by the computer will follow in Chapter 4.

1.1 Microprocessors and the 8086 family

In any microcomputer, the component which actually processes data is entirely contained on a single silicon chip called a **microprocessor**. There are many different kinds of microprocessor just as there are different makes of computer.

Table 1.1 gives a short list of some microcomputers popular at the time of writing and the type of microprocessor each uses. Incidentally, microprocessors tend to have mysterious sounding names like QB99*4 but just as the name of a car tells you little about the car itself, so it often is with microprocessors.

We call the family of microprocessors on which the IBM-PC range is based, the 8086 family. Intel Corporation, the manufacturer of these microprocessors, first produced the 8086 microprocessor as an updated version of one which was used in many of the microcomputers on sale in the late 1970s. The other members of the family are the 8088 microprocessor (which, as we shall see, is less powerful than the 8086 microprocessor but was introduced to enable computer designs with lower manufacturing costs) and then the 80186, 80188, 80286, 80386, 80386SX and 80486 microprocessors, the last of which is one of the most powerful on the market at the time of writing. Figure 1.1 shows the relationship between them.

Table 1.1 Microcomputers and the microprocessors on which they are based.

Microcomputer	*Microprocessor it uses*
IBM Personal Computer	8088
Apricot	8086
Research Machines Nimbus	80186
IBM PC AT	80286
Tandy 5000	80386
IBM Model 70-A21	80486
Acorn Archimedes	ARM
Apple Macintosh	68000
Olivetti M-20	Z8000
Atari ST	68000
Commodore Amiga	68000

Increasing computer power ↓	
	8086 (8088 is functionally the same but less powerful)
	80186 (80188 is functionally the same but less powerful)
	80286
	80386 (80386SX is functionally the same but less powerful)
	80486

Figure 1.1 Major members of the 8086 family and the relationship between them.

We use the term 'family' because there is a great deal of compatibility between the microprocessors: software written to be executed by the 8088 microprocessor will work just as well if executed by the 80386 microprocessor. This is because they all share the same set of instructions, but later additions to the family have an extended and more sophisticated repertoire. Chapter 2 explains some of these differences and Chapter 23 will consider instructions unique to the more sophisticated processors such as the 80386 microprocessor.

In the meantime, we shall cover some of the necessary background, starting with the preferred language for programming microprocessors, assembly language.

1.2 Assembly language

Most computer programs these days are written in high-level languages such as BASIC, COBOL and Pascal. Writing programs in any of these is quicker and easier (and therefore cheaper if you are paying somebody to do it) than in the machine's own language – **machine code**. There are some occasions, however, when a high-level language just cannot be used. Pascal may be able to do the job from a logical point of view, but the machine code generated from it may be too slow for the application in question. For example, when a computer is being used to control a nuclear reactor in a power station, if the controlling program cannot respond very quickly to changes in the reactor's state the reactor may go critical and there will be danger of an explosion. Also, if it happens to be your lot to write programs to control peripherals such as disk drives, then a high-level language such as Pascal will neither work fast enough to give users the rapid response they expect, nor will it give you close enough control over the hardware to do the job efficiently. Indeed, using a high-level language in this sort of context is often like trying to eat a bar of chocolate with a knife and fork while wearing a thick pair of mittens – just about possible but not much fun if you have to do it every day.

Regrettably, then, there are occasions when the programmer must program at the machine's own level though very few programmers actually use machine code, the language of 0s and 1s which the computer's circuits understand directly. Machine code programs are tedious to write and highly error-prone. Imagine the errors likely to arise from an interdepartmental telephone conversation about the following machine code program:

```
0010101111000011
1000101111001000
101110100000000000000000
```

In situations where a high-level language is inappropriate we avoid working in machine code most of the time by making the computer do more of the work. We humans write our programs in a more readable form – **assembly language** – and then get the computer to turn this assembly language program into machine code. The above machine code program was produced by a computer from the following assembly language version:

```
SUB AX,BX
MOV CX,AX
MOV DX,0
```

Here, as you may guess, the mnemonic (memory aid) `SUB` is short for SUBtract and `MOV` represents a MOVe instruction. It is much easier to remember `SUB AX,BX` than 0010101111000011 – the actual instruction code the machine uses.

Assembly languages are an intermediate step between high-level languages and machine code. For example, the actual execution of a Pascal program is sometimes achieved by automatically converting the program into assembly language form and then finally converting that into machine code which is executed. This process is illustrated in Figure 1.2. Conversion between these languages is performed at each stage by computer programs: from high-level language to assembly language by a compiler and from assembly language to machine code by an assembler.

Pascal programmers work in a cushioned environment as do most high-level language programmers. In Pascal, variables can be of integer, real, char, array or record types – or even one of the programmer's own defined types – but machine code has just binary numbers. Modern versions of assembly language do now handle some of the data types high-level languages provide

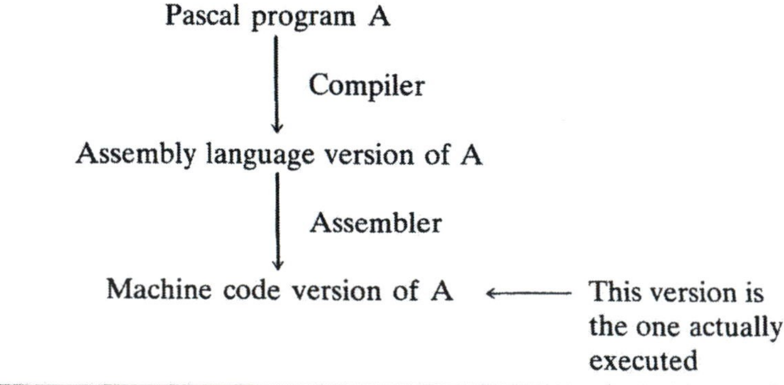

Figure 1.2 The relationship between high-level languages and machine code.

but the accompanying programming facilities to handle objects of these types are often very limited. Indeed the main advantage of high-level languages is that the effect of each programmable operation is at a higher functional level than in assembly language programming. Thus, printing the result of the addition of two numbers is a one line instruction in Pascal whereas the equivalent in assembly language involves several instructions. In APL, a given array can be assigned to the product of two other arrays by a single instruction. Generally, a much greater level of detail is involved in using assembly language to make even simple things happen.

All this makes writing big programs in assembly language harder and more error-prone than high-level language programming. Unfortunately assembly language sometimes *has* to be used – for example, because of the loss of speed experienced when using a compiled language such as Pascal. Thus, in a commercial environment, assembly language is used only when no other higher level programming language is deemed able to give the necessary performance from the hardware. But then there is an even greater penalty for using assembly language than the extra costs involved. Assembly language programs are very much more dependent upon the precise design of the computer they are to run on than their high-level language equivalents. In consequence, it is usually much easier to get a Pascal program, written originally for machine A, up and running on machine B than it is to transport an assembly language program from machine A to machine B. Indeed, if the architecture of machine B differs in any considerable way from that of machine A, virtually a complete rewrite may be necessary.

More often than not, operating systems have to be written in assembly language as do programs to control external devices such as printers and plotters. But even this use of assembly language may sometimes be avoided by using high-level languages such as C, in which the vast majority of the UNIX operating system, including even the disk drive controllers, was originally written for the (now obsolescent) DEC PDP/11 series of computers. Within a Pascal type of programming environment, C allows programmers the efficient access to actual memory locations – and hence hardware devices – denied them by Pascal. More recent implementations of UNIX for DEC VAX and IBM AS/400 series minicomputers and several microcomputers have used the same idea.

If C is not available to the programmer for some reason, it may be that linking assembly language modules with a high-level language main program is the best way to avoid doing the whole job in assembly language. Different versions of the same high-level language vary enormously in both the provision they make for doing this and the complexity involved in making it all work, but overall this will almost certainly be quicker than developing a large program entirely in assembly language.

Hopefully the message is clear: for real-life problems use assembly language only as a last resort. Sometimes you don't have any choice, as is the case if you want to modify an operating system already written in assembly language. From now on we assume that circumstances force you to read this book (!) and it is now time to commence our detailed study of assembly language.

1.3 Number systems used in assembly language

As was remarked earlier, binary numbers are the only data type available in machine code. Assembly language frees us from this constraint in some respects, not least by allowing us to work with one of three **number systems** – **binary**, **decimal** or **hexadecimal** – the assembler making any necessary conversions into binary. Thanks to our 10 fingers and 10 toes the decimal number system is the one with which we are all most familiar. Unfortunately, assembly language cannot allow us just to stick to decimal numbers: computer designers have seen to that! Also, letters of the alphabet and punctuation marks have to be coded up into numeric form so that text can be processed by assembly language programs. In this section a brief overview of these three number systems and the ASCII text coding system which has become the de facto standard on microcomputers is presented. It is intended only as a summary and a reader familiar with this material can move directly on to Section 1.4. Readers needing more information on these topics should consult *Introduction to Computer Science* by Neil Graham, West Publishing Co., St. Paul, Minnesota, 1985.

1.3.1 Binary numbers

As we learned at school, the decimal number 294 means

$$
\begin{aligned}
& 2 \text{ hundreds} + 9 \text{ tens} + 4 \text{ units} \\
= {} & 2 * 100 \quad + 9 * 10 + 4 * 1 \\
= {} & 2 * 10^2 \quad + 9 * 10^1 + 4 * 10^0
\end{aligned}
$$

All that is different about the binary number system is that only the digits 0 and 1 are used and each place to the left represents a higher power of 2 (instead of 10). Thus the binary number 11011 is

$$
\begin{aligned}
& 1 * 2^4 + 1 * 2^3 + 0 * 2^2 + 1 * 2^1 + 1 * 2^0 \\
= {} & 16 \quad + 8 \quad + 0 \quad + 2 \quad + 1 \\
= {} & 27
\end{aligned}
$$

in decimal.

To avoid any possible confusion between the decimal number 10 and the binary number 10 (which is just 2 in decimal) we shall in future write the letter B after a binary number and D after a decimal number where there is any possible ambiguity. Thus 10B = 2D and 11011B = 27D as we saw above.

The number 11011B contains five binary digits (or **bits**). Since computers are largely concerned with performing arithmetic on binary numbers and with moving such numbers from one place in memory to another, it simplifies matters greatly if a fixed number of bits is moved each time. Members of the 8086 family of microprocessors move data around in multiples of eight bits, a collection of eight bits being called a **byte**. Often two bytes (known as a **word**) are moved at the same time. For example:

0	a bit
1011	4 bits (sometimes called a **nibble**)
11100010	a byte
1010111001110010	a word

In a byte or word (for example, 1010110001110010) the rightmost digit is referred to as the **least significant digit** (in the example it is a 0) and the leftmost digit is referred to as the **most significant digit** (1 in the example).

Amongst the programming instructions for the 8086 family are several concerned with performing arithmetic, including those with mnemonics `ADD`, `SUB`, `MUL` and `DIV`. Arithmetic can be performed between either two bytes or two words, whichever the programmer chooses. Moreover, just as a programmer must decide whether to represent a numerical quantity by an integer or real variable in Pascal, in assembly language programmers choose whether to represent a value in a byte or word and whether as a **signed** or **unsigned** binary number. Unsigned binary numbers are the ones we have met so far and, while they do not admit the possibility of representing negative decimal numbers such as −8147 and −1 in binary, they are adequate for many purposes. Signed numbers allow both positive and negative numbers to be represented, but every signed number must be given a sign. This is done by taking the most significant digit in a byte or word as corresponding not to 2^7 or 2^{15} respectively, but to -2^7 or -2^{15}. Thus, as a signed number the byte 10110000 is, in decimal,

$$\begin{aligned}
&1 * (-2^7) + 0 * 2^6 + 1 * 2^5 + 1 * 2^4 + 0 * 2^3 + 0 * 2^2 + 0 * 2^1 + 0 * 2^0 \\
&= -128 + 32 + 16 \\
&= -80
\end{aligned}$$

and as a signed number the byte 00110000 is, in decimal,

$$\begin{aligned}
&0 * (-2^7) + 0 * 2^6 + 1 * 2^5 + 1 * 2^4 + 0 * 2^3 + 0 * 2^2 + 0 * 2^1 + 0 * 2^0 \\
&= 32 + 16 \\
&= 48
\end{aligned}$$

It follows that the most significant digit of a byte or word representing a signed number will be 0 if the number is positive and 1 if it is negative.

The signed representation of a negative number can be found in the following way. If x is positive, $-x$ is represented by $2^{16} - x$ (word) or $2^8 - x$ (byte) ignoring the most significant bit of the result of the subtraction. In binary the necessary arithmetic is surprisingly easy. For example, to represent the decimal −42 in signed 16-bit form we subtract 42 from 2^{16} as follows:

$$\begin{aligned}
2^{16} &= 1\ 0000000000000000 \\
42 &= 0000000000101010 \\
\text{Difference} &= (0)\ 1111111111010110
\end{aligned}$$

and hence the 16-bit signed representation of −42 is 1111111111010110. This is

Table 1.2 Examples of two's complement representations.

Decimal	*One byte signed binary representation*	*Two's complement of binary no. in column 2*	*Decimal*
0	00000000	00000000	0
+1	00000001	11111111	−1
+2	00000010	11111110	−2
+3	00000011	11111101	−3
+4	00000100	11111100	−4

called the **two's complement** representation of −42.

Another way of working out the two's complement of a number is to carry out the following procedure on its positive equivalent: change all the 0s to 1s and all the 1s to 0s; then add 1 to the result forgetting any carry digit which goes beyond the number of bits in the representation you are seeking. Thus +37 in signed 8-bit form is 00100101 so −37 in the same form is 11011010 + 1 = 11011011 and −2 is 11111110 so +2 is 00000001 + 1 = 00000010. If you are not familiar with two's complement representation, check the entries in Table 1.2 using both methods.

The range of signed numbers which can be held in a byte goes from −128 to +127 as follows:

```
−128   10000000
−127   10000001
   .
   .
   .
 −37   11011011
   .
   .
   .
  −2   11111110
  −1   11111111
   0   00000000
  +1   00000001
  +2   00000010
   .
   .
   .
 +37   00100101
   .
   .
   .
+126   01111110
+127   01111111
```

Table 1.3 Comparison of signed and unsigned numbers.

Binary	*Value in decimal*	
	Unsigned	*Signed*
00000011	3	3
11111101	253	−3
01000110	70	70
11000110	198	−58
0010110110001100	11 660	11 660
1010110110001100	44 428	−21 108

For a word the corresponding range is as follows:

−32 768	100000000	00000000
−32 767	100000000	00000001
.		
.		
.		
−2	11111111	11111110
−1	11111111	11111111
0	00000000	00000000
+1	00000000	00000001
+2	00000000	00000010
.		
.		
.		
+32 766	01111111	11111110
+32 767	01111111	11111111

For unsigned numbers the ranges are 0 to 255 (byte) and 0 to 65535 (word). It is interesting to compare signed and unsigned representations, as shown in Table 1.3.

In general a given byte or word can represent one of two decimal numbers depending on whether it is to be regarded as signed or unsigned. Consequently, for each numeric data item in a program, the programmer must take a decision to use either a signed or unsigned representation and must stick to that choice: the two forms must not be mixed. This is rather like deciding in Pascal whether to store a date of birth as a number or as a string: both may be of use for certain applications but the two cannot be used interchangeably!

Numbering the bits in a byte or word

In subsequent chapters we shall often have occasion to refer to the individual bits in a given byte or word. Tradition has it that these are numbered from the least significant end of the byte or word, and from zero upwards. Thus, given the byte 01101100 individual bits are numbered as follows:

bit number	7 6 5 4 3 2 1 0
byte	0 1 1 0 1 1 0 0

and given the word 0110001110000111 individual bits are numbered as:

bit number	15 14 13 12 11 10 9 8 7 6 5 4 3 2 1 0
word	0 1 1 0 0 0 1 1 1 0 0 0 0 1 1 1

1.3.2 Hexadecimal numbers

Given that 0000000000000111 is one of the possible forms in which the computer handles the 'harmless' decimal number 7, there is a strong motivation for a shorthand for all those 0s and 1s. An essential feature of any shorthand is that it must be easy to go from the full form to the shorthand and vice versa. This is why a third number system, hexadecimal, is introduced.

In the hexadecimal number system we use the ordinary decimal digits 0,1,2,3,. . .,9 together with the first six letters of the alphabet – A, B, C, D, E and F. A stands for 10 in decimal, B for 11 and so on up to F which stands for 15 in decimal. Otherwise everything works in the same way as for decimal and binary except that, in this case, each place to the left represents a higher power of 16. Thus the hexadecimal number 3FA04 is equivalent to the decimal

$$\begin{aligned} & 3 * 16^4 + F * 16^3 + A * 16^2 + 0 * 16^1 + 4 * 16^0 \\ = & 3 * 16^4 + 15 * 16^3 + 10 * 16^2 + 0 * 16^1 + 4 * 16^0 \\ = & 196\,608 + 61\,440 + 2560 + 0 + 4 \\ = & 260\,612 \end{aligned}$$

Table 1.4 Hexadecimal conversion table.

Decimal	*Binary*	*Hexadecimal*
0	0000	0
1	0001	1
2	0010	2
3	0011	3
4	0100	4
5	0101	5
6	0110	6
7	0111	7
8	1000	8
9	1001	9
10	1010	A
11	1011	B
12	1100	C
13	1101	D
14	1110	E
15	1111	F

At first sight the idea of a number with létters in it may appear rather strange, but it should always be borne in mind that the letters stand for numbers which in decimal require two digits (Table 1.4).

Conversion between hexadecimal and binary is very easy. To convert from hexadecimal to binary involves replacing each hexadecimal digit by its binary equivalent written as a 4-bit number. Thus, to represent hexadecimal 3FA04 in binary:

3	F	A	0	4
0011	1111	1010	0000	0100

so the binary equivalent of 3FA04 is 00111111101000000100. Going the other way is just as easy:

1011	0110	0011	1001	1110
B	6	3	9	E

so that the hexadecimal equivalent of binary 10110110001110011110 is B639E. Hopefully this justifies the use of the hexadecimal number system as a shorthand for binary.

Pronunciation

It you're not sure how to pronounce hexadecimal numbers such as 1A, 1B. . ., you could always follow Bilbo Baggins and refer to 1A as onety-A and so on. More often than not, however, hexadecimal numbers like B639E are read as 'bee-six-three-nine-ee'.

1.3.3 Converting decimal to hexadecimal

To convert a decimal number to hexadecimal we repeatedly divide the decimal number by 16 until a zero quotient is obtained. The remainders from the divisions then give you the equivalent hexadecimal number, the last remainder obtained being the highest order digit of the hexadecimal number. For example, the conversion of decimal 1103 to hexadecimal looks like:

1103 ÷ 16 = 68 remainder F
68 ÷ 16 = 4 remainder 4
4 ÷ 16 = 0 remainder 4

so that the hexadecimal equivalent of 1103 is 44F.

Converting decimal numbers to binary is carried out in a similar fashion except that you divide by 2 each time. Thus, to find the binary equivalent of decimal 46:

46 ÷ 2 = 23 remainder 0
23 ÷ 2 = 11 remainder 1
11 ÷ 2 = 5 remainder 1
5 ÷ 2 = 2 remainder 1

Table 1.5 Decimal and hexadecimal equivalence table.

Decimal	*Hexadecimal*
1	1
10	0A
100	64
1000	3E8
10000	2710
100000	186A0
1000000	F4240
10000000	989680

$2 \div 2 = 1$ remainder 0
$1 \div 2 = 0$ remainder 1

so the binary equivalent of decimal 46 is 101110.

For future use, some equivalences between decimal and hexadecimal numbers are shown in Table 1.5. As an exercise in converting decimal numbers to hexadecimal form the reader is invited to verify as many of the entries as time allows.

Further practice in conversion from hexadecimal to binary can be obtained by converting the right-hand entries to binary and then checking that the decimal value of the binary numbers obtained is that given in the left-hand column. For instance, 3E8 in hexadecimal is 001111101000 in binary which is $512 + 256 + 128 + 64 + 32 + 8 = 1000$ in decimal so that row four of Table 1.5 is verified.

1.3.4 Hexadecimal addition and subtraction

We need to be able to do hexadecimal addition and subtraction in order to verify the results of running assembly language programs during the debugging phase. Because we are so used to thinking in decimal, hexadecimal multiplication and division are best done by converting the numbers to decimal, multiplying or dividing, and then converting the result back to hexadecimal.

In order to distinguish between hexadecimal and decimal numbers, we write the letter H after a hexadecimal number. Thus, at the end of a number, a B denotes a binary number, a D denotes a decimal number and an H denotes a hexadecimal number.

Addition and subtraction are relatively easy. When adding or subtracting two hexadecimal numbers, the secret is to think of the decimal equivalent of each digit, to add or subtract the decimal equivalents, and then to reconvert the results. Thus, to perform the addition:

```
  3A6CH
+ B2E1H
  -----
  -----
```

we think of the decimal equivalents of the first pair of digits (12 and 1 respectively), add those (giving 13), and convert this back (giving the hexadecimal digit D):

```
  3A6CH
+ B2E1H
  -----
      D
  -----
```

For the next pair of hexadecimal digits to be added, we think of their decimal equivalents (6 and 14 respectively), add these (giving 20), and convert this back to hexadecimal (giving 14H) so we write down the 4 and carry the 1:

```
  3A6CH
+ B2E1H
  -----
     4D
  -----
    1
```

Now we think of the decimal equivalents of the next pair of digits (10 and 2 respectively), add these and the carry (giving 13), and convert this back (giving the hexadecimal digit D):

```
  3A6CH
+ B2E1H
  -----
    D4D
  -----
    1
```

Finally we think of the decimal equivalents of the remaining pair of digits (3 and 11 respectively), add these (giving 14), and convert this back (giving the hexadecimal digit E):

```
  3A6CH
+ B2E1H
  -----
   ED4D
  -----
    1
```

Subtraction is performed in a similar way.

1.3.5 Representing text

Computers are able to handle non-numeric data as well as numbers. In fact, most 'real world' computer use at the moment involves non-numeric computing, such as searching a file of accounts to find all outstanding invoices in the name of J.S. Gruntfuttock. The ability to handle text derives from coding the alphabet and punctuation marks into numbers. For example, we could use the number 41H as a code for the letter A, 42H for the letter B, 43H for the letter C, 2CH for the symbol ',' (comma), 3BH for the symbol ';' (semicolon), and so on. Given a numerical code, the processing of text is reduced to processing numbers. Thus searching a file for an invoice under the name BACCA actually involves searching for an invoice beginning with 42H, 41H, 43H, 43H and 41H.

In microcomputers such as the IBM-PC the code most often used is the **ASCII** (pronounced ass-key) code – the American Standard Code for Information Interchange – from which the above examples were taken. The complete ASCII code is given in Appendix 1 for ease of reference. By the time you have finished reading this book that appendix will be well-thumbed. Take a first look at it now and verify that the examples given above conform to the ASCII code.

Besides the alphabetic characters A,B,C,. . ., Z,a,b,. . ., z and punctuation marks, the ASCII code also includes codes for certain characters which are never printed but rather are used to control devices external to the main computer, such as a printer. Other codes are used to control communications between the computer and a remote device, rather like the 'over and out' communications protocol used by aeroplane pilots. Thus, in Appendix I there is an ASCII code to get a printer to move onto a new line – LF (Line Feed); to send the printing head back to the beginning of the line – CR (Carriage Return); to signal an ENQuiry – ENQ; and to signal the End Of Transmission – EOT.

Originally ASCII codes contained just seven bits and could thus be used to represent 128 (2^7) characters. When placing data in memory, multiples of eight bits are used and so it is natural to use a single byte for each character. The additional eighth bit (added at the most significant end of the code) is put to use in two different ways.

First, in order to extend the range of characters which the PC can display on its screen, IBM has extended the ASCII code by using this eighth bit to represent an additional 128 characters. This permits such weird and wonderful display characters as Greek letters, playing-card suits, square root signs and smiling faces to be represented.

Second, when data is transmitted over relatively long distances, for example over telephone lines, there is the possibility of corruption due to electrical noise. The eighth bit can be used to afford protection against such data corruption by setting it to 0 or 1 as necessary to ensure that the code for every character has an even number of bits set to 1 (**even parity**) or to ensure that every character's code has an odd number of bits set to 1 (**odd parity**).

For example, the 7-bit ASCII code for the letter A is 1000001. If even parity is used this becomes 01000001 while odd parity would give 11000001. Hardware can be designed to check for parity discrepancies. Thus, if we were using odd parity and 11000011 were received by the computer over a telephone line, the hardware would detect that this could not be the code of any real data (since it contains an even number of bits set to 1) and would signal an error.

To summarize, inside the PC itself the eighth bit is used to give extra characters. When communicating with external devices – another computer or a printer perhaps – the eighth bit can be used to guard against transmission errors if we do not want to transmit or receive these extra characters.

EXERCISES

1.1 Complete the following table:

16-bit binary (unsigned)	*4-digit hexadecimal*	*Decimal*	*16-bit binary (signed)*
0000000000011111	001F	31	
			0101010101010101
	AE2B		
0001110001110000			
	1E1E		
		2345	
	ABCD		

1.2 Complete the following table:

16-bit (signed)	*Decimal*
1000000000111111	
1000111000111001	
0000100100100000	
0100000000000000	
1100000000000000	

1.3 Find the two's complement of the 16-bit signed number 0110110110110111. Regard the result as a binary number x and find the two's complement of x.

1.4 Decipher the following ASCII-coded secret message:

02 4D 45 65 54 20 6D 45 20 41 74 20 43 41 52 4E 45
67 49 65 20 48 41 6C 4C 20 31 34 2E 33 30 20 03

1.5 Perform the following hexadecimal additions and subtractions:

(a) 23ABH + 0AC34H
(b) 9458H + 9977H
(c) 0F0BH + 8FFFH
(d) 296BH + 7A4FH
(e) 6901H + 996FH
(f) 1111H + 0FFFFH

(g) 734BH – 9F3BH
(h) 9938H – 34FFH
(i) 290DH – 1FA8H
(j) 0FE43H – 0E229H
(k) 5FEFH – 1212H
(l) 89CBH – 123CH

1.4 Some simple 8086-family assembly language instructions

Since we have now covered the number systems used in assembly language we can start to explore the 8086-family's instructions which permit arithmetic to be performed. The majority of these instructions involve **registers** in some way or other and it is to a description of four of the registers possessed by all members of the 8086 family that we turn first.

1.4.1 Registers

My pocket calculator is one of the simplest and cheapest available. To get it to add two numbers, say 3 and 2, you have to follow the three steps of Figure 1.3.

A calculator display is a good model for a register in a microprocessor. Registers are places where data can be processed particularly quickly. Members of the 8086 family are very well endowed in this respect. One of their registers is called the AX register and this can be used to add 3 and 2 in much the same way as the simple calculator just discussed. Here is the program:

```
MOV AX,3 ;put 3 into register AX
ADD AX,2 ;add 2 to contents of register AX
```

(Here, anything appearing after a semicolon (;) is a comment to help humans understand the program. Only the instructions to the left of the ; are obeyed

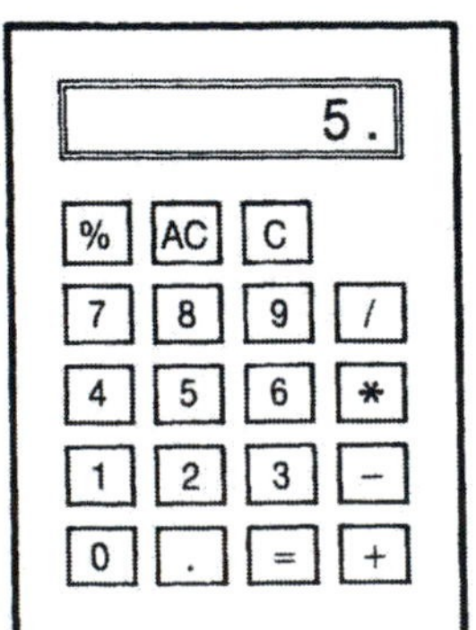

Figure 1.3
A simple calculator.

by the microprocessor.) As was the case with the calculator example above, the answer '5' would be left in the register AX.

Actually the members of the 8086 family have four general-purpose registers: AX, BX, CX and DX, each of which holds one 16-bit number. Our simple addition program could have used any one of these four by replacing AX with the name of one of the other registers throughout. Moving data between registers is accomplished by the `MOV` instruction. Appending the following instructions to the addition program would result in the value 5 being put into all the registers AX, BX, CX and DX.

```
MOV BX,AX ;copy what's in register AX into register BX
MOV CX,AX ;copy what's in register AX into register CX
MOV DX,CX ;copy what's in register CX into register DX
```

So often in programming do we want to add 1 to the contents of a register that the 8086-family have an instruction specially for that purpose: the INC instruction. Thus,

```
INC DX
```

would add 1 to the current contents of register DX.

But we can do more than just add! Subtraction and three sorts of multiplication and division are possible as well. Consider the following little program:

```
MOV AX,5 ;put 5 into the AX register
MOV BX,4 ;put 4 into the BX register
SUB AX,2 ;subtract 2 from the AX register
MUL BX   ;multiply the unsigned 16-bit number in the BX
         ;register by the unsigned 16-bit number in the
         ;AX register. Leave the 32-bit answer
         ;in the DX and AX registers, DX
         ;containing the binary digits
         ;corresponding to 2^16 = 65536 and
         ;higher powers of 2
```

It will calculate $(5 - 2) * 4$ and leave the answer (12 in decimal, C in hexadecimal, 00000000 00000000 00000000 00001100 in unsigned 32-bit form) in 32-bit form in registers DX and AX: thus DX will contain 0000000000000000 and AX will contain 0000000000001100. The stages of the calculation are illustrated in Figure 1.4 in which we have adopted the convention which will often be followed in this book, namely, the contents of registers are given in hexadecimal notation. Note that in the `MUL`tiply instruction, AX is one of the

	AX	BX	CX	DX
	?	?	?	?
`MOV AX,5`	5	?	?	?
`MOV BX,4`	5	4	?	?
`SUB AX,2`	3	4	?	?
`MUL BX`	C	4	?	0

Figure 1.4 Stages of the calculation of $(5 - 2) * 4$. ? denotes a value which we do not know in advance. (Before our program starts the registers will contain whatever the previous program left in them.)

operands even though the assembly language mnemonic does not mention it: `MUL BX` causes 8086-family microprocessors to work out BX multiplied by AX. It would be a reasonable criticism of 8086-family assembly language instruction mnemonics to say that each and every instruction should have explicit operands. Some versions of 8086-family assembly language do require this, but we shall adopt the most popular version, MASM, which does not.

Removing ambiguity

Calculators work in decimal of course, but microprocessors use binary arithmetic. Thanks to assembly language we can write instructions like

```
MOV AX,7
```

and leave it to the assembler to convert the number 7 into its appropriate binary equivalent. However, there is now the possibility of ambiguity. For example, does

```
MOV AX,26
```

refer to the decimal number 26, or hexadecimal 26 ($2 * 16^1 + 6 * 16^0 = 38$ in decimal)?

To remove any ambiguity as far as the assembly language conversion is concerned we write 26H for hexadecimal 26 and 26D for decimal 26. Likewise 10B is binary, 10D is decimal and 10H is hexadecimal. Actually, assembly language instructions are usually assumed to specify numbers in decimal unless the programmer decides otherwise by adding a code letter after the number (or in some other way). For the time being it is better always to add a letter explicitly indicating which sort of number it is that you are talking about. In this way you will become used to thinking about the problem of ambiguity of meaning.

1.4.2 Size of registers

Given the benefits of assembly language, we still cannot ignore completely the fundamental reliance of microprocessors upon the binary number system. A pocket calculator has a limit to the number of decimal digits you can enter – mine accepts 98 765 432 (eight digits) but not 198 765 432 (nine digits), for example. Likewise the registers AX, BX, CX and DX are limited to 16 binary digits (bits) so that in an instruction

```
MOV AX,n
```

the number *n* must not need more than 16 bits for its binary representation. In other words, in decimal *n* must be non-negative and less than or equal to 65 535 for an unsigned number, or between −32 768 and 32 767 for a signed number. This also means that all four registers are limited to four hexadecimal digits.

Program	*Trace*			
	AX	BX	CX	DX
	?	?	?	?
MOV AX,0	0	?	?	?
ADD AX,6	6	?	?	?
MOV BX,4	6	4	?	?
MOV CX,5	6	4	5	?
ADD AX,BX	0A	4	5	?
SUB AX,3	7	4	5	?
MUL BX	1C	4	5	0

Figure 1.5
Making a program trace.

Unlike most pocket calculators, the number entered into AX, BX, CX or DX must consist of exactly 16 binary digits. Thus, the assembly language

```
MOV AX,7H
```

would actually be converted to the machine code equivalent of

```
MOV AX,0000000000000111B
```

since the binary for 7H is 111. Fortunately this is done for you automatically.

1.4.3 Making traces

Following through the execution of any assembly language program consisting of more than a couple of lines can be a difficult undertaking. It helps to keep a trace of register contents as we did in Figure 1.4. As another demonstration of this technique we now give an assembly language program involving `ADD`, `SUB` and `MUL` together with a trace of its execution. In the trace, an entry '?' will denote a value which we do not know. Thus, the contents of all four registers are indicated as '?' at the beginning of the trace when a particular program makes no assumption about the contents of registers before it is executed.

To make the trace we simply write down the contents of each of the registers before the program starts and then again after each instruction has been executed (Figure 1.5). Notice that the program uses the instruction:

```
ADD CX,BX ; add the number in register CX to the number
          ; in register BX. Put the answer in register CX
          ; and leave BX unchanged
```

There are similar forms of the ADD instruction involving each of the 12 possible combinations of two different registers chosen from AX, BX, CX and DX, with a similar effect in each case.

EXERCISES

1.6 What will be the contents of the AX, BX, CX and DX registers after executing each of the following program fragments?

(a)
```
MOV CX,3
ADD CX,5
MOV BX,CX
INC BX
MOV AX,BX
```

(b)
```
MOV DX,8
MOV AX,9
SUB DX,4
MUL DX
MOV CX,DX
INC CX
SUB CX,1
MOV BX,CX
```

1.7 Write a program to leave the result of 5 * (7+1)−6 in register CX.

1.8 By making a careful trace determine the post-execution contents of all the registers involved in each of the following program fragments.

(a)
```
MOV AX,0F1H
MOV BX,0ABCH
ADD AX,BX
MOV CX,3BH
SUB AX,0FH
MUL BX
```

(b)
```
MOV AX,2
MUL AX
MUL AX
MUL AX
MOV BX,3
ADD AX,BX
ADD AX,BX
MUL BX
```

(c)
```
MOV AX,0H
MOV BX,34H
MOV CX,35H
MOV DX,0FH
ADD BX,DX
SUB CX,01CH
ADD AX,BX
INC CX
MUL CX
```

1.5 Eight 'new' registers

This section could have been entitled 'New Lamps for Old' because the promised eight new registers actually come from our four familiar ones, AX, BX, CX and DX. We already know that each of these is a 16-bit register, but

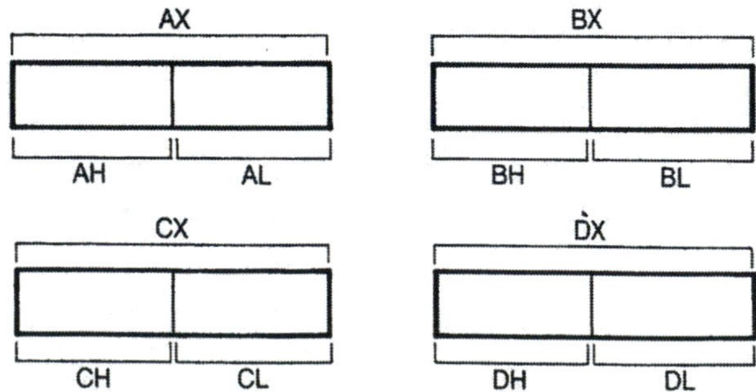

Figure 1.6
Each 16-bit register AX, BX, CX, and DX can be used as two 8-bit registers.

the 8086 family allows each of them to be used as two 8-bit registers as well. The leftmost eight bits of AX form an 8-bit register, AH, and the rightmost eight bits of AX form an 8-bit register, AL. Similarly, we get BH and BL from BX, CH and CL from CX, and DH and DL from DX (see Figure 1.6).

One can use instructions like `MOV AL,BH`; `MOV DL,CL`; `MOV BH,3`; `ADD BL,DH`; and `ADD DL,DH`, which have effects similar to those for their 16-bit register equivalents. If `MUL` is used with an 8-bit register as one of its operands, then the other operand is AL and the result is left in AX. Thus, `MUL BH` will multiply the unsigned number in BH by the unsigned number in AL and leave a 16-bit unsigned product in AX.

Any instruction must either operate entirely with 8-bit registers or entirely with 16-bit registers. Thus, `MOV AX,DL` is *not* allowed. (By the way, the H in AH stands for High and the L in AL stands for Low since if AX contains a 16-bit number, AH will contain the highest order bits and AL the lowest.)

It is important to remember that changing the value of one of the 8-bit registers will affect the corresponding 16-bit register and vice versa. Thus, after execution of:

```
MOV DH,98H
MOV DX,23ABH
ADD DH,1
```

DH will contain 24H (*not* 99H) and DX will contain 24ABH.

To see why, first note that 98H = 1001 1000B. `MOV DH,98H` therefore sets register DH to 10011000 with register DL containing whatever value it had previously:

```
┌───DX───┐
10011000????????
└─DH─┘└─DL─┘
```

But `MOV DX,23ABH` affects the whole of DX and so affects both DH and DL. Since

23ABH = 0010 0011 1010 1011B

the effect of `MOV DX,23ABH` is to leave DX containing

```
┌───DX───┐
0010001110101011
└─DH─┘└─DL─┘
```

Now `ADD DH,1` will add 1 to the eight most significant bits of DX, that is to say 00100011, giving 00100100, and put this result in place of the original eight bits. As a result, DX will then contain:

```
┌───DX───┐
0010010010101011
└─DH─┘└─DL─┘
```

and 0010 0100 1010 1011B = 24ABH.

Danger – ambiguity

There is now the risk of confusion as to whether

```
MOV DL,AH
```

means 'copy the contents of register AH into register DL' or 'put the hexadecimal number A into register DL'. To eliminate such ambiguity there is a rule in assembly language programming that all hexadecimal numbers beginning with a letter (for example A123H and E1FCH) must be written with a zero preceding them (so that our examples become 0A123H and 0E1FCH). Hence 'copy the contents of register AH into register DL' is now unambiguously

```
MOV DL,AH
```

and 'put the hexadecimal number A into register DL' becomes

```
MOV DL,0AH
```

EXERCISES

1.9 Complete the following:

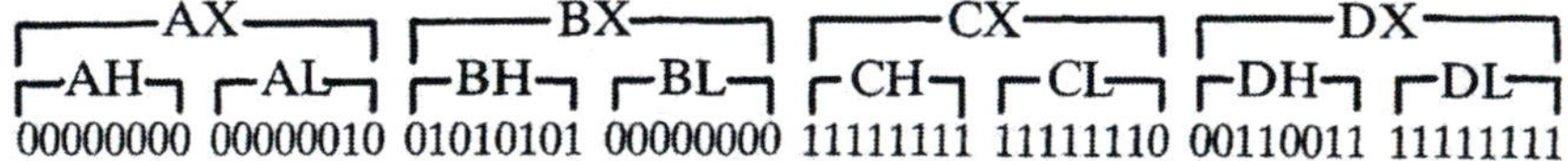

to make a trace of the execution of the following program fragment:

```
MOV DL,3
MOV CX,5
MOV BH,DL
SUB CX,7
ADD AH,2
ADD CH,5
MOV DX,AX
```

1.10 By making a careful trace determine the post-execution contents of all the registers involved in each of the following program fragments.

(a)
```
MOV DL,0F1H
MOV BL,0BCH
ADD DL,BL
MOV CH,3BH
SUB DL,0FH
```

(b)
```
MOV AH,2
MOV BH,3
ADD AH,BH
ADD AH,BH
MOV AL,2
MOV BL,1
MUL BX
```

(c)
```
MOV AX,0H
MOV BL,34H
MOV CH,35H
MOV DX,0FH
MOV CL,DL
MOV BH,CH
ADD BX,DX
SUB CX,01CH
ADD BL,CH
INC CX
MUL CX
```

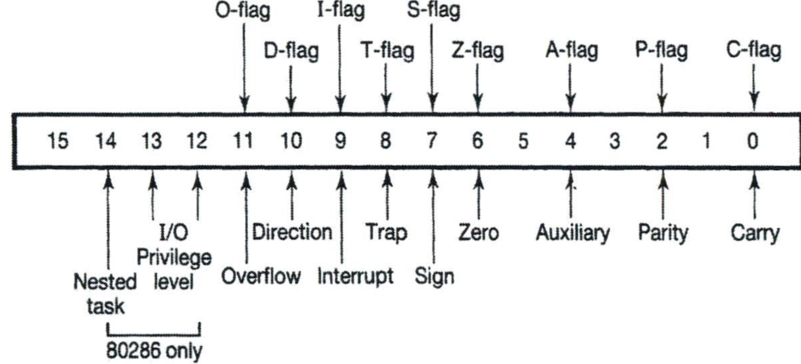

Figure 1.7
The flags register.

1.6 The flags register

The 8086-family microprocessors have a special 16-bit register called the **flags register** because the individual bits are used as flags to indicate the result of executing certain instructions. Thus, just as the British flag flies above London's Buckingham Palace only when the Queen is in residence (as tourists in England hoping to catch a glimpse of Her Majesty soon learn), so the Z-flag in the flags register can be set to 1 by any of a certain group of instructions to indicate that the result of executing that instruction was zero.

Altogether, five of the bits in the flags register (Figure 1.7) are used to indicate the results of arithmetic and related operations and are referred to as the **arithmetic flags**. These are the O-flag (overflow), the S-flag (sign), the Z-flag (zero), the A-flag (auxiliary carry) and the C-flag (carry). The P-flag indicates the parity of a result and is primarily used in data communications while three other bits are used to control processor actions like the direction in which large blocks of data are to move. The rest of the bits in the flags register are unused except that the 80286 microprocessor uses bits 12, 13 and 14 to organize **multitasking** (see Section 2.2).

To see how the flags work in relation to arithmetic instructions let us consider the carry flag. This is often used to hold the carry bit (either 0 or 1) resulting from an arithmetic operation. Thus, the sequence of instructions:

```
MOV AL,3H
MOV BL, 0FFH
ADD AL,BL
```

will try to set AL to the result of 3H + 0FFH = 102H. But 102H = 100000010H which is nine bits in total and therefore too much to be held in AL. Because of the particular values in AL and BL when it is executed, `ADD AL,BL` will therefore set the carry flag to 1 to indicate that the total is too big to fit in AL. Flags will be dealt with in more detail in Chapter 6, which examines their role in arithmetic operations, and in Chapter 7, which looks at how we can take different actions depending on the current value of a flag.

SUMMARY

In this chapter we have seen that assembly language is a last resort for most programming tasks. High-level languages offer environments in which the programming of a task can proceed much more efficiently. Assembly language offers two basic data types – binary signed or unsigned numbers – and all data items for a given problem have to be represented in numeric form before they can be used in a machine code program; in particular, text is represented using the ASCII code.

We met the idea of a microprocessor register which enables the programmer to store binary numbers and perform various operations on them, including arithmetic. These operations are determined by 8086-family instructions and we encountered the `MOV`, `ADD`, `SUB`, `INC` and `MUL` instructions for the first time.

To understand what happens during the execution of a sequence of 8086-family instructions the technique of tracing was presented as being particularly useful to the beginner. As we shall see in due course, much more sophisticated facilities exist to help the programmer, but even very experienced assembly language programmers use tracing as the last-resort method for locating errors.

We saw how AX, BX, CX and DX can also be thought of as eight 8-bit registers. While a large number of registers can sometimes seem unnecessarily complicated to the beginner, just a little more assembly language programming experience will soon lead you to believe the professional programmer's maxim that 'you can never have too many registers' (though, as with most maxims, there are plenty of exceptional cases).

Finally, we briefly introduced the flags register which is very important because individual flags within it indicate the outcome of arithmetic operations, and because which instruction is executed next can be made to depend on certain flag settings – as we shall see in Chapters 6 and 7.

SELF-CHECK QUIZ

1. For each of the following programming tasks, say whether you think it would be more appropriate to write the corresponding program in Pascal or assembly language:

   (a) A college student record system to ensure that all students pay their fees and to record each student's academic progress at the college.

   (b) A spreadsheet.

   (c) A system to record rainfall directly from an electronic rain detector placed on the roof of the main campus administration block and connected directly to the computer. Monthly printed reports on the levels of daily rainfall are required.

2. The following extract shows part of a program written for a computer based on a member of the 8086 family. Is it in machine code? If you think it is, explain why. If you think it isn't, explain what changes would have to be made to the program extract for it to be in machine code.

```
1 E  3 6
2 A  1 2
3 D0 3
4 D1 3
5 C  0
6 J  2
```

3. Convert the following numbers as required:

   (a) from decimal to binary

   (i) 18 (ii) 78 (iii) 364 (iv) 14,241

   (b) from hexadecimal to binary

   (i) 1AB8H (ii) 2EFAH (iii) 1364H
   (iv) 14AAH

   (c) to hexadecimal

   (i) 1011001101000111B
   (ii) 0011010110101111B
   (iii) 849D (iv) 7134D

   (d) from hexadecimal to decimal

   (i) 19A26H (ii) 0AFFFH (iii) 1364H
   (iv) 2CH

4. Given that

   (a) P = 11001001B Q = 01110001B
   P and Q are signed numbers

   (b) P = 01111001B Q = 11100001B
   P and Q are unsigned numbers

   (c) P = 3ABCH Q = 0CD2FH

   evaluate the following arithmetic expressions in each case:

   (i) P + Q (ii) P − Q (iii) P + P − Q
   (iv) Q + Q − P

   (Use two's complement arithmetic between signed numbers.)

5. Write an explanation of the difference between signed numbers and unsigned numbers. Your explanation must *not* contain any kind of numeric example: use words only!

6. (a) Write the following messages as sequences of ASCII codes:

   (i) PETER GRIMES
   (ii) The Burning Fiery Furnace
   (iii) Opus 64B No 3
   (iv) −273

   (b) Decode the following ASCII sequences into the corresponding text equivalent:

   (i) 6C 75 78 75 72 79 20 63 61 72
   (ii) 41 4E 41 4C 59 53 49 53
   (iii) 31 39 38 39 31 39 39 30 31 39 39 31

7. Write sequences of 8086-family assembly language instructions which use registers AX, BX, CX and DX to evaluate the following expressions:

   (a) $36 - (4 + 8)$

   (b) $(41 - 26) + (83 - 69)$

   (c) $(8 * 2) - 7$

   (d) $(9 * 8) - (4 * 7)$

8. Use the 8-bit registers AH,AL,. . .,DH, and DL to evaluate the following expressions:
   (a) $(16 - 5) - (8 + 11) - (2 * (9 - 4))$

   (b) $(11 * 4) + (2 * 5) + ((3 * 4) * (2 * 3))$

   Try to repeat this exercise using only registers AX, BX, CX and DX and hence explain an advantage of having eight registers rather than four. Can you describe any disadvantages of having many registers?

9. What will be the contents of AX, BX, CX, DX, AH, AL, BH, BL, CH, CL, DH and DL after execution of the following program fragment?

```
MOV AX,4C0DH
MOV BX,2AAFH
MOV CX,2
MUL CX
SUB BX,AX
ADD AL,BL
ADD DL,CL
```

10. Write assembly language instruction sequences to evaluate each of the expressions:

    11001001B + 01110001B

    01011101B + 00110101B

    01111001B + 11100001B

    using 8-bit registers. What will be the contents of the carry flag after executing each such sequence?

2

Organization of Computers Based on a Member of the 8086 Family

Contents

This chapter focuses on the architectural aspects of computers which are based on a member of the 8086 family of microprocessors. Here, and in the rest of this book, we shall rarely consider the electrical details involved and, instead, concentrate on the functionality of the components. The term usually used to refer to such a functional consideration of computer architecture is **computer organization**.

Assembly language programmers need to study computer organization for several reasons:

- it is essential to understand the memory addressing mechanism used by members of the 8086 family in order to write programs which access data items stored in memory;
- input/output programming requires an understanding of the way in which computer components are interconnected;
- many features of assembly language closely reflect the underlying computer organization; and

- it is necessary in order to understand the differences between individual members of the 8086 family

Our study of the organization of computers based on a member of the 8086 family will begin with a building-block view of the architecture of such a computer. We shall then study memory and input/output organization in a little more detail, including a key concept for the whole book; namely, segmented memory. Next follows an outline description of the bus interface unit which to a large extent controls communication between the microprocessor and memory. We then relate our diagrammatic view of computer organization to the actual electrical connections which must be made to an 8086 microprocessor (the 8086 pin-out). This leads to a description of the functions of the main chips used to build a microcomputer based on an 8086 microprocessor. We then take a similar but even briefer look at the 80286 and 80386 pin-out and support chips. Finally, we summarize some of the properties of the different members of the 8086 family.

2.1 Building-block microcomputer architecture

When people look at the architecture of a building, they are not normally concerned with the composition of the building blocks used to make the building: they might note the clever use of some red bricks here, and a stone pillar there, but the actual chemical content of the red bricks is not important. On the other hand, professional architects require this kind of knowledge for many reasons, such as to assess the strength of a certain type of brick – and it is similarly the case for us. Consequently we shall eventually need to look, not just at the organization of computers based on a member of the 8086 family, but also, at a deeper level, at how to program some of the other chips which support the microprocessor (see Chapters 20, 21 and 22 for example). We begin our study in this section by considering only the main building blocks.

Inside any computer based on a member of the 8086 family the basic arrangement of the main components is the same, as shown in Figure 2.1. Information is sent from one main component to another along the communication channel, which is often called the **system bus** by electrical engineers. Since you can put information 'on the bus' at the keyboard and take it off again at the bus interface unit or memory or . . . the analogy is quite a good one.

Both programs and data are stored in the memory, the **bus interface unit** within the microprocessor fetching new instructions or data as necessary. It is also the bus interface unit's job to interpret or decode instructions and to route results to their proper destinations. The microprocessor's **execution unit** carries out any arithmetic which is required, including memory address calculations.

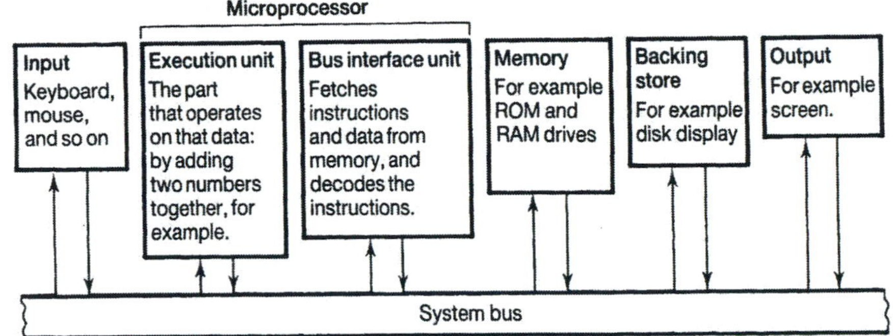

Figure 2.1
Data flow between the main components of an 8086 family computer.

Microcomputer memories consist of collections of chips of two kinds – **Read Only Memory (ROM)** and **Random Access Memory (RAM)**. ROMs have data written into them only once during their lifetime, usually during manufacture. This data is then resident in ROM memory forever. This memory is used to store programs and data which the programmer is not permitted to change and which must be available immediately the computer is turned on – such as the basic input and output system of the computer that controls, among other things, the operation of the keyboard and video display screen. RAM chips provide program and data storage for the ordinary programmer. Whatever is stored in RAM chips is lost when the computer is turned off.

2.2 Memory and input/output

The general organization of memory and input/output for 8086 family-based computers in shown in Figure 2.2. The figure shows the electrical interconnections between the major components, the functions of which will be described in this and later sections. Notice that the system bus is in fact made up of three separate buses – the **control bus**, the **data bus** and the **address bus**. In order to explain the number of individual electrical highways which make up the data and address buses, we shall also give a conceptual view of the manner in which data is held in memory and introduce the key concept of segmented memory.

Data items to be stored in memory or which are retrieved from memory to be used in a calculation are sent along the data bus. The address in which that data item is to be stored, or from which it is to be retrieved, is sent along the address bus. All activity within the microcomputer, including the storage and retrieval of data items, is initiated by the microprocessor but managed by the control bus. It is the responsibility of the control bus, for example, to switch the direction of travel on the data bus depending on whether a data item is to be stored or retrieved from memory.

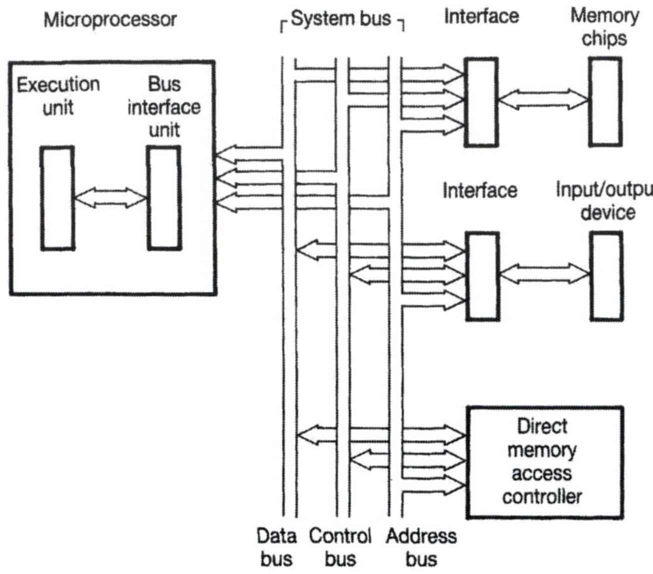

Figure 2.2 Memory and input/output organization.

2.2.1 Memory

Computer memory is best thought of as a collection of numbered pigeon-holes (called **locations**), each capable of storing *exactly* eight binary digits (a byte), as in Figure 2.3.

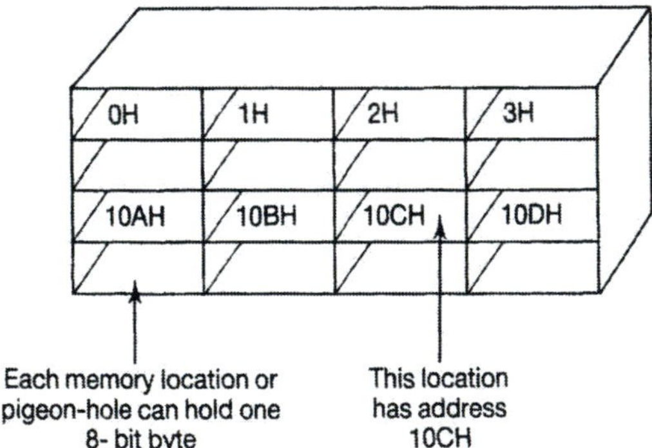

Figure 2.3 Computer memory. (Notice that the pigeon-holes are numbered from zero onwards.)

2.2.2 Input/output

In an 8086 family-based computer, all communication must involve the system bus. Thus, if you want to connect a printer to the computer, one possibility is to connect the printer directly to the system bus, but this is impractical in two respects. First, the amount of electrical power used to send signals along the bus is very, very low. This means that using a printer cable longer than a few centimetres would be out of the question – there just would not be enough driving force to push the bits along. The second impracticality arises from the fact that, if you did connect a printer in this way, there would be a direct electrical path from the printer to the microprocessor and other parts of the microcomputer. Consequently, if something were to go wrong with the printer so that a relatively high voltage were sent back along the bus, it would be possible for the microprocessor and other chips to be destroyed.

External devices are therefore almost always connected not directly to the system bus but to an **interface** (see Figure 2.2). Sending a character to a printer then involves putting the ASCII code for that character on to the data bus which is connected to the interface for that printer. The interface then arranges for that ASCII code to be sent to the printer, taking such steps as necessary (including boosting the power of the signal) to ensure that the printer receives the correct code. But it isn't just printers that are connected to the microprocessor in this way. Interfaces are used to control all I/O devices including the keyboard and the video display.

Direct memory access

Direct Memory Access (DMA) is where input and output take place directly to and from memory without any involvement of the microprocessor other than starting the process off, thus speeding up operations. Output to the screen display is handled in this way, for example. The programmer has simply to arrange that the ASCII codes for the characters making up whatever message is to be displayed are placed in a certain location (or locations) in memory. A DMA controller chip in the microcomputer will then arrange that the message is displayed without any reference to the microprocessor at all. Exactly where on the screen the message will appear depends on the actual memory locations used.

2.2.3 The data bus

Data items which are either to be used in some action by the microprocessor, or to be stored in memory, are sent in either direction along the data bus (see Figure 2.2). Since memory locations hold exactly eight bits, the data bus consists of a minimum of eight lines: one for the transmission of each bit. One member of the 8086 family employs this minimum 8-bit data bus, namely the 8088 microprocessor.

However, most programs which involve arithmetic calculations require numbers to be represented by at least 16-bits. For such programs, an 8-bit data bus implies slower execution speeds because storing a 16-bit number requires two separate operations. It is for this reason that the 8086 and 80186 microprocessors are more powerful than their sibling rivals (the 8088 and 80188 microprocessors, respectively), since both the 8086 and 80186 have a 16-bit data bus – as does the 80286. The 80386 and 80486 have a 32-bit data bus which therefore allows signed integers with magnitude in excess of 1 000 000 000 to be stored and retrieved from memory in a single operation.

2.2.4 Segmented Memory

In order to understand the important concept of **segmented memory**, which is used by all members of the 8086 family, let us fix our attention on just one microprocessor for a moment, namely the 8086 microprocessor. It allows memory addresses to consist of 20 bits. Thus, when executing an instruction which involves fetching a data item from memory, the 20-bit address of that item will be sent along the computer's address bus (see Figure 2.2) to tell the memory circuits where the required data item is to be found. Hence the address bus has 20 lines, one for the transmission of each bit of the address. The use of a 20-bit address means that the 8086 microprocessor has the ability to access:

$$2^{20} = 1\ 048\ 576$$

different memory locations, numbered from:

0000 0000 0000 0000 0000 (0 in decimal)

to:

1111 1111 1111 1111 1111 (1 048 575 in decimal)

We must recall at this point that the instructions in a machine code program are themselves stored in memory. The 8086 microprocessor instructions were designed to take up a maximum of six bytes given that two bytes were allowed for the 'name' of a particular instruction. It follows that if a 20-bit address such as 20BAFH were allowed, then an instruction of the form 'check if the value stored at address 20BAFH is 365' would require:

2 bytes for the instruction's name;
2 bytes to represent 365 as an unsigned 16-bit number; and
3 bytes for the address 20BAFH

thus exceeding the designers' self-imposed 6-byte instruction length limit. To avoid this (and because there are other advantages, as shall be pointed out later), it was decided that the 8086 family would employ the segmented memory concept.

Rather than representing each address as a 20-bit unsigned number, memory is thought of as being divided up into **segments** each of which contains 2^{16} locations. In this way an address can be thought of as consisting of two parts: a 16-bit segment address and a 16-bit offset from the start of that segment. This is similar to identifying a particular day in the year by means of the month in which it occurs (which corresponds to the segment address) and the day of that month (which corresponds to the offset):

'February	'segment 2000H,
11th	offset 0BAFH
is the	corresponds to the actual address
42nd day in the year'	20BAFH'

month: 2	*segment number: 2000H*
day of month: 11	*offset within that segment: 0BAFH*
day in year: 42	*actual address: 20BAFH*

However, the analogy breaks down for two reasons:

(1) all segments are 64K bytes long, whereas the length of the months of the year vary; and

(2) the programmer can *choose* where in the whole of available memory each segment is to begin, whereas the commencement of each month in the year is predetermined by the Julian calendar.

With many programs it may be possible for both machine code and data to be contained in just one 64K segment of memory – as is the case for all the programs in this book. But even then, there is a logical advantage in clearly separating the two. Consequently our programs will always have a code segment (a segment containing the program instructions themselves *in machine code*) and a (possibly empty) data segment.

Specifying addresses

To represent a segment address and its relative offset we use the notation:

<segment address> : <offset address>

Thus, 020A:1BCD denotes offset 1BCDH from segment 020AH. The actual address it refers to is obtained in the following way:

1.	Add a zero to the right-hand side of the segment address.	0 2 0 A 0 H
2.	Add to this the offset.	1 B C D H
	Total	0 3 C 6 D H

Hence the actual address referred to by 020A:1BCD is 03C6DH.

EXERCISES

2.1 For each of the following pairs of addresses given in segment:offset form, decide if the two addresses correspond to the same memory location.

(a) 74D6:0100	74C6:0110
(b) 4E50:F10F	4C50:0FF0
(c) 1234:1234	1358:0040
(d) 0500:ABCD	0EB0:10CD

2.2 If a given data item is stored only in each of the locations in the range 0AB1CH to 0AB2CH inclusive, how many copies of that data item will be held in memory? What are the corresponding answers if the range is:

(a) 1BCD:1BCD to 1DEF:1DEF

(b) 8ABC:0100 to 8DEF:0CEF

(c) 2421:ABCD to 2422:ABCD

2.3 For each of the following pairs of addresses given in segment:offset form say which of the pair represents the higher absolute address:

(a) BCEF:0123 and BCFE:2412

(b) DE12:AB1C and DD12:BB1D

(c) 0AEB:C1D2 and 0DFB:024B

2.2.5 Addresses and the more advanced 8086-family members

Like the 8086 microprocessor, both the 80188 and 80186 microprocessors have 20-bit address buses. The 80286 microprocessor has a 24-bit address bus (which allows it access to over 16 million bytes of memory) and the 80386 and 80486 microprocessors have a 32-bit address bus (permitting 4 294 967 296 bytes of memory). However, all members of the 8086 family can work with instructions based on 20-bit segmented memory addresses so this is a key concept for them all: the 80286 microprocessor can run all 8086 programs and the 80386 and 80486 microprocessors have various operating modes which allow them to act like 80286 or multiple 8086 microprocessors. But the more powerful members, such as the 80286, 80386 and 80486 microprocessor, have extra memory addressing capability which extends their performance considerably.

By way of an example, let us consider the 80286 microprocessor. It can be put into one of two modes of operation: **real address mode** or **protected virtual address mode**. When started up, the 80286 microprocessor works in real address mode and obeys only the same instructions as the 80186 microprocessor. This means that it essentially operates as a fast 8086 microprocessor with a 24-bit address bus and a 16-bit data bus.

In protected virtual address mode (we shall say 'virtual mode' for short), the 80286 microprocessor permits **multitasking**. During multitasking, the codes for two or more programs (**tasks**) is in memory at the same time and each code is executed in turn for a small period of time, thus giving the *impression* that several programs (tasks) are being executed simultaneously (of course, a single microprocessor can only execute one instruction at a time). The advantage of multitasking stems from the fact that it allows more programs to be run over a given period of time; if task 1 needs to wait for a relatively lengthy I/O operation to be completed, task 2 can be run in the meantime (Figure 2.4).

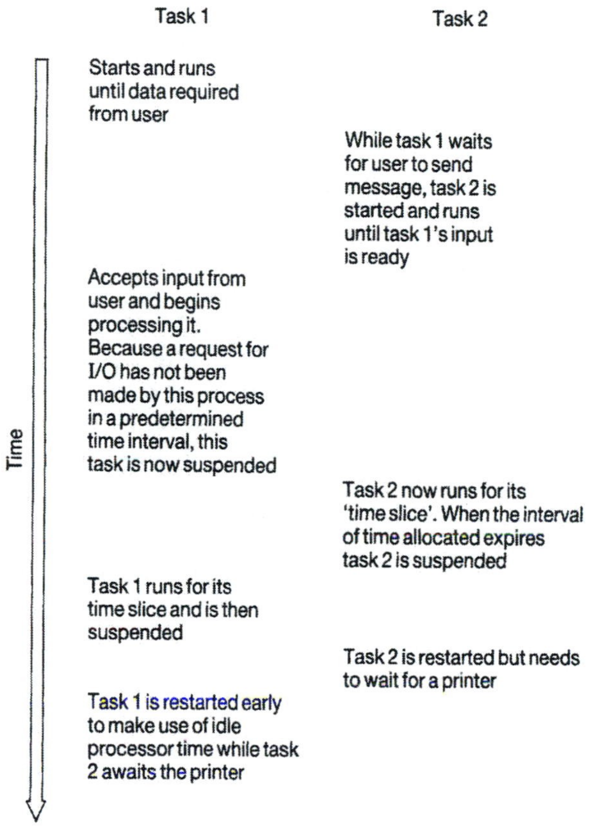

Figure 2.4 Multitasking.

In virtual mode, the 80286 microprocessor has instructions that enable the memory management and task switching necessary for multitasking. These instructions must ensure that: the operating system knows which task is stored where; each task has sufficient memory; there is adequate protection between application tasks (such as collecting data from an industrial process monitoring device) and the operating system which controls multitasking; the tasks are separated from one another; program instructions and data are kept separate; and that unauthorized accessing or changing of program instructions or data is not possible.

The name 'virtual mode' derives from the fact that in virtual mode the 80286 microprocessor works with virtual addresses that are translated into physical addresses by the memory management hardware. Virtual addresses are addresses in the normal sense, but are not constrained by there having to be one location in memory for every virtual address: usually there are more virtual addresses than real memory locations. For example, each 80286 task is allowed up to 2^{30} locations of virtual memory whereas there are only a maximum 2^{24} locations of real memory. If a task does require more memory than is physically available, the contents of virtual locations not required for the execution of the current instruction are kept on disk and then swapped back into memory as needed. Special instructions and registers within the 80286 microprocessor control this swapping process.

2.3 The bus interface unit

In principle, the bus interface unit is nothing other than an intricate collection of electronic switches which break down every machine code instruction into a sequence of relatively small steps. These steps are carried out by the opening and closing of switches to allow data to flow from one part of the computer to another along the system bus.

It is the responsibility of the bus interface unit to decode an instruction into its constituent parts and arrange for the instruction to be executed. The sequence of operations this involves is called the **fetch, decode and execute cycle** and we shall now examine each of the components of this cycle in turn.

2.3.1 Fetching data from memory

The first stage in the execution of a machine code instruction is to copy the instruction from memory into a 6-byte queue in the bus interface unit (exceptionally, for the 8088 microprocessor the queue is only two bytes long). Indeed, it is a design feature of the 8086 family of microprocessors, which distinguishes these microprocessors from others, that the bus interface unit continuously tries to keep this instruction queue filled. Thus, in parallel with activity within the execution unit, the bus interface unit attempts to retrieve the instruction stored in memory immediately following the last one fetched. If possible, this is placed in the queue so that it will be ready directly the execution unit has completed its current task.

Overlapping bus interface unit and execution unit operation in this way eliminates many of the delays caused by the execution unit running out of work. However, if the execution unit requires operands from memory to finish a given operation then fetching operands takes priority over fetching new instructions. Also, if the next instruction to be executed is not the one stored in memory immediately after the last one executed, the bus interface unit effectively clears its instruction queue and restarts the fetching and queuing process from the correct memory location.

For reasons of electronic design economy, members of the 8086 family always move data between the execution unit and memory *one word at a time*. If the execution unit requires a word stored in two locations, the first having an even-numbered address, then the bus interface unit need only organize one memory access. Similarly, only one memory access is required if the execution unit requires a byte stored at an even-numbered address – though a whole word will be put on to the data bus and the superfluous byte will be ignored.

Two memory accesses are necessary if the execution unit requires a word, the first byte of which is stored at an odd-numbered address. One memory access is required for the low-order byte and another for the high-order byte. In each access, a full word is placed on the data bus and the unwanted data ignored. (It follows that in execution time-critical applications, time can be saved by placing data words in memory at even addresses only).

The clock

Synchronizing operations within any computer is an electronic clock which sends out **pulses** (or **cycles**) much like an army drill sergeant shouts left–right–left–right to synchronize a parade. For the 8086 microprocessor the original manufacturer's declared maximum clock rate was 5 megahertz (5 million cycles per second), which we write as 5 MHz. A later version of the 8086 microprocessor, identical in all operational respects, allowed a clock rate of 8 Mhz (8 million cycles per second). As manufacturing technology and microprocessor design advances, more modern production versions of microprocessors in the 8086 family allow faster clock speeds making it difficult for a book such as this to specify limits. However, for the purposes of comparison, knowledge of the actual clock speeds is not always necessary. For example, as we shall see later in this book, the execution of an 8086-family eight bit multiplication instruction takes at least 71 clock cycles whereas only 4 clock cycles are needed to fetch a word from memory. Consequently, the bus interface unit would have ample time to fill its 6-byte instruction queue in the time it takes the execution unit to complete such a multiplication.

System bus timing

Each basic system bus operation takes at least four clock cycles. If we call these T1, T2, T3 and T4 then the relevant address is emitted from the microprocessor during T1. T2 is the period during which the direction of the bus is changed if a read operation is to be performed. The actual transfer between the memory or I/O interface and the microprocessor is carried out during T3 and T4. If the addressed device is not ready to supply or receive the relevant item, then the system will pause between T3 and T4. Such pauses are called **wait states** and they always last a whole number of clock cycles.

2.3.2 Decoding an instruction

Of course, the computer never sees instructions of the form:

SUBTRACT this data item
                     from that data item
                     and place the result so-and-so

but rather instructions arrive at the microprocessor in the form:

0010101111000011

Since even the simplest member of the 8086 family, the 8088 microprocessor, can execute more than 300 different instructions, up to two bytes are required to specify which operation is required. In the example above, the first eight bits are the machine code for specifying the SUBTRACT operation. The other bits identify the source of the two data items to be subtracted and the destination of the result of the subtraction.

Having fetched an instruction from memory, it is the job of the bus interface unit to decode the instruction by separating the operation type from the specification of its operands, then to initiate the fetching of any operands required from memory, and finally to set the appropriate execution in motion.

2.3.3 Execution

If the instruction is solely concerned with the movement of data to or from memory then the sequence of operations necessary for its execution will resemble that for fetching an instruction from memory. The movement of data between registers necessary for the execution of `MOV AX,BX` and the execution of arithmetic required in `ADD AX,2` takes place in the execution unit within the microprocessor. It houses the **arithmetic and logic unit** which actually performs any arithmetic or logical operation.

The time it takes to execute a given instruction depends on the number of clock cycles needed for its execution together with the time required to calculate the effective address if memory is involved. This information is summarized in Appendix V. It follows that for an 8086 microprocessor with a 5 MHz clock, we have the following execution times:

Instruction	*No. of clock cycles*	*Execution time (seconds)*
`ADD AX,2`	4	0.000 000 8
`MOV AX,CX`	2	0.000 000 4
`MOV DX,3`	4	0.000 000 8
`MUL BX`	133	0.000 026 6

2.4 The 8086-family chips

2.4.1 The 8086 microprocessor

By way of example of the electrical attachments which must be made to an actual 8086-family microprocessor chip for the various functions, Figure 2.5 shows these for the 8086 microprocessor. The details of many of the attachments are beyond the scope of this book, but the groupings clearly show how the control, address and data bus concepts shown in our schematic diagrams (Figures 2.1 and 2.2) relate to an actual 8086 chip.

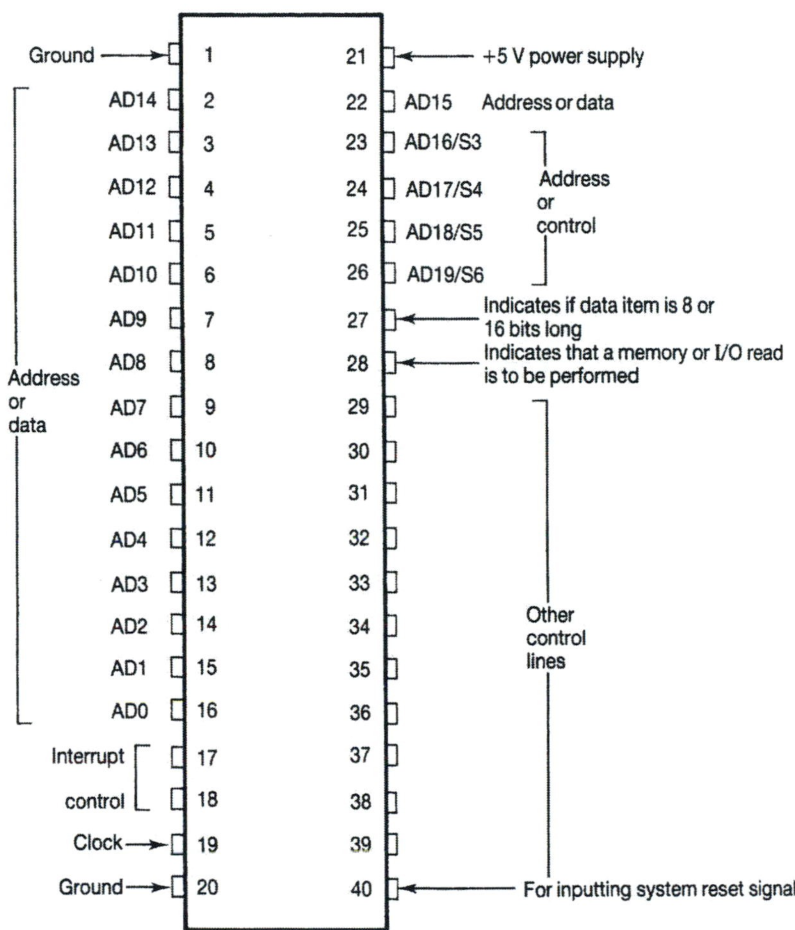

Figure 2.5
8086-chip pin assignments.

Note that the address and data bus share 16 of the same connectors on the chip. During a data transfer, the relevant address is output first on lines AD0–AD15 and AD16–AD19. The circuitry attached to the address bus must receive and maintain this address on the address bus (we say, **latch** the address), pending the arrival of the data item. If, to be definite, we assume the transfer involves writing an item in memory, then after the address has been output, the 8086 microprocessor will output the data item on the AD0–AD15 pins, using the control bus to indicate whether the data item consists of 8 or 16 bits. Once again, it is the responsibility of circuitry attached to the 8086 chip to latch the value of the data item on the data bus.

Connectors 17 and 18 allow the input of an electrical signal to change the normal program execution sequence. By applying an appropriate signal to these connectors to interrupt normal execution, a branch can be made into another sequence of instructions (such as part of the operating system) and then a return to normal execution made where execution left off when it was interrupted.

Line 40 allows a microcomputer based on the 8086 microprocessor to be started up. If an appropriate signal is received on this line by the microprocessor, an instruction is fetched automatically from location FFFF: 0000 which the microcomputer's designers will have arranged to be in ROM. That instruction then normally causes execution to continue from the beginning of the microcomputer's operating system – in our case, the Basic Input/Output System (BIOS) – which in turn calls up the Disk Operating System (DOS) if the computer has disk drives.

Starting up a computer in this way is called **bootstrapping** because of a resemblance to pulling yourself upright from a horizontal sleeping position by tugging at your bootlaces – which, like all the best programmers, you had omitted to remove before going to sleep.

2.4.2 Some of the other chips used in an 8086-based microcomputer

Any microcomputer contains a range of standard chips as well as the basic microprocessor itself. Figure 2.6 shows a schematic diagram of the layout for one based on the 8086 microprocessor. The general scheme is fairly typical of microcomputers based on a member of the 8086 family, though the actual chips used for the various functions may vary.

The quartz crystal supplies timing pulses to the Intel **8284 clock generator** chip which provides synchronizing pulses for the whole computer's operations. The **8288 bus controller** chip controls the interface between the microprocessor and the system bus. It is this chip which controls the interconnection between extra circuit boards (called **adapter cards**) which may be slotted into the main circuit board so that extra functions such as voice input/output, music synthesis, very high resolution graphics or a printer interface can be provided.

Addresses are latched on to the address bus by means of the **8283 latch** chip and then passed on to the intended recipient by an **8287 bus driver**. This latter chip is known as a **transceiver** because it can both transmit and receive signals. Another 8287 bus driver is used on the data bus.

The **8259 interrupt controller** arbitrates between several calls for the program the microprocessor is currently executing to be interrupted. For example, two different peripheral devices may simultaneously signal that they need the microprocessor's attention and the interrupt controller chip must decide which one to pass on to the microprocessor.

While this completes a functional description of the chips shown in Figure 2.6, the connections to ROM and RAM and peripheral devices involve many other standard chips. In order to write our own programs for input and output with different facilities from those provided by DOS we shall require a more detailed knowledge of the operation of some of these chips (and others), as we shall see in Chapter 21. For the time being only the most important of those remaining will be listed. A more detailed consideration of some of them will be made later.

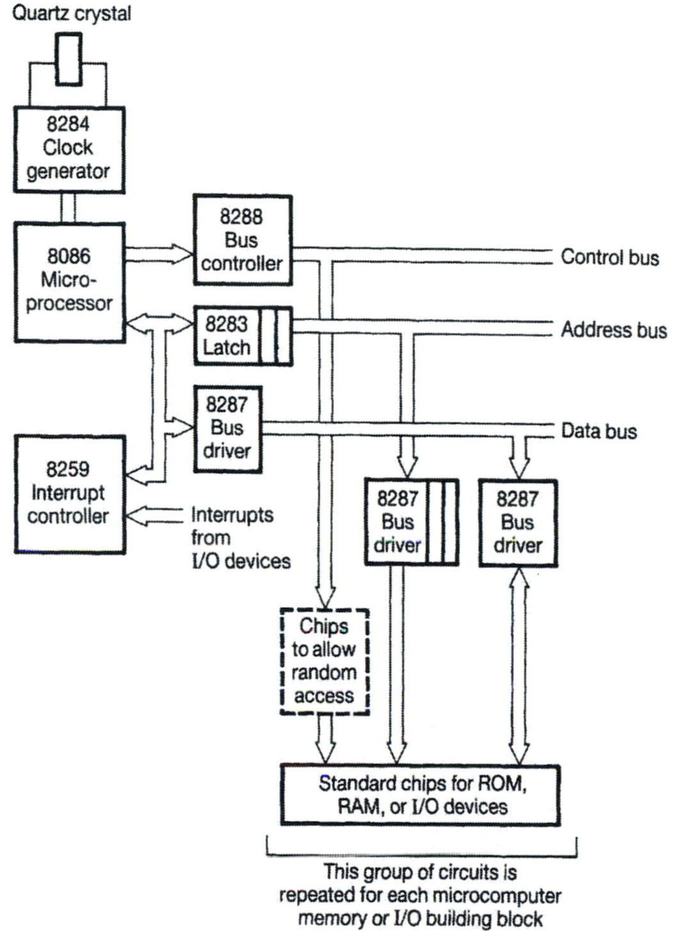

Figure 2.6
Basic construction of an 8086-based microcomputer.

- **Keyboard controller** This chip decodes patterns of signals sent from the keyboard when a key is pressed. It is actually a small computer in its own right, with its own RAM and ROM. Its ROM holds the decoding program and the RAM stores incoming keypresses so that if the user types at a faster rate than the software can cope with, no characters are lost.
- **Programmable interval timer** The main memory RAM chips in today's microcomputers are constructed from **dynamic RAM**. This is a type of memory which requires that its contents are refreshed regularly in order to retain what has been stored there. The programmable interval timer produces the timing signal which generates the request for the RAM to be refreshed. It also produces the signal which drives the internal loudspeaker.
- **DMA controller** This chip enables Direct Memory Access (DMA), that

is, it allows input and output to take place directly to and from memory without any involvement of the microprocessor other than starting the process off, thus speeding up operations.

- **Programmable peripheral interface** Controls the operation of system peripherals such as the keyboard.
- **Real-time clock** Has a clock and calendar which keeps the current time, day and date in some internal RAM. It is battery powered so that the real-time clock keeps going when the computer's power is switched off.

2.4.3 The 80186 chip

The **80186** chip is an enhanced version of the 8086 microprocessor which has a clock generator, a DMA controller, a programmable interrupt controller, a timer unit and a chip select unit incorporated into the microprocessor chip itself. Since the design of a microcomputer normally requires these supporting devices, the 80186 can reduce the overall number of chips (the 'chip count') needed in a microcomputer based on it and simplify its design. As with the 8086 microprocessor, the address and data lines AD0–AD15 are shared and address lines AD16–AD19 are shared with the control bus.

2.4.4 The 80286 chip

For the **80286** chip the address, control and data pins are quite separate, unlike both the 8086 and 80186 chips. Similar supporting chips are required to interface an 80286 chip to the system bus as with the 8086 configuration shown in Figure 2.6. For this, the microcomputer designer may use the **82284 clock generator** and the **82288 bus controller** which are the counterparts of the 8284 clock generator and 8288 bus controller used there. The 8283 address latch chip, the 8287 bus driver and the 8259 interrupt controller may all be used in an 80286 system as well.

As indicated above, the 80286 chip was derived from the original 8086 microprocessor with the intention of enabling computers designed around it to operate in a multitasking mode. Until that time, microprocessors permitted multitasking through support circuitry and various layers of controlling software. But the 80286 chip has all the necessary mechanisms to support multitasking on the chip itself. Consequently the 80286 chip design is significantly more complex than that for the 8086 chip.

Figure 2.7 shows the 80286 internal structure. It is this structure which enables the 80286 chip to operate in its two modes. When the chip is first powered up, it goes automatically into real address mode in which it can access a maximum of 1 megabyte of memory using 20-bit addresses which are formed from a segment and offset as described in Section 2.2. In this mode, therefore, the 80286 chip appears to the programmer as an 8086 microprocessor which executes faster and has an extended range of instructions.

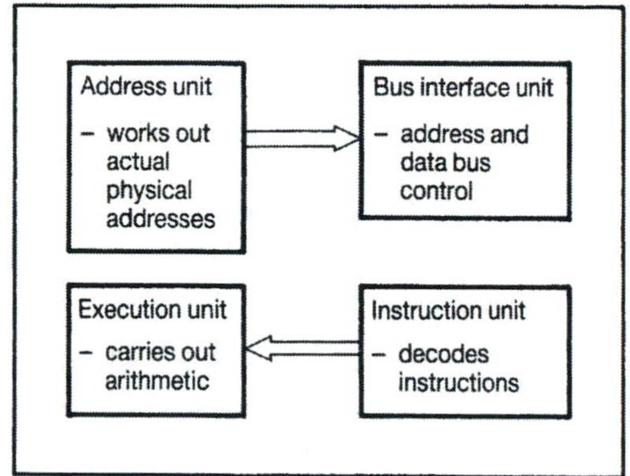

Figure 2.7 80286 internal structure.

The bus interface unit and execution unit were described above. The **instruction unit** gets instructions from the queue of six bytes fetched by the bus interface unit, decodes these instructions and stores the decoded form in a queue containing up to three fully decoded instructions.

When in protected virtual address mode, multitasking is controlled through the **address unit** in that it organizes the addressing of the (up to) 16 megabytes of real memory in the computer and implements the protection mechanisms in protected virtual address mode. The address unit has a private memory of its own which is used to accelerate address translation and permission checking.

2.4.5 The 80386 chip

The **80386** chip is three or four times more powerful than the 80286 chip but offers the same choice of real address and protected virtual address modes. When it is started up, the 80386 chip operates in real mode. Effectively it is then a very fast 8086 microprocessor and so is limited to 1 megabyte of memory and uses the 20-bit segmented memory addressing scheme described earlier.

A full range of support chips are available for the 80386 chip but a comparison of the actual chips used in the original 8088-based IBM-PC and a more recent 80386 machine reveals a surprising degree of similarity (Table 2.1).

2.4.6 The 80486 chip

At the time of writing the **80486** chip is the most recent member of the 8086 family. It integrates the 80386 chip and three of the its main support chips all on one chip and has several performance enhancements. The instruction set of the 80486 chip is completely compatible with that of the 80386 chip and a program which runs on the 80386 chip will run on the 80486 chip. Frequently used instructions such as `MOV` (which would take four clock cycles on an 80386 chip) have been designed to execute in just a single clock cycle on the 80486

Table 2.1 Comparison of support chips.

Microprocessor	*IBM-PC* *Intel 8088*	*80386-based microcomputer* *Intel 80386*
Support chips:		
8284 clock generator	1	1
6818 real-time clock		1
82284 clock generator/ready interface		1
8288 bus controller	1	
82288 bus controller		1
8259 programmable interrupt controller	1	2
8237 programmable DMA controller	1	2
8253 programmable interval timer	1	
8254 programmable interval timer		1
8255 programmable peripheral interface	1	1
8278 programmable keyboard interface	1	
8742 keyboard controller		1

chip. Memory accessing is speeded up so that wait states necessary to execute instructions on earlier 8086-family microprocessors are eliminated in many instances.

SUMMARY

This chapter began with an overview of 8086-family microcomputer organization. We then saw how the address bus is used to communicate addresses within a microcomputer and how the data bus is used to transmit data items. In order to shorten the overall length of an instruction which involves fetching data from, or storing data in, memory the 8086 family uses the concept of segmented memory. With segmented memory, all addresses are given in the form segment:offset. As we shall see in later chapters, we quite often wish to work with data entirely contained within one memory segment. The use of the segment:offset format for addresses then allows us to specify an address uniquely by reference only to the offset, a 16-bit number.

Fetching instructions from memory, breaking them down into their constituent parts and initiating execution are the main functions of the bus interface unit, one of the components of the microprocessor chip.

The construction of any microcomputer based on a member of the 8086 family relies on readily available support chips designed for the purpose by chip manufacturers. We described the functions of the main support chips used in an 8086-based microcomputer: microcomputers

Table 2.2 Some members of the 8086 family.

Microprocessor	*Width of data bus (bits)*	*Width of address bus (bits)*	*Instruction queue length (bytes)*	*Maximum clock rate* (MHz)	*Notes*
8086	16	20	6	5	
8088	8	20	4	5	Functionally identical to 8086, lower performance.
80186	16	20	6	8	Runs all 8086 and 8088 software but has 10 new instructions.
80188	8	20	4	8	Functionally identical to 80186, lower performance.
80286	16	24	6	10	Runs all 8086 and 80186 programs but has extra instructions. Several times more powerful than the 8086. Has special instructions to enable multitasking and the use of virtual memory.
80836	32	32	6	16	Has various operating modes which allow it to act like an 80286 chip or multiple 8086 chips, as well as a set of instructions capable of 32-bit operations such as arithmetic.
80386SX	16	32	6	16	Functionally identical to 80386 chip, lower performance.
80846	32	32	6	16	Acts like a superfast 80386 chip. Floating-point arithmetic operations are built into the 80486 chip as are the functions of three of the main 80386 support chips.

based on other members of the 8086 family are of similar construction. Finally we made a brief comparison of the main members of the 8086 family itself: some of the main features are summarized in Table 2.2.

However, most important of all is that all members of the 8086 family effectively start up in a mode in which they appear to the programmer as an 8086 microprocessor (usually faster, but in the case of the 8088 chip, rather slower). Consequently Chapters 3 through 22 will describe the assembly language instructions available with the 8086 chip (and therefore common to all members of the 8086 family) while Chapter 23 examines instructions specific to more powerful members of the 8086 family such as the 80286, 80386 and 80486 chips.

SELF-CHECK QUIZ

1. Write the following absolute addresses in segment:offset form where the segment address is 4AB1H:

   (a) 4AB10H (c) 4FFFFH

   (b) 51000FH (d) 55555H

2. Write the following segment:offset addresses as absolute addresses:

   (a) 26AB:1234 (d) 1234:26AB

   (b) FEDC:AAAA (e) 1991:1992

   (c) A5B9:9999 (f) 9FA1:800C

3. If it is required to store a byte in each of the following ranges of memory locations, how many bytes will be stored in total:

   (a) 6723:0ABC to 7100:0010 inclusive

   (b) 7BCA:2300 to 7BCA:2400

   (c) 0000:0000 to FFFF:FFFF

4. Explain the difference between the bus interface unit and the execution unit by summarizing the different functions they have to carry out.

5. What is the maximum number of memory locations a microprocessor can address if it has (a) an 8-bit address bus and (b) a 32-bit address bus?

6. Would there be any advantage in having a 64-bit data bus version of one of the 8086-family microprocessors? Can you list any disadvantages?

7. How would you decide whether extending the instruction queue in the bus interface unit to 12 bytes, rather than 6 bytes, would increase the overall speed at which an 8086-family microprocessor could operate, and how would you calculate any efficiency gain?

8. Explain the fetch, decode and execute cycle with reference to the program fragment:

```
MOV AX,3
MOV BX,the contents of memory location n
ADD BX,AX
```

   (`the contents of memory location n` is not real assembly language. We shall see in the next chapter how to express this properly in assembly language.)

9. Work out the time taken to execute:

```
MOV AX,2
MOV BX,3
MUL BX
ADD AX,BX
```

   given that (a) when assembled into machine code, the first two instructions are 3 bytes long and the second two are 2 bytes long, (b) the computer on which the program fragment is to be executed has a 12 MHz clock and (c) that four clock cycles are needed to fetch a word from memory.

10. Can you think of any reasons why address and data bus lines are shared on an 8086-family microprocessor chip? Why not just have separate sets of lines for each?

3 Addresses and Instructions Which Affect Memory

Contents

This chapter begins by examining just three of the 8086-family's rich supply of jump instructions. These are the mechanism by which loops can be created in assembly language programs – just as **for**, **repeat** and **while** make this possible in Pascal.

However, since the great majority of assembly language programs require the storage and retrieval of data items in memory, the main focus of this chapter is on a version of the `MOV` instruction which makes this possible, and on the actual mechanism used for storing and retrieving the contents of registers. Register BX has a special role to play in this: this chapter describes how it allows us to access a group of memory locations which are only determined during program execution rather than in advance by the programmer. Because this material is so fundamental to understanding the contents of later chapters several detailed examples (including traces) of programs which access memory are given.

The 8086-family microprocessors use segmented memory, so all addresses must be given in segment:offset form. Four special 16-bit registers are used to specify the segment involved in the storage or retrieval of instructions and data, namely the segment registers CS, DS, SS and ES; the offset of an instruction or data item is then given either explicitly or in an appropriate register. The penultimate section describes how actual memory locations are determined in this way.

Reflecting the fact that an instruction stored in memory has its segment specified by the Code Segment (CS) register, and a data item has its segment specified by the Data Segment (DS) register, an assembly language program must make it quite clear what is to be stored relative to each of these segment registers, and the others (SS and ES). Consequently, the final section in this chapter describes how to do this by adopting a conventional layout for assembly language programs. This skeleton program structure will be used throughout the book except where it is necessary to depart from it in order to describe particular features of 8086-family assembly language.

3.1 Jumps

Jump instructions allow members of the 8086 family to take decisions according to information provided by the flags register: for example, if registers AX and BX contain the ASCII code for the same letter then do one thing, if not then do another.

Generally speaking, instructions in an assembly language program are obeyed one after another. Jumps can enable execution to continue from an instruction further on in the program. Thus, in the following example, the

```
JZ MISSLOTS
```

instruction can be interpreted to mean, 'Jump if execution of the previous instruction resulted in Zero (`JZ`) to the instruction labeled `MISSLOTS` and continue execution in the normal way from there':

```
               .
               .
               .
           MOV AX,3
           SUB BX,AX
           JZ  MISSLOTS
           INC DX        ;obey this and the following
               .         ;instructions only if subtracting
               .         ;the contents of AX from BX did
               .         ;not give zero
MISSLOTS:  MOV CX,DX
               .
               .
               .
```

Also, jumps can enable execution to continue from an earlier instruction in a similar fashion:

```
                  .
                  .
                  .
BACKAGAIN: MOV BX,DX
                  .
                  .
                  .
           SUB DX,AX
           JZ  BACKAGAIN
           INC DX
                  .
                  .
                  .
```

As we shall see in Chapter 7, 8086-family processors have a rich supply of jump instructions. For the time being just three of them will suffice:

JZ *<label>*
JNZ *<label>*
JMP *<label>*

The precise meaning of these instructions will be discussed in Chapter 7. For now we can simply interpret them as follows:

JZ jump to *<label>* if the result of the last arithmetic instruction was zero;

JNZ jump to *<label>* if the result of the last arithmetic instruction was *non*-zero; and

JMP jump to *<label>*

The *<label>* is a luxury facility available thanks to assembly language. In machine code jump instructions you must either specify the precise address in memory where the instruction you want to jump to can be found or indicate how many instructions before or after the current one you want to jump. During the conversion process from assembly language to machine code all the *<label>*s in jump instructions are replaced by the appropriate numbers.

To make this conversion possible, there are certain rules governing the way in which *<label>*s are made up. A *<label>* must contain only alphabetic characters (A,B,. . .,Z,a,b,. . .,z), digits (0,1,2,3,4,. . .,9) or underline characters (_) and begin with an alphabetic character. *<label>*s can be as long as you like though the assembler cannot differentiate between two labels both beginning with the same 31 characters. Thus,

```
process_gr
remove_12
step_19
list56
```

are allowable <*label*>s but

```
3rdmonth
tues+weds
mylabelwhichcontains;asemicolon
```

are not.

3.1.1 An example program using jump instructions

Let us write an assembly language program for the 8086 family to compare the contents of registers AX and BX. If they both contain the same number we shall put a 1 in register DX; otherwise we shall put a 0 in DX. Further, suppose that the contents of both AX and BX are to be unaltered at the end of the program. The following satisfies our design constraints. (It is certainly not the best program possible but has been chosen to illustrate the use of jump instructions.)

```
        MOV CX,AX ;take a copy of the contents of AX as the next
                  ;instruction will destroy what is in AX
        SUB AX,BX
        JZ  MAKE1 ;if AX and BX contained the same number this
                  ;instruction will cause execution to continue
                  ; from the instruction labeled MAKE1
        MOV DX,0  ;otherwise execution continues sequentially,
                  ;so set DX to 0 indicating that the contents
                  ;of AX and BX were different
        JMP RESET ;jump unconditionally to the instruction
                  ;labelled RESET (this is to avoid obeying
                  ;the following instruction automatically)
MAKE1:  MOV DX,1  ;we only obey this instruction if the
                  ;contents of AX and BX were the same
RESET:  MOV AX,CX ;restore the original contents of AX from CX
```

EXERCISES

3.1 Write an assembly language program fragment which puts the ASCII code for the letter Y in register DX if the sum of the contents of registers AX and BX is the same as the current contents of register CX. If not, put the ASCII code for N in register DX. Lastly, put 0 in registers AX, BX and CX.

3.2 Given that on entry register AX contains 3H and register BX contains 4H, what will be the contents of registers AX, BX and CX after execution of the following program fragment:

```
      MOV CX,0
AGAIN:ADD CX,AX
      SUB BX,1
```

```
        JZ DONE
        JMP AGAIN
   DONE:MOV AX,0
        MOV BX,0
```

If registers AX and BX contained 2H and 5H respectively, can you say what registers AX, BX and CX would contain after execution of the above program fragment without doing any more work?

3.3 Write an assembly language program which will examine the contents of register AX and leave 0 in register DX if AX contains 47H and leave 0FFH in register DX otherwise. The program should preserve the contents of register AX, that is, after the program has been run the contents of AX should be the same as at the beginning.

3.2 Storing and retrieving data from memory

Until now our programs have only used some of the 8086-family registers and flags. Any 'real' program will necessitate the use of memory to store (possibly large amounts of) data. Data can be transferred from memory into a register one or two bytes at a time. The instruction

```
MOV AL,[10H]
```

will transfer the contents of location 10H into register AL whereas the instruction

```
MOV BX,[20H]
```

will transfer the contents of locations 20H and 21H into BX. The symbol `[20H]` is read as 'the contents of location 20H' to distinguish between

`MOV AL,20H` (put the hexadecimal number 20H in AL)

and

`MOV AL,[20H]` (put the contents of location 20H in AL)

Storing data in memory can also be done one or two bytes at a time. `MOV [20H],CL` would copy the contents of register CL into location 20H; `MOV [20H],DX` would copy the contents of register DX into locations 20H and 21H.

If register AX contained 2A8BH and the instruction

```
MOV [20H],AX
```

were executed, location 20H would contain 8BH and location 21H would contain 2AH. It is rarely the case that the programmer needs to be aware of

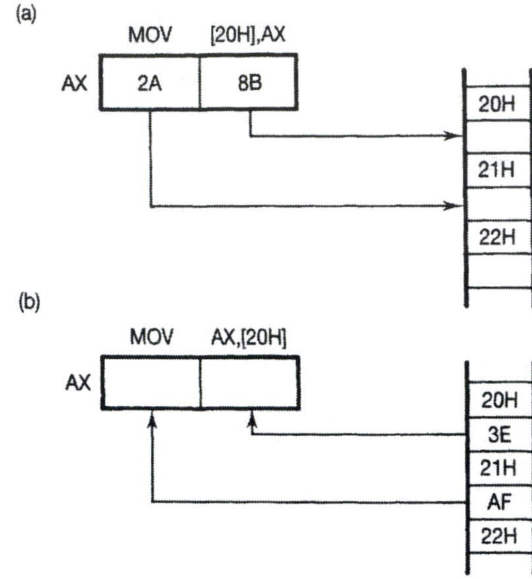

Figure 3.1 Storing data in memory:
(a) `MOV [20H],AX`
(b) `MOV AX,[20H]`.

this as moving data the other way – from memory to register – reverses this 'swap', as in Figure 3.1.

3.2.1 Changing addresses

Varying an address while a program is running involves specifying the location concerned in a register. The following program adds 1 to each of the 8-bit numbers stored in locations 200H–202H inclusive. At the core of the program is the instruction

```
MOV AL,[BX]
```

which moves into AL the contents of the location whose address is given in register BX, and its counterpart

```
MOV [BX],AL
```

which saves what is in register AL as the contents of the location whose address is given in BX.

The program will work by repeating the same basic group of instructions three times – once each for locations 200H, 201H and 202H. In order to count the number of repeats, we shall use CX to record the number of repetitions left to be done. At the beginning of the program, CX will be initialized to 3 therefore. After execution of the basic group of instructions, we shall arrange to have CX reduced by 1 by using the

```
DEC CX
```

instruction. DEC can be used in a similar form with any of the 16-bit general-purpose registers AX, BX, CX or DX and their 8-bit constituent registers. On

			Location		
AL	BX	CX	200H	201H	202H
?	200	?	2A	B4	51
?	200	3	2A	B4	51
2A	200	3	2A	B4	51
2B	200	3	2A	B4	51
2B	200	3	2B	B4	51
2B	201	3	2B	B4	51
2B	201	2	2B	B4	51
B4	201	2	2B	B4	51
B5	201	2	2B	B4	51
B5	201	2	2B	B5	51
B5	202	2	2B	B5	51
B5	202	1	2B	B5	51
51	202	1	2B	B5	51
52	202	1	2B	B5	51
52	202	1	2B	B5	52
52	203	1	2B	B5	52
52	203	0	2B	B5	52

Figure 3.2
Trace of program to increment the contents of locations 200H–202H by 1.

execution, the contents of the named register are decremented by 1.

The program now follows. Once again this is not necessarily the best or easiest way of going about the task – the choice of instructions has been dominated by the desire to explain.

```
            MOV BX,200H     ;BX will specify the location to
                            ;be worked on
            MOV CX,3H       ;CX will maintain a count of how
                            ;many more locations to be done
ALTER_NEXT: MOV AL,[BX]
            INC AL
            MOV [BX],AL     ;the preceding three instructions
                            ;add 1 to the contents of the
                            ;location whose address is given
                            ;in BX
            INC BX          ;advance BX to the next location
            DEC CX          ;one less location to be done
                            ;now
            JNZ ALTER_NEXT  ;do some more unless none left
                            ;to do
```

Assuming that before this program is run locations 200H–202H have the contents

Location	200H	201H	202H
Contents	2A	B4	51

then a trace of the execution of the program will look like Figure 3.2.

There are corresponding instructions whereby two bytes are moved instead of one. For example

```
MOV AX,[BX]
```

transfers two bytes, one from the location whose address is given in register BX and one from the location after that.

BX is different from AX, CX and DX

There is no equivalent of the [BX] part of instructions like

```
MOV CX,[BX]
```

for registers AX, CX and DX. For example,

```
MOV CX,[DX] ;is illegal
```

is not allowed because of the [DX]. Only register BX may be used in this way.

EXERCISE

3.4 What will be the contents of locations 200H, 201H, 202H and 203H after execution of each of the following program fragments (use ? to describe a value which is unknown):

(a)
```
MOV AL,6
MOV AH,5
MOV BX,0ABDCH
MOV [200H],AX
MOV [202H],BX
```

(b)
```
MOV AX,43BCH
MOV BX,0FE01H
MOV [200H],AX
MOV [202H],BX
MOV AL,[201H]
MOV BL,[203H]
MOV CL,BL
MOV BL,AL
MOV AL,CL
MOV [201H],AL
MOV [203H],BL
```

(c)
```
MOV CX,34H
MOV [201H],CX
MOV DX,808H
MOV [202H],DX
MOV AX,[201H]
ADD AX,14H
MOV [200H],AX
```

(d)
```
MOV BX,200H
MOV AX,2A3BH
MOV [BX],AX
MOV CX,[BX]
ADD AX,CX
ADD BX,2
MOV [BX],CX
```

3.3 Programs which affect memory – some examples

Example 1

A program to swap the contents of locations 20H and 21H is:

```
MOV AL,[20H]
MOV BL,[21H]
MOV [20H],BL
MOV [21H],AL
```

Example 2

A program to store 0 in locations 200H–300H inclusive. (This is part of a technique used to test if the memory chips in a microcomputer are working properly. Every location is filled with 0 and then after a fraction of a second pause the contents of each location are checked to verify they are still set at 0. If not, then one of the chips is malfunctioning.)

Since locations 200H–300H inclusive are to be filled, there are 101H locations to fill. (Compare this with being asked to deliver mail to addresses 0 to 7 – if you do, you'll visit eight houses in total.)

```
            MOV BX,200H     ;BX records the address of the next
                            ;location to be done
            MOV CX,101H     ;CX will keep a count of the
                            ;number of locations left to do
DO_ANOTHER: MOV [BX],0H     ;fill the location
            INC BX          ;move on to the next address
            DEC CX          ;one less to do now
            JNZ DO_ANOTHER
```

Example 3

Count the number of occurrences of a given 16-bit number and leave this count in register DX. If locations 200H–24FH inclusive contain 28H 16-bit numbers (that is, 28H numbers having 4 hexadecimal digits), the program in Figure 3.3 will count the number of them which are equal to 0127H.

In order to give part of a trace for the program we will assume that the contents of locations 200H–205H are as follows:

Location	200	201	202	203	204	205
Contents	2A	B5	27	01	6C	1B

Thus, as far as the 8086-family microprocessor is concerned, the 16-bit number in locations 200H and 201H is 0B52AH; that in 202H and 203H is 0127H; and that in 204H and 205H is 1B6CH.

Example 4

Making a total of 16-bit numbers stored in memory. If locations 500H to 54FH contain 28H 16-bit numbers, the program below will add up these numbers and leave the total in register AX.

The program makes use of the instruction

```
ADD AX,[BX]
```

which takes the two bytes stored starting at the address given in register BX as

		AX	BX	CX	DX
	MOV BX,200H	?	200	?	?
	MOV CX,28H	?	200	28	?
	MOV DX,0	?	200	28	0
NEXTLOC:	MOV AX,[BX]	B52A	200	28	0
	SUB AX,127H	B403	200	28	0
	JNZ MISSING_COUNT				
	INC DX	B403	201	28	0
MISSING_COUNT:	INC BX	B403	202	28	0
	INC BX	B403	202	27	0
	DEC CX	0127	202	27	0
	JZ DONE	0	202	27	0
	JMP NEXTLOC	0	202	27	1
DONE:					
		0	203	27	1
		0	204	27	1
		0	204	26	1
		1B6C	204	26	1
		1A45	204	26	1
		1A45	205	26	1
		1A45	206	26	1
		1A45	206	25	1
			.		
			.		
			.		

Figure 3.3
Program and trace to count occurrences of 16-bit numbers.

a 16-bit number (stored with its least significant byte in the lower address, the most significant byte in the higher address) and then adds that number to the contents of register AX leaving the answer in AX.

Before:			*Location*	*Location*
	AX	BX	2011	2012
	0115	2011	3A	1B
After:			*Location*	*Location*
	AX	BX	2011	2012
	1C4F	2011	3A	1B

(since 0115H + 1B3AH = 1C4FH)

In order that a partial trace of the execution of the totalling program (Figure 3.4) can be given we assume that the contents of locations 500H–505H before execution are as follows:

Location	500	501	502	503	504	505
Contents	00	01	00	01	E2	00

		AX	BX	CX
	MOV AX,0	0	?	?
	MOV BX,500H	0	500	?
	MOV CX,28H	0	500	28
ADD_IN_NEXT:	ADD AX,[BX]	100	500	28
	INC BX			
	INC BX	100	501	28
	DEC CX	100	502	28
	JNZ ADD_IN_NEXT	100	502	27
		200	502	27
		200	503	27
		200	504	27
		200	504	26
		2E2	504	26
		2E2	505	26
		2E2	506	26
		2E2	506	25
			.	
			.	
			.	

Figure 3.4 Program (and trace) to total 16-bit numbers stored in memory.

					Memory locations					
		BX	AX	CX	200	201	202	203	204	205
	MOV BX,200H	200	?	?	?	?	?	?	?	?
	MOV AX,0H	200	0	?	?	?	?	?	?	?
	MOV CX,101H	200	0	100	?	?	?	?	?	?
NEXT_LOC:	MOV [BX],AX	200	0	100	0	0	?	?	?	?
	INC BX									
	INC BX	201	0	100	0	0	?	?	?	?
	INC AX	202	0	100	0	0	?	?	?	?
	INC AX	202	1	100	0	0	?	?	?	?
	DEC CX	202	2	100	0	0	?	?	?	?
	JNZ NEXT_LOC	202	2	0FF	0	0	?	?	?	?
		202	2	0FF	0	0	2	0	?	?
		203	2	0FF	0	0	2	0	?	?
		204	2	0FF	0	0	2	0	?	?
		204	3	0FF	0	0	2	0	?	?
		204	4	0FF	0	0	2	0	?	?
		204	4	0FE	0	0	2	0	?	?
		204	4	0FE	0	0	2	0	4	0
					.					
					.					
					.					

Figure 3.5 Program and trace storing 16-bit numbers in memory.

Example 5

The next example is rather academic but illustrates how 16-bit numbers are stored in memory. The program will store 0H as a 16-bit number in locations 200H,201H; 2H in locations 202H,203H; 4H in locations 204H,205H; and so on, up until 200H has been stored in 400H and 401H (Figure 3.5).

EXERCISE

3.5 Write 8086-family assembly language program fragments to achieve each of the following tasks.

(a) Fill locations 200H, 202H, 204H,. . .,300H inclusive with the 8-bit unsigned number 0FFH.

(b) Swap the contents of location 200H with those of location 300H, those of 201H with 2FFH, and so on. Thus:

	Location	*Contents*		*Location*	*Contents*
	200	2A		200	3F
	201	56		201	AB
	.	.		.	.
Before	.	.	*After*	.	.
	2FF	AB		2FF	56
	300	3F		300	2A

(c) Count the number of locations in the range 200H–300H inclusive which contain the ASCII code for the letter X.

(d) Locations 200H–03FFH inclusive contain 100H 16-bit numbers. Leave in register AX the number of them which are equal to 1984H.

(e) Store

500H in locations 200H,201H
4FEH in locations 202H,203H
4FCH in locations 204H,205H
.
.
.
400H in locations 300H,301H

3.4 The code and data segment registers

Recall from Section 2.2 that the machine code version of a program is stored in a segment in memory which we call the code segment. Usually, the operating system decides exactly where in memory this code segment should be. While we can override the operating system's decision and specify precisely where in memory our program is to be stored, for our purposes we shall be very glad of the operating system's help. This is also the case regarding the storage of any data which a machine code program needs, for (provided we don't object) the operating system will also choose where our data segment should be.

By leaving the location of our programs and data to it, we can be sure that we still have easy access to all the utilities that the operating system provides. These include several easily exploitable ready-made routines, for example, to read a character from the keyboard and print a character on the display screen (see Chapter 4). However, we do need to understand the mechanism by which members of the 8086 family access instructions and data from wherever they have been stored in memory.

Members of the 8086 family have four 16-bit registers called **segment registers** which form an essential part of this mechanism. These are the **Code Segment** (CS), **Data Segment** (DS), **Stack Segment** (SS) and **Extra Segment** (ES) registers. Their purposes can be roughly summarized as follows:

- CS used to access the memory segment containing program *instructions*.
- DS used to access the memory segment containing *data items* knowing the exact whereabouts of which is crucial to the program's design.
- SS used to access the memory segment containing *working memory* in which the precise location of a temporary data item (perhaps used as an intermediary step in some complicated calculation) is not crucial to the design of the program.
- ES used during the *manipulation of sequences of characters* by special 8086-family instructions.

Later chapters will explain more about the SS and ES registers: for now we concentrate on CS and DS.

3.4.1 Offsets within segments referred to by segment registers

The segment registers are thus titled because they specify the segment to which a particular object belongs. It follows that an offset within that segment must also be given in order to specify the complete memory address of that object (see Section 2.2).

Table 3.1 Specifying offsets in relation to segment registers.

Object	*Segment given by*	*Offset given by*
instruction	CS	IP
program data item	DS	explicitly or in BX, SI or DI
working storage item	SS	SP or BP
member of character sequence	ES	DI

For instructions the offset is given by a 16-bit register called the **Instruction Pointer** (IP) register. At any instant in time, the complete address of the next instruction to be executed is specified by the contents of CS (its segment) and the contents of IP (its offset within that segment).

The offset of data items may be specified by values given explicitly in the program, by the contents of BX, or by the contents of two other 16-bit registers: SI and DI (see Sections 8.2, 10.6 and 11.1). Among other things, SI and DI are used to index the elements of arrays and for string manipulation.

Items for which the segment is specified by SS can have their offset specified by two 16-bit registers, SP and BP (see Sections 8.3 and 8.7), and in other ways. When ES is used to give the segment address of sequences of characters, DI is used for the offset address. Table 3.1 summarizes this information.

During normal execution of a program, instructions are automatically fetched from memory so, as programmers, we generally do not have to worry about the particular values of CS and IP, or indeed, about the actual values of any of the segment registers. And, for the time being, the *precise* purpose of SI,DI,SP and BP will not concern us: these registers will feature large in later chapters.

3.4.2 Arrangement of registers inside the execution and bus interface units

Apart from the 8086-family registers we have already mentioned, the Execution Unit (EU) contains a set of circuits which actually carry out the arithmetic: the Arithmetic and Logic Unit (the ALU). Consequently registers which are frequently involved in arithmetic operations, such as AX, BX, CX and DX, are located there. As was pointed out in Chapter 2, it is the job of the Bus Interface Unit (BIU) to determine instruction and data memory addresses. It follows that the segment registers are located there, as shown in Figure 3.6.

3.4.3 Accessing the next instruction in the code segment

Even though the actual order in which the instructions in a program are executed is arranged automatically by the microprocessor, it will be important later for the reader to have an understanding of the mechanism used. As was

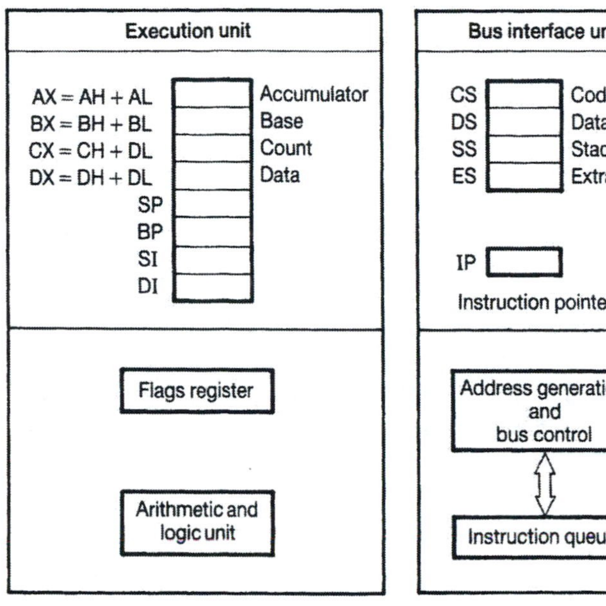

Figure 3.6 Location of registers within the BIU and EU.

mentioned above, the address of any program instruction is specified via CS (segment) and IP (offset). Given:

Contents of CS: 3B12H   Contents of IP: 12EFH

we can determine the precise location in memory of the next instruction to be executed from the addition:

```
3B120H
 12EFH
------
3C40FH
------
```

which indicates that it begins at location 3C40FH.

Different instructions may vary in length. For example, `INC AX` consists of just one byte whereas `MOV AX,[100H]` consists of three bytes. To be explicit, let us consider execution of the following program fragment by the 8086 microprocessor:

```
.
.
.
INC DX
MOV AX,[100H]
INC AX
.
.
.
```

and assume that somehow we have discovered that it is stored in memory as follows:

```
.
.
.
1023:20AA INC DX
1023:20AB MOV AX,[100H]
1023:20AE INC AX
.
.
.
```

Now let us focus attention on what happens just before execution of the MOV AX,[100H] instruction. Once INC DX has been moved into the instruction queue within the BIU, CS and IP will have been set to 1023H and 20ABH respectively. During execution of INC DX (or, possibly, even earlier) the three bytes of the MOV instruction will be moved into the instruction queue within the BIU and IP advanced to point to the next instruction in sequence, INC AX at 1023:20AEH. IP will therefore be set to 20AEH and as soon as it is possible, the INC AX instruction will be fetched from memory and put into the instruction queue in the BIU.

Once execution of INC DX is complete, execution of MOV AX,[100H] will commence. Since the MOV cannot be executed until the contents of location 100H is fetched from memory, fetching this data item will take priority over any further instruction fetches necessary to keep the instruction queue filled.

3.4.4 Addressing data items in memory

At this point we have to admit to telling a little white lie in respect of instructions which address memory; or at least not telling the whole truth. In fact, the actual address from which data is fetched when an instruction like

```
MOV AL,[200H]
```

is obeyed is not location 200H but *location 200H relative to the contents of the data segment register.* Any explicit address specified in an 8086-family instruction is, in fact, taken relative to the DS register's contents.

To see how this works out, suppose the DS register contains 0500H. The actual whereabouts of the byte which will be moved into AL on execution of the instruction:

```
MOV AL,[200H]
```

can be calculated as follows:

1.	Add a zero to the right-hand side of the contents of the DS register.	5000H
2.	Add to that the address given.	200H
	Total	5200H

Thus, the actual location accessed by the `MOV AL,[200H]` instruction is 5200H in this case.

Loading the DS register (or any of the segment registers) cannot be done in the same way as loading registers like AX, BX, CX or DX. *DS must be loaded indirectly*. Thus,

```
MOV BX,500H
MOV DS,BX
```

would set the DS register to 500H.

In the following program fragment, the right-hand column shows in parentheses the actual location(s) addressed by each instruction in hexadecimal.

```
MOV BX,1275H
MOV DS,BX
MOV AX,5H
MOV DX,17H
MOV BH,[100H]   (12750 + 100  = 12850)
MOV BL,[30H]    (12750 +  30  = 12780)
MOV BX,DX
MOV CX,[BX]     (12750 +  17  = 12767 and
                 12750 +  18  = 12768)
ADD BX,CX
ADD AX,BX
MOV [75H],AX    (12750 +  75  = 127C5 and
                 12750 +  76  = 127C6)
MOV [204H],BL   (12750 + 204  = 12954)
MOV [31A5H],BH  (12750 + 31A5 = 158F5)
```

However, usually the computer's operating system sets the DS register to a suitable value before a program is run. In absolute terms, it (the operating system!) decides where in memory to locate both our programs and data. By setting the DS register with a `MOV` instruction like the one above it is possible to insist on using a collection of specific locations for data but it is rare that one wants to do this. On the contrary, with our knowledge of the 8086 family in its present state we are only too grateful for all the help the operating system can provide.

EXERCISE

3.6 In the following program fragments, some of the instructions transfer data between registers or move a number into a register whereas others involve the transfer of data to and from memory. For each instruction involving a transfer of data to or from memory, make a list of the actual absolute 20-bit memory address(es) used for each data transfer.

(a)
```
MOV CX,23ABH
MOV DS,CX
MOV AX,[31AH]
MOV BX,[34BH]
ADD AX,BC
ADD AX,CX
MOV [33BH],AX
```

(b)
```
MOV DX,0ABCDH
MOV DS,DX
MOV AL,[2DEH]
MOV BL,[2FFH]
DEC BL
DEC AL
ADD AL,BL
MOV [3DFH],AL
MOV AH,BL
MOV [222H],AX
```

3.7 Given the following program fragment stored in the locations specified:

```
BC1A:0000 ADD AX,3
BC1A:0003 INC AX
BC1A:0004 MOV DX,AX
BC1A:0006 SUB DX,3
BC1A:0009 MUL DX
BC1A:000B ADD AX,DX
```

and assuming that prior to its execution by the 8086 microprocessor (in which the BIU instruction queue has length six bytes) the operating system has set the contents of CS to 0BC1AH and IP to 0000H, make a trace of the execution of the program in which the sequence of values of CS and IP are carefully recorded and show the contents of the BIU instruction queue at each stage.

3.5 Defining segments in an assembly language program

The most common assembler for 8086-family assembly language is called **MASM**. It requires that every program should have at least three segments: a data segment, a stack segment to provide working storage, and a code segment.

When any computer program is executed, both the program and any necessary data must be in memory. MASM gives the programmer absolute control over the memory so that exactly where both program and data are stored is the programmer's choice. Normally one would have the program and data stored in completely separate areas of memory so that there is less chance of the program interfering with the data. There are occasions, however, where program and data can be mixed to advantage and it is to allow for this possibility that MASM insists that code and data segments in an assembly language program be clearly labeled.

3.5.1 Stacks: providing working storage

Most large programs require temporary working storage and for members of the 8086 family this is provided by means of a **stack**. A stack is a storage structure in which data items are stored in memory on a last-in, first-out basis, rather like the storage of plates in a cafeteria plate dispenser (see Figure 3.7). Items can be stored on the stack and retrieved from it during program execution without reference to any particular addresses.

Figure 3.7 The operation of a cafeteria plate dispenser models that of a stack: the plates are removed in the reverse order from that in which they were inserted.

Selection of stack size depends on the particular program. All the programs in this book will be adequately served by a 100H word stack which we shall conventionally allocate in a **stack segment**.

3.5.2 Telling the assembler which segments are which

Data segments, stack segments and code segments are distinguished by including assembler **pseudo-ops** in the assembly language program. These are not 8086-family instructions. Rather they are instructions to the assembler itself to assist it in its task of converting assembly language to machine code. Thus the pseudo-ops `SEGMENT. . .ENDS` tell MASM that everything which they enclose belongs to the same segment. In addition, each segment must be given a name:

<*my_segment_name*> `SEGMENT`

.

.

.

<*my_segment_name*> `ENDS`

Thus, for example,

```
MYPROGRAM SEGMENT
        MOV AX,4H
```

```
        SUB AX,5H
           .
           .
           .
MYPROGRAM ENDS
```

could be the bare bones of a code segment with name MYPROGRAM.

The programmer is free to make up <*my_segment_name*> subject to similar restrictions to those on jump label names in Section 3.1. In this book we shall adopt a convention that our data segment will be called DATA, our stack segment WORKING_STORAGE, and the code segment CODE. Thus, the instructions in our programs will be written between CODE SEGMENT and CODE ENDS pseudo-ops.

We shall call the stack segment in our programs the WORKING_STORAGE segment. The stack segment in a program must be clearly marked for the assembler by means of the STACK pseudo-op which must be appended to the WORKING_STORAGE SEGMENT pseudo-op. Thus, the working store in our programs will be achieved by:

```
WORKING_STORAGE SEGMENT STACK
   DW 100H DUP(?)
WORKING_STORAGE ENDS
```

The stack segment of our programs will have addresses relative to the SS register because 8086-family instructions which operate on the stack (see Chapter 8) use SS to calculate the corresponding actual addresses (which, as we have observed, the programmer does not need to know about during normal execution).

MASM must also be told to which segment register a named segment belongs. This is achieved via the ASSUME pseudo-op. Hence, if our program had segments called MYDATA, MYSTACK and MYPROGRAM then:

```
ASSUME DS:MYDATA
ASSUME SS:MYSTACK
ASSUME CS:MYPROGRAM
```

would inform MASM that the DS register must be used for address calculation in the MYDATA segment (that is, MYDATA is a data segment), that the SS register must be used for address calculation in the MYSTACK segment (that is, MYSTACK is a stack segment) and that the CS register must be used to calculate all addresses in the MYPROGRAM segment (that is, MYPROGRAM is a code segment). The alternative form:

```
ASSUME DS:MYDATA,SS:MYSTACK,CS:MYPROGRAM
```

has the same effect.

Following our naming convention, we want DS associated with DATA, SS with WORKING_STORAGE and CS with CODE. This is arranged by using the ASSUME pseudo-op as follows:

```
ASSUME DS:DATA,SS:WORKING_STORAGE,CS:CODE
```

which is included as the first line of the code segment:

```
CODE SEGMENT
ASSUME DS:DATA,SS:WORKING_STORAGE,CS:CODE
    .  <———————— The 8086-family instructions
    .            to perform the required
    .            task go here
CODE ENDS
```

Throughout this book, we will adopt a conventional format for our assembly language programs which incorporates this code segment proforma. Thus, our programs will conventionally take the shape shown in Figure 3.8.

```
DATA SEGMENT
  .
  .  <———————— Definitions of data items
  .              go here
DATA ENDS

WORKING_STORAGE SEGMENT STACK
  .
  .  <———————— This program's requirement for
  .              working storage goes here
WORKING_STORAGE ENDS

CODE SEGMENT
ASSUME DS:DATA,SS:WORKING_STORAGE,CS:CODE
    .  <———————— The 8086-family instructions
    .              to perform the required
    .              task go here
CODE ENDS
```

Figure 3.8 The conventional format to be used for an assembly language program in this book.

SUMMARY

Jump instructions allow us to alter the flow of control during program execution. The chapter began with an informal introduction to three of the 8086-family jump instructions: JZ, JNZ and JMP. Chapter 7 contains a more detailed consideration of jump instructions.

We also saw that data can be transferred between registers and memory by means of versions of the MOV instruction which, among others, can take one of the forms:

(a) MOV *register_name*, [*n*]

(b) MOV [*n*],*register_name*

where *n* is a 16-bit unsigned number specifying an offset relative to the DS segment register and thus determining a unique location in memory. If the *register_name* refers to one of the 8-bit registers, the contents of that location is copied into the named register (format (a)), or the contents of the named register copied into that location (format (b)).

If a 16-bit *register_name* is employed then, in format (a), the 16-bit data item to be moved into the register is constructed from the contents of the uniquely determined memory location (let us call this *m*) and the following one ($m + 1$). The contents of location *m* goes into the eight lower order bits of the 16-bit register, and the contents of $m + 1$ into the eight higher order bits. With format (b) the lower order eight bits of the register go into location *m* and the higher order eight bits go into location $m + 1$.

The `MOV` instruction formats:

(c) `MOV` *register_name*,`[BX]`

(d) `MOV [BX]`,*register_name*

can be used to access memory in a similar way by setting the contents of BX to the offset of the required address. Thus, if BX contains the 16-bit offset *n*, instructions in the above two formats will be executed in an equivalent way to:

`MOV` *register_name*,[*n*]
`MOV` [*n*],*register_name*

respectively. BX is special in this respect, however, for there are no equivalents of (c) and (d) involving AX, CX or DX.

The segment registers CS, DS, SS and ES determine the segment to which an address used in one of the above instructions corresponds. Segment registers are given values automatically by DOS, but we can override this if we wish. However, segment registers cannot be loaded with a value directly.

In order that the segment registers can be correctly associated with instructions and data in our assembly language programs, the assembly language programs in this book will usually conform to a conventional layout which was described in Section 3.4. It is possible to use other layouts – indeed the MASM manual recommends a much simpler looking format – but we have chosen ours as the best compromise between ease of use and scope for illustration of 8086-family assembly language features.

SELF-CHECK QUIZ

1. Which of the following are valid label names and which are not? For those which are not, give a reason.

   (a) MUL

   (b) TESTING&CHECKING

   (c) ZERO CHECK

   (d) 12_STEPS_LEFT_TO_GO

   (e) PRICES_IN_$

   (f) PPPPPPPPPPP

2. What would be the contents of locations 200H, 201H, . . ., 210H after execution of the following program fragment:

```
      MOV CX,200
      MOV AX,32ABH
NEXT: MOV BX,CX
      MOV [BX],AX
      INC AX
      INC BX
      MOV [BX],AX
      MOV CX,BX
      SUB BX,210H
      JNZ NEXT
```

3. Given that the contents of locations 200H and 201H are 4AH and 8FH respectively, what will be the contents of the specified register or memory location(s) after execution of the following instructions?

   (a) AX, after `MOV AX,[200H]`

   (b) AH after `MOV AX,10AH`
   `ADD [200H],AX`

   (c) locations 200H and 201H after

```
MOV AX,[200H]
MOV BL,AL
MOV AL,AH
MOV AH,BL
MOV [200H],AX
```

4. Why are segment registers necessary in an 8086-family microprocessor? Could segment registers be dispensed with entirely or, if not, how could we provide the facilities they provide without using segment registers?

5. What would be the advantages of having more segment registers? What would be the disadvantages?

6. Write an 8086-family assembly language fragment that would fill a complete segment of memory (the data segment?) with zeros.

7. Given that owing to previous instructions, locations 300H to 600H inclusive contain either 0 or 1, write an assembly language fragment which will set AL to 0 if the number of locations containing a 1 is even or to 0FFH if it is odd.

8. If DS contains 3AB5H, which absolute location(s) in memory will be addressed by each of the following:

   (a) `MOV BX,2AB1H`
   `MOV CL,[BX]`

   (b) `MOV BX,1A9CH`
   `ADD AX,[BX]`

9. How would you arrange for a 250H byte stack to be included in an assembly language program?

10. Explain the positioning of registers within the execution unit and bus interface unit. Why do you think the 8086-family designers arranged things the way they are?

4

Assembling, Linking and Running Programs

Contents

The ultimate aim of this chapter is to demonstrate how to have an assembly language program converted to machine code and executed by the host 8086-family based microcomputer. The process will be illustrated by means of a specific example program, namely one which turns the computer into a very simple adding machine. But there is much to describe before even this is intelligible, so actual program execution is very much the climax of the chapter.

Before that, because we want our very simple adding machine to be able to display a message on the screen and return to DOS control when it has finished, we examine some of the DOS operating system functions, a set of ready-made routines which carry out jobs such as displaying characters on the screen automatically – provided we bring them into action in the appropriate way. One of these will even display a complete message at one go, so long as the message has first been stored in memory. Consequently, the chapter begins by explaining how storage is assigned to fixed items of data (such as a message which is to be displayed repeatedly during the execution of a program) in an assembly language program.

4.1 Allocating storage space

The allocation of storage in an assembly language program is carried out by use of **pseudo-ops**. Pseudo-ops give extra information to the assembler, beyond the raw program instructions for the task to be carried out, which it uses to convert our assembly language into machine code. The main pseudo-op used to allocate storage is the **define** pseudo-op which takes five basic forms:

```
DB    Define Byte
DW    Define Word
DD    Define Doubleword
DQ    Define Quadword
DT    Define Tenbytes
```

These allow, respectively, multiples of one, two, four, eight and ten bytes of storage to be allocated and initialized at one time. Thus:

```
DB 16H   ;allocates one byte of store with initial value 16H

DB ?     ;allocates one byte of store with indeterminate
         ;initial value

DB 'Z'   ;allocates one byte of store with initial value
         ;the ASCII code for the letter Z

DW 1992D ;allocates two bytes of storage, 1992D
         ;being automatically converted into the
         ;signed 16-bit form (07C8H) and the two bytes
         ;initialized to that value consistent with the
         ;low-order byte in the lowest memory address
         ;principle described in Chapter 3:

              address    n    n+1
              contents   C8    07

DD 1294967295D ;allocates four bytes of storage, 1294967295D
               ;being automatically converted into signed
               ;32-bit form and the four bytes
               ;initialized to that value (0FFA12F4DH)
               ;consistent with the low-order
               ;byte in the lowest memory address
               ;principle described in Chapter 3:

              address    n    n+1    n+2    n+3
              contents   4D    2F     A1     FF
```

If several define pseudo-ops are used one after another, then consecutive memory locations are allocated for the objects defined. Thus, given the sequence:

```
DB 14H
DW 1000D
```

```
DB 'H'
DB 'E'
DB 'L'
DB 'L'
DB 'O'
DW 10D
```

if the first value (14H) is stored in location 200H relative to DS (say) then the contents of the ten locations 200H, 201H, to 209H will be as follows (all values are hexadecimal):

Location	200	201	202	203	204	205	206	207	208	209
Contents	14	E8	03	48	45	4C	4C	4F	0A	00

since 1000D = 03E8H, 10D = 000AH, and the ASCII codes for the letters in HELLO are 48H, 45H, 4CH and 4FH respectively.

Abbreviated multiple definitions are also permissible. Thus:

```
DB 21H,45H,73H, 'A' , 'B' ,11H, 'Z'
```

allocates seven bytes, with initial values determined just as if seven separate DB pseudo-ops had been used one after the other:

```
DB 21H
DB 45H
DB 73H
DB 'A'
DB 'B'
DB 11H
DB 'Z'
```

Similarly,

```
DB 'HELLO'
```

allocates five bytes of storage in exactly the same way as:

```
DB 'H'
DB 'E'
DB 'L'
DB 'L'
DB 'O'
```

and

```
DW 1,10,100,1000,10000
```

allocates ten bytes of storage, initialized to the signed 16-bit forms of 1D, 10D, 100D, 1000D and 10000D.

Note that:

```
DB 'ALL GOOD MEN'
```

is equivalent to:

```
DB 'A','L','L',' ','G',. . .
```

so that the fourth and ninth bytes allocated will be initialized to the ASCII code for a space, namely 20H.

The DUP(. . .) pseudo-op permits multiple initializations to the same value. Thus we have:

```
DB 10H DUP('A')    ;allocates the next 10H locations with
                   ;initial value 41H (the ASCII code for
                   ;the letter A)

DB 80H DUP(?)      ;allocates the next 80H locations with
                   ;initial value indeterminate

DW 50H DUP(100D)   ;the next 50H words are set to 0064H (the
                   ;signed 16-bit form of 100D)
```

4.1.1 Common confusions about storage allocations

There are three very common pitfalls in understanding how storage allocation is made in 8086-family assembly language. Consider the program fragment:

```
DATA SEGMENT
    MY_BYTE   DB 32H
    MY_DIGITS DB '3','2'
        .
        .
        .
```

The first thing to emphasize is that in associating offsets with the corresponding memory locations for our data, MASM starts at *zero*. Thus, the offset of MY_BYTE from the start of the DATA segment will be zero. Moreover,

```
MY_BYTE DB 32H
```

reserves just a *single* byte of store (containing 00110010B = 32H) and *not* two. Lastly,

```
MY_DIGITS DB '3','2'
```

reserves *two* bytes of store containing 00110011B = 33H and 00110010B = 32H respectively – the ASCII codes for the digits 3 and 2. To summarize, as a result of the above DATA segment pseudo-ops, storage will be allocated as shown in Figure 4.1.

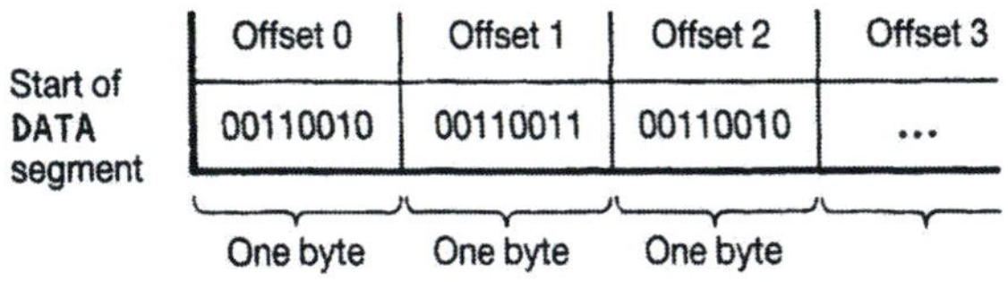

Figure 4.1 Allocation of storage as a result of certain DATA segment pseudo-ops.

Start of DATA segment	Offset 0	Offset 1	Offset 2	Offset 3
	00110010	00110011	00110010	...
	One byte	One byte	One byte	

EXERCISES

4.1 How many bytes in total are defined by the following groups of define pseudo-ops:

(a)
```
DB 13H DUP('%')
DB 'SYNTAX ERROR$'
DW 1991,1992,1993,1994
```

(b)
```
DW 150H DUP(?)
DD 1,10,100,1000,10000,100000,1000000
```

4.2 If the first location which is to be used to store the data items defined in the following sequence of define pseudo-ops has offset 200H relative to DS, complete the table:

Location	200	201 . . .
Contents	41	41 . . .

showing the outcome of these definitions.

```
DB 'AA.BBB,CCC','h','e','l','l','o',24H
DW 1024,2048,65535
DW 5 DUP(1066D)
```

4.3 Give suitable define pseudo-ops to initialize a group of locations to specify each of the months in the year in calendar order by means of:

(a) the name of the month (using the same fixed number of bytes for each such name); and
(b) an unsigned 8-bit number representing the number of days in the month.

4.2 Accessing data items in assembly language programs

4.2.1 Specifying addresses

In a large payroll program written in Pascal it is better to declare the rates of tax as constants at the beginning of the program and then refer to them via the corresponding variable names rather than to use the actual values. For then, if the tax rates change (as they inevitably will!), updating the program would simply involve changes to the dozen or so constant declarations rather than searching through the entire 30 000 lines of Pascal for every occurrence of a tax rate (and quite possibly missing several of them).

Similarly, having written a large assembly language program which makes some complicated calculations based on the contents of a certain group of memory locations, if we avoid using actual numeric addresses in the program itself, changing the program to work on a different group of locations will be much easier. Consequently, 8086-family assembly language does not allow addresses of the form [200] as in the perfectly valid instruction MOV

AX,[200] – all addresses must be represented by **variables** which are assigned to the locations to which they refer in the appropriate segment of the program.

To see how this is done in practice, suppose we wish to store two very simple messages in memory ready to be output to the display screen. If the messages are Y and N (for Yes and No) then we allocate storage using DB as above:

```
DB 'Y'
DB 'N'
```

In this case, it does not matter which actual memory locations are used to store the message since it makes no difference to the outcome we are after (provided, of course, that the message is not stored so that it interferes with either DOS or our program). Since it is quite sufficient to have a name by which to refer to them we assign a **variable name** to each DB statement:

```
AFFIRM_MESSAGE DB 'Y'
DENY_MESSAGE   DB 'N'
```

Notice the difference between a label (which ends with a colon) and a variable (which does not). Otherwise names for variables and labels are constructed in exactly the same way.

This variable name may subsequently be used (rather than an actual address inside [and]) to refer to the location in which each message is stored. Thus:

```
MOV AL,AFFIRM_MESSAGE
```

will load AL with the ASCII code for the letter Y. Similarly, to overwrite the Y which stands for Yes with a J standing for the German 'Ja' we could use:

```
MOV AL,4AH              ; the ASCII code for the letter J
MOV AFFIRM_MESSAGE,AL
```

This is a luxury afforded us by assembly language. During conversion to machine code, the actual address corresponding to AFFIRM_MESSAGE will be worked out and, if we suppose this to be 12AB:9876, then

```
MOV AL,AFFIRM_MESSAGE
```

will be converted into the machine code equivalent of

```
MOV AL,[9876]
```

automatically.

The same idea is used for a longer message such as HAPPY NEW YEAR so that:

```
DEC_31_MESSAGE DB 'HAPPY NEW YEAR'
```

will associate the variable name DEC_31_MESSAGE with the beginning of the message, that is to say, the location in memory in which the ASCII code for the letter H is stored.

4.2.2 Linking data items with the DS register

The definitions made using define statements will most often be given in the data segment definition in our assembly language program. Following our conventional layout, the data segment of an assembly language program containing our definitions of AFFIRM_MESSAGE and DENY_MESSAGE, the message 'Good morning readers' and the signed 16-bit forms of 1066 and 1984 would be written:

```
DATA SEGMENT
AFFIRM_MESSAGE  DB 'Y'
DENY_MESSAGE    DB 'N'
                DB 'Good morning readers'
                DW 1066
                DW 1984
DATA ENDS
```

4.2.3 Establishing data segment addressability

If a program uses items of data stored in a data segment, the DS register must be set to the value DOS chooses for that data segment before execution can commence. The start of the data segment of a program which follows our naming conventions is easily accessed since the segment name DATA has the relevant address as one of its attributes. We need simply make sure that the sequence:

```
MOV AX,DATA
MOV DS,AX
```

is executed before any data is transferred to or from the data segment defined in DATA.

4.2.4 OFFSET

There are occasions when we don't need to access actual addresses but we do need to know such things as the difference between two addresses. For example, this might be the case if we were trying to count the number of locations containing some given letter of the alphabet by subtracting the address of the first location containing the letter from the address of the last location which contains it.

To make this kind of thing possible, associated with each variable are two values: the address of the segment to which the location it denotes belongs, and the offset within that segment. Consequently the assembler can be told to use one of these two numbers in arriving at the machine code form of an instruction. To specify that the offset is what is required we use the pseudo-op OFFSET.

To be explicit about what happens, let us suppose that AFFIRM_MESSAGE in fact corresponds to the actual address 102A:0200 and DENY_MESSAGE to the actual address 102A:0201. Then the assembly language statements:

```
MOV BX,OFFSET AFFIRM_MESSAGE
MOV CX,OFFSET DENY_MESSAGE
```

would load BX with 200H and CX with 201H.

Having now seen how to allocate storage to a message, the next section will show how DOS provides facilities to have such a message printed on the display screen with very little further work on our part.

EXERCISE

4.4 Given:

```
START_DATA  DB 2,3,5,7,11,13,17,19
            DB 1,2,4,8,16,32,64,128
TEST_DATA   DB 11,21,31,41,51,61,71,81
RESULTS     DB 8 DUP(?)
```

and that the location to which the variable START_DATA refers has offset 50H relative to DS, make a trace of the execution of the following program fragment showing clearly the values of all registers and memory locations involved:

```
      MOV DX,OFFSET RESULTS
      MOV CX,OFFSET TEST_DATA
      MOV AH,8
      MOV BX,0
NEXT: ADD BX,OFFSET START_DATA
      MOV AL,[BX]
      SUB BX,OFFSET START_DATA
      ADD BX,CX
      ADD AL,[BX]
      SUB BX,CX
      ADD BX,DX
      MOV [BX],AL
      SUB BX,DX
      INC BX
      DEC AH
      JNZ NEXT
```

4.3 DOS functions

DOS provides a whole range of **functions** which can be brought into action by assembly language programs. These functions work by allowing the programmer to interrupt the normal, line-by-line execution of an assembly language program. It is then possible to branch into the operating system's own machine code instructions. Within the operating system are routines to read a character from the keyboard, print a character on the screen, read some data from a disk, . . . After the execution of one of these routines, control is returned to the program which caused the interruption. Execution then resumes on the usual line-by-line basis.

The 8086-family instruction which allows this to happen is the INT instruction (INT is short for INTerrupt). Altogether 256 different sorts of interruption are allowed so it is necessary to specify which one is required. The interrupt instruction which allows operations such as reading a character from the keyboard, printing a character on the display screen and handling files on disk is number 21H. Other software interrupts are discussed in Chapter 21.

Thus, executing the instruction INT 21H gives you access to a whole range of input and output functions. Specifying which function you want involves putting a code number in register AH. Table 4.1 specifies the effects of more than a dozen of the functions available under software interrupt 21H. Others are listed in Chapter 19.

Table 4.1 Specifications of DOS functions available under software interrupt 21H.

Function number	*Description*	*What it does*
1	Keyboard input	Wait until a character is typed at the keyboard and then put the ASCII code for that character in register AL. Whatever is typed is also printed on the display screen wherever printing last left off. If CTRL-BRK is pressed, an automatic return is made to DOS control.
2	Output on the display screen	Print on the display screen the character whose ASCII code is contained in register DL. The character is displayed immediately after the last character displayed.
3	Asynchronous input	Waits for a character to be input via the asynchronous communications adapter card and places the received character in AL.
4	Asynchronous output	The character in DL is sent to the asynchronous communications adapter card.
5	Print character	The character in DL is sent to the printer.
6	Keyboard input/ character display	If DL = 0FFH, the zero flag is set to 0 if a keyboard character is ready and the character is placed in AL. If no character is available the zero flag is set to 1. No waiting takes place. If DL <> 0FFH the contents of DL are interpreted as ASCII code and the appropriate character is displayed on the screen.
7	Keyboard input/no display	Waits for an input character from the keyboard and, when it arrives, places it in AL. The character is not automatically printed on the

Table 4.1 *(cont.)*

Function number	*Description*	*What it does*
		display screen. CTRL-BRK cannot be used to return to DOS.
8	Keyboard input/no display	As in function 7 except that normal CTRL-BRK service is provided.
9	Display string	Prints a whole series of characters stored in memory starting with the one in the address given in DX (relative to DS). Stop when a memory location containing the ASCII code for a $ sign is encountered. Does not print the $ sign.
A	Read keyboard string	A character string is read into store beginning at the address given in DS:DX. The first byte typed by the user specifies the maximum number of bytes which have been made available for the string and the second byte the length of the string. The actual characters of the string are stored in the third and following bytes of the designated group of locations until either the ENTER key is pressed or one less than the stated maximum number of locations has been filled. If the ENTER key is pressed, then the second byte of the storage pointed to by DS:DX is set to the number of characters read (excluding the ENTER). The last byte of the string is set to CR. Extra characters are ignored and the bell is rung if an overflow condition is about to occur.
B	Keyboard status	AL is set to 0FFH if a character is available from the keyboard. Otherwise AL is set to 0. A check for CTRL-BRK is made.
C	Keyboard buffer clear	The keyboard buffer within the keyboard is cleared, and the `INT 21H` function (only 1,6,7,8 and 0AH are allowed) specified in AL is performed.
4C	Return to DOS	Terminates program execution and returns control to DOS. An 'error level' may be set in AL: for normal use it is best to set AL to 0.

At this stage, the `INT 21H` functions in Table 4.1 which are of most interest to us are function 1 (keyboard input), function 2 (output on the display screen) and function 9 (display string).

The following sequence of instructions causes the microprocessor to wait for a character to be typed at the keyboard and then displays the character that was typed on the display screen and leaves the ASCII code for that character in AL:

```
MOV AH,1 ;specifies function number 1
INT 21H  ;do it
```

Similarly, the following sequence causes the letter A (ASCII code 41H) to be printed on the display screen straight after the last character displayed there:

```
MOV DL,41H ;ASCII code for the letter A
MOV AH,2   ;specifies function number 2
INT 21H    ;do it
```

The combination

MOV DX,*offset relative to DS of starting address of message*
MOV AH,9
INT 21H

will output the characters whose ASCII codes are stored in the locations with the given starting address (relative to the DS register) and following until the ASCII code for a $ sign is encountered. At this point the INTerrupt will cease and execution will continue as normal from the instruction after INT 21H.

Thus, given

```
DATA SEGMENT
  .
  .
  .
DEC_31_MESSAGE DB 'HAPPY NEW YEAR$'
  .
  .
  .
DATA ENDS
```

then the sequence

```
MOV AX,DATA
MOV DS,AX
  .
  .
  .
MOV DX,OFFSET DEC_31_MESSAGE
MOV AH,9
INT 21H
```

will cause HAPPY NEW YEAR to be output on the display screen starting wherever output last finished.

As a final example, the following sequence will turn the computer into a stuttering typewriter. It repeatedly: waits for a lower-case letter a,b,c,. . .,z to be typed at the keyboard, outputs that character on the display screen and then outputs the upper-case equivalent of that letter A,B,C,. . .,Z. To do so it uses the fact that the ASCII codes for lower-case letters are 20H greater than those for upper-case letters (see Appendix I):

```
NEXT_CHARACTER: MOV AH,1          ;read a character into AL
                                  ;(simultaneously
                INT 21H           ;displaying it on the screen)
                SUB AL,20H        ;convert it
                MOV DL,AL         ;display the converted character
                MOV AH,2
                INT 21H
                JMP NEXT_CHARACTER
```

4.3.1 Printing new lines

When using an old-fashioned mechanical typewriter, starting a new line involves two operations; returning the carriage which holds the paper to the beginning of the line (carriage return) and moving the paper up one line (line feed). The display of text on a computer's screen has been designed to emulate this, so taking a new line involves 'printing' the ASCII codes for carriage return (in the table in Appendix I as CR) and line feed (in Appendix I as LF). As with a typewriter, the operations of carriage return and line feed can be done in either order, but there may be problems with some makes of printer if the carriage return is not done first.

The following sequence of instructions therefore outputs the message HI to the display screen followed by a new line:

```
MOV AH,2   ;select output to screen function
MOV DL,48H ;ASCII for H
INT 21H    ;display it

MOV DL,49H ;ASCII for I
INT 21H    ;display it

MOV DL,0DH ;ASCII code for CR
INT 21H    ;do it

MOV DL,0AH ;ASCII code for LF
INT 21H    ;do it
```

EXERCISE

4.5 Write assembly language program fragments using DOS functions and incorporating all necessary pseudo-ops as follows:

(a) The user types any of the characters A,B,. . .,Z and it and the next character in the ASCII code definition (Appendix I) are displayed on the screen followed by a new line. Then the sequence of events is repeated. Thus, if the user types the letters S,T,R,A,N,G,E the resulting display should be:

```
ST
TU
RS
AB
NO
GH
EF
```

(b) The user types one of the digits 1,2 or 3 and the corresponding message in:

```
1 – HELLO
2 – GOODBYE
3 – HAVE A NICE DAY
```

is displayed followed by a new line, and then the sequence of events is repeated. Thus, if the user types 1,3,2 the resulting display should be:

```
1HELLO
3HAVE A NICE DAY
2GOODBYE
```

(c) The user types two digits in the range 0,1,2,3,. . .,9 and then either the character Y or the character N is displayed followed by a new line. If two digits are equal then Y should be displayed, otherwise N should be displayed. Then the sequence of events is repeated. Thus, if the user types 8 ,8 ,4 ,5 the resulting display should be:

```
88Y
45N
```

4.4 Returning to DOS control

Through one particular function of INT 21H, DOS provides a mechanism whereby a program can be called into action in such a way that, when the program has been executed, control can once again be returned to the operating system. All that is required is that function 4CH of INT 21H is called into action with AL set to 0. The following example shows how this can be carried out in a program:

```
MOV AX,4C00H
INT 21H
```

To emphasize: execution of these two instructions terminates the current program and returns control to DOS.

EXERCISES

4.6 Write and test an assembly language program which asks its user to type in a name and then prints out:

```
Roses are red
Violets are blue
How are you
<the name typed in>?
```

and then returns to the operating system.

4.7 Rewrite the programs in Exercise 4.5 so that control returns to the operating system immediately after each task has been carried out rather than looping round again.

4.5 Running assembly language programs

We have already covered enough of the instruction set of the 8086 family to enable the reader to write some powerful programs, but we have yet to describe how to get programs into the computer and actually executed by the machine. When you have written your 8086-family assembly language program, three steps are involved in actually converting the program to machine code and then having it executed in such a way that you can check that it has performed according to plan:

- *Step 1* In order that the assembler knows where to store the program and any data, extra statements will have to be added to the bare 8086-family instructions – as first described in Section 4.4. Having added these extra assembler directives, run the assembler program with your prepared assembly language program as input. The output from the assembler will be a machine code version of your assembly language original.
- *Step 2* As with high-level language programs, a large machine code program is best developed in modules which can be independently tested and then linked together to provide the final desired result. The linking together is done by a program known as the **linker**. Because the assembler outputs machine code in a form suitable for the linker but not ready for immediate

execution, even a single program module must be submitted to the linker for final conversion into executable form.

- *Step 3* Run the executable machine code form of your program under the control of a debugging program.

Step 1 Preparing for the assembler

File names

We shall use one of the most popular 8086-family assemblers: MASM. MASM requires that your assembly language program is already in a disk file. It will be assumed that the reader already knows how to organize this. Using MASM is easiest when the file containing your assembly language program has the second name ASM. Thus you should put programs for conversion into files called

```
EXAMPLE.ASM
CALCS123.ASM
TEST.ASM
```

but not in files called

```
JUNK.TYP
WROT37.AB4
DONT.TRY
```

Should you want to, it is possible to override this convention. For details see the MASM manual.

Contents of the assembly language file

The contents of the file containing the assembly language program to be converted should be as follows:

```
DATA SEGMENT
Insert here any necessary allocation
and/or initialization of data storage
DATA ENDS

WORKING_STORAGE SEGMENT STACK
    DW 100H DUP(?)
WORKING_STORAGE ENDS

CODE SEGMENT
ASSUME CS:CODE,DS:DATA,SS:WORKING_STORAGE

PROG_START:Insert here the 8086-family instructions
           to perform the task which is to be
           carried out

CODE ENDS
END PROG_START
```

The `END` pseudo-op tells the assembler that it has now come to the end of the assembly language statements requiring conversion to machine code. Immediately after the `END` pseudo-op we must specify a label which identifies the first instruction in the program which is to be executed – in our case we shall conventionally use `PROG_START` for this purpose. (Of course, with just one program the assembler does not need to be told that the first instruction to be executed is the one at the beginning. But if a large program is built up out of several modules, each contained in a separate file, then it will no longer be obvious which module contains the first instruction to be executed.)

Conversion to machine code

We now assume that your assembly language program (with all the necessary pseudo-ops) is contained in a file of the right type. For the purposes of illustration we shall assume the file is called `FIRSTEX.ASM`. Remember that it is just the name of the file type which must be fixed; you can choose the file's first name.

Is everything on the right disk?

It simplifies matters considerably if your assembly language program and the assembler program which is going to do the conversion are both on the same disk in drive A or in the same directory on a hard disk. For practical purposes it is a good idea to make yourself up a disk or directory with MASM, an editor program (EDIT, WORDSTAR or whatever you use), a linker (that supplied with MASM is called LINK and comes in a file called LINK.EXE), and a debugging program (see Chapter 5) all in the same directory before you start trying to work in assembly language. (Check that this does not break anyone's copyright – one day you may be a software author yourself and value every cent of royalties).

From now on it will be assumed that this is the case. Thus, if you issue a `DIR` command to DOS, the response should at least include the following files together with an editor or word-processing program:

```
MASM.EXE
LINK.EXE
```

Invoking the assembler is easy. You type the name of the assembler after the operating system prompt, then a space, and then the first name of the file containing your assembly language program and a few extra characters at the end. For example, if your assembly language program is in a file in the root directory on drive A: then you type:

```
A>MASM FIRSTEX,,,,
```

Once the assembler has finished its job the operating system prompt will be displayed again and two new files will have been created because of the MASM options selected by the four commas. The contents of these files are described in Table 4.2.

Table 4.2 Contents of files created by `MASM FIRSTEX,,,,`

Name of file	*Contents of the file*
FIRSTEX.LST	A printout showing your assembly language program, its machine code equivalent in hexadecimal notation and a list of any errors detected in your assembly language.
FIRSTEX.OBJ	The machine code equivalent of your assembly language program, not quite in a state in which it can be executed.

Step I reviewed

Let us illustrate with a simple assembly language program which accepts two digits in the range 0 to 4 typed at the keyboard and displays the result of adding them up. It then returns to DOS. Thanks to the define pseudo-op

```
GOODBYE_MESSAGE DB 'CALCULATION COMPLETE',ODH,OAH,'$'
```

the message CALCULATION COMPLETE will be displayed after the result and output to the display screen will continue on a new line:

```
DATA SEGMENT
        GOODBYE_MESSAGE DB 'CALCULATION COMPLETE',ODH,OAH,'$'
DATA ENDS

WORKING_STORAGE SEGMENT STACK
      DW 100H DUP(?)
WORKING_STORAGE ENDS

CODE SEGMENT
ASSUME DS:DATA,SS:WORKING_STORAGE,CS:CODE
       ;establish data segment addressability
PROG_START:MOV AX,DATA
           MOV DS,AX
          ;read a digit
           MOV AH,1
           INT 21H
          ;convert to a number
           SUB AL,30H
          ;save it in DL
           MOV DL,AL
          ;read second digit
           INT 21H
          ;convert it to a number
           SUB AL,30H
          ;add the two
           ADD DL,AL
          ;convert to a digit
           ADD DL,30H
          ;display the answer
           MOV AH,2
           INT 21H
          ;and a message
```

```
                MOV DX,OFFSET GOODBYE_MESSAGE
                MOV AH,9
                INT 21H
               ;return to DOS
                MOV AX,4C00H
                INT 21H
CODE ENDS
END PROG_START
```

Putting this complete text into a file of the right type (call it ADDER.ASM), we next invoke the assembler:

```
MASM ADDER,,,,
```

As the conversion proceeds, the messages shown in Figure 4.2 are printed on the display.

```
Microsoft (R) Macro Assembler Version 5.10
Copyright (C) Microsoft Corp 1981, 1988. All rights reserved.


  47482 + 412225 Bytes symbol space free

      0 Warning Errors
      0 Severe  Errors
```

Figure 4.2 Messages displayed during conversion of assembly language program to machine code.

When the conversion is complete, the A> prompt will be displayed. The file ADDER.LST now contains a fairly complete record of the assembler's work, the first page of which is shown in Figure 4.3.

This shows, among other things, that the machine code equivalent of SUB AL,30H is 2C30 in hexadecimal notation or 0010110000110000 in binary and that the first of these subtraction instructions is to be stored in locations 9H and 0AH relative to the program's starting point and the second in locations 0FH and 10H.

Page 2 of the contents of the file ADDER.LST is not very meaningful to us at this stage but at least it says there are no errors. It is shown in Figure 4.4.

Step 2 Invoking the linker

To convert the 'rough and ready' machine code version the assembler has produced into its final form, just one more command is needed:

```
A>LINK FIRSTEX,,,;
```

The linker produces two more files, FIRSTEX.MAP and FIRSTEX.EXE. FIRSTEX.MAP contains a list of the starting and finishing addresses of the various program segments, relative to a zero initial location:

```
Microsoft (R) Macro Assembler Version 5.10    Page    1-1

 1 0000                    DATA SEGMENT
 2 0000 20 20 20 43 41 4C GOODBYE_MESSAGE DB 'CALCULATION COMPLETE',0DH,0AH,'$'
 3      43 55 4C 41 54 49
 4      4F 4E 20 43 4F 4D
 5      50 4C 45 54 45 0D
 6      0A 24
 7 001A                    DATA ENDS
 8
 9 0000                    WORKING_STORAGE SEGMENT STACK
10 0000 0100 [                   DW 100H DUP(?)
11           ????
12                    ]
13 14 0200                 WORKING_STORAGE ENDS
15 16 0000                 CODE SEGMENT
17                         ASSUME DS:DATA,SS:WORKING_STORAGE,CS:CODE
18                         ;establish data segment addressability
19 0000 B8 ---- R PROG_START: MOV AX,DATA
20 0003 8E D8                 MOV DS,AX
21                         ;read a digit
22 0005 B4 01                 MOV AH,1
23 0007 CD 21                 INT 21H
24                         ;convert to a number
25 0009 2C 30                 SUB AL,30H
26                         ;save it in DL
27 000B 8A D0                 MOV DL,AL
28                         ;read second digit
29 000D CD 21                 INT 21H
30                         ;convert it to a number
31 000F 2C 30                 SUB AL,30H
32                         ;add the two
33 0011 02 D0                 ADD DL,AL
34                         ;convert to a digit
35 0013 80 C2 30              ADD DL,30H
36                         ;display the answer
37 0016 B4 02                 MOV AH,2
38 0018 CD 21                 INT 21H
39                         ;and a message
40 001A BA 0000 R             MOV DX,OFFSET GOODBYE_MESSAGE
41 001D B4 09                 MOV AH,9
42 001F CD 21                 INT 21H
43                         ;return to DOS
44 0021 B8 4C00               MOV AX,4C00H
45 0024 CD 21                 INT 21H
46 0026                    CODE ENDS
47                         END PROG_START
```

Figure 4.3
Page 1 of a record of the assembler's work.

```
Segments and Groups:

          Name                          Length   Align Combine Class

CODE . . . . . . . . . . . . . . . . .  0026     PARA     NONE
DATA . . . . . . . . . . . . . . . . .  0001A    PARA     NONE
WORKING_STORAGE    . . . . . . . . . .  0200     PARA     STACK

Symbols:

          Name                        Type     Value   Attr

GOODBYE_MESSAGE  . . . . . . . . . .L BYTE     0000    DATA

PROG_START . . . . . . . . . . . . .L NEAR     0000    CODE

CPU. . . . . . . . . . . . . . . . .TEXT   0101h
FILENAME  . . . . . . . . . . . . . .TEXT   new
VERSION . . . . . . . . . . . . . . .TEXT   510

       40 Source    Lines
       40 Total     Lines
       14 Symbols
    47482 + 412225 Bytes symbol space free

        0 Warning   Errors
        0 Severe    Errors
```

Figure 4.4
Page 2 of the record of the assembler's work.

```
Start   Stop    Length   Name     Class
00000H  00019H  0001AH   DATA
00020H  0021FH  00200H   STACK
00220H  00245H  00026H   CODE

Program entry point at 0022:0000
```

In our present context, the actual locations used for a program and its data are determined by DOS or the debugger (see Chapters 3 and 5) but the relative displacements in the linker's `.MAP` file are preserved.

The file `FIRSTEX.EXE` contains the EXEcutable machine code version which can now be executed by typing:

```
FIRSTEX
```

Provided the reader has entered the program *exactly* as it was given above, it will then be possible to type 2 and 3 and have 5 displayed as the result of 2 + 3, and so on. However, if even a fairly minor typing error has been made, the program may 'hang' the computer and/or not work at all. Indeed, it is more usual when developing a program oneself that this is the stage where debugging begins.

Step 3 Running a program under debug control

Experience with other languages such as Pascal should indicate that programs of any reasonable length will not work first time – a little 'fine tuning' is invariably necessary. With assembly language programming, matters are actually a little worse in that a slight change in the contents of a register may be the only outcome of a program. Without a device that tells you what is going on in the registers and memory it will therefore be impossible to determine if your program has worked! Consequently DOS provides a special tool for debugging assembly language or machine code programs.

Taking a look at your program and/or data in memory, modifying either of them and actually running the program are all handled by **debugger** commands, the most important of which we shall describe in the next chapter.

EXERCISES

4.8 Verify your solutions to Exercises 4.5–4.7 by assembling and running them. (If anything has gone wrong, the computer may exhibit very strange behaviour and you may have to switch off and turn on again to bring things back under control. Chapter 5 will explain how to locate errors.)

4.9 Write, assemble and test-run assembly language programs as follows:

(a) The user types a digit and the program displays Y if twice that digit is equal to 18 or N otherwise, followed by a new line. Then the sequence of events is repeated two more times before returning to DOS.

(b) The user types two letters and if either of them is Y the program displays the word YES followed by a new line, otherwise it displays NO followed by a new line. Then the sequence of events is repeated three more times before returning to DOS.

4.10 Type the following error-ridden program into a file, being careful to type it exactly as it appears below:

```
DATA SEGMANT
        TEST_DATA DB 50,100,150,200
        ANSWERS: DW 34H DUP( )
DATA END

WORKING_STORAGE SEGMENT STACK
        DW 100H DUP( )
WORKING_STORAGE ENDS

CODE SEGMENT
ASSUME CS_CODE,DS_DATA,SS_STACK
```

```
establish data segment addressability
            MOV DS,DATA
PROG_START MOV AX,4K
           MOV AH,AX
           SUB AX,2
           SUB AH,0123456H
           MOV BX,AX
           ADD AX,BL
           SUB 3,AX
           MOV BX,OFFSET DATA
           MOV AX,(BX)
  CODE END
END PROG_START
```

Try to assemble it and see what error messages you get. Can you say what has caused each error?

4.6 Insisting upon exact addresses

If necessary we can insist that certain absolute locations in memory are used for program or data storage. Care must be taken when using absolute addresses in this way as it is possible to overwrite DOS or your debugger (or both) and have the system hang up on you.

We can load any segment register (indirectly) with any value we choose to specify a segment. Thus, to swap the contents of actual locations 9FF00H and 9FF01H we could load DS with 9FF0 via

```
MOV AX,9FF0H
MOV DS,AX
```

and then swap the contents of locations 0 and 1 relative to DS using `MOV` instructions in the ordinary way.

Within a given segment, allocation of storage will begin from offset zero by default. To change this we use the pseudo-op `ORG`. It tells MASM to continue the allocation of storage to instructions or data as if it had already reached the offset specified in the `ORG` command.

For example, the following little program swaps the contents of locations 200H and 201H (relative to the start of the data segment of our program). We reach these specific locations by using the `ORG` pseudo-op. Thus the combination

```
ORG 200H
FIRST_LOCATION DB ?
```

in a segment addressed by the DS register makes the variable `FIRST_LOCATION` refer to location 200H relative to the start of the data segment `DATA`.

```
DATA SEGMENT
     ORG 200H
     FIRST_LOCATION DB ?
     ORG 201H
```

```
        SECOND_LOCATION DB ?
DATA ENDS

WORKING_STORAGE SEGMENT STACK
          DW 100H DUP(?)
WORKING_STORAGE ENDS

CODE SEGMENT
ASSUME DS:DATA,SS:WORKING_STORAGE,CS:CODE
;establish data segment addressability
PROG_START: MOV AX,DATA
            MOV DS,AX
;swap the contents
            MOV AL,FIRST_LOCATION
            MOV BL,SECOND_LOCATION
            MOV FIRST_LOCATION,BL
            MOV SECOND_LOCATION,AL
CODE ENDS
END PROG_START
```

SUMMARY

In this chapter we have explained what must be done to have an assembly language program converted to machine code. The next chapter covers debugging, the final stage necessary to obtain a correctly working program. We illustrated the initiation of the conversion process by means of a very simple adding-machine simulator which was largely constructed from DOS functions: routines accessible within the operating system's own program by means of the INT instruction. These DOS functions are of crucial importance later in this book. In the context of utilizing them for our specific example we learnt how to arrange the storage of data items in an assembly language program and studied the mechanism by which the assembly language versions of 8086-family instructions must refer to such data items. One DOS function allows us to terminate execution of our program and return to DOS Control.

SELF-CHECK QUIZ

1. Using a single suitable DB or DW pseudo-op in each case, write an assembly language statement to initialize the contents of a group of locations, the first of which is to be referred to by MY_BYTES, as follows:

   (a) The decimal numbers 0,1 ,2,. . .,10 as unsigned 8-bit numbers.

   (b) The decimal numbers -10,-20,-30,. . .,-100 as signed 8-bit words.

(c) All the characters in the play title: 'Long Day's Journey Into Night'.

2. Draw a diagram showing the storage space allocated and its contents byte by byte, given the following assembly language statements:

(a) `MY_BYTES DB 'NUMBER',16,-16H,6 DUP(0,?,2,?)`

(b) `MY_WORDS DW 6 DUP(0,1,2),?,-5,'WO','ORD', 347H`

3. Given the following data segment:

```
DATA SEGMENT
   D1 DW 1600
   D2 DW 4800
   D3 DW 1300
   D5 DW 3900
   D6 DW 7200
   D7 DW 1300
   D8 DW 5600
   D9 DW  750
   DA DW 1500
DATA ENDS
```

make a trace of the execution of the following program fragment:

```
MOV AX,DATA
MOV DS,AX
MOV BX,2
MOV AX,[BX]
MOV CX,D6
SUB AX,CX
ADD BX,6
MOV AX,[BX]
ADD AX,D9
ADD BX,8
MOV AX,[BX]
SUB AX,D9
```

4. Given

```
ITEMA DB 26H
ITEMB DW -123
ITEMC DB 'Welcome'
```

which of the following would be legal assembly language statements:

(a) `MOV AX,ITEMA`

(b) `MOV ITEMB,AL`

(c) `MOV AX,ITEMC`

(d) `MOV ITEMC,AL`

(e) `MOV ITEMC,AX`

(f) `ADD ITEMA,AL`

(g) `ADD ITEMA,AX`

5. Given

```
CCC DW 2BAFH
DDD DW A441H
BBB DW 289AH
```

what will be the contents of AX after execution of:

```
MOV AX,CCC
ADD AX,BBB
SUB DDD,AX
```

6. Given the following data segment:

```
DATA SEGMENT
   DAT1 DW 16 DUP(3)
   DAT2 DW 11 DUP(21)
   DAT3 DB 13,14,17,19
   DAT4 DB 'Welcome'
   DAT5 DW 1300,5600,750,1500
DATA ENDS
```

make a trace of the execution of the following program fragment:

```
MOV AX,DATA
MOV DS,AX
MOV AX,OFFSET DAT1
MOV BX,OFFSET DAT5
MOV CX,[BX]
ADD CX,DAT5
ADD BX,OFFSET DAT2
MOV BX,OFFSET DAT3
MOV AL,[BX]
```

7. Write a sequence of assembly language instructions and corresponding `DB` pseudo-op to display the message `CALIFORNIA WELCOMES CAREFUL DRIVERS` on the display screen on each of four separate lines.

8. Write a sequence of assembly language instructions and corresponding `DB` pseudo-op which would allow the user to type in a 20 letter message (possibly including spaces) and store the message in a group of memory locations the first of which is to be referred to by `USER_MESSAGE`.

9. What is wrong with the following attempt at a complete assembly language program which is intended to add together the two stored digits and print the answer on the display, and then return to DOS control:

```
DATA SEGMENT
 M1 DB 3
 M3 DB 2
ENDS

CODE
ASSUME CS,DS:DATA,CODE
         MOV AL,M1
         ADD AL,M3
         ADD AL,30
         MOV AH,2
         INT 21H
ENDS
```

10. Write a sequence of assembly language instructions to add the contents of absolute locations 23579H and 40AAFH.

5

Debugging Programs

Contents

It is indeed rare that an assembly language program will assemble and eventually run as predicted at the first attempt. Typically several approximations to the truth will have to be made before a final working program is produced, and the following scheme is nearly always adopted:

While the machine code program (if any) does not match the desired specification:

(1) Write or amend the assembly language program (as necessary) and submit it to the assembler.

(2) While the assembly language program contains things the assembler cannot understand, correct it by editing the file which contains the program and resubmit the corrected program to the assembler.

(3) Now that a version has been obtained which contains no errors of

assembly language, assemble and LINK it. Run the executable machine code version under debugger control.

On completion of this chapter, the reader should be able to locate the errors in an 8086-family assembly language program, using either DEBUG, among the simplest of the tools for locating errors in machine code programs, or the more recent Code View debugger, which has many more comprehensive and sophisticated features and allows sight of the original assembly language program during debugging. Because the easiest way in which to get to know Code View is to use a subset of its facilities very similar to those available from DEBUG, Sections 5.2, 5.3 and 5.4 combine introductions to both of these debugging aids. Then we examine the more sophisticated facilities which only Code View provides.

Readers who possess only DEBUG should just glance over the section specifically describing Code View and need not feel too disadvantaged: assembly language programmers have managed with just the facilities provided by DEBUG for almost a decade. However, in more advanced work, especially that involving programs consisting of several modules in different high-level programming languages besides assembly language, there is no doubt that Code View can make debugging a great deal easier. But to derive the fullest possible benefits from it you will need to have version 5.0 of MASM (or later) and version 3.6 of LINK (or later). We shall assume this to be the case in what follows.

As indicated in Chapter 3, the labels used in assembly language are replaced with numbers by the assembler to obtain machine code instructions. Before we commence our consideration of the debugging process, this chapter begins with a description of the some of the actual mechanisms used to replace the labels. We describe these here because it is necessary to understand the mechanics of this replacement in order to understand the on-screen output from either of the two debuggers.

5.1 The jump mechanism

As we have pointed out before, the <*label*> in a jump instruction is a luxury facility available thanks to assembly language. In machine code, jump instructions must either:

(1) specify the precise address in memory where the instruction you want to jump to can be found; or

(2) indicate how many instructions before or after the current one you want to jump.

During the conversion process from assembly language to machine code all the

<*label*>s in jump instructions are replaced by the appropriate numbers.

Viewed as machine code, there are three basic forms of 8086-family jump instruction. The first can be illustrated with reference to conditional jumps like the instruction `JZ` <*label*>. If the instruction indicated by the <*label*> is stored within +127 or −128 locations of the last of those containing the `JZ` instruction itself, the assembler replaces the <*label*> with an appropriate number. When the `JZ` is executed, that number is added to the contents of the IP register. Note that all conditional jumps follow this pattern, that is, *all conditional jumps must be to an address within +127 or −128 locations from the place where the conditional jump instruction is stored.*

If in:

```
JMP <label>
```

the <*label*> points to an instruction between 0 and 0FFFFH locations from the last of those containing the `JMP` instruction itself, the assembler can replace the <*label*> by the unsigned 16-bit form of the distance between the two. On execution of the JMP, that unsigned 16-bit displacement is added to the IP register.

The following extract from an assembler listing demonstrates both these possibilities:

```
3000 8B C3                   MOV AX,BX
3002 74 0A                   JZ NEAR_BY
                              .
                              .
                              .
300E B1 02          NEAR_BY:MOV CL,2
3010 03 C3                   ADD AX,BX
3012 2A C1                   SUB AL,CL
3014 E9 2D 14                JMP FAR_AHEAD
                              .
                              .
                              .
4444 8A C3       FAR_AHEAD: MOV AL,BL
```

Here, we see that location 3002H contains 74H and 3003H contains 0BH. 74H is the machine code form of the `JZ` instruction. 0AH specifies that the target for the jump – the instruction labeled `NEAR_BY` – is just 0AH locations ahead of the `JZ` instruction itself, in locations 300EH and 300FH. Similarly, location 3014H contains the machine code form of the `JMP` <*label*> instruction, 0E9H. The next two locations contain the unsigned 16-bit displacement of the instruction labeled `FAR_AHEAD`, namely 142DH, but stored with its bytes in reverse order: 2DH at offset 3015H and 14H at offset 3016H.

MASM assumes that all jumps are **intra-segment**, that is, within the same segment (or, what is the same thing, never more than 0FFFFH locations between the location being jumped from and the location to which you are jumping) unless a label has been specifically declared as a `FAR` away label via the `LABEL` pseudo-op. Thus,

```
LONG_WAY_OFF LABEL FAR
```

in conjunction with

```
JMP LONG_WAY_OFF
```

would mean that the `JMP` would be coded into the **inter-segment** form in which the target address would be specified by four bytes (as for `CALL` in Section 8.6).

5.2 The basic debugging commands of DEBUG and Code View

Debuggers are software tools that allow us to run machine code programs in such a way that the programmer can observe the changes a program makes to 8086-family registers and memory. In this section we describe the action of some of the most important commands common to DEBUG and Code View. The next section illustrates their use during an actual debugging session. Because the method of bringing each debugger into action is slightly different, we first describe how to do this in each case; thereafter the discussion is exactly the same whichever you are using.

We shall assume for simplicity and convenience that the reader has a copy of the program to be debugged in a file called `FIRSTEX.ASM` together with MASM, LINK, a text editor or word processor and either DEBUG or Code View on the same disk and/or in the same directory.

5.2.1 Starting up DEBUG

First, assemble and link the program in the manner described in Chapter 4. To commence debugging you type

```
DEBUG FIRSTEX.EXE
```

after the DOS prompt and the next thing you see will be the DEBUG prompt which is just a dash at the edge of the screen.

5.2.2 Starting up Code View

In order to use Code View, extra options must be declared when assembling the program using MASM and when linking with LINK. Thus, you should assemble and link the program by means of the following sequence of commands after the DOS prompt. First:

```
MASM /ZI FIRSTEX,,,,
```

and then

```
LINK /CO FIRSTEX,,,;
```

and then finally call Code View into action by:

```
CV /T FIRSTEX
```

Code View will respond with an introductory message of the form:

```
Microsoft (R) CodeView (R) Version 2.2
(C) Copyright Microsoft Corp. 1986-1988. All rights reserved.
>
```

The > symbol is the Code View command prompt.

To make Code View work with hexadecimal numbers a default *radix* must be set to specify the kind of numbers Code View must expect. In decimal, a radix of 16 corresponds to hexadecimal numbers, a radix of 10 to decimal numbers and a radix of 2 to binary numbers. Thus, to set a radix of 16 for hexadecimal numbers we type the command `N16` and press the ENTER key:

```
>N16
>
```

Also, because Code View is capable of executing program instructions in three different modes we must set it into mixed mode (mixed between source and assembly language) by giving the command `S&` followed by pressing the ENTER key:

```
>S&
mixed
>
```

We are now ready to begin debugging with Code View.

5.2.3 Basic commands for DEBUG and Code View

Note:

(1) All debugger commands are obeyed once the ENTER key has been pressed to indicate the end of the command;

(2) Both debuggers assume that all numbers are in hexadecimal so there is no need to type H (for hexadecimal) when entering numbers. Indeed, if you do you will get an error message; and

(3) We have used the DEBUG command prompt (-) and not the Code View command prompt (>) in the following descriptions. Apart from this minor difference, the text applies to both throughout.

R Display the contents of registers

The `R` command can be used in two forms. On its own, the contents of 8086-family registers are displayed on the screen. The display will be similar to the following:

```
-R
AX=0000 BX=0000 CX=0000 DX=0000 SP=0200 BP=0000 SI=0000 DI=0000
DS=04B5 ES=04B5 SS=04D9 CS=04C5 IP=0000 NI UP DI PL NZ PE NC
04C5:0000 B505              MOV     CH,05
-
```

Table 5.1 Flag name abbreviations used by DEBUG and Code View.

Flag name	*Flag set to one*	*Flag set to zero*
Overflow	OV	NV
Direction	DN	UP
Interrupt	EI	DI
Sign	NG	PL
Zero	ZR	NZ
Auxiliary carry	AC	NA
Parity	PE	PO
Carry	CY	NC

Here, the current setting of register CX is 0000H and CS is set to 04C5H. NV, UP, and so on, are abbreviations for the current flag settings as given in Table 5.1. For example, NG means that the sign flag has been set to 1 by the last instruction to affect it.

The other form of the `R` command is used to inspect and/or change the contents of a single register. If, for example, you type `RCX` after the command prompt:

```
-RCX
```

the debugger responds by typing out the current contents of register CX, for example

```
CX 2347
:
```

and then waits for you either to type in a new value to which you would like CX to be set after the colon (followed by the ENTER key) or just to press ENTER, indicating that you do not want to change the contents of the CX register.

U*n* Unassemble the contents of memory from location *n* (relative to CS)

Of course, the memory locations containing your program store the full binary version of the instructions. But when the debugger prints out what is in each location under this option, the assembly language format is reconstituted as far as is possible. The actual memory location from which the listing starts is obtained from the contents of the CS register and the offset address *n* in the usual way. Thus if the CS register contains 7BA4, then `U23A` would list from 7BA40 + 23A = 7BC7A.

Normally we do not have to bother about the CS register at all since we have arranged that either debugger will set this to the start of our programs automatically. Consequently, our programs may be listed directly after the starting up procedure described above by giving the debugger command `U0` or just `U`. Typically a listing in a format similar to the following will be obtained:

```
-U0
04C5:0127 51     PUSH CX
04C5:0128 52     PUSH DX
04C5:0129 B8C900 MOV AX,00C9
04C5:012C BB2D01 MOV BX,012D
04C5:012F 58     POP AX
04C5:0130 5B     POP BX
04C5:0131 01D0   ADD AX,DX
04C5:0133 83EB7B SUB BX,+7B
04C5:0136 BBC601 MOV BX,01C6
04C5:0139 49     DEC CX
04C5:013A 4B     DEC BX
04C5:013B 0000   ADD [BX+SI],AL
04C5:013D 0000   ADD [BX+SI],AL
04C5:013F 0000   ADD [BX+SI],AL
04C5:0141 0000   ADD [BX+SI],AL
04C5:0143 0000   ADD [BX+SI],AL
04C5:0145 0000   ADD [BX+SI],AL
-
```

If `U0` does not result in a version of your program being displayed, check that the last line of your assembly language program is of the form

```
END PROG_START
```

and that the label (`PROG_START` in this example) is indeed attached to the first instruction in your program.

As described in Chapter 2, the notation 04C5:0129 denotes the actual address

04C50 + 0129 = 04D79

which, the above listing tells us, is the first of three locations where the instruction `MOV AX,00C9` is stored. The same notation is also used in the more general formats illustrated by:

(1) `CS:12AB`

(2) `DS:F02A`

If the CS register currently contains 39F2 and the DS register 81EC then the actual address referred to by (1) is 39F20 + 12AB = 3B1CB and by (2) is 81EC0 + F02A = 90EEA. Thus

```
UCS:12AB
```

would cause either debugger to list the assembly language instructions stored at absolute address 3B1CB and following.

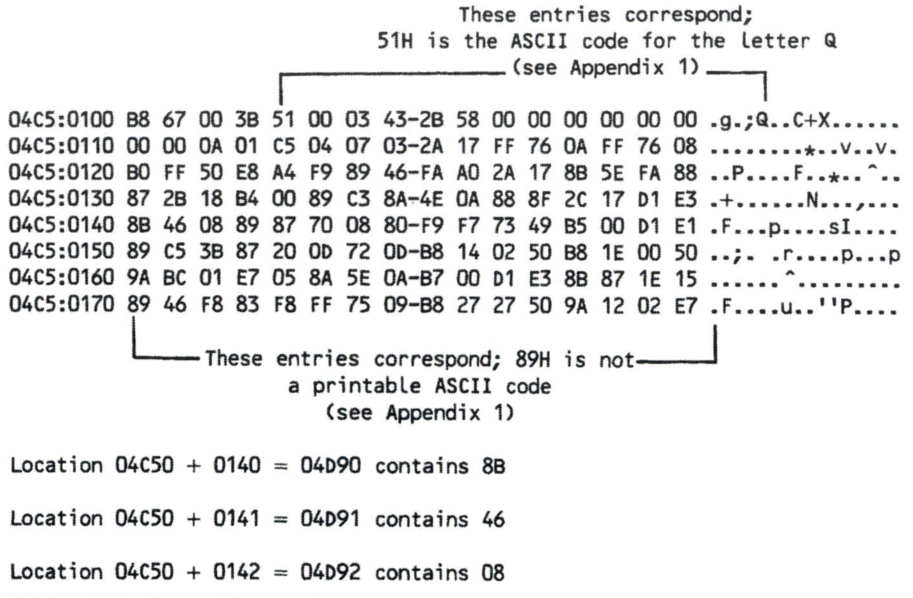

```
                          These entries correspond;
                     51H is the ASCII code for the letter Q
                                (see Appendix 1)
04C5:0100 B8 67 00 3B 51 00 03 43-2B 58 00 00 00 00 00 00 .g.;Q..C+X......
04C5:0110 00 00 0A 01 C5 04 07 03-2A 17 FF 76 0A FF 76 08 .........*..v..v.
04C5:0120 B0 FF 50 E8 A4 F9 89 46-FA A0 2A 17 8B 5E FA 88 ..P....F..*..^..
04C5:0130 87 2B 18 B4 00 89 C3 8A-4E 0A 88 8F 2C 17 D1 E3 .+......N...,...
04C5:0140 8B 46 08 89 87 70 08 80-F9 F7 73 49 B5 00 D1 E1 .F...p....sI....
04C5:0150 89 C5 3B 87 20 0D 72 0D-B8 14 02 50 B8 1E 00 50 ..;. .r....p...p
04C5:0160 9A BC 01 E7 05 8A 5E 0A-B7 00 D1 E3 8B 87 1E 15 ......^.........
04C5:0170 89 46 F8 83 F8 FF 75 09-B8 27 27 50 9A 12 02 E7 .F....u..''P....
          These entries correspond; 89H is not
                 a printable ASCII code
                    (see Appendix 1)

Location 04C50 + 0140 = 04D90 contains 8B

Location 04C50 + 0141 = 04D91 contains 46

Location 04C50 + 0142 = 04D92 contains 08
```

Figure 5.1 Typical output from a command `Dn`. (Note: all these numbers are in hexadecimal notation.)

`Dn` Display memory contents from offset *n* (relative to DS) in hexadecimal and as ASCII codes

This command option gives two listings of memory contents at the same time. The content of each location is displayed in hexadecimal form on the left-hand side of the display screen. If a given location contains the ASCII code for a printable character then that character is displayed on the right-hand side of the screen. If not then a period (`.`) is displayed in the appropriate place. The actual address from which the listing commences is obtained by combining the contents of the DS register with the offset given in the command. Thus if the DS register contains 12E3 then the debugger command D27A4 would begin listing from memory location 12E30 + 27A4 = 155D4.

Our two debuggers initialize things so that any data items used in our programs will be stored starting at offset 0H from the automatically initialized segment value in DS (we shall see later that there are good reasons for this). It follows that the debugger command D0 should be used to get a hexadecimal listing of any stored data items.

Some typical output from such a command is shown in Figure 5.1.

`Ga` Go and execute up to the instruction at address a (relative to CS)

This command causes execution to begin at the instruction contained in location CS:IP and stop just before executing the instruction at address CS:*a*. The address of the instruction just before which execution is to stop is taken relative to the current contents of the CS register which will be automatically preset to the required value for our program. Thus, to run the first eight instructions of the following program fragment:

```
04C5:0127 51     PUSH CX
04C5:0128 52     PUSH DX
04C5:0129 B8C900 MOV AX,00C9
04C5:012C BB2D01 MOV BX,012D
04C5:012F 58     POP AX
04C5:0130 5B     POP BX
04C5:0131 01D0   ADD AX,DX
04C5:0133 83EB7B SUB BX,+7B
04C5:0136 BBC601 MOV BX,01C6
04C5:0139 49     DEC CX
04C5:013A 4B     DEC BX
04C5:013B 0000   ADD [BX+SI],AL
04C5:013D 0000   ADD [BX+SI],AL
04C5:013F 0000   ADD [BX+SI],AL
04C5:0141 0000   ADD [BX+SI],AL
04C5:0143 0000   ADD [BX+SI],AL
04C5:0145 0000   ADD [BX+SI],AL
```

it is first necessary to set the IP register correctly. This is done with the R command as described above. You type RIP after the debugger prompt

```
-RIP
```

and the debugger will respond by typing out the current contents of register IP:

```
IP 2347
:
```

and then waits for you to type in the new value followed by the ENTER key. We require 0127:

```
:0127
```

and now we check that IP has been correctly set by using the R command on its own:

```
-R
AX=0000 BX=01C6 CX=0147 DX=0000 SP=0200 BP=0000 SI=0000 DI=0000
DS=04B5 ES=04B5 SS=04D9 CS=04C5 IP=0136 NV UP DI PL NZ PE NC
04C5:0127 51 PUSH CX
-
```

Since it has and assuming that the CS register has been set automatically, the command:

```
G136
```

will cause the execution of the desired eight instructions. After execution, the debugger prints the address of the next instruction and an assembly language version of that instruction:

```
AX=0000 BX=00CC CX=0147 DX=0000 SP=0200 BP=0000 SI=0000 DI=0000
DS=04B5 ES=04B5 SS=04D9 CS=04C5 IP=0136 NV UP DI PL NZ PE NC
04C5:0136 BBC601 MOV BX,01C6
-
```

Checking that the instructions have had the desired effect now involves examining the contents of memory and registers using the `D`, `R` and `U` commands.

`T`*n* Trace the execution of *n* instructions

Both debuggers provide facilities for making traces much as we did by hand in Chapter 1. The instruction has the form `T`*n* where *n* is the number of instructions (in hexadecimal) to be obeyed before tracing stops. The new state of all the registers is displayed after each instruction is obeyed. The address of the first instruction to be obeyed in a `T` command is taken to be CS:IP so it is generally necessary to set the IP register before beginning a trace.

`E`*a* Enter the contents of memory location DS:*a* directly

If a program requires data to be held in memory it is important to be able to change that data when testing a program (so that special cases can be tried out, for example). The `E` debugger command allows you to alter the contents of a memory location by typing in a new value in hexadecimal form. `E` always works relative to the current contents of the DS register. On receipt of the command `E`*a* after the prompt, the debugger prints the current contents of that location and waits for the new value to be typed in after a period:

```
-E203
04B5:0203 AB.
```

Having typed a new value (suppose we want to replace 0ABH by 99H), you can either press the spacebar, in which case the debugger now similarly waits for a new value for the next location (in this case, to replace 5FH) to be entered after the colon:

```
-E203
04B5:0203 AB.99 5F.
```

or we can just press the ENTER key which will terminate the `E` command.

`A`*a* Assemble the instruction entered and store starting at address CS:*a*

Given the following output from a `U` debugger command:

```
-U0
592F:0000 B86700 MOV AX,0067
592F:0003 BB5100 MOV BX,0051
592F:0006 01C8   ADD AX,CX
592F:0008 2BD8   SUB BX,AX
592F:000A 4E     DEC SI
592F:000B 42     INC DX
```

```
592F:000C 3030    XOR Byte Ptr [BX+SI],DH
592F:000E 44      INC SP
-
```

the `A` command would allow us to change the `ADD AX,CX` instruction to an add `ADD AX,BX` as follows. We give the debugger command

```
-A6
```

to which the debugger responds:

```
592F:0006
```

and then we type the required new assembly language instruction after the address followed by the ENTER key.

```
592F:0006 ADD AX,BX
```

Having typed a new value followed by the ENTER key, the debugger now similarly waits for a new value for the next location to be entered:

```
592F:0006 ADD AX,BX
592F:0008
```

We can now either type another new instruction to be stored starting at location 592F:0008 and go on to enter more new instructions in the same way, or just press the ENTER key which will terminate the `A` command.

The US Government now attaches a health warning to every pack of cigarettes to warn smokers of the possible dangers of smoking. The `A` debugger command should come with a similar warning to all programmers. We mention it here because it can be used sensibly in the development of programs involving just a few instructions to control hardware. But its use in larger scale programming (that is, for any program of more than about 10 instructions) should be outlawed except for *very* minor modifications which use of the other debugger facilities have indicated are necessary. Thus, a good use of the `A` command would be to temporarily amend *one* `JZ` instruction to a `JNZ` instruction. A bad use would be to employ it to add instructions to deal with a whole case of possibilities you had not realized existed until debugging began. In short: the `A` command can lead to programs which are very badly structured (see Chapter 8) and which are therefore especially expensive to maintain; while its use often seems to be speeding things up, more often than not it actually slows development time down, and as a result good assembly language programmers avoid it. This ends the health warning.

`Q` Quit using the debugger and return to DOS

Type `Q` and then press the ENTER key.

5.3 A sample debugging session

We now demonstrate the debuggers in action, applied to the following little example program:

```
DATA SEGMENT
        LOC_ONE DW 1ABH
        LOC_TWO DW 32ACH
        LOC_THREE DW ?
DATA ENDS

WORKING_STORAGE SEGMENT STACK
    DW 100H DUP(?)
WORKING_STORAGE ENDS

CODE SEGMENT
ASSUME DS: DATA,SS:WORKING_STORAGE,CS:CODE
           ;establish data segment addressability
PROG_START: MOV AX,DATA
            MOV DS,AX
            ;main program
            MOV AX,LOC_ONE
            ADD AX,2
            ADD AX,LOC_TWO
            MOV LOC_THREE,AX
CODE ENDS
END PROG_START
```

We shall assume that the executable machine code version of this program now lies in the file EXAMPLE.EXE having been obtained in the manner appropriate to the debugger (DEBUG or Code View) in use and that the appropriate initialization of the debugger has been made – as described in the last section. Having done so, our program should be in location 0 and following (relative to the contents of the CS register), so let's check:

```
-U0
5930:0000 B80F59    MOV AX,590F
5930:0003 8ED8      MOV DS,AX
5930:0005 A10000    MOV AX,[0000]
5930:0008 050200    ADD AX,0002
5930:000B 03060200 ADD AX,[0002]
5930:000F A30400    MOV [0004],AX
5930:0012 4E        DEC SI
5930:0013 42        INC DX
-
```

(Only the first six instructions are significant. The U command always prints out the instructions occupying about 20 bytes and those at the end of our program were either left in memory by a previous program or are the result of random memory settings which occurred when the computer was switched on.)

To have our program executed, we must first set the IP register to the address (relative to the CS register) of the first instruction (0 in this case). To do this we use the R command:

```
-RIP
```

The debugger responds by typing the current setting of the IP register

```
IP 0000
:
```

and normally we would then type in the desired setting. Since IP is already correctly set in this case we simply press the ENTER key. To check all this we use the R command again:

```
-R
AX=0000 BX=0000 CX=0000 DX=0000 SP=0200 BP=0000 SI=0000 DI=0000
DS=58FF ES=58FF SS=5910 CS=5930 IP=0000 NV UP EI PL NZ NA PO NC
5930:0000 B80F59 MOV AX,590F
-
```

We discovered from the output of the U command that the last instruction in our program resides in locations having offsets 0FH,10H and 11H relative to the CS register so we want to stop execution just before the instruction in the location with offset 0012 is obeyed. Thus, to run our program we use the command

```
-G12
```

which, when execution has stopped, displays another debugger prompt. To check the register contents now and to discover the next instruction to be executed we use the R debugger command once again:

```
-R
AX=3459 BX=0000 CX=0000 DX=0000 SP=0200 BP=0000 SI=0000 DI=0000
DS=590F ES=58FF SS=5910 CS=5930 IP=0012 NV UP EI PL NZ NA PE NC
5930:0012 4E DEC SI
-
```

If our program has worked correctly, AX should contain 01AB + 2 + 32AC = 3459H. By inspection of the output from the R command above that much at least is easily verified. Also locations 4 and 5 relative to DS should contain the 16-bit equivalent of 3459H. To check this let us use the D debugger command. Since our program actually resets DS during execution so that our program's data has offset 0 from DS, we simply need to give the D0 command:

```
-D0
590F:0000 AB 01 AC 32 59 34 00 00-00 00 00 00 00 00 00 00...2Y4..........
590F:0010 00 00 00 00 00 00 00 00-00 00 00 00 00 00 00 00................
590F:0020 00 00 00 00 00 00 00 00-00 00 00 00 00 00 00 00................
590F:0030 00 00 00 00 00 00 00 00-00 00 00 00 00 00 00 00................
590F:0040 00 00 00 00 00 00 00 00-00 00 00 00 00 00 00 00................
590F:0050 00 00 00 00 00 00 00 00-00 00 00 00 00 00 00 00................
590F:0060 00 00 00 00 00 00 00 00-00 00 00 00 00 00 00 00................
590F:0070 00 00 00 00 00 00 00 00-00 00 00 00 00 00 00 00................
-
```

from the first line of which we can see that this part of the program has also worked according to plan.

As another example, let us replace the contents of LOC_ONE and LOC_TWO with two new values and verify the result of that. Since after execution of our program these correspond to the words stored starting at DS:0000 and DS:0002 respectively we can do this by using the E command as follows:

```
-E0
590F:0000 AB.
```

We type 11 and press the spacebar:

```
590F:0000 AB.11 01.
```

and now type 02 and press the spacebar:

```
590F:0000 AB.11 01.02 AC.
```

and now finish the entry by typing 3A, spacebar, 03 and the ENTER key:

```
590F:0000 AB.11 01.02 AC.3A 32.03
```

and then check that the values are stored as we intended:

```
-D0
590F:0000 11 02 3A 03 59 34 00 00-00 00 00 00 00 00 00 00..:.............
590F:0010 00 00 00 00 00 00 00 00-00 00 00 00 00 00 00 00................
590F:0020 00 00 00 00 00 00 00 00-00 00 00 00 00 00 00 00................
590F:0030 00 00 00 00 00 00 00 00-00 00 00 00 00 00 00 00................
590F:0040 00 00 00 00 00 00 00 00-00 00 00 00 00 00 00 00................
590F:0050 00 00 00 00 00 00 00 00-00 00 00 00 00 00 00 00................
590F:0060 00 00 00 00 00 00 00 00-00 00 00 00 00 00 00 00................
590F:0070 00 00 00 00 00 00 00 00-00 00 00 00 00 00 00 00................
-
```

Next we need to reset IP:

```
-RIP
IP 0012
:0
-
```

and then execute until just before the instruction stored starting in offset 12 relative to CS:

```
-G12
-
```

Now let us check the outcome, first in memory:

```
-D0
590F:0000 11 02 3A 03 4D 05 00 00-00 00 00 00 00 00 00 00..:.M...........
590F:0010 00 00 00 00 00 00 00 00-00 00 00 00 00 00 00 00................
590F:0020 00 00 00 00 00 00 00 00-00 00 00 00 00 00 00 00................
590F:0030 00 00 00 00 00 00 00 00-00 00 00 00 00 00 00 00................
590F:0040 00 00 00 00 00 00 00 00-00 00 00 00 00 00 00 00................
590F:0050 00 00 00 00 00 00 00 00-00 00 00 00 00 00 00 00................
590F:0060 00 00 00 00 00 00 00 00-00 00 00 00 00 00 00 00................
590F:0070 00 00 00 00 00 00 00 00-00 00 00 00 00 00 00 00................
-
```

and next the AX register:

```
-R
AX=054D BX=0000 CX=0000 DX=0000 SP=0200 BP=0000 SI=0000 DI=0000
DS=590F ES=58FF SS=5910 CS=5930 IP=0012 NV UP EI PL NZ NA PE NC
5930:0012 4E DEC SI
-
```

Since 0211 + 2 + 033A = 054D, the outcome is verified.

5.3.1 If it all hangs up

Once things go radically wrong with a machine code program – which is often the case – it is all too easy to 'kill off' the operating system completely. The main symptom is the keyboard going dead – it will accept neither debugger commands nor any control keys such as CTRL-ALT-DELETE to restart DOS. If this happens there is just the slightest chance that one of your disk files could be spoiled, but generally speaking it is nothing to worry about. Remove any floppy disks from the disk drives, switch off the computer and then reboot the operating system as at the beginning of a normal session. You may then turn to the task of finding out why it all happened in the first place.

There are a variety of possible causes of such a system crash. Sometimes a loop that is designed to stop after a certain number of executions never actually stops because the terminating condition is never satisfied (BX never gets to zero, or AX never gets more than 37H or . . .). Perhaps the terminating address given to the `G` debugger command was wrong – often one instruction too many – or perhaps the IP register had not been set to the correct value to start with. If you are using Code View, be sure *not* to leave a space between the command and the address (for example, it should be `G12` and *not* `G 12`). Also, when tracing with Code View, make sure that you have given the `S&` command. Verify that all the jump instructions are aimed at the right place. (Checking this is easier from the assembly language listing. Look out for `JZ` which should be `JNZ` and vice versa.)

5.4 Automatic tracing

For the sake of illustration we shall now trace the execution of our program under debugger control. As a first step we must once again set the IP register to the address of the location (relative to the CS register) containing the instruction from which the trace of execution is to commence:

```
-RIP
IP 0012
:
```

We now type in the desired setting for IP, namely `0`

```
:0
-
```

and once again use the R command to check:

```
-R
AX=054D BX=0000 CX=0000 DX=0000 SP=0200 BP=0000 SI=0000 DI=0000
DS=590F ES=58FF SS=5910 CS=5930 IP=0000 NV UP EI PL NZ NA PE NC
5930:0000 B80F59 MOV AX,590F
-
```

Now we can begin the trace proper. First we trace a single step. After executing that step the debugger prints out the new state of the registers:

```
-T1
AX=590F BX=0000 CX=0000 DX=0000 SP=0200 BP=0000 SI=0000 DI=0000
DS=590F ES=58FF SS=5910 CS=5930 IP=0003 NV UP EI PL NZ NA PE NC
5930:0003 8ED8 MOV DS,AX
-
```

(MOV DS,AX is the next instruction to be executed.) Let us do another step:

```
-T1
AX=590F BX=0000 CX=0000 DX=0000 SP=0200 BP=0000 SI=0000 DI=0000
DS=590F ES=58FF SS=5910 CS=5930 IP=0005 NV UP EI PL NZ NA PE NC
5930:0005 A10000 MOV AX,[0000]                          DS:0000=0211
-
```

Notice that we are told that the next instruction to be executed is MOV AX,[0000] and that the content of the location referred to by this MOV instruction (DS:0000) is 0211H. Now let us do the four final steps to finish off:

```
-T4
AX=0211 BX=0000 CX=0000 DX=0000 SP=0200 BP=0000 SI=0000 DI=0000
DS=590F ES=58FF SS=5910 CS=5930 IP=0008 NV UP EI PL NZ NA PE NC
5930:0008 050200 ADD AX,[0002]

AX=0213 BX=0000 CX=0000 DX=0000 SP=0200 BP=0000 SI=0000 DI=0000
DS=590F ES=58FF SS=5910 CS=5930 IP=000B NV UP EI PL NZ NA PO NC
5930:000B 03060200 ADD AX,[0002]                        DS:0002=033A

AX=054D BX=0000 CX=0000 DX=0000 SP=0200 BP=0000 SI=0000 DI=0000
DS=590F ES=58FF SS=5910 CS=5930 IP=000F NV UP EI PL NZ NA PE NC
5930:000F A30400 MOV [0004],AX                          DS:0004=054D

AX=054D BX=0000 CX=0000 DX=0000 SP=0200 BP=0000 SI=0000 DI=0000
DS=590F ES=58FF SS=5910 CS=5930 IP=0012 NV UP EI PL NZ NA PE NC
5930:0012 4E DEC SI
-
```

In fact, Code View gives us more information than this since the trace output refers, for example, not to MOV AX,[0000] but rather to

```
MOV AX,Word Ptr [LOC_ONE (0000)]
```

indicating that offset 0000 relative to DS is the first location of two in which a 16-bit word is stored (Word Ptr) and that the variable name which was used for this word in the original assembly language program was LOC_ONE.

EXERCISES

5.1 Using your own machine, assemble, link and then run under debugger control the following assembly language program:

```
MOV AX,7H
SUB AX,3H
MOV BX,AX
MOV CX,AX
MOV DX,AX
```

Try tracing the machine code version, one instruction at a time, and also execute the whole program in one go using the `G` command.

5.2 Using your own machine, assemble, link and run under debugger control:

```
     MOV AH,0
LOOP:INC AH
     JMP LOOP
```

Trace 10H steps of the execution of this program to check that you understand how it works. Then discover what happens when you obey `INC AH` and the contents of AH is OFFH.

5.5 Code View

The Code View debugger can operate in sequential mode or in window mode. Thus far, we have only used Code View in sequential mode. This is no great restriction, for any debugging operation which can be done in window mode can also be done in sequential mode. But in window mode, Code View displays up to four windows enabling us to see registers, program and data simultaneously. Consequently, if you have Code View, it is usual practice to run it in window mode. Doing so involves calling it up without the `/T` command option as described in Section 5.2. Thus, the following sequence of DOS commands should be given to use Code View in window mode to debug an assembly language program stored in the file `EXAMPLE.ASM`:

```
MASM /ZI EXAMPLE,,,,
LINK /CO EXAMPLE,,,;
CV EXAMPLE
```

We shall assume that this has been done and work through a simple session with Code View in window mode. Assuming the contents of `EXAMPLE.ASM` is the example program from Section 5.3, once Code View has been started up, the screen looks as shown in Figure 5.2. Notice that the first instruction in our program has been highlighted because CS and IP have automatically been set to the beginning of it.

```
File View Search Run Watch Options Language Calls Help F8=Trace F5=Go

----------------------------| example.ASM |----------------------------
5931:0000 B81059      MOV     AX,5910                         AX=0000
5931:0003 8ED8        MOV     DS,AX                           BX=0000
5931:0005 A10000      MOV     AX,Word Ptr [0000]              CX=0000
5931:0008 050200      ADD     AX,0002                         DX=0000
5931:000B 03060200    ADD     AX,Word Ptr [0002]              SP=0200
5931:000F A30400      MOV     Word Ptr [0004],AX              BP=0000
5931:0012 4E          DEC     SI                              SI=0000
5931:0013 42          INC     DX                              DI=0000
5931:0014 3030        XOR     Byte Ptr [BX+SI],DH             DS=5900
5931:0016 94          XCHG    AX,SP                           ES=5900
5931:0017 0000        ADD     Byte Ptr [BX+SI],AL             SS=5911
5931:0019 0000        ADD     Byte Ptr [BX+SI],AL             CS=5931
5931:001B 0000        ADD     Byte Ptr [BX+SI],AL             IP=0000
5931:001D 0000        ADD     Byte Ptr [BX+SI],AL
5931:001F 0000        ADD     Byte Ptr [BX+SI],AL              NV UP
5931:0021 0000        ADD     Byte Ptr [BX+SI],AL              EI PL
5931:0023 0000        ADD     Byte Ptr [BX+SI],AL              NZ NA
5931:0025 000B        ADD     Byte Ptr [BP+DI],CL              PO NC
-----------------------------------------------------------------
  Microsoft (R) CodeView (R) Version 2.2
  (C) Copyright Microsoft Corp. 1986-1988. All rights reserved.
  >
```

Figure 5.2 Screen layout for Code View in window mode.

5.5.1 Window mode

Using the keyboard (mouse owners can consult the Code View manual) commands are entered in the command window (bottom left) after the > Code View prompt. Since it is still necessary to type the `S&` and `N16` commands, each followed by pressing the ENTER key, you should enter these next. When we type the `S&` Code View command for setting mixed mode the register window disappears (having previously occupied all of the right-hand edge of the screen), but it can be brought back by pressing the F2 key which toggles the register window on and off. Note also that, given the small amount of space in the command window, Code View allows us to scroll up through past commands, and back again, by using the up-arrow and down-arrow cursor control keys.

All the commands already described are allowed in window mode. These are typed in the command window and have the same effect in window mode as in sequential mode except that some commands will also affect the program window (occupying most of the centre of the screen) and the register window. The register window always shows the current settings of both registers and flags, and the program window shows the group of instructions pointed to by CS:IP. Use the `R` command as before to reset IP to 8 and look at the effect on the program window. You will see that the third instruction in the program window is now highlighted instead of the first because it is stored beginning at CS:IP.

Now reset IP to 0 and then trace the execution of the program in EXAMPLE.ASM, one instruction at a time. At each stage, the next instruction to be executed is highlighted in the program window. Notice that if an instruction involves something stored in memory then the appropriate contents are displayed at the very bottom right of the screen.

During the execution of our program in order to make this trace, DS was set to point to our program's data segment. Code View tries to give information as closely resembling the original program which we wrote as possible. Having executed the second instruction DS now points to our program's data segment. As a result, Code View can deduce that, in an instruction such as

```
MOV AX,Word Ptr [0000]
```

the location referred to is that which was given the name LOC_ONE in the original assembly language program. Consequently, if you now give a U0 command the display in the program window changes to reflect the original assembly language program. For example,

```
MOV AX,Word Ptr [0000]
```

becomes

```
MOV AX,Word Ptr [LOC_ONE (0000)]
```

5.5.2 Working with data types

Code View allows us to display data items stored in memory not just in byte format but also as words, unsigned decimal integers or as ASCII codes.

DW*n* Display memory contents from DS:*n* as Words

DB*n* Display memory contents from DS:*n* as Bytes

DU*n* Display memory contents from DS:*n* as Unsigned decimal integers

As an example, initiate Code View ready to debug the program in EXAMPLE.ASM, and give the command DW0:

```
>DW0
5900:0000 20CD A000 9A00 FEF0 F01D 0715 299E 07D9
5900:0010 299E 0AB5 299E 208F 0101 0001 0102 0301
>
```

Here, the contents of 5900:0000 and 5900:0001 are 0CDH and 20H respectively, but regarded as a signed or unsigned 16-bit number this represents 20CDH. Code View has saved us the mental twist which would otherwise be necessary because of the way in which the 8086 family store words in memory.

The advantage of this will become even clearer if we first trace a couple of steps of the program in EXAMPLE.ASM so that DS is reset to point to the data segment of our program:

```
>T2
```

and then inspect our data:

```
>D0
5910:0000 01AB 32AC 0000 0000 0000 0000 0000 0000
5910:0010 0000 0000 0000 0000 0000 0000 0000 0000
>
```

The data looks just like what we gave in the data segment definition in our assembly language program. (Notice also, that Code View remembers the last type of data display requested and uses this unless you tell it otherwise. The default is for data to be displayed in bytes. We changed that to words with our `DW` command, and so `D0` in this case displayed our data as words.)

Let us trace four more steps and inspect our data segment again:

```
>T4
>D0
5910:0000 01AB 32AC 3459 0000 0000 0000 0000 0000
5910:0010 0000 0000 0000 0000 0000 0000 0000 0000
>
```

How much easier it is to check that the program has worked properly when the data is presented in this form! We simply read off that 01AB + 2 + 32ACH should be 3459H. Compare this with what we get when the same data is displayed in byte format:

```
>DB0
5910:0000 AB 01 AC 32 59 34 00 00-00 00 00 00 00 00 00 00...2Y4.........
5910:0010 00 00 00 00 00 00 00 00-00 00 00 00 00 00 00 00................
>
```

(This is harder to read not least because each word such as 01AB is, of course, actually stored with the lower order bits in the lowest address; that is, AB is stored in the lower address, 01 in the next address.)

To verify that Code View does indeed remember whether it is supposed to be displaying words or bytes or whatever, let us give a straight `D` command:

```
>D
5910:0020 00 00 00 00 00 00 00 00-00 00 00 00 00 00 00 00................
5910:0030 00 00 00 00 00 00 00 00-00 00 00 00 00 00 00 00................
>
```

Even with `DW` we still need to carry out hexadecimal arithmetic in order to verify the outcome of our program. But thanks to the `DU` command we can avoid that also. `DU` displays the contents of memory as words, but gives the value of the words as unsigned decimal integers. Thus:

```
>DU0
5910:0000    427 12972 13401     0     0     0     0     0
5910:0010      0     0     0     0     0     0     0     0
>
```

shows that 01ABH is 427 in decimal, and that 32ACH is 12972 in decimal. And it is even easier now to check that 427 + 2 + 12972 = 13401 given that everything is in decimal.

EW*n* Enter memory contents starting at DS:*n* as Words

EB*n* Enter memory contents starting at DS:*n* as Bytes

EI*n* Enter memory contents starting at DS:*n* as Integers

Thanks to this group of Code View commands, we can also enter test data for a program in a variety of formats. Let us continue with `EXAMPLE.ASM` and enter new test data with `EI`. We first give the command `EI0` and then Code View shows the existing contents of DS:0 as an unsigned decimal integer and waits for a new decimal integer to be typed:

```
>EI0
5910:0000    291
```

We type our desired new value, namely decimal 100 followed by the ENTER key:

```
>EI0
5910:0000    291  100
5910:0002  17767
```

Code View now waits for us to type another new value, this time for the word to be stored starting at 5910:0002, or to press the ENTER key to terminate the `EI` command. We shall enter 200 this time, press the ENTER key, and then press the ENTER key once more to finish:

```
>EI0
5910:0000    291  100
5910:0002  17767  200
5910:0004  13401
>
```

Now let us re-run the program with this new test data:

```
>RIP
IP 0012
:0
>G12
>
```

and take a look at the result:

```
>DI0
5910:0000  100  200  302    0    0    0    0    0
5910:0010    0    0    0    0    0    0    0    0
>
```

from which it is immediately obvious that the answer is correct. Compare this with working with hexadecimal words:

```
>DW0
5910:0000 0064 00C8 012E 0000 0000 0000 0000 0000
5910:0010 0000 0000 0000 0000 0000 0000 0000 0000>
>
```

As with the `D` command, Code View remembers whether you entered decimal integers, words, bytes, or whatever, last time you used an E command. Thus, if we enter two words as test data using, as before, the spacebar to terminate each entry and the ENTER key to terminate the current use of the E command:

```
>EWO
5910:0000  01AB.123  32AC.4567  3459.
>
```

and then change our minds about the first item of test data, we need only say EO and Code View remembers that we were entering words:

```
>EO
5910:0000  0123.
```

If we have been working with integers or words, EB allows us to return to working with bytes so that the E command then operates as described in Section 5.2.

? Display the value of a symbol or expression

? allows us the closest possible interaction with our original assembly language program. We can ask, what is the value currently stored in the memory location corresponding to LOC_ONE:

```
>? LOC_ONE
0x01ab
>
```

which in this case indicates that it is 01ABH. We can also request this information in integer format:

```
>? LOC_ONE,I
427
>
```

or in decimal format:

```
>? LOC_ONE,D
427
>
```

We can ask for the contents of the byte pointed to by SS:SP by qualifying ? with BY which is short for BYte:

```
>?BY SP
0x0000
>
```

and for the contents of the word at DS:0 by qualifying ? with WO which is short for WOrd:

```
>? WO DS:0
0x01ab
>
```

```
File View Search Run Watch Options Language Calls Help F8=Trace F5=Go

---------------------------| adder.ASM |---------------------------

5921:0000 B8FF58     MOV    AX,58FF                       AX=0000
5921:0003 8ED8       MOV    DS,AX                         BX=0000
5921:0005 B401       MOV    AH,01                         CX=0000
5921:0007 CD21       INT    21                            DX=0000
5921:0009 2C30       SUB    AL,30                         SP=0200
5921:000B 8AD0       MOV    DL,AL                         BP=0000
5921:000D CD21       INT    21                            SI=0000
5921:000F 2C30       SUB    AL,30                         DI=0000
5921:0011 02D0       ADD    DL,AL                         DS=58EF
5921:0013 80C230     ADD    DL,30                         ES=58EF
5921:0016 B402       MOV    AH,02                         SS=5901
5921:0018 CD21       INT    21                            CS=5921
5921:001A BA0000     MOV    DX,0000                       IP=0000
5921:001D B409       MOV    AH,09
5921:001F CD21       INT    21                            NV UP
5921:0021 B8004C     MOV    AX,4C00                       EI PL
5931:0024 CD21       INT    21                            NZ NA
5931:0026 0000       ADD    Byte Ptr [BX+SI],AL           PO NC
-----------------------------------------------------------
   Microsoft (R) CodeView (R) Version 2.2
   (C) Copyright Microsoft Corp. 1986-1988. All rights reserved.
   >
```

Figure 5.3
Ready to debug ADDER.ASM.

5.5.3 Debugging a program which uses I/O

The menu which appears at the top of the main Code View debugging screen will not be discussed in detail here. It provides many important advanced features and its use is described fully in the Code View manual. However, one feature which can be selected from this menu can also be obtained directly by pressing the F4 function key and it is of crucial importance when debugging a program which uses I/O.

By way of example, let us illustrate with the very simple adding machine example of Chapter 4 which we kept in a file called ADDER.ASM. If we call up Code View in the normal way ready to debug this program then the Code View screen appears as in Figure 5.3.

If we trace the first five instructions of this program with a T5 debugger command, the Code View debugging screen of Figure 5.3 disappears and we return to the DOS screen. There we type the first of our digits in the range 0 to 4 which the program is to add up. Having done so, we are returned to the Code View debugger screen ready for any necessary debugging actions. How are we to see the DOS screen again? Well, by pressing F4 which toggles between the two. Try it now a few times and then trace the rest of the program, each time stopping just after the user was expected to provide an input value.

5.5.4 Other Code View features

Each of the Code View commands we have described in this section is much richer in capability than we have indicated here. All Code View commands are fully described in the MicroSoft Code View and Utilities manual and it is not our intention to replicate that here. Rather, we have given a useful basic subset of commands with which readers can first gain confidence before getting to know Code View in greater detail in their own good time. However, we shall return to discuss some further features of Code View later in this book.

EXERCISES

5.3 Write and fully test an assembly language program which will perform subtraction between two digits in the range 0 to 4 inclusive and display the result on the screen in the form:

```
4 - 3 = 1
```

followed by a new line and then return to DOS. If the result is negative then the display should take the form:

```
1 - 3 = -2
```

5.4 Write and fully test an assembly language program which accepts an upper-case letter (A,B,. . .,Z) from its user and prints out the rest of the alphabet starting with that letter. Thus if the user types `T` then the display should be:

```
TUVWXYZ
```

followed by a new line and the program should then return to DOS.

SUMMARY

Assembly language programming is highly prone to errors because so much detailed work is involved. In this chapter we learned how to use DEBUG and Code View to locate errors in our assembly language programs. DEBUG and Code View provide good facilities for locating errors, and a summary of the debugger commands introduced in this chapter is given in Table 5.2. As ever, prevention is better than cure. In chapter 8, therefore, we look into programming techniques specifically aimed at minimizing the number of errors in an assembly language program.

Table 5.2 A summary of debugger commands introduced in Chapter 5.

Command	*Purpose*	*Format*
R	Display the contents of all registers. Alter the contents of a register.	R R *register_name*
U	List the instructions contained in the given address and following in assembly language form (the address is relative to the contents of the CS register).	U *address*
D	Display the contents of memory in hexadecimal format and as ASCII characters, starting with the address given (the address is relative to the contents of the DS register).	D *address*
G	Execute the instructions starting with the one in address CS:IP and stop just before executing the instruction in the *stop_address* (the address is relative to the contents of the CS register).	G *stop_address*
T	Trace the execution of the given number of instructions starting with the one having the address given in CS:IP.	T *number*
E	Enter values into memory, starting with *start_address*.	E *start_address*
Q	Finish this session with DEBUG or Code View.	

SELF-CHECK QUIZ

After assembling and linking the following assembly language program:

```
DATA SEGMENT
        LOC1 DW 2
        LOC2 DW 4
        LOC3 DW 6,8
             DB 500H DUP(0)
DATA ENDS

WORKING_STORAGE SEGMENT STACK
        DW 100H DUP(?)
WORKING_STORAGE ENDS

CODE SEGMENT
ASSUME CS:CODE,DS:DATA,SS:WORKING_STORAGE
   START:MOV AX,DATA
         MOV DS,AX
   AGAIN:MOV AX,LOC1
         ADD AX,LOC2
         SUB AX,LOC3
         MOV BX,OFFSET LOC3
         ADD BX,2
         MOV [BX],AX
         JMP AGAIN
CODE ENDS
END START
```

a user invoked either the DEBUG or Code View debugger and obtained the following screen display:

```
-U0
2465:0000 B8F423    MOV   AX,23F4
2465:0003 8ED8      MOV   DS,AX
2465:0005 A10000    MOV   AX,[0000]
2465:0008 03060200  ADD   AX,[0002]
2465:000C 2B060400  SUB   AX,[0004]
2465:0010 BB0400    MOV   BX,0004
2465:0013 83C302    ADD   BX,+02
2465:0016 8907      MOV   [BX],AX
2465:0018 EBEB      JMP   0005
2465:001A 8946FC    MOV   [BP-04],AX
```

1. What will be the contents of each of locations 23F4:0000 to 23F4:0007 inclusive?

2. What would be the result of issuing the `D0` debugger command?

3. What would be the contents of AX after execution of `G8` by the debugger?

4. If the user then issues the debugger command `T2` what will be the contents of AX afterwards?

5. What two commands could the user now issue to complete execution of the program up to and including the `JMP AGAIN` instruction?

6. How could the user arrange to execute the program again from the start without recourse to re-invoking the debugger?

7. If the user issues the debugger command `A8` and then types `SUB AX,[02]`, what will be the contents of AX after resetting IP to 0 and issuing the debugger command `G16`?

8. How could we change the program so that

```
JMP AGAIN
```

would be assembled as a `FAR` jump?

9. How could we change the contents of memory so that the first four instructions calculate the value of 2 + 3?

10. What would have happened if we had not executed the first two instructions in the program?

6

Arithmetic Flags and Operations

Contents

In this chapter the 8086-family instructions for the addition, subtraction, multiplication and division of signed and unsigned numbers and certain related instructions will be described. We shall also see how to resolve ambiguity as to whether the object of certain operations (not just arithmetic) is to be a word or a byte. We start by showing how the flags can be used to monitor the outcome of arithmetic operations and finish with a complete example program which shows several of the arithmetic instructions in a typical application. A complete summary of all the 8086-family arithmetic instructions discussed is given at the end of the chapter.

6.1 Using flags to monitor the outcome of arithmetic operations

Recall that, altogether, five of the bits in the flags register (Figure 6.1) are used to indicate the results of arithmetic and related operations: the O-flag (overflow), the S-flag (sign), the Z-flag (zero), the A-flag (auxiliary carry) and the C-flag (carry).

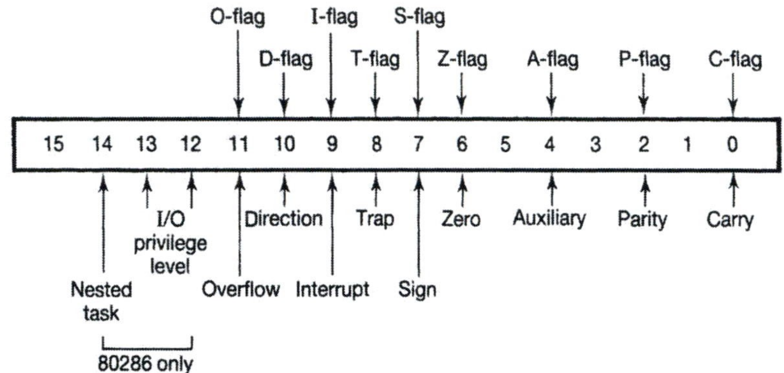

Figure 6.1
The flags register.

Each time an arithmetic instruction is executed, certain flags will be set either to 0 or to 1 to indicate the outcome of that arithmetic operation. Full details of which instructions affect which flags can be found in Appendix V but it is important to note that *not all instructions affect the flags register*. Indeed, different instructions affect different flags. Some instructions do not affect any of the flags; others affect all the flags we have mentioned. Remembering which instructions affect which flags comes with practice since, at first, there seems to be no obvious pattern: `ADD` and `SUB` affect all the arithmetic flags but `INC` affects all of them except the carry flag; `MOV` affects none of the flags.

We shall now consider each of the arithmetic flags in turn and describe which aspect of an arithmetic operation each of them monitors. In the course of this discussion, whether we are working with *signed* or *unsigned* numbers is crucial (see Section 1.3).

6.1.1 The carry flag

During arithmetic operations with unsigned numbers, the **carry flag** records whether certain instructions produced an unsigned number which was too big (or too small) to be held in the specified register or memory location. For example, executing:

```
MOV AL,0FFH
ADD AL,4
```

will set the carry flag to 1 because 0FFH + 4 produces a carry as the result,

103H (= 100000011B), is too large to be correctly represented in the 8-bit register AL. It is important to note, however, that AL will in fact contain 03H after execution – the correct answer without the carry bit:

```
    1111 1111  (= 0FFH)
    0000 0100  (= 4H)
    ---------
(1) 0000 0011  (= 103H)
```

Similarly, executing

```
MOV DH, 2
SUB DH, 0FFH
```

will set the carry flag to 1 because 2 − 0FFH produces a borrow since 0FFH is bigger than 2. But in this case after execution DH will contain 03H, *not* −0FDH which cannot all be represented using only eight bits. This is because `SUB` performs

$x - y$

as

$x + (-y)$

where $(-y)$ is represented in two's complement form. Thus, to calculate

2 − 0FFH

`SUB` has the microprocessor work out the two's complement of 0FFH, namely 00H + 1H = 1H (see Section 1.3), and then adds that to 2, resulting in 3H:

2 − 0FFH −> 2 + (two's complement of 0FFH) −> 2 + 1 −> 3

It follows that care is needed when working with unsigned numbers to ensure that the results of arithmetic operations are kept within range to maintain accuracy. Since the carry flag tells us when things have gone wrong, this is one of its most important uses.

6.1.2 The overflow flag

One of the main uses of the **overflow flag** is to ensure that the results of operations with *signed* numbers are within range. First note that the largest signed number which can be held in a byte is +127 in decimal or 7FH. After execution of:

```
MOV BL, 4H
ADD BL, 7FH
```

the overflow flag will be set to 1 to indicate that the result is out of the range of byte-sized signed numbers. (In fact, after execution, BL will contain 83H – the correct result for an unsigned addition, but representing −7DH as a signed number.)

Similarly, the smallest negative number representable in 8-bit signed form is −128 in decimal or 80H. Given that −2 represented as an 8-bit signed number is 0FEH and +127 in decimal is 7FH as an 8-bit signed number, then after execution of:

```
MOV BL, 0FEH
SUB BL, 07FH
```

the overflow flag will be set to 1 indicating that the result is out of range for 8-bit signed numbers. After execution, BL will contain 7F, the correct answer for an unsigned subtraction. But this does not represent the correct answer when 0FFH and 80H are interpreted as signed numbers: in that case the result should be −2 − 127 = −129.

6.1.3 The sign flag

The **sign flag** is only useful when operating with *signed* numbers. It indicates whether the result of an operation on signed numbers is positive (in which case the sign flag is set to 0) or negative (in which case it is set to 1). Thus, executing the program fragment

```
MOV AL,2
SUB AL,5
```

would set the S-flag to 1 indicating a negative result (and leave AL containing 0FDH, the signed 8-bit form of −3 in decimal), whereas:

```
MOV AL,3
SUB AL,0FFH
```

would set the S-flag to 0 indicating a positive result (for 0FFH is the 8-bit signed representation of −1) and leave AL containing 4.

6.1.4 The zero flag

The **zero flag** records whether an operation produced a zero result. Thus, executing the program fragment

```
MOV AX,2
SUB AX,2
```

would set the zero flag to 1 indicating that the result of `SUB AX,2` was 0 whereas

```
MOV AX,3
SUB AX,2
```

would set the zero flag to 0 indicating that the result of `SUB AX,2` was not 0. Remember:

- If the Z-flag = 0 it means that the result of the last instruction which affected the Z-flag was not 0.
- If the Z-flag = 1 it means that the result of the last instruction which affected the Z-flag was 0.

It follows that testing if two registers, for example CX and DX, both contained the same number would involve subtracting the contents of one register from the other and checking to see if the result was 0, this latter check being carried out by inspecting the Z-flag.

6.1.5 The parity flag

The **parity flag** simply records whether the result of an operation contains an even number of 1s (in which case the parity flag is set to 1) or an odd number of 1s (in which case the parity flag is set to 0). Thus, after executing

```
MOV AL,3
ADD AL,7
```

the parity flag will be set to 1 because the 8-bit binary form for 10 decimal is 00001010 which contains an even number of 1s. Similarly, after

```
MOV AH,8
SUB AH,1
```

the parity flag will be set to 0 because the 8-bit binary form for 7 decimal is 00000111 which contains an odd number of 1s.

For ease of reference, the purposes of the flags which are most important for simple programming tasks are summarized in Table 6.1.

Table 6.1 Purpose of each arithmetic flag.

Flag	*Purpose*
Carry Flag CF	CF is set to 1 if an arithmetic operation on *unsigned* numbers gives a result which is out of range: if an addition has produced a carry then CF is set to 1, otherwise it is set to 0; if a subtraction has produced a borrow then CF is set to 1, otherwise it is set to 0; CF also indicates: the result of a CoMPare operation (see Section 6.2.4); the bit which has been shifted or rotated out of a register or memory location (see Chapter 9); and in conjunction with OF, the result of a multiplication.
Overflow Flag (OF)	OF is set to 1 if an arithmetic operation on *signed* numbers gives a result which is out of range. Thus OF: is set to 1 if adding two like-signed numbers or subtracting two opposite-signed numbers gives a result which requires more bits for an accurate representation than the operands themselves, otherwise it is set to 0; is set to 1 if the sign bit of an operand changes during a shift operation (see Chapter 9), otherwise it is set to 0.

Table 6.1 *(cont.)*

Flag	*Purpose*
	In combination with CF, OF indicates the size of the result of a multiplication: both CF and OF are set to 1 if the upper half of a product is non zero, otherwise both CF and OF are set to 0. Is set to 1 if a division operation produces a quotient that is too big for the register which is to contain the result.
Sign Flag (SF)	Indicates the outcome – positive or negative – of operations on *signed* numbers. SF takes the same value as the most significant (sign) bit of the result.
Zero Flag (ZF)	If the result of an operation is zero, ZF is set to 1, otherwise it is set to 0.
Parity Flag (PF)	If the result of an operation has an even number of bits then PF is set to 1, otherwise it is set to 0. It is mainly useful when transmitting data between devices (see Chapter 20).
Direction Flag (DF)	If DF is set to 0, the 8086-family special string manipulation instructions (see Chapter 11) increment the appropriate index registers and so progress forward through memory, whereas if DF is set to 1 the index registers are decremented and so progress is backward through memory.
Auxiliary Carry Flag (AF)	Similar to CF except that it indicates the presence or absence of a carry or borrow based on a 4-bit numeric representation in bits 0,1,2, and 3. It is useful for operations on 'packed decimal' numbers (see Chapter 15).
Trap Flag (TF)	By setting TF to 1 the 8086-family microprocessors can be forced to operate in single step mode (see Chapter 21).
Interrupt Enable Flag (IF)	Allows interruption to normal 8086-family operation to be initiated from peripherals and other sources (see Chapter 21).

6.1.6 Many instructions affect several flags simultaneously

The preceding examples may have left the impression that a given instruction only affects one of the flags. In fact, as mentioned earlier, a particular instruction may affect a number flags simultaneously – or none at all. For example, both `ADD` and `SUB` affect the carry, overflow, sign, zero and parity flags. `INC` and `DEC` affect all of these *except* the carry flag, and `MOV` affects none of the flags at all. Which flags are affected by which arithmetic instructions is summarized in Table 6.2. Some of the instructions listed there we have yet to

Table 6.2 Summary of the effect on the flags of the arithmetic instructions (see also Appendix V).

Instruction	*Flag affected*				
	Z-flag	*C-flag*	*S-flag*	*O-flag*	*A-flag*
ADD	Yes	Yes	Yes	Yes	Yes
ADC	Yes	Yes	Yes	Yes	Yes
SUB	Yes	Yes	Yes	Yes	Yes
SBB	Yes	Yes	Yes	Yes	Yes
INC	Yes	No	Yes	Yes	Yes
DEC	Yes	No	Yes	Yes	Yes
NEG	Yes	Yes	Yes	Yes	Yes
CMP	Yes	Yes	Yes	Yes	Yes
MUL	No	Yes	No	Yes	No
IMUL	No	Yes	No	Yes	No
DIV	No	No	No	No	No
IDIV	No	No	No	No	No
CBW	No	No	No	No	No
CWD	No	No	No	No	No

meet, but by the end of the chapter we shall have encountered all of them. Appendix V contains complete information about the flags affected by all 8086-family instructions.

To see what actually happens, let us trace the state of the flags through the execution of a short program sequence involving arithmetic operations. Following our notational convention established earlier, a ? denotes a flag value which we do not know.

Instruction	*Flags*					*Comment*
	Carry	*Overflow*	*Sign*	*Zero*	*Parity*	
	?	?	?	?	?	When execution begins we do not know what the flags have been set to already
`MOV BL,3`	?	?	?	?	?	MOV does not affect the flags
`ADD BL,2`	0	0	0	0	1	Decimal 5 = 00000101 in binary
`SUB BL,5`	0	0	0	1	1	Since 3 + 2 − 5 = 0
`SUB BL,2`	0	0	1	0	0	Result (−2) is now negative

Instruction	*Flags* Carry	Overflow	Sign	Zero	Parity	*Comment*
MOV DH,2	0	0	1	0	0	MOV does not affect the flags
ADD DH,0FFH	1	0	0	0	0	Carry because 2 + 0FFH = 101H
MOV AL,4	1	0	0	0	0	MOV does not affect the flags
ADD AL,7FH	1	1	1	0	0	Signed number overflow

EXERCISES

6.1 For each of the following program sequences, make a similar trace of the values taken by the flags as the program is executed. Verify your answers by using a debugger.

(a)
```
MOV DH,3
ADD DH,2
ADD DH,1
SUB DH,73H
ADD DH,79H
ADD DH,2
ADD DH,0FAH
ADD DH,3
```

(b)
```
MOV AX, 0FEH
INC AX
MOV BX,0
ADD BX,AX
DEC BX
SUB AX,BX
INC AX
INC BX
SUB AX,BX
DEC AX
ADD BX,BX
SUB AX,BX
INC BX
INC AX
```

(c)
```
MOV CL,1
SUB CL,65H
SUB CL,21H
SUB CL,86H
SUB CL,33H
```

(d)
```
MOV AX,2
SUB AX,0FFFFH
MOV BX,AX
DIV BX
ADD AX,AX
```

(e)
```
MOV AX,0FFFH
MUL AX
SUB AX
ADD AX,1
SUB DX,DX
```

(f)
```
MOV AX,0110H
ADD AX,1000H
MOV CL,4
SUB AL,CL
MOV CH,2
ADD CX,AX
```

(g)
```
MOV AX,0F24FH
MOV BX,0A3F5H
ADD BX,AX
SUB AX,0F24EH
MOV CX,1000H
ADD CX,0E14CH
ADD CX,0EEEEH
```

(h)
```
MOV AX,9000H
SUB AX,0FFFFH
MOV CX,5750H
ADD CX,0AABBH
MOV DX,0EBB3H
ADD DX,144CH
MOV BX,2H
ADD BX,0EFFEH
```

6.2 For a certain application, a programmer wanted to regard `BL,AX` as containing a 24-bit signed number and `DL,CX` as containing another signed 24-bit number with BL and DL respectively containing the higher order bits. Explain how the programmer could add these signed numbers using the `ADD` instruction and how it would be possible to check whether the result was zero, or involved a carry or overflow.

6.3 Design some program fragments to carry out arithmetic on signed 10D-bit numbers held in the general-purpose 8086-family registers. Explain how you would detect overflow, record any carry from an arithmetic operation and detect if the outcome of an arithmetic operation were zero.

6.2 Addition and subtraction

The 8086-family instructions for the addition and subtraction of signed and unsigned numbers comprise `INC`, `ADD`, `ADC` (ADd with Carry), `DEC`, `SUB`, `SBB` (SuBtract with Borrow), `CMP` (CoMPare) and `NEG` (NEGate).

6.2.1 INC and DEC

`INC` and `DEC` we have already met. They both affect all of the arithmetic flags except the carry flag. `INC` increments its operand by one; `DEC` decrements its operand by one. `INC` and `DEC` take the following general forms:

`INC` *register* `DEC` *register*
`INC` *memory* `DEC` *memory*

where *register* denotes any non-segment register and *memory* any valid byte or word memory pointer.

Thus, if AX contains 03ABH before execution of:

```
INC AX
```

then afterwards AX will contain 03ACH. If AX contains 0FFFFH before execution of `INC AX`, then afterwards it will contain 0000H.

We can also increment bytes or words stored in memory. But to do so it is necessary to make it clear to the assembler whether a memory reference, such as that in the incorrect instruction

```
INC [BX] ;incorrect instruction
```

is to a word or a byte. This is done by means of the pseudo-ops `BYTE PTR` and `WORD PTR` respectively (PTR is short for PoinTeR). Thus:

```
INC BYTE PTR [BX]
```

will increment the *byte* stored at DS:BX by 1, whereas:

```
INC WORD PTR [BX]
```

will increment the word stored at DS:BX by 1.

Suppose that we have defined a word in memory in the data segment of a program (following our layout convention established in Chapter 4) as follows:

```
KEEP_COUNT DW ?
```

Then if the word referred to by KEEP_COUNT contains 0FABCH before execution of:

```
DEC KEEP_COUNT
```

then, afterwards, that word will contain 0FABBH. (This latter instruction is unambiguous because the assembler knows from the definition of KEEP_COUNT that it refers to a word).

6.2.2 ADD and ADC

Both ADD and ADC affect all of the arithmetic flags, but the effect they have is defined only for the carry and auxiliary carry flags. The ADD and ADC instructions may take the forms:

```
ADD register,number       ADC register,number
ADD memory,number         ADC memory,number
ADD register,register     ADC register,register
ADD register,memory       ADC register,memory
ADD memory,register       ADC memory,register
```

Here, a format such as:

```
ADD register,register
```

is really an abuse of notation for we actually mean

```
ADD register1,register2
```

where *register1* and *register2* both denote any one of the execution unit registers including AX, BX, CX, DX and their 8-bit counterparts. Thus, typical examples of instructions of the form

```
ADD register,register
```

are ADD AL,BL, ADD CX,DX, and ADD BH,BH.

number stands for any signed or un-signed number of an appropriate size, either 8 or 16 bits long, or any assembly language expression which results in a number. Typical examples of the format

```
ADD register,number
```

are therefore ADD AL,27H, ADD DH,00011011B, and ADD CX,0ABCFH. Moreover, thanks to assembly language, we can write expressions such as:

```
ADD AL,'N'
```

and the assembler will replace 'N' by the ASCII code for the letter N (4EH) and so convert this to the machine code equivalent of

```
ADD AL,4EH
```

memory stands for any allowed specification of an address in memory.

The range of permissible specifications will grow in the course of later chapters. With that available now, typical examples of the formats

```
ADD register,memory
ADD memory,register
```

are `ADD AX,[BX]`, `ADD AL,MYBYTE`, and `ADD MYBYTE,CL`.

The instruction

```
ADD DX,CX
```

adds the contents of register DX to the contents of register CX and leaves the result in DX. Thus, if before execution DX contained 1234H and CX contained 6AB1H then after execution of

```
ADD DX,CX
```

DX would contain 1234H + 6AB1H = 7CE5H and CX would contain 6AB1H.

If `MYBYTE` corresponds to an offset of 300H relative to DS then

```
ADD AL,MYBYTE
```

adds the contents of AL and location 300H (relative to the contents of DS). `ADC` is similar to `ADD` except that the current value of the carry flag is included in any addition. For example:

```
ADC AX,[BX]
```

adds the contents of the word in memory pointed to by register BX to the contents of register AX, *and then adds the current value of the carry flag to that* and leaves the result in register AX. Thus if AX contains 0AEFFH, BX contains 1023H, the word at DS:1023H in memory contains 4BBCH and the carry flag is set to 1, then after execution of

```
ADC AX,[BX]
```

AX will contain 0AEFFH + 4BBCH + 1 = 0FABCH, BX will contain 1023H, the word at DS:1023H in memory will contain 4BBCH and the carry flag will be set to 0.

In the latter case it was clear to the assembler that the *word* pointed to by BX was required since we wanted something to add to AX and we always add like quantities. However, as with `INC` and `DEC`, it is necessary to resolve the ambiguity in an incorrect instruction like:

```
ADD [BX],3 ;incorrect instruction
```

by means of `BYTE PTR` and `WORD PTR`. Thus, in:

```
ADD WORD PTR [BX],3
```

3 will be added to the word at DS:BX whereas in:

```
ADD BYTE PTR [BX],3
```

3 will be added to the byte at DS:BX.

6.2.3 SUB and SBB

The SUB and SBB instructions have the same general formats as the ADD and ADC instruction described above, namely:

SUB *register,number*	SBB *register,number*
SUB *memory,number*	SBB *memory,number*
SUB *register,register*	SBB *register,register*
SUB *register,memory*	SBB *register,memory*
SUB *memory,register*	SBB *memory,register*

where *register* denotes any non-segment register and *memory* any valid byte or word memory pointer. Both affect all the arithmetic flags and set them according to the outcome of the arithmetic operation except that the effect of SUB on the auxiliary carry flag is indeterminate.

An instruction

```
SUB TOTAL,AL
```

is unambiguous because AL determines that 8-bit arithmetic will be performed (and because of the definition of TOTAL, which must be as a byte). If, before execution, the value stored at TOTAL is 37H and AL contains 21H then after execution the value stored at TOTAL will be 16H and AL will contain 21H.

An instruction of the form

```
SBB DX,BX
```

adds the current contents of the carry flag (0 or 1) to the contents of register BX and subtracts the resulting total from the contents of register DX, leaving the result in DX.

The other formats for SBB follow this pattern. Thus, if DS:BX contains 1FH, AL contains 23H and the carry flag is set to 1, then after execution of

```
SBB AL,[BX]
```

AL will contain 3H, DS:BX will contain 1FH and the carry flag will be set to 0.

6.2.4 CMP

As we shall see in Chapter 7, the main use of CMP (CoMPare) is in decision making in conjunction with conditional jumps. It takes one of the following forms (where we assume that comparisons are always made between numbers of the same size):

CMP *register,number*
CMP *register,register*
CMP *memory,number*
CMP *register,memory*
CMP *memory,register*

The CMP instruction does not change the value of any of the 8086-family registers but simply sets the flags according to the outcome of subtracting its second operand from the first. Thus if AL contained 38H before execution of

```
CMP AL,38H
```

then, after execution, AL would contain 38H still but the zero flag would be set to 1 indicating that 38H subtracted from the contents of AL gave zero. Similarly, if AL contained 1AH before execution of

```
CMP AL,41H
```

then AL would still contain 41H afterwards, but the carry and sign flags would be set to 1 indicating that the result was negative. (In fact the flags are always set exactly as they would be by a SUB instruction but CMP does not change the value of the register or memory location(s) involved.)

6.2.5 NEG

NEG turns positive 8-bit and 16-bit signed numbers into their negative two's complement equivalent and vice versa (NEG is short for NEGate). It takes the general forms

NEG *register*
NEG *memory*

where *register* denotes any non-segment register and *memory* any valid byte or word memory pointer. It affects all the arithmetic flags and sets the carry flag to 1 unless the value in *register* or *memory* is zero in which case it sets the carry flag to 0.

Thus, if CX contains 00000001 00011001B (the 16-bit signed representation of +25) to begin with, then after the instruction

```
NEG CX
```

has been executed, CX contains 11111111 11100111B (the 16-bit two's complement representation of −25) and the carry flag will be set to 1. Similarly, if DS:BX contains 11111111 11110001B (the 16-bit two's complement representation of −15), after

```
NEG WORD PTR [BX]
```

it will contain 00000001 00001111B (the 16-bit signed representation of +15) and the carry flag will be set to 1.

EXERCISES

6.4 Add the necessary assembler pseudo-ops, assemble, link and run under debugger control the following simple program:

```
MOV AL,3
INC AL
MOV BL,0FEH
DEC BL
ADD AL,BL
SUB AL,BL
SBB AL,BL
NEG AL
```

and hence complete the following table of flag values after the execution of each instruction in this program. Try to account for what you find.

Instruction	*Flag values* AF	SF	OF	ZF	PF	CF
MOV AL,3						
INC AL						
MOV BL,0FEH						
DEC BL						
ADD AL,BL						
SUB AL,BL						
SBB AL,BL						
NEG AL						

6.5 Hand trace the execution of the following program fragments showing what happens to the flags in each case.

(a)
```
MOV DH,3
NEG DH,2
SUB DH,1
SUB DH,73H
ADD DH,79H
ADD DH,2
CMP DH,0FAH
ADD DH,3
```

(b)
```
MOV AX,0FEH
INC AX
MOV BX,0
ADD BX,AX
NEG BX
SUB AX,BX
NEG AX
NEG BX
SBB AX,BX
DEC AX
ADC BX,BX
SUB AX,BX
NEG BX
NEG AX
```

(c)
```
MOV CL,1
SUB CL,65H
NEG CL,21H
ADD CL,86H
SBB CL,33H
```

(d)
```
MOV AX,0F24FH
MOV BX,0A3F5H
ADD BX,AX
SBB AX,0F24EH
MOV CX,1000H
ADD CX,0F14CH
ADC CX,0EEEEH
```

(e)
```
MOV AX,9000H
SUB AX,0FFFFH
MOV CX,5750H
ADC CX,0AABBH
MOV DX,0EBB3H
ADC DX,144CH
MOV BX,2H
ADD BX,0EFFEH
```

6.6 Can you write a sequence of 8086-family instructions which is *exactly* equivalent to `SBB AL,BL` (of course, you should not use the `SBB` instruction to do so)?

6.7 Repeat Exercise 6.6 for the `SUB` instruction:

(a) without using `SUB`; and

(b) without using `SUB` or `SBB`.

6.8 Can you write a sequence of 8086-family instructions which is *exactly* equivalent to `ADC AL,BL` (of course, you should not use the `ADC` instruction to do so)?

6.9 Repeat Exercise 6.8 for the `ADD` instruction:

(a) without using `ADD`; and

(b) without using `ADD` or `ADC`.

6.3 Multiplication

While the `ADD` and `SUB` instructions will work with both signed and unsigned numbers, the 8086 family provides separate instructions for the multiplication and division of signed and unsigned numbers. Thus for signed multiplication and division we have `IMUL` (Integer MULtiplication) and `IDIV` (Integer DIVision), and for unsigned multiplication and division we have `MUL` and `DIV`.

6.3.1 Multiplication of signed numbers

The `IMUL` instruction takes one of the forms:

`IMUL` *register*
`IMUL` *memory*

where *register* denotes any non-segment register and *memory* any valid byte or word memory pointer.

Either two 8-bit numbers are multiplied together, or two 16-bit numbers. If two 8-bit numbers are to be multiplied together, one of them must be in the AL register and the other is specified by the *register* or *memory* operand in the instruction. The 16-bit result is then left in AX. For example, if AL contains 61H and CL contains 4H then after execution of

```
IMUL CL
```

AX will contain 0184H and CL will contain 4H:

```
AL      01100001 (= 61H)
CL      00000100 (=  4H)
    ----------------
AX 0000000110000100 (= 0184H)
    ----------------
```

If two 16-bit numbers are to be multiplied together, one of them must be in the AX register and the other is specified by the *register* or *memory* operand in the instruction. The 32-bit result is then left in DX and AX with DX containing the higher order bits. Thus

```
IMUL CX
```

will multiply the signed 16-bit number in register AX by the signed 16-bit number in register CX and leave the signed 32-bit result in registers AX and DX, DX containing the higher order bits. If AX contains 2003H (8195 in decimal) and CX contains 0011H (the signed equivalent of 17 in decimal), then after execution of

```
IMUL CX
```

DX will contain 0002H and AX will contain 2033H so that DX,AX contains 00022033H (the 32-bit signed equivalent of 8195 * 17 = 139315 in decimal) and CX will be unchanged:

```
                AX 0010000000000011B
                CX 0000000000010001B
----------------------------------------
                0010000000000110000B
                    0010000000000011B
----------------------------------------
00000000000000100010000000110011B
└──── DX ────┘└──── AX ────┘
```

Similarly:

```
IMUL WORD PTR LIMIT
```

would multiply the signed 16-bit number in register AX by the signed 16-bit number stored at the word referred to by `LIMIT` and leave the signed 32-bit result in DX,AX with the contents of the word at LIMIT being unchanged.

6.3.2 Multiplication of unsigned numbers

In this case the formats are:

`MUL` *register*
`MUL` *memory*

where *register* denotes any non-segment register and *memory* any valid byte or word memory pointer. Both of these work in exactly the same way as the corresponding `IMUL` instruction but the result is unsigned.

EXERCISES

6.10 Write fragments of 8086-family assembly language which will:

(a) Leave in DX,AX the value of $(a * (b - c) * d)$ where a, b, c, d denote the signed 8-bit contents of AL, BL, CL and DL respectively. (Assume that the result can be accurately represented as a signed 32-bit number.)

(b) Leave $(a + b) * (a + b) * (c - d)$ in DX,AX where a, b, c and d are as in (a) above.

6.11 Write an assembly language program which will accept as input from its user a digit in the range 0,1,. . .,9 inclusive and then print a new line on the display screen, print the value of double that digit, followed by a new line and then return to the operating system. Thus, if the user types `6`, then the program should display `12 (= 2 * 6)`.

6.12 Write an assembly language program which allows its user to type in two digits in the range 0,1,. . .,9 inclusive and then prints out their product followed by a new line and then returns to the operating system. Thus, the program should be capable of the following dialogue with its user:

```
First digit: 3
Second digit: 7
Product is: 21
```

6.4 Division

As for multiplication, there are separate instructions for signed and unsigned division – `IDIV` and `DIV` respectively. Moreover, both `IDIV` and `DIV` allow the alternatives of dividing an 8-bit number into a 16-bit number or of dividing a 16-bit number into a 32-bit one. Both do elementary school 'long division with whole numbers' so that dividing 7D into 36D would give a quotient of 5D and a remainder of 1D.

Both `IDIV` and `DIV` operate according to whichever of the following schemes the programmer chooses:

(1) *Division into a 32-bit number*
The 32-bit number must be placed in registers DX and AX (DX containing the higher order bits). It will then be divided by the contents of the specified 16-bit *register* or the corresponding *memory* word. The result will be left in registers AX and DX: quotient in AX, remainder in DX (see Figure 6.2).

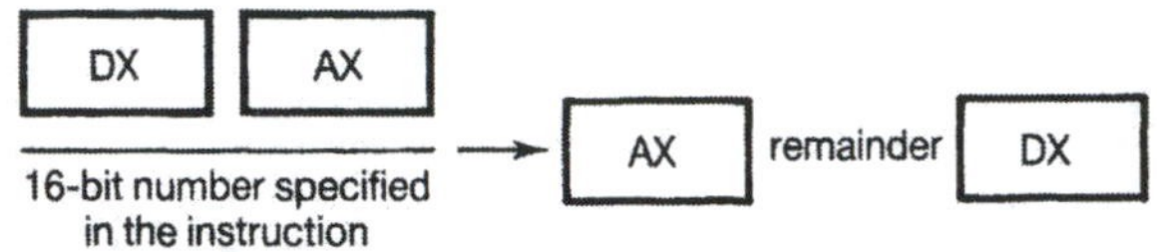

Figure 6.2 Division into a 32-bit number.

(2) *Division into a 16-bit number*
The 16-bit number in register AX is divided by the contents of the specified 8-bit register or memory location and the result left in registers AL and AH: quotient in AL, remainder in AH (see Figure 6.3).

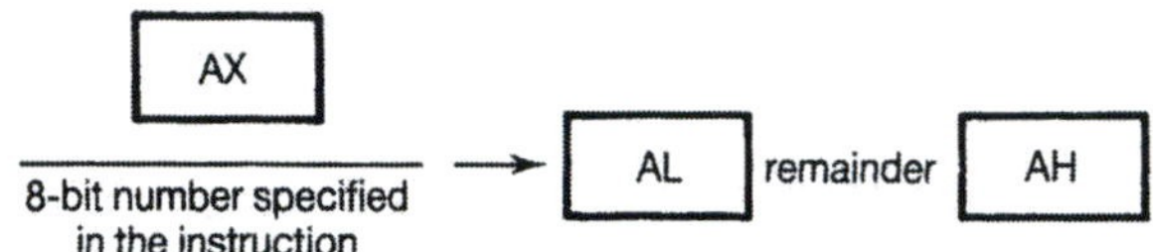

Figure 6.3 Division into a 16-bit number.

6.4.1 Division of signed numbers

`IDIV` takes one of the forms:

`IDIV` *register*
`IDIV` *memory*

where *register* denotes any non-segment register and *memory* any valid byte or word memory pointer.

Thus, if AX contains 0056H and CL contains 11H then after execution of

```
IDIV CL
```

AL will contain 5 and AH will contain 1 because 56H = (5 * 11H) + 1 that is, dividing 11H into 56H gives 5 remainder 1. (CL will be unchanged.)

Similarly, if DX,AX contains 000244ACH and the word pointed to by TOTAL contains 3H, then after execution of

```
IDIV TOTAL
```

AX will contain 0C18BH and DX will contain 1H because 244ACH divided by 3H is 0C18BH remainder 1. (The contents of the word pointed to by TOTAL will be unchanged.)

Note that `IDIV` always arranges that the sign of the remainder will be the same as that of the number into which you are dividing. Thus if we divide decimal −26 by decimal +7 using `IDIV` the result will be −3 remainder −5.

6.4.2 Division of unsigned numbers

`DIV` takes one of the forms:

`DIV` *register*
`DIV` *memory*

where *register* denotes any non-segment register and *memory* any valid byte or word memory pointer. Both of these work in exactly the same way as the corresponding `IDIV` instruction but the results are unsigned.

Warning – division by zero

Any attempt to divide by zero will cause your computer to resort to all manner of strange behaviour – exactly what will depend on the particular make – and you will probably have to switch it off and start running your program all over again. Consequently, great care must be taken within a program to ensure that division by zero is never attempted. (To be completely honest, the disastrous results of dividing by zero can be brought under programmer control – see Chapter 21).

6.4.3 CBW and CWD

The 8086-family multiplication and division instructions were designed so that the double-length result of a multiplication could be used in a division later in the same program. But facilities are also provided to enable numbers which did not arise from a former multiplication to be used easily in a division. For example, if we want to divide the 8-bit unsigned equivalent of decimal 35 (00100011) by 7 (00000111) then the `DIV` instruction expects the number we want to divide into (35) to be in 16-bit form in AX. We cannot just put 35 into AL, therefore, or whatever was in AH will form part of the number we shall divide into. What is required is an instruction to convert the 8-bit signed number in AL into a 16-bit signed equivalent in AX. Enter `CBW`.

The instruction:

```
CBW
```

tests the leftmost bit of AL. If it is a 1 (so that the content of AL regarded as a signed number is negative), then AH is set to 0FFH so that AX now contains the 16-bit signed equivalent of what is in AL. If it is a 0 (so that the contents of AL regarded as a signed number is positive), then AH is set to zero so that AX now contains the 16-bit signed equivalent of what was in AL.

For example, if AL contains 0F1H (the signed 8-bit form of −15 in decimal) before execution of

```
CBW
```

then after execution, AX contains 0FFF1H which is the signed 16-bit equivalent of −(0000000000001110B + 1) = −(0000000000001111B) = −15 in decimal.

For a 32-bit division which did not arise as the result of a multiplication we require an instruction which will similarly convert the signed 16-bit number in AX to a signed 32-bit equivalent in DX,AX. Enter `CWD`.

The instruction

```
CWD
```

stores 0FFFFH in DX if the highest order bit of AX (that is, the sign bit in a signed 16-bit representation) is 1 and stores 0000H in DX otherwise. This allows us to regard DX and AX as containing the signed 32-bit form of what was in AX, with DX containing the higher order bits.

EXERCISES

6.13 Write fragments of 8086-family assembly language which will:

(a) Leave in AX the value of $(a - b) / (c - d)$ where a, b, c, d denote the signed 16-bit contents of AX, BX, CX and DX respectively and where we assume that $c - d$ is not zero.

(b) Leave the average value $(a + b + c) / 3$ in register DX where a, b, c are as in (a) above.

(c) Leave the value of $(b * c) / a$ in register DX where a, b, c are as in (b) above and it is assumed that the content of AX is not zero.

6.14 Write a program to find the average of a collection of at most 10D digits 0,1,2,. . .,9 typed in at the keyboard. The program first asks the user to type the number of digits to be averaged:

```
Type number of digits:
```

and waits for this to be entered and for the ENTER key to be pressed. The program then prints a new line on the display screen and requests each digit in the form

```
Please enter digit 1:
```

and waits for that digit to be typed followed by the ENTER key. When all of the digits have been typed, a new line is printed on the display screen and then the average of the digits is displayed to the nearest whole number. It then prints another new line and returns to the operating system.

For example, your program should be capable of generating the following dialogue:

```
Type number of digits:3
Please enter digit 1:4
Please enter digit 2:5
Please enter digit 3:7
Average is:5
```

6.15 As part of an investigation into the properties of the first 12 prime numbers (2,3,5,7,11,13,17,19,23,29,31 and 37) a student came up with the hypothesis that if you multiply a prime number by itself and then subtract 1, the result is always divisible by 2 or 3. Thus:

$(2 * 2) - 1 = 3$; $(3 * 3) - 1 = 8$; $(4 * 4) - 1 = 15$;

Write an assembly language program which checks this hypothesis out for the first 12 prime numbers and prints YES on the display screen if it is true for all of them and NO if it is not, followed by a new line and a return to the operating system.

6.5 A complete program example using the arithmetic instructions

We shall write a program which will find all decimal 3-digit numbers which are equal to the sum of the cubes of their digits. Thus:

$153 = 1^3 + 5^3 + 3^3$

The numbers to be considered are those in the range 100D to 999D. We shall store each of the three digits in a separate word in memory and initialize the three digits to the first number in the range, 100D:

```
FIRST_DIGIT  DW 1
SECOND_DIGIT DW 0
THIRD_DIGIT  DW 0
```

The main sequence of operations in the program can be described informally by mimicking the **repeat** . . . **until** loop in Pascal:

repeat
cube each of the digits and add up the cubes in BX;
put the binary version of the number the digits represent in AX;
compare AX and BX;
if they are the same: display the digits by first converting each digit to ASCII and then display them using `INT 21H`, *and then display a new line;*
think of the stored digits as a decimal number and increment that number;
until *999D has been tried*

To this we need to add instructions to establish data segment addressability and to return to DOS control when we have found all the desired three digit numbers. The complete program is given in Figure 6.4. As usual, the manner in which it has been implemented has been determined by the desire to illustrate concepts in as straightforward a way as possible – there are more beautiful ways of doing the same thing. But nevertheless, if you take the trouble to run the program, the output is quite a surprise.

At the very end of the program, note the use of

```
NEW_NUMBER: .
            .
            .
            JZ FINISH
            JMP NEW_NUMBER
    ;return to dos
     FINISH:MOV AX,4C00H
```

rather than the more obvious construction:

```
NEW_NUMBER: .
            .
            .
           JNZ NEW_NUMBER
   ;return to dos
            MOV AX,4C00H
```

This is necessary because in the second version the target for the JNZ (the instruction labeled NEW_NUMBER) is more than 128 bytes away from the JNZ instruction itself, and so would be out of range. The interested reader may replace the first version in our example program with the second to discover how MASM reports such an error.

```
DATA SEGMENT
         FIRST_DIGIT   DW 1
         SECOND_DIGIT DW 0
         THIRD_DIGIT   DW 0
DATA ENDS

WORKING_STORE SEGMENT STACK
         DW 100H DUP(?)
WORKING_STORE ENDS

CODE SEGMENT
ASSUME DS:DATA, SS:WORKING_STORE, CS:CODE
;establish data segment addressability
     START:MOV AX,DATA
           MOV DS,AX
;cube digits and add into BX
NEW_NUMBER:MOV AX,FIRST_DIGIT
           MOV CX,AX
           MUL CX
           MUL CX
           MOV BX,AX
           MOV AX,SECOND_DIGIT
           MOV CX,AX
           MUL CX
           MUL CX
           ADD BX,AX
           MOV AX,THIRD_DIGIT
           MOV CX,AX
           MUL CX
```

Figure 6.4 Finding decimal 3-digit numbers which are the sum of the cubes of their digits.

```
          MUL CX
          ADD BX,AX
;binary version of the number the digits represent in AX
          MOV AX,FIRST_DIGIT
          MOV CX,10D
          MUL CX
          ADD AX,SECOND_DIGIT
          MUL CX
          ADD AX,THIRD_DIGIT
;compare
          CMP AX,BX
;if they are the same then display the digits
          JNZ NEW_DIGITS
;convert each digit to ASCII and display
          MOV DX,FIRST_DIGIT
          ADD DL,30H
          MOV AH,2H
          INT 21H
          MOV DX,SECOND_DIGIT
          ADD DL,30H
          INT 21H
          MOV DX,THIRD_DIGIT
          ADD DL,30H
          INT 21H
;display a new line
          MOV DL,0DH
          INT 21H
          MOV DL,0AH
          INT 21H
;next three digits
NEW_DIGITS: INC THIRD_DIGIT
          CMP THIRD_DIGIT,10D
          JNZ NEW_NUMBER
          MOV THIRD_DIGIT,0
          INC SECOND_DIGIT
          CMP SECOND_DIGIT,10D
          JNZ NEW_NUMBER
          MOV SECOND_DIGIT,0
          INC FIRST_DIGIT
          CMP FIRST_DIGIT,10D
          JZ  FINISH
          JMP NEW_NUMBER
;return to dos
    FINISH: MOV AX,4C00H
          INT 21H
CODE ENDS
END START
```

Figure 6.4
(cont.)

EXERCISE

6.16 Write 8086-family assembly language programs to find:

(a) All possible sets of three decimal digits in which the digits make up a Pythagorean triple. Thus, {3, 4, 5} is a Pythagorean triple because $3^2 + 4^2 = 5^2$

(b) All 3-digit decimal numbers for which the sum of the digits is an exact divisor of the product of its digits. For example, this property holds for 862 because:

$8 + 6 + 2 = 16$ and $8 * 6 * 2 = 96$

and $96 / 16 = 6$.

(c) All 2-digit decimal numbers which are the sum of the squares of two of the decimal numbers in the set {2, 3, 5, 7}. Thus,

$34 = 5^2 + 3^2$

(d) All decimal numbers which are the product of three of the numbers in the set {2, 3, 5, 7}. Thus,

$42 = 2 * 3 * 7$

(e) The number of values of the expression $x^2 + x + 41$ which are prime numbers (that is, they are larger than 1 and exactly divisible only by themselves and 1) when x is chosen from the range 1, 2,. . .,20. For example, if x is 1 then the value of the expression is $1 + 1 + 41 = 43$ which is a prime number.

SUMMARY

This chapter has featured the 8086-family arithmetic instructions (which are summarized in Table 6.3) and the use of some of them in a complete program example. Chapter 10 will provide an illustration of the use of almost all of the 8086-family arithmetic instructions in a fairly large assembly language program. Table 6.2 summarized the effect on the flags of the arithmetic instructions (see also Appendix V).

Table 6.3 A summary of 8086-family arithmetic instructions.

Instruction	*Effect*
Addition	
`ADD` op1,op2	op1 := *op1* + *op2*. Allowed formats: *op1* *op2* *register* *number* *memory* *number* *register* *register* *memory* *register* *register* *memory*
`ADC` *op1,op2*	ADd with Carry: if CF = 0, then `ADD` as above. If CF = 1, then *op1* := *op1* + *op2* + 1.
`INC` *op*	INCrement: *op* := *op* + 1. The operand may be in either a register or in memory.
Subtraction	
`SUB` *op1,op2*	*op1* := *op1* − *op2*. Allowed formats as in `ADD` above.
`SBB` *op1,op2*	SuBtract with Borrow: if CF = 0, then `SUB` as above. If CF = 1 then *op1* := *op1* − *op2* − 1.
`DEC` *op*	DECrement: *op* := *op* − 1. The operand may be in either a register or in memory.
`NEG` *op*	NEGate: *op* := 0 − *op*. Operand as in `DEC`.
`CMP` *op1,op2*	CoMPare: set flags according to the result of *op1* − *op2* but do not change either operand.
Multiplication	
`MUL` *op*	MULtiplication (unsigned): if op is a byte, then AH,AL := *op* * AL. If op is a word, then DX,AX := *op* * AX. If the upper half of the result is not zero then CF and OF are set to 1. *op* can be either in a register or in memory.
`IMUL` *op*	Integer MULtiplication (signed): as with `MUL` except that signed multiplication takes place.
Division	
`DIV` *op*	DIVision (unsigned): if *op* is a byte, then (AH,AL) / *op* = AL remainder AH. If *op* is a word, then (DX,AX) / *op* = AX remainder DX. If the quotient exceeds the capacity of AL or AX, then both quotient and remainder are undefined (and a type 0 interrupt is generated – see Chapter 21). *op* can be as in `MUL` above.
`IDIV` *op*	Integer DIVision (signed): as with `DIV` above except that a signed division takes place.
Sign extension	
`CBW`	Convert Byte to Word: the 8-bit signed number in AL is converted to 16-bit signed equivalent in AX.
`CWD`	The 16-bit signed number in AX is converted to a 32-bit signed equivalent in DX,AX with DX containing the higher order bits.

SELF-CHECK QUIZ

1. If AX contains 00BBH and BX contains 00BCH and then `SUB AX,BX` is executed, which of the following would be possible contents of the flags register:

   (a) 0211H (b) F221H (c) 0221H

2. Where possible, give short assembly language sequences using arithmetic instructions which perform an arithmetic operation and, as a result, will *simultaneously* set the named flags to the required values. If the required settings are not simultaneously possible, give a reason why not.

   (a) Z and C flags to 0

   (b) Z and C flags to 1

   (c) C and S flags to 0

   (d) C and S flags to 1

3. If AL contains a signed number in the range 20D to 30D, what is the largest number that can be added to it without causing overflow?

4. If a `CMP` instruction is used to compare two values, explain how the values of the S-flag and the O-flag can tell you if one operand were *less* than the other. Which combination of flag values will tell you whether one operand is *less than or equal* to another after a `CMP` instruction has been executed?

5. To double a value n, we can calculate either $n + n$, or $2 * n$, or $n - (-n)$. Write three sequences of assembly language instructions each of which doubles the contents of AX using each of these expressions respectively.

6. Because of overflow, arithmetic with signed numbers can fail the mathematical law which says that $(a + (b + c)) = ((a + b) + c)$. Can you find an example of this for 8-bit signed numbers? Can you find a corresponding example involving unsigned 8-bit numbers?

7. Repeat exercise 6 but for the mathematical law which says that $((a * b) * c) = (a * (b * c))$.

8. Write an assembly language sequence which will change the signed number in AL which represents a student's score out of 20D, into a whole-number percentage in AL.

9. Explain in detail the effect of the instruction sequence:

   ```
   CBW
   CWD
   ```

   on AL.

10. Does the instruction sequence:

    ```
    ADC AX,BX
    SBB AX,BX
    ```

    always leave AX unchanged? Explain your answer.

7

Jumps and Loops

Contents

Normally, assembly language instructions are executed in the order in which they are given to the microprocessor (or, what often amounts to the same thing, in the order that they occur in the program). The programmer can use jump instructions to alter this mechanism. Conditional jump instructions cause execution to continue not from the next instruction in sequence, but from some remote instruction *provided some condition is satisfied*. In this chapter we shall introduce all 18 of the different conditional jumps which the 8086-family members can execute and describe the actions of many of them.

The most important ways in which conditional jumps can be used to change the flow of control in a program are in the implementation of loops similar to **for**, **repeat** and **while** loops in Pascal and in taking decisions. Sections 7.2 and 7.3 discuss how to program loops in 8086-family assembly language using both conditional jumps and the instructions LOOP, LOOPZ and LOOPNZ which 8086-family assembly language provides especially for this purpose. It is necessary to consider both of these approaches since the simplicity and efficiency gains from using LOOP, LOOPZ and LOOPNZ may only be obtained when there are a fixed maximum number of repetitions of a loop and a single condition can be used to determine whether the end of a loop has been reached.

The use of conditional jumps to implement decision-taking in programs is discussed in the penultimate section and this is followed by a complete example program which illustrates several of the ideas in this chapter.

7.1 Conditional jumps

The execution of **conditional jumps** depends on the 8086-family flags, since whether or not a certain condition is met is dependent on the current setting of a particular flag. Thus, the precise meaning of

JZ *<label>*

is 'if the Z-flag is currently set to 1, then jump to the instruction labeled *<label>* and continue execution from there'. Another, slightly less formal interpretation, is 'jump to *<label>* if the result of the last instruction to affect the Z-flag was zero'. For

JNZ *<label>*

the precise meaning is similarly, 'if the Z-flag is currently set to 0, then jump to the instruction labeled *<label>* and continue execution from there'. Slightly less formally, 'jump to *<label>* if the result of the last instruction to affect the Z-flag was not zero'.

Instructions such as JZ allow the programmer to change the order of instruction execution depending on whether the result of the last instruction to affect the flags was zero or non-zero or, equivalently, whether when the contents of two registers were compared, it turned out that they contained the same thing. Provision has also been made for jumps conditional upon comparing signed numbers and unsigned numbers, and for jumps conditional upon the settings of particular flags and conditional upon the value of the CX register.

Altogether, the 8086 family has 18 different kinds of conditional jump instructions allowing the execution sequence to be altered and these are summarized in Table 7.1. In the table, CF stands for the Carry Flag, ZF for the Zero Flag and so on. Under 'flags tested' an entry of the form

(CF or ZF) = 0

means that the jump is made if either one of CF and ZF is currently set to 0.

Table 7.1 8086-family conditional jumps and the flags tested by them.

Name	*Jump if*	*Flags tested*
Testing for zero		
JZ	Zero	ZF = 1
JNZ	Not Zero	ZF = 0
Comparing unsigned numbers		
JA	Above	(CF and ZF) = 0
JB	Below	CF = 1
JAE	Above or equal	CF = 0
JBE	Below or equal	(CF or ZF) = 1
JNC	No carry	CF = 0
Comparing signed numbers		
JG	Greater	ZF = 0 and SF = OF
JL	Less	SF<>OF
JGE	Greater or equal	SF = OF
JLE	Less or equal	(ZF = 1) or (SF<>OF)
Testing for overflow		
JO	Overflow	OF = 1
JNO	Not overflow	OF = 0
Testing signs		
JS	Sign	SF = 1
JNS	No sign	SF = 0
Testing parity		
JPO	Parity odd	PF = 0
JPE	Parity even	PF = 1
Checking CX for zero without inspecting the flags		
JCXZ	CX is equal to zero	none

7.1.1 Aliases for conditional jumps

There is one further complication which need not detain us very much at this point in the text. This arises because possibilities for the outcome of comparisons other than those listed in Table 7.1 may come to mind. For example, the table mentions a 'jump if above or equal', but what about a corresponding 'jump if *not* above or equal'? In fact, the latter would be exactly equivalent to 'jump if below'. Instead of arbitrarily fixing on one of these expressions rather than another, the designers of 8086-family assembly language decided to allow several names for conditional jumps as alternatives to those given in Table 7.1. These are listed in Table 7.2.

7.1.2 A jump 'survival kit'

While there may seem a daunting number of jump instructions to remember, this is because jumps are provided to deal with conditions arising from signed

Table 7.2 Aliases for conditional jumps.

Name	*Alias(es)*	
Testing for zero		
JZ	JE	Jump if Equal
JNZ	JNE	Jump if Not Equal
Comparing unsigned numbers		
JA	JNBE	Jump if Not Below or Equal
JB	JNAE	Jump if Not Above or Equal
	JC	Jump if Carry
JAE	JNB	Jump if Not Below
JBE	JNA	Jump if Not Above
JNC	no alias	
Comparing signed numbers		
JG	JNLE	Jump if Not Less or Equal
JL	JNGE	Jump if Not Greater nor Equal
JGE	JNL	Jump if Not Less
JLE	JNG	Jump if Not Greater
Testing for overflow		
JO	no alias	
JNO	no alias	
Testing signs		
JS	no alias	
JNS	no alias	
Testing parity		
JPO	JNP	Jump if Not Parity
JPE	JP	Jump if Parity
Checking CX for zero without inspecting the flags		
JCXZ	no alias	

and unsigned arithmetic, from the settings of individual flags such as the parity flag, and from other considerations.

The main reason for there being so many arithmetic conditional jump instructions is that we want to be able to jump depending on whether one number is bigger than another as well as whether two numbers are equal. But this poses a problem, for the 8-bit binary number 11111111 is bigger than the 8-bit binary number 00000000 provided the former is interpreted as an *unsigned* number. If, however, 11111111 is interpreted as an 8-bit *signed* number then it is less than 00000000 (for its decimal value is then -1). So 'jump if bigger' and 'jump if smaller' need to be interpreted differently for signed and unsigned numbers.

To make the necessary distinction, the designers of the 8086 family of microprocessors decided to use the terms **above** and **below** when comparing *unsigned* numbers and to use the terms **greater than** and **less than** when comparing *signed* numbers. Thus, JA and JB are jumps which are made as a result of comparisons of unsigned numbers whereas JG and JL are jumps depending on signed number comparisons.

To save memorizing the whole of Table 7.1 at once, it is sufficient for now to work with a 'survival-kit' of jump instructions – just seven of them. If we first remind ourselves of two points, we can state these very simply. The two points are:

(1) decisions whether to jump are usually made upon the settings of the flags when the jump instruction is executed, and

(2) this decision therefore depends on the outcome of the last instruction executed prior to the jump instruction itself *which affected the flags*.

The seven 'survival-kit' jump instructions are:

```
JMP Jump (no matter what)
JZ  Jump if the result was Zero
JNZ Jump if the result was Not Zero
JA  Jump if the result was Above zero      ;unsigned
JB  Jump if the result Below zero          ;arithmetic
JG  Jump if the result was Greater than zero ;signed
JL  Jump if the result was Less than zero  ;arithmetic
```

and these should enable the reader to cope until Table 7.1 has been fully absorbed.

EXERCISES

7.1 Three numbers held in AX, BX and CX respectively are to be put into ascending numerical order with AX containing the smallest, BX the next largest and CX the largest of all. Write two different assembly language fragments to do this. In the first, assume that AX, BX and CX contain unsigned 16-bit numbers and in the second assume that they contain signed 16-bit numbers.

7.2 Write an assembly language program fragment which will add two signed 8-bit numbers. If the result is too large to represent as an 8-bit signed number then the message:

```
overflow during signed addition
```

should be displayed on the screen.

7.3 Write an assembly language program which will add together the two signed 8-bit numbers stored in locations referred to by `FIRST_NO` and

SECOND_NO, and print out the answer in decimal, including either a + or a − sign. Thus, if before execution FIRST_NO and SECOND_NO contain 10000111B and 11111101B respectively (that is, −120D and −3D) then your program should print out:

```
-123
```

(*Hint:* in order to calculate the digits of a signed 8-bit number notice, for example, that 123D / 10D = 12D remainder 3D and that 12D / 10D = 1D remainder 2D).

7.4 As part of a secret communications program designed for use by a major world bank, a sequence of 100H coded bytes is stored in memory starting at the location referred to by BUFFER. If the signed 8-bit number represented by a coded byte is x, then:

$$((17 * x) - 29) \text{ modulo } 7$$

should have even parity if the coded byte has been received correctly. Write an assembly language program which will check that each of the coded bytes stored in memory has been received correctly and, if not, displays the message

```
error in transmission
```

7.2 Implementing loops

This section considers in turn how to implement equivalents of the different kinds of loop statements available in Pascal (or a similar high-level language) using conditional jumps.

7.2.1 repeat . . . until

Thanks to jump instructions, a **repeat . . . until loop** similar to that found in Pascal:

repeat *action 1*
action 2
action 3
.
.
.
action n
until *<condition>*

can be implemented by assembly language of the form:

```
START_REPEAT: implementation of action 1
              implementation of action 2
              implementation of action 3
                        .
                        .
                        .
              implementation of action n
              if <condition> not true jump to START_REPEAT
```

To see how, let us allow ourselves to extend Pascal informally so that register names can be incorporated in Pascal statements. Then the Pascal:

```
repeat AX := AX - 1;
       BX := BX + 1;
       CX := AX - BX
until AX = 0
```

could be implemented in assembly language as follows:

```
START_REPEAT: DEC AX
              INC BX
              MOV CX,0
              ADD CX,AX
              SUB CX,BX
              CMP AX,0
              JNZ START_REPEAT
```

7.2.2 while . . . do

Similarly, a Pascal **while . . . do loop**:

```
while <condition> do begin
                        action 1
                        action 2
                          .
                          .
                          .
                        action n
                     end
```

is roughly equivalent to the assembly language structure:

```
START: if <condition> not true, jump to STOP
       action 1
       action 2
         .
         .
         .
       action n
       JMP START
 STOP:
```

Thus:

while $AX < 100\text{D}$ **do begin**
$AX := AX + BX;$
$BX := BX + 1$
end

could be implemented in assembly language as:

```
START:CMP AX,100D
      JNB STOP
      ADD AX,BX
      INC BX
      JMP START
 STOP:
```

7.2.3 for . . . do

A Pascal **for . . . do loop**:

for *i* := *initial_value* **to** *final_value* **do begin**
action 1
action 2
.
.
.
action n
end

is likewise roughly equivalent to the following assembly language structure in which the byte in memory referred to by the name LOOP_COUNTER is used to record the value of the **for** loop counter *i*:

```
       MOV LOOP_COUNTER,initial_value
START: CMP LOOP_COUNTER,final_value
       JA STOP
       action 1
       action 2
       .
       .
       .
       action n
       INC LOOP_COUNTER
       JMP START
 STOP:
```

Thus, the Pascal:

for *i* := 3 **to** 25D **do begin**
$AX := AX + BX;$
$BX := BX - 1$
end

could be implemented in assembly language as:

```
        MOV LOOP_COUNTER,3
START:  CMP LOOP_COUNTER,25D
        JA STOP
        ADD AX,BX
        DEC BX
        INC LOOP_COUNTER
        JMP START
STOP:
```

EXERCISES

7.5 A sequence of numbers can be generated by starting with a whole number n, $n > 0$, and then applying the rules:

(1) if $n = 1$ then stop

(2) if n is even, then the next number in the sequence, m, is $n / 2$

(3) if n is odd then the next number in the sequence, m, is $(3 * n) + 1$

and then applying these rules to generate the next number in the sequence from m, and so on. Thus, the sequence beginning with $n = 5$ is 5, 16, 8, 4, 2, 1.

Write a program which, given an initial n in AX, $1 \leqslant n \leqslant 20D$, generates the appropriate sequence and stores it in memory.

7.6 In the planet Nebucron, well-formed sentences are those in which, when scanning through from the beginning of the sentence to the end, the number of letter As encountered never exceeds the number of letter Os. Thus:

HOW GOOD YOU ARE.

is well formed but:

OH AWFUL ANSWERS WON'T HELP.

is not. Write a program to check whether a sentence stored in memory (and containing upper-case text and punctuation only) is well formed in this sense.

7.7 One way of verifying that a coded message has been coded correctly is to check that it conforms to the following rules when scanning through each coded sentence starting at the beginning:

(1) Before a letter P is encountered, any letter may occur.

(2) Once a letter P has occurred in a coded sentence, the letter A may occur until an L occurs after which neither an A nor an E may occur in the rest of the sentence.

Thus:

ALL HOPE IS LOST

is correctly coded whereas

ALL HOPE EVAPORATED QUICKLY AND QUIETLY

is not.

Write a program to check whether a coded sentence (containing just upper-case text and punctuation) stored in memory is correctly coded.

7.8 Write a program to convert a normal English sentence held in memory (and consisting of just upper-case text and punctuation) into an advertising slogan by replacing any occurrence of the sequence of letters QU by the sequence KW. Thus:

OUR TRANSPORTATION IS QUICK, QUIET AND QUOTABLE

would become

OUR TRANSPORTATION IS KWICK, KWIET AND KWOTABLE

Assume that in the English language a letter Q is always followed by a letter U.

7.3 The LOOP family of instructions

This section introduces the 8086-family assembly language instructions provided specially for implementing loops when there is a fixed maximum number of repetitions and just a single condition for terminating the loop. Clearly, many loops will fall outside of this more restricted class, which is why we discussed the more general case first: often we have no choice but to use conditional jump implementations of loops instead.

The three special instructions for the 8086 family which are designed to help in the efficient implementation of loops are LOOP, LOOPZ (alias LOOPE) and LOOPNZ (alias LOOPNE). LOOP is used for loops involving a predetermined number of iterations – as with a **for** loop. LOOPZ and LOOPNZ are used to implement similar such loops which have an additional single condition for termination.

The LOOP instruction can perhaps be best explained by considering the **for** loop:

for i := 23D **downto** 1 **do begin**
$AX := AX + BX;$
$BX := BX - 1$
end

Using register CX for the **for** loop counter *i* rather than a location in memory we could implement this as:

```
        MOV CX,23D
START:  ADD AX,BX
        DEC BX
        DEC CX
        JNZ START
 STOP:
```

The instruction:

```
LOOP START
```

is, in effect, equivalent to

```
DEC CX
JNZ START
```

but LOOP affects none of the flags.

Thus:

```
        MOV CX,23D
START:  ADD AX,BX
        DEC BX
        LOOP START
```

is a better implementation of the original **for** . . . **downto** loop in that it is both shorter and easier to read.

The following example illustrates the use of the LOOP instruction in another context. It converts the 128H upper-case letters stored in memory starting at the location referred to by LETTERS to lower case. To do so, a glance at the table of ASCII codes in Appendix I will confirm that the lower-case letters a,b,c,. . .,z all have ASCII codes which are 20H more than their upper-case equivalents A,B,. . .,Z. For simplicity, therefore, we simply add 20H to each of the 128H values stored starting at LETTERS.

```
          MOV  BX,OFFSET LETTERS
          MOV  CX,128H          ;the number of bytes to be moved
NEXTLOC:  MOV  AL,[BX]          ;move the next byte into AL
          ADD  AL,20H           ;convert into lower case
          MOV  [BX],AL          ;store it back
          INC  BX               ;ready to access next location
          LOOP NEXTLOC          ;if more to do, go back
```

LOOPZ *<label>* decrements the CX register without affecting the flags and jumps to the *<label>* if CX<>0 and the Z-flag is 1. It can be thought of as meaning 'loop while the outcome is zero and CX is non-zero'.

Suppose in the above example involving conversion of letters to lower case that the stored text begins with a certain number of letter Xs (at least one!) and that only these Xs are to be converted to lower case. Once a letter different from X is encountered, the text thereafter is to be left unchanged. As before, the total number of text characters is 128H. In this case LOOPZ can be used to control the loop which effects the conversion:

```
          MOV    BX,OFFSET LETTERS
          MOV    CX,128H             ;the number of bytes to be moved
          MOV    AL,[BX]             ;move the first byte into AL
NEXTLOC:  ADD    AL,20H              ;convert into lower case
          MOV    [BX],AL             ;store it back
          INC    BX                  ;ready to access next location
          MOV    AL,[BX]
          CMP    AL,'X'
          LOOPZ  NEXTLOC             ;if an 'X' then repeat provided CX<>0
```

The LOOPZ NEXTLOC instruction causes execution to continue from NEXTLOC provided that the Z-flag is 1 and that CX is non-zero after being decremented by 1.

LOOPNZ <*label*> works similarly. It decrements the CX register without affecting the flags and jumps to the <*label*> if CX<>0 and the Z-flag is 0. By way of example, suppose in this case that the first letter is to be converted to lower case no matter what, but that thereafter conversion of the text is to stop when a letter W is first encountered. Then the following program fragment could be used to effect the conversion:

```
          MOV BX,OFFSET LETTERS
          MOV CX,128H             ;the number of bytes to be moved
          MOV AL,[BX]             ;move the first byte into AL
NEXTLOC:  ADD AL,20H              ;convert into lower case
          MOV [BX],AL             ;store it back
          INC BX                  ;ready to access next location
          MOV AL,[BX]
          CMP AL,'W'
          LOOPNZ NEXTLOC          ;if not a 'W' then repeat provided CX<>0
```

7.3.1 JCXZ

Consideration of the conditional jump JCXZ has been delayed until now because it is very often useful in conjunction with LOOP; specifically, when a condition must be checked at the beginning of a loop rather than at the end. Note that unlike LOOP, however, JCXZ does not decrement CX.

By way of example, suppose that the number of repetitions in a **for** loop is given in CX which was set by an earlier part of the program, and that the repetition is to stop when CX gets down to zero. CX must be tested before being decremented for, otherwise, if it is zero it will be decremented to −1 in the first iteration and so 65 535 iterations will be carried out before CX gets down to 0 again.

```
            .
            .      ; instructions which set CX to the number
            .      ; of repetitions to be carried out


        JCXZ DONE ; check that CX is not zero
NEXT:     .
          .
          .
        LOOP NEXT
DONE:
```

Finally, we should note that LOOP, LOOPZ, LOOPNZ and JCXZ all require the corresponding label to refer to an instruction within +127 or −128 locations.

EXERCISES

7.9 Write some Pascal statements – including a **for** loop – corresponding to the first example program fragment concerned with the conversion of text to lower case.

7.10 Could LOOP, LOOPZ or LOOPNZ be used to provide an alternative implementation for any of the Exercises 7.5 – 7.8?

7.11 Write an assembly language program which calculates the first 20D values of the Fibonacci series which begins with two 1s and then each successive number is the sum of the preceding two numbers: 1,1,2,3,5,8, ... Use LOOP and leave each value in a group of memory locations starting with that referred to by FIB_NOS.

7.12 Use LOOP to write a program to store in memory the values of:

$$2^n - 1$$

for n taking values from 2 to 10D.

7.13 100D decimal digits are stored in memory, one per byte. Starting with that stored in the location with the lowest address, these are to be summed up in AX until the total is an even number, when the summation stops. Thus, if the first few digits were 1,2,6,8,2,6,7,8,9,3,2, 1,. . . then the summation would stop when the first 7 digit is encountered, with AX containing 25. Write a program to carry out this summation using either a LOOP, LOOPZ or LOOPNZ instruction.

7.14 100D locations in memory contain 20D five-digit codes representing prices. Each five-digit code consists of four digits representing the price in dollars followed by a check digit to guard against errors. The check digit is found by adding up the price digits and then reducing the total modulo 4. Thus, if the price of an item were $3679 then the check digit would be

$$(3 + 6 + 7 + 9) \text{ modulo } 4 = 25 \text{ modulo } 4 = 1$$

and the code stored would be 36791 with the 3 in the lowest address, 6 in the next lowest address, and so on. Write a program to find the first stored digit code for which the check digit does not correspond with the associated price.

7.4 Decisions

Once again mirroring Pascal's decision-taking apparatus, we need to consider the implementation of assembly language equivalents of **if. . .then. . .else** and **case. . .of. . ..**

7.4.1 if . . . then . . . else

A Pascal statement of the form:

if <*condition*> **then** *actions1* **else** *actions2*

can be implemented by assembly language of the form:

```
            test <condition> and if false jump to ACTIONS_2
              .    assembly language instructions
              .    to implement actions1
              .
            JMP DONE
ACTIONS_2:    .
              .    assembly language instructions
              .    to implement actions2
     DONE:
```

Thus,

if $AX = 0$ **then** $CX := CX - AX$; $INC\ AX$; $DX := DX + AX$
else $CX := CX - 23D$

could be implemented:

```
           CMP AX,0
           JNZ ACTIONS_2
           SUB CX,AX
           INC AX
           ADD DX,AX
           JMP DONE
ACTIONS_2: SUB CX,23D
     DONE:
```

7.4.2 case . . . of . . .

Using `CMP`, a statement of the form:

case *variable* **of**
value_1 : *action_1*

```
value_2 : action_2
        .
        .
        .
value_n : action_n
        end
```

can be implemented by assembly language of the form:

```
          CMP value,value_1
          JZ ACTION_1
          CMP value,value_2
          JZ ACTION_2
             .
             .
             .
          CMP value,value_n
          JZ ACTION_N
          JMP END_CASE
ACTION_1:
             .
             .
             .
          JMP END_CASE
ACTION_2:
             .
             .
             .
          JMP END_CASE
ACTION_3:
             .
             .
             .
          JMP END_CASE
ACTION_n:
             .
             .
             .
END_CASE:
```

For example,

```
case AL of
  'A':CL := 'h';DL := 'a' ;DH := 'y'
  'E':CL := 'e';DL := 'e' ;DH := ' '
  'I' :CL := 'e';DL := 'y' ;DH := 'e'
  'O':CL := 'o';DL := 'w';DH := 'e'
  'U':CL := 'y';DL := 'o' ;DH := 'u'
     end
```

could be implemented:

```
             CMP AL,'A'
             JZ ACTION_1
             CMP AL,'E'
             JZ ACTION_2
             CMP AL,'I'
             JZ ACTION_3
             CMP AL,'O'
             JZ ACTION_4
             CMP AL,'U'
             JZ ACTION_5
             JMP END_CASE
ACTION_1:    MOV CL,'h'
             MOV DL,'a'
             MOV DH,'y'
             JMP END_CASE
ACTION_2:    MOV CL,'e'
             MOV DL,'e'
             MOV DH,' '
             JMP END_CASE
ACTION_3:    MOV CL,'e'
             MOV DL,'y'
             MOV DH,'e'
             JMP END_CASE
ACTION_4:    MOV CL,'o'
             MOV DL,'w'
             MOV DH,'e'
             JMP END_CASE
ACTION_5:    MOV CL,'y'
             MOV DL,'o'
             MOV DH,'u'
             JMP END_CASE
END_CASE:
```

EXERCISES

7.15 Write a program which accepts two decimal digits from its user, prints a new line on the display screen, and if the first digit is larger than the second, displays the average of the two digits (to the nearest whole number) and otherwise displays the square root of the product of the two digits (to the nearest whole number). Then the program should return to DOS control. Thus, if the user types

```
93
```

then the program displays

```
6
```

and if the user types

```
39
```

then the program displays

```
5
```

(*Hint:* do not become involved in fancy square root calculations. Think of an easier way for this simple example).

7.16 Write a program which accepts a three-letter assembly language mnemonic typed by the user and displays a new line, an appropriate message, and another new line before returning to DOS control. The messages are as follows:

mnemonic	*message*
SUB	SUBtract
SBB	SuBtract with Borrow
all others	A mnemonic a day helps you program away

7.17 Write a program which accepts lower-case letters typed by the user and for each such letter displays a message according to the following scheme and then prints a new line:

letter	*message to be displayed*
a	hay for horses
b	beef for strong bones
c	see if there's anyone outside
d	differential
e	either you or me
f	effervescence
g	chief of police
all other letters	no comment

If the user types any character other than a lower-case letter, control returns to DOS.

7.5 A complete example program involving a loop and decisions

We shall write a program which will 'help' individuals decide if they should become a computer programmer, an accountant, or go into advertising. The program will ask users three questions and then recommend a suitable career based on these answers as follows:

Answer to question	*1*	*2*	*3*	*Career*
	Yes	?	?	advertising
	No	Yes	Yes	programmer
	No	?	No	accountant

where ? means that the user's answer to this question does not affect whether or not this career would be suitable for the user.

The three questions are:

(1) Do you like flower arranging?

(2) Do you like drinking lots of coffee?

(3) Do you like parties?

The user will be expected to type either Y (for Yes) or N (for No). Thus a typical interaction with the program will be:

Do you like flower arranging?
N
Do you like drinking lots of coffee?
Y
Do you like parties?
Y
You are obviously a programmer – howdy partner!

The program then asks if another user would like some career advice. If so, then the user presses Y (for Yes please) and the question–answer cycle is repeated, otherwise the user presses N (for No thanks) whereupon control is returned to DOS. This part of the dialog is:

Does another user wish to have some help with career choice?
Y
Do you like flower . . .

If the program cannot decide on a suitable career, then the message:

Programming, advertising and accountancy are not for you

will be displayed rather than a career recommendation.

The structure of the program can be described informally making use of the **repeat. . .until** structure from Pascal as follows:

repeat
  ask the 1st question;
  record the answer;
  ask the 2nd question;
  record the answer;
  ask the 3rd question;

record the answer;
display a new line;
if *answer1 = yes then career := advertising*
else if answer2 = yes **and** *answer3 = yes*
then *career := programmer*
else if *answer3 = no*
then *career := accountant*
else *career := none found;*
display the career we have determined;
ask if another user wants help;
get answer
until *answer = no;*
return to DOS

Because there is not a fixed number of repetitions, we shall use the general implementation of **repeat. . .until** from Section 7.2 rather than any of the special LOOP instructions. The complete program is given in Figure 7.1. In it, we have used the MASM pseudo-op EQU for the first time. EQU admits a facility in some ways similar to the constant data type of PASCAL. Thanks to EQU, a program heavily dependent on certain numerical values need not be spattered with those values, since they can be declared as constants at the beginning of a program. In this way, a tax calculation program can be amended to accommodate a new rate of tax by altering one single EQU statement rather than (possibly) tens of individual instructions.

```
CR EQU 0DH
LF EQU 0AH
DATA SEGMENT
     QUEST1 DB CR,LF,'Do you like flower arranging?',CR,LF,'$'
     QUEST2 DB CR,LF,'Do you like drinking lots of coffee?',CR,LF,'$'
     QUEST3 DB CR,LF,'Do you like parties?',CR,LF,'$'

     ANSWER1 DB ?
     ANSWER2 DB ?
     ANSWER3 DB ?

     ADVERTISING DB 'Being creative, you should be in advertising',CR,LF,'$'
     PROGRAMMER  DB 'You are obviously a programmer - howdy partner!',CR, LF,'$'
     ACCOUNTANT  DB 'You should feel at home in accountancy',CR,LF,'$'
     NOT_KNOWN   DB 'Programming, advertising and accountancy are '
                 DB 'not for you',CR,LF,'$'
     NEW_USER    DB CR,LF,CR,LF,'Does another user wish to have '
                 DB 'some help with career choice?',CR,LF,'$'
 DATA ENDS
 WORKING_STORE SEGMENT STACK
         DW 100H DUP(?)
 WORKING_STORE ENDS
```

Figure 7.1
Help with choosing a career.

```
CODE SEGMENT
ASSUME DS:DATA, SS:WORKING_STORE, CS:CODE
    ;establish data segment addressability
     START:MOV AX,DATA
           MOV DS,AX ;repeat
  ;ask the 1st question
 ANALYSIS:MOV DX,OFFSET QUEST1
          MOV AH,9
          INT 21H
  ;record the answer
          MOV AH,1
          INT 21H
          MOV ANSWER1,AL
  ;ask the 2nd question
          MOV DX,OFFSET QUEST2
          MOV AH,9
          INT 21H
  ;record the answer
          MOV AH,1
          INT 21H
          MOV ANSWER2,AL
  ;ask the 3rd question
          MOV DX,OFFSET QUEST3
          MOV AH,9
          INT 21H
  ;record the answer
          MOV AH,1
          INT 21H
          MOV ANSWER3,AL
  ;display a new line
          MOV AH,2
          MOV DL,CR
          INT 21H
          MOV DL,LF
          INT 21H
  ;if answer1 = yes then career := advertising
          CMP ANSWER1,'Y'
          JNZ TRY_PROG
          MOV DX,OFFSET ADVERTISING
          JMP DISPLAY
  ;else if answer2 = yes and answer3 = yes then career := programmer
 TRY_PROG:CMP ANSWER2,'Y'
          JNZ TRY_ACC
          CMP ANSWER3,'Y'
          JNZ TRY_ACC
          MOV DX,OFFSET PROGRAMMER
          JMP DISPLAY
  ;else if answer3 = no then career := accountant
  TRY_ACC:CMP ANSWER3,'N'
          JNZ NO_CAREER
          MOV DX,OFFSET ACCOUNTANT
          JMP DISPLAY
  ;else career := none found
NO_CAREER:MOV DX,OFFSET NOT_KNOWN
  ;display the career which has been determined
```

Figure 7.1 *(cont.)*

```
DISPLAY:MOV AH,9
        INT 21H
;ask if another user wants help
        MOV DX,OFFSET NEW_USER
        INT 21H
;get answer
        MOV AH,1
        INT 21H
;until answer = no
        CMP AL,'N'
        JNZ ANALYSIS ;return to DOS
        MOV AX,4C00H
        INT 21H
CODE ENDS
END START
```

Figure 7.1 (*cont.*)

EXERCISES

7.18 Write a computer dating program similar to our career choice example program.

7.19 Write a program which will display all possible menus made up by choosing one item from each of the following groups:

appetizers: soup, melon

main course: meat, fish, nuts

dessert: fresh apples, chocolate sundae, baked alaska

subject to the following rules:

if the meal includes meat then it must not also include chocolate sundae or baked alaska;

fish can only follow melon; and

if the first two courses are melon and nuts then the third course must be fresh apples.

7.20 Write a program which asks its user to think of either a dog or a cat without revealing which and then asks three questions to try to guess which animal they are thinking about. Use the following animal database:

cat: docile, furry, affectionate

dog: fierce, active, affectionate

SUMMARY

In this chapter we have explored the mechanism used in assembly language programming to alter the execution flow through a set of instructions. The mechanism is based around the flags register. The 8086-family microprocessors can respond to 18 different conditional jump instructions which are the means whereby the programmer can ask for execution to continue, not with the next instruction in sequence, but with a remote instruction – provided the relevant entries in the flags register say that a certain condition has been met.

Using conditional jumps we have described a general assembly language implementation of Pascal's **for**, **while** and **repeat** loops. We also saw that the `LOOP`, `LOOPZ` and `LOOPNZ` instructions allow efficient implementation of loops for which there is a predetermined maximum number of repetitions and, possibly, just one further additional condition for terminating the loop.

Finally, we considered how conditional jumps may be used to implement decision taking structures such as **if. . .then. . .else** and **case. . .of. . ..**

Throughout the chapter an increasing emphasis was placed on the use of the Pascal programming language, informally extended to the assembly language domain, as a device for describing the way in which an assembly language program should work. In the next chapter we take this idea a stage further and make it an essential part of our software development method.

SELF-CHECK QUIZ

1. Consider the sequence:

```
CMP AX,BX
conditional jump to somewhere
```

for each of the following possibilities and say what flags are set to 1 as a result of executing the `CMP` instruction, and whether the transfer to the jump address is made.

	AX	*BX*	*Conditional jump*
(a)	6	0FCH	JA
(b)	6	0FCH	JG
(c)	0F1H	0F0H	JNBE
(d)	0	0F0H	JLE

2. If AX and BX contain signed 16-bit numbers and CX and DX contain unsigned 16-bit numbers, how would you find out if

(a) the number in DX is greater than that in CX

(b) the number in BX exceeds that in AX

(c) the number in DX is zero

(d) the number in BX is equal to or smaller than that in AX

(e) the number in DX is equal to or smaller than that in CX

using `CMP` and conditional jumps?

3. Show how to implement (a) **repeat. . .until**, (b) **while. . .do**, and (c) **for. . .do** loop structures without using `CMP` or any of the `LOOP` family of instructions.

4. With reference to the specific example of **for** *i* **in** [2,4,6,8] **do** . . . in which *i* successively takes the values 2, 4, 6, and 8, show how to implement loops of this kind in general.

5. Generalize the **case**. . .**of**. . . structure given in the text to include numerical ranges as in:

   case *i* **of**
   [2,3,4]:<*actions1*>
   [5,6,7,8]:<*actions2*>
   .
   .
   .
   end

   in which <*actions1*> are carried out if *i* has the value 2, 3 or 4, <*actions2*> are carried out if *i* has the value 5, 6, 7 or 8, and so on.

6. How could an **if**. . .**then**. . .**else** statement involving an **or** be implemented in assembly language. Illustrate with reference to:

   if *AX* < 3 **or** *BX* < 2 **then**. . .

7. How could an **if**. . .**then**. . .**else** statement involving an **and** be implemented in assembly language. Illustrate with reference to:

   if *AX* < 3 **and** *BX* < 2 **then**. . .

8. What will be in AX, BX and CX after execution of:

```
      MOV CX,11D
      MOV AX,9D
      MOV BX,7D
NEXT: INC BX
      SUB AX,BX
      LOOPNZ NEXT
```

9. What will be in AX, BX and CX after execution of:

```
      MOV CX,11D
      MOV AX,9D
      MOV BX,8D
NEXT: INC BX
      INC AX
      SUB AX,BX
      LOOPZ NEXT
```

10. What will be in AX and CX after executing the sequence:

```
      MOV AX,10D
      MOV CX,14H
NEXT: SUB AX,1
      LOOP NEXT
      LOOPZ NEXT
      LOOPNZ NEXT
```

8

Controlling Program Development

Contents

This chapter describes a method that can be used to develop the reader's own assembly language programs. The method helps to contain the occurrence of errors by mimicking some of the facilities of a structured programming language like Pascal. It also relies on the use of subroutines wherever sensible. Subroutines are assembly language's version of Pascal's procedures and make it possible for a large program to be built up out of smaller components which are already known to be working. These subroutines are set to work by placing any values that they require before being called into operation in predetermined registers or memory locations; or, as we say, by passing them any necessary parameters. The chapter ends with a description of two of the most important subroutine parameter-passing mechanisms.

8.1 Structured assembly language programming

Experience has shown that it is possible to contain the number of errors in an assembly language program if program development is carried out in a controlled manner. Indeed, a systematic approach to program development is essential for the efficient production of software which is verifiable, reliable and understandable by programmers other than its author. Pascal is rich in control structures which make this easier to achieve than is possible with assembly language, but it is possible to mimic some of these facilities quite readily.

For any given problem we first map out a solution using the normal combination of top-down and bottom-up methodologies, as appropriate. We write this solution in an extension of the Pascal language which we shall call **pseudo-Pascal**. Then the assembly language program is built up from the pseudo-Pascal outline on almost a statement-by-statement (and largely routine) basis. Thanks to our consideration of loops and decision-taking structures in Chapter 7, we know this to be possible.

It should be emphasized that there is no formal definition of pseudo-Pascal – it is something that each programmer can adapt to his or her own style of working. Thus, you are free to change any or all of the statements we use. The only essential thing is that your own version of pseudo-Pascal should contain ad hoc extensions to the Pascal programming language sufficient to allow almost a statement-by-statement assembly language implementation of the pseudo-Pascal original.

Apart from the relatively easy transition from pseudo-Pascal to assembly language, the main advantage of this approach is that use of pseudo-Pascal enforces a structured approach to the assembly language programming task. Moreover, if the pseudo-Pascal is used to comment the assembly language program, a high standard of program documentation is assured.

8.1.1 A program developed using pseudo-Pascal

The advantages of using pseudo-Pascal for program development will now be illustrated by working through the solution to a specific example problem. If, after studying it, the reader still needs convincing of the value of this approach, he or she should try tackling the problem without this methodology: without the support of pseudo-Pascal it is all too easy to create a confused mess of loops.

The problem

We are given as data the ASCII codes for an extract from the book *David Copperfield* by Charles Dickens. All punctuation except periods (.) has been removed from the extract and the words of the text are separated by single ASCII space characters (code 20H). When represented in this manner the complete extract is contained within the memory segment specified by the DS register.

An assembly language program is required which will leave in register AX the length of the longest sentence (in characters, including spaces) and in CX the starting address of that sentence (relative to DS). The maximum length of any sentence is 255 characters (including spaces) and an ASCII code for a $ sign indicates the end of the extract.

A solution

Imagine solving a corresponding problem in Pascal. One of the first things to do is to decide which variables are required and of what type they should be. Since we shall have to examine the length of each sentence in the extract in relation to the lengths of previous sentences, variables are required:

- to record the maximum sentence length so far;
- for the starting address of the sentence having the maximum length amongst those already considered;
- the address of the character currently under consideration;
- to keep count of the number of characters in the sentence currently being examined;
- to hold each character of the text as we examine it to see if it is a period (.) denoting the end of a sentence or a dollar sign ($) denoting the end of the text.

In Pascal, the next stage would be to decide on the type of these variables – should they be integer, real or char? A corresponding set of decisions has to be made in assembly language: for example, should the variables occupy a byte or a word and should signed or unsigned representations be used for numeric work?

For the problem under consideration both variables representing addresses may be unsigned 16-bit numbers since it suffices to work with just offsets and, since we were told that the maximum length of any sentence is 255 characters, unsigned 8-bit numbers will be adequate for the sentence length variables. The variable which holds each character of the text as it is inspected will occupy one byte. It remains to decide whether to use registers or memory locations to store these variables. In this instance all the variables could be stored in registers, so that is what we shall do, given that the two answers to the problem must be left in AX and CX. Table 8.1 gives our allocation of registers to variables. (It is rare indeed for us to be so lucky – most often, variables have to be stored in memory!)

Table 8.1 Allocations of registers to variables for the text-processing problem.

Variable	*Register*	*Comment*
maxaddress	CX	Offset of start address of sentence of maximum length encountered so far.
maxlength	AL	Length (in characters) of the sentence of which the starting address is given in CX (that is, length of the sentence so far considered to be the longest).
address	BX	Address of the character currently under consideration.
charcount	DH	The number of characters encountered in a given sentence so far.
char	DL	The particular character being examined.

Using these variables, it is easy to give a complete solution to the problem in pseudo-Pascal:

```
address := address of first character in text
maxlength := 0; maxaddress := address; read(char);
while char <> '$' do
  begin

  (* count to the end of this sentence *)
  charcount := 0;
  while char <> '.' do
    begin
    charcount := charcount + 1;
    address := address + 1;
    read(char)
    end;

  (* compare length with biggest so far *)
  if charcount > maxlength then
    begin
    maxlength := charcount;
    maxaddress := address-charcount
    end;

  (* now at the end of a sentence, so read on *)
  address := address + 1;
  read(char)
  end
```

We can now use this to finish the solution, assuming that the start of the text has been associated with a variable by a pseudo-op of the form:

```
START_OF_TEXT DB. . .
```

and using the pseudo-op OFFSET to extract from the variable START_OF_TEXT its offset from the segment register associated with the segment in which it was defined (in this case DS) so that:

```
MOV BX,OFFSET START_OF_TEXT
```

in effect, loads BX with the actual starting address (relative to DS) of the start of the text.

Here is an assembly language solution to the *David Copperfield* problem obtained by converting the pseudo-Pascal outline, line by line using the correspondence between variables and registers given in Table 8.1 and the implementation of Pascal constructs described in Section 8.1.

```
    ;set up data segment address in DS
       MOV AX,DATA
       MOV DS,AX
    ;address := address of first character in text
       MOV BX,OFFSET START_OF_TEXT
    ;maxlength := 0; maxaddress := address;
       MOV AX,0 ;zeros AH and AL
       MOV CX,BX
    ;read(char)
       MOV DL,[BX]
    ;while char <> '$' do
            ;begin
CHECK_DOLLAR_SIGN: CMP DL,'$'
                   JZ END_OF_TEXT

            ;(* count to the end of this sentence *)
            ;charcount := 0
                  MOV DH,0
            ;while char <> '.' do
                 ;begin
          CHECK_FULL_STOP:CMP DL,'.'
                         JZ END_OF_SENTENCE
                   ;charcount := charcount + 1
                         INC DH
                   ;address := address + 1
                         INC BX
                   ;read(char)
                         MOV DL,[BX]
                   ;end
                         JMP CHECK_FULL_STOP

            ;(* compare length with biggest so far *)
            ;if charcount < maxlength then
  END_OF_SENTENCE: CMP DH,AL
                   JB NEXT_SENTENCE
                   ;begin
                   ;maxlength := charcount
                         MOV AL,DH
                   ;maxaddress := address-charcount
                         MOV CX,BX ;copy address into maxaddress
```

```
                           MOV DL,DH ;convert charcount to
                           MOV DH,0  ;unsigned 16-bit form
                           SUB CX,DX ;subtract
                      ;end of comparison with biggest so far

               ;(* now at the end of a sentence, so read on *)
               ;address := address + 1; read(char)
        NEXT_SENTENCE: INC BX
                       MOV DL,[BX]
               ;end of dealing with a sentence
                       JMP CHECK_DOLLAR_SIGN
               ;end of whole text
          END_OF_TEXT: HLT
```

(HLT is an 8086-family instruction which causes microprocessors in the 8086 family to HaLT completely. Once a HLT instruction has been obeyed, the microcomputer will have to be switched off and the operating system reloaded, since the HLT suspends operation and cannot be overridden by software. Consequently, if you enter this program and run it under debugger control you must be careful to terminate execution *before* the HLT instruction is executed.)

EXERCISES

8.1 Add the necessary pseudo-ops to the above fragment so that it can be assembled by MASM, and run the result under debugger control. Use the following extract from *David Copperfield* as test data.

> I could think of the past now gravely but not bitterly and could contemplate the future in bright spirit. Home in its best sense was for me no more. She in whom I might have inspired a dearer love I had taught to be my sister. She would marry and would have new claimants on her tenderness and in doing it would never know the love for her that had grown in my heart. It was right that I should pay the forfeit of my headlong passion. What I reaped I had sown.$

You can either type the data in every time you do a debugger test run (laborious!) or use DB pseudo-ops in the assembly language program and enter it just once.

8.2 Use the above method (preparing an outline solution in pseudo-Pascal and then mimicking the resulting Pascal-like fragment in assembly language) to solve the following problems. Test your solutions carefully.

(a) You are given a piece of text from which all punctuation has been removed and in which all upper-case letters have been converted to lower case. The total length of text thus produced is less than 255 characters. Leave in DX the start address (relative to DS) of the longest sequence of letters which occur in the text in alphabetical order, and leave the length of this sequence in CL. (If there is more than one sequence of maximum length, set DX to the start address of the first such sequence.) Thus if the text was:

a mathematician confided
the mobius band is one sided
if you cut it in half
youll get quite a laugh
for it stays in one piece though divided

then the longest sequence of letters in alphabetical order contains three letters and DX should be set to point to the 'b' of 'mobius'.

(b) Following inspiration from real-estate advertisements, secret agent Clotsky decided to code all messages by omitting all vowels (a,e,i,o, and u) except those which occurred at the beginning of a word. Thus:

come quickly before all is lost

would be coded as

cm qckly bfr all is lst

Write an assembly language program to carry out this coding procedure. Assume that the text to be coded consists of 255 characters or less and is stored by means of a DB statement:

```
MESSAGE_TO_BE_SENT DB '. . .'
```

The coded message is to overwrite the original text stored in memory.

8.2 Subroutines

In Pascal, **procedures** make it possible to break a large program down into smaller pieces so that each piece can be shown to work correctly without reference to any of the others. In this way the final program is built up out of lots of trusty bricks and is easier to debug since, if there is an error, it can only be caused by the interlinking of the bricks. In 8086-family assembly language the nearest equivalent to Pascal's procedures are **subroutines**.

Making a sequence of assembly language instructions into a subroutine is easy – we simply label the first instruction in the sequence as if we were going to make it the object of a jump instruction, and add the 8086-family instruction `RET` to the end of the sequence. Consider the example below, which contains a program fragment which leaves the sum of the unsigned 16-bit numbers in AX, BX, CX and DX (assuming this sum can be represented in 16-bit form) in SI, a 16-bit register, new to us, the special purpose of which will be introduced in Chapter 10.

```
MOV SI,0
ADD SI,AX
ADD SI,BX
ADD SI,CX
ADD SI,DX
```

Let us make this into a subroutine called REGISTER_SUMMATION:

```
REGISTER_SUMMATION: MOV SI,0
                    ADD SI,AX
                    ADD SI,BX
                    ADD SI,CX
                    ADD SI,DX
                    RET
```

Having done so, we can call the subroutine into action via the 8086-family CALL instruction, thus: CALL REGISTER_SUMMATION. This causes the microprocessor to begin executing the instruction sequence starting with the label REGISTER_SUMMATION until a RET instruction is encountered, at which point execution RETurns to the instruction next in sequence after the CALL instruction itself (see Figure 8.1).

In the program fragment below, comments show the sequence of values taken by SI during the execution of the given program fragment:

```
MOV AX,0
MOV BX,0
MOV CX,0
MOV DX,1
CALL REGISTER_SUMMATION ;SI has now been set to 1
MOV AX,2
CALL REGISTER_SUMMATION ;SI has now been set to 3
MOV BX,3
MOV CX,4
CALL REGISTER_SUMMATION ;SI has now been set to 0AH
```

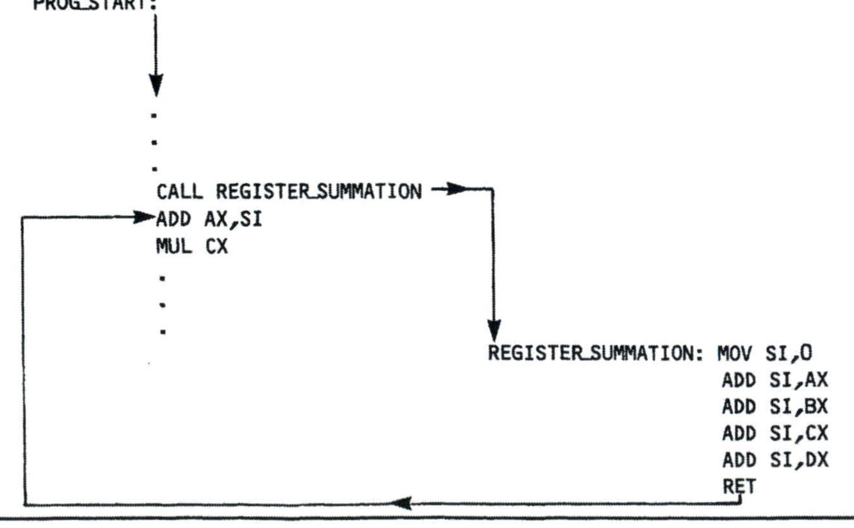

Figure 8.1 Execution of a subroutine.

EXERCISES

8.3 Make a hand trace of the execution of the following program fragment, assuming that the subroutine PRINT_ON_SCREEN prints on the display screen the character whose ASCII code is in register AL and does not change any register values. Give a clear indication of what appears on the display screen.

```
                 MOV  CX,5H
                 MOV  AX,40H
    NEXT_STEP:   INC  AX
                 CALL PRINT_ON_SCREEN
                 CALL CODE_AND_PRINT
                 DEC  CX
                 JNZ  NEXT_STEP
                 HLT

CODE_AND_PRINT:  MOV  BX,20H
                 ADD  BX,AX
                 MOV  DX,AX           ;save the value of AX
                 MOV  AX,BX
                 CALL PRINT_ON_SCREEN
                 MOV AX,DX            ;restore the value to AX
                 RET

PRINT_ON_SCREEN:  .
                  .
                  .
                 RET
```

Notice that, as with procedures in Pascal, one subroutine may call another.

8.4 Write an assembly language subroutine called CALC_FRANC_EQUIV which, given an unsigned 16-bit number in AX representing a value in dollars, will leave in AX an unsigned 16-bit number representing the nearest whole number of French francs equivalent to this amount using the hypothetical conversion rate of \$1 = 8FF.

8.3 The stack and its role in the subroutine mechanism

As stated in Chapter 3, a stack is a group of locations in memory which the programmer reserves for the (temporary) storage of important items of data. The mechanism by which subroutines are implemented in the 8086 family uses a stack. Briefly, when a subroutine is called up, the address of the instruction following the call is saved on a stack until the RET instruction in the body of the subroutine is encountered. Then execution continues from the instruction following the call by retrieving the return address from that stack. Before examining the mechanism in detail, a thorough discussion of 8086-family stack implementation is necessary, and it is to that which we now turn.

8.3.1 The stack

The method by which the 8086 family provides a stack facility is a common one. Given our conventional format for an assembly language program, MASM, LINK and DOS arrange that the stack begins just before the start of our program and grows backwards in memory as demand warrants, as shown in Figure 8.2.

Copies of the contents of registers can be stored on and retrieved from a stack thanks to the PUSH and POP instructions which have the general forms:

PUSH <16-bit register name>

(for example PUSH AX) and

POP <16-bit register name>

(for example POP DX). PUSH stores the copy in memory, and POP loads it back again. For the flags register (a 16-bit register in its own right) special forms of the PUSH and POP instructions must be used: PUSHF stores and POPF retrieves.

The top of a stack is where items are added and removed – compare with the dinner plate dispenser model of Chapter 3. In order that PUSH and POP can operate successfully it is necessary only to: specify how big a memory stack is required; set the stack segment register SS to the segment address of the start of the stack; and set the 16-bit **Stack Pointer** (SP) register to the offset address of the top of the stack. Both SS and SP are initialized automatically by MASM and LINK thanks to the pseudo-ops:

```
WORKING_STORAGE SEGMENT STACK
   DW 100H DUP(?)
WORKING_STORAGE ENDS
```

which instruct the linker to set SS to a value compatible with the memory allocation plan of Figure 8.2 and to initialize SP to the appropriate top of stack value (2 * 100H = 200H, relative to SS). Of course, reserving more words of store for the stack – up to 64 Kbytes is allowed – will alter the value to which SP is initialized.

Let us suppose that the stack pointer register, SP, has been initialized to 0200H (relative to the SS register) and consider the effect of the instruction PUSH BX in detail. Suppose further that register BX contains 1A9EH. Then the action of PUSH BX is as follows:

(1) The SP register is decremented by 1.

(2) The high-order byte of BX is stored in the memory location addressed by SP (relative to the SS register).

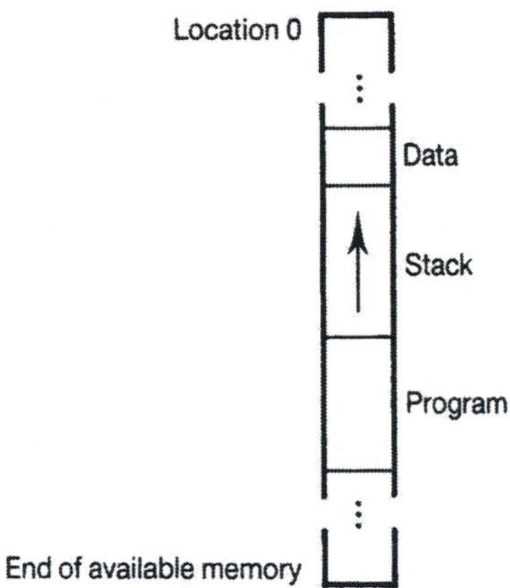

Figure 8.2 Typical memory allocation when using a stack.

(3) The SP register is decremented by 1.

(4) The low-order byte of BX is stored in the memory location now addressed by SP (relative to the SS register).

(Notice that SP is thus left pointing to the last element stored in the stack, that is, to the top of the stack.)

Before			*After*	
SP	0200		SP	01FE
BX	1A9E		BX	1A9E
01FE	??		01FE	9E
01FF	??		01FF	1A
0200	??		0200	??

On the other hand, the action of an instruction such as `POP DX` releases memory from the stack, in that the SP register is incremented. Its action is as follows:

(1) Copy the byte stored at the address given in the SP register (relative to SS) into DL.

(2) Increment the SP register by 1.

(3) Copy the byte now pointed to by the SP register (relative to SS) into DH.

(4) Increment the SP register by 1.

Assuming that the SP register currently contains 009EH, and that locations 009EH and 009FH relative to the SS register contain 0A2H and 0B3H respectively, then the effect of `POP DX` will be to put 0B3A2H into DX and to change the contents of the SP register to 00A0H.

8.3.2 PUSH and POP in daily use

Once everything is initialized, PUSH and POP can be used freely wherever temporary storage is required. It is necessary to remember just two points:

(1) It is essential that any subroutine should leave the stack in the same state as when that subroutine started using the stack. Otherwise, strange things may happen when your program is executed since, for example, a value which you have PUSHed but not POPped could be taken as the return address for that subroutine – see Section 8.6.

(2) The last item put on the stack is the first off. Thus:

```
PUSH AX ;copy AX onto stack
PUSH BX ;copy BX onto stack
POP  AX ;copy the item currently on the top
        ;of the stack into register AX and
        ;then remove that item from the stack
POP  BX ;copy what is on the top of the stack
        ;into register BX and then remove
        ;that item from the top of the stack
```

effectively swaps the contents of registers AX and BX.

EXERCISES

8.5 Make a detailed trace of the execution of the following program fragment, giving the contents of all the registers and memory locations involved. Assume that before execution begins the SS register contains 1000H, and the SP register 0200H, and that the contents of AX, BX, CX and DX are (respectively) 0100H, 123AH, 0FE1BH and 0A981H.

```
PUSH AX
PUSH BX
PUSH CX
POP  DX
POP  CX
PUSH DX
POP  AX
POP  BX
```

8.6 Registers AX, BX and CX all contain the ASCII codes for two letters as follows:

AX		BX		CX	
AH	AL	BH	BL	CH	CL
S	O	R	T	M	E

Using PUSH and POP, write a subroutine called REARRANGE which leaves AX, BX and CX containing the letters in alphabetical order:

AX		BX		CX	
AH	AL	BH	BL	CH	CL
E	M	O	R	S	T

8.4 A complete program using subroutines

To make matters absolutely clear, this section gives a complete assembly program which uses subroutines and which prints a small message on the computer's display screen. The actual printing on the screen is done – as before – by one of the DOS functions, but this time we incorporate it into a subroutine.

```
PRINTCHAR: MOV AH,02H ;function number 2
           INT 21H    ;of INTerrupt 21H
           RET
```

The program given below is a complete program which uses the subroutine PRINTCHAR to print the three-letter message IBM on the screen. (It uses the fact that with PRINTCHAR, each time something is printed, printing continues from wherever it finished last time.) Type it into your machine and verify that it works. Try to amend it so that the message printed out is ABC and check your work by re-assembling your amended version.

In the program we have used a new MASM pseudo-op, COMMENT. COMMENT lets you enter comments about your program without having to precede each comment line with a semicolon. Instead, the actual comment is enclosed by the first non-blank character after the COMMENT pseudo-op and the next occurrence of that character.

```
COMMENT *This program prints a three-letter message
        on the PC screen. The message can be changed
        by altering the values of FIRSTLETTER,
        SECONDLETTER and THIRDLETTER.*

FIRSTLETTER  EQU 49H ;49H is the ASCII code for the letter I
SECONDLETTER EQU 42H ;42H is the ASCII code for the letter B
THIRDLETTER  EQU 4DH ;4DH is the ASCII code for the letter M
PRINTFUN EQU  2H
CHARFNS  EQU 21H
```

```
DATA SEGMENT
DATA ENDS

WORKING_STORAGE SEGMENT STACK
    DW 100H DUP(?)
WORKING_STORAGE ENDS

CODE SEGMENT
ASSUME CS:CODE,DS:DATA,SS:WORKING_STORAGE
PROG_START: MOV  DL,FIRSTLETTER
            CALL PRINTCHAR
            MOV  DL,SECONDLETTER
            CALL PRINTCHAR
            MOV  DL,THIRDLETTER
            CALL PRINTCHAR
            ;return to DOS
            MOV AX,4C00H
            INT 21H

PRINTCHAR: MOV AH,PRINTFUN
           INT CHARFNS
           RET

CODE ENDS
END PROG_START
```

EXERCISE

8.7 Type the above program into your computer and verify that it works. Inspect the `.LST` file produced by MASM to see the effect of `EQU`. Amend the program so that the message printed is:

```
DOS
RULES
OK !!
```

8.5 CALL and RET – the mechanism of the basic (intra-segment) forms

As pointed out in Section 3.3 it is from the IP register (relative to the contents of the CS register) that the 8086 family gets the address of the next instruction to be obeyed. Generally speaking, the programmer does not access the IP register directly. Before execution of a program the operating system initializes CS:IP to the first of the locations containing that program. After execution of any particular instruction, IP is automatically incremented to point to the

	Before		After
		CALL 0001	
IP	010DH		0111H
SP	01E4H		01E2H
01E1H	??		??
01E2H	??		10H
01E3H	??		01H
01E4H	??		??
		RET	
IP	0125H		0110H
SP	01E2H		01E4H
01E1H	??		??
01E2H	10H		10H
01E3H	01H		01H
01E4H	??		??

Figure 8.3 The effect of CALL and RET on the contents of the IP register.

address of the next instruction. CALL and RET disturb this mechanism by changing the contents of the IP register (and sometimes the CS register).

As a specific example let us consider the following extract from the listing of an assembler:

```
                              .
                              .
                              .
010B 8B C1                    MOV   AX,CX
010D E8 01 00                 CALL A_SUB
0110 F4                       HLT
0111 F7 E3          A_SUB:    MUL   BX
0113 8B D0                    MOV   DX,AX
                              .
                              .
                              .
0124 C3                       RET
```

By the time these instructions come to be executed the assembler will have replaced the label A_SUB in CALL A_SUB with one of two things. If the subroutine with first instruction labeled A_SUB is stored within 0FFFFH locations of the CALL instruction, then the label A_SUB is replaced by a 16-bit unsigned number. This number specifies what will need to be added to the contents of the IP register after execution of the CALL has begun in order for CS:IP to point to the instruction labeled A_SUB. Thus, in this case, the label in CALL A_SUB will be replaced by 0001. This is shown in Figure 8.3.

Notice from the assembler listing above that the instruction CALL A_SUB (really, CALL 0001) has the machine code equivalent E8 01 00. When execution of the CALL begins, IP will – as normal – be incremented to point to the next instruction in sequence (in this case it is a HLT instruction). But during execution of CALL 0001, the 16-bit unsigned number following the code for the CALL instruction itself (0E8H) is added to the current contents of the IP register. Since the next instruction to be obeyed after the CALL will be taken from the location specified by the IP register (relative to the contents of CS), the next instruction executed will indeed be that labeled A_SUB. But this is not the only effect of CALL. In order that a return to the main program can be effected once a RET instruction is encountered, CALL also pushes the address of the instruction which follows it on to the stack. Execution of the RET instruction simply entails popping the top 16-bit element of the stack into the IP register. Provided as many PUSHes as POPs have occurred within the body of the subroutine, the word at the top of the stack will be the address of the instruction following the CALL.

CALL and RET instructions of this type are known as **intra-segment** (or within segment) instructions, since the body of the subroutine is in the same segment (that is, in the same collection of 10000H memory locations) as the CALL.

To summarize the effect of CALL and RET intra-segment instructions:

- CALL *<label>* The *<label>* following the instruction is replaced by an unsigned 16-bit number which is the difference between the address of the first location after those containing the CALL instruction and the address of the first location containing the body of the subroutine (both relative to CS).

  When the CALL instruction is executed, the unsigned 16-bit number is added to the contents of the IP register and the address of the instruction following the CALL instruction is pushed onto the stack.
- RET When the RET instruction is executed, the top of the stack is popped into the IP register.

8.6 The inter-segment subroutine mechanism

If the instruction following the CALL and the body of the subroutine called are more than 0FFFFH locations apart, the **inter-segment** form of both CALL and RET must be used. Fortunately MASM keeps track of which form is necessary so we never actually have to count locations ourselves. The format of the CALL instruction does not change but CALL *<label>*, where the *<label>* refers to a subroutine in another segment, will be translated by MASM into the form CALL *<address>* where the *<address>* is a 4-byte quantity representing the address of the body of the subroutine. Of these four bytes, the first two are the offset of the subroutine from the CS register and the second two the setting of the CS register for the segment containing the CALL instruction. When the inter-segment CALL instruction is executed the full (4-byte) address of the instruction following the CALL is placed on to the stack, CS value first. Then the 4-byte address in the CALL instruction itself is transferred to the IP and CS registers so that the next instruction to be executed will be the first in the appropriate subroutine.

To return from an inter-segment subroutine a different form of the RET instruction is used. On execution it pops the top two stack bytes into IP and the next two bytes into the CS register.

To know in advance whether a given CALL is to be converted into the machine code form of an inter-segment CALL or an intra-segment CALL, MASM insists that the programmer who wants to work in several segments must cloak each part of the program in such a way that what is near and what is far is obvious to the assembler. Unless explicitly told otherwise, it assumes that all CALL and RET instructions are intra-segment.

Inter-segment CALLs and RETs are achieved thanks to the idea of a procedure, which is simply a subroutine labeled in a careful way and given one of the attributes near or far. Thus:

```
(1)   MY_SUBROUTINE: MOV AX,4
                     INC BX
                      .
                      .
                      .
                     RET
(2)   MY_SUBROUTINE  PROC NEAR
                     MOV AX,4
                     INC BX
                      .
                      .
                      .
                     RET
      MY_SUBROUTINE  ENDP
(3)   MY_SUBROUTINE  PROC FAR
                     MOV AX,4
                     INC BX
                      .
                      .
                      .
                     RET
      MY_SUBROUTINE  ENDP
```

all result in exactly the same machine code, except that the RET instruction in (1) and (2) will be coded as intra-segment and that in (3) as inter-segment (and likewise CALL MY_SUBROUTINE in the first two cases will be translated into an intra-segment CALL whereas CALL MY_SUBROUTINE in case (3) will be inter-segment).

Both popular debuggers, DEBUG and Code View, use different names for the CALL and RET instructions if inter-segment operation is involved. Thus CALLF is used to CALL a Far away subroutine and RETF to RETurn from a Far away subroutine.

EXERCISES

8.8 Rewrite, assemble and run our complete program example above containing subroutines so that it uses procedures (a) in such a way that all CALL and RET instructions are assembled as *near* and (b) so that all CALL and RET instructions are assembled as *far*. Compare the .LST files thus obtained.

8.9 Write and test an assembly language program which draws a 4 * 4 chess board on the screen with the 'black' squares made up from a 4 * 4 grid of letter Xs:

```
XXXX    XXXX
XXXX    XXXX
XXXX    XXXX
XXXX    XXXX
    XXXX    XXXX
    XXXX    XXXX
    XXXX    XXXX
    XXXX    XXXX
XXXX    XXXX
XXXX    XXXX
XXXX    XXXX
XXXX    XXXX
    XXXX    XXXX
    XXXX    XXXX
    XXXX    XXXX
    XXXX    XXXX
```

8.7 Subroutines with parameters

The PRINTCHAR subroutine of Section 8.4 was an example of the technique of using registers to pass a parameter across to a subroutine: register AL contained the ASCII code for the character to be printed by PRINTCHAR. In this way, general-purpose registers can be used to hold the parameters themselves or they may hold the addresses where parameters are located in memory. The main advantages of such an approach are that it is relatively easy to pass a small number of parameters and that, when a register is used to pass the initial (or base) address of a group of memory locations, the calling subroutine does not need its own copy of the data.

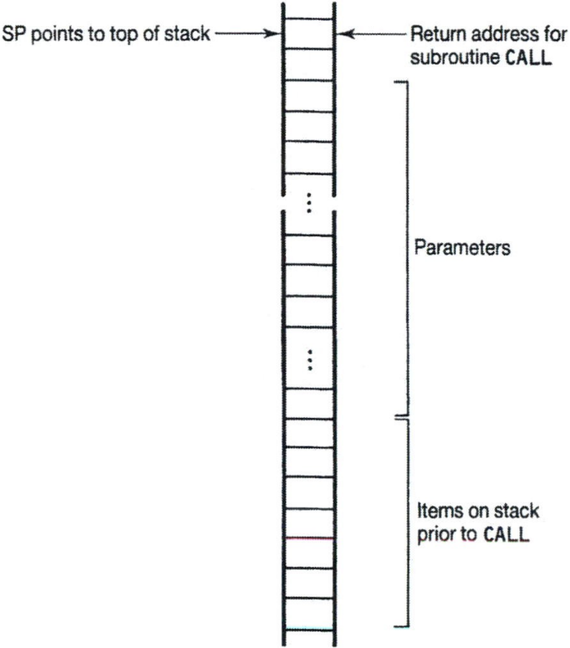

Figure 8.4 Accessing parameters placed on the stack cannot easily be done using PUSH and POP.

Since the number of general-purpose registers is limited (really there are just four – AX, BX, CX and DX), if it is required to pass several parameters it is better to use the stack. Before the subroutine CALL the parameters are simply PUSHed onto the stack, but because the CALL then stores its own return address also on the stack, these parameters cannot then easily be retrieved by PUSH and POP instructions (see Figure 8.4).

The problem is overcome by using the **BP register**, a 16-bit register, to access the contents of memory locations in the same way as BX in an instruction such as

```
MOV AX,[BX]
```

Whereas BX works relative to the DS register, addresses accessed via BP are taken relative to the SS register so that

```
MOV DL,[BP]
```

moves the byte at SS:BP into DL.

Both BX and BP have a further property, namely they can both be used as base registers. Thus, while the instruction:

```
MOV AX,[BP]
```

loads AX with the word at the address (relative to SS) given in BP,

```
MOV AX,[BP+2]
```

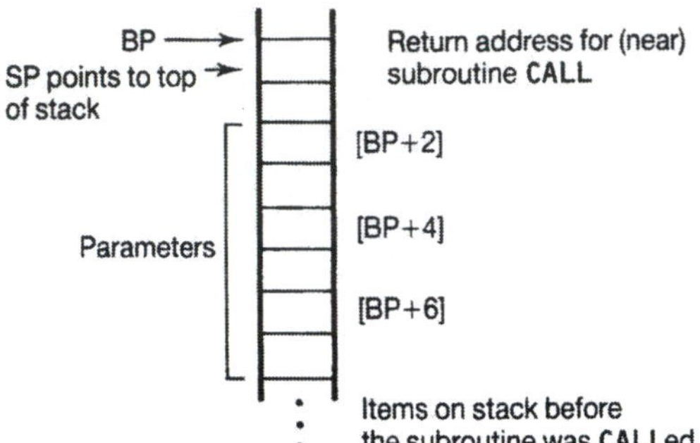

Figure 8.5
Use of BP to access parameters.

loads AX with the word at the address (relative to SS) formed by taking what is in BP and adding 2 to it. In general,

```
MOV register,[BP + n]
MOV [BP + n],register
```

(where *n* is either a signed 8-bit number or an unsigned 16-bit number) will transfer the contents (byte or word as appropriate) from or to the location having address (relative to SS) found by adding *n* to the contents of BP. Similarly, though perhaps less often useful as one normally needs the BX register for other duties, the instructions

```
MOV register,[BX + n]
MOV [BX + n],register
```

perform equivalent transfers, though all addresses are taken relative to the DS register in this case.

Returning now to the problem of passing subroutine parameters placed on the stack before the subroutine was called, an easy solution is provided by setting BP to the same value as SP (so that BP now also points to the top of the stack) and then using instructions

```
MOV. . .,[BP+2]
MOV. . .,[BP+4]
MOV. . .,[BP+6]
```

and so on to access the parameters (see Figure 8.5).

MASM allows the use of instructions of the form

```
MOV AX,[BP+'A'] ;equivalent to MOV AX,[BP+41H]
MOV BX,[BP+'b'] ;equivalent to MOV CX,[BP+62H]
MOV CX,[BP+'W'] ;equivalent to MOV BX,[BP+57H]
```

so that, for example, one parameter could be specified for every letter of the alphabet, or for each printable character in the ASCII code. **Local variables** (that is, variables whose values are needed *only* within the subroutine itself) can be provided through BP under these circumstances by instructions of the form:

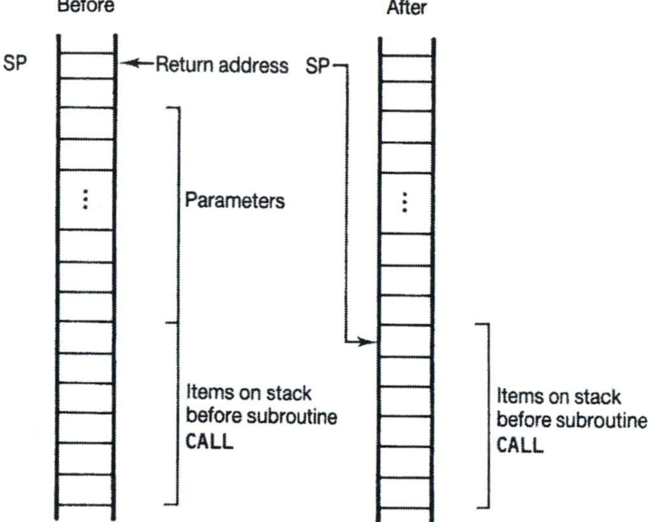

Figure 8.6
The effect of `RET` x.

```
MOV [BP-2],AX
ADD [BP-4],DX
```

and so on, provided that use of the stack within the subroutine itself does not interfere with this.

Upon return to the calling program after execution of a subroutine which accesses its parameters in this way, the top items on the stack will be these very same parameters. Quite often, the parameters are no longer required after the execution of the subroutine and so must be `POP`ped and discarded. To make such discarding of parameters easier, there is a special form of both intra- and inter-segment `RET` instructions:

```
RET x
```

which allows return from a subroutine in the normal manner, but which – after the return – increments SP by x, where x is an unsigned 16-bit number (see Figure 8.6).

To illustrate much of this we shall now give a complete example program which uses BP and `RET` x. The program adds a fixed value to each element of an array of values and then returns to DOS. It most certainly does not follow the best method of accomplishing this task, but is, rather, intended to illustrate subroutine parameter passing using the stack without masses of other details getting in the way. In the program we have used the pseudo-op `.RADIX` which allows us to set the **default radix** assumed by MASM to be any number between 2 and 16 (inclusive). Thus, after a `.RADIX 16` pseudo-op, all numbers not explicitly marked as being in a certain base are assumed by MASM to be hexadecimal. Nevertheless, it is still necessary that every number begins with a digit (possibly 0), so that there is no chance of confusion between labels, variables, registers and numbers.

8.7.1 Adding a fixed value to each element of a numerical array

In the promised program using BP and RET x which follows, the original array of nine unsigned 16-bit values is stored in the group of locations beginning with that corresponding to TEST_ARRAY. The program adds 9 to each of these values using the subroutine ARRAY_INC. It requires three parameters which should have been placed on the stack in unsigned 16-bit form in the following order: the start address of the array (relative to DS); the number which is to be added; and the size of the array.

```
            .RADIX 16
            ADDNUMBER  EQU 12
            ARRAY_SIZE EQU  9

            DATA SEGMENT
                TEST_ARRAY DW 3A,4A,5A,6A,7A,1234,5678,9ABC,0DEF
            DATA ENDS

            WORKING_STORAGE SEGMENT STACK
              DW 100 DUP(?)
            WORKING_STORAGE ENDS

            CODE SEGMENT
            ASSUME CS:CODE,DS:DATA,SS:WORKING_STORAGE
            ;establish data segment addressability
PROG_START: MOV  AX,DATA
            MOV  DX,AX
            ;main program
            MOV  AX,OFFSET TEST_ARRAY
            PUSH AX
            MOV  AX,ADDNUMBER
            PUSH AX
            MOV  AX,ARRAY_SIZE
            PUSH AX
            CALL ARRAY_INC
            MOV  AX,4C00
            INT  21         ;return to DOS

            ARRAY_INC PROC NEAR
               MOV BP,SP         ;initialize BP to value of SP
               MOV CX,[BP+2]     ;CX is the size of the array
               MOV AX,[BP+4]     ;AX is the number to be added
               MOV BX,[BP+6]     ;BX is the start address
ALTER_THIS_LOC: MOV DX,[BX]      ;bring contents of next location
               ADD DX,AX         ;add the increment to it
               MOV [BX],DX       ;store away again
               ADD BX,2          ;set BX to next address
               DEC CX            ;reduce count
```

```
    JNZ ALTER_THIS_LOC
    RET 6               ;if done, return and add 6 to SP
ARRAY_INC ENDP

CODE ENDS
END PROG_START
```

EXERCISES

8.10 Write a subroutine which adds up the five unsigned 16-bit numbers which have been placed on the stack and leaves their total in AX. (Assume that this total can be accurately represented in unsigned 16-bit form.) Write also a main program which calls up your subroutine, and test the complete program carefully.

8.11 Write a subroutine which will add together the corresponding entries in two arrays, each containing 10D signed 16-bit numbers, and leave the result in a third similar array, assuming in every case that the result of the addition can be accurately represented in signed 16-bit form. Your subroutine should take its parameters from the stack, given that they were placed on the stack in the following order:

starting address of first array
starting address of second array
starting address of array to hold the sums

Write a main program to accompany the subroutine so that it can be properly tested.

8.12 Repeat Exercise 8.11 but with the subroutine in this case swapping the elements of the two given arrays. Use two local variables accessed via BP to effect the swap.

SUMMARY

This chapter has been concerned with the artifacts of good assembly language programming technique: a controlled program development methodology, mimicking the sophisticated features for structured programming which are found in languages such as Pascal, and the use of subroutines – with and without parameters – so that difficult, large programs can be built up out of smaller, proven building blocks.

Chapter 10 will apply this methodology to produce a fairly substantial complete example program. Before we can do this, however, in Chapter 9 we must first make a detailed study of the 8086-family instructions which allow us to access individual bits in a register.

SELF-CHECK QUIZ

1. Text is stored in a group of 1000H locations in memory. These locations are to be searched for the first occurrence of two consecutive letter As, upper or lower case, or mixed. Write a pseudo-Pascal outline of an assembly language routine to find them. Say how you would assign variables in your outline to memory and registers.

2. If we insist on using only the registers AX, BX, CX and DX (and their 8-bit counterparts) for variables in a pseudo-Pascal outline, what limitations does this place on the kinds of program we can write?

3. Write a subroutine which given the value of n as an unsigned 8-bit number in AL will leave the value of 2^n in DX,AX as a 32-bit unsigned number, DX containing the higher order bits.

4. Using only `PUSH` and `POP` instructions, is it possible to rearrange the unsigned 16-bit numbers in AX, BX and CX so that AX contains the largest, BX the next largest and CX the smallest?

5. Give a sequence of assembly language instructions which put the offsets of `MY_BYTE` and `MY_WORD` on the stack.

6. A certain subroutine requires its own stack, quite separate from the normal program stack. How could this be arranged?

7. Can the *first* instruction in a subroutine ever be a `POP` instruction? Justify your answer.

8. Draw a diagram to show the contents of the stack during the following execution sequence, assuming that all stack activity arises from the calls and returns we describe:

   `MAIN` calls `NEAR` subroutine `SUB1` – the return offset is 300H

   `SUB1` then calls `NEAR` subroutine `SUB2` – the return offset is 04A0H

   `SUB2` then calls `FAR` subroutine `SUB3` – the return offset is 500H and the return segment address is 0B0AH

   return from `SUB3` to `SUB2`

   `SUB2` now calls `NEAR` subroutine `SUB4` – the return offset is 01ABH

   return from `SUB4` to `SUB2`

   return from `SUB2` to `SUB1`

   return from `SUB1` to `MAIN`

9. If parameters are passed to a subroutine via the stack, how can a result be passed to the calling program via the stack?

10. Write a subroutine which calculates p^n given p and n represented as unsigned 8-bit numbers passed to the subroutine via the stack. The result should be left in DX,AX as a 32-bit unsigned number, DX containing the higher order bits.

9

Getting at Individual Bits

Contents

Microprocessors are not just used as the foundation stone of microcomputer architecture. They are also used to make control devices for a range of equipment including large-scale manufacturing production machinery on the one hand and traffic light controllers on the other. All of these require the ability to manipulate individual bits since, for example, a given bit can be set to 1 to turn a traffic light on, or to 0 to turn it off.

Consequently, the designer of a microprocessor must include in its instruction set an appropriate repertoire for these types of microprocessor applications. This chapter discusses a subset of those available for this purpose in the 8086 family. In fact, we shall discuss three different families of instructions: the logical family, the shift family and the rotate family.

Certain members of the rotate family of instructions can use the carry flag to save some information which would otherwise be lost. Usually, the values of flags are only changed indirectly by instructions. But to make the fullest possible use of these instructions without recourse to tricks, the 8086 family provides instructions to change the value of the carry flag directly and these are also described in this chapter.

Finally, we briefly consider the execution efficiency of programs. Years ago, this issue was the mainstay of assembly language programming technique. But with today's high labor costs, producing programs as quickly as possible and in a form which can be maintained cheaply have replaced it as the dominant consideration.

9.1 The family of 'logical' instructions

We have seen that the contents of a register like AX or AL can be thought of as a signed or unsigned number and as the ASCII code for some character. There is a third important way of viewing the binary digits in a register in which each bit gives certain information depending on its position in the register. For example, in a 16-bit register the 16 bits could represent the result of an electronic quality control test on 16 product items – a 1 in a particular position indicating that the corresponding item was satisfactory, a 0 indicating failure. Thus, if the contents of AX was

0000100100000010

then items 1, 8 and 11 were **not** faulty (numbering from zero from the right-hand side in the usual way). Accessing individual bits could also be useful when a microcomputer based on some member of the 8086 family is being used to control an external device – a set of traffic lights, for example. In that case the setting of a given bit might determine whether a light is turned on or off.

The 8086 family has several instructions which enable one to process information of this kind including `AND`, `OR`, `NOT`, `XOR` and `TEST`. These are known as the **logical family** of instructions because they operate bit by bit on the contents of either one or two registers and the outcome reflects the interpretation of 1 as representing the logical value TRUE and 0 as representing the logical value FALSE.

An instruction

```
AND AX,BX
```

changes the contents of register AX in the following way. The contents of registers AX and BX are combined bit by bit. If, in a given position, both AX and BX contain a 1 then the result of `AND AX,BX` will have a 1 in that position, otherwise there will be a 0. For example:

Contents of AX	0000101011100011
Contents of BX	1001100000100001
	————————
Contents of AX after `AND AX,BX`	0000100000100001

(the result has a 1 only in those positions in which both AX and BX contain a 1)

The AND instruction affects all the arithmetic flags and can be used to check if the bit in a particular position is 0 or 1. For example, to check if the bit in position 7 of register AX is a 1 we would first put 0000000010000000B into register BX and then execute an AND AX,BX instruction. Because of all the 0s in register BX the result of the AND can have at most one non-zero entry – in position 7. If AX contains a 1 in that position, so will the result which will then be 0000000010000000B, otherwise the result will be 0.

Thus, if AX does have bit 7 set to 1:

```
AX     1000101011001110
BX     0000000010000000
       ----------------
result of 0000000010000000
AND AX,BX
```

and if AX does not have bit 7 set to 1:

```
AX     0101010101010101
BX     0000000010000000
       ----------------
result of 0000000000000000
AND AX,BX
```

Hence, with the given setting of BX, if after AND AX,BX register AX is 0 (in which case the Z-flag will be set to 1) then there was a 0 in position 7 of register AX initially and if not then there was a 1 in that position.

This is an instance of a general technique called **masking**. As another example, let us consider the problem of recouping the numeric value from the ASCII code for a digit. Consider Table 9.1 and notice the correlation between the last two columns.

Table 9.1 Recouping a numeric value from an ASCII code.

Decimal digit	*ASCII code* *Hex* *Binary*	*8-bit unsigned number with same value as the decimal digit*
0	30H = 0011 0000	00000000
1	31H = 0011 0001	00000001
2	32H = 0011 0010	00000010
3	33H = 0011 0011	00000011
4	34H = 0011 0100	00000100
5	35H = 0011 0101	00000101
6	36H = 0011 0110	00000110
7	37H = 0011 0111	00000111
8	38H = 0011 1000	00001000
9	39H = 0011 1001	00001001

Whenever a digit is typed in at the computer keyboard and accepted via the DOS function 1 of interrupt number 21H, the ASCII code for that digit will end up in AL. Before the value of that digit can be used in a calculation it must be transformed from ASCII into a numeric format. One method of effecting this transformation would be to enter 00001111B into register BL and execute an `AND AL,BL` which would leave the numerical value of the digit in register AL.

For example, if register AL contains the ASCII code for the digit 7:

Contents of AL	0011 0111	
Contents of BL	0000 1111	
Contents of AL after `AND AL,BL`	0000 0111	(an unsigned binary number equivalent to decimal 7)

As mentioned earlier, there are four other members of the logical family of bit manipulating instructions: `OR`, `NOT`, `XOR` and `TEST`. An instruction `OR AX,BX` changes the contents of register AX in the following way. The contents of registers AX and BX are compared bit by bit. If, in a given position, either AX or BX contains a 1 then the result of `OR AX, BX` will have a 1 in that position, otherwise a 0. For example

Contents of AX	0011001101011010
Contents of BX	0101010100000111
Contents of AX after `OR AX,BX`	0111011101011111

While the `AND` and `OR` instructions operate with two registers, `NOT` requires only one. `NOT BX`, for example, simply changes every bit in BX which is a 1 to a 0 and every 0 to a 1:

Initial contents of BX	0101111100001001
Contents of BX after `NOT BX`	1010000011110110

The format of the `XOR` instruction is exactly the same as that of the `OR`. An instruction

```
XOR AX,BX
```

changes the contents of register AX in the following way. The contents of registers AX and BX are combined bit by bit. If, in a given position, both AX and BX contain a 1 or both AX and BX contain a 0 then the result of `XOR AX,BX` will have a 0 in that position, otherwise there will be a 1. In other words, after execution of `XOR AX,BX`, register AX will have a 1 in a given position if either AX or BX has a 1 in that position, but not both (XOR stands for eXclusive OR).

For example:

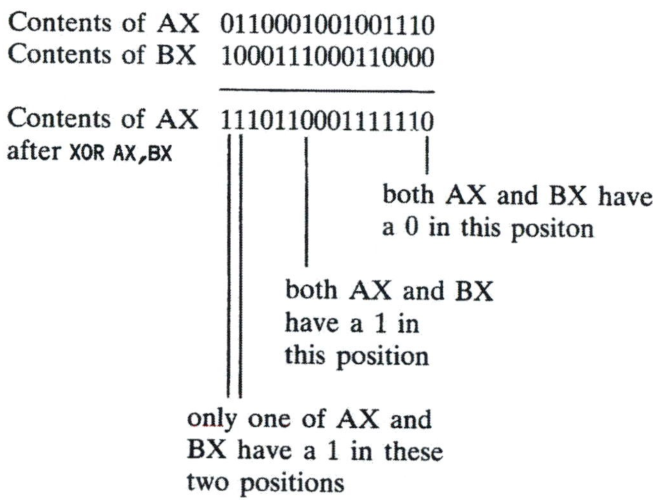

The TEST instruction is very similar to the AND instruction in that they both have the same format and both perform the same operation between their operands, but TEST does not affect the main registers and only changes the flags. Thus,

	AH	*DH*	*Z-flag*
Before	01010011	10001100	?
After AND DL,AH	01010011	00000000	1
After TEST DL,AH	01010011	10001100	1

Figure 9.1 gives a trace of a program fragment involving members of the logical family of instructions and Table 9.2 summarizes the uses of the instructions.

Program	*Trace* AL	BL	CL	DL
	?	?	?	?
MOV AL,10111111	10111111	?	?	?
MOV BL,01010111	10111111	01010111	?	?
MOV CL,0	10111111	01010111	0	?
AND AL,BL	00010111	01010111	0	?
OR AL,BL	01010111	01010111	0	?
JZ EXIT	01010111	01010111	0	?
NOT BL	01010111	10101000	0	?
AND AL,BL	00000000	10101000	0	?
JZ CHANGE				
MOV DL,1				
JMP EXIT				
CHANGE: MOV DL,0	00000000	10101000	0	0
EXIT: MOV CL,1	00000000	10101000	1	0

Figure 9.1
A trace of a program fragment using logical family instructions.

Table 9.2 Logical family instructions.

Instruction	*Use*
AND	Setting specified bit position of the first operand to 0, the other operand specifying the bit positions. Thus, AND BH,00011100B will set bits 0,1,5,6 and 7 of BH to 0 leaving the others unchanged.
OR	Setting specified bit positions of the first operand to 1, the other operand specifying the bit positions. Thus, OR CL,11000000B will set bits 6 and 7 of CL to 1 leaving the others unchanged.
NOT	Changing every bit in its operand to the opposite of what it was initially.
XOR	Changing specified bits of its first operand to the opposite of their current settings, the other operand specifying the bit positions. Thus, XOR AH,00000011B will change bits 0 and 1 of AH to the opposite of their previous setting and leave the others unchanged.
TEST	Testing whether specified bit positions of the first operand are set to 0, the other operand specifying the bit positions. Thus TEST DL,01010101B will set the Z-flag to 1 only if bits 0,2,4 and 6 of DL are all 0.

9.1.1 General forms of the logical family instructions

This is the first occasion on which some indication of the general form of an instruction has been offered and we shall use some fairly informal notation. Should any ambiguities or other confusion arise from our notation, the precise definitions of all the 8086-family instructions are given in Appendix V.

The AND, XOR, OR and TEST instructions may all be used in the same forms which will be illustrated with the AND instruction. These are:

AND *register,number*
AND *memory,number*
AND *register1,register2*
AND *register,memory*
AND *memory,register*

The NOT instruction may be used in the formats:

NOT *register*
NOT *memory*

EXERCISES

9.1 Make traces of the execution of each of the following program fragments:

(a)

```
        MOV AL,38H
        MOV BL,2AH
        MOV CL,0ABH
        AND AL,BL
        AND BL,CL
        NOT CL
        OR  CL,BL
```

(b)

```
        MOV AX,0001110001110001B
        MOV BX,1110001110001111B
        AND AX,BX
        NOT AX
        OR  AX,BX
        NOT BX
        JZ  NEWTRY
        AND BX,AX
        NOT BX
        JMP EXIT
NEWTRY: AND AX,BX
  EXIT: NOT AX
```

(c)

```
         MOV  AL,23H
         MOV  CH,6BH
         XOR  AL,CH
         TEST AL,77H
         JZ   MISSAND
         AND  CH,33H
MISSAND: XOR  CH,0AAH
         TEST CH,AL
         JZ   MISSOR
         NOT  AL
         OR   CH,AL
 MISSOR: NOT  CH
```

9.2 Write program fragments which *use registers only, not memory* to carry out each of the following tasks:

(a) Change every other bit of AL to its opposite value, starting with bit 7. Thus, if AL contained 01101010B before execution of the program fragment it should contain 11000000B afterwards.

(b) Swap the two nibbles in AL around. Thus if AL contained 01101010B before execution it should contain 10100110B afterwards.

(c) Change bit 3 of AL according to the values of bits 0,1 and 2; set bit 7 according to the values of bits 4,5 and 6; and leave all the other bits alone. If all three preceding bits have the same value, bit 3 or 7 (respectively) should be set to 1; otherwise to 0. Thus if AL contained 01111010B before execution, it should contain 11110010B afterwards.

9.2 The shift family

Because microprocessors in the 8086 family work with binary numbers, they can easily provide facilities for multiplying and dividing a signed or unsigned number by 2. As we shall see in the final section of this chapter – which deals with issues of efficiency – it turns out that these special facilities work much faster than using the ordinary multiply and divide instructions.

The principle used is an easy one. Consider Table 9.3. In the binary column, the first three entries differ only in that entry 2 is the first entry shifted left one bit and entry 3 is the second entry shifted left one bit. From the decimal column we see that the decimal equivalents of these binary entries double after each left shift. On the other hand, binary column entries 4 to 8 (inclusive) differ only by a shift right of one bit and the corresponding decimal values are halved after each right shift.

There are two different sets of 8086-family **shift instructions**, one set for doubling and halving unsigned binary numbers, the other for doubling and halving signed binary numbers. The instructions which perform the doubling and halving of unsigned numbers are SHL (SHift Left) and SHR (SHift Right) and those which do the same for signed numbers are SAL (Shift Arithmetic Left) and SAR (Shift Arithmetic Right).

9.2.1 SHL and SHR

SHL doubles an unsigned number by shifting all bits one position to the left and filling in the vacated right-most bit with a 0. To test if the doubling has resulted in a number which is too big to be represented in the number of bits available in the particular register or memory location being operated on, the bit which is shifted out of the left-hand end is moved into the carry flag.

The general forms of the SHL instruction are:

SHL *register*,1
SHL *memory*,1

Table 9.3 Binary and decimal equivalents.

Entry	*Binary*	*Decimal*
1	00011111	31
2	00111110	62
3	01111100	124
4	00110000	48
5	00011000	24
6	00001100	12
7	00000110	6
8	00000011	3

Suppose that register AL contains 01001111B and that we execute the instruction:

```
SHL AL,1
```

After execution the contents of AL will be 10011110B and the carry flag will be set to 0. If register CX contains 1010101011111111B, then after execution of

```
SHL CX,1
```

CX will contain 0101010111111110B and the carry flag will be set to 1.

Halving unsigned numbers can be carried out via the SHR instruction which has the general forms:

SHR *register*,1
SHR *memory*,1

and operates by shifting all bits one position to the right, filling the then vacated left-most position with a 0 and placing the bit that was shifted off the right-hand end into the carry flag. In this case, the carry flag being set to 1 indicates that the number just halved was not even (and therefore that the 'halving' is only approximate).

If register DX contains 1010101011111110B before execution of

```
SHR DX,1
```

then after execution DX will contain 0101010101111111B and the carry flag will be set to 0. With register BL containing 01100111B beforehand, the execution of

```
SHR BL,1
```

will leave 00110011B in BL and the carry flag will be set to 1 (01100111 in binary is equivalent to decimal 207).

9.2.2 SAL and SAR

Doubling and halving signed numbers involves the slight complication of ensuring that the sign of the number is not changed. Thus, doubling +8 (00001000) should result in +16 (00010000) and doubling −20 (11101100) should result in −40 (11011000). Likewise, halving +6 (00000110) should give +3 (00000011) and halving −120 (10001000) should give −60 (11000100).

SAL (Shift Arithmetic Left) doubles signed numbers and SAR (Shift Arithmetic Right) halves them. These instructions have the general forms:

SAL *register*,1
SAL *memory*,1

SAR *register*,1
SAR *memory*,1

SAL operates in precisely the same way as SHL, since the sign bit of a positive signed number is 0. It is up to the programmer to ensure that the result

Table 9.4 Effect of SAR.

Contents of AL before execution of SAR AL,1		*Contents of AL after execution of* SAR AL,1	
Binary	*Decimal*	*Binary*	*Decimal*
01101100	+108	00110110	+54
00101011	+43	00010101	+21
10000010	−126	11000001	−63
10101111	−81	11010111	−41
11000010	−62	11100001	−31

of such doubling is in range (for otherwise, doubling a positive signed number like 01101100 may well result in a negative signed number, namely 11011000). In general, it is better if the programmer plans in advance to avoid such an eventuality, but on occasions planning ahead is impossible. In these cases the sign flag enables detection of the phenomenon, for when the SAL or SAR instruction is executed the sign flag is set to 0 or 1 corresponding to the sign of the result.

SAR halves signed binary numbers by shifting all bits one position to the right but at the same time leaving the sign bit unchanged (see Table 9.4), that is, a copy is made of the original sign bit and after everything has been shifted to the right that copy is used to fill the vacated left-most bit. Suppose, for example, that the contents of AL is 11011011. When the contents of AL is viewed as an 8-bit signed number, the sign bit is 1. Shifting the contents of AL one bit to the right gives:

?1101101

If we now use the sign bit to fill the vacated bit:

11101101

it follows that the result of SAR AL,1 in this case leaves AL containing 11101101. To check that this does indeed give the right answer note that 11011011 is −37 in decimal and 11101101 is −19 in decimal. (Notice that halving a signed number always results in a signed number which is less than or equal to half the given number. Hence, when an odd number like +43 is halved the result is +21, and similarly halving −81 gives −41).

EXERCISE

9.3 Make execution traces of the contents of each of the registers involved in the following program fragments:

(a)
```
MOV CX,0303H
SHL CH,1
SHR CX,1
SHR CH,1
SHL CL,1
SHL CH,1
```

(b)
```
MOV DX,1101101101010011B
SAR DX,1
SAR DX,1
SAL DH,1
SAL DL,1
SAR DX,1
SAL DX,1
```

(c)
```
MOV DL,4
MOV BX,10110111B
SAR DL,1
SAL DL,1
SHL DL,1
SHR DL,1
SAR BX,1
SAL BH,1
SAL BL,1
SAR BX,1
```

9.2.3 Quadrupling, octupling and all that

All the shift family instructions have another form which allows shifting up to eight places left or right at a time. Shifting left two bits corresponds to multiplying by 4D and shifting left five bits to multiplying by 32D. Shifting right two bits corresponds to dividing by 4D and shifting right six bits to dividing by 64D. In each case, the only change to the instruction format is the addition of a register to hold the (unsigned) number of places to shift. This register must be CL:

SHL *register/memory*,CL
SHR *register/memory*,CL

SAL *register/memory*,CL
SAR *register/memory*,CL

Thus, if AL contains 10110111B before execution of:

```
MOV CL,3
SHR AL,CL
```

then after execution AL will contain 00010110. Similarly, if BX contains 1011011100000000B before execution of:

```
MOV CL,4
SAR BX,CL
```

then after execution BX will contain 1111101101110000.

EXERCISES

9.4 Write and test an 8086-family assembly language program to multiply the unsigned number in the AL register by 10D using shift instructions. Assume that the result can be represented as an 8-bit unsigned number. (*Hint:* calculate eight times the contents of AL and twice the contents of AL and add.)

9.5 Expand the program you developed for Exercise 9.4 so that the result is left as an unsigned 16-bit number in AX and the program works for any unsigned number in AL. (*Hint:* shift one bit at a time and use the carry flag to make decisions about the contents of AH after each shift.)

9.6 Repeat Exercises 9.4 and 9.5 for division by 8D.

9.3 The rotate family

When a 4-bit shift left is performed, the 4 left-most bits 'fall off the end' and are lost forever (one of them may possibly end up in the carry flag). There are occasions when we do not wish to throw away information with such abandon. The **rotate family** of instructions provides the ability to rearrange bits without losing information. Two types of rotation are possible: one which simply affects the register or memory location nominated in the instruction, and one which involves the carry flag in an essential way.

9.3.1 Rotate

The rotate instructions take the following general forms:

ROL *memory/register*,1
ROL *memory/register*,CL

ROR *memory/register*,1
ROR *memory/register*,CL

ROL (ROtate Left) and ROR (ROtate Right) permit left or right rotation of the bits respectively and any bits which fall off one end are rotated around to fill the vacated positions at the other end. Thus, if AL contains 01000111B then execution of ROR AL,1 will leave 10100011 in AL:

begin with	AL	01000111	
rotate one place to the right	AL	?0100011	and 1 'falls' off the right-hand end

1 rotates round to the other end	AL	10100011	

Similarly, if AL contains 01000111B execution of `ROL AL,1` will leave 10001110 in AL:

begin with	AL	01000111	
rotate one place to the left	AL	1000111?	and 0 'falls' off the left-hand end
0 rotates round to the other end	AL	10001110	

In diagrammatic form, `ROR` can therefore be represented:

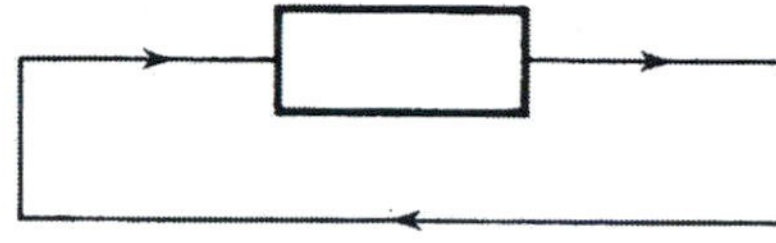

and `ROL`:

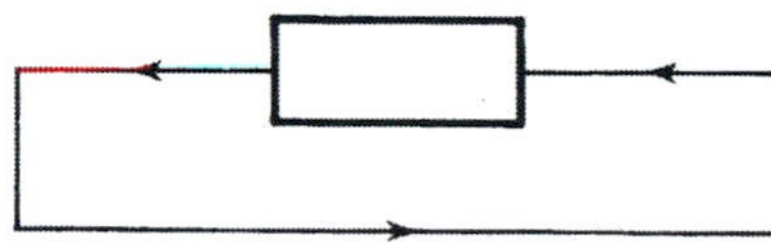

9.3.2 Rotate through the carry flag

Because the flags are not involved in `ROL` and `ROR` it is difficult to keep track of the value of a particular bit and so there are alternative forms of the rotate instructions involving the carry flag. Thus, `RCL` (Rotate through Carry Left) and `RCR` (Rotate through Carry Right) include the carry flag in the rotation: the bit that falls off one end goes into the carry flag, the bit that was in the carry flag goes into the vacated bit (Figure 9.2).

(a)

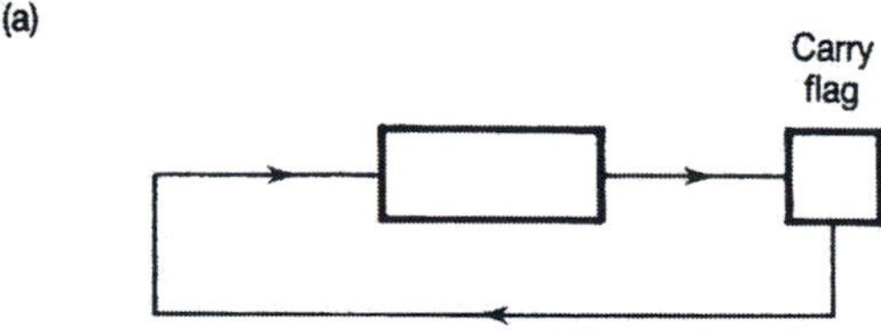

(b)

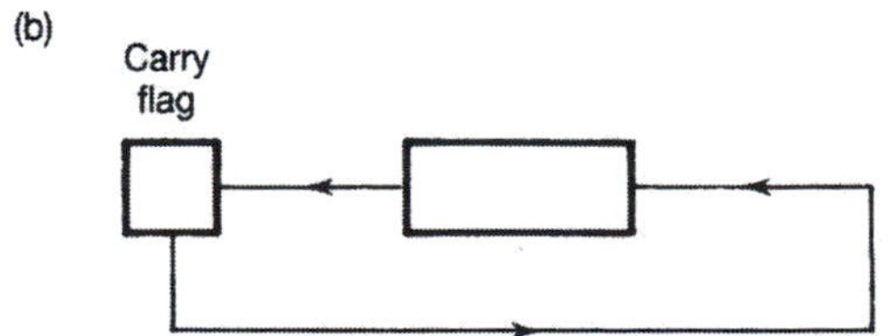

Figure 9.2
The (a) `RCR` and (b) `RCL` instructions.

The rotate family instructions take the following general forms:

RCL *memory*/register,1
RCL *memory/register*,CL
RCR *memory/register*,1
RCR *memory/register*,CL

Hence, if the carry flag is 0 and BL contains 01101100B before execution of RCL BL,1 then after execution BL contains 11011000 and the carry flag will be set to 0. If the carry flag is 0 and AL contains 10101101 before execution of RCR BL,1, then afterwards AL will contain 11010110 and the carry flag will be set to 1.

9.3.3 Setting and clearing the carry flag

For the fullest possible control over rotation through the carry flag we need instructions which allow us to set and clear the carry flag directly. These are provided in the form of STC (SeT Carry flag) and CLC (CLear Carry flag) respectively. Thus, if AL contains 10101110B before execution of:

```
STC
RCR AL,1
```

then after execution AL will contain 11010111 and the carry flag will be set to 0. Similarly, if AL contains 00110011B before execution of:

```
CLC
RCR AL,1
```

then after execution AL will contain 00011001 and the carry flag will be set to 1.

EXERCISES

9.7 Make execution traces of the contents of each of the registers involved in the following program fragments:

(a)
```
MOV CL,4
MOV BX,10110111B
ROR BX,1
ROR BX,CL
```

(b)
```
MOV DX,1101101101010011B
MOV CL,7
STC
RCR DX,1
RCR DX,CL
SHR DX,1
SHL DX,CL
```

```
SAL DX,1
CLC
RCL DX,CL
```

(c)
```
MOV CX,0303H
SHL CH,CL
STC
ROL CX,1
RCL CH,CL
SAR CX,1
RCR CX,CH
```

9.8 Using only SHL, RCL and MOV instructions devise routines to:

(a) multiply the 32-bit unsigned number stored in registers DX and AX by 4 (register DX contains the higher order bits so that

00001111000000001111111101010101B

would be stored with DX containing 0000111100000000B and AX containing 1111111101010101B). Assume that the result can be accurately represented as an unsigned 32-bit number;

(b) repeat (a) but for division by 4; and

(c) repeat (a) and (b) for the 48-bit unsigned number in DX, AX and BX.

9.4 Analyzing beliefs – a complete program example

This section illustrates some of the bit manipulation instructions introduced in this chapter in a complete example program. Perhaps the best illustration would have been a program to control a hardware device such as a set of traffic lights. But such an example would restrict the ability to run the program to those with access to the relevant device. Consequently, we shall illustrate instead with an example program, which could be used in the course of undertaking some market research about the general public's perception of products and for which it is natural to store the users' input in bit form.

In fact, the program will implement a Kelly grid system for analyzing how similar an individual regards four different makes of car – Chevrolet, Volkswagen, Volvo and Porsche – with regard to five pairs of **attributes** in which each pair represents two opposite extremes:

luxury car – family car
expensive – good value for money
exclusive – common
aggressive image – sedate image
for the young – for the old

For each make of car we shall ask the user to type a 1 if he or she thinks the given make of car has the left-hand attribute or 0 if the given make of car has the right-hand attribute. Suppose the replies for a particular user can be summarized as follows:

	chevrolet	volkswagen	volvo	porsche	
luxury car	0	0	0	1	family car
expensive	0	0	0	1	good value for money
exclusive	0	0	0	1	common
aggressive image	0	1	0	1	sedate image
for the young	1	1	0	1	for the old

Then we compare the makes of car, pair by pair. For each pair, we count the number of attributes for which the user's attribute values are the same. We do this for all possible pairwise combinations of different makes of car: Volkswagen and Chevrolet, Volkswagen and Volvo, Volkswagen and Porsche, and so on. Since, in our example, the columns for Chevrolet and Volkswagen have the same entry (both 0 or both 1) four times, there are four agreements between them. Similarly, because the columns for Volvo and Porsche have no entries the same, there are zero agreements between them. The position for all possible pairs can be summarized as follows:

	volkswagen	volvo	porsche
chevrolet	4	4	1
volkswagen		3	2
volvo			0

From this we can deduce that, on the basis of our chosen attributes, the individual whose replies are summarized above thinks that there is little difference between a Chevrolet, a Volkswagen and a Volvo but that a Porsche is very different from the other three.

Our program will be a tool written for the market researcher who wishes to discover an individual user's perceptions of the four makes of car in this way. The dialog to obtain a user's opinions about these products with regard to the given attributes from the user will be as follows (where the user types the chosen value after the colon):

luxury car – score 1
family car – score 0
  chevrolet: 0
  volkswagen: 0
  volvo: 0
  porsche: 1

expensive – score 1
good value for money – score 0
  chevrolet: 0
  volkswagen: 0
  volvo: 0
  porsche: 1

exclusive – score 1
common – score 0
chevrolet: 0
volkswagen: 0
volvo: 0
porsche: 1

aggressive image – score 1
sedate image – score 0
chevrolet: 0
volkswagen: 1
volvo: 0
porsche: 1

for the young – score 1
for the old – score 0
chevrolet: 1
volkswagen: 1
volvo: 0
porsche: 1

ANALYSIS

	volkswagen	*volvo*	*porsche*
chevrolet	*4*	*4*	*1*
volkswagen		*3*	*2*
volvo			*0*

We shall store all the user responses for a given car in one byte. The four bytes for the four cars are assigned in the data segment by:

```
REPLIES DB 4 DUP(0)
```

In each byte, the attribute value typed by the user is stored as a 0 or 1 in a position corresponding to the order in which values for attributes are requested:

Attribute pair	*Order in which value requested in dialog with user*	*Bit position occupied in relevant* REPLIES *byte*
luxury/family	first	7
expensive/good value	second	6
exclusive/common	third	5
aggressive/sedate	fourth	4
young/old	fifth	3

Thus, if the user's replies are those given above, then the four bytes referred to by REPLIES will contain 00001000B, 00011000B, 00000000B, and 11111000B respectively.

The basic outline of the program is entirely straightforward:

```
establish data segment addressability;
for i := 1 to 5 do
  begin
  display a new line;
  display attribute definitions;
  for j := 1 to 4 do
    begin
    display car name;
    get user response;
    store user response;
    display a new line;
    end
  end;
display analysis headings;
for p := 1 to 3 do
  begin
  display row label;
  display (p - 1) * 9 spaces;
  for q := p + 1 to 4 do
    begin
    DL := users' attributes for car p;
    DH := users' attributes for car q;
    count agreements between DL and DH;
    display 8 spaces;
    display number of agreements
    end
  print a new line;
  end;
return to dos
```

There are two points of detail in the implementation which are especially worthy of note. The 0 or 1 typed by the user is first converted from ASCII to a binary 0 or 1 and PUSHed on to the stack while we point BX to the relevant byte of REPLIES. Then it is POPped off the stack and shifted left until it is in the correct position for the given attribute. To store the reply for this attribute we OR the shifted value with the user's values for the other attributes which are already stored in the relevant REPLIES byte (accessed via BX), and store the new value back via BX.

For a precise example suppose that, for a Volvo, the user has already typed 0 for the first attribute pair and 1 for the second. Then the byte of REPLIES corresponding to a Volvo will so far have been set to 01000000B. Suppose next that the user is now asked for a value for the attribute pair *exclusive – common* for a Volvo and types 1 – indicating that he or she believes that a Volvo is an exclusive car. The ASCII code for a 1 will then arrive in AL and we arrange for it to be converted to binary so that, afterwards, AL contains 00000001B. We shift this left five places, giving 00100000B, and OR the result with the byte of REPLIES which corresponds to a Volvo, giving 01100000B. Finally, this value is stored back in the relevant byte of REPLIES, and so on.

The 8086-family bit manipulation instructions are also used to work out the number of attribute pairs on which the user's replies for two different cars agree. Suppose the relevant bytes of REPLIES for a Porsche and a Volvo are 10101000B and 01101000B respectively. These are to be interpreted as:

	porsche	volvo	
luxury car	1	0	family car
expensive	0	1	good value for money
exclusive	1	1	common
aggressive image	0	0	sedate image
for the young	1	1	for the old

If these values are held in DH and DL then to calculate the number of agreements we first execute:

```
XOR DL,DH
NOT DL
```

which leaves DL containing a 1-bit for every instance of agreement:

```
    10101000B
    01101000B
    ---------
XOR 11000000B

NOT 00111111B
```

and then we simply count the number of bits set to 1 in positions 7,6,5,4 and 3 via:

```
             MOV CX,5
             MOV AL,0
   NEXT_BIT: RCL DL,1
             JNC SKIP_COUNT
             INC AL
 SKIP_COUNT: LOOP NEXT_BIT
```

which in our example gives 3.

The complete program is given in Figure 9.3.

Figure 9.3 Which cars are similar?

```
CR EQU 0AH
LF EQU 0DH
DATA SEGMENT
   ATTRIBUTES DB 'luxury car - score 1             ',CR,LF
              DB 'family car - score 0             ',CR,LF,'$'
```

```
                DB 'expensive — score 1             ',CR,LF
                DB 'good value for money — score 0,CR,LF,'$'
                DB 'exclusive — score 1             ',CR,LF
                DB 'common — score 0                ',CR,LF,'$'
                DB 'aggressive image — score 1      ',CR,LF
                DB 'sedate image — score 0          ',CR,LF,'$'
                DB 'for the young — score 1         ',CR,LF
                DB 'for the old — score 0           ',CR,LF,'$'

           CARS DB '   chevrolet:','$'
                DB '  volkswagen:','$'
                DB '       volvo:','$'
                DB '     porsche:','$'

       ANALYSIS DB '    ANALYSIS =======================',CR,LF
                DB '                    volkswagen volvo porsche', CR,LF,'$'
           ROWS DB '  chevrolet','$'
                DB ' volkswagen','$'
                DB '      volvo','$'

        REPLIES DB 4 DUP(0)

      ATT_COUNT DB ?
      CAR_COUNT DB ?
      ROW_COUNT DB ?
      COL_COUNT DB ?
DATA ENDS

WORKING_STORAGE SEGMENT STACK
        DW 100H DUP(?)
WORKING_STORAGE ENDS

CODE SEGMENT
ASSUME DS:DATA, SS:WORKING_STORAGE, CS:CODE
;establish data segment addressability
       START:MOV AX,DATA
             MOV DS,AX
;for i:= 1 to 5 do
          MOV ATT_COUNT,1
          ;begin
          ;display a new line
         NEXT_ATT:CALL PRINT_NEWLINE
          ;DX:= OFFSET ATTRIBUTES + (ATT_COUNT - 1) *  65D
                 MOV DX,OFFSET ATTRIBUTES
                 MOV AL,ATT_COUNT
                 DEC AL
                 MOV BL,65D
                 MUL BL
                 ADD DX,AX
          ;display attribute definitions
                 MOV AH,9
                 INT 21H
          ;for j:= 1 to 4 do
                 MOV CAR_COUNT,1
                 ;begin
                 ;DX:= OFFSET CARS + (CAR-COUNT - 1) * 14D
```

Figure 9.3
(cont.)

```
                NEXT_CAR:MOV DX,OFFSET CARS
                         MOV AL,CAR_COUNT
                         DEC AL
                         MOV BL,14D
                         MUL BL
                         ADD DX,AX
                ;display car name
                         MOV AH,9
                         INT 21H
                ;get user response
                         MOV AH,1
                         INT 21H
                         SUB AL,30H
                         PUSH AX
                ;BX:= CAR_COUNT-th byte of REPLIES
                ;that is, BX:= OFFSET REPLIES + (CAR_COUNT - 1)
                         MOV BX,OFFSET REPLIES
                         MOV AL,CAR_COUNT
                         DEC AL
                         MOV AH,0
                         ADD BX,AX
                ;by shifting it left 8 - ATT_COUNT bits and OR-ing
                ;with what is there already
                         MOV CL,8
                         SUB CL,ATT_COUNT
                         POP AX
                         SHL AL,CL
                ;store it
                         OR [BX],AL
                ;display a new line
                         CALL PRINT_NEWLINE
                         ;end
                INC CAR_COUNT
                CMP CAR_COUNT,4
                JLE NEXT_CAR
          ;end
          INC ATT_COUNT
          CMP ATT_COUNT,5
          JLE NEXT_ATT
;display analysis headings
          CALL PRINT_NEWLINE
          CALL PRINT_NEWLINE
          MOV DX,OFFSET ANALYSIS
          MOV AH,9
          INT 21H
;for p:=1 to 3 do
          MOV ROW_COUNT,1
          ;begin
          ;display row label
          ;DX:= OFFSET ROWS + (15D*(ROW_COUNT-1))
        NEXT_ROW:MOV DX,OFFSET ROWS
                 MOV AL,ROW_COUNT
                 DEC AL
                 MOV BL,15D
```

Figure 9.3
(cont.)

```
                    MUL BL
                    ADD DX,AX
                    MOV AH,9
                    INT 21H
               ;display (p-1) * 9 spaces
                    MOV AL,9
                    MOV CL,ROW_COUNT
                    DEC CL
                    MUL CL
                    CMP AX,0
                    JZ NO_INIT_SPACES
                    MOV CX,AX
                    MOV AH,2
                    MOV DL,' '
           NEXT_SP: INT 21H
                    LOOP NEXT_SP
               ;for q:=p+1 to 4 do
    NO_INIT_SPACES: MOV AL,ROW_COUNT
                    MOV COL_COUNT,AL
                    INC COL_COUNT
                    ;begin
                    ;DL:= user's attributes for car p
                      NEXT_COL:MOV BX,OFFSET REPLIES
                               MOV AL,ROW_COUNT
                               CBW
                               DEC AX
                               ADD BX,AX
                               MOV DL,[BX]
                      ;DH:=user's attributes for car q
                               MOV BX,OFFSET REPLIES
                               MOV AL,COL_COUNT
                               CBW
                               DEC AX
                               ADD BX,AX
                               MOV DH,[BX]
                      ;count agreements
                               CALL COUNT_AGREEMENTS
                               PUSH AX
                      ;display 8 spaces
                               MOV AH,2
                               MOV DL,' '
                               MOV CX,8
                  ANOTHER_SP:  INT 21H
                               LOOP ANOTHER_SP
                      ;display number of agreements
                               POP DX
                               ADD DL,30H
                               INT 21H
                      ;end
                               INC COL_COUNT
                               INC COL_COUNT,4
                               JBE NEXT_COL
               ;print a new line
                               CALL PRINT_NEWLINE
               ;end
```

Figure 9.3
(cont.)

```
                  INC ROW_COUNT
                  CMP ROW_COUNT,3
                  JBE NEXT_ROW
;return to dos
FINISH:MOV AX,4C00H
       INT 21H

    COUNT_AGREEMENTS:XOR DL,DH
                     NOT DL
                     ;now count 1 bits in positions 7,5,4,3,2
                     MOV CX,5
                     MOV AL,0
            NEXT_BIT:RCL DL,1
                     JNC SKIP_COUNT
                     INC AL
          SKIP_COUNT:LOOP NEXT_BIT
                     RET

    PRINT_NEWLINE:MOV AH,2
                  MOV DL,CR
                  INT 21H
                  MOV DL,LF
                  INT 21H
                  RET

    CODE ENDS
    END START
```

Figure 9.3 *(cont.)*

EXERCISE

9.9 Extend the Kelly grid program so that:

(a) views from a number of users could be collected by the program and then a summary printed indicating the average number of agreements between the four cars on the given attribute pairs. Try to allow for up to 100D users; and

(b) the program is not limited to the given objects (cars) or the given attribute pairs. Instead, the market researcher should type these in and set the program up before the users are allowed access to it. Try to allow for up to 8 objects and up to 16 attributes.

9.5 Efficiency

In a commercial programming environment the single most expensive resource is programming staff. Efficient working in this case involves maximizing the amount of correct programming they can do in a given period of time. The best way of achieving this is to ensure that programs are developed in small, independent blocks which are then glued together – as was promoted in the previous chapter. In this way, the location of errors in programs is speeded up by the ability to trust previously proven blocks to work exactly according to their specification: new errors can only be as a result of the gluing process.

Some practical applications of computing may require a minimum speed of execution: a program to detect nuclear reactor failure must be capable of working out that a disaster is about to occur because of a fault in less time than it takes for the fault to cause a disaster. Other applications can involve restrictions on the amount of memory available, possibly to contain costs in a commercial product. Just because members of the 8086-family can address more than one million locations, it does not mean that a computer system based on such a microprocessor will necessarily have more than a few bytes of memory.

In the commercial world, then, writing a program for a particular task may involve a trade-off between the amount of time required to write the program in a particular way (which influences the cost of producing the program radically), the speed at which the program executes (which must conform to the user's desired minimum) and the amount of memory occupied by the program. Minimizing the memory use by a program often comes down to giving careful thought to the way any graphics are implemented. However, there are some considerations which can save more than the odd byte or two, the most important being to choose a good algorithm and related data structures for the program. After that the programmer must resort to dirty tricks, but because these make a program hard to read for a person not directly involved in its production, these are eschewed in commercial programming environments. A good algorithm is also the basis of producing a program which performs within certain speed constraints. If the best possible algorithm is already in use and speed requirements are still not satisfied, it may be that a more careful choice of 8086-family instructions can solve the problem.

To examine a specific example, let us suppose we are working with the humblest PC based on an 8088 chip with a system clock which works at 4.75 million pulses a second. Each 8088 instruction takes a certain number of clock pulses or cycles to be executed. The details of the number of cycles each instruction takes to execute can be found in Appendix V. `RCR CX,1` takes two; the `NOP` (No OPeration) instruction does nothing and takes three cycles – it is normally used to enable a program to wait for a certain amount of time before continuing; and `MUL BX` takes between 118 and 133 cycles.

Cycle times give us a means, should we really need one, of comparing the speed of two program fragments. Let us prove that a program which uses shift instructions to perform multiplication by powers of two executes faster than it would if using the `MUL` instruction. Consider the program fragment:

```
MOV CL,3
SAL AX,CL
```

which has the effect of multiplying the contents of AX by 8. The two instructions take up four bytes of store when converted to machine code and it takes 24 cycles to execute them. On the other hand, consider:

```
SAL AX,1
SAL AX,1
SAL AX,1
```

This takes up two extra bytes of storage but executes in a mere six cycles. Use of the 8086-family multiplication instruction `MUL` is slower than both of these 'shifty' alternatives since `MUL` requires a minimum of 118 cycles to execute if a 16-bit register is involved. However `MUL` occupies just two bytes of store for the instruction itself and two more bytes would be needed for a `MOV` instruction to initialize a register to 8.

As has been indicated, with programming time usually accounting for most of the costs involved in establishing a computer solution to a real-world problem, we would have to be in a tight corner indeed before looking for clever ways to avoid the otherwise obvious choice of `MUL`. But were we in such a rare situation, the second of our three solutions would be preferable unless program size were the predominant consideration; in that case the first solution would be the best.

SUMMARY

This chapter covered three families of instructions most useful when a program needs to manipulate individual bits within a register.

The logical family comprises the `AND`, `OR`, `NOT`, `XOR` and `TEST` instructions and enables individual bits to be set to a value or tested to see if they are set to a given value.

The `SHL`, `SHR`, `SAL`, and `SAR` instructions form the shift family. All of these are instructions provided for doubling and halving numbers: `SHL` and `SHR` for unsigned numbers and `SAL` and `SAR` for signed numbers. There are also versions for quadrupling, octupling and so on.

Finally, we met the rotate family of instructions. These allow us to rearrange bits within a byte or word. Two of them, `ROL` and `ROR`, simply rotate the byte or word to the left or right respectively. The other two, `RCL` and `RCR`, involve the carry flag in the rotation so we also have instructions to set (`STC`) and clear (`CLC`) the carry flag.

In the final section in this chapter it was explained how, in these days of high labor costs, it is the actual programming process which is the key to efficiency rather than the execution speed of a particular program fragment.

SELF-CHECK QUIZ

1. Write a sequence of assembly language instructions which will examine the memory location referred to by INPUT_BYTE and jump to:

   the instruction labeled READY if one of bits 2, 4, or 8 is set to 1;

   otherwise to NOT_READY if both bits 1 and 3 are 1;

   otherwise to ERROR

2. 100H locations contain ASCII text. Write a subroutine to set bit 2 of AL to 1 if these locations do *not* contain the letter X and to 0 otherwise. Only bit 2 of AL is to be changed.

3. Let us agree that an *ugly* unsigned number is one in which the number of bits set to 1 is different from the number of bits set to 0. Write a program fragment to test if the contents of AL is ugly.

4. Explain why *any* 16-bit multiplication operation – not just multiplying by 2 – could in fact be done using just shifts and addition.

5. Write a subroutine to reverse the order of the bits in AL.

6. Write program sequences *not* using shift instructions which will simulate the effect of each of the 8086-family shift instructions.

7. Is it true that any two of the logical instructions AND, OR, XOR and NOT can be simulated by combinations of the other two?

8. Write sequences of assembly language instructions which are exactly equivalent to AND, OR, and XOR respectively, but which do not use any of the logical family of instructions (other bit manipulation instructions are allowed).

9. Write a sequence of assembly language instructions to multiply the 48-bit number in CX,BX,AX by 2 using bit manipulation instructions.

10. 200H locations, the first of which is referred to by SMALL_NUMS, each contain an 8-bit signed number. Write a subroutine using bit manipulation instructions to convert each of these to 16-bit signed numbers, to be stored in a group of locations starting with that referred to by BIG_NUMS.

10

Large Program Development – Simulating a Simple Calculator

Contents

This chapter illustrates the use of the program development methodology outlined in Chapter 8 to produce a substantial machine code program which simulates the operation of a simple four-function electronic calculator. The final exercises in this chapter assume that the reader has become sufficiently familiar with the architecture of the calculator-simulating program to make modifications and extensions to its basic structure. On the way, we meet the use of the SI register as an index register – a topic to which we shall return in Chapter 13.

10.1 Specification

Users of our calculator simulator will type in a simple arithmetic expression involving just one of the arithmetic operations addition, subtraction, multiplication or division (+, −, * and /), two decimal numbers having at most four digits and an equals sign (=). The calculator simulator will then evaluate the expression and type the result after the equals sign. Thus, if the user types:

```
6000 + 1999 =
```

the calculator simulator will then print 7999 after the equals sign and wait to be given another arithmetic expression to evaluate.

Users have to enter their expressions in one of four formats:

(1) number + number =

(2) number − number =

(3) number * number =

(4) number / number =

and the simulating program will then print the answer after the equals sign. Once it has been started up our simulator will do sums forever, or at least until the computer is switched off.

As far as our calculator simulator is concerned the only characters which are legal are the digits 0,1,2,. . .,9; the operation signs +, −, *, /; the equals sign =; and spaces. Only positive decimal whole numbers will be accepted. Each such number may be preceded or followed by any number of spaces but will be terminated by the first non-digit character encountered. Also, there must be at least one digit before and after the operation sign (+, −, * or /, whichever it is). If we denote space characters typed by the user by the # symbol, then:

```
####24+########96=
```

is allowed because the spaces before the number 24 will be ignored, as will those after the + sign. Similarly, both of

```
####22+317=
9148##*##8866#=
```

are allowed.

However,

```
3###7##-14=
```

is *not* allowed because spaces are not allowed within a number. Also,

```
#######-#999###=
```

is not allowed because there must be a number before the operator sign (in this case a − sign),

```
+2169  * 417=
```

is not allowed because exactly one of +, −, * and = must appear in the arithmetic expression to be evaluated and that must be between two numbers, and

```
4.16/2.72=
```

is not allowed because only decimal whole numbers may be entered.

If either of the numbers typed in has too many digits the simulator will display the message:

```
NUMBER TOO BIG — RESTART CALCULATION
```

on the computer's screen and expect the person using our calculator simulator to enter the whole of that sum again. If an illegal character is entered due to mistyping (or malice!) the calculator simulator will display:

```
ILLEGAL CHARACTER — RESTART CALCULATION
```

and once again expect the user to start afresh.

Division by zero is not allowed: an attempt to divide by zero will gain the response:

```
DIVISION BY ZERO NOT ALLOWED
```

and the whole of that calculation will be ignored. For a successful division, the answer will be printed in quotient and remainder form, as in:

```
13/2=6R1
```

meaning that 13 divided by 2 is 6, remainder 1.

10.2 Program design

Step 1 Choose data structures and types

We have only to deal with numbers, so data structuring is not a problem. Only whole numbers of up to four decimal digits are allowed, so the biggest number which can be entered into our calculator is 9999. This means that the biggest number of digits in an answer will come from 9999 * 9999 = 99 980 001. If we use signed 16-bit numbers in the program the biggest number we can have is 0111111111111111B, that is, 32767D. Thus signed 16-bit numbers are quite adequate for storing our 4-digit, positive, decimal whole numbers. The answer which results from combining two such decimal numbers can similarly be accommodated as a 32-bit signed number, since the largest positive number representable in that form is 2147483647D.

Step 2 Top-down program design

While the user of our calculator simulator will simply type in an arithmetic expression (possibly including some space characters) followed by an equals sign, the program behind the calculator simulator has to work character by character and break the user's input up into its various components: two numbers and an operation sign. It also has to check that the user's input is correctly formed.

A basic outline of the program is easy to write:

repeat
read in a decimal number and an operator;
store the decimal number in AX;
store the operator in DL;
read in a second decimal number and store it in BX;
when the user has typed an equals sign **then**
print the result of the operator applied to AX and BX
forever

Each number will be obtained from the user's input by essentially the same process. Any spaces typed preceding the number will be ignored. Then we shall read the number itself and ignore any spaces following it. We shall regard the process of obtaining that particular number as complete when we encounter the first non-space character after it. For the first of the two numbers in the user's arithmetic expression, this terminating non-space character should be one of +, −, * or / whereas for the second number it should be an = sign. This process is shown in Figure 10.1, where the first line is what the user types (with spaces shown as # symbols) and underneath that is shown the process by which our program will 'understand' the user's input character by character.

It follows that we need a subroutine:

```
GET_OK_NUM_AND_TERM_NON_SPACE_CHAR
```

which performs the following functions:

(1) Waits for the user to type in a single decimal number of not more than four digits at the keyboard.

(2) Skips any preceding and trailing spaces in the user's input.

(3) Leaves in BX the binary form of the decimal number entered (if it was valid).

(4) Leaves in CL a coded value signifying the type of terminating non-space character:

the value 1 signifying that the first non-space character typed after the decimal number was one of +, −, *, /
the value 2 signifying that the first non-space character typed after the decimal number was an = sign
the value 3 signifying that the first non-space character typed after the decimal number was neither +, −, *, / nor an = sign

(5) Leaves in AL the ASCII code for the terminating non-space character.

(6) Returns the number of digits read in CH.

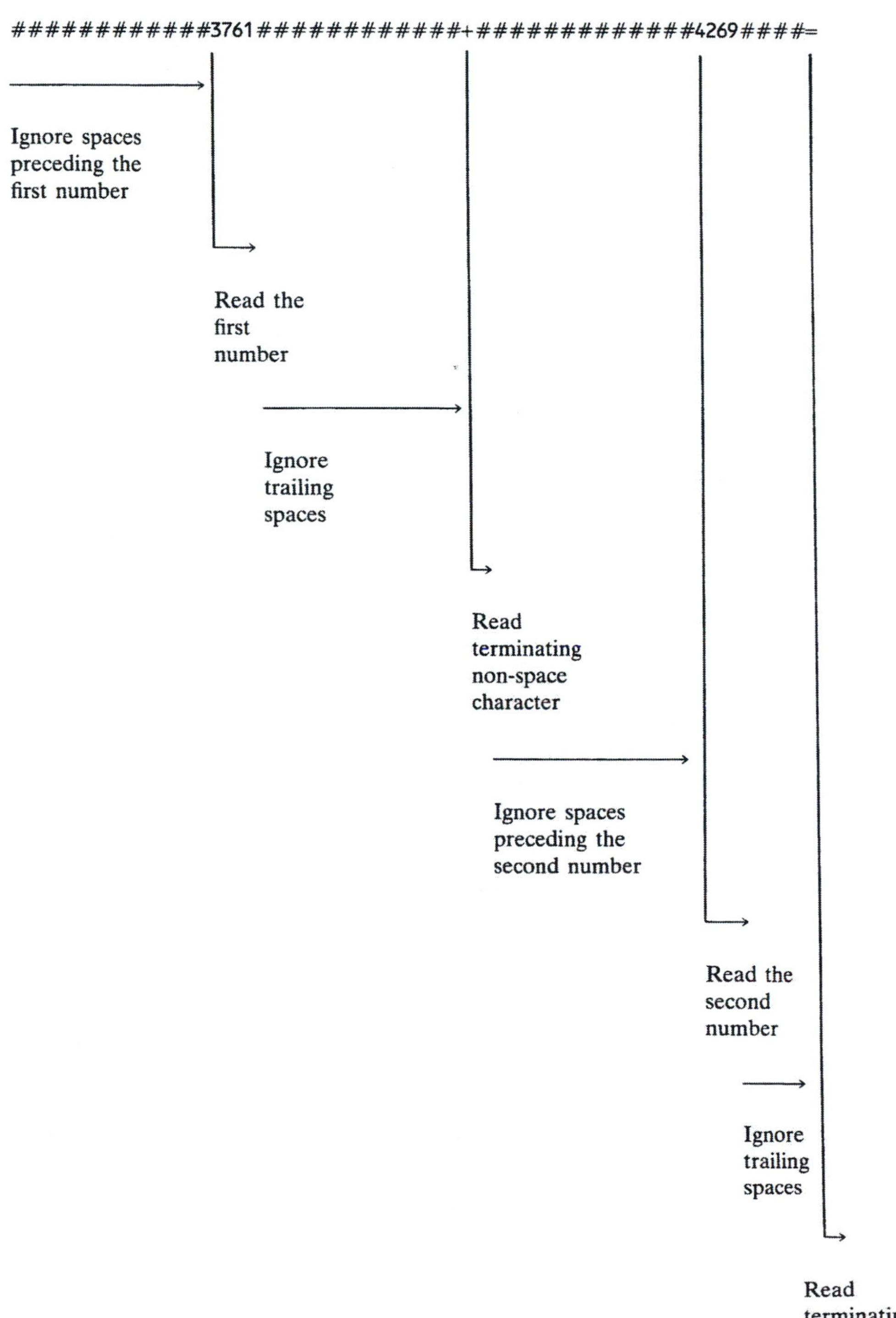

Figure 10.1 Understanding the user's input

```
repeat
  digits_read := 5;
  while digits_read= 5 or code <> 1 do
    begin
    print (new line);
    call get_ok_num_and_term_non_space_char;
    if digits_read = 5 then print(too_long);
    if code <> 1 then print(illegal_character);
    if digits_read = 0 then
      begin
      print(illegal character);
      code := 0
      end
    end;
  PUSH AX (*to preserve the operator on the stack*)
  PUSH BX (*save user's first decimal number on stack*)
  call get_ok_num_and_term_non_space_char;
  if digits_read = 5 then begin POP AX; POP BX; print(too_long) end
  else if digits_read > 0 and code = 2 then
    begin
    POP AX ; (*restore first user number*)
    POP DX ; (*restore operator to DL*)
    case DL of
    '+' : call doplus;
    '–' : call dosub;
    '*' : call domult;
    '/' : call dodivision;
      end
    end
  else begin POP AX; POP BX; print(illegal character) end
forever
```

Figure 10.2 Outline of the calculator simulator program.

Using this subroutine we can develop a version of the program which is sufficiently refined to identify the building-block subroutines of the final program. This is shown in Figure 10.2 where the subroutines *DOPLUS*, *DOSUB*, *DOMULT* and *DODIVISION* carry out the appropriate arithmetic between the numbers in AX and BX and print the result on the display screen.

EXERCISE

10.1 Make a trace of the execution of the calculator simulator program by following through the outline given in Figure 10.2 for each of the following sequences of user input (where, once again, we have used # to indicate that the user typed a space character):

(a) `12+21=` (b) `2#+###=` (c) `2&`

(d) `3` (e) `3#+#+`

Record the values of registers and pseudo-variables by completing a table with the following headings:

AL	*BX*	*CH (=digits_read)*	*CL (= code)*	*DX*

10.2.1 The subroutines we need

From Figure 10.2 it follows that we must write subroutines which carry out the following tasks:

(1) Wait for a character to be typed at the keyboard and leave the ASCII code for that character in AL.

(2) Print the character whose ASCII code is in register DL.

(3) Print a new line on the display.

(4) Print error messages on the screen as follows:

(a) `NUMBER TOO BIG — RESTART CALCULATION`
(b) `ILLEGAL CHARACTER — RESTART CALCULATION`
(c) `DIVISION BY ZERO NOT ALLOWED`

(5) Assuming the unsigned 16-bit forms of the two decimal numbers typed in by the user are in AX and BX (AX containing the first number typed), a routine to perform each of the four basic arithmetic operations on the contents of those registers. The operations performed will be as follows:

(a) Addition
(b) Subtraction
(c) Multiplication
(d) Division

In every case the answer will be left as a signed 32-bit number in registers DX and CX with DX containing the higher order bits. Thus, if the user gives the calculator the expression `9999 * 22` to evaluate, then the answer (219978 = 00035B36H as a 32-bit signed number) will be left in DX and CX as shown in Figure 10.3.

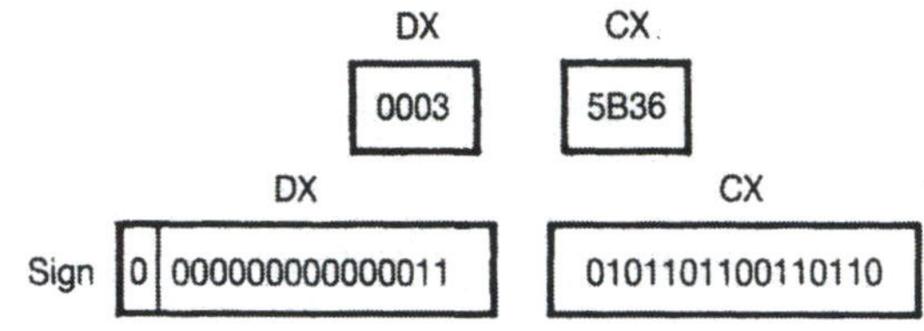

Figure 10.3 219978 = 00035B36H = 00000000000000011-0101101100110110B as a signed 32-bit number, represented with register DX containing the higher order bits.

(6) Implement `GET_OK_NUM_AND_TERM_NON_SPACE_CHAR`.

(7) Convert the signed 32-bit binary number held in registers DX and CX into a decimal number and print it on the screen.

(8) Implement `DOPLUS`, `DOMINUS`, `DOMULT`, `DODIVISION`.

These subroutines will be developed in the following sections.

10.3 Reading and printing characters

10.3.1 Reading a character from the keyboard (READCHAR)

Thanks to function number 1 provided by INTerrupt 21H there is very little work to do.

```
READCHAR: MOV AH,1H
          INT 21H
          RET
```

10.3.2 Printing a character on the display screen (PRINTCHAR)

Exactly the same subroutine as that introduced in Chapter 8 will do:

```
PRINTCHAR: MOV AH,2H
           INT 21H
           RET
```

10.3.3 Printing the error messages

When the user of our calculator simulator goes wrong we want to be able to print out helpful messages such as `NUMBER TOO BIG` and `ILLEGAL CHARACTER`. Since the combination

`MOV DX,`*starting address of message*

```
MOV AH,09H
INT 21H
.
.
.
```

will print the characters whose ASCII codes are stored in the locations with the given starting address (relative to the DS register) and following until the ASCII code for a $ sign is encountered (see Section 4.4), all that remains to do is:

(1) put the message into an appropriate place in memory, terminated by a $ sign; and
(2) specify its starting address.

To do this, in the CODE segment we must add the subroutine:

```
ILLEGAL_CHAR: CALL PRINT_NEWLINE
              MOV  AH,09H
              MOV  DX,OFFSET ILLEGAL_MESS
              INT  21H
              RET
```

and in the DATA segment:

```
ILLEGAL_MESS DB 'ILLEGAL CHARACTER – RESTART CALCULATION', ODH,OAH,'$'
```

Appendix II gives a complete listing of the calculator simulator program and it would be worth glancing through that appendix at this point to see the subroutines we have developed so far in their actual places in the final program. To encourage you to do this we shall present here neither the bodies of the other two subroutines which print error messages – TOO_LONG and DIVISION_BY_ZERO – nor the necessary data pseudo-ops. Instead you are requested to turn to Appendix II.

EXERCISES

10.2 The following fragment is part of a program which will wait for 10D characters to be typed at the keyboard and then print those characters in reverse order. Complete the program, type it into your computer and assemble and run it. Modify the program so that once the 10D characters have been typed in they are printed out with each pair of characters in the correct order. Thus, if the 10D characters typed were A, then B, then C,. . ., and then J, the output from the modified program would be IJGHEFCDAB.

```
            MOV  BX,0AH
READ_NEXT:CALL  READCHAR
            PUSH AX
            DEC  BX          ;read another if BX
            JNZ  READ_NEXT   ;not zero yet
            MOV  BX,0AH      ;set up new count for printing
PRINT_NEXT: POP  AX          ;restore the last item stacked
            MOV  DL,AL       ;transfer the character ready
            CALL PRINTCHAR   ;for printing
            DEC  BX
            JNZ  PRINT_NEXT  ;done 10D yet?
```

10.3 Write an assembly language program to read in four letters (A,B,. . .,Z) from the keyboard, print a space (ASCII code 20H) and then print the four letters in alphabetical order followed by a new line. Keep the four letters typed in registers BH, BL, DH and DL.

10.4 Write an assembly language program to read in three letters (A,B,. . .,Z) from the keyboard, print a new line, and then print the whole alphabet excluding those letters.

10.4 Subroutines for the arithmetic

10.4.1 Addition of two unsigned 16-bit numbers, both between 0 and 9999 D

Our requirement is as follows:

(1) given the first 16-bit number typed by the user in AX, call it a;

(2) given the second 16-bit number typed by the user in BX, call it b;

(3) then the sum $a + b$ is to be left in signed 32-bit form in CX and DX, DX to contain the higher order bits.

The implementation is easy because $a + b$ will be at most $9999 + 9999 = 19\,998$ and so is accurately representable as an unsigned 16-bit number. Hence, we can have the addition performed using `ADD AX,BX` and then we need only sign extend the answer in AX to a 32-bit signed version in DX,AX and then move that into DX,CX:

```
ADDITION: ADD AX,BX
          CWD
          MOV CX,AX
          RET
```

10.4.2 Subtraction of two unsigned 16-bit numbers both between 0 and 9999D

Our requirement in this case is as follows:

(1) given the first unsigned 16-bit number typed by the user in AX, call it *a*;

(2) given the second unsigned 16-bit number typed by the user in BX, call it *b*;

(3) the difference, $a - b$, is to be left in signed 32-bit form in CX and DX, DX to contain the higher order bits;

and the implementation is similar to that for ADDITION:

```
SUBTRACTION: SUB AX,BX
             CWD
             MOV CX,AX
             RET
```

As we saw in Chapter 6, the CWD instruction stores 0FFFFH in DX if the highest order bit of AX (that is, the sign bit in a signed 16-bit representation) is 1 and stores 0000H in DX otherwise. This ensures that DX, AX contains the signed 32-bit form of the result of the subtraction even when this is negative.

If the result of the subtraction is negative the sign flag will be set to 1, otherwise it will be set to 0. Since the RET instruction does not affect any of the flags, the sign flag will still indicate whether the result of the subtraction was negative or not even after the return to the main program has been effected. We shall use this fact when writing the routine which prints out the result of the subtraction, for we shall want to print a minus sign only if the result is negative.

10.4.3 Multiplication of two unsigned 16-bit numbers both between 0 and 9999D

We require:

(1) the first unsigned 16-bit number typed by the user in AX, call it *a*;

(2) the second unsigned 16-bit number typed by the user in BX, call it *b*;

(3) the product $a * b$ to be left in signed 32-bit form in CX and DX, DX to contain the higher order bits.

The implementation is:

```
MULTIPLICATION: MUL BX
                MOV CX,AX
                RET
```

10.4.4 Division of two unsigned 16-bit numbers, both between 0 and 9999D

For the division routine of our calculator simulator we shall assume that a check for division by zero has been made before it is entered from the main program. Our working specification is therefore:

(1) given the first unsigned 16-bit number typed by the user in AX, call it a;

(2) given the second unsigned 16-bit number typed by the user in BX, call it b;

(3) if $a / b = x$ remainder y, then x is to be left in signed 32-bit form in DX and CX, DX to contain the higher order bits; and y is to be left in signed 32-bit form in AX and BX, BX to contain the higher order bits;

with the implementation:

```
DIVISION: MOV DX,0
          DIV BX
          MOV CX,AX
          MOV AX,DX
          MOV DX,0
          MOV BX,0
          RET
```

10.5 Reading and converting decimal numbers to signed 16-bit form

10.5.1 The GET_OK_NUM_AND_TERM_NON_SPACE_CHAR subroutine

Characters are read from the keyboard one at a time, so while we think of typing in the number 7231 the computer actually gets a stream of single digits: first a 7, then a 2, then a 3 and then finally a 1. One of the main components of GET_OK_NUM_AND_TERM_NON_SPACE_CHAR is the conversion of such a stream of digits into a binary number stored in one of the 8086-family registers.

Retrieving the binary form of any one digit is easy. Our READCHAR subroutine will be used to read the digit from the keyboard and it leaves the ASCII code for that digit in register AL. The ASCII codes for the digits 0,1,. . .,9 are as shown in Table 10.1.

Each ASCII code is precisely 30H bigger than the actual numerical value of the digit concerned. Hence, if in register AL we have the ASCII code of a digit, subtracting 30H from register AL will leave the digit's numerical value in that register.

So much for single digits. Here now is how we deal with a stream of digits (for example, 7 then 2 then 3 then 1). First initialize register BX to 0. Then, having read the first digit 7 and converted the resulting ASCII-coded

Table 10.1 ASCII codes for digits 0–9.

Digit	*ASCII code*
0	30H
1	31H
2	32H
3	33H
4	34H
5	35H
6	36H
7	37H
8	38H
9	39H

contents of AL to the numeric value 7, we add that to the current contents of BX. If there is another digit to be read we now multiply the contents of BX by 10 and add in the numeric value of the next digit. (At this stage in our example, register BX contains the binary for decimal 72.) Again, if there's another digit to be read we now multiply the contents of BX by 10 and add the numeric value of the next digit (BX now contains the binary for decimal 723). And so on until there are no more digits to be read in. (In our example, multiplying the contents, 723, of BX by 10 and adding in the numerical value of the last digit read, 1, leaves the desired result, 7231, in binary form in register BX.)

Now we can give a structured outline of the subroutine `GET_OK_NUM_AND_TERM_NON_SPACE_CHAR`:

```
BX := 0 (* ready for the conversion to binary *)
code := 3;
digits_read := 0;
repeat read(char) until char <> ' '; (*skip spaces*)
while char in ['0' .. '9'] and digits_read <> 4 do
  begin
  digits_read := digits_read +1;
  BX := BX * 10 + binary_value_of(char);
  read(char)
  end;
while char = ' ' do read(char); (*skip trailing spaces*)
if char in ['0' .. '9'] then digits_read := digits_read +1
else if char in ['+','−','*','/'] then CL := 1
else if char = '=' then CL := 2
```

The implementation of the above outline will use registers for the variables as shown in Table 10.2.

Table 10.2 Assignment of registers.

Register	*Variable*
BX	binary value of user's decimal number
CH	digits_read
AL	char – each character read from the keyboard
CL	the code indicating the type of the terminating non-space character

EXERCISE

10.5 Work through the above outline of GET_OK_NUM_AND_TERM_NON_SPACE_CHAR for each of the following calculator simulator inputs where the user's spaces have been replaced with # symbols:

(a) ####17+2138= (c) ####+#1

(b) ####4###2 (d) 2#&

State clearly what will be in registers AL, BX, CH and CL at the end of each call.

Separating numbers and operators

First, we initialize variables, skip over any preceding spaces and form the body of the main **while** loop:

```
GET_OK_NUM_AND_TERM_NON_SPACE_CHAR: MOV BX,0H
;code:=3
       MOV CL,3
;digits_read := 0;
       MOV CH,0
;repeat read(char) until char <> ' ';
SKIP_SPACES: CALL READCHAR
             CMP AL, ' '
             JZ SKIP_SPACES
;while char in ['0' .. '9'] and digits_read <> 4 do
CHECK_NUMERIC: CMP AL,'0'
               JB MISS_TRAIL_SPACES
               CMP AL,'9'
               JA MISS_TRAIL_SPACES
               CMP CH,4
               JZ MISS_TRAIL_SPACES
               ;begin
               ;digits_read := digits_read + 1;
               ;BX := BX * 10 + binary_value_of(char);
               ;read(char)
               ;end
               JMP CHECK_NUMERIC
MISS_TRAIL_SPACES:
```

Once the body of this **while** loop has been filled in, that leaves us with a **while** loop to skip any trailing spaces and an **if** statement to set CL and *digits_read* appropriately. Let us complete these last two statements first:

```
;while char = ' ' do read(char)
 MISS_TRAIL_SPACES: CMP  AL,' '
                    JNZ  IS_THIS_FIFTH_DIGIT
                    CALL READCHAR
                    JMP  MISS_TRAIL_SPACES
;if char in ['0' .. '9'] then digits_read := digits_read + 1
IS_THIS_FIFTH_DIGIT: CMP  AL,'0'
                    JB   TRY_OPERATOR
                    CMP  AL,'9'
                    JA   TRY_EQUALS
                    INC  CH
                    JMP  DONE_THIS
;else if char in ['+', '-', '*', '/'] then CL := 1
       TRY_OPERATOR: CMP  AL,'+'
                    JZ   GOT_OPERATOR
                    CMP  AL,'-'
                    JZ   GOT_OPERATOR
                    CMP  AL,'*'
                    JZ   GOT_OPERATOR
                    CMP  AL,'/'
                    JZ   GOT_OPERATOR
;else if char = '=' then CL := 2
         TRY_EQUALS: CMP  AL,'='
                    JNZ  DONE_THIS
                    MOV  CL,2
                    JMP  DONE_THIS
       GOT_OPERATOR: MOV  CL,1
          DONE_THIS: RET
```

EXERCISE

10.6 Work through the two parts of the above (incomplete) implementation outline of GET_OK_NUM_AND_TERM_NON_SPACE_CHAR for each of the following calculator simulator inputs where # denotes that the user typed a space:

(a) ####17+2138=

(b) ####4###2

(c) ####+#1

(d) 2#&

State clearly what will be in registers AL, BX, CH and CL at the end of each call.

The numeric conversion on input

Our requirement is for instructions which will multiply the contents of register BX by 10D and add into BX the numeric value of the character whose ASCII code is in register AL. The contents of register CH should be the same at the end of the conversion as they were at the beginning.

```
;BX := BX * 10D + binary_value_of(char)
MOV CL,AL  ;copy the contents of AL for safe keeping
MOV AX,10D
MUL BX
MOV BX,AX  ;BX now contains 10D times its previous contents
MOV AL,CL  ;restore AL
SUB AL,30H ;retrieve numeric value from character
MOV AH,0H  ;prepare AX for 16-bit addition
ADD BX,AX
```

Even though the result of `MUL BX` is held in registers DX and AX, DX cannot be non-zero since the largest decimal number we are to read in is 9999 which is easily represented in signed 16-bit form. Thus we can ignore the contents of DX after the multiplication instruction has been executed. Figure 10.4 gives the complete `GET_OK_NUM_AND_TERM_NON_SPACE_CHAR` subroutine.

```
GET_OK_NUM_AND_TERM_NON_SPACE_CHAR: MOV BX,0H
;code := 3
        MOV CL,3
;digits_read := 0;
        MOV CH,0
;repeat read(char) until char <> ' ';
SKIP_SPACES: CALL READCHAR
             CMP  AL, ' '
             JZ   SKIP_SPACES
;while char in ['0' .. '9'] and digits_read <> 4 do
CHECK_NUMERIC: CMP AL,'0'
               JB  MISS_TRAIL_SPACES
               CMP AL,'9'
               JA  MISS_TRAIL_SPACES
               CMP CH,4
               JZ  MISS_TRAIL_SPACES
               ;begin
               ;digits_read := digits_read + 1;
               INC CH
               ;BX := BX * 10D + binary_value_of(char)
               MOV CL,AL  ;copy the contents of AL for safe-
                          ;keeping
               MOV AX,10D
               MUL BX
               MOV BX,AX  ;BX now contains 10D times its
                          ;previous contents
               MOV AL,CL  ;restore AL
               SUB AL,30H ;retrieve numeric value from character
               MOV AH,0H  ;prepare AX for 16-bit addition
```

Figure 10.4
The GET_OK_NUM_AND_TERM_NON_SPACE_CHAR subroutine.

```
                ADD BX,AX
                ;read(char)
                CALL READCHAR
                ;end
                JMP CHECK_NUMERIC
;while char = ' ' do read(char)
MISS_TRAIL_SPACES: CMP  AL,' '
                   JNZ  IS_THIS_FIFTH_DIGIT
                   CALL READCHAR
                   JMP  MISS_TRAIL_SPACES
;if char in ['0' .. '9'] then digits_read := digits_read + 1
IS_THIS_FIFTH_DIGIT: CMP AL,'0'
                     JB  TRY_OPERATOR
                     CMP AL,'9'
                     JA  TRY_EQUALS
                     INC CH
                     JMP DONE_THIS
;else if char in ['+','-','*','/'] then CL := 1
TRY_OPERATOR: CMP AL,'+'
              JZ  GOT_OPERATOR
              CMP AL,'-'
              JZ  GOT_OPERATOR
              CMP AL,'*'
              JZ  GOT_OPERATOR
              CMP AL,'/'
              JZ  GOT_OPERATOR
;else if char = '=' then CL := 2
 TRY_EQUALS:  CMP AL,'='
              JNZ DONE_THIS
              MOV CL,2
              JMP DONE_THIS
GOT_OPERATOR: MOV CL,1
   DONE_THIS: RET
```

Figure 10.4 *(cont.)*

EXERCISES

10.7 Write an assembly language program which will accept a 2-digit decimal number typed at the keyboard and then print out a new line followed by the remainder when that decimal number is divided by 9.

10.8 Write an assembly language program which will read in a 3-digit decimal number and print a new line followed by whichever of the following messages is appropriate: `ABOVE 100`, `EQUALS 100`, or `BELOW 100`.

10.6 Converting a positive signed 32-bit number to decimal and printing the answer

In this section we shall construct the PRINTOUT subroutine which will print on the display screen the decimal equivalent of the 32-bit unsigned number held in registers DX and CX (DX containing the higher order bits). We shall assume that the unsigned 32-bit number in DX and CX is in the range 0 to +99 999 999 inclusive.

Thus, if the contents of DX and CX are:

DX	CX
0000000000000010	0000000000001111

then we want to print 131079 on the screen since

00000000000000100000000000001111 = 0002000FH = 131079

in decimal.

We shall adopt the following method for determining the decimal digits of the number held in registers DX and CX. Suppose for the sake of illustration that DX and CX contain 21030087D. Subtract 10000000D (seven zeros) from DX and CX until DX and CX is negative and count the number of subtractions. Thus:

21030087 − 10000000 − 10000000 − 10000000

is negative and we have subtracted three times. Hence the first decimal digit of the contents of DX and CX is 2 in this case. Now add the last 10000000D subtracted back again, so making the contents of DX and CX positive. This gives 1030087D in our example. Now subtract 1000000D (six zeros) repeatedly until DX and CX becomes negative. Thus:

1030087 − 1000000 − 1000000

is negative and we have subtracted twice. Thus the next decimal digit of the decimal equivalent of the contents of DX and CX is 1. Now make DX and CX positive again by adding back the last 1000000D subtracted. This gives 30087D. Now subtract 100000D (five zeros) until DX and CX becomes negative. Since:

30087 − 100000

is already negative and we have subtracted only once, the next decimal digit of DX and CX is 0. Add the 100000D back and then subtract 10000D (four zeros) giving the next digit as 3. Add back and subtract 1000D (three zeros) giving the decimal digit 0; add back to make DX and CX positive and then subtract 100D (two zeros) and so on until finally subtracting 1 until DX and CX is negative. Since:

7 − 1 − 1 − 1 − 1 − 1 − 1 − 1 − 1

is negative, the final decimal digit of the decimal equivalent of the number in DX and CX is 7. (Notice that this method destroys the contents of DX and CX.)

10.6.1 Subroutines for 32-bit addition and subtraction

Implementing this method in 8086-family assembly language will require a subroutine which enables numbers such as the binary equivalent of 10000000D to be subtracted from DX and CX, and a corresponding subroutine for addition. These subroutines will be called `BIG_SUB` and `BIG_ADD` respectively.

`BIG_ADD` signed 32-bit addition

This subroutine will treat the register pairs DX,CX and BX,AX as 32-bit registers (DX and BX containing the higher order bits in each case). The current contents of the pair DX,CX as a 32-bit signed number will be added to the 32-bit signed number in BX,AX and the result left in DX,CX. After a call to the subroutine the pair BX,AX will be unaltered.

To implement the subroutine we follow the time-honoured elementary school method for the decimal addition of, say, 37 + 15. Add the units, so that 7 add 5 is 2 down, carry 1. Then add the tens: 3 add 1 is 4 plus the carry makes 5. Hence the answer is 52. `BIG_ADD` will first add CX and AX leaving the result in CX. Next it will add DX and BX together with any carry from the previous addition.

```
BIG_ADD: ADD CX,AX
         ADC DX,BX
         RET
```

`BIG_SUB` signed 32-bit subtraction

This is very similar to `BIG_ADD` in that we follow the method of decimal subtraction which allows us to 'borrow then pay back'. For example, to work out 46 − 19 (in decimal) we borrow 10D and do 16 − 9 which leaves 7. Then we pay back 1 to the tens and do 4 − 2 which leaves 2, so that 46 − 19 is 27. `BIG_SUB` first subtracts AX from CX. If the result is negative (that is, a borrow was necessary) the carry flag is set to 1. Next the contents of BX are subtracted from the contents of DX once any borrow has been paid back. (The `SUB CX,AX` instruction will set the carry flag to 1 if a borrow was necessary and to 0 otherwise.)

```
BIG_SUB: SUB CX,AX
         SBB DX,BX
         RET
```

Powers of 10

According to our method for extracting the digits of the decimal equivalent of the contents of DX,CX we first repeatedly subtract 10000000; then 1000000;

then 100000; and so on. Consequently we shall need the signed 32-bit equivalent of all these various powers of 10 stored in memory. This is easily organized thanks to the DD (Define Doubleword) pseudo-op first mentioned in Chapter 4. We simply add the following pseudo-ops to the data segment of our program:

```
POWERS_TABLE DD 10000000
             DD 1000000
             DD 100000
             DD 10000
             DD 1000
             DD 100
             DD 10
             DD 1
```

and MASM does all the necessary conversions for us and stores the results in the location labeled POWERS_TABLE and following.

10.6.2 The SI and DI registers

When writing the body of the PRINTOUT subroutine we shall want to access the powers of 10 one by one. To enable us to work through such a list it is convenient to use either the **SI (Source Index)** or **DI (Destination Index) register**. For our current purpose, SI and DI are interchangeable so we will use SI. (Chapter 11 describes the different roles SI and DI have in 8086-family microprocessors.)

By initializing SI to the address of the first entry in the list:

```
MOV SI,OFFSET POWERS_TABLE
```

the first two bytes of the signed 32-bit equivalent of 10000000D can be loaded into AX by the instruction

```
MOV AX,[SI]
```

demonstrating that SI is similar to BX and BP in this respect (though SI always specifies offsets relative to DS). What is new, however, is that the instruction

```
MOV BX,2[SI]
```

will load BX with the 16-bit number to be found in the location with offset 2 + (current value in the SI register). Together then, these three instructions accomplish the loading of the signed 32-bit form of 10000000D (the first power of 10 on our list) into BX,AX ready for subtraction from DX,CX. When the time comes to load BX,AX with the next power of 10 (1000000D) all we need do is obey an ADD SI,4 instruction and jump back to the MOV AX,[SI] instruction, and so on:

```
                MOV SI,OFFSET POWERS_TABLE
                  .
                  .
                  .
REMOVE_POWER:   MOV AX,[SI]
                MOV BX,2[SI]
                  .
                  .
                  .
                ADD SI,4
                JMP REMOVE_POWER
                RET
```

EXERCISES

10.9 You are given two strings of characters, which we shall refer to as *X* and *Y*. *X* is at most 3 characters long and *Y* at most 255 characters long. Write an assembly language program which will count the number of occurrences of the string *X* in the string *Y*, leaving the result in AL. Thus, if *X* were the string 'on' and *Y* were the string 'once upon a time' your program should leave 2 in AL.

10.10 Write an assembly language program which, given a pattern *P* and a piece of ASCII coded text *T*, will count the number of those words in *T* which match *P*. The pattern *P* may contain up to three characters comprising:

any of the letters (A,B,C,. . .,Z) which match only themselves; and

two special characters:

? matches any single character;
* matches any sequence of characters (including the empty string).

For example, the pattern DOG matches the word DOG, the pattern D?G matches the words DOG, DUG and DIG, the pattern ?G* matches the words AGO, EGO, EGGS and IGLOO.

10.6.3 Finishing the PRINTOUT subroutine

We can now complete the **PRINTOUT** subroutine by implementing the repeated subtraction plan. The only remaining complication is that we do not want to print zeros at the beginning of a number. Thus we prefer to print 1286 rather than 00001286. To achieve this, in our pseudo-Pascal design for the subroutine we shall use a variable *digit_printed_yet* as an indicator of whether we have had a non-zero decimal digit to print yet. What happens after the next digit to be printed has been worked out depends on the setting, true or false, of this

```
power := 7;
digit_printed_yet := false;
repeat
  count := 0;
  while DX,CX >= 0 do
    begin
    DX,CX := DX,CX - 10^power;
    count := count + 1
    end;
  DX,CX := DX,CX + 10^power;
  count := count - 1;
  if count <> 0 then
    begin
    digit_printed_yet := true;
    print(count)
    end;
  if (count = 0 and digit_printed_yet) or (power = 0) then print(count);
  power := power - 1
until power = 0
```

Figure 10.5 A structured outline for the PRINTOUT subroutine.

variable. If it is false and the digit just calculated is zero then we do not print the digit unless it is the very last to be printed. If it is the last digit to be printed, then the number in DX,CX must itself have been zero and we do print a zero in this case. A structured outline for the PRINTOUT subroutine is given in Figure 10.5.

EXERCISE

10.11 Complete the following execution trace table by working through the structured outline for PRINTOUT given in Figure 10.5 assuming that the 32-bit unsigned content of DX and CX is (a) the equivalent of decimal 15, (b) the equivalent of decimal 512, (c) the equivalent of 0.

DX,CX	*power*	*count*	*digit_printed_yet*	*what is printed on the display screen*

Table 10.3 Assignation of variables.

Register	*Variable*
BP	*power*
BH	*digit_printed_yet* 0 indicates FALSE 1 indicates TRUE
BL	*count*

The assignation of variables to registers in our implementation of the pseudo-Pascal outline in Figure 10.5 will be as shown in Table 10.3.

We begin by initializing registers:

```
  ;power := 7;
    PRINTOUT:MOV BP,7
             MOV SI,OFFSET POWERS_TABLE
;digit_printed_yet   := false;
             MOV BH,0
;repeat count := 0
  NEXT_POWER:MOV BL,0
```

The **while** loop which repeatedly subtracts a power of 10 is straightforward, except that we need our powers of 10 in BX,AX so that we can use BIG_SUB and BIG_ADD. It is necessary, therefore, to preserve the contents of BX (= BH,BL) on the stack before reading a power of 10 into BX,AX. To test if DX,CX is negative we rotate the sign bit into the carry flag.

```
     ;while DX,CX >= 0 do
REMOVE_POWER: MOV  AX,DX
              RCL  AX,1
              JB   ADD_BACK
        ;begin
        ;DX,CX := DX,CX_10^power;
                   PUSH BX
                   MOV  AX,[SI]
                   MOV  BX,2[SI]
                   CALL BIG_SUB
        ;count := count + 1
                   POP  BX
                   INC  BL
        ;end;
                   JMP  REMOVE_POWER
```

If the result of the call to BIG_SUB is below zero then we are ready to add back and print this digit. If the digit is non-zero there are no complications.

```
     ;DX,CX := DX,CX + 10^power;
ADD_BACK: PUSH BX
          MOV  AX,[SI]
          MOV  BX,2[SI]
          CALL BIG_ADD
```

```
;count := count - 1;
    POP  BX
    DEC  BL
;if count <> 0 then
    CMP  BL,0
    JZ   TRY_COUNT_ZERO
    ;begin
    ;digit_printed_yet := true;
         MOV BH,1
;print(count)
```

The printing is easy: we need only convert the digit in BL to ASCII by adding 30H, and print the digit by a call to the PRINTCHAR subroutine of Section 8.4. Since PRINTCHAR assumes that the code for the thing to be printed is in register DL, we first preserve the contents of DX on the stack and then restore those contents after printing.

```
         ADD  BL,30H
         PUSH DX
         MOV  DL,BL
         CALL PRINTCHAR
         POP  DX
    ;end;
```

Finally we deal with the digits which are zero:

```
        ;if count = 0 and (digit_printed_yet or power = 0)
    TRY_COUNT_ZERO: CMP BL,0
                    JNZ DONE_THIS_POWER
                    CMP BH,1
                    JZ  PRINT_THIS_ZERO
    TRY_POWER_ZERO: CMP BP,0
                    JZ  PRINT_THIS_ZERO
                    JMP DONE_THIS_POWER
            ;then print(count);
   PRINT_THIS_ZERO: PUSH DX
                    MOV  DL,BL
                    ADD  DL,30H
                    CALL PRINTCHAR
                    POP  DX
           ;power := power - 1
   DONE_THIS_POWER: ADD SI,4
                    SUB BP,1
   ;until power = 0
              JAE   NEXT_POWER
DONE_ALL_DIGITS: RET
```

EXERCISES

10.12 Work out a complete trace for a call to the PRINTOUT subroutine with DX,CX containing 00000027H. Record carefully the data items stored on the stack and list each digit as it would be printed by the call to PRINTCHAR under a column headed 'digits printed'.

10.13 Enhance the PRINTOUT subroutine so that it handles *signed* 32-bit numbers.

10.14 Write an 8086-family assembly language program which accepts a 4-digit decimal number from its user and then types out that number and its negative. Thus, if the user types 7291, the output from your program should be:

```
7291      -7291
```

Use the NEG instruction to perform the actual negation.

10.15 Suppose that locations 700H–7FFH inclusive contain the exam marks for 20H students in each of four subjects. Thus:

Location	700	702	704	706	708	70A	70C	70E	710
Contents of word stored starting at that location	41	63	22	38	4B	60	5A	1F	5C

would indicate that student number 1 achieved marks of 65D, 99D, 34D and 56D for the four subjects, student 3 has the highest mark in the first subject out of students 1, 2 and 3, and so on.

Here is a program fragment which leaves the total of each student's marks in AX ready for printing by a subroutine called PRINTMARK (the details of which do not concern us at the moment):

```
              MOV  BX,0
              MOV  SI,700H
NEXT_STUDENT: MOV  AX,0
              ADD  AX,[SI]
              ADD  AX,2[SI]
              ADD  AX,4[SI]
              ADD  AX,6[SI]
              CALL PRINTMARK
              ADD  SI,8
              INC  BX
              CMP  BX,20H
              JNZ  NEXT_STUDENT
```

Produce a detailed trace of the execution of this program fragment for the first two students, using the exam marks specified above.

10.7 Doing the arithmetic and printing the answer

We now have all but four of the building blocks necessary for the outline in Figure 10.2. The missing subroutines are DOPLUS, DOSUB, DOMULT and DODIVISION each of which has to call up ADDITION, SUBTRACTION, MULTIPLICATION or DIVISION (as appropriate) to carry out the arithmetic on the numbers in AX and BX and then print out the value of the 32-bit signed result stored in DX,CX.

We shall print out the answer by using the PRINTOUT subroutine constructed in the last section. It is not exactly what we require: it prints out in decimal the value of the unsigned 32-bit number in DX and CX, given that this is in the range 0 to +99 999 999. Since the largest possible answer our calculator will have to deal with is 9999 * 9999 = 99 980 001 every positive answer will be well in range but we also need to deal with the printing of negative numbers.

The way round this is easy: we first test the number in DX,CX to see if it is negative. If it is not, there is no problem, just use PRINTOUT. If it is, print a minus sign, negate the number in DX,CX and then use PRINTOUT to print that.

With this proviso, we can begin implementation of DOPLUS, DOSUB, DOMULT and DODIVISION directly. DOPLUS is simple because the result will always be positive:

```
DOPLUS: CALL ADDITION
        CALL PRINTOUT
        RET
```

DOSUB is a little more complicated because if DX,CX is negative, we print a minus sign, convert DX,CX to its positive equivalent by subtracting DX,CX from zero (using BIG_SUB) and then use that as a parameter for PRINTOUT.

```
          DOSUB: CALL SUBTRACTION
                 ;check if result was negative
                 JNB  RESULT_NOT_NEG
                 ;if so print minus sign
                 PUSH DX
                 MOV  DL,'-'
                 CALL PRINTCHAR
                 POP  DX
                 ;then negate DX,CX
                 MOV  BX,DX
                 MOV  AX,CX
                 MOV  DX,0
                 MOV  CX,0
                 CALL BIG_SUB
                 ;now convert to decimal and print
RESULT_NOT_NEG:  CALL PRINTOUT
                 RET
```

DOMULT involves no special cases and is easy to handle:

```
DOMULT: CALL MULTIPLICATION
        CALL PRINTOUT
        RET
```

Now we come finally to DODIVISION. Before it invokes DIVISION we must check for division by zero. If division by zero is attempted then the user who perpetrated this crime must be admonished by a suitable error message. Having invoked DIVISION for a correctly posed division problem we must print the quotient, then the letter R (for Remainder), and then the remainder itself so that 14 divided by 4 appears in the format:

```
14 / 4 = 3R2
```

After a call to DIVISION, registers DX and CX contain the quotient and registers BX and AX contain the actual numeric remainder. When we use PRINTOUT to print the quotient it will destroy the contents of BX and AX. To avoid losing the remainder the values of BX and AX must therefore be preserved on the stack before PRINTOUT is called to print the quotient.

```
    DODIVISION: CMP  BX,0               ;check for division by zero
                JZ   DIVISION_ERROR
           ;otherwise do the division
                CALL DIVISION
           ;print the quotient
                PUSH AX                 ;preserve remainder
                PUSH BX                 ;on stack
                CALL PRINTOUT
                MOV  DL,'R'
                CALL PRINTCHAR          ;print R for Remainder
                POP  DX
                POP  CX                 ;now restore and print
                CALL PRINTOUT           ;remainder
                JMP  DONE_DIV
DIVISION_ERROR: CALL DIVISION_BY_ZERO   ;prints error message
      DONE_DIV: RET
```

10.8 Putting it all together

At last we can complete the main program as outlined in Figure 10.2. by implementing a CASE statement as in Section 7.4. The main program begins with register initialization and a while loop:

```
;digits_read := 5;
        START:MOV CH,5
;while digits_read = 5 or code <> 1 do
        TEST:  CMP CH,5
               JZ  READ_FIRST_DECIMAL
               CMP CL,1
               JNZ READ_FIRST_DECIMAL
               JMP READ_SECOND_DECIMAL
```

```
                    ;begin
                        .
                        .
                        .
                    ;end;
END_FIRST_WHILE: JMP TEST
```

The body of the while loop is performed if we have not read a valid first operand yet:

```
;print(new line);
READ_FIRST_DECIMAL: CALL PRINT_NEWLINE
                    CALL GET_OK_NUM_AND_TERM_NON_SPACE_CHAR
;if digits_read = 5 then print(too long);
                    CMP  CH,5
                    JNZ  TRY_CODE
                    CALL TOO_LONG
;if code <> 1 then print(illegal character);
          TRY_CODE: CMP  CL,1
                    JZ   NO_NUM_BEFORE_OPERATOR
                    CALL ILLEGAL_CHAR
;if digits_read = 0 and code = 1 then NO_NUM_BEFORE_OPERATOR:
                    CMP  CL,1
                    JNZ  END_FIRST_WHILE
                    CMP  CH,0
                    JNZ  END_FIRST_WHILE
                    ;begin
                    ;print(illegal character);
                         CALL ILLEGAL_CHAR
                    ;code := 0
                         MOV   CL,0
          END_FIRST_WHILE:JMP   TEST
```

After successful execution of the program so far we are ready to process the user's second decimal number.

```
;preserve operator and operand on the stack
;call GET_OK_NUM_AND_TERM_NON_SPACE_CHAR
READ_SECOND_DECIMAL: PUSH AX
                     PUSH BX
                     CALL GET_OK_NUM_AND_TERM_NON_SPACE_CHAR
;if digits_read = 5 then begin clear stack;print(too long) end
                     CMP  CH,5
                     JNZ  TRY_DO_SUM
                     POP  BX
                     POP  AX
                     CALL TOO_LONG
                     JMP  REPEAT_LOOP
 ;else if digits_read <> 0 and code = 2 then begin
          TRY_DO_SUM: CMP  CH,0
                     JZ   NO_DIGITS
                     CMP  CL,2
                     JNZ  NO_DIGITS
 ;pop operand and operator
                     POP  AX
                     POP  DX           ;operand into DL
```

```
;case operator of . . .
                        CMP  DL,'+'
                        JZ   PLUS
                        CMP  DL,'-'
                        JZ   MINUS
                        CMP  DL,'*'
                        JZ   STAR
                        CMP  DL,'/'
                        JZ   SLASH
                        JMP  REPEAT_LOOP
                 PLUS:  CALL DOPLUS
                        JMP  REPEAT_LOOP
                MINUS:  CALL DOSUB
                        JMP  REPEAT_LOOP
                 STAR:  CALL DOMULT
                        JMP  REPEAT_LOOP
                SLASH:  CALL DODIVISION
                        JMP  REPEAT_LOOP
;else begin clear stack; print(illegal character) end
NO_DIGITS: POP  AX
           POP  BX
           CALL ILLEGAL_CHAR
;forever
REPEAT_LOOP: JMP START
```

Now we really have completed our first major assembly language program. You are invited to type it into your own computer, assemble it and then try it out under debugger control. At the very least you should turn to Appendix II where (as has often been advertised) you will find a complete listing of the program.

EXERCISES

10.16 If you did go to the trouble of typing in the whole calculator simulator program, try to make small alterations to the assembly language version which satisfy the following conditions. Reassemble and debug the resulting machine code programs.

(a) Change the error messages so that they are very rude to the user. (In general we know that the users of any computer program respond better if the error messages are Kind and Understanding but you can let your hair down here, just this once.)

(b) Instead of just printing R for Remainder after a division print the whole word. Thus:

```
110/9 = 12 REMAINDER 2
```

(c) Change the program so that multiple operators are allowed. Thus:

11 * 2 + 4 = 26
5 + 8 − 3 + 7 + 9 + 11 = 37
5 − 1 + 14 / 2 − 3 + 7 * 6 = 78

(Expressions are to be evaluated from left to right. Beware of numbers which are so large that they are no longer within the scope of the program. For example 9999 * 9999 * 9999 should cause an error message to be printed out.)

(d) As it stands, our simulator program could not be used by people unfamiliar with its constraints and limitations. Add instructions so that messages are printed out which make the program completely self-contained in this respect.

10.17 List in detail the changes you would have to make so that the simulator could handle up to twice the number of digits. If you are feeling energetic, have a go at implementing the changes.

10.18 Write an assembly language program which, when run, will allow its user to type in a number M between 1 and 100D and then print out the M times table in the form:

$0 * M = 0$
$1 * M = M$
$2 * M = \ldots$
.
.
.
$10 * M = \ldots$

10.19 Write an assembly language program to print out a conversion table from Celsius to Fahrenheit for temperatures in the range −100 to 100 degrees Celsius inclusive, in steps of 10 degrees. Set out the table as follows:

Celsius	Fahrenheit
−100	−148
−90	−130
.	.
.	.
.	.
0	32
10	40
.	.
.	.
.	.
100	212

10.20 A collection of locations in memory contains signed 16-bit numbers. The first address of these locations is given in register AX and the final address in BX. Find the maximum positive number in those locations and print this number on the display.

10.21 The modulus of a negative number is the number you are left with when the minus sign is dropped. Thus the modulus of −71 is 71 and of −8 is 8. Find and print the negative number in the same range of locations as above which has maximum modulus. In each case, if the range specified does not contain a number of the given type, print out a suitable message.

SUMMARY

Thanks to our pseudo-Pascal development methodology, we have been able to develop a quite complicated program incrementally. We could test the logic of the pseudo-Pascal outlines to see, not only if they would work, but also to check that they embraced all possible cases. Should they have been wrong, rewriting pseudo-Pascal is a lot easier than rewriting a largish batch of assembly language instructions. But once correct, implementing them in assembly language was then not only a relatively mechanical task but also allowed us to proceed with confidence that we would not become lost in all the details. Incorporating the pseudo-Pascal as our assembly language documentation allows anyone to see how the thinking that developed the assembly language programming went – making program maintenance easier. Chapter 12 provides another relatively large program development example.

We also touched upon the special property of the SI register – namely, its use as an index register; there will be more of this in Chapter 13.

SELF-CHECK QUIZ

1. Write a simulator for a binary calculator which accepts only the single binary digits 0 and 1 and the four arithmetic operators +, − , * and /.

2. Write a subroutine which will accept a sequence of four digits representing a year in this millenium (1000 to 1999) typed by the user and terminated by the ENTER key. Spaces are allowed in the user's input and can be ignored.

3. Write a subroutine which accepts 4-bit unsigned

binary numbers typed at the keyboard and leaves AL set to the 8-bit unsigned equivalent.

4. Write a subroutine which accepts 4-digit unsigned hexadecimal numbers typed at the keyboard and leaves AX set to the 16-bit unsigned equivalent.

5. One innovative way of awarding final student grades is to mark each paper with just 0, + or – where: 0 indicates satisfactory, + indicates above average and – indicates unsatisfactory. The final grade is then the 'sum' of a set of such individual marks on the basis that:

   if the number of + grades and – grades is the same (possibly none of either) then the overall grade is 0;

   otherwise the grade is the same as whichever occurs most frequently.

   Write a subroutine to accept a string of individual grades from a user and leave AL containing the ASCII code for the overall grade.

6. Write a subroutine which prints out the value of AL as an unsigned binary number on the display screen.

7. Write a subroutine which prints out the value of AX as an unsigned hexadecimal number on the display screen.

8. Write a subroutine using SI which verifies that AL contains one of the numbers stored in the group of 50H locations, the first of which is referred to by `VALID_NUMS`. If it does not, the contents of AL should be overwritten with 0FFH. Otherwise the contents of AL should not be altered on return from the subroutine.

9. Write a subroutine to check that the contents of every location in a range of 100H bytes is a positive signed number and set AL to 1 if this is the case and to 0FFH if not.

10. Each of the unsigned 8-bit numbers in a group of 100H locations should satisfy the following condition:

    the sum of the number in a given location n and that in the next location $n + 1$ should be bigger than that in the following location $n + 2$.

    Write a subroutine to verify this, using SI.

11 Text and Tables

Contents

The vast majority of commercial computer use involves non-arithmetic work such as word processing, searching files for invoices relating to BLOGGS Ltd and sorting payments received into customer file order. Consequently, the 8086 family is well endowed with instructions for handling text or, more precisely, **strings**. A string is any arbitrary sequence of characters, such as

12;"[[hhM<ABX

or

123

or

HELLO, HELLO, HELLO WHAT'S ALL THIS THEN.

In the first part of this chapter each of the 8086-family string manipulation instructions will be described in detail (and the related, special-purpose instructions CLD, STD, and the family of instructions based on REP) and we shall illustrate their use via some short example programs.

These string manipulation instructions also facilitate the handling of tabular data. But special table manipulation instructions are provided as well, including the XLAT table translation instruction and the XCHG (eXCHanGe) instruction – both of which are featured in the later sections of this chapter in complete example programs.

Once the reader has had a chance to assimilate them through the briefer examples and exercises in this chapter, Chapter 12 uses all of the instructions introduced here in a substantial example program.

11.1 Primitive string manipulation instructions

There are five primitive 8086-family **string manipulation** instructions:

- MOVS MOVe a String
- LODS LOaD a String
- STOS STOre a String
- SCAS SCAn a String
- CMPS CoMPare Strings

Using these instructions, it is possible to move strings around in memory and to compare two strings to see if they are the same or to find the first place in which they differ. All of this could be done using the instructions we have already encountered but the special string manipulation instructions work much faster than anything we programmers could put together. Moreover, they facilitate the programming of tasks involving the manipulation of text. This has the commercial advantage that if the task is made easier, the time taken to carry it out will be reduced and so the cost will be lower.

Each of the string manipulation instructions enables a certain basic operation (such as moving one or two bytes from a certain place in memory to another location or locations) to be repeated without our having to organize lots of little details. It is possible, for example, to move the contents of locations 200H–300H (relative to the DS register) *en bloc* into locations 500H–600H. In addition, we can easily determine whether the move is to be done in the forwards direction (that is, the contents of location 200H are moved to location 500H, then the contents of location 201H to 501H, and so on) or in reverse order (so that the contents of location 300H are first moved into location 600H, then the contents of 2FFH into 5FFH, and so on). The CLD (CLear Direction flag) instruction sets the direction flag to zero and thereby determines that any string instruction following it should work forwards through memory. STD (SeT the Direction flag) causes reverse order working.

The primitive string instructions are controlled with the CX, SI and DI registers. CX is used to keep a count of the number of locations left to be operated on and we think of SI as holding the **Source Index** and DI the **Destination Index**.

11.1.1 REP and MOVS

Given that register CX contains *n*, moving a sequence of *n* bytes starting at the address given in the SI register to the collection of locations whose first address is given in the DI register involves the following operations:

while *CX* <> 0 **do**
1. MOV *register*,[SI]
2. MOV [DI],*register*
3. INC SI
4. INC DI
5. DEC CX

Actions 1–4 of the body of this **while** loop can be accomplished by a single 8086-family instruction, namely MOVS. Better still, there is an instruction REP which, when used as a prefix for the MOVS instruction, implements the **while** loop and action 5 of its body. To emphasize: REP MOVS is equivalent to the complete **while** loop above.

However, all the necessary details have not yet been given. In steps 1 and 2 above it must be made clear whether the MOV is to be an 8-bit move or a 16-bit move. Both are possible but a different form of the MOVS instruction is used for each. Thus if 8 bits are to be moved at a time we use the format MOVSB and if 16 bits are to be moved at a time we use the format MOVSW.

Another detail omitted so far is that MOVS treats the address given in SI as being relative to the contents of the DS register (as do all the primitive string instructions), whereas that in DI is relative to the ES (**Extra Segment**) register. The ES register belongs to the family of segment registers which contains CS, DS and SS. Often we initialize DS and ES to the same value so that, for example, MOVS can be used to relocate a string within a program's data segment. In more advanced applications, however, the extra segment addressed by ES will be different from that addressed by DS.

(We have mentioned before that the screen display of a PC is memory mapped. This means that there are a certain group of locations such that the act of storing the ASCII code for a byte in one of these locations will cause the character corresponding to that byte to be displayed on the screen. Exactly where the character appears on the screen depends on the address of the location. When programming the memory-mapped screen display, we shall use ES to address the screen locations and DS to address the program's data segment proper so that characters can easily be moved from main memory to the part of memory from which they can be displayed on the screen. The details are given in Chapter 22.)

For reference purposes the properties of REP and MOVS are summarized as follows:

- REP Causes the primitive string instruction following it to be repeated while CX is not zero. After each step of the execution of the string instruction, CX is decremented.
- MOVS Moves 8 or 16 bits from the location whose address is given in the SI register (relative to the contents of DS) to the address given in the DI register (relative to the contents of ES). The SI and DI registers are then incremented if the direction flag is 0 or decremented if the direction flag is 1.

Example 1

The following little program copies the contents of the group of locations labeled FIRST_GROUP to those labeled SECOND_GROUP and following.

```
        DATA  SEGMENT
              FIRST_GROUP DB 56H DUP('A')
              SECOND_GROUP DB 56H DUP(?)
        DATA  ENDS

        WORKING_STORAGE SEGMENT STACK
              DW 100H DUP(?)
        WORKING_STORAGE ENDS

        CODE  SEGMENT
        ASSUME DS:DATA,SS:WORKING_STORAGE,CS:CODE
  PROG_START:MOV AX,DATA
             MOV DS,AX        ;address our program's data segment
             MOV ES,AX        ;initialize ES to same value as DS
             MOV SI,OFFSET FIRST_GROUP  ;source address
             MOV DI,OFFSET SECOND_GROUP ;destination
             MOV CX,56H                 ;there are 56H bytes to be moved
             CLD              ;move them in the forward direction
             REP MOVSB
        CODE ENDS
        END PROG_START
```

As always, the reader is invited to type the program into a computer and to try it out.

A new debugger command

Testing a program such as that in Example 1 under debugger control is facilitated by the DEBUG and Code View command F (Fill). Using the F command a whole range of locations can be filled with a given value. Thus:

```
F 21A 324 41
```

would store the ASCII code for the letter A (41H) in each of locations 21AH,21BH,. . .,324H. Individual locations can, of course, be accessed more easily by the E command.

EXERCISE

11.1 Write an assembly language program with a data segment as follows:

```
START_OF_RANGE DB 'AA'
ORIGINAL_STRING DB 100H DUP(?)
BEFORE_COPY DB 'BB'
COPY_STRING DB 100H DUP(?)
END_OF_RANGE DB 'CC'
```

The program should copy the contents of the 100H locations starting with that labeled `ORIGINAL_STRING` into the locations starting with that labelled `COPY_STRING`. Test your program under debugger control by first using the `F` command to fill `ORIGINAL_STRING` with the ASCII code for the letter X, then run your program and verify that the locations in `COPY_STRING` have been set appropriately. Verify carefully that your program has performed correctly at the end points of the range concerned. These are the places where things are most likely to go wrong, since first attempts at programs often work with one location too few or one too many due to the programmer miscounting.

11.1.2 STOS

Filling blocks of memory with the same byte is one of the functions of the second primitive string operation, `STOS`. It stores the contents of AL (8-bit operation) or AX (16-bit operation) in the memory location addressed by the DI register (relative to the ES register) and then the DI register is incremented or decremented depending on the setting of the direction flag. As with the `MOVS` instruction, two formats, `STOSB` and `STOSW`, are used depending on whether an 8-bit (`STOSB`) or 16-bit (`STOSW`) store is to be performed.

Example 2

The following assembly language program fragment fills locations 200H–20FH (relative to the ES register) inclusive with 0H.

```
MOV DI,200H ;destination address
MOV CX,10H  ;number of locations to be filled
MOV AL,0H   ;fill them with 0H
CLD         ;fill them forwards
REP STOSB
```

EXERCISE

11.2 Add the necessary assembler pseudo-ops to the program fragment in Example 2 and assemble and test the result under debugger control.

11.1.3 LODS

The LODS primitive string operation moves 8 (LODSB) or 16 (LODSW) bits at a time, from the location given in the SI register (relative to the contents of the DS register) into the AL or AX register as appropriate. The SI register is then incremented or decremented depending on the value of the direction flag.

REP is hardly ever used in conjunction with LODS. This is because it is unlikely that we should want to move the contents of a particular location into register AL and then straight away move the contents of the next location into the same register. On the other hand, LODS and STOS are often used together when we want to move a collection of bytes or words from one area of memory to another, making changes during the move. In that case the number of repetitions is not controlled by a REP instruction but by the LOOP instruction in the ordinary way.

The next example illustrates the combined use of STOS and LODS and shows the use of the LOOP instruction to control the number of repetitions.

Example 3

A glance at the table of ASCII codes in Appendix I will confirm that the lower-case letters a,b,c,. . .,z all have ASCII codes which are 20H more than their upper-case equivalents A,B,. . .,Z. The following program fragment moves the contents of locations 154H–27BH (relative to the DS register) to locations 300H–427H inclusive (relative to the ES register) and assumes that the bytes to be moved are all ASCII codes for upper-case letters. During the move the entire text is converted to lower case.

```
          MOV SI,154H  ;source address
          MOV DI,300H  ;destination address
          MOV CX,128H  ;the number of bytes to be moved
          CLD          ;forwards direction
NEXTLOC:  LODSB        ;move the next byte into AL
          ADD AL,20H   ;convert into lower case
          STOSB        ;store it in the new location
          LOOP NEXTLOC ;if more to do, go back and repeat
```

11.1.4 CMPS and REPZ

We come now to an instruction for comparing two strings. CMPS subtracts the byte or word specified by the memory location whose address is given in the DI register (relative to the ES register) from the byte or word specified by the location whose address is given in the SI register (relative to DS), and sets the flags accordingly. (The contents of memory are not affected by the CMPS instruction.) Then both the SI and DI registers are incremented or decremented depending upon the current setting of the direction flag. CMPS takes the form CMPSB if two 8-bit quantities are to be compared and CMPSW when we are comparing two 16-bit quantities.

If two strings are being searched in an attempt to determine if they are the same or not, the search can come to a halt in one of two ways. Either a place has been found where they differ, or the strings agree because all the locations that needed to be checked have been. As usual, the REP instruction can be used to control the number of repetitions, but to stop the search through the two strings once a difference between them has been identified we use a slightly modified form – REPZ.

When used in conjunction with any one of the five primitive string operations, REPZ causes that operation to be repeated *while CX is not 0 and the Z-flag is 1*. Thus

```
REPZ CMPSB
```

will stop for one of two reasons. The first possibility is that the count in CX has been reduced to zero. In this case the Z-flag will still be 1 since the subtractions performed by CMPS on each iteration will always have resulted in zero. On the other hand, REPZ CMPS may have stopped because the Z-flag has been set to 0, indicating that the two strings being compared disagree at some point.

The only way of telling which of these two possibilities obtains is to test the Z-flag and jump accordingly after the REPZ CMPS instruction. Thus

```
                REPZ CMPS. . .
                JNZ  STRINGS_DIFFER
                CALL PRINT_STRINGS_EQUAL
                   .
                   .
                   .
STRINGS_DIFFER:
```

makes the jump only if the strings disagree.

Example 4

The following program fragment compares the string in locations 200H–24FH inclusive (relative to the DS register) with that in locations 300H–34FH inclusive (relative to the ES register). If they are the same, the ASCII code for the letter Y is left in AL; if not then the ASCII for the letter N is left in AL.

```
                CLD                 ;forward direction
                MOV  CX,50H         ;length of the two strings
                MOV  SI,200H        ;start of first string
                MOV  DI,300H        ;start of second string
                REPZ CMPSB          ;compare the two strings
                JNZ  STRINGS_DIFFER
                MOV  AL,'Y'
                JMP  DONE
STRINGS_DIFFER: MOV  AL,'N'
                DONE:
```

11.1.5 SCAS and REPNZ

SCAS is the primitive string instruction which enables us to scan memory for a particular byte or word, held in AL or AX. The memory byte or word specified by the address given in register DI (relative to the ES register) is subtracted from AL or AX and the flags set accordingly. (Neither the contents of the relevant memory location(s) nor the AL or AX register are affected.) Then the DI register is incremented or decremented depending on the value of the direction flag. The formats of the SCAS instruction are SCASB (when searching for an 8-bit object) and SCASW (when searching for a 16-bit object).

As with CMPS, repeated applications of SCAS may stop for one of two reasons. Either the locations to be searched have been exhausted (that is, CX has been reduced to zero) or the required byte or word has been found, in which case the Z-flag will be set to 1. Used in conjunction with a primitive string operation, REPNZ causes the operation which follows it to be repeated *while CX is not zero and the Z-flag is zero.*

Thus in

```
        REPNZ SCASB
        JZ    FOUND
          .
          .
          .
FOUND:
```

the jump will only be made if the byte or word being searched for has been found.

Example 5

In the following program fragment, the contents of each location in the range 200H–400H inclusive (relative to the ES register) which contains the ASCII code for the letter X is replaced by the ASCII code for the letter Y. After the REPNZ SCASB instruction we test to see if the Z-flag has been set to 1, indicating that a location containing the ASCII code for the letter X has been found. If so, then we want DI to contain the address of this location in order that the STOS instruction can be used to store the ASCII code for Y there, afterwards. But the last repetition of SCASB will have incremented DI so we must decrement DI before the STOS instruction is executed. Similarly, CX will be reduced by REPNZ SCASB before it stops, having located the code for the letter X. Consequently CX must be incremented after replacement of X by Y if we are to loop back ready to search for another letter X without missing a location.

```
      CLD            ;forward direction
      MOV   DI,200H  ;first location to be searched
      MOV   CX,201H  ;the number of locations to be searched
NEXT: MOV   AL,'X'
      REPNZ SCASB    ;do the search
      JNZ   DONE     ;more locations to check? Go check them!
      DEC   DI
```

```
        MOV   AL,'Y'
        STOSB         ;substitute 'Y'
        INC   CX      ;restore CX
        LOOP  NEXT    ;try to find another X if
                      ;all the locations have not been
                      ;exhausted
DONE:
```

To make things clear, let us suppose that the contents of the first few locations with offset 200 or more from the start of the segment pointed to are as follows:

Offset	200	201	202	203	
	A	Q	X	B	

and trace through the execution of our example program fragment. The first few steps are straightforward:

Instruction	*CX*	*DI*	*AL*	*Z-flag*	*D-flag*	*Location 202*
`CLD`	?	?	?	?	0	X
`MOV DI,200H`	?	200	?	?	0	X
`MOV CX,201H`	201	200	?	?	0	X
`MOV AL,'X'`	201	200	X	?	0	X

Next comes `REPNZ SCASB` which causes the following sequence of actions:

(1) compare what is in AL with the byte at ES:DI and set the flags accordingly;

(2) increment DI;

(3) decrement CX. If CX is zero stop. Check if the Z flag is set. If not, and if CX is not zero, go back to step 1. If the Z-flag is set, then execution of `REPNZ SCASB` is to stop.

This leads to the following trace:

Instruction	*CX*	*DI*	*AL*	*Z-flag*	*D-flag*	*Location 202*
`REPNZ SCASB`	200	201	X	0	1	X
	1FF	202	X	0	1	X
	1FE	203	X	1	1	X

The rest of the trace is straightforward provided that we remember that `STOSB` will increment DI and that `REPNZ` had decremented CX before it found that the Z-Flag had been set:

Instruction	*CX*	*DI*	*AL*	*Z-flag*	*D-flag*	*Location 202*
`JNZ DONE`	1FE	203	X	1	1	X
`DEC DI`	1FE	202	X	1	1	X
`MOV AL,'Y'`	1FE	202	Y	1	1	X
`STOSB`	1FE	203	Y	1	1	Y
`INC CX`	1FF	203	Y	1	1	Y
`LOOP NEXT`	1FE	203	Y	1	1	Y
`MOV AL,'X'`	1FE	203	X	1	1	Y

11.1.6 Changing direction

This far, every one of our examples works independently of the direction in which the primitive string operation is performed. We could replace `CLD` by `STD` in any of them, amend the initial values of SI and DI where necessary, and still each program fragment would have its desired effect. There are occasions, however, when the ability to move the relevant bytes or words in reverse order is crucial.

Consider the problem of moving the string stored in locations 100H–120H to locations 102H–122H (see Figure 11.1). Because of the overlap, it is impossible to make this move in a forward direction. The bytes at 100H and 101H are easily copied into locations 102H and 103H, but when it comes to

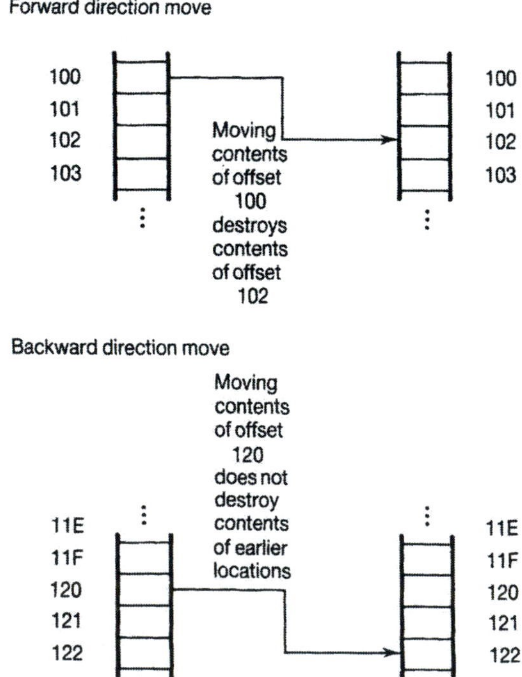

Figure 11.1 Moving a string to an overlapping group of locations.

moving the byte originally at location 102H into 104H we find that we have just replaced the contents of location 102H!

Moving in reverse order eliminates the problem since the bytes at 120H and 11FH are copied into 122H and 121H respectively. Then, when we come to move the byte at 11EH into 120H, the byte which was at 120H has already been moved into its new position.

11.1.7 Handling two bytes at a time

While none of our examples has employed the 16-bit form of a string operation, the ability to move a word at a time or search for a given pair of bytes has advantages both in handling coded external data and in straight numeric work. The following program fragment, for example, searches locations 200H–24BH (each pair of which contains a 16-bit signed number) for 0128H and leaves the appropriate address in DI.

```
            MOV   AX,0128H ;search for 0128H
            MOV   DI,200H  ;the address of the first of them
            MOV   CX,26H   ;there are 26H 16-bit numbers to check
            REPNZ SCASW
            JNZ   NOT_FOUND
            DEC   DI
              .
              .
              .
NOT_FOUND:
```

11.1.8 REP and its variants

REPZ and REPNZ have aliases: REPZ can also be called REPE (REPeat while Equal to zero); REPNZ can also be called REPNE (REPeat while Not Equal to zero). Moreover, the earlier illustrative examples may have given the impression that REPZ can only be used with CMPS, and REPNZ only with SCAS, and so on. In fact, the programmer is free to combine any of the string primitives with REP, REPZ or REPNZ as the task in hand dictates. Since MOVS, LODS and STOS have no effect on the flags it is unlikely that one would want to use REPZ or REPNZ in conjunction with those instructions, but it is not forbidden.

Table 11.1 gives a summary of the 8086-family string manipulation instructions.

EXERCISE

11.3 Write assembly language programs to carry out the following tasks. Test the programs thoroughly.

(a) In a certain string of known length, replace every occurrence of the

Table 11.1 8086-family primitive string instructions.

Instruction	*Effect*
MOVSB MOVSW	The byte or word at address DS:SI is moved to address ES:DI. IF DF = 0, then SI := SI + x and DI := DI + x. If DF = 1, then SI := SI − x and DI := DI − x. x = 1 for byte moves, x = 2 for word moves.
REP	REPeat next string instruction while CX <> 0.
REPE/REPZ	REPeat next string instruction while CX <> 0 and ZF = 1.
REPNE/REPNZ	REPeat next string instruction while CX <> 0 and ZF = 0.
STOSB STOSW	STOre String Byte; STOre String Word. The byte or word in AL or AX is transferred to the address in ES:DI. DI is modified as for MOVSB and MOVSW above.
LODSB LODSW	LOaD String Byte; LOaD String Word. The byte or word in address DS:SI is transferred to AL or AX. SI is modified as for MOVSB and MOVSW above.
CMPSB CMPSW	CoMPare String – Byte;CoMPare String – Word. The byte or word in address ES:DI is subtracted from that at DS:SI and the flags are set accordingly. SI and DI are modified as for MOVSB and MOVSW above.
SCASB SCASW	SCAn String – Byte;SCAn String – Word. The byte or word at address ES:DI is subtracted from AL or AX and the flags are set accordingly. DI is modified as for MOVSB and MOVSW above.

string LTD with the string PLC. (*Hint:* use the string operations to locate the letter L and then check if the next two locations contain T and D. Then repeat.)

(b) At the first place where two strings of known (and equal) length differ, insert the string YES in each of them. (Obviously this will involve increasing the length of each string.) If the two strings are identical then leave them both unchanged.

(c) Leave a copy of the FIRST string in the SECOND string but with the characters in reverse order. Thus, if the original string begins ONCE. . . and ends . . .UNLIKELY, the copy will begin YLEKILNU. . . and end . . .ECNO.

11.2 Simple table look-up

The primitive string manipulation instructions also have an important role to play in the handling of tabular data. In this and the following sections we shall examine their use in programs which access entries in tables.

We begin with a very simple illustration which makes use of LODSB once the required entry has been located. It is an 8086-family assembly language program which waits for the user to type in a two-digit decimal number in the range 00 to 12 and then prints out a space, the name of the corresponding month of the year, and a new line. Thus, if the user types `02` then the program displays

```
FEBRUARY
```

and if the user types `11` then the program displays

```
NOVEMBER
```

The names of the months will be kept in a table defined in the data segment of our program:

```
MONTHS DB 'JANUARY ','FEBRUARY ','MARCH     ',. . .
```

Since the month with the longest name is September (nine letters), every entry in the table will be allocated nine letters to make accessing individual entries easier.

We shall store the ASCII codes for the two decimal digits typed by the user in two memory bytes referred to by the name `NUMERIC_MONTH`:

```
NUMERIC_MONTH DB ?,?
```

It then follows that when looking up month 04 we have to convert the two ASCII codes '04' to the binary equivalent of 4 and work out the offset of that month's table entry from the beginning of the table. For the former, we recall that the ASCII codes for the digits are 30H greater than the numeric values of the digits themselves. Thus, if the user types `04` then `NUMERIC_MONTH` will point to 30H and 34H, and if the user types `11` then `NUMERIC_MONTH` will refer to 31H and 31H. Consequently, if the month number is in the range 00 to 09 it is sufficient to mask out the extra 3s; otherwise we have to mask out the extra 3s and add 10 to the result. Thus:

```
              MOV AH,NUMERIC_MONTH
              MOV AL,NUMERIC_MONTH+1
              XOR AX,3030H
              CMP AH,0
              JZ  LESS_THAN_10
              MOV AH,0
              ADD AL,10D
LESS_THAN_10:
```

leaves the binary equivalent of the month number typed by the user in AL.

To work out the offset of the given month's table entry from the beginning of the table we have to remember that the table entry for month 1 has offset $0 * 9$ from the beginning of the table, the entry for month 2 has offset $1 * 9$ from the beginning of the table, and so on. It follows that the sequence below leaves SI set to the offset address (relative to DS) of the first letter of the name of the month corresponding to the binary month number in AL:

```
MOV SI,OFFSET MONTHS
DEC AL
MOV BL,9
MUL BL
ADD SI,AX
```

The complete program is given in Figure 11.2. Note the use of expressions such as

```
MOV NUMERIC_MONTH+1,AL
```

which the assembler replaces with an instruction of the form

```
MOV [n],AL
```

where n is obtained by adding 1 to the offset address of NUMERIC_MONTH.

```
CR EQU ODH
LF EQU OAH
DATA SEGMENT
MONTHS          DB 'JANUARY  ','FEBRUARY ','MARCH    '
                DB 'APRIL    ','MAY      ','JUNE     '
                DB 'JULY     ','AUGUST   ','SEPTEMBER'
                DB 'OCTOBER  ','NOVEMBER ','DECEMBER '
NUMERIC_MONTH   DB  ?,?
DATA ENDS

WORKING_STORAGE SEGMENT STACK
        DW 100H DUP(?)
WORKING_STORAGE ENDS

CODE SEGMENT
ASSUME DS:DATA,SS:WORKING_STORAGE,CS:CODE,ES:DATA
;establish data segment addressability
  START: MOV AX,DATA
         MOV DS,AX
;get a month number
        MOV AH,1
        INT 21H
        MOV NUMERIC_MONTH,AL
        INT 21H
        MOV NUMERIC_MONTH+1,AL
;convert month number to binary
        MOV AH,NUMERIC_MONTH
        MOV AL,NUMERIC_MONTH+1
        XOR AX,3030H
        CMP AH,0
        JZ  LESS_THAN_10
        MOV AH,0
        ADD AL,10D;
;find corresponding entry in the table
LESS_THAN_10: MOV SI,OFFSET MONTHS
        DEC AL
```

Figure 11.2
Searching a table for the name of a month.

```
            MOV BL,9
            MUL BL
            ADD SI,AX
    ;display it
            CLD
            MOV CX,9
NEXT_LETTER: LODSB
            MOV DL,AL
            MOV AH,2
            INT 21H
            LOOP NEXT_LETTER
    ;print a new line
            MOV DL,CR
            INT 21H
            MOV DL,LF
            INT 21H
    ;return to DOS
            MOV AX,4C00H
            INT 21H
    CODE ENDS
    END START
```

Figure 11.2
(*cont.*)

11.3 Translation tables and XLAT

Replacing one character in a string with another according to a corresponding entry in a table is, like comparing and moving strings, a frequently required operation. For example, before sending details of a customer's account along telephone lines from a branch to head office, a bank will encode the account details to prevent fraud and infringement of privacy. The 8086 family provides the XLAT instruction to facilitate translation between one character code and another, and to enable tasks involving table look-up to be carried out efficiently.

If the starting address of a table is held in the location specified by register BX, and a particular entry in the table is specified by giving a number in AL relative to the start of the table (for example, entry 0,1,2,3,. . .) the XLAT instruction will load the AL register with the contents of the address obtained by adding what is in AL to what is in BX (relative to the DS register). Thus XLAT is equivalent to the *illegal* move instruction:

```
MOV AL,[BX+AL]    ;illegal instruction
```

11.3.1 Conversion from ASCII to EBCDIC

By way of illustration of the use of XLAT a complete example program is now presented which allows users to type several upper-case letters A,B,C,. . .,Z one at a time and, for each of them, displays the EBCDIC code for that letter, followed by a new line. The program is terminated (and control returns to DOS) when the user types a #. All other user keypresses are ignored.

Table 11.2 EBCDIC coding.

Letter	*EBCDIC code (in hex)*	Letter	*EBCDIC code (in hex)*	Letter	*EBCDIC code (in hex)*
A	C1	J	D1	S	E2
B	C2	K	D2	T	E3
C	C3	L	D3	U	E4
D	C4	M	D4	V	E5
E	C5	N	D5	W	E6
F	C6	O	D6	X	E7
G	C7	P	D7	Y	E8
H	C8	Q	D8	Z	E9
I	C9	R	D9		

The EBCDIC code is a way of coding textual material into binary, most often used in big, mainframe computers. It begins as shown in Table 11.2.

We shall store this table via the data segment pseudo-op:

```
EBCDIC DB 0C1,0C2,0C3,0C4,0C5,0C6,0C7,0C8,0C9
       DB 0D1,0D2,0D3,0D4,0D5,0D6,0D7,0D8,0D9
       DB 0E2,0E3,0E4,0E5,0E6,0E7,0E8,0E9
```

Then, given the ASCII code for an upper-case letter in AL, the corresponding EBCDIC code will be left in AL by the sequence:

```
MOV BX,OFFSET EBCDIC
SUB AL,41H
XLAT
```

To print out this value we shall use XLAT once again. Looking at Table 11.2 it is clear that the EBCDIC code for a letter has two hexadecimal digits, the first of which is either C, D or E and the second of which is a decimal digit in the range 1 to 9. Consequently we shall arrange for the value of the first hexadecimal digit of the code to be in AL via:

```
AND AL,0F0H
MOV CL,4
SHR AL,CL
```

and then translate to the ASCII code for the value of that digit using the data segment pseudo-op:

```
PRINT_CODES DB 'C','D','E'
```

and the sequence:

```
SUB AL,12D
MOV BX,OFFSET PRINT_CODES
XLATB
```

This leaves in AL (ready for printing on the display screen) the ASCII code for the first hexadecimal digit of the EBCDIC code for the letter typed by the user.

In order to print the second hexadecimal digit of the EBCDIC code on the display screen, if the EBCDIC code is in AL we shall first extract the digit itself via:

```
AND AL,0FH
```

and then convert it to ASCII with:

```
ADD AL,30H
```

The complete program has the following pseudo-Pascal outline:

set BX to address table;
repeat
  read(*char*);
  if *it is an upper-case letter* **then**
    begin
    look up EBCDIC code;
    print it out;
    end
until *char* = '#'

and is given in Figure 11.3.

```
.RADIX 16
CR EQU 0DH
LF EQU 0AH
DATA SEGMENT
EBCDIC      DB 0C1,0C2,0C3,0C4,0C5,0C6,0C7,0C8,0C9
            DB 0D1,0D2,0D3,0D4,0D5,0D6,0D7,0D8,0D9
            DB 0E2,0E3,0E4,0E5,0E6,0E7,0E8,0E9
PRINT_CODES DB 'C','D','E'
DATA ENDS

WORKING_STORAGE SEGMENT STACK
        DW 100H DUP(?)
WORKING_STORAGE ENDS

CODE SEGMENT
ASSUME DS:DATA,SS:WORKING_STORAGE,CS:CODE
MAIN PROC FAR
;establish data segment addressability
            MOV AX,DATA
            MOV DS,AX
;set BX to address table
            MOV BX,OFFSET EBCDIC
;repeat read(char)
   NEXT_LETTER: CALL READCHAR
        ;if it is an upper-case letter
              CMP AL,'A'
              JB  TRY_HASH
              CMP AL,'Z'
              JA  TRY_HASH
```

Figure 11.3
A program to display the EBCDIC codes of upper-case letters in hexadecimal.

```
          ;then begin
             ;look up EBCDIC code
                    SUB AL,41H
                    XLAT
             ;print it out
                    CALL EBCDIC_PRINT
             ;end
;until char= '#'
  TRY_HASH: CMP AL,'#'
            JNZ NEXT_LETTER
;then terminate program
            MOV AX,4C00
            INT 21H
MAIN ENDP

EBCDIC_PRINT PROC NEAR
;print a space
            MOV DL,' '
            CALL PRINTCHAR
;preserve AL and BX
            PUSH BX
            PUSH AX
;access first hex digit of EBCDIC code
            AND AL,0F0H
            MOV CL,4
            SHR AL,CL
;translate to corresponding ASCII code
            SUB AL,12D
            MOV BX,OFFSET PRINT_CODES
            XLAT
;print the ASCII letter
            MOV DL,AL
            CALL PRINTCHAR
;restore AL
            POP AX
;access second hex digit of EBCDIC code
            AND AL,0FH
;convert to ASCII
            ADD AL,30H
;print the ASCII digit
            MOV DL,AL
            CALL PRINTCHAR
;print a new line
            MOV DL,CR
            CALL PRINTCHAR
            MOV DL,LF
            CALL PRINTCHAR
;restore BX
            POP BX
            RET
EBCDIC_PRINT ENDP

READCHAR PROC NEAR
            MOV AH,1
            INT 21H
```

Figure 11.3
(cont.)

```
            RET
READCHAR ENDP

PRINTCHAR PROC NEAR
            PUSH AX
            MOV AH,2
            INT 21H
            POP AX
            RET
PRINTCHAR ENDP

CODE ENDS
END MAIN
```

Figure 11.3
(*cont.*)

EXERCISES

11.4 In a certain Secret Society a secret code is used for all communications. Under the code, each letter of the alphabet is replaced by another letter arrived at by considering the diagram in Figure 11.4. A given letter is substituted by a letter which is five places further round the circle in a clockwise direction. Using the XLAT instruction, write an assembly language program to encode messages of up to 25 letters typed in by the user under this procedure.

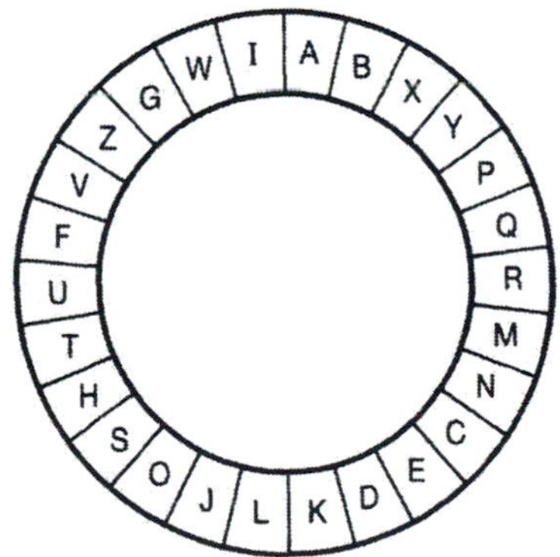

Figure 11.4
Encoding diagram for a Secret Society.

11.5 Write an assembly language program which will accept a decimal digit (0,1,2,. . .,9) from the user and then draw that digit on the display screen in the form in which a 7-segment LED display would represent that digit. Thus, if the user typed the decimal digit 5 then the program should print:

and if the user typed the decimal digit 8 then the program should print:

Make use of a table that defines which segments should and should not be drawn by labeling the segments as follows:

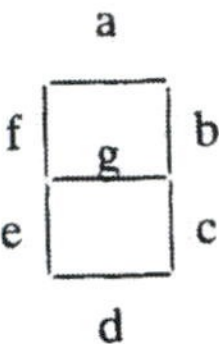

representing 'draw' as a 1 and 'don't draw' as a 0, and coding the result as the seven least significant bits in a byte:

0abcdefg

Thus, the table entry for drawing the picture of the decimal digit 5 should be:

01011011

and that for the decimal digit 8 should be:

01111111

Your program should look up entries in this table and use the appropriate entry to draw the picture corresponding to the digit the user typed.

11.4 Searching tables with gaps

Translation tables are special in that the entries in them are in consecutive order – there are no gaps. Many other kinds of tables do not contain consecutive entries. Consider, for example, the table:

```
INSTRUCTION_CODES DB '42','INC DX '
                  DB '4E','DEC SI '
                  DB '56','PUSH SI '
                  DB '58','POP AX '
                  DB 'AC','LODSB  '
                  DB 'FC','CLD    '
```

which might form part of a larger table in a debugger program, and gives the assembly language equivalents corresponding to certain 8086-family machine code instructions.

We shall write an assembly language program which will be given two

XCHG has three basic forms:

(1) XCHG 16-bit register for example, XCHG BX
(2) XCHG register,memory for example, XCHG CX,[SI]
(3) XCHG register, register for example, XCHG BL,CH

In form (1) the contents of the specified (non-segment) register are swapped with the contents of AX.

In forms (2) and (3) the contents of the register are swapped with the contents of the (8-bit or 16-bit non-segment) register or memory location(s). Thus XCHG CX,[SI] exchanges the contents of the CX register with the word stored at the location specified by SI (relative to DS).

Figure 11.5
The XCHG instruction.

hexadecimal digits representing a machine code instruction via the pseudo-op:

```
SEARCH_VALUE DW. . .
```

and will leave the corresponding assembly language instruction in the variable:

```
INSTRUCTION_NAME DB 7D DUP(?)
```

Thus, if the program contains the pseudo-op:

```
SEARCH_VALUE DW '58'
```

then after execution, INSTRUCTION_NAME should contain the string 'POP AX '.

The program will make use of the XCHG instruction (see Figure 11.5). The need for XCHG arises because, as first described in Section 4.4, when MOV is used to move a word into a register from memory, it swaps the two bytes around. Thus, given:

```
SEARCH_VALUE DW '58'
```

the location pointed to by SEARCH_VALUE will contain 35H and the next byte will contain 38H. But then:

```
MOV AX,SEARCH_VALUE
```

will leave AX containing 3835H. If we then execute:

```
XCHG AL,AH
```

AX will then contain 3835H ready to begin the search with the digits stored in the same order as in the table.

The program is otherwise quite straightforward and is given in Figure 11.6.

```
DATA SEGMENT
INSTRUCTION_CODES DB '42','INC DX  '
                  DB '4E','DEC SI  '
                  DB '56','PUSH SI '
                  DB '58','POP AX  '
                  DB 'AC','LODSB   '
                  DB 'FC','CLD     '
SEARCH_VALUE      DW '58'
INSTRUCTION_NAME  DB 7D DUP(?)
DATA ENDS

WORKING_STORAGE SEGMENT STACK
          DW 100H DUP(?)
WORKING_STORAGE ENDS

CODE SEGMENT
ASSUME DS:DATA,SS:WORKING_STORAGE,CS:CODE,ES:DATA
;establish data and extra segment addressability
START:  MOV AX,DATA
        MOV DS,AX
        MOV ES,AX
;get machine code in AX
        MOV AX,SEARCH_VALUE
        XCHG AL,AH
;search table
        MOV CX,6
        MOV SI,OFFSET INSTRUCTION_CODES
COMPARISON:CMP AX,[SI]
        JE  FOUND
        ADD SI,9H
        LOOP COMPARISON
        JMP DONE
;transfer table entry into INSTRUCTION_NAME
  FOUND:MOV CX,7
        MOV DI,OFFSET INSTRUCTION_NAME
        INC SI
        INC SI
        REP MOVSW
   DONE:HLT
CODE ENDS
END START
```

Figure 11.6
Table searching.

11.5 Sorting table entries

This section briefly describes a program which accepts 20 names typed by the user, each consisting of up to thirty **lower-case** letters, stores these in a table in memory, and then prints out the names in alphabetical order on the display screen. To keep the program as concise as possible and thereby focus on the use of the primitive string manipulation instructions there has been no attempt at any kind of user interface. Indeed, it is assumed throughout that users do exactly what they are supposed to do. It is an exercise for the reader to add an appropriate user interface.

Entries in a table will be sorted by the **bubblesort** method which is so called because the smaller entries are gradually bubbled up to the top of the table. For a table with n entries a bubblesort proceeds as follows:

```
repeat
for i := 1 to n - 1 do
  if entry[i] should be after entry[i + 1] then
    begin
    swap entry[i] and entry[i + 1];
    swap_made := TRUE
    end
until swap_made = FALSE
```

Let us see how this proceeds with a table having just four entries:

Initial table	*1st repeat execution of* **for** *loop* $i = 1$	$i = 2$	$i = 3$	*2nd repeat execution of* **for** *loop* $i = 1$	$i = 2$	$i = 3$	
jon	jon	jon	jon	bill	bill	bill	
tom	tom	bill	bill	jon	fred	fred	Table
bill	bill	tom	fred	fred	jon	jon	is now
fred	fred	fred	tom	tom	tom	tom	sorted
swap_made	TRUE	TRUE	TRUE	TRUE	TRUE	FALSE	

Our main assembly language program is entirely sequential thanks to the use of three subroutines: `READNAMES`, `SORT` and `PRINTNAMES`. `READNAMES` reads the names typed by the user into a table held in memory via the data segment pseudo-op:

```
TABLE DB 20D DUP(30D DUP(' '))
```

and `PRINTNAMES` displays the 20 entries in the table pointed to by `TABLE`. `SORT` bubblesorts the 20 entries in the table pointed to by `TABLE` and itself calls a subroutine `SWAPENTRIES` which swaps table entries and uses

```
TEMP DB 30D DUP(?)
```

to provide temporary store to effect the swap. The main program is shown in Figure 11.7.

```
CR EQU ODH
LF EQU OAH

DATA SEGMENT
        TABLE DB 20D DUP(30D DUP(' '))
        TEMP  DB 30D DUP(?)
DATA ENDS

WORKING_STORAGE SEGMENT STACK
     DW 100H DUP(?)
WORKING_STORAGE ENDS

CODE SEGMENT
ASSUME DS:DATA,SS:WORKING_STORAGE,CS:CODE,ES:CODE
MAIN PROC FAR
;establish data and extra segment addressability
        MOV AX,DATA
        MOV DS,AX
        MOV ES,AX
        CALL READNAMES
        CALL SORT
        ;print a new line
        MOV AH,2
        MOV DL,CR
        INT 21H
        MOV DL,LF
        INT 21H
        CALL PRINTNAMES
;return to DOS
        MOV AX,4C00H
        INT 21H
MAIN ENDP
      .
      .
      .
CODE ENDS
END MAIN
```

Figure 11.7 Main program for table sorting.

The implementation of READNAMES is just as straightforward:

```
READNAMES PROC NEAR
MOV DI, OFFSET TABLE
;for i:= 0 to 19 do
    MOV BX,0H
              ;read entry[i+1]
READ_NEXT_ENTRY:PUSH DI
                MOV CX,30D
      NEXT_CHAR:MOV AH,1
                INT 21H
                CMP AL,CR
                JZ NEXT_NAME
                STOSB
                LOOP NEXT_CHAR
        ;print a new line
      NEXT_NAME:MOV AH,2
                MOV DL,CR
                INT 21H
```

```
                        MOV DL,LF
                        INT 21H
                ;point DI to next entry in table
                        POP DI
                        ADD DI,30D
            ;end of for loop
                CMP BX,19D
                JZ  DONE_ALL_NAMES
                INC BX
                JMP READ_NEXT_ENTRY
DONE_ALL_NAMES: RET
            READNAMES ENDP
```

SORT is a direct implementation of the pseudo-Pascal description of bubblesort given above. Yet again the 8086-family primitive string manipulation instructions simplify the task enormously:

```
        SORT PROC NEAR
        ;repeat
            ;swap_made:=FALSE
NEXT_REPEAT:MOV DL,0
            MOV SI,OFFSET TABLE
            ;for i:=1 to 19 do
                MOV DH,1
            ;if entry[i] should be after entry[i+1]
    NEXT_COUNT: PUSH SI
                MOV CX,30D
                MOV DI,SI
                ADD DI,30D
                REPZ CMPSB
                JBE NO_SWAP_NEEDED
                    ;then begin swap contents;
                            ;swap_made:=TRUE
                            ADD SI,CX
                            SUB SI,30D
                            CALL SWAPENTRIES
                        ;end
NO_SWAP_NEEDED: POP SI
                ADD SI,30D
                CMP DH,19D
                JZ  DONE_FOR
                INC DH
                JMP NEXT_COUNT
    ;until swap_made = FALSE
      DONE_FOR: CMP DL,0
                JNZ NEXT_REPEAT
                RET
        SORT ENDP
```

Thanks to primitive string instructions, SWAPENTRIES is entirely sequential:

```
SWAPENTRIES PROC NEAR
;move entry i to TEMP
        MOV BX,SI
        MOV CX,30D
```

```
        MOV DI,OFFSET TEMP
        REP MOVSB
;move entry i+1 to i
        MOV CX,30D
        MOV DI,BX
        REP MOVSB
;move entry in TEMP to i+1
        MOV CX,30D
        MOV SI,OFFSET TEMP
        REP MOVSB
;swap_made := true
        MOV DL,1
        RET
SWAPENTRIES ENDP
```

PRINTNAMES uses a single for loop:

```
PRINTNAMES PROC NEAR
           MOV SI, OFFSET TABLE
     ;for i:= 0 to 19 do
           MOV BX,0H
           ;print entry[i+1]
       PRINT_NEXT_ENTRY: MOV CX,30D
             PRINT_NEXT: LODSB
                         MOV DL,AL
                         MOV AH,2
                         INT 21H
                         LOOP PRINT_NEXT
                ;print a new line
                         MOV DL,CR
                         INT 21H
                         MOV DL,LF
                         INT 21H
    ;end of for loop
           CMP BX,19D
           JZ  PRINT_DONE
           INC BX
           JMP PRINT_NEXT_ENTRY
PRINT_DONE: RET
PRINTNAMES ENDP
```

EXERCISES

11.6 Type the table-sorting program into your computer, assemble, link and test run it. Then add a better user interface. In particular:

(a) Demand each table entry with a prompt. Thus, for the tenth entry the prompt might be:

```
please type name 10:
```

(b) If the user tries to specify a name of more than 30 letters then issue an appropriate error message, ignore what has been typed, print a new line on the display screen and issue the prompt for that entry afresh.

(c) Allow the optional termination of the list of names. Thus, if the user types a `$` then any remaining entries are set to the ASCII code for a space character and the table is sorted as normal.

(d) Allow mixed upper- and lower-case names and sort them so that names in lower case only precede both those in upper case only and in a mixture of cases.

11.7 Write and test a family of subroutines which mimic the string manipulation facilities in a language like Turbo Pascal for strings of 255 characters and less. Thus, there should be a subroutine `CONCATENATE` which joins two strings together, a subroutine `LENGTH` which leaves the length of a string in CL, a subroutine `INSERT` which inserts one string in another starting at the character position in the second string given in CL, and a subroutine which returns in CL the position of the first occurrence (if any) of the first string in the second. Assume that DS:SI and ES:DI point to the first and second string respectively and that, on entry, AH contains the length of the first string and AL the length of the second string.

11.8 Rewrite your solution to Exercise 11.7 so that all parameters are passed on the stack, including the two strings.

11.9 Try to re-code the table-sorting program without using primitive string manipulation instructions.

11.10 You are to write an assembly language program with a `DATA SEGMENT` which begins as follows:

```
DATA SEGMENT
.RADIX 10
        ARRAY_A  DB 2,3,4,7,9,11,13,17,19,23
        ARRAY_B  DB 3,7,15,31,63,127,255,511,1023,2047
        RESULTS  DW 10 DUP(?)
        .
        .
        .
```

The program should compare `ARRAY_A` and `ARRAY_B` byte by byte and set the corresponding entry of `RESULTS` according to the following formula:

If the sum of corresponding entries is an even number then the result should be a 16-bit signed equivalent of the negated value in `ARRAY_A`;

If the sum of the corresponding entries is odd then examine the difference between corresponding entries to determine the result instead. If this difference (subtract `ARRAY_A` values from `ARRAY_B` values) is negative then the corresponding entry in `RESULT` is the *sum* (in 16-bit signed form) of all the entries in ARRAY_A up to and including the present one. Otherwise it is the sum (in 16-bit signed form) of all the entries in ARRAY_B from the present one up to and including the last.

(*Hint:* write three separate subroutines to deal with each of the three cases.) Test your program carefully under debugger control.

SUMMARY

In this chapter we have learned how to use the powerful 8086-family string and table manipulation instructions MOVS, LODS, STOS, CMPS, SCAS, XCHG and XLAT together with the associated control instructions in the REP family (the LOOP family also have a role in this connection, of course). We have seen that these simplify the programming task by reducing complexity. (Anyone who doubts this has not tried Exercise 11.9!) In the next chapter we shall use these instructions in a large example program both for further illustration of their utility and also to give another substantial example of program development with our pseudo-Pascal based methodology.

SELF-CHECK QUIZ

1. Write a subroutine to reverse the order of the bytes in a group of 40H locations in memory, the offset of the start address of the group of bytes being passed to your subroutine in AX.

2. Show how to simulate the operation of CMPS using any of the string manipulation instructions except CMPS and SCAS.

3. Show how to simulate the operation of SCAS using any of the string manipulation instructions except CMPS and SCAS.

4. Write a subroutine which compacts a string stored in memory by removing all spaces and punctuation.

5. Two text strings stored in memory are said to be in **lexicographic order** if they are the same or if, in the first place in which they differ, the corresponding letters are in alphabetical order. Write a subroutine to verify that two strings are in lexicographic order.

6. What will be in AX, BX and CX and locations 200H to 220H (relative to DS) after execution of:

```
      MOV DI,OFFSET MY_BYTES
      MOV CX,11D
      MOV AL,9D
      MOV BX,7D
NEXT: REPZ SCASB
      ADD AL,2
      STOSB
      LOOP NEXT
```

   given that the offset (relative to DS) of MY_BYTES is 200H and that before execution locations 200H to 220H all contain 9D.

7. What will be in AX, BX and CX and locations 200H to 220H (relative to DS) after execution of:

```
      MOV SI,OFFSET MY_WORDS
      MOV DI,OFFSET MY_NEWWORDS
      MOV CX,5D
      MOV AX,9D
```

```
        MOV BX,8D
   NEXT:REPNZ CMPSW
        INC BX
        ADD AX,BX
        LOOP NEXT
```

given that the offset (relative to DS) of MY_WORDS is 200H, the offset of MY_NEW_WORDS (relative to DS) is 210H and that before execution locations 200H to 220H all contain 9D.

8. Prime numbers are stored in memory as follows:

```
PRIMES DW 2,3,5,7,11,13,17,19,23,29,31,37,41
```

Write a subroutine using XLAT which given a number *n* in AL between 1 and 13D inclusive, returns with the *n*th prime number in AX.

9. Give four different ways of simulating the XCHG instruction.

10. Using only the XCHG instruction is it possible to reverse the order of a group of unsigned 16-bit numbers stored in memory? Explain your answer.

12

A Simple Text Editor

Contents

This chapter is devoted to the construction of a simple text editor program featuring the string manipulation instructions introduced in Chapter 11 and using the program development methodology of Chapter 8. Our simple text editor will allow the user to type in a text and modify it in various ways – by adding a new line or deleting an existing one, for example. Since the mechanisms for copying data held in memory on to disk and for copying from disk into memory will not be described until Chapter 19, our text editor will lack many features vital to a real editor program. In particular, the user will not be able to save text on disk. Thus our text editor will be a long way from being a practical tool; indeed, even its basic design is not appropriate for a real editor. However, our aim is to illustrate the use of the 8086-family string manipulation instructions introduced in the first part of the last chapter in an appropriate environment, rather than to compete with professionally produced products.

12.1 Specification

Our **text editor** will handle up to nine lines of text at any one time. These will be stored in memory and may each contain up to 72D characters. **Editor commands** will have one of the formats:

```
Pm
Dm
Nm
Smn
F%any string%
P
E
```

where the letter (P,D,N,S,F,E) specifies the type of command and *m* and *n* are single digits (1,2,. . .,9) which specify to which line or lines that command is to be applied. Commands are typed straight after the editor's prompt character – an asterisk (*). Each command is obeyed when the person using the text editor presses the ENTER key after typing it. Table 12.1 summarizes the commands and the actions they cause.

If the ENTER key is not pressed immediately after a command the message

```
A COMMAND MUST BE TERMINATED BY PRESSING THE ENTER KEY
```

will be displayed and that command ignored. Indeed, if anything is wrong with the format of a command, then that command is ignored.

Also, to simplify the printing out of the text we shall assume that no line of text entered by the user contains a dollar sign ($). This is not essential to the design of the text editor and in due course it will be an exercise for the reader to eliminate this restriction.

12.2 Top-down implementation

As in Chapter 8, the task will be broken down into independent building blocks. Before that, however, it is necessary to decide on a strategy for storing the text in memory.

Table 12.1 Command summary for the text editor program.

Command	*Action*

N*m*	This command allows the user to specify New text for line *m*. The previous line *m* is completely eliminated by this command.
	Once the ENTER key has been pressed for the N command to be obeyed, a colon (:) is printed as a prompt to the user. The line of text typed by the user after the colon prompt then becomes the new line number *m*. If *m* is not one of 1,2,. . .,9 then the error message
	`NO SUCH LINE EXISTS.`
	`ILLEGAL CHARACTER IN LINE NUMBER?`
	is printed out. If the new line of text contains more than 72D characters, the old text is retained and the error message
	`STRING TOO LONG`
	is displayed.

D*m*	This is the editor command to Delete the *m*th line of text. Again, if *m* is not one of 1,2,. . .,9 then the message
	`NO SUCH LINE EXISTS.`
	`ILLEGAL CHARACTER IN LINE NUMBER?`
	is displayed.

P*m*	Print the *m*th line of text. If *m* is out of range then the same error message as for the N and D commands is displayed.
P	This is a short form of the Print command which causes all nine lines of text to be printed out.
S*mn*	This allows the user to Swap lines *m* and *n* of the text. The command is abandoned if *m* or *n* is out of range (and the usual error message is printed). There must be no spaces between the first line number, *m*, and the second, *n*.
F%any string%	Finds all the lines which contain the string inside the per cent signs (%). (This string must not itself contain per cent signs – it will be an exercise for the reader later on to remove this restriction.) The line number of each line containing the search string is printed on the display. If one (or both) of the per cent signs is (are) missing the error message `%SIGN(S) MISSING IN FIND COMMAND` will be displayed.
E	End the editing session and return to the operating system. (Since we are not yet able to save the text on disk, the text stored in memory will be lost after this command.)

12.2.1 Text storage – the strategy

Once again we depart from practical considerations and allow ourselves the luxury of reserving separate groups of memory locations for each of the nine lines of text. With the first location of the first line of text we shall associate the

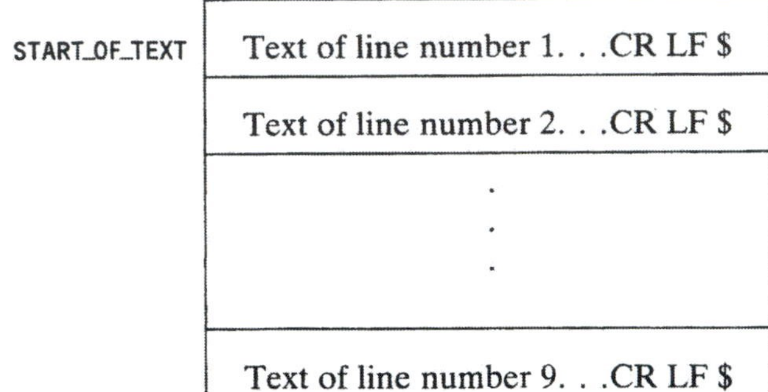

Figure 12.1 Text storage in our simple text editor.

name START_OF_TEXT. For each line we shall reserve a total of 75D locations (that is, 72D maximum for the actual text, to which we shall then add Carriage Return and Line Feed characters and finally a $ sign, so that each line can be printed out by using the operating system 'print string' function). This is shown in Figure 12.1.

Since 9 * 75D = 675D, the first pseudo-op in the data segment of our program will be

```
START_OF_TEXT DB 675D DUP(?)
```

If the N (New text) command is called up it must then prompt the user with a colon to indicate that the user may now type in the new text. If we were to replace the old text by the new as each character was typed in by the user, we would run the risk of having ruined the old text despite the fact that the new line is too long and therefore unacceptable. Consequently, we read the proposed new text into a **buffer** (or temporary store) and move it into place only when we know everything is as it should be.

Since the maximum allowed length of any text line in our editor is 72D characters, we shall know that the maximum has been exceeded if 73D characters have been entered by the user and the last one is not a Carriage Return (CR) character. Hence we reserve 80D bytes for the buffer (more than we actually need) by adding the directive

```
READ_LINE_BUFFER DB 80D DUP(?)
```

to the data segment of our program.

After a new line of text has been entered we want to calculate and record its length once and for all so that the same calculation is not necessary every time we call up the F(ind) command. To record the lengths of the nine lines of text as signed 8-bit numbers we use the directive

```
LINE_LENGTHS DB 9 DUP(0)
```

in the data segment of our program. This initializes the nine lengths to zero in each case.

12.2.2 An outline of the text editor program

For each possible command we shall implement that command by means of a self-contained subroutine. Let us assume that these have names as follows:

Command	*Subroutine which implements that command*
P	PRINT_ALL_TEXT
P*m*	PRINT_A_LINE
S*mn*	SWAP
N*m*	NEW_TEXT
D*m*	DELETE
F%. . .%	FIND

We shall also require a subroutine – which we shall call INITIALIZE – which sets all nine lines to blank initially. Given these subroutines, it is then fairly easy to write an outline of the program and this is shown in Figure 12.2. The only variables required at this stage of the design are *char*1 and *char*2 to store the first two characters typed by the user as part of an editor command (for E and the short form of P these are the only user input characters which need to be stored).

```
call INITIALIZE;
print(prompt);
read(char1,char2);
while not (char1 = E and char2 = CR) do
  begin
  if char1 = P and char2 = CR then call PRINT_ALL_TEXT
  else if char1 = P then call PRINT_A_LINE
  else if char1 = S then call SWAP
  else if char1 = N then call NEW_TEXT
  else if char1 = D then call DELETE
  else if char1 = F then call FIND
  else call ILLEGAL_CHARACTER
  print(new line);
  print(prompt);
  read(char1,char2)
  end;
return to DOS
```

Figure 12.2 Outline of the text editor program.

EXERCISE

12.1 Work through the pseudo-Pascal outline in Figure 12.2 for each of the following sequences of user input typed at the keyboard. The sequences show the characters corresponding to the keys pressed by the user, nothing more.

(a) `N1<ENTER>EAT MORE FRUIT<ENTER>P<ENTER>P1<ENTER>E<ENTER>`

(b) `H2<ENTER>K<ENTER>E<ENTER>` (c) `TEST`

Assume that `PRINT_ALL_TEXT`, `SWAP`, and so on implement the relevant command completely so that, on exit, we are ready to receive and complement another command.

12.3 Implementation of the main program

For reading characters from the keyboard and printing characters on the display screen we shall use the `READCHAR` and `PRINTCHAR` subroutines (respectively) of Chapter 10. Furthermore, the `PRINT_STRING` subroutine for printing strings on the display screen given a starting address in DX (relative to DS) will be a similar adaptation of DOS function 9 from Chapter 4. These apart, we have to write the subroutines `PRINT_ALL_TEXT`, `PRINT_A_LINE`, `SWAP`, `NEW_TEXT`, `DELETE` and `FIND` given in Figure 12.2. Before attempting these, however, we shall code the main body of the program. The text editor program is a good example of a program wherein the subroutines to be written are completely independent, but where testing can be facilitated by choosing a sensible order of implementation. Thus, if we implement `PRINT_ALL_TEXT` first it can be used in testing `NEW_TEXT` and so on.

Testing of our implementation of the skeletal main program is carried out by implementing all missing subroutines (not counting `INITIALIZE` and those for reading and writing borrowed from other chapters) as a single `RET` instruction. For example, for the purpose of testing the main program, `NEW_TEXT` could be implemented as

```
NEW_TEXT PROC NEAR
      RET
NEW_TEXT ENDP
```

Figure 12.3 gives our implementation in which *char*1 of the pseudo-Pascal outline in Figure 12.2 is assigned to CL and *char*2 is assigned to AL. Note that we have defined the two prompt characters `STAR` and `COLON` along with Carriage Return (CR) and Line Feed (LF) via `EQU` definitions so that these may easily be changed to different characters. The complete text editor program can be found in Appendix III, which can be referred to for further clarification as and when the reader desires it.

```
LF      EQU 0AH
CR      EQU 0DH
STAR    EQU '*'
COLON   EQU ':'
DOLLAR EQU '$'

DATA SEGMENT
START_OF_TEXT     DB 675D DUP(?)
READ_LINE_BUFFER  DB 80D DUP(?)
LINE_LENGTHS      DB 9 DUP(0)

ILLEGAL_MESS      DB 'ILLEGAL CHARACTER IN INPUT',CR,LF,DOLLAR
   .
   .
   .
DATA ENDS

WORKING_STORAGE SEGMENT STACK
        DW 100H DUP(?)
WORKING_STORAGE ENDS

CODE SEGMENT
ASSUME DS:DATA,SS:WORKING_STORAGE,CS:CODE

MAIN PROC FAR
;address our program's data segment
      MOV AX,DATA
      MOV DS,AX
      MOV ES,AX ;for string manipulation instructions
;call initialize
       CALL INITIALIZE
;print(prompt)
       MOV  DL,STAR
       CALL PRINTCHAR
;read(char1, char2);
       CALL READCHAR
       MOV  CL,AL
       CALL READCHAR ;CL = char1, AL = char2
;while not (char1 = E and char2 = CR) do
PROCESS: CMP CL,'E'
         JNZ NOT_END
         CMP AL,CR
         JNZ NOT_END
         JMP DONE
   ;begin
   ;if char1 = P and char2 = CR
      NOT_END: CMP  CL,'P'
               JNZ  TRY_LINE
               CMP  AL,CR
               JNZ  TRY_LINE
   ;then print all the text
               CALL PRINT_ALL_TEXT
               JMP  GET_COMMAND
   ;else if char1 = P then print a line
```

Figure 12.3
Implementation of the main program.

```
 TRY_LINE:    CMP  CL,'P'
              JNZ  TRY_S
              CALL PRINT_A_LINE
              JMP  GET_COMMAND
 ;else if char1 = S then call swap
 TRY_S:       CMP  CL,'S'
              JNZ  TRY_N
              CALL SWAP
              JMP  GET_COMMAND
 ;else if char1 = N then call new_text
 TRY_N:       CMP  CL,'N'
              JNZ  TRY_D
              CALL NEW_TEXT
              JMP  GET_COMMAND
 ;else if char1 = D then call delete
 TRY_D:       CMP  CL,'D'
              JNZ  TRY_F
              CALL DELETE
              JMP  GET_COMMAND
 ;else if char1 = F then call find
 TRY_F:       CMP  CL,'F'
              JNZ  ILLEGAL
              CALL FIND
              JMP  GET_COMMAND
       ;else print(illegal character);
      ILLEGAL: CALL ILLEGAL_CHARACTER
;print(new line);
  GET_COMMAND: CALL PRINT_NEWLINE
;print(prompt);
               MOV  DL,STAR
               CALL PRINTCHAR
  ;read(char1, char2);
               CALL READCHAR
               MOV  CL,AL
               CALL READCHAR
  ;end;
               JMP  PROCESS
;return to DOS
     DONE: MOV AX,4C00H
           INT 21H
MAIN ENDP

ILLEGAL_CHARACTER PROC NEAR
     CALL  PRINT_NEWLINE
     MOV   DX,OFFSET ILLEGAL_MESS
     CALL  PRINT_STRING
     RET
ILLEGAL_CHARACTER ENDP
  .
  .
  .
CODE ENDS
END MAIN
```

Figure 12.3
(cont.)

EXERCISE

12.2 Trace the execution of the program in Figure 12.2 (making suitable assumptions about the effects of the subroutines which have yet to be defined) for each of the following sequences of user input typed at the keyboard. The sequences show the characters corresponding to the keys pressed by the user, nothing more. Your trace should clearly show the contents of all registers involved and any output displayed on the screen.

(a) `N1<ENTER>EAT MORE FRUIT<ENTER>P<ENTER>P1<ENTER>E<ENTER>`

(b) `H2<ENTER>K<ENTER>E<ENTER>`

(c) `TEST`

12.4 Initialization

When the program starts up, each line of text must be set to blank. In fact we shall organize things so that each line contains just the CR and LF characters. (Note that, throughout the program, these two characters will not be included in line length calculations.) The `INITIALIZE` subroutine creates nine blank lines in the appropriate places by storing CR and LF characters and a $ sign in the first three storage locations allocated to each of the nine lines. Its basic structure is a simple **for** loop:

for *i* := 1 **to** 9 **do** *line*[*i*] := (*CR*,*LF*,*DOLLAR*);

and its implementation follows the simpler of the two schemes given in Chapter 7:

```
INITIALIZE PROC NEAR
;for i := 1 to 9 do line[i] := (CR,LF,DOLLAR);
                    MOV CX,9
                    MOV SI,OFFSET START_OF_TEXT
INIT_NEXT:          MOV [SI],BYTE PTR CR
                    MOV 1[SI],BYTE PTR LF
                    MOV 2[SI],BYTE PTR DOLLAR
                    ADD SI,75D
                    LOOP INIT_NEXT
                    RET
INITIALIZE ENDP
```

(It is probably better to avoid initializing data in this way by defining `START_OF_TEXT` in the `DATA` segment as:

```
START_OF_TEXT DB CR,LF,DOLLAR
          DB 72D DUP(' ') ;1st text line initialized
          DB CR,LF,DOLLAR
```

```
DB 72D DUP(' ') ;2nd text line initialized
.
.
.
```

But doing it via the INITIALIZE subroutine has allowed us another opportunity to illustrate the use of SI as an index register prior to a more formal description of addressing modes in Chapter 13).

12.5 Printing the whole text

Printing the whole text is carried out by the PRINT_ALL_TEXT subroutine and is relatively straightforward to implement using the PRINT_STRING subroutine.

```
          PRINT_ALL_TEXT PROC NEAR
          ;for i := 1 to 9 do print(line[i]);
               CALL PRINT_NEWLINE
               MOV CX,9
               MOV DX,OFFSET START_OF_TEXT
NEXT_LINE:CALL PRINT_STRING
               ADD DX,75D ;set address pointer to next line
               LOOP NEXT_LINE
               RET
          PRINT_ALL_TEXT ENDP
```

12.6 VERIFY_RANGE_AND_FORMAT

The main program checks that a valid command *name* has been given but passes the responsibility for ensuring both that the command format is correct and that the line number(s) typed by the user is (are) meaningful to the subroutines which implement the commands. We shall put both of these functions into a subroutine called VERIFY_RANGE_AND_FORMAT which will be called by each of the subroutines implementing editor commands involving line numbers – PRINT_A_LINE, SWAP, NEW_TEXT, and DELETE.

It examines the two characters typed after the command letter and expects to find first a valid line number and then an ASCII carriage return code corresponding to the ENTER key having been pressed. When VERIFY_RANGE_AND_FORMAT is called up from within PRINT_A_LINE, SWAP, NEW_TEXT, or DELETE, the first of these characters will already be in AL thanks to the operation of the main program (see Figure 12.2). So VERIFY_RANGE_AND_FORMAT examines the character in AL and then accepts another character from the user and verifies that this third character is indeed a carriage return. It then returns three parameters in registers AH, BL and DX as follows:

- AH Indicates whether or not there is a command format error:

0 indicates correct format
0FFH indicates a format error

- DX If there is a format error then DX is set to the offset address of a suitable error message.
- BL If the format is correct, BL contains the ASCII code for the number of the line which is to be affected by this command.

The first job of VERIFY_RANGE_AND_FORMAT is to check that the second character typed by the user (supplied to it as a parameter in AL) is a valid line number. If not, then we set register AH to 0FFH to denote an error, set register DX to the address of the NO_SUCH_LINE error message and exit from the subroutine.

Once we are sure that the line number is in range, we save its ASCII code in BL and read the next character. If that character is not a carriage return character then once again there has been an error so we set register AH to 0FFH and register DX to the address of the ENTER_ERROR message and exit. Otherwise we set register AH to 0 to indicate that all is well and we are done:

```
if char2 not in ['1'..'9'] then
   begin
   DX := address of NO_SUCH_LINE message
   AH := 0FFH
   end
else begin
     read(char3)
     if char3 <> CR then
        begin
        DX := address of ENTER_ERROR message;
        AH := 0FFH
        end
     else AH := 0
     end
```

Our implementation of this outline is given in Figure 12.4.

Of course, we must also add the definition of the error messages to the data segment. They are as follows:

```
FORMAT_ERROR DB 'SPACE MISSING AFTER COMMAND',CR,LF,DOLLAR

NO_SUCH_LINE DB 'NO SUCH LINE EXISTS.'
             DB 'ILLEGAL CHARACTER IN LINE NUMBER?',CR,LF,DOLLAR

ENTER_ERROR  DB 'A COMMAND MUST BE TERMINATED BY '
             DB 'PRESSING THE ENTER KEY',CR,LF,DOLLAR
```

To summarize: after a call to the VERIFY_RANGE_AND_FORMAT subroutine, register AH either contains 0FFH, indicating that an error has occurred, or it contains 0H, indicating that a valid line number followed by a CR have been read and the ASCII code for the line number is in register BL. If an error has occurred, register DX will be set to the address of a suitable error message.

```
VERIFY_RANGE_AND_FORMAT PROC NEAR
;if char2 not in ['1'..'9'] then
    CMP AL,'1'
    JB  OUT_OF_RANGE
    CMP AL,'9'
    JBE IN_RANGE
       ;begin
       ;set DX to address of error message
OUT_OF_RANGE: MOV   DX,OFFSET NO_SUCH_LINE
       ;set AH to indicate error
            MOV   AH,0FFH
       ;end
            JMP RF_ERROR
 ;else begin
       ;read(char3)
IN_RANGE:MOV   BL,AL          ;char2 now in BL
       CALL READCHAR
    ;if char3 <> CR then
       CMP AL,CR
       JZ   RF_OK
          ;begin
          ;set DX to address of error message
               MOV DX,OFFSET ENTER_ERROR
          ;set AH to indicate error
               MOV AH,0FFH
          ;end
               JMP RF_ERROR
    ;else set AH to indicate OK
  RF_OK:MOV AH,0
RF_ERROR:  RET
VERIFY_RANGE_AND_FORMAT ENDP
```

Figure 12.4 Implementation of VERIFY_RANGE_AND_FORMAT.

12.7 PRINT_A_LINE

Having done all this work in advance, completing the PRINT_A_LINE subroutine now comes down to calculating the starting address of the relevant line from the ASCII code stored in BL:

call VERIFY_RANGE_AND_FORMAT;
if *AH <> 0FFH* **then begin**
*DX := (BL − 31H) * 75D + (OFFSET START_OF_TEXT)*
call PRINTSTRING
end

Notice that, while subtracting 30H from the ASCII code for the line number would give the actual line number, what we want is the offset address of the first character in that line. Since each line of text is allocated 75D bytes of store, this address will be found by adding the appropriate number of 75D blocks to the offset address of START_OF_TEXT: 0 blocks for the first line of text, 1 block for the second line, and so on. Hence we subtract 31H from BL and not 30H. The actual implementation is now easy:

```
PRINT_A_LINE PROC NEAR
        CALL VERIFY_RANGE_AND_FORMAT
        CALL PRINT_NEWLINE
;if AH <> 0FFH
        CMP  AH,0FFH
        JZ   PRINT_DONE
        ;then begin
              ;DX:= (BL - 31H) * 75D + (OFFSET START_OF_TEXT)
                  SUB BL,31H
                  MOV AL,75D
                  MUL BL
                  MOV DX,AX
                  ADD DX,OFFSET START_OF_TEXT
              ;call PRINT_STRING
        PRINT_DONE:CALL PRINT_STRING
        RET
PRINT_A_LINE ENDP
```

12.8 NEW_TEXT

The plan for the NEW_TEXT subroutine is also relatively straightforward. NEW_TEXT is brought into action after the first command character has been entered and recognized as an N. Hence the first thing which must happen in the body of NEW_TEXT is a call to VERIFY_RANGE_AND_FORMAT to check that the next character is a valid line number and that the command is terminated properly. If all is well, we print a colon prompt at the beginning of a new line and, using the STOS instruction, move the new text into the READ_LINE_BUFFER as it is typed. (Thus, a colon prompts for an input line, a star prompts for an editor command.) Reading finishes as soon as either more than 72D characters have been typed or a carriage return (CR) character is typed. If more than 72D characters have been typed and character number 73D is not a CR character, the new text line is too long and we print an error message and exit from the subroutine.

Assuming that the new text in the buffer is within the allowed length we must ensure that there is a CR, LF, DOLLAR sequence at the end of it so that the complete new text line can be moved into its proper place by a MOVS instruction. The CR typed by the user at the end of the text will already have been stored in the buffer so we need only add the LF and DOLLAR characters.

All that remains to be done then is to calculate the starting address of the buffered text's destination (using the fact that the ASCII code for the appropriate line number is still in register BL), to calculate and store the length of the text (not counting the CR, LF, DOLLAR sequence) and to move the new text into place. This is shown in the outline in Figure 12.5.

---

call VERIFY_RANGE_AND_FORMAT;
call PRINT_NEWLINE;
if *AH* = *0FFH* **then** *print error message*
  else begin
    print(*colon prompt*);
    DI := *address of READ_LINE_BUFFER*;
    CX := *73D*;
    repeat *read*(*char*); *decrement CX*;
        store char in READ_LINE_BUFFER
    until *CX* = 0 **or** *char* = *CR*;
    if *char* <> *CR* **then** *print*(*TOO_LONG*)
    else begin
      append LF and $ to text in READ_LINE_BUFFER;
      set DI to starting address of buffered text's destination:
        – *work out number of 75D blocks from START_OF_TEXT*
        – *use this to work out start address relative to START_OF_TEXT*;
        – *set DI to the actual offset address*;
      calculate the length of the text in READ_LINE_BUFFER;
      store the text length in LINE_LENGTHS;
      set SI to point to the buffer;
      move the text into place using MOVS;
      end
    end;

Figure 12.5 Pseudo-Pascal outline of the NEW_TEXT subroutine.

When the new text is too long the error message to be printed out is specified by adding the following pseudo-op to the data segment:

```
TOO_LONG DB 'STRING TOO LONG',CR,LF,DOLLAR
```

Much of the implementation of the outline in Figure 12.5 is now routine. Let us first consider the reading of the proposed new line of text into the buffer:

```
NEW_TEXT PROC NEAR
        CALL VERIFY_RANGE_AND_FORMAT
        CALL PRINT_NEWLINE
;if AH = 0FFH then print error message
        CMP  AH,0FFH
        JNZ  OBEY_NEW
        CALL PRINT_STRING
        JMP  NEW_DONE
    ;else begin
          ;print (colon prompt)
      OBEY_NEW: CLD
                MOV  DL,COLON
                CALL PRINTCHAR
```

```
               ;DI := address of READ_LINE_BUFFER
                      MOV DI,OFFSET READ_LINE_BUFFER
               ;CX := 73D
                      MOV CX,73D
            ;repeat read(char)
        READ_MORE:  CALL READCHAR
                      ;store char in buffer
                      STOSB
            ;until  CX = 0 or char = CR
                      CMP   AL,CR
                      LOOPNZ READ_MORE
                      JZ    END_OF_LINE
            ;if char <> CR then print(TOO_LONG)
                      MOV   DX,OFFSET TOO_LONG
                      CALL PRINT_STRING
                      CALL PRINT_NEWLINE
                      JMP   NEW_DONE
END_OF_LINE:;else begin
            ;append LF and $ to text in READ_LINE_BUFFER;
;set DI to starting address of buffered text's destination:
                      - work out number of 75D blocks from START_OF_TEXT
                      - use this to work out start address relative to
                        START_OF_TEXT;
                      - set DI to the actual offset address;
            ;calculate the length of the text in READ_LINE_BUFFER;
            ;store the text length in LINE_LENGTHS;
            ;set SI to point to the buffer;
            ;move the text into place using MOVS;
            ;end
        ;end
NEW_DONE: RET
NEW_TEXT ENDP
```

Since the STOSB instruction will have automatically incremented DI and will have stored the CR typed by the user at the end of the text in the buffer, preparation of the new line of text within the buffer will be completed if we add the LF and $ characters:

```
        ;append LF and $ to text in READ_LINE_BUFFER;
END_OF_LINE: MOV BYTE PTR [DI],LF
             INC DI
             MOV BYTE PTR [DI],DOLLAR
```

Finally, we must calculate the starting address of the buffered text's destination:

```
;set DI to starting address of buffered text's destination
;step 1 — work out number of 75D blocks from START_OF_TEXT
        SUB BL,31H
;step 2 — use this to work out start address relative
;to START_OF_TEXT
        MOV AL,75D
        MUL BL          ;start address relative to
                        ;START_OF_TEXT now in AX
;set DI to the actual offset address
        MOV DI,AX
        ADD DI,OFFSET START_OF_TEXT
```

calculate and store the length of the text (not counting the CR, LF, $ sequence) in LINE_LENGTHS:

```
;calculate the length of the text in READ_LINE_BUFFER
          MOV DX,75D
          SUB DX,CX         ;length now in DX
          MOV CX,DX         ;save length ready for text move
;store the text length in appropriate place
          SUB DL,3          ;remove CR,LF,$ from count
          MOV BH,0          ;BX now contains the line no.-1
          ADD BX,OFFSET LINE_LENGTHS
          MOV [BX],DL       ;save the line length
```

and move the text into place:

```
;set SI to point to the buffer
          MOV SI,OFFSET READ_LINE_BUFFER
;move the text into place
          REP MOVSB
;end
;end
 NEW_DONE:RET
NEW_TEXT ENDP
```

12.9 DELETE

The DELETE subroutine is somewhat similar in structure to NEW_TEXT:

call VERIFY_RANGE_AND_FORMAT;
call PRINT_NEWLINE;
if *AH* = *0FFH* **then** *print error message*
  else begin
    find start address of line to be deleted;
    insert CR, LF, DOLLAR at this address and following;
    reset entry in LINE_LENGTHS to zero;
    print DELETE_OK message
    end;

Once the deletion has been completed we print out the message DELETION COMPLETED by adding to the data segment the pseudo-op:

```
DELETE_OK DB 'DELETION COMPLETED',CR,LF,DOLLAR
```

it being just as important to keep users of your programs informed when things go right as it is when they go wrong. (It is another exercise for the reader to modify previous subroutines in which this has not been done.)

Because the implementation of the above pseudo-Pascal outline for DELETE is so similar to parts of that for NEW_TEXT the whole thing is given now without further comment:

```
DELETE PROC NEAR
          CALL VERIFY_RANGE_AND_FORMAT
          CALL PRINT_NEWLINE
;if AH = OFFH then print error message
          CMP  AH,OFFH
          JNZ  DO_DELETE
          CALL PRINT_STRING
          JMP  DELETE_DONE
;else begin
        ;find start address of line to be deleted
     DO_DELETE: SUB  BL,31H ;our line is this many 75D blocks
                             ;from start
               MOV  AL,75D
               MUL  BL
               ADD  AX,OFFSET START_OF_TEXT
        ;start address now in AX
        ;insert CR, LF, DOLLAR at beginning of line with this address
               MOV  SI,AX
               MOV  BYTE PTR [SI],CR
               MOV  BYTE PTR 1[SI],LF
               MOV  BYTE PTR 2[SI],DOLLAR
        ;reset line length to zero
               MOV  SI,OFFSET LINE_LENGTHS
               MOV  BH,0H ;BX now contains the line no.-1
               ADD  SI,BX
               MOV  [SI],BH
        ;print deletion OK message
               MOV  DX,OFFSET DELETE_OK
               CALL PRINT_STRING
        ;end
DELETE_DONE: RET
DELETE ENDP
```

12.10 SWAP

Recall that the format of the S(wap) command is:

S*mn*

where *m* and *n* are valid line numbers. The SWAP subroutine is to be called up once the S command has been identified and the second character typed by the user (the ASCII code value corresponding to *m*) is stored in AL. Consequently, SWAP must begin by checking that the contents of AL do indeed correspond to a line number between 1 and 9. Having checked this, we preserve the contents of AL in register CL.

SWAP now expects another valid line number followed by a CR. This is just the situation after we have recognized the D or N command, for example. Consequently, we can read the next character (which we hope is indeed the second line number required by SWAP) into AL and call up VERIFY_RANGE_AND_FORMAT as usual so that the second line number, if valid, is left in BL.

The next step is to calculate the starting addresses of the actual text for the line numbers whose ASCII codes are in BL and CL, and to swap the corresponding recorded line lengths. To keep the structure simple we relegate the actual instructions for this to a subroutine which we shall call `LENGTH_SWAP`. It assumes that the contents of BL and CL both denote an offset from the location pointed to by `LINE_LENGTHS`. The lengths of the corresponding text lines are then swapped.

To effect the swap we set DX to the offset address of the beginning of the text corresponding to the line number in BL and AX to the start address of the text corresponding to the line number in CL. We then move the string whose starting address is in AX into the `READ_LINE_BUFFER`, copy the string starting at the offset address in DX into the locations starting with the offset address given in AX and then finally copy the contents of the `READ_LINE_BUFFER` into the locations starting with the offset address given in DX.

Thus a complete pseudo-Pascal outline for the `SWAP` subroutine is as follows:

> **if** *AL* **not in** ['1' .. '9'] **then** *print*(*no such line*)
> **else begin**
>   *MOV CL,AL*
>   *read*(*char*);
>   *call VERIFY_RANGE_AND_FORMAT*;
>   *print*(*new line*);
>   **if** *AH* = *0FFH* **then** *print*(*error message*)
>   **else begin**
>   *call LENGTH_SWAP*
>   *DX* := *start address of text with line number in BL*;
>   *AX* := *start address of text with line number in CL*;
>   *move string pointed to by AX into READ_LINE_BUFFER*;
>   *copy string pointed to by DX into that pointed to by AX*;
>   *copy READ_LINE_BUFFER string into that pointed to by DX*;
>   *print*(*SWAP COMPLETED*)
>   **end**
>   **end**

Here again, we inform the user once the editing command has been carried out, this time via the pseudo-op:

```
SWAP_OK DB 'SWAP COMPLETED',CR,LF,DOLLAR
```

The complete `SWAP` subroutine follows. Its relative simplicity owes a great deal to the power of 8086-family string manipulation instructions:

```
SWAP PROC NEAR
;if AL not in ['1' .. '9'] then print(no such line)
            CMP  AL,'1'
            JB   TOO_LOW
            CMP  AL,'9'
            JBE  LINE_NO_OK
```

```
 TOO_LOW:    CALL PRINT_NEWLINE
             MOV  DX,OFFSET NO_SUCH_LINE
             CALL PRINT_STRING
             JMP  SWAP_DONE
 ;else begin
LINE_NO_OK:  MOV  CL,AL
      ;read(char)
             CALL READCHAR
             CALL VERIFY_RANGE_AND_FORMAT
      ;print(new line)
             CALL PRINT_NEWLINE
      ;if AH = 0FFH then print error message
             CMP  AH,0FFH
             JNZ  DO_THE_SWAP
             CALL PRINT_STRING
             JMP  SWAP_DONE
      ;else begin
                 ;swap the recorded line lengths
       DO_THE_SWAP:    SUB  CL,31H
                       SUB  BL,31H
                       CALL LENGTH_SWAP
           ;DX := address of first text line
                       MOV  AL,75D
                       MUL  BL
                       ADD  AX,OFFSET START_OF_TEXT
                       MOV  DX,AX
           ;AX := address of second text line
                       MOV  AL,75D
                       MUL  CL
                       ADD  AX,OFFSET START_OF_TEXT
           ;move string pointed to by AX into READ_LINE_BUFFER
                       MOV  SI,AX
                       MOV  DI,OFFSET READ_LINE_BUFFER
                       MOV  CX,75D
                       REP  MOVSB
           ;move string pointed to by DX to locations
           ;pointed to by AX
                       MOV  SI,DX
                       MOV  DI,AX
                       MOV  CX,75D
                       REP  MOVSB
           ;copy string in READ_LINE_BUFFER to locations
           ;pointed to by DX
                       MOV  SI,OFFSET READ_LINE_BUFFER
                       MOV  DI,DX
                       MOV  CX,75D
                       REP  MOVSB
           ;print(swap complete)
                       MOV  DX,OFFSET SWAP_OK
                       CALL PRINT_NEWLINE
                       CALL PRINT_STRING
           ;end
        ;end
 SWAP_DONE: RET
 SWAP ENDP
```

12.10.1 LENGTH_SWAP

It remains to define the LENGTH_SWAP subroutine which provides a natural opportunity to illustrate a use of the 8086-family instruction XCHG (first described in Chapter 11). Before giving the instructions for LENGTH_SWAP let us quickly recapitulate: we require a subroutine which swaps the recorded line lengths for the text lines whose offsets from the start of the LINE_LENGTHS block of memory are in registers BL and CL. Moreover, the subroutine must preserve the latter two registers. Since the flow of control through the subroutine is entirely linear we shall give the full version of it at once:

```
LENGTH_SWAP PROC NEAR
;preserve BL on the stack
          PUSH BX
          MOV SI,OFFSET LINE_LENGTHS
;set BX to point to offset of the location where
;the length of the line referred to by BL is kept
          MOV BH,0
          ADD BX,SI
;set SI to point to offset of the location where
;the length of the line referred to by CL is kept
          MOV CH,0
          ADD SI,CX
;swap the lengths
          MOV AL,[SI]
          XCHG AL,[BX]
          MOV [SI],AL
;restore the value of BL
          POP BX
          RET
LENGTH_SWAP ENDP
```

12.11 Implementation of the FIND subroutine

The structure of a F(ind) command line is a little different from that required by the other editor commands. For example, to search the text for the string HULLABALLOO the command line would be

```
F%HULLABALLOO%
```

Since our FIND subroutine is called up after the F command has been recognized, on entry to FIND, AL will contain the ASCII code for the character the user typed immediately after the F command itself. We must first verify that this was a % sign. If this is not the case we must display an appropriate error message via the addition of the pseudo-op

```
SEARCH_ERROR DB '%SIGN(S) MISSING IN FIND COMMAND',CR,LF,DOLLAR
```

to the data segment of our program.

After the % sign we accept characters until another % sign is encountered, or the ENTER key has been pressed, or until 73D characters have been typed, the last of which is not a % sign. In the latter two cases an error has occurred (because we do not allow the ENTER character in the FIND string or because the maximum length of a line – and hence of a string to be found – is 72D characters) and we display an appropriate error message.

As the characters are entered we copy them into the READ_LINE_BUFFER ready to begin the search if the command line is correct. Next we check that the command line is terminated with the ENTER key and then finally we can set things up for the search itself.

The actual search will be carried out by a new subroutine, LOCATE, which will search each text line for the string contained in the READ_LINE_BUFFER, the length of which has been passed to it in the BP register. Once the search has been completed we display the message SEARCH COMPLETED via the pseudo-op

```
FIND_OK DB 'SEARCH COMPLETED',CR,LF,DOLLAR
```

Putting all this into pseudo-Pascal gives the outline in Figure 12.6.

```
if AL <> '%' then DX := address of SEARCH_ERROR message
else begin
  count := 73D;
  repeat read(char);
         store char in next free location in READ_LINE_BUFFER;
         count := count - 1
  until (char = '%') or (count = 0);
  if count = 0 then DX := address of TOO_LONG message
  else begin
    read(char);
    if char <> CR then DX := address of ENTER_ERROR message
    else begin
      BX := length of text in READ_LINE_BUFFER (not
              counting the final % sign);
      if BX <> 0 then
              begin
              MOV BP,BX;
              CALL PRINT_NEWLINE;
              CALL LOCATE
              DX := address of FIND_OK message
              end
      end
    end
  end;
CALL PRINT_NEWLINE;
CALL PRINT_STRING
```

Figure 12.6 Pseudo-Pascal outline of the FIND subroutine.

EXERCISE

12.3 Text has already been stored in memory using the `N` command of our simple text editor so that if a `P` command is given the response is:

```
JACK AND JILL
WENT UP THE HILL
TO GET A PAIL OF WATER
JACK FELL DOWN
AND BROKE HIS CROWN
AND JILL CAME TUMBLING AFTER
```

and three blank lines.

Starting with the main program in Figure 12.3 and then moving on to the pseudo-Pascal outline in Figure 12.6 as necessary, make an execution trace for each of the following `F` commands as if issued to our simple text editor after the above `P` command has been completely executed. Show clearly the contents of all registers and memory locations involved, including the `READ_LINE_BUFFER`.

(a) `F%%<ENTER>`

(b) `F%A%<ENTER>`

(c) `F*A*<ENTER>`

12.11.1 Completing FIND

Using the outline of Figure 12.6 it is now straightforward to complete `FIND`:

```
        FIND PROC NEAR
        ;if AL <> '%' then DX := address of SEARCH_ERROR message
                CMP  AL,'%'
                JZ   GET_FIND_STRING
                MOV  DX,OFFSET SEARCH_ERROR
                JMP  FIND_DONE
        ;else begin
            ;count := 73D;
GET_FIND_STRING: MOV   CX,73D
          ;point DI to start of READ_LINE_BUFFER
                  MOV   DI,OFFSET READ_LINE_BUFFER
         ;repeat
                  ;call readchar
        MORE_STRING: CALL READCHAR
                  ;store char
                     STOSB
          ;until char = % or count = 0;
                  CMP  AL,'%'
                  LOOPNZ MORE_STRING
          ;if count = 0 then DX := address of TOO_LONG message
```

```
          JZ    END_OF_STRING
          MOV   DX,OFFSET TOO_LONG
          JMP   FIND_DONE
         ;else begin
               ;read(char);
         END_OF_STRING: CALL READCHAR
               ;if char <> CR then DX := address of ENTER_ERROR
                                                  ;message
                        CMP   AL,CR
                        JZ    START_SEARCH
                        MOV   DX,OFFSET ENTER_ERROR
                        JMP   FIND_DONE
                      ;else begin
                           ;BX := length of search text
                    START_SEARCH:MOV BX,73D
                                 SUB BX,CX
                                 DEC BX          ;ignore final % sign
                           ;if BX <> 0 then
                                  CMP BX,0
                                  JZ   FIND_DONE
                                       ;begin
                                        MOV   BP,BX
                                        CALL  PRINT_NEWLINE
                                        CALL  LOCATE
                                       ;DX := address of FIND_OK message
                                        MOV DX,OFFSET FIND_OK
                                       ;end
                           ;end
              ;end
         ;end
FIND_DONE:CALL PRINT_NEWLINE
          CALL PRINT_STRING
          RET
FIND ENDP
```

12.12 The LOCATE subroutine

The hard work is nearly over. It remains now to produce the subroutine LOCATE which must print the line number of every text line containing the string in the READ_LINE_BUFFER which has its length given in register BP. Our strategy is simple-minded. Suppose we are searching for an occurrence of the string HULLABALLOO in the text line, 'HULLO HULLO WHAT'S ALL THIS THEN': we reposition HULLABALLOO alongside the text until we either find a match or come to the end of the text line:

```
HULLO HULLO WHAT'S ALL THIS THEN
                     HULLABALLOO
                    HULLABALLOO
                   HULLABALLOO
                        .
                      .
                    .
HULLABALLOO
```

Once we have found a match, we print the relevant line number. If no match is found, we try the next line – if there is one. This basic structure is summarized by the pseudo-Pascal:

```
for i := 9 downto 1 do
  begin
  found := false;
  j := length(line[i]) - BP + 1;
  while (not found) and j > 0 do
    begin
    compare string in position j of line[i] with search text;
    if strings are equal then begin
                                print(i);
                                found := true
                                end
    else j := j - 1
    end
  end
```

Let us try the body of this **for** loop out on some test data. Suppose that one of the lines of text – call it line i – stored in our simple text editor is:

```
TEA FOR TWO
```

and that the string to be searched for in this line (and the other lines of text) is

```
OR
```

so that our subroutine LOCATE is called up with OR in the READ_LINE_BUFFER and BP containing 2. A trace is given in Figure 12.7. Notice that line *i* has length 11 (nine letters and two spaces).

In the LOCATE subroutine itself, instead of working with actual line numbers, it is easier if we effectively work with the offset address of a given text line from START_OF_TEXT. Thus, DL is used to hold a number specifying how

found	*j*	Comparison with line *i*
FALSE	11 − 2 +1 = 10	TEA FOR TWO `         OR`
FALSE	9	TEA FOR TWO `        OR`
FALSE	8	TEA FOR TWO `       OR`
FALSE	7	TEA FOR TWO `      OR`
FALSE	6	TEA FOR TWO `     OR`
TRUE		

Figure 12.7
Trace of the basic search operation.

many blocks of 75D bytes the line of text currently being searched is from the START_OF_TEXT. Register CL will be set to 0FFH to represent the FALSE state of the pseudo-Pascal variable found and set to 0H to represent the TRUE state. Bearing in mind that the length of the search text is passed to LOCATE in register BP we can now give a more detailed pseudo-Pascal outline of it:

```
for DL := 8 downto 0 do
  begin
  AX := length of line DL + 1;
  if AX < BP then AX := 0
  else AX := AX - BP + 1(max necessary number
                          of scans of this text line);
  BX := DL * 75 (offset address of the (DL + 1)th
                 line of text);
  CL := 0FFH;
  while CL <> 0 and AX <> 0 do
    begin
    PUSH AX (make AX and CX available);
    PUSH CX (as working registers);
    CX := BP (length of search string);
    DI := AX + BX + 1 (next position in text
                        being searched);
    SI := start of search string;
    compare the strings with CMPS;
    if strings are equal then
      begin
      print line number DL + 1;
      POP CX
      CL := 0;
      POP AX
      end
    else begin
        POP CX
        POP AX
        DEC AX
        end
  end (*of while loop*)
end (*of for loop*);
set DX to address of completion message;
```

Let us use this more detailed outline to make an execution trace similar to that produced earlier in this section. To do so, it will be assumed that START_OF_TEXT has offset 0 from DS and that text line 9 is

```
AMAZING
```

text line 8 is

```
I
```

and that the search string is

```
IN
```

The trace is given in Figure 12.8.

AX	BX	CX = CHCL	DL	BP	SI	DI	Stack
?	?	????	8	2	?	?	?
7	?	????	8	2	?	?	?
6	?	????	8	2	?	?	?
6	600D	????	8	2	?	?	?
6	600D	??FF	8	2	?	?	?
6	600D	??FF	8	2	?	?	?,6
6	600D	??FF	8	2	?	?	?,6,??FF
6	600D	0002	8	2	?	?	?,6,??FF
6	600D	0002	8	2	?	607D	?,6,??FF
6	600D	0002	8	2	675D	607D	?,6,??FF

comparison: AMAZING
IN

so comparison fails

AX	BX	CX = CHCL	DL	BP	SI	DI	Stack
6	600D	??FF	8	2	675D	607D	?,6
6	600D	??FF	8	2	675D	607D	?
5	600D	??FF	8	2	675D	607D	?
5	600D	??FF	8	2	675D	607D	?,5
5	600D	??FF	8	2	675D	607D	?,5,??FF
5	600D	0002	8	2	675D	607D	?,5,??FF
5	600D	0002	8	2	675D	606D	?,5,??FF

comparison: AMAZING
IN

so comparison succeeds
so print line number 8 + 1 = 9

AX	BX	CX = CHCL	DL	BP	SI	DI	Stack
5	600D	??FF	8	2	675D	606D	?,5
5	600D	??00	8	2	675D	606D	?,5
5	600D	??00	8	2	675D	606D	?
5	600D	??00	7	2	675D	606D	?
1	600D	??00	7	2	675D	606D	?
0	600D	??00	7	2	675D	606D	?
0	525D	??00	7	2	675D	606D	?
0	525D	??FF	7	2	675D	606D	?
0	525D	??FF	6	2	675D	606D	?

.
.
.

Figure 12.8 Trace of pseudo-Pascal version of LOCATE.

Completing the actual subroutine from our pseudo-Pascal outline is again relatively straightforward, largely thanks to 8086-family string manipulation instructions.

```
        LOCATE PROC NEAR
         ;for DL:= 8 downto 0 do
                  MOV DL,8
                 ;begin
                 ;AX := length of line DL + 1
    SEARCH_NEXT_LINE:       MOV  BX,OFFSET LINE_LENGTHS
                            MOV  AL,DL
                            XLAT BX
                            MOV  AH,0
                 ;if AX < BP then AX := 0
                            CMP  AX,BP
                            JAE  SET_SCANS
                            MOV  AX,0
                            JMP  SET_ADDRESS
                 ;else AX := max necessary scans of this line;
                 SET_SCANS: SUB  AX,BP
                            INC  AX
                 ;BX:= offset address of the (DL + 1)th line
               SET_ADDRESS: PUSH AX
                            MOV  BL,DL
                            MOV  AL,75D
                            MUL  BL
                            ADD  AX,OFFSET START_OF_TEXT
                            MOV  BX,AX
                            POP  AX
                 ;found := false
                            MOV  CL,0FFH
                 ;while not found and AX <> 0 do
           CHECK_THIS_LINE: CMP  AX,0
                            JZ   END_FOR
                            CMP  CL,0FFH
                            JNZ  END_FOR
                     ;begin
                                 PUSH AX
                                 PUSH CX
                     ;CX := length of search string
                                 MOV CX,BP
                     ;set DI to start of text being searched
                     ;DI := AX + BX - 1
                                 DEC   AX
                                 ADD   AX,BX
                                 MOV   DI,AX
                     ;set SI to start of search text
                                 MOV   SI,OFFSET READ_LINE_BUFFER
                     ;compare the strings
                                 REPZ CMPSB
                     ;if strings equal then
                                 JNZ   TRY_FURTHER_ALONG
                            ;begin
                            ;print line number DL + 1
                                        ADD  DL,31H
```

```
                              CALL PRINTCHAR
                              CALL PRINT_NEWLINE
                              SUB  DL,31H
                   ;found := true
                              POP  CX
                              MOV  CL,0
                              POP  AX
                              DEC  AX
                   ;end
                              JMP  END_WHILE
                   ;else begin
                 TRY_FURTHER_ALONG:POP CX
                                POP AX
                                DEC AX
                        ;end
             ;end (*of while*)
             END_WHILE: JMP CHECK_THIS_LINE
     ;end (*of for loop*)
     END_FOR:    SUB DL,1
                 JB   LOCATE_DONE
                 JMP SEARCH_NEXT_LINE
     ;set DX to address of completion message
    LOCATE_DONE: MOV DX,OFFSET
                 FIND_OK
                 RET
    LOCATE ENDP
```

This completes our second major program. Once again, we invite the reader to inspect the full program in Appendix III, to type it into a computer and to verify that it does indeed work. Exercises 12.4–12.10 suggest some of the simpler improvements which could be made to the program.

EXERCISES

12.4 Make the improvements to our simple text editor which were suggested in the text. Namely:

(a) Remove the restriction that no line of text may contain a dollar sign (`$`).

(b) Display a message after the successful completion of every command.

12.5 Modify the simple text editor program so that an arbitrary number of spaces can be used in command lines (except inside the `%` signs of an `F` command).

12.6 Add an extra command called `A` to the simple text editor which allows the user to type nine new lines at once, each terminated by pressing the ENTER key. The first line typed becomes the new text line number 1, the second becomes new text line number 2, and so on. Print out suitable error messages if things go wrong.

12.7 By using suitable `EQU` pseudo-ops, make it possible to change the letter names of the commands by changing just a few lines at the start of the program.

12.8 Add pattern-matching facilities to the `F` command so that, for example, the command:

```
F%D?G%
```

would locate all three-letter words beginning with D and ending with G.

12.9 Tidy up the design of the simple text editor so that:

(a) If the command

```
S11
```

is given, no swap is actually carried out.

(b) If a user tries to include a `%` sign in the search string in an `F` command, as in:

```
F%30% INCREASE%
```

then the error message correctly reports that this is what has been done. (Try the above command to see what response the editor gives at the moment.)

12.10 Make the text find and replacement facilities more like those available from your own particular text editor or word processing software.

SUMMARY

This chapter has demonstrated the considerable advantage that the 8086-family primitive string manipulation instructions afford the programmer: not because they execute faster than the equivalent self-programmed instructions (which they do), but because they simplify the coding of complicated algorithms so much. `SWAP`, `FIND` and `LOCATE` were particular examples of this. Hopefully, to the diligent reader, this chapter will also have further vindicated the use of pseudo-Pascal both as a creative tool and as an efficient and effective means of program documentation.

SELF-CHECK QUIZ

1. Write a subroutine which allows a new character to be inserted as the *n*th character of a string stored in memory.

2. Write a subroutine which displays the *n*th character of a string stored in memory.

3. Write a subroutine which deletes the *n*th character of a string stored in memory.

4. Write a subroutine which swaps two characters of a string stored in memory.

5. Write a subroutine which mimics the operation of `SHL` for a string stored in memory.

6. Write a subroutine which mimics the operation of `ROL` for a string stored in memory.

7. Write a subroutine which mimics the operation of `TEST` for two strings stored in memory, the two operands being of the same length.

8. Which other string manipulation instructions would you like there to be in the 8086-family instruction set? Give reasons.

9. How many different ways can you think of for initializing a collection of locations to the ASCII code for a space (20H)? Illustrate each method.

10. How many different ways can you think of for searching one string for the first occurrence of another? Illustrate each method.

13 Addressing Modes and Instruction Encoding

Contents

This chapter examines the different ways in which an 8086-family microprocessor instruction can specify the data items on which an instruction is to operate. These different ways are referred to as **addressing modes**. We shall study 8086-family addressing modes in relation to the problem of implementing the machine code generation phase of a compiler for a high-level language such as Pascal. The 8086-family machine code instruction formats are highly dependent on these addressing modes and so in turn is the way in which 8086-family assembly language instructions are encoded into binary. Section 13.2 describes the encoding process itself, since an understanding of it is vital to someone who has to write an 8086-family assembler or debugger.

13.1 Addressing modes

The designers of the 8086 family of microprocessors had the convenient implementation of high-level language data types, control constructs and sub-program mechanisms as one of their major objectives. This is reflected in the

General-purpose 16-bit registers		*General purpose 8-bit registers*		
AX	=	AH	+	AL
BX	=	BH	+	BL
CX	=	CH	+	CL
DX	=	DH	+	DL
SI				
DI				
SP				
BP				

Segment registers	*Other 16-bit registers*
At least: CS	IP
DS	
SS	Flags
ES	

Figure 13.1
A summary of registers common to all members of the 8086 family.

choice of **addressing modes** which the designers made available, namely: **register**, **immediate**, **direct**, **register indirect**, **direct indexed**, **base relative** and **base indexed** addressing modes. In this section each of them will be considered in turn.

13.1.1 Register addressing

Microprocessors in the 8086 family have eight general-purpose 16-bit registers, eight general-purpose 8-bit registers related to four of the 16-bit registers, at least four segment registers, the flags register and the IP register (which the programmer cannot access directly) as summarized in Figure 13.1.

If every instruction operand is fetched from or moved into a register then an instruction is said to employ **register addressing** mode. Thus:

```
MOV AL,BL
INC BX
DEC AL
SUB DX,CX
```

are all examples of instructions using register addressing.

Instructions which affect only registers execute faster than instructions involving memory access, as no time is spent fetching operands. Consequently, a good Pascal compiler will endeavour to ensure that data items required in repeatedly executed sections of a program are held in registers whenever possible.

Thus, if *a* and *b* are identifiers corresponding to integer variables, then by the time it comes to executing:

a := 4; *b* := 3;
for *i* := 1 **to** 10000 **do**
begin
code[*i*] := *code*[*a*] + *code*[*b*];
a := *a* + 2;
b := *b* + 1
end

a Pascal compiler would have already assigned memory locations to *i*, *a* and *b*, but would *try* to arrange that the values of *i*, *a*, and *b* are moved into registers for the duration of the **for** loop execution.

13.1.2 Immediate addressing

In **immediate addressing** mode the data item on which the instruction is to operate is stored as part of the instruction in memory. Thus, the instruction

```
MOV CL,61H
```

uses immediate addressing mode because the data item on which it operates, 61H, is stored as part of the machine code version of the instruction which, in hexadecimal, is:

B1 61

0B1H being the **opcode**, the binary code which corresponds to assembly language statements of the form:

`MOV CL,`*8-bit number*

and 61H being the 8-bit number.

During the normal 8086-family execution sequence, `MOV CL,61H` is moved into the instruction queue from memory prior to actual execution. Since the immediate operand (61H) is stored as part of the instruction itself (0B161H) the immediate operand is thus fetched from memory at the same time as the instruction itself, once again reducing execution time.

The same is true for 16-bit immediate operands. For example, in:

```
MOV DI,2AB4H
```

the immediate operand 2AB4H forms part of the machine code version of this assembly language instruction:

BF 2AB4

and so the operand is fetched from memory at the same time as the instruction itself.

13.1.3 Direct addressing

Direct addressing mode is similar except that in this case the effective *address* of one of the operands is taken directly from the instruction. Consider the instruction

```
MOV AX,TOTAL
```

in which TOTAL corresponds to the location with offset 210H relative to DS. The machine code version of this instruction is

A1 1002

Since 1002 is the memory representation of 0210H, MOV AX,TOTAL is an instruction which uses direct addressing mode.

Only one operand of an instruction may be directly addressed, so that if *total* and *item_sum* are identifiers of two Pascal integer variables which we assume are represented in signed 16-bit form then, for optimal execution speed not involving arithmetic in registers, the Pascal

total := *total* + *item_sum*

could be coded by a compiler using two directly addressed instructions:

```
MOV AX,ITEM_SUM
ADD TOTAL,AX
```

(where ITEM_SUM and TOTAL are the locations corresponding to the Pascal identifiers *item_sum* and *total* respectively).

Also, given

const *taxrate* = 30;
var *total*:*integer*;

.
.
.

begin

.
.
.

end

the Pascal statement *total* := *taxrate* could be coded using immediate and direct addressing thus:

```
MOV AX,30D
MOV TOTAL,AX
```

(where we assume that TOTAL is a word in memory corresponding to the Pascal integer *total*).

13.1.4 Register indirect addressing

In an instruction which employs **register indirect addressing** mode, the effective address is found in either the BX, BP, SI or DI register. In other words, the effective address is not found directly from the instruction itself but *indirectly* by accessing a register, as in

```
SUB DX,[BX]
```

A Pascal compiler may use indirect addressing for manipulating pointers. For example, given:

type *customer* = *record*
name:**array**[1..30] **of** *char*;
address:**array**[1..50] **of** *char*
end;

customers= *file of customer*;

var *mail_list*:*customers*;

then BX could be used to point to successive records in the *mail_list* file so that the assembly language `[BX]` corresponds to the Pascal *mail_list*^.

13.1.5 Direct indexed addressing

We should first observe that authors often differ in the names they give to the various addressing modes. Of course, the correct names are those given to the modes by the creators of the 8086 family, Intel Corporation. But writers often believe they can makes things clearer to their readers by choosing their own names. The addressing mode described in this section which we will call **direct indexed addressing** is a good example. While we are certainly not alone in using this name, many other authors call this **indexed addressing**. Our name allows us to emphasize the relation between this addressing mode and another one, called based indirect addressing, which shall be described in due course.

An instruction which uses *direct indexed addressing* mode obtains its data item from, or stores its data item in, an address which is the sum of the contents of an index register (DI or SI) and a signed 8-bit number or an unsigned 16-bit number. Thus,

```
MOV AX,[SI+4]
ADD [DI-6],CX
MUL WORD PTR [SI-192]
```

are all examples of instructions which use direct indexed addressing.

In `MOV AX,[SI+4]`, the offset (relative to DS) of the data item to be moved into AX is found by adding 4 to the contents of SI. In `ADD [DI-6],CX` the offset relative to DS specifying the data item to which the contents of CX are to be added is found by subtracting 6 from the contents of DI.

Alternative forms

8086-family assembly language actually requires instructions which use direct indexed addressing mode to be written in forms such as:

```
MOV AX,[SI+36]
MOV [SI-27],AX
```

but MASM also allows the alternative forms

```
MOV AX,36[SI]
MOV -27[SI],AX
MOV AX,[SI]36
MOV [SI]-27,AX
```

Moreover, if `TOTAL` is defined by a pseudo-op of the form

```
TOTAL DW. . .
```

and corresponds to offset 204H (say) from DS, then given the instruction

```
MOV AX,TOTAL[BX]
```

MASM will assemble this into the machine code equivalent of

```
MOV AX,[BX+204]
```

Some justification for the existence of direct indexed addressing mode

Consider implementing the Pascal assignment

account[*i*] := *total*

where we have

var
i,*total*:*integer*;
account,*daily_balance*:**array**[1..*limit_constant*] **of** *integer*;

Suppose further that the array *account* is stored in signed 16-bit form in consecutive locations corresponding to the MASM variable `ACCOUNT` starting with *account*[1]; that the value of *i* is in register SI; and that the MASM variable `TOTAL` corresponds to *total*. Then

```
MOV AX,TOTAL
MOV ACCOUNT[SI],AX
```

is equivalent to

account[*i*] := *total*

The facilitation of the compilation of such high-level language array accesses is precisely the reason that the 8086 family has direct indexed addressing mode, where the effective address is calculated as '*index register contents* + *displacement*'. An assignment of the form

account[*i*] := *daily_balance*[*j*]

requires two index registers (which is one reason why the 8086 family has SI and DI), and if we assume the value of *j* is in register DI, then

```
MOV AX,DAILY_BALANCE[DI]
MOV ACCOUNT[SI],AX
```

is the assembly language equivalent of *account*[*i*] := *daily_balance*[*j*] (assuming suitable arrangements with regard to segment registers). Similarly

for *i* := 1 **to** 10 **do** *balance*[*i*] := *balance*[*i*] − *credit*[*i*] + *debit*[*i*];

could be implemented

```
              MOV  CX,10D
              MOV  SI,1
NEXT_BALANCE: MOV  AX,BALANCE[SI]
              SUB  AX,CREDIT[SI]
              ADD  AX,DEBIT[SI]
              MOV  BALANCE[SI],AX
              INC  SI
              INC  SI
              LOOP NEXT_BALANCE
```

13.1.6 Base relative addressing

In **base relative addressing** mode, the offset of a data item is found by adding a signed 8-bit or unsigned 16-bit number to the contents of a base register (BX or BP). Thus

```
MOV AX,[BX-3]
SUB [BP+4],5
```

are examples of instructions which employ base relative addressing mode. MASM also allows these instructions to be written in the alternative forms, such as

```
MOV AX,[BX]-3
MOV AX,-3[BX]
```

Of course, addresses given in BX are taken relative to DS whereas those in BP are taken relative to SS.

In order to see why this addressing mode is provided, consider the Pascal declarations:

type *marks* = *record*
student_number:*integer*;
math:*integer*;
french:*integer*;
physics:*integer*;
geography:*integer*;
biology:*integer*;
end;
exam = *file of marks*;
var *year*1:*exam*;

and a related Pascal program fragment to find the average physics mark in year 1:

sum := 0; *count* := 0;
while not *eof* **do**
begin
get(*year*1);
sum := *sum* + *year*1^.*physics*;

```
    count := count + 1
    end;
  if count <> 0 then
    writeln('average physics mark is', sum/count)
```

To access the record component *year*1^.*physics* in the machine code equivalent of this fragment, base relative addressing mode is used.

The *physics* component of a marks record will be stored in the word corresponding to the 6th and 7th bytes of that record (see Figure 13.2), numbering bytes in a record as 0,1,2,3,. . . Hence, if BX is used to point to the beginning of successive records in the *year*1 file so that [BX] corresponds to *year*1^, then the word at [BX+6] corresponds to *year*1^.*physics* and

```
sum := sum + year1^.physics
```

could be implemented as:

```
MOV AX,SUM
ADD AX,[BX+6]
MOV SUM,AX
```

For the less powerful members of the 8086 family, direct indexed addressing and base relative addressing amount to the same thing: both involve the format *register + displacement*. However, there is actually a big *conceptual* advantage to be gained by thinking of them as different. And when we come to study the 80386 chip and more powerful members of the 8086 family in Chapter 23 we shall see that, for these microprocessors, there is a genuine difference between the two modes.

The best way to think of direct indexed addressing is that it is used to

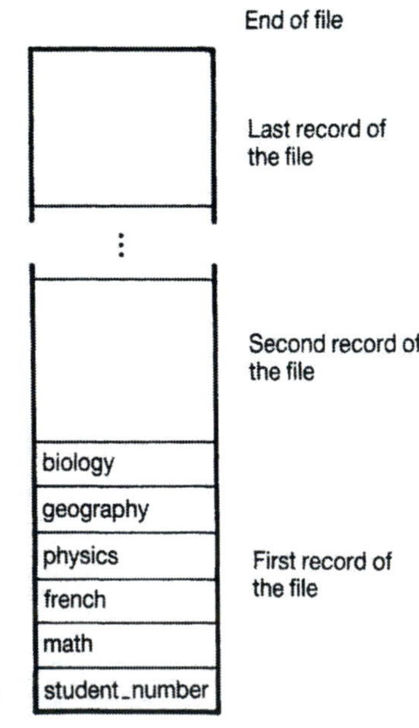

Figure 13.2
The file *year*1.

access successive elements of an array, the displacement corresponding to the start of the array and the register specifying the particular element within that array. Base relative addressing, on the other hand, allows access to an individual component of a record in a file, the base register corresponding to the start of the record and the displacement specifying the particular component in that record.

13.1.7 Base indexed addressing

An instruction which uses **base indexed addressing** mode obtains its data item from, or stores its data item at, an address which is obtained by adding together the contents of a base register and an index register and, optionally, an 8-bit (or 16-bit) signed (respectively, unsigned) number added to that. Thus

```
MOV AX,[BX+DI]
MOV [BX+SI+2],AX
INC BYTE PTR [BP+SI-45]
```

are all examples of instructions which use base indexed addressing mode.

In `MOV AX,[BX+DI]` the data item will be moved from the location having offset relative to DS obtained by adding the contents of the BX and DI registers. In `INC BYTE PTR [BP+SI-45]` the location whose contents are to be incremented will have offset relative to SS obtained by adding the contents of BP to the contents of SI and then subtracting 45.

As with the direct indexed and base relative addressing modes, MASM allows alternative forms of instruction which employ base indexed mode. Thus, all three terms may be in brackets in any order or the signed 8- or 16-bit number may be combined with either register. Thus:

```
MOV AX,[BX+SI+2]
MOV AX,[SI+BX+2]
MOV AX,[SI][BX+2]
MOV AX,[BX][SI+2]
MOV AX,2[BX][SI]
```

would all be assembled by MASM into the same machine code instruction.

Based indexed addressing mode is provided to assist in the accessing of records in a file which contain array fields. Consider the Pascal declarations

> **type** *classrecord* = *record*
> *student_number*:*integer*;
> *age*:*integer*;
> *coursework_marks*:**array**[1..20] **of** *integer*;
> *exam_average*:*integer*
> **end**;
>
> **var** *class_file*:**file of** *classrecord*;

and suppose that we want to find the average total coursework mark for all students whose details are held in *class_file* (see Figure 13.3.).

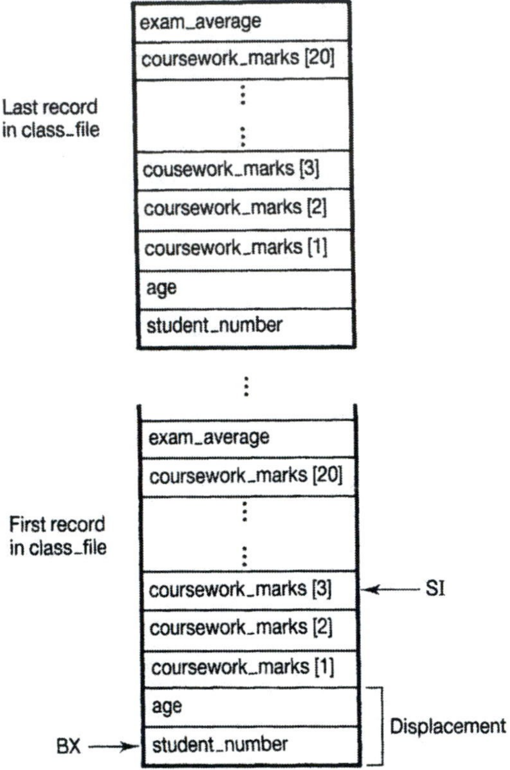

Figure 13.3 `ADD AX,[BX+SI+`*displacement*`]` used to access elements of a record of a file.

Assuming that, within each record, the array *coursework_marks* is held in bytes 4 to 43 inclusive (numbering bytes in a record 0,1,2,3,4,. . . as usual), then the body of the **for** loop in:

> *get*(*class_file*); *no_of_students* := 0; *sum* := 0;
> **while not** *eof* **do**
> **begin**
>   *no_of_students* := *no_of_students* + 1;
>   **for** *i* := 1 **to** 20 **do**
>   *sum* := *sum* + *class_file*ˆ.*course_work_marks*[*i*];
>   *get*(*class_file*)
> **end**

could be implemented by using the base register BX to hold the starting address of this particular record (that is, corresponding to *class_file*ˆ), and having the index register SI point to each particular array element to be added. Thus:

```
ADD AX,[BX+SI+4]
```

would correspond to

sum := *sum* + *class_file*ˆ.*course_work_marks*[*i*];

(see Figure 13.3).

13.1.8 A summary of 8086-family addressing modes

This completes our introduction to the 8086-family addressing modes. The details are summarized for easy reference in Table 13.1.

13.1.9 Addressing modes involving BP

In a Pascal compiler, indirect addressing can be useful for matching formal parameters and actual parameters and controlling the allocation of memory to procedures. Procedures in Pascal are **re-entrant**: that is, they may be **invoked** (called up) while already in execution from a previous invocation. This could occur, for example, if a procedure were recursive (and so invoked itself) or if it invoked some other procedure which in turn invoked the original procedure.

The main consequence of this is that both the parameters and any local variables must be assigned to a unique set of memory locations – one for each concurrent invocation. Otherwise the data being used by one invocation might be corrupted by a subsequent invocation. Thus, memory must be allocated for

Table 13.1 8086-family addressing modes.

Addressing mode	*Operand format*	*Example*
register	*reg*	MOV AX,BX
immediate	*data*	MOV AX,31
direct	*disp*	MOV AX,TOTAL
register indirect	[BX]	
	[BP]	
	[SI]	
	[DI]	MOV AX,[BX]
direct indexed	[SI]+*disp*	
	[DI]+*disp*	MOV AX,TOTAL[SI]
base relative	[BX]+*disp*	
	[BP]+*disp*	MOV AX,[BP]4
base indexed	[BX][SI]+*disp*	
	[BX][DI]+*disp*	
	[BP][SI]+*disp*	
	[BP][DI]+*disp*	MOV AX,[BX+SI+3]

Note: *reg* is any 8- or 16-bit register except IP
data is an 8- or 16-bit constant value
disp is an 8- or 16-bit signed number, and is optional for base indexed addressing.

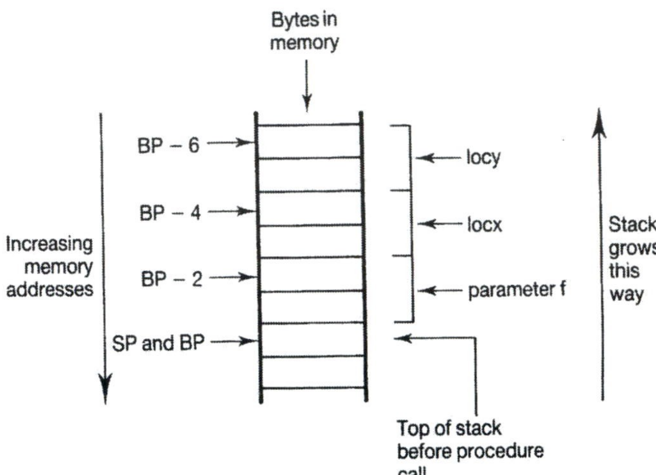

Figure 13.4 Activation record implementation for *proc example*.

a procedure's data items (parameters and local variables) every time the procedure is called. The collection of memory locations allocated in this way is called an **activation record**. Because the memory used by a procedure is released when execution of that procedure terminates, Pascal compilers usually arrange to keep activation records on the stack: this is a natural consequence of the fact that the last procedure invoked will be the first to finish execution. (We have already encountered this idea in all but name when we discussed the passing of parameters to subroutines via the stack, in Section 8.7).

Each time a Pascal procedure is invoked, an appropriate block of memory is reserved for the activation record on the top of the stack by changing the contents of the SP register. During execution, BP is used to remember where the activation record begins. Access to items within the activation record can then be arranged by the addressing modes which use BP. For example, as we saw in Section 8.7, [BP+*disp*] can be used to access a simple parameter within the activation record.

To be specific, consider the declarations

proc example(**var** *f*:*integer*);
var *locx*,*locy*:*integer*
begin
.
.
.
end;
var *a*:*integer*;

Clearly, the assembly language or machine code equivalent of *example* produced by a compiler cannot use any specific address corresponding to the variable *f* since this will not be known until a call such as

example(*a*)

Table 13.2 Use of memory addressing modes to implement Pascal and similar high-level languages (*disp* is an unsigned 16-bit number).

	Ordinary	*Pointer*	*Activation Record*
Variables of type *integer* and *char*	direct	BX	BP+*disp*
Arrays	SI+*disp* DI+*disp*	BX+SI BX+DI	BP+SI+*disp* BP+DI+*disp*
Individual records	direct	BX+*disp*	BP+*disp*
Arrays within records	SI+*disp* DI+*disp*	BX+SI+*disp* BX+DI+*disp*	BP+SI+*disp* BP+SI+*disp*

occurs and the actual parameter (*a*) corresponding to the formal parameter (*f*) is known.

At the point of invocation, code will be generated by the Pascal compiler to put an activation record on the stack consisting of just three words: one for the *integer* parameter and two for the local integer variables *locx* and *locy*. If the address of the start of the activation record is put into BP then indirect addressing can be used to refer to the parameter in the form `[BP]` (using the fact that indirect addressing with BP is relative to SS) and the local variables can be referred to using `[BP-4]` and `[BP-6]` (see Figure 13.4).

The uses of addressing modes in the implementation of high-level languages like Pascal are summarized in Table 13.2. It has three columns, one for ordinary variables of each type, one for pointers to variables of that type, and one for a corresponding activation record.

EXERCISES

13.1 For each of the following say whether it is a valid 8086-family assembly language instruction and then submit the whole text to MASM to verify your answers.

```
ADD AX,[BX+CX+2]
SUB DX,[BX+BP+8]
SUB CH,[BX+20487]
MOV [BX+SI+2],AL
MOV [BH+SI+32],DL
MOV AX,[12+SI+BP]
ADD [SI]TOTAL,3
SUB [DI+3+BP],2
ADD 3[DI+BP],2
ADC 3[DI][BP],2
SBC TOTAL[DI][BP],2
```

13.2 Make a survey of the number of times each addressing mode is used in each of the complete example programs given in Appendices II and III. (If you want to do this in a really sophisticated way, write an 8086-family assembly language program to do it automatically.)

13.3 Find a Pascal (or other, similar, high-level language) textbook and choose a few example programs spread throughout the book. For every executable statement in each of your chosen programs decide which would be the most appropriate addressing mode(s) for a compiler's 8086-family code generation phase to adopt for that statement.

13.4 In Pascal, or another, similar, high-level language with which you are familiar, write programs for each of the following tasks and then write, test and debug 8086-family assembly language equivalents using addressing modes which a compiler's machine code generation phase might be expected to employ:

(a) Given a collection of ages in the range 1 to 101 terminated by the sentinel −99, print out the number of occurrences of each age.

(b) Input a series of dates expressed in the form ddmmyy and print the most frequently occurring year, month and day.

(c) Input a series of dates in the form ddmmyy and, for each date, the sales of each of 50 different products. For each product print the date on which sales of that product were highest. If the highest sales figure was achieved on more than one day, print the most recent date.

13.2 Instruction encoding

This section takes a brief look at 8086-family machine code instruction formats. From the point of view of learning about the architecture of the 8086 family this is interesting in its own right, but the inclusion of this section has three other motivating factors. First, the implementor of a new 8086-family assembler or debugger (with, of course, all kinds of fancy programmer productivity aids not available in those already on the market) needs to know about them. Second, it does help to explain the decoding process – mnemonic to binary – carried out by MASM. Last, but not least, encoding is one of the essential tasks carried out by an assembler – as we shall see in the next chapter.

Full details of how 8086-family microprocessor instructions are encoded in binary are given in Appendix V. There, an encoding pattern is shown for each instruction. This pattern needs completion depending on the actual operands and addressing mode used. Consequently, it is only necessary to

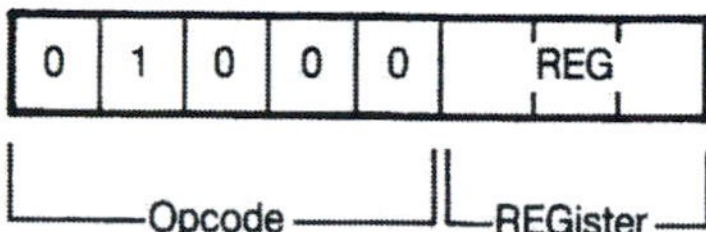

Figure 13.5 Format of single operand instruction where the operand is in a 16-bit register.

explain here how to complete one of these patterns for a given instruction. In fact there are two types of pattern: one for single operand instructions and one for two operand instructions. We shall consider each of these two types in turn.

13.2.1 Single operand instructions

Instructions such as `INC`, `DEC`, `MUL`, `DIV` and `NOT` require a single operand. To illustrate how to complete the patterns in Appendix V for such single operand instructions we shall consider `INC` which is quite typical. Our first illustration will be the encoding of `INC` when it is used in register addressing mode and then the encoding of `INC` employed in direct or indirect addressing mode.

In fact there are two encoding patterns for `INC` given in Appendix V, a short form for when `INC` is used in register addressing mode and the register concerned is a 16-bit register (in which case the encoded instruction occupies just a single byte), and a more general pattern. The first of these is reproduced in Figure 13.5.

The five left-most bits in the byte are used as a code – in this case 01000 – to denote the `INC` instruction used in this addressing mode with a 16-bit operand. The remaining three bits – the REG field – specify which register is to be used as an operand according to Table 13.3. Thus, the encoded form of `INC BX` is 01000 011 or 43H.

As we know, in its most general form `INC` can increment the contents of 8- and 16-bit registers as well as the contents of directly and indirectly addressed memory locations. The encoding pattern for this more general form occupies two bytes and can also be found in Appendix V: we have reproduced the second, more general, pattern shown there as Figure 13.6.

Table 13.3 Encoding of the REG instruction field.

REG	*16-bit register operand*	*8-bit register operand*
000	AX	AL
001	CX	CL
010	DX	DL
011	BX	BL
100	SP	AH
101	BP	CH
110	SI	DH
111	DI	BH

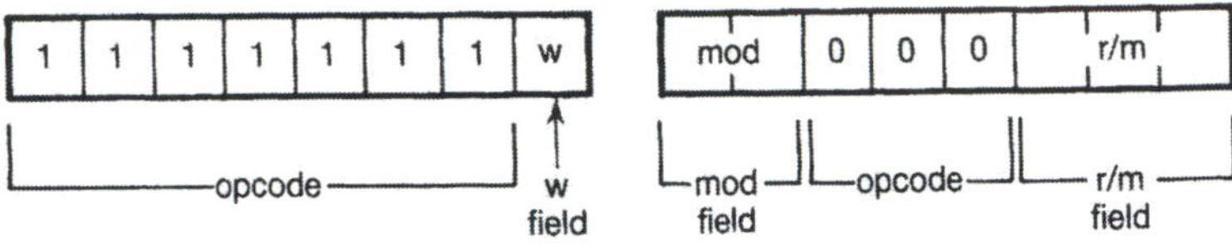

Figure 13.6 General form of a single operand instruction where the operand is in a register or memory.

In this case the opcode (1111111000) is split into two blocks, the first block of seven bits being contained in the first byte and the remaining three bits in the second byte. The **w field** specifies whether the operand is 8 (w = 0) or 16 (w = 1) bits (w specifies the *width* of the operand) whereas the **mod field** specifies whether the operand is in a register (mod = 11) or memory (mod <> 11).

If the operand is in a register, the **r/m field** is interpreted as a REG field and so specifies which register is to contain the operand using the encoding in Table 13.3. For example, `INC DH` is encoded 11111111 11000111 (w = 1, mod = 11, r/m = 110 and the `INC` opcode is 1111111000).

If the operand is in memory (that is, we are using direct or indirect addressing) the r/m field specifies base and index registers (as shown in Table 13.4) and the mod field specifies the displacement from a base or index register or from DS if direct addressing is being used (as shown in Table 13.5).

To summarize:

w	specifies the width of the operand
mod	specifies whether the operand is in a register or memory and where any displacement is to be found
r/m	specifies which register or which addressing mode

Thus, `INC BYTE PTR [BX-4]` is encoded as 0FE47FCH:

1111111	0	01	000	111	11111100
opcode	w	mod	opcode	r/m	additional third byte specifying displacement (−4 in two's complement)

and `INC MY_LOCATION`, where `MY_LOCATION` is a MASM byte variable with offset 01A3H from DS, as 0FE0601A3H:

1111111	0	00	000	110	00000001 10100011
opcode	w	mod	opcode	r/m	16-bit offset

Addressing modes field encoding is summarized in Table 13.6.

Table 13.4 Encoding of the r/m field when mod <> 11 (otherwise code r/m as for the REG field in Table 13.3).

r/m	*Base register*	*Index register*
000	BX	SI
001	BX	DI
010	BP	SI
011	BP	DI
100	–	SI
101	–	DI
110 if mod = 00	the instruction contains two additional bytes specifying an offset address from DS	
else	BP	–
111	BX	–

Table 13.5 Encoding of the mod field.

mod	*displacement (if any)*
00	0000H
01	instruction contains an additional byte and the displacement is the 8-bit signed contents of that byte sign-extended to 16-bits
10	instruction contains two additional bytes specifying an unsigned 16-bit displacement
11	operand is in a register

Table 13.6 Use of registers in direct and indirect addressing modes (*d* is a signed 8-bit number; *n* is an unsigned 16-bit number; and *address* is an unsigned 16-bit offset derived from a MASM variable).

	mod				
	00	01	10	11	
r/m				*w* = 0	*w* = 1
000	[BX+SI]	[BX+SI+d]	[BX+SI+n]	AL	AX
001	[BX+DI]	[BX+DI+d]	[BX+DI+n]	CL	CX
010	[BP+SI]	[BP+SI+d]	[BP+SI+n]	DL	DX
011	[BP+DI]	[BP+DI+d]	[BP+DI+n]	BL	BX
100	[SI]	[SI+d]	[SI+n]	AH	SP
101	[DI]	[DI+d]	[DI+n]	CH	BP
110	address	[BP+d]	[BP+n]	DH	SI
111	[BX]	[BX+d]	[BX+n]	BH	DI

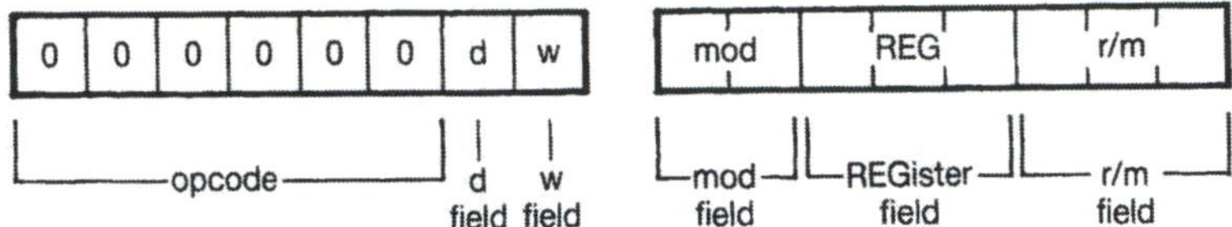

Figure 13.7 General form of the ADD instruction for register addition.

13.2.2 Two operand instructions

Instructions such as MOV, ADD and TEST all take two operands. At the design stage of the 8086-family it was decided to insist that, in any instruction requiring two operands, one of them would have to be a register. In this way the maximum length of an 8086 instruction was restricted to six bytes. As before, we can look up the general pattern for encoding a register-to-register ADD instruction from Appendix V. This is reproduced in Figure 13.7. and contains a new encoding field – the **d** (destination) **field**.

The d field determines whether the REG field specifies where an operand should be obtained *from* (d = 0) or whether the result should be sent *to* the place specified by the REG field (d = 1). Thus, the encoding of ADD BL,DH is 02DEH:

000000	10	11	011	110
opcode	dw	mod	REG	r/m

(the d field indicating that the result is to be sent *to* the operand referred to by the REG field) and the encoding of ADD MY_LOCATION,DX (where MY_LOCATION is a MASM variable having offset 0A2BCH from DS) is 0116A2BCH:

000000	01	00	010	110	10100010 10111100
opcode	dw	mod	REG	r/m	offset address

(the d-field indicating that an operand is to be obtained *from* the place specified by the REG field).

Two operand instructions have only one w field so the operands must either both be 8 bits or both be 16 bits wide. For the purposes of arithmetic, immediate operands are often representable in signed 8-bit form, so to reduce the length of some 8086-family immediate-operand instructions, the **s** (sign-extend) **field** is used. The field only has significance for 16-bit operands (that is, when w = 1) and specifies whether all 16 bits of the immediate operand are contained in the instruction (s = 0) or whether only the eight least significant bits are contained in the instruction (s = 1) which must therefore be sign-extended to a signed 16-bit equivalent.

To summarize:

d = 0 result goes *from* the operand specified by REG

d = 1 result goes *to* the place specified by REG

and if w = 1 then

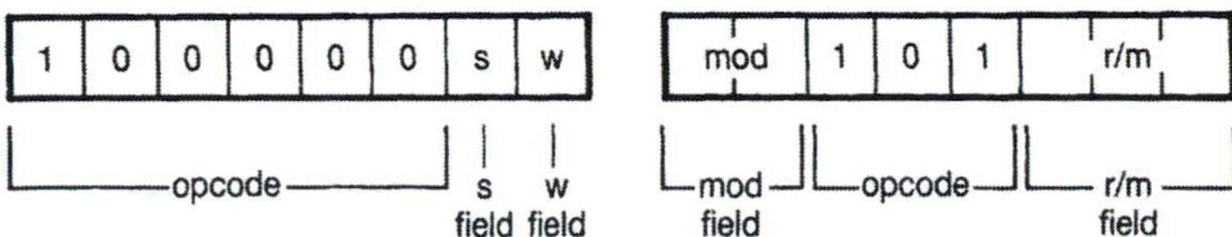

Figure 13.8 Encoding of a SUB instruction when the two operands are an immediate operand and a register (not AX) or memory operand.

s = 0 indicates all 16 bits of the immediate operand are present

s = 1 sign-extend the eight given bits of the immediate operand to get a full 16-bit operand

Consider the general encoding of the SUB instruction in the case where the two operands are an immediate operand and a register (not AX) or memory operand, as shown in Figure 13.8 (which, once again, has been copied from Appendix V).

From this, it follows that the encoding of `SUB BX,14H` is

100000	11	11	101	011	00001110
opcode	sw	mod	opcode	r/m	immediate operand

and that the encoding of `SUB MY_LOCATION,31H` (where `MY_LOCATION` is a MASM word variable with offset 0200H from DS) is:

100000	11	00	101	110	00000010 00000000	00110001
opcode	sw	mod	opcode	r/m	address-offset	immediate operand

Similarly, for the encoding of `SUB MY_LOCATION,SI` we need the appropriate general pattern from Appendix V, as reproduced in Figure 13.9. From the figure it follows that the encoding of `SUB MY_LOCATION,SI` (where `MY_LOCATION` is a MASM word variable with offset 0200H from DS) is:

001010	01	00	110	110	00000010 00000000
opcode	dw	mod	REG	r/m	address-offset

and that the encoding of `SUB SI,MY_LOCATION` is:

001010	11	00	110	110	00000010 00000000
opcode	dw	mod	REG	r/m	address-offset

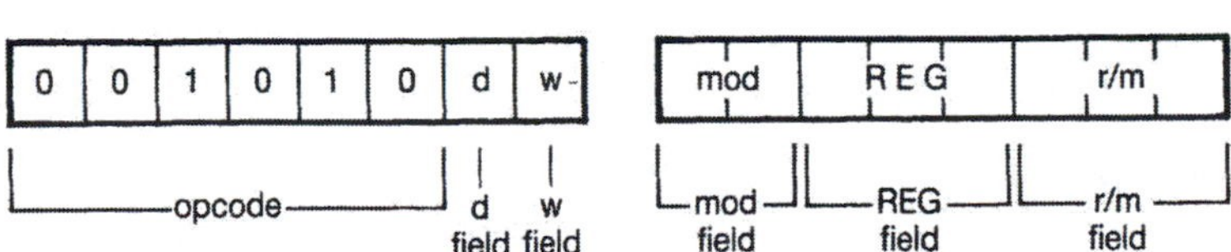

Figure 13.9 Encoding of a SUB instruction when neither of the two operands is an immediate operand.

EXERCISES

13.5 Appendix V contains a summary of 8086-family instruction coding. Use it to encode the following program fragment. Check your answer using MASM.

```
      INC  SI
      MOV  CX,0
      INC  AH
      MOV  CL,4
      SUB  AH,CL
      JZ   TEMP
      MOV  MY_LOCATION,CX
      AND  BX,[BP+SI+14]
      CALL TEMP
      IDIV BX
TEMP: SBB  BX,MY_LOCATION
      SUB  CX,[BX]
      ADD  BYTE PTR MY_LOCATION[DI],21
      LOOP TEMP
      RET
```

13.6 Encode the following assembly language instructions:

```
           MOV  BH,0
           SUB  SI,6D
           MOV  DI,23ABH
           ADC  CX,17D
MOVE_NEXT:MOV   AL,[SI]
           OR   AL,30H
           CMP  BH,1
           JZ   LABEL3
           TEST AL,30H
           JNZ  LABEL2
           MOV  AL,' '
           JMP  LABEL3
   LABEL2: MOV  BH,1
   LABEL3: MOV  [DI],AL
           DEC  SI
           DEC  BYTE PTR [DI]
           CMP  CX,3D
           JLE  LABEL4
           MUL  DI
   LABEL4: LOOP LABEL1
```

13.7 Decode each of the following 8086-family machine code instructions into equivalent assembly language instructions:

FE C8
B3 41
F6 E3
D3 D0
B4 09

```
CD 21
C6 06 0202 01
BA 0145
A0 0202
FE C8
B3 0E
B4 01
2C 30
50
```

SUMMARY

In this chapter we have studied 8086-family addressing modes in the context of implementing a compiler for a high-level language such as Pascal, and 8086-family instruction encoding – one of the vital processes undertaken by an 8086-family assembler like MASM. Both of these are features to which the 8086-family designers will have given considerable thought, since the ultimate utility and power of a microprocessor is highly dependent upon the range and nature of its addressing modes and on the related instruction encoding scheme.

SELF-CHECK QUIZ

1. Identify the addressing mode used in each of the following instructions:

   (a) `MOV AX,BX`

   (b) `MOV AX,[BX]`

   (c) `MOV CX,[BX+10]`

   (d) `MOV AL,[BP+SI+2]`

   (e) `MOV AL,24H`

   (f) `MOV AL,MY_LOC`

2. For each of the seven addressing modes, write a subroutine which examines a string representing an assembly language instruction stored in memory and determines whether or not the instruction uses that addressing mode.

3. Are all the addressing modes absolutely essential? Which, if any, could be removed from the 8086-family instruction repertoire without restricting the range of programs that could be executed (though possibly at the cost of some programmer inconvenience).

4. Which (if any) of the following are true statements:

   (a) The roles of BP and BX are completely interchangeable.

   (b) The roles of BP and SP are completely interchangeable.

   (c) The roles of SI and DI are completely interchangeable.

(d) The roles of BX and SI are completely interchangeable.

5. Consider a computerised hotel room booking system in which a record is kept for each customer with details of name, address, nationality, room number, meals consumed, and so on. Write program fragments to illustrate how each of the 8086-family addressing modes can be of use in constructing such a system.

6. The cost of manufacturing *n* items of a certain commodity is given by the formula:

   cost of manufacture in dollars =
   $(((a + b) * n)/100) + 1375$

   Write a subroutine to leave this cost as an unsigned 32-bit number in DX,AX, given the parameters *a*,*b*, and *n* on the stack as unsigned 16-bit numbers.

7. Encode the instructions:

```
ADC AX,BX
```

and

```
ADC BX,AX
```

8. Which assembly language instructions would generate the following encoded `MOV` instructions:

   (a) 8B 07 (b) 8B 00 (c) 8B 42 02
   (d) B8 24 10

9. Assuming that `MY_LABEL` has offset address 30B0H, give the machine code for the following instructions, assuming that each instruction has an offset of 30A0H :

   (a) `JNZ MY_LABEL`

   (b) `JB MY_LABEL`

   (c) `JMP MY_LABEL`

   What changes will be necessary if the instruction has an offset of 30C0 instead?

10. Encode the instructions:

   (a) `SUB AX,BX`

   (b) `SUB AX,[BX]`

   (c) `SUB CX,[BX+10]`

   (d) `SUB AL,[BP+SI+2]`

Modular Programming

14

Contents

This chapter studies modular programming which simplifies the programming task by allowing us to construct a large program by combining smaller ones called **modules**. These modules are then linked together by the linker to form the final executable program. Consequently, the linker and the pseudo-ops used to control its operation will be examined in more detail. Before this, the operation of an 8086-family assembler is examined as an essential step in understanding certain assembly language instructions, as well as in appreciating the role of the linker sufficiently to comprehend its role in achieving modular programming. (Knowledge of the assembly process is also vital in order to use some of the more advanced features provided by 8086-family assembly language.)

14.1 8086-family assemblers – how they work

This section examines the assembly process by giving a much simplified account of the way an assembler such as MASM converts assembly language source programs into **object modules** ready for the linker. Even though reference is continually made to MASM, much of what is said applies to other popular 8086-family assemblers too.

14.1.1 The assembly process

MASM scans the source assembly language program we give it twice, and hence is called a **two-pass assembler**. Consider the assembly language fragment:

```
DATA SEGMENT
        EXAM_RESULTS DB 100H DUP(?)
        SUM   DB ?
        TOTAL DW ?
        COUNT DB 23H
      .
      .
      .
DATA ENDS
      .
      .
      .
CODE SEGMENT
ASSUME CS:CODE,DS:DATA,SS:WORKING_STORAGE
START: MOV AX,DATA
       MOV DS,AX
       MOV CX,COUNT
 NEXT: DEC CX
      .
      .
      .
```

This contains various **symbols** which represent numeric or character values. These include EXAM_RESULTS, SUM, TOTAL, COUNT, DATA, START and NEXT. The purpose of MASM's first pass is to work out the locations corresponding to these symbols, and then the second pass uses this information to generate the **object code** equivalent. Object code is machine code in which some actual addresses (as opposed to offsets) have yet to be determined.

To work out the locations corresponding to symbols in the source assembly language, MASM uses a variable known as the **location counter**. Before assembly of each segment begins the location counter is set to zero. As each statement in that segment is scanned, the location counter is incremented by the number of bytes required by that statement. During the first pass, MASM uses the location counter to construct a table called the **symbol table** which records the relative offsets of data items or instructions within each segment. This information is used in the second pass to generate operand addresses.

To be specific, consider the first pass through the code segment of the above fragment:

Location counter		*Length of this instruction in bytes*
0H	`CODE SEGMENT`	0
0H	`ASSUME CS:CODE,DS:DATA,SS:WORKING_STORAGE`	0
0H	`START: MOV AX,DATA`	3
3H	`MOV DS,AX`	2
5H	`MOV CX,COUNT`	4
9H	`NEXT: DEC CX`	1
0AH	. . .	

The location counter is set to zero at the beginning of the segment. The first two statements are pseudo-ops, which do not take up memory space in the object program, so the location counter does not change as MASM passes over them. However, as MASM knows from tables permanently stored within itself, `MOV AX,DATA` translates into a machine code instruction requiring 3 bytes of storage. Consequently the location counter is incremented by 3. Similarly, the next three instructions require 2, 4 and 1 bytes of storage respectively so the location counter will, in turn, be incremented by 2, 4 and 1 to 5, 9 and 0AH respectively.

Likewise, the first pass through the data segment of the above program fragment will give:

Location counter		*No. of bytes assigned*
0	`DATA SEGMENT`	0
0	`EXAM_RESULTS DB 100H DUP(?)`	100H
100H	`SUM DB ?`	1
101H	`TOTAL DW ?`	2
103H	`COUNT DB 23H`	1
104H	. . .	

The successive values of the location counter are used to construct the symbol table which takes the form shown in Table 14.1.

Notice that the symbol table also includes the type of each symbol and the name of the segment in which that symbol was defined. Figure 14.1 outlines the major features of MASM's pass 1 in pseudo-Pascal.

Table 14.1 Symbol table constructed from first pass through the data segment.

Symbol	*Offset from start of defining segment (in hexadecimal)*	*Name of defining segment*	*Type*
DATA	0		Segment
EXAM_RESULTS	0	DATA	Variable: byte
SUM	100H	DATA	Variable: byte
TOTAL	101H	DATA	Variable: word
COUNT	103H	DATA	Variable: byte
.			
.			
.			
CODE	0		Segment
START	0	CODE	Label: near
NEXT	9	CODE	Label: near
.			
.			
.			

To see how the second pass uses symbol table information when constructing the machine code equivalents of assembly language instructions, let us consider the third instruction in the code segment of the program fragment given earlier: namely, `MOV CX,COUNT`. MASM can read off from the symbol table that `COUNT` has offset 103H from the start of the `DATA` segment referred to by DS and so knows it must in fact convert `MOV CX,[103]` into machine code. Given that all the necessary information for this latter conversion is stored in permanent tables within MASM, this is now a very straightforward matter.

Machine code generation in pass 2 is not always so simple, however. First, as we shall see in Chapter 16, MASM assembly language allows instructions and pseudo-ops to contain arithmetic expressions. Pass 2 will need to evaluate these expressions before code generation can take place. Second, there is the problem of forward references. Consider the program fragment:

```
              .
              .
              .
              JNE TRY_B
              ADD AX,20H
              JMP DONE
      TRY_B:  CMP AX,'B'
              .
              .
              .
      DONE:
```

```
location counter:=0;
read next source statement;
while source statement is not an END pseudo-op do
  begin
  if the source statement defines a MASM variable or a label
  then begin
        if variable or label already in symbol table
        then write error message
        else enter symbol, current value of location counter
          and information about the symbol's type (and so on)
          into symbol table
        end;
  case source statement uses of
        DB, DW, DD,..: begin
                       determine length of reserved storage;
                       increment location counter by this number
                       end;
             SEGMENT:  begin
                       location counter:= 0;
                       enter segment name in symbol table
                       end
                        .
                        .
                        .
                       end;
  if source statement is valid 8086-family instruction
  then begin
        determine instruction length from internal table;
        increment location counter by instruction length
        end
  else write error message
  end;
call pass 2;
```

Figure 14.1 Pseudo-Pascal outline of MASM pass 1.

When MASM encounters `JNE TRY_B`, the label `TRY_B` will not have been entered in the symbol table because MASM will not meet the place where it is defined until it has scanned three more lines. Thus, `JNE TRY_B` contains a **forward reference** to the label `TRY_B`. Pass 1 cannot replace `TRY_B` by the correct corresponding signed 8-bit number so it assumes this is 0 for the duration of pass 1. By the time pass 2 commences, pass 1 will have scanned

```
TRY_B: CMP AX,'B'
```

and recorded `TRY_B` in the symbol table so that it is clear that the correct value by which `TRY_B` should be replaced in

```
JNE TRY_B
```

is 5. Pass 2 will correct the false assumption made in pass 1.

The above program fragment contains another, potentially damaging, forward reference in the instruction `JMP DONE`. In this case, the label `DONE` is not defined until much later in the program. When it meets such an instruction, MASM assumes a **near jump** unless it already has information to the contrary. Consequently pass 1 will reserve three bytes for the machine code equivalent of `JMP DONE`. If, however, pass 1 subsequently determines in the source statements between `JMP DONE` and the definition of `DONE` that the jump must be a **far jump**, then pass 2 will record a **phase error** when it meets `JMP DONE`: thus implying that the information available to pass 1 and pass 2, respectively, was inconsistent.

If MASM is called into action using the `/D` option as in:

```
MASM /ZI /D MYPROG,,,;
```

then the `.LST` file produced will contain both an assembler output listing for pass 1 as well as for pass 2 (which is the normal listing that we have been working with for some considerable time now). Using the `/D` option we can see how pass 1 flags up the forward references:

```
 0000  75 00                                        JNE   TRY_B
myprog.ASM(7): error A2009: Symbol not defined:  TRY_B
 0002  05 0020                                      ADD   AX,20H
 0005  E9 0000                                      JMP   DONE
myprog.ASM(9): error A2009: Symbol not defined:  DONE
 0008  3D 0042                                      TRY_B:CMP AX,'B'
```

Even though these are recorded as errors by pass 1, at the end of pass 2 everything may have been satisfactorily resolved if `DONE` is indeed a *near* label:

```
10 0000 75 06           JNE TRY_B
11 0002 05 0020         ADD AX,20H
12 0005 EB 06 90        JMP DONE
13 0008 3D 0042   TRY_B:CMP AX,'B'
    .
    .
    .
0 Warning Errors
0 Severe Errors
```

14.2 Modular programming

There are two key reasons for undertaking modular programming: to break a task down into smaller, more manageable components which can relatively easily be integrated after separate design, implementation and testing; and to ensure that the maximum possible benefit is derived from the effort expended in software creation by enabling the reuse of tried and tested software components in other applications.

It is often the case that, when writing a program, certain routines have to be written which could be used in other applications. Whenever possible, these routines will be written in a high-level language. But if it has been found essential to write them in assembly language, it is even more important that their use should not be confined to the application for which they were written. This is part of the fundamental philosophy of software engineering which favors the formation of new systems by integrating previously produced programs. Consequently, reusable routines are often not built into a particular application program but, rather, are built as independent **modules** which can be used in the formation of many different programs.

In our present context, this modularity is achieved through MASM pseudo-ops which communicate with the linker. A collection of assembly language statements assembled as a single unit is referred to as a **source module** which, after assembly, becomes an object module. Thus, a module can be a part of a segment, a segment, parts of several segments, several segments, or a combination of these. The linker can then be told to 'join' together a certain named collection of object modules, thereby forming a single, larger, executable module.

If a source module is in a file MYPROG.ASM then the object module created by the assembler is called MYPROG.OBJ by default. Apart from the names of the files containing the object modules it is to link together, the linker must also know the address of the first instruction to be executed. This information is determined by the assembler (which passes it to the linker through the object module) from the END pseudo-op. Thus

```
END PROG_START
```

tells the assembler that execution is to begin at the instruction labeled PROG_START. When several modules are linked together in this way only one END statement may specify the starting location of the combined module.

To allow one module to refer to labels and variables in another module, MASM provides the EXTRN (EXTeRNal) and PUBLIC pseudo-ops. An EXTRN pseudo-op takes the form:

EXTRN *name1*:*type1*, *name2*:*type2*, *name3*:*type3*,. . .

and lists the names of those MASM variables which are defined in another module but which you want to use in this module. *name1*, *name2*, *name3*, and so on, are the names of MASM variables or labels. For a variable, *type1*, *type2*, *type3*, and so on, must be one of BYTE, WORD or DWORD. For a label, they must be either NEAR or FAR. For a constant defined via EQU they must be ABS.

Thus a module which contained the pseudo-op:

```
EXTRN RANDOM:FAR
```

could contain the instruction

```
CALL RANDOM
```

even though the subroutine RANDOM is not defined in that module.

Similarly, a module which contained the pseudo-op:

```
EXTRN FIRST_LOCATION:WORD
```

could contain the instruction

```
INC FIRST_LOCATION
```

even though the data item `FIRST_LOCATION` is not defined in that module. Also, given

```
EXTRN CR:ABS, LF:ABS
```

a module could use the symbols `CR` and `LF` as in

```
MY_MESSAGE DB 'WELCOME',CR,LF
```

even though that module did not contain `EQU` pseudo-ops defining `CR` and `LF`.

Correspondingly, a name which is to be used in another module must be declared to be available for public use in the module which defines that name. This is carried out by using the `PUBLIC` pseudo-op which takes the form:

`PUBLIC` *symbol1*, *symbol2*, *symbol3*,. . .

Thus, to continue with the previous examples, the module which defines the subroutine `RANDOM` would contain the pseudo-op

```
PUBLIC RANDOM
```

to allow it to be used by other modules, and the module which defines the data item `FIRST_LOCATION` would contain the pseudo-op

```
PUBLIC FIRST_LOCATION
```

to allow it to be used by other modules.

To illustrate the use of `PUBLIC` and `EXTRN` in context we shall now give two complete examples of modular programming.

Example 1 Linking modules not sharing data

Suppose that we wish to develop a program which will add a random number in the range 0 to 15D to single decimal digits typed by the user until the user types the digit 0. Thus, a typical dialogue might be

```
2  2
4 10
6 18
8 10
1  6
0
```

in which the user typed the digit `2` to which the random number 0 was added, then the user typed `4` to which the random number 6 was added, and so on until the user typed a `0`.

In order that we can use it as a module in other programs, let us suppose further that we want to have the random number generating subroutine in a separate module. Figures 14.2 and 14.3 show the contents of two files (which

```
NAME RANDFUNC

WORKING_STORAGE SEGMENT STACK
        DW 100H DUP(?)
WORKING_STORAGE ENDS

CODE SEGMENT
RANDOM PROC FAR
PUBLIC RANDOM
ASSUME CS:CODE
        MOV BX,251D
        MUL BX
        ADD AX,138D
        MOV AH,0
        AND AL,0FH
        RET
RANDOM ENDP
CODE ENDS
END
```

Figure 14.2 Contents of the file RANDFUNC.ASM.

we shall call ADDRANDS.ASM and RANDFUNC.ASM respectively) that contain the two source modules which are to be assembled separately and then combined by the linker.

Because we need a way of labeling the text form of a module in order to be clear which is which, MASM provides the NAME pseudo-op which simply allows us to give modules names within the program text. MASM is very liberal in that it allows you to choose module names independently of the file names containing the modules, and this does have its advantages. But at this stage we shall always make the name given to a module via NAME the same as the first part of the name of the file containing it. Thus, the module in ADDRANDS.ASM will be given the name ADDRANDS and the module in RANDFUNC.ASM will be given the name RANDFUNC.

Let us consider first the pseudo-random number generating module. Pseudo-random numbers will be generated by the subroutine RANDOM of Figure 14.2 which produces a new random number r_n (which is left in AX) from the previous one (or an initial seed), r_{n-1} (also in AX), using the formula

$$r_n = ((r_{n-1} * 251) + 138) \bmod 16$$

Since the RANDOM subroutine will be required by another module at link time, the PUBLIC pseudo-op is used to inform the assembler of this fact.

The main module (Figure 14.3) contains a small test program which accepts a single digit in the range 1 to 9 from the user, adds a pseudo-random number in the range 0 to 15 to that, and displays the result. The process is then repeated. If the user types 0 at any time then a return is made to DOS. Thus, the main module has the following pseudo-Pascal outline:

establish data segment addressability;
read a digit;
while *digit* <> 0 **do**
  begin
  convert to 16-bit form;
  add a random number to it;
  convert result to digits;
  display the digits;
  read a digit
  end;
return to DOS

Within the code segment of our assembly language implementation of this outline, the EXTRN pseudo-op informs the assembler that there is a symbol which is not completely defined within the current module but whose definition will be provided at link time. Also, the END PROG_START pseudo-op informs the linker that any program formed from modules combined with this one should begin execution at the instruction labeled PROG_START.

```
        NAME ADDRANDS

        CR EQU ODH
        LF EQU OAH

        DATA SEGMENT
        DIGITS DB ' ',?,?,CR,LF,'$'
        DATA ENDS

        WORKING_STORAGE SEGMENT STACK
                DB 100H DUP(?)
        WORKING_STORAGE ENDS

        CODE SEGMENT
        ASSUME CS:CODE,DS:DATA,SS:WORKING_STORAGE
        EXTRN RANDOM: FAR
        ;establish data segment addressability
PROG_START: MOV AX,DATA
            MOV DS,AX
        ;read a digit
            MOV AH,1
            INT 21H
        ;while digit<>0 do
            CMP AL,'0'
            JZ  DONE
            ;begin
            ;convert to 16-bit form
                   SUB AL,30H
                   CBW
            ;add a random number to it
```

Figure 14.3
Contents of the file ADDRANDS.ASM.

```
                 MOV CX,AX
                 CALL RANDOM
                 ADD AX,CX
          ;convert result to digits
                 SUB AX,10D
                 JAE MORE_THAN_10
                 MOV DIGITS[1],' '
                 ADD AX,10D
                 JMP OTHER_DIGIT
   MORE_THAN_10: SUB AX,10D
                 JAE MORE_THAN_20
                 MOV DIGITS[1],'1'
                 ADD AX,10D
                 JMP OTHER_DIGIT
   MORE_THAN_20: MOV DIGITS[1],'2'
    OTHER_DIGIT: ADD AX,30H
                 MOV DIGITS[2],AL
         ;display the digits
                 MOV AH,9H
                 MOV DX,OFFSET DIGITS
                 INT 21H
         ;end
                 JMP PROG_START
      ;return to DOS
DONE: MOV AX,4C00H
      INT 21H
CODE ENDS
END PROG_START
```

Figure 14.3 (*cont.*)

After separate assembly in the normal manner via:

```
MASM ADDRANDS,,,;
```

and

```
MASM RANDFUNC,,,;
```

(the order of assembling individual modules is immaterial) the modules are then linked together via the command:

```
LINK ADDRANDS+RANDFUNC,,,;
```

and trial runs may then be carried out by running the executable program which the linker creates in the file ADDRANDS.EXE as a result by typing ADDRANDS after the operating system prompt in the normal way. As usual the reader is urged to type in the two modules and to carry out this procedure at the earliest opportunity.

Having assembled and linked the two modules, it is informative to take a look at the linker-created file ADDRANDS.MAP. Its contents will be similar to the following:

```
Start  Stop   Length Name   Class
00000H 00005H 00006H DATA
00010H 0020FH 00200H STACK
00210H 00261H 00052H CODE
00270H 0027CH 0000DH CODE
```

```
Program entry point at 0021:0000
```

clearly showing how the linker has assigned storage to the two modules (Figure 14.4).

However, even though five byte addresses are used in the **.MAP** file, these are not necessarily the addresses which will be used when the program is executed. In fact, when the program is loaded by DOS for execution, these addresses are added to a 5-byte base address allocated by DOS – as can be seen by running the program in **ADDRANDS.EXE** under the control of a debugger. This is so that when the program is loaded, DOS can relocate it to an area of memory where it will not interfere with the operation of DOS.

Example 2 Linking modules which share data

This example has been chosen to illustrate how to arrange for two modules to share data. We shall describe a program which calculates the tax payable on incomes stored as unsigned 16-bit numbers in a group of locations labeled **INCOMES**. The tax payable is a fixed percentage of income, the actual percentage used being stored as an unsigned 16-bit number in the word referred to by **TAXRATE**. The results are left in locations corresponding to **TAX_PAYABLE** – one for each entry in **INCOMES**. Thus, if before program execution we have:

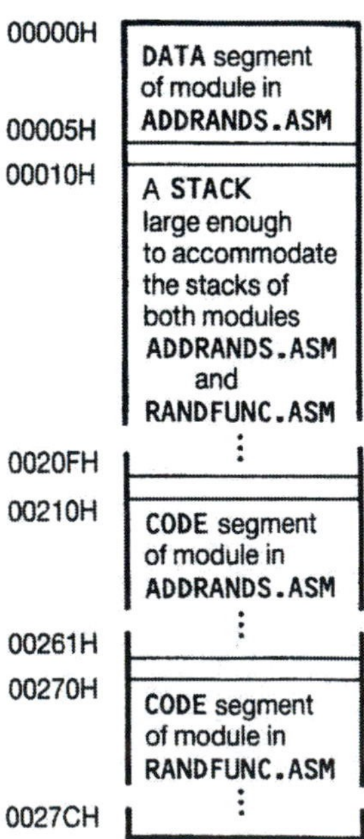

Figure 14.4 Assignment of storage for both modules.

Location	*Contents*
TAXRATE	15
INCOMES	2000 4500 1700

then, after execution, the contents of TAX_PAYABLE will be:

Location	*Contents*
TAX_PAYABLE	300 675 255

because 15% of 2000 is 300, 15% of 4500 is 675 and 15% of 1700 is 255.

We shall organize the program as two modules: TAXCALCS and TAXPROG. We shall assume that the TAXCALCS module is in a file called TAXCALCS.ASM. It contains a subroutine CALCULATE_TAX which calculates the tax payable at TAXRATE per cent on the amount AX, as shown in Figure 14.5. The TAXPROG module (which we shall assume is in a file called TAXPROG.ASM) contains the details of the INCOMES for which tax is to be calculated, organizes appropriate calls to CALCULATE_TAX and leaves the tax payable in TAX_PAYABLE. It is shown in Figure 14.6.

Because the TAXCALCS module accesses the variable TAXRATE from the main TAXPROG module, TAXRATE must be declared as EXTRN in TAXCALCS and the data segment in which this declaration is made must be put on PUBLIC access.

In the TAXPROG module (Figure 14.6), on the other hand, TAXRATE must be declared PUBLIC after its definition, and once again the containing data segment made PUBLIC. Similar arrangements for accessing the subroutine CALCULATE_TAX must be made as for accessing RANDOM in the previous example.

```
NAME TAXCALCS

DATA SEGMENT PUBLIC
EXTRN TAXRATE:WORD
DATA ENDS

CODE SEGMENT
CALCULATE_TAX PROC FAR
PUBLIC CALCULATE_TAX
ASSUME CS:CODE,DS:DATA
          PUSH CX
          MOV  BX,TAXRATE
          MUL  BX
          MOV  CX,100D
          DIV  CX
          POP  CX
          RET
CALCULATE_TAX ENDP
CODE ENDS
END
```

Figure 14.5 The module TAXCALCS.

```
        DATA SEGMENT PUBLIC
            INCOMES DW 2000D,4500D,1700D
            TAX_PAYABLE DW ?,?,?
            TAXRATE DW 15D
            PUBLIC TAXRATE
        DATA ENDS

        WORKING_STORAGE SEGMENT STACK
             DW 100H DUP(?)
        WORKING_STORAGE ENDS

        CODE SEGMENT
        ASSUME CS:CODE,DS:DATA,SS:WORKING_STORAGE
        EXTRN CALCULATE_TAX:FAR
PROG_START: MOV  AX,DATA
            MOV  DS,AX
            MOV  CX,3
            MOV  DI,OFFSET TAX_PAYABLE
            MOV  SI,OFFSET INCOMES
  NEXT_LOC: MOV  AX,[SI]
            CALL CALCULATE_TAX
            MOV [DI],AX
            ADD SI,2
            ADD  DI,2
            DEC  CX
            JNE  NEXT_LOC
         ;return to DOS
            MOV  AX,4C00H
            INT  21H
        CODE ENDS

        END  PROG_START
```

Figure 14.6 The module TAXPROG.

The two modules are assembled individually via the DOS commands

```
MASM TAXPROG,,,,
```

and

```
MASM TAXCALCS,,,,
```

(once again, the order here is immaterial) and then linked with the command:

```
LINK TAXPROG+TAXCALCS,,,;
```

which will leave an executable program in TAXPROG.EXE.

The linker also produces the file TAXPROG.MAP which contains information similar to the following about the manner in which it has combined the modules:

```
Start  Stop   Length Name   Class
00000H 0002FH 00030H DATA
00030H 0012FH 00100H STACK
```

```
00130H 00154H 00025H CODE
00160H 0016DH 0000EH CODE

Program entry point at 0013:0000
```

EXERCISES

14.1 Link the two modules TAXPROG and TAXCALCS using the following linker command:

```
LINK TAXCALCS+TAXPROG,,,;
```

and explain the error message that results.

14.2 Write and test a module CONVERT which, given a length in inches in AX, will leave in BX the nearest equivalent length expressed as a whole number of centimeters. Thus, for example, if AX contained 123D then, after execution, BX would contain 312D (using 1 inch = 2.54 cm). Combine this with another module MAIN which, given a length of *m* feet and *n* inches, stores *m* in a location referred to by FEET and *n* in a location referred to by INCHES, converts (*m* feet, *n* inches) to inches, calls CONVERT to do a conversion to centimeters and leaves the result in a location referred to by METRIC.

14.3 Write and, as far as is possible, test independently two modules which together allow the ratio of consonants to vowels in a given piece of text to be calculated. The main module should work out and print the ratio from counts of consonants and vowels supplied by the other module.

14.4 Write and test a module which calculates the simple interest payable on a sum of $*m* at *n* per cent interest over *r* years (assume that *m*, *n* and *r* are whole numbers). Use this module in conjunction with another module to print tables showing the interest which could be earned on sums of $1000, $2000,. . .,$30 000 invested for 5 or 10 years at rates of interest of 10%, 11% and 15%.

14.3 The linker

This section examines the role of the linker in a little more detail. In particular, **relocation** and **memory management** are considered. Together, these aspects of the linker's operation allow us to control the format of the executable program which is constructed by the linker from our individual modules.

14.3.1 Relocation

The **linker** has three main tasks. It must:

(1) find the object modules to be linked;

(2) match each reference to a name defined externally with a module containing the definition corresponding to that name; and

(3) construct an executable program by combining all the object modules into a single program.

We have seen in the previous section how EXTRN and PUBLIC are used to match references in a module to names defined externally with the appropriate definitions. But the linker also has somehow to connect the modules into a single executable unit.

To allow the linker to carry out this task, the assembler does not assign values to all the addresses used in an assembly language program. Wherever possible – that is, unless the programmer has stated that certain absolute locations must be used – it leaves this to the linker and DOS. (DOS needs to have some say in the matter, not least because unless programmed to do so, user programs should not interfere with DOS.)

When MASM has finished with a module, both segment and offset values may be marked as **relocatable**: that is, the linker is free to determine the actual addresses used. To see this, let us first look at part of the assembler listing for the program fragment:

```
NAME MODULE2

DATA SEGMENT
        HOURS DB ?
        SECS  DB ?
DATA ENDS

WORKING_STORAGE SEGMENT STACK
        DW 100H DUP(?)
WORKING_STORAGE ENDS

CODE SEGMENT
ASSUME CS:CODE,DS:DATA,SS:WORKING_STORAGE
EXTRN LABEL1:FAR,MY_SUB:FAR
START:  MOV AX,DATA
        MOV DS,AX
        MOV CL,HOURS
        MOV DL,SECS
        CALL MY_SUB
        JMP LABEL1
```

It is as follows:

```
1 0000                     DATA SEGMENT
2 0000 ??                  HOURS DB ?
3 0001 ??                  SECS DB ?
```

```
4 0002                   DATA ENDS
5
6 0000                   WORKING_STORAGE SEGMENT STACK
7 0000 0100 [            DW 100H DUP(?)
8           ????
9                ]
10
11 0200                  WORKING_STORAGE ENDS
12
13 0000                  CODE SEGMENT
14                       ASSUME CS:CODE,DS:DATA,SS:WORKING_STORAGE
15                       EXTRN LABEL1:FAR,MY_SUB:FAR
16 0000 B8 ---- R        START: MOV AX,DATA
17 0003 8E D8                   MOV DS,AX
18 0005 8A 0E 0000 R            MOV CL,HOURS
19 0009 8A 16 0001 R            MOV DL,SECS
20 000D 9A 0000 ---- E          CALL MY_SUB
21 0012 EA 00EC ---- E          JMP LABEL1
```

In line 2 we are told that the location assigned to the byte referred to by HOURS will be at offset 0000 from the start of the DATA segment, and that the byte referred to by SECS will be at offset 0001 from the start of the DATA segment. Which actual locations are used will depend on the choice of segment address for the DATA segment. While the linker will place constraints on this choice depending on the other modules to be linked with this one to form the executable program, the choice of segment address will finally be made by DOS.

Next, notice that in line 16 the machine code version of MOV AX,DATA has an R next to it:

B8 ---- R

This indicates that the actual segment address associated with DATA and hence required by this instruction is Relocatable. Here again, the assembler is informing the linker that provided the programmer's relationships between data items are preserved, the program will have its intended effect regardless of the actual segment address chosen for DATA. Consequently, the linker can freely determine the specific segment address chosen in conjunction with DOS.

Similarly, line 18 shows the machine code version of MOV CL,HOURS to be relocatable:

8A 0E 0000 R

This is in case the module containing our program fragment (MODULE2) is linked to another one (which we shall assume is called MODULE1) via:

```
LINK MODULE1+MODULE2,,,;
```

in which there are two DATA segments which have to be combined (see Figure 14.7).

In order to form one larger data segment in which the storage allocated to the DATA segment of MODULE2 comes last, the offsets corresponding to HOURS

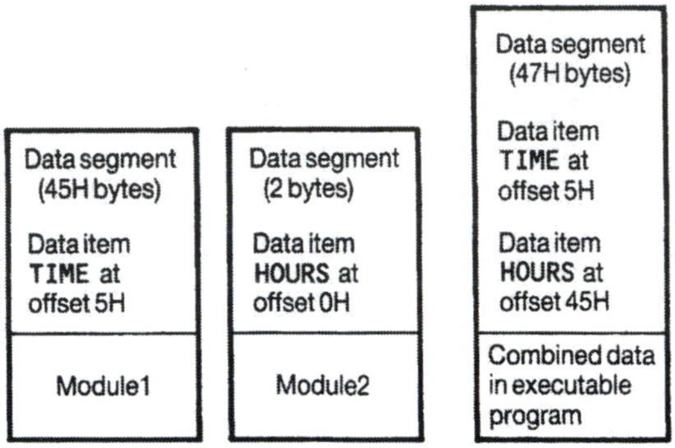

Figure 14.7
A simple data segment relocation.

and SECS will have to be changed. But lines 18 and 19 of the assembler listing show that instructions which would be affected as a consequence are also flagged as being Relocatable, and the linker will therefore ensure that these are adjusted appropriately before execution.

In lines 20 and 21 the incomplete machine code is marked as E (for External). Since both concern the relocation of code, we shall just consider line 21 (similar remarks hold for line 20). Line 21 does not assign a destination to the jump:

```
EA 00EC ---- E JMP LABEL1
```

because at this stage the assembler simply cannot do so: LABEL1 is an externally declared label. Only when the code segments in MODULE2 and the module defining LABEL1 (which we shall assume is MODULE1) are combined can a destination value be given (see Figure 14.8).

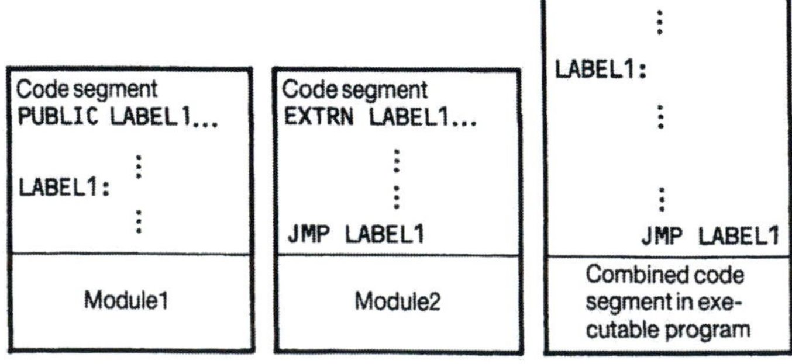

Figure 14.8
Determining the destination for a jump to an external label.

Table 14.2 Combine-type options for the SEGMENT pseudo-op.

Option	*Purpose*
blank	Segment is non-combinable (this is the default option).
PUBLIC	All PUBLIC segments with the same name as this one are to be concatenated to form one physical segment when linked.
STACK	All STACK segments having the same name will be treated as if they were PUBLIC.The linker requires that a program has at least one STACK segment.
COMMON	All COMMON segments with the same name as this one are to begin at the same physical address and thus occupy common storage.The length of the single combined segment will be the length of the largest segment of that name.
MEMORY	A MEMORY segment is to be placed in memory at a higher address than all the other segments.If several segments having the MEMORY combine-type are being linked together then the first one encountered by the linker will be processed as such; the rest are processed as COMMON segments.
AT expression	The segment is placed AT the absolute equivalent of the segment address given in the expression.

14.3.2 Memory management

MASM allows us to tell the linker how to allocate storage in the final executable program by adding a **combine type** to the SEGMENT pseudo-op:

<segment name> SEGMENT *<combine type>*

One segment may be combined with other segments in the same module and/or with segments defined in other modules. When combined, these segments will form the actual physical segments located in memory that are pointed to by the segment registers in the final executable program.

The combine type specified in a given segment's definition tells the linker how it is to combine this particular segment with segments from other modules to form a single physical segment in memory in the final executable program. If present, the combine type must be one of PUBLIC, STACK, COMMON, MEMORY or AT. These options and their effects are summarized in Table 14.2 (see also Figure 14.9). Typical uses are:

```
WORKING_STORAGE SEGMENT STACK

DATA SEGMENT PUBLIC

MY_SEGMENT SEGMENT COMMON
```

The SEGMENT pseudo-op can be followed by two other optional entries specifying an **align type** and a **class name**, respectively. These take the general formats:

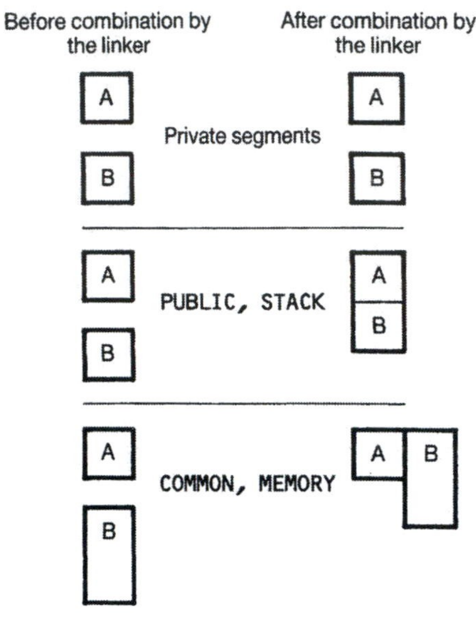

Figure 14.9
SEGMENT combine types.

<segment name> SEGMENT *<align type>*

and

<segment name> SEGMENT *<class name>*

The align-type parameter must be one of PARA, PAGE, WORD, or BYTE and specifies on which type of boundary in memory the linker should locate the segment. In effect, the align type poses conditions on the absolute address at which the given segment may be loaded, as shown in Table 14.3. Typical examples of the use of an align type are:

```
CODE SEGMENT PARA

DATA SEGMENT WORD

MY_SEGMENT SEGMENT PAGE
```

The various align types are designed to overcome one of the shortcomings of segmented memory. Namely, that because the last four bits of an absolute segment address are always zero (since segment addresses are left-shifted four bits to get absolute addresses), memory segments defined via segment registers always start on 16-byte boundaries.

While a segment can be up to 64K bytes long, if a segment does not use all of its bytes, some other segment could start just beyond the last byte used by the first segment. But since the second segment must also start on a 16-byte boundary, there could be up to 15 bytes wasted between segments – which may be important in situations where memory is scarce. Align types allow us to overcome this restriction and other, related, consequences of segmented memory.

Table 14.3 Align-type options for the SEGMENT pseudo-op.

Align-type	*Effect*	*Form of absolute address at which segment may be loaded*
PARA	(This is the default setting if this parameter is blank.) A PARA segment must begin on a paragraph boundary (that is, with address divisible by 16D).	XXXX0H
PAGE	A PAGE segment must begin on a page boundary (that is, with address divisible by 256D).	XXX00H
WORD	A WORD segment begins on a word boundary (that is, at an even address).	XXXXYH (Y even)
BYTE	A BYTE segment can begin anywhere.	XXXXXH

The align types PAGE, WORD and BYTE give more control than the default (PARA) align-type parameter in that they allow the linker to begin a segment at various absolute addresses, not just those with last hexadecimal digit zero. As a consequence of the PC architecture which is beyond the scope of this book, the PAGE align type can be very useful when preparing 8086-family ROM programs since a PAGE segment must begin on a page boundary (that is, with address divisible by 256D). A segment with the WORD align type begins on a word boundary (that is, at an even address). As pointed out in Chapter 2, because all memory accesses involve one word at a time and all memory access starts on an even boundary, retrieving a word stored starting at an odd-numbered location involves two memory accesses, not one. WORD allows us to avoid unnecessary extra memory accesses of this type. But to allow absolute control of segment allocation, a segment with the BYTE align type can begin anywhere.

The class-name parameter consists of a name enclosed in single quotes (for example, 'TIMER'). When constructing the executable program from individual modules, the linker groups together segments with the same class name parameter value so that they occupy contiguous memory locations. Within the memory allocation to a class, segments are loaded in the order that the linker encounters the segments in the object files. Thus, one might give the class-name 'CODE' to all program segments, 'DATA' to all data segments and 'STACK' to all stack segments in various modules, depending on whether the combine type implies that this would make sense. A typical example of the use of a class-name parameter is:

```
DATA SEGMENT 'OURDATA'
```

Using more than one option

The SEGMENT pseudo-op can include any combination of align-type, combine-type and class-name parameters but, if present, they must come in that order (align type must precede combine type which must precede class name). Thus possible examples include:

```
MY_SEGMENT SEGMENT PARA COMMON 'VIDEO'
```

which uses all three;

```
DATA SEGMENT AT 3CB0H 'DISPLAY'
```

which uses a combine type and a class name; and

```
CODE SEGMENT BYTE 'EXAMPLE'
```

which uses an align type and a class name.

EXERCISES

14.5 With the module EXMOD1 of Figure 14.10 in a file EXMOD1.ASM and that of Figure 14.11, EXMOD2, in EXMOD2.ASM, the linker invocation

```
LINK EXMOD1+EXMOD2,,,;
```

produces an executable program in the file EXMOD1.EXE. By careful study of the two modules, predict what will be printed out if this program is run and then check your answer by typing in the modules, assembling and linking them, and finally actually running the program. You may find it helpful to consider the contents of the file EXMOD1.MAP produced by the linker which will be similar to the following:

```
Start  Stop   Length Name   Class
00000H 0005FH 00060H DATA
00060H 006FFH 006A0H STACK  OUR_STACK
00700H 0072EH 0002FH CODE   CODE
00730H 0073DH 0000EH CODE   CODE

Program entry point at 0070:0000
```

14.6 By making a few changes to the pseudo-ops in the two modules EXMOD1 and EXMOD2 (and in some cases to the STACK segment definitions), produce four versions of this pair of modules so that, when assembled and linked, the contents of EXMOD1.MAP are as shown in (a)–(d) below. In each case, state the changes necessary to the originals given in Figures 14.10 and 14.11. State clearly what will be printed out when the modules are combined into a program and that program is run. Check your answers on the computer.

```
NAME EXMOD1

DATA SEGMENT PARA COMMON
CR EQU ODH
LF EQU OAH
PUBLIC CR,LF
MESSAGE_ONE DB 'HELLO. THIS IS MESSAGE ONE IN THE MAIN MODULE',CR,LF,'$'
MESSAGE_TWO DB 'THIS IS MESSAGE TWO IN THE MAIN MODULE (TWO)',CR,LF,'$'
DATA ENDS

WORKING_STORAGE SEGMENT PARA STACK 'OUR_STACK'
     DW 100H DUP(?)
WORKING_STORAGE ENDS

CODE SEGMENT PARA 'CODE'
ASSUME CS: CODE,DS:DATA,SS:WORKING_STORAGE
           EXTRN PRINT_STRING:FAR
           EXTRN MAIN:FAR
         ;establish data segment addressability
PROG_START:MOV   AX,DATA
           MOV   DS,AX
         ;print some messages
           MOV   DX,OFFSET MESSAGE_ONE
           CALL PRINT_NEWLINE
           CALL PRINT_STRING
           CALL PRINT_NEWLINE
           CALL MAIN
         ;return to DOS
           MOV   AX,4C00H
           INT   21H

PRINT_CHAR PROC NEAR
      MOV AH,2H
      INT 21H
      RET
PRINT_CHAR ENDP

PRINT_NEWLINE PROC NEAR
      PUSH DX
      MOV  DL,CR
      CALL PRINT_CHAR
      MOV  DL,LF
      CALL PRINT_CHAR
      POP  DX
      RET
PRINT_NEWLINE ENDP

CODE ENDS
END PROG_START
```

Figure 14.10
Contents of the file EXMOD1.ASM.

```
NAME EXMOD2

DATA SEGMENT PARA COMMON
EXTRN CR:ABS,LF:ABS
MESSAGE_ONE DB 'NOW THIS IS MESSAGE ONE, MODULE 2 (TWO)',CR,LF,'$'
DATA ENDS

WORKING_STORAGE SEGMENT STACK 'OUR_STACK'
       DW 250H DUP(?)
WORKING_STORAGE ENDS

CODE SEGMENT PARA 'CODE'
ASSUME CS:CODE,DS:DATA,SS:WORKING_STORAGE
PUBLIC PRINT_STRING,MAIN
    PRINT_STRING PROC FAR
          MOV  AH,9H
          INT  21H
          RET
     PRINT_STRING ENDP

     MAIN PROC FAR
          MOV  DX,OFFSET MESSAGE_ONE
          CALL PRINT_STRING
          RET
     MAIN ENDP
CODE ENDS
END
```

Figure 14.11
Contents of the file EXMOD2.ASM.

14.6 *(cont.)*

(a)

```
Start  Stop   Length Name  Class
00000H 0005FH 00060H DATA
00060H 0025FH 00200H STACK SOME_STACK
00260H 0028EH 0002FH CODE  CODE
00290H 0029DH 0000EH CODE  CODE
002A0H 0073FH 004A0H STACK OUR_STACK

Program entry point at 0026:0000
```

(b)

```
Start  Stop   Length Name  Class
00000H 0005FH 00060H DATA
00060H 006FFH 006A0H STACK OUR_STACK
00700H 0072EH 0002FH CODE  CODE
00800H 0080DH 0000EH CODE  CODE

Program entry point at 0070:0000
```

(c)

```
Start  Stop   Length Name  Class
00000H 0005FH 00060H DATA
00060H 00089H 0002AH DATA
00090H 0072FH 006A0H STACK OUR_STACK
00730H 0075EH 0002FH CODE  CODE
00760H 0076DH 0000EH CODE  CODE

Program entry point at 0073:0000
```

(d)
```
Start  Stop   Length Name   Class
00000H 0005FH 00060H DATA
00100H 00129H 0002AH DATA
00130H 007CFH 006A0H STACK  OUR_STACK
007D0H 007FEH 0002FH CODE   CODE
00800H 0080DH 0000EH CODE   CODE

Program entry point at 007D:0000
```

14.3.3 The GROUP pseudo-op

The GROUP pseudo-op enables the programmer to instruct the linker to collect together a list of segments so that they all reside in one 64K physical segment (this limit is not checked by the assembler). For example, it is possible to have

```
SMALL_MEMORY GROUP CODESEG1,CODESEG2
      CODESEG1 SEGMENT
               ASSUME CS:SMALL_MEMORY
                 .
                 .
                 .
      CODESEG1 ENDS

      CODESEG2 SEGMENT
               ASSUME CS:SMALL_MEMORY
                 .
                 .
                 .
      CODESEG2 ENDS
END
```

in one module and

```
SMALL_MEMORY GROUP OTHER_MODULE_SEG
      OTHER_MODULE_SEG SEGMENT
                       ASSUME CS:SMALL_MEMORY
                         .
                         .
                         .
      OTHER_MODULE_SEG ENDS
END
```

in another module so that CODESEG1, CODESEG2 and OTHER_MODULE_SEG are collected together into the same physical 64K segment of memory under the name SMALL_MEMORY. Once a group name has been defined in this way, it can be used like any segment name.

SUMMARY

This chapter has focused on a crucial technique for the design and construction of large programs: modular programming. It began with a brief overview of the operation of an 8086-family assembler such as MASM: in particular, we drew attention to its use of two passes over the source assembly language program in order to produce an object program ready for the linker. There followed a similarly brief overview of the way in which the linker uses the object code output from MASM to create an executable file.

The PUBLIC pseudo-op allows data definitions to be made available to other modules and the EXTRN pseudo-op allows a module to make use of externally defined data items. Among the main responsibilities of the linker are the resolution of external references with definitions, and the combination of individual modules into a single executable unit. But through appropriate pseudo-ops it also affords the programmer control over the organization in memory of this final executable program.

In the next chapter we return to 8086-family instructions; in particular, to a consideration of those which make it possible to perform arithmetic on decimal numbers with a fractional part.

SELF-CHECK QUIZ

1. By encoding instructions by hand if necessary, describe the assembler's symbol table after both passes over the following assembly language program:

```
DATA SEGMENT
         LOC1 DW 2
         LOC2 DW 4
         LOC3 DW 6,8
              DB 500H DUP(0)

              AGAIN LABEL FAR
DATA ENDS

WORKING_STORAGE SEGMENT STACK
         DW 100H DUP(?)
WORKING_STORAGE ENDS

CODE SEGMENT
ASSUME CS:CODE,DS:DATA,SS:WORKING_STORAGE
  START:MOV AX,DATA
        MOV DS,AX
  AGAIN:MOV AX,LOC1
        ADD AX,LOC2
        SUB AX,LOC3
        MOV BX,OFFSET LOC3
        ADD BX,2
        MOV [BX],AX
        JMP AGAIN
CODE ENDS
END START
```

2. During assembly, certain addresses are identified as being relocatable. Explain why. What happens when a label is identified as EXTRN? What is the function of the PUBLIC pseudo-op?

3. If I want to combine three existing programs into one by regarding them as three source modules, what are the least possible changes I will have to make to each program to make this possible?

4. Given that:

   the word MY_WORD, the collection of bytes referred to by BYTE_ARRAY and the NEAR label MY_LABEL are defined in source module 1 but are used by source modules 2 and 3;

   the word NEW_WORD and the FAR label MY_FAR_LABEL are defined in source module 2, and NEW_WORD is used in source module 1 and MY_FAR_LABEL is used in source module 3

   write down the necessary EXTRN and PUBLIC pseudo-ops for each module.

5. Under what circumstances is an externally declared label given the NEAR attribute?

6. Is the use of EXTRN and PUBLIC avoidable, albeit quite possibly at the expense of program readability?

7. Write a program which finds the average of three numbers stored in memory. The program should consist of two modules and all addition should take place outside the main module, and all division in the main module.

8. A full-scale electronic calculator simulator is to be programmed, including such functions as statistical calculations, sines and cosines, and so on. Describe how your design would break the program up into modules to ensure maximum reuseability of each part of the calculator simulator.

9. Are the align types the only way of controlling where in memory our programs and data are stored? Is each one essential in that the result of using it cannot be achieved in any other way?

10. Is the use of the COMMON pseudo-op avoidable? That is, could the storage overlapping it facilitates be arranged in another way?

15 BCD Arithmetic

Contents

This chapter introduces the 8086-family instructions for performing arithmetic on numbers represented in **Binary Coded Decimal** (BCD) form. BCD can save us much of the trouble of converting decimal numbers into binary on input and has the advantage that it can easily represent numbers of arbitrary precision. It is also useful when dealing with decimal numbers which must have many digits before the decimal point and a few after the decimal point. For example, even though banks deal with accounts running to many millions of dollars, the cents must also be accurately recorded. There are other situations in which amounts have to be rounded to the nearest cent and BCD representation is also an appropriate vehicle for this. It follows that BCD representation has many applications in large-scale accounting software.

The first section in this chapter examines the different ways of representing numbers in BCD form. Then separate sections cover addition and subtraction, multiplication and division. The penultimate section gives a complete example program using BCD arithmetic and we conclude the chapter with programs which illustrate how to convert between BCD and binary numbers and vice versa.

15.1 BCD representation

One of the disadvantages of reading in numbers as a series of ASCII codes for digits is that, before any arithmetic can be performed with such numbers, their binary equivalents have to be calculated. Thus, if the decimal number 37 were typed at the keyboard, the ASCII codes for 3 and 7 (33H and 37H respectively) would have to be converted to their corresponding binary equivalents, and then the binary equivalent of the first digit multiplied by 10 and added to the second. (We had to do all this – and worse – in the GET_OK_NUM_AND_TERM_NON_SPACE_CHAR subroutine of Chapter 10.)

BCD is a way of representing numbers which avoids the need for conversions of this sort. The principle used is to encode each decimal digit separately and to use as many bits as necessary to represent the complete number exactly. To encode each of the digits 0,1,2,. . .,9 their unsigned 4-bit equivalents are used (see Table 15.1). Thus, rather than adopt the above procedure, we can read the ASCII codes for 3 and 7 (33H and 37H respectively) and convert them to their BCD equivalents (3H and 7H) and store these instead of the signed or unsigned binary equivalent of decimal 37.

The remaining details of a BCD representation are left up to the programmer though there are some conventions, such as 01H being used to represent that a BCD signed number is positive and 8H or 80H to represent that it is negative.

Table 15.1 BCD representation of the digits 0,1,. . .,9.

Digit	*BCD representation*
0	0000
1	0001
2	0010
3	0011
4	0100
5	0101
6	0110
7	0111
8	1000
9	1001

Typically, one or more bytes will be used at the beginning of a representation to indicate the total number of BCD digits used. Another four bits may be used for the sign. Thus, one way of obtaining a BCD representation of a decimal number such as −125 is to first glue together the BCD representation of each of its digits: 0001 0010 0101; then add a sign (0001B for a +, 1000B for a −): 1000 0001 0010 0101; and finally add on the number of digits in the representation (three!):

0011	1000	0001	0010	0101
3 digits	sign is −	1	2	5

Since we have packed two BCD digits into each byte this is known as a **packed BCD** representation.

Unpacked BCD representation involves storing one BCD digit per byte. Thus an unpacked BCD representation of 2619 might be:

0000 0100	0000 0001	0000 0010	0000 0110	0000 0001	0000 1001
4 digits	sign is +	2	6	1	9

In an unpacked BCD representation it often also makes sense to store the least significant BCD digit in the location with the lowest address, the next least significant BCD digit in the next lowest address, and so on. With packed BCD representations the convention is to store the least significant *pair* of BCD digits in the location with the lowest address, the next least significant *pair* of BCD digits in the next lowest address, and so on. (In this case each pair of digits occupies a byte and the BCD digits are stored with the least significant digit in the least significant bits.)

In order to focus more specifically on the problems involved, in most of what follows unsigned BCD numbers are used and it is left to the reader to produce equivalent versions of programs for signed BCD representations.

EXERCISES

15.1 Write (a) packed and (b) unpacked BCD representations of the decimals 29, −3091, 1066, 1812, −273 and 11 111 111.

15.2 Write an 8086-family assembly language routine to add a pair of packed BCD digit numbers together. Test your routine. (As we shall see in the next section, there are special 8086-family instructions to do this, but trying it for yourself will help you understand how these instructions will need to work.)

15.2 Addition and subtraction

We have already seen one disadvantage of representing numbers in BCD form. A BCD representation is generally less compact than the straight binary (signed or unsigned) form. Thus, decimal 125 is 000100100101 in unsigned packed BCD form compared with a signed 8-bit representation of 01111101. At first sight, another disadvantage is that, when we add two BCD representations, the result is not necessarily the BCD form of the sum of the two numbers represented. Consider the following addition. On the left-hand side we have written the decimal equivalent of the packed BCD numbers on the right.

```
24   0010 0100
13   0001 0011
--   ---------
37   0011 0111
```

Here, everything works. Adding the BCD form of 24 and 13 results in the BCD form of the correct answer, 37. But now consider:

```
19   0001 1001
24   0010 0100
--   ---------
3?   0011 1101
```

The problem is that 1101 is not the BCD for any digit. A 4-bit coding can represent up to 16 different things, but there are only 10 decimal digits. This means that if we add the BCD form of any two digits which give a number in this range of non-codes (such as 9D + 4D or 1001 + 0100), the result cannot be correct.

All is not lost, however. If we add 6 to the sum in any digit position that steps into the forbidden range we compensate for the non-existent digits which must be passed over:

```
19   0001 1001
24   0010 0100
--   ---------
3?   0011 1101
06   0000 0110   (adjust forbidden range digits)
43   0100 0011
```

Besides adding 6 when the sum steps into the forbidden range, it turns out that we also need to add 6 whenever there is a carry resulting from the addition of two digit codes. Consider:

```
19   0001 1001
28   0010 1000
--   ---------
41   0100 0001
```

The answer is wrong! In this case the right-most digit passed completely through the forbidden range and so again we need to adjust by adding 6:

```
41    0100 0001
06    0000 0110   (adjust for digits passing through the forbidden range)
--    ---------
47    0100 0111
```

If we are adding two BCD numbers in an 8-bit register, the auxiliary carry flag is set to 1 if there was a carry from adding the two least significant BCD digits and to 0 otherwise. The carry flag indicates whether a carry has resulted from adding the two most significant BCD digits. Thus, in:

```
            Auxiliary
              carry
                |
19        0001  |  1001
18        0001  |  1000
--        ----  |  ----
31        0011  |  0001
                |
               (1)
```

the auxiliary carry flag would be set to 1.

Although the above discussion has considered only packed BCD representations, there are corresponding problems with unpacked BCD representations. Thankfully, we do not have to worry about all these details in the course of normal programming, since there are 8086-family instructions which do the adjusting for us. These are `DAA` (Decimal Adjust for Addition) which makes adjustments for packed representations, and `AAA` (ASCII Adjust for Addition) which makes adjustments for unpacked representations. Based on the settings of the carry and auxiliary carry flags and on whether the sum of two digits has entered the forbidden range, `DAA` adds 6 to the appropriate BCD digit of the BCD number held in AL. `AAA` works in a similar way.

`DAA` and `AAA` have counterparts for subtraction – `DAS` (Decimal Adjust for Subtraction) and `AAS` (ASCII Adjust for Subtraction) – which make the corresponding adjustments when subtracting two BCD numbers via the AL register.

Example 1 Adding and subtracting packed BCD numbers

The program extract

```
MOV AL,52H
MOV BL,29H
ADD AL,BL
DAA
```

loads the AL register with the packed representation of the decimal 52 and the BL register with the corresponding BCD equivalent of 29 in decimal. The two numbers are added by an ordinary 8086-family ADD instruction, leaving the result in AL. Finally DAA is used to adjust AL so that the sum is left in packed BCD form.

Subtraction of BCD numbers is carried out in a similar way. Thus:

```
MOV AL,56H
MOV BL,28H
SUB AL,BL
DAS
```

leaves 28H in register AL.

Of course, in each case the programmer would also have to ensure that the sign and number-of-digits fields of the BCD representation were manipulated appropriately.

Example 2 Adding two packed BCD numbers having lots of digits

Up to now the discussion has centered on BCD representations involving just two BCD digits. In practice, most BCD numbers we would want to handle will have more than two BCD digits, and so we turn our attention to writing an 8086-family program fragment which can add together two numbers represented in *packed* BCD form, each having the same number of BCD digits.

Programmers normally arrange to store BCD numbers in a form which occupies an exact number of bytes, since 8086-family microprocessors are designed to handle multiples of eight bits at a time. Thus the packed BCD representation of 123 (which requires at least 12 binary digits of storage – not counting the sign and number-of-digits fields) would be stored in the equivalent form: 0123H. In our example, there will be very little restriction on the number of BCD digits allowed in either of the packed BCD numbers to be added. As many as 131 072 BCD digits can be handled but, however many BCD digits are involved, we shall assume that there is an even number of them. It follows that the length of a packed BCD number is completely specified by stating the number of bytes it occupies: for example, a BCD number occupying five bytes has 10 BCD digits.

Our program fragment for adding two multi-digit packed BCD numbers will assume that both numbers occupy the same number of bytes and that this is given in register CX. The first BCD number is assumed to be stored in the collection of locations starting at that given in the SI register (relative to the contents of the DS register), and the second in the location given in the DI register (relative to DS) and following. Both BCD numbers are further assumed to have been stored with their least significant pair of BCD digits in the lowest address, the next least significant pair of BCD digits in the next lowest address, and so on. Within each location, the two BCD digits are stored as in our illustrative examples above: the most significant BCD digit occupies the most significant binary digits.

The sum of the two BCD numbers to be added will be left in the group of locations beginning with that given in the DI register, and will be stored in the same form as each of the original two numbers. Thus, if before executing the program fragment we have:

	Location	Contents
CX:0003H	400H	41
SI:0400H	401H	98
DI:0500H	402H	01
	403H	??
	.	.
	.	.
	.	.
	500H	64
	501H	71
	502H	02
	403H	??

(? indicates 4 bits of a byte whose contents are not known)

then after execution we would have

	Location	Contents
CX:0000H	400H	41
SI:0403H	401H	98
DI:0503H	402H	01
	403H	??
	.	.
	.	.
	.	.
	500H	05
	501H	70
	502H	04
	503H	00

since, as decimals, 019841 + 027164 = 047005.

The program fragment itself affords a natural opportunity to demonstrate that **DAA** and **DAS** can just as well be used with **ADC** and **SBB** (respectively) as with **ADD** and **SUB**. The method used is to sum two BCD digits at a time, adding in any BCD carry digit which resulted from the previous two digits. Thus, to calculate the sum of the BCD numbers 1234H and 5678H the program fragment proceeds as follows. Given:

```
12  34
56  78
—   —
??  ??
```

add the first pair of BCD digits:

```
      carry
        |
   12   |  34
   56   |  78
   —    |  —
   ??   |  12
        |
       (1)
```

add the next pair of digits together with any previous carry:

```
                    12   34
                    56   78
previous carry       1
                    —    —
                    69   12
```

so that the sum is 6912.

In pseudo-Pascal this method is:

clear carry;
repeat *move next two digits of first number into AL*;
add corresponding digits of second number;
add current carry;
do BCD adjustment;
save the sum digit;
until *no more digits to do*;
save the final carry

Programming this method into 8086-family assembly language under the aforementioned assumptions we obtain the program fragment in Figure 15.1.

EXERCISES

15.3 Two packed BCD numbers of the same length are stored in memory, one – call it x – starting at the address given in SI, the other – call it y – at the address given in DI (both relative to the DS register). The format in which these numbers are stored is the same as in Example 2 above. Write an 8086-family assembly language program which will leave $x - y$ stored in BCD in the same format in the group of locations beginning at the address given in DI.

15.4 Incorporate the program fragment of Example 2 and your solution to Exercise 15.3 into a program which will calculate the sum or difference

```
        ;clear carry;
                CLC
        ;repeat move next two digits of first number into AL;
NEXT_DIGITS:    MOV AL,[SI]
                ;add corresponding digits of second number;
                ;add current carry;
                ADC AL,[DI]
                ;do BCD adjustment;
                DAA
                ;save the sum digit;
                MOV [DI],AL
                ;adjust pointers to positions of next digits;
                INC SI
                INC DI
        ;until no more digits to do;
                DEC CX
                JNZ NEXT_DIGITS
        ;save the final carry;
                MOV AL,0
                ADC AL,0
                MOV [DI],AL
```

Figure 15.1 Addition of two unsigned packed BCD representations.

of any two positive numbers typed in at the keyboard. Each number should be terminated by the user pressing the ENTER key. Both numbers should be stored in memory in packed BCD format, the appropriate answer calculated as a packed BCD number, and finally the decimal equivalent of the BCD number printed out on a new line. Make any reasonable simplifying assumptions you like. (*Hint:* work out the number of bytes, *n*, needed to store the larger of the two numbers in packed BCD format and then store both numbers as *n*-byte packed BCD numbers.)

15.5 Produce an equivalent program fragment to that given in Figure 15.1 for packed, *signed* BCD representations.

15.6 Repeat Exercises 15.3 and 15.5 for unpacked BCD representations.

15.3 Multiplication

It is not possible to perform multiplication and division by using the ordinary 8086-family multiply and divide instructions and then adjusting the result unless an *unpacked* BCD representation is used. In that case, multiplying two unpacked BCD digits, one in AL and the other in BL, is carried out by the two instructions:

```
MUL BL
AAM
```

`MUL BL` multiplies the two unpacked BCD digits in AL and BL as binary numbers, leaving the result in AX. `AAM` (ASCII Adjust for Multiplication) converts this result into two unpacked BCD digits and leaves the most significant digit in AH and the least significant in AL. Thus, if AL contains 04H and BL contains 09H before execution of these two instructions, register AX would contain 0000 0011 0000 0110 = 0306H, the unpacked BCD representation of 36D, after execution.

Example 3 A subroutine to multiply unpacked BCD numbers

Any program which requires the multiplication of unpacked BCD numbers will almost certainly need a subroutine to multiply two such numbers with several digits, not just one. This example takes the first step towards providing such a subroutine; the reader is invited to complete the task in an exercise. Once again we confine our attention to unsigned BCD representations.

We shall construct an assembly language program fragment which will multiply an unpacked BCD number having a more or less arbitrary number of digits by a single unpacked BCD digit. The program fragment expects the multi-digit unpacked BCD number to be stored at the sequence of locations beginning with the address given in the SI register (relative to the contents of DS). We shall assume that the BCD digits of this number are stored with the least significant digit in lowest address, next least significant digit in next lowest address, and so on. We shall further assume that the number of BCD digits of this number is in the CX register, and that the DL register contains the single unpacked BCD digit by which the other number is to be multiplied. The result of the multiplication will be stored starting at the address given in DI (relative to DS) in the same form as the two multiplicands. Thus, if before executing the program fragment we have:

	Location	*Contents*
CX:004H	0400H	01H
DL:06H	0401H	09H
DI:0600H	0402H	02H
SI:0400H	0403H	08H
	.	.
	.	.
	.	.
	0600H	?
	0601H	?
	0602H	?
	0603H	?
	0604H	?

then after execution we shall have

	Location	*Contents*
CX:0000H	0400H	01H
DL:06H	0401H	09H
DI:604H	0402H	02H
SI:404H	0403H	08H
	.	.
	.	.
	.	.
	0600H	06H
	0601H	04H
	0602H	07H
	0603H	09H
	0604H	04H

since 8291 * 6 = 49746.

The program fragment itself uses the schoolchild's multiplication algorithm, which applied to 8291 * 6 is:

Step 1 6 times 1 is 6 so write down 6 and carry 0;

Step 2 6 times 9 is 54, add the carry is 54, so write down 4 and carry 5;

Step 3 6 times 2 is 12, add the carry is 17, so write down 7 and carry 1;

Step 4 6 times 8 is 48, add the carry is 49, so write down 9 and since this is the last digit to be multiplied, write down 4 also.

Very informally in pseudo-Pascal this is:

last_carry := 0;
repeat *move the next digit of the big number into AL*;
multiply this by the contents of DL;
adjust the result;
add last_carry;
adjust the result;
save the sum digit as the current product digit;
move pointers to next digits;
last_carry := *current carry*
until *no more digits of the multiplicand left*;

This leads to the 8086-family assembly language version given in Figure 15.2.

EXERCISES

15.7 Make a detailed trace of the execution of the program fragment given in Example 3 above for the following initial contents of registers and memory locations.

```
          ;last_carry := 0;
                MOV BYTE PTR [DI],0
          ;repeat move the first digit of the big number into AL;
NEXT_DIGIT:     MOV AL,[SI]
                ;multiply this by the contents of DL;
                MUL DL
                ;adjust the result;
                AAM
                ;add last_carry;
                ADD AL,[DI]
                ;adjust the result;
                AAA
                ;save the sum digit as the current product digit;
                MOV [DI],AL
                ;move pointers to next digits;
                INC DI
                INC SI
                ;last carry := current carry;
                MOV [DI],AH
          ;until no more digits of the multiplicand left;
                DEC CX
                JNZ NEXT_DIGIT
```

Figure 15.2 Multiplication of a multi-digit unsigned unpacked BCD number by a single unpacked BCD digit.

Register	*Contents*	*Location*	*Contents*
CX	0005H	0400H	6
DL	07H	0401H	1
SI	0400H	0402H	9
DI	0600H	0403H	2
		0404H	8

15.8 Use the program fragment in Example 3 to construct a subroutine which will multiply two unpacked BCD numbers – x and y – each having the number of BCD digits given in the CX register. Assume that x and y are stored in the same format as the multi-digit unpacked BCD number in Example 3, and that y is stored in the sequence of locations beginning with that having the address given in the BX register (relative to DS). Test your program carefully. (*Hint:* you may need to use a (slightly) modified version of the program fragment in Example 2.)

15.9 Construct equivalents for *signed*, unpacked BCD numbers of the program fragment in Figure 15.2 and for the program you constructed in Exercise 15.8.

15.4 Division

Division of two unpacked BCD digits can be accomplished by using the ordinary (binary) 8086-family divide instruction after the dividend (the thing to be divided into) has been suitably adjusted. The AAD (ASCII Adjust for Division) instruction takes the unpacked two BCD digit number in AX and converts it to a form so that DIV may be used to leave an unpacked BCD quotient in AL and an unpacked BCD remainder in AH. Thus if AX contains 0604H and DL contains 09H then after execution of

```
AAD
DIV DL
```

register AL will contain 07H and register AH will contain 01H.

Example 4 Dividing a single unpacked BCD digit into an unpacked BCD number

Predictably, we shall now construct a program fragment which will divide one single unpacked BCD digit into an unpacked BCD number with (almost) arbitrarily many digits. As before, we shall assume that the SI register (relative to DS) points to the unpacked BCD number, whose number of digits is recorded in register CX, and that this number is stored with its least significant digit in the lowest address, the next least significant digit in the next lowest address, and so on. The quotient of the division will be stored in the same form as the dividend, but at the sequence of locations beginning with that having the address given in DI (relative to DS). AH will contain the remainder. DL will contain the single unpacked BCD digit divisor. Thus, if before execution of the program fragment we have:

Register	*Contents*	*Location*	*Contents*
SI	0400H	0400H	01H
DI	0600H	0401H	09H
CX	0005H	0402H	09H
DL	08H	0403H	07H
AH	?	0404H	02H
		.	.
		.	.
		.	.
		0600H	?
		0601H	?
		0602H	?
		0603H	?
		0604H	?

then after execution we will have:

Register	*Contents*	*Location*	*Contents*
SI	03FFH	0400H	01H
DI	05FFH	0401H	09H
CX	0000H	0402H	09H
DL	08H	0403H	07H
AH	07H	0404H	02H
		.	.
		.	.
		.	.
		0600H	08H
		0601H	09H
		0602H	04H
		0603H	03H
		0604H	00H

because 27991/8 = 3498 remainder 7.

Once again the algorithm used by the program fragment will mirror the schoolchild's method. For example, to divide decimal 231 by decimal 6: 6 into 2 won't go, so carry the 2 forward and try 6 into 23; 6 into 23 is 3 remainder 5, so write down 3 and carry the 5 forward; 6 into 51 is 8 remainder 3, so write down 8 and, since there are no more digits to divide into, 3 is the remainder for the whole division. Thus, 231 divided by 6 is 38 remainder 3.

This gives us the program fragment of Figure 15.3 (in which register AH contains the digit to be carried forward at each stage) and completes our discussion of the 8086-family BCD instructions.

```
                 MOV AH,0
         ;point SI to highest order BCD digit of dividend;
                 ADD DI,CX
         ;point DI to highest order BCD digit of result;
                 ADD SI,CX
         ;repeat move next unpacked digit into AL;
NEXT_DIGIT:      MOV AL,[SI]
                 DEC SI
                 ;adjust AL and AH;
                 AAD
                 ;divide DL into AL; (*remainder now in AH,
                 ;quotient in AL*)
                 DIV DL
                 ;store quotient at address pointed to by DI;
                 MOV [DI],AL
                 DEC DI
         ;until no more digits left;
                 DEC CX
                 JNZ NEXT_DIGIT
```

Figure 15.3 Division of a multi-digit unsigned, unpacked BCD number by a single unpacked BCD digit.

EXERCISES

15.10 Make a detailed trace of the execution of the program fragment in Example 4 for the following initial data:

AH	AL	CX	DL	DI	SI	Locations 400H	401H	402H	403H	404H
?	?	05H	07H	300H	400H	07H	04H	00H	02H	09H

(Set out your trace across the page as here and make one trace entry for each instruction executed, except that `AAD` and `DIV DL` should be regarded as a single instruction.)

15.11 Devise, implement and thoroughly test a program which accepts two unsigned, unpacked BCD numbers typed in at the keyboard and divides the first number typed by the second, then prints out the quotient and remainder. Assume that each of the two numbers is terminated by pressing the ENTER key. (*Hint:* try to imitate the schoolchild algorithm for long division.)

15.12 Using the routines you have developed in Exercises 15.3–15.9 and Exercise 15.11 as a basis, write a multi-length arithmetic equivalent to the calculator simulator of Chapter 10. In other words, your new version should accept non-negative whole numbers of up to, say, 100 digits.

15.13 An alternative means of implementing multi-length integer arithmetic is to store each integer in signed binary form, allowing the maximum number of bits in the representation to be a multiple of 8 and to be determined by the integers with which you are calculating. Thus, to calculate 125 784 361 * 5 522 110 000 193 667 832 both integers would first be represented in signed 64-bit form and the multiplication would be carried out between these signed representations. Write such subroutines for each arithmetic operation and compare execution times with their BCD equivalent.

15.5 Recording sales – a complete example program using BCD arithmetic

15.5.1 Numbers with a decimal point

BCD arithmetic is often used when dealing with sums of money, or other quantities involving numbers with a decimal point. As every schoolchild knows, arithmetic with such numbers is exactly the same as for numbers without a decimal point; the only additional complication is placing the decimal point in the correct place in the answer.

To illustrate this, and to show the flavour of how BCD arithmetic routines are incorporated into a complete program, this section gives a complete example program using BCD arithmetic, based on the idea of calculating the total income from the sales of replacement parts for cars. For reference, the program itself can be found in Appendix IV. While it would be more typical of the real world for such a program to be written entirely in a high-level language, if a very large number of types of parts had to be dealt with in conjunction with other processing-intensive operations, then at least the actual arithmetic might be implemented in assembly language. But, of course, the main aim here is to teach the use of a particular group of 8086-family instructions – which excuses this slight break from reality.

15.5.2 Recording sales

The Dubinsky Engineering Corp. sells replacement parts for cars. At any one time it has at most 10 000 different types of parts (brake discs, spark plugs, gas tanks, radiator hoses, . . .) in stock. A program is required that will calculate the total value of sales of different subsets of these parts each week. This program should allow its user to type in the total number of different types of parts to be considered and, for each type of part, the unit price for that part and the quantity of those parts sold in the relevant week. Unit prices are entered in dollars in the form

dddd.dd

and the quantity sold is entered in the form

nnnn

The number of types of parts is entered as a number between 0 and 10000, followed by pressing the ENTER key.

Thus, for just two types of parts, the user's dialog with the system will take the form shown in Figure 15.4 where the user's input is given in italics.

Note that a unit price must always consist of exactly four digits before the decimal point and exactly two after (thus, 15 dollars and 50 cents must be entered as 0015.50) and that the quantity must always consist of exactly four

```
No of items in list? 2<ENTER>

Unit price? 3500.00

Quantity? 2034

RUNNING TOTAL OF SALES:                 7119000.00

Unit price? 0015.50

Quantity? 0275

RUNNING TOTAL OF SALES:                 7123262.50

**************************** GRAND TOTAL OF SALES ****************************
                                        7123262.50
```

Figure 15.4 A sample run with the sales calculation program.

digits (so that 275 must be entered as 0275). It will be an exercise for the reader to remove these limitations which have been adopted to allow the example program to focus on matters concerning BCD arithmetic rather than on user interface. When the program has finished, it returns control to DOS.

15.5.3 Choosing data types

Unit price and quantity will be represented in the program as (respectively) 6- and 4-digit unpacked BCD numbers. This is achieved via the data segment pseudo-ops:

```
PRICE    DB 6D DUP(?)
QUANTITY DB 4D DUP(?)
```

Up to 10 000 part types have to be dealt with. For each of these, up to 9999 may be sold in a week and each may cost a maximum of 9999.99 dollars. It follows that the maximum possible sales figure in a week is:

10 000 * 9999 * 9999.99

dollars. Including the two digits after the decimal point, it follows that it will be sufficient to work with 17-digit unpacked BCD numbers. Print operations will have to allow for such numbers to contain 18 characters – 17 digits plus the decimal point itself.

The program handles most of the dialog with the user via the DOS print string operating system function (function 9 of `INT 21H`). In order to do so, we define a dialog framework in the data segment and fill in the missing numeric entries as and when necessary. The framework used will be as follows:

```
CR EQU 0DH
LF EQU 0AH

INITIAL_DISPLAY     DB CR,LF,'No of items in list? ','$'
NORMAL_DISPLAY      DB CR,LF,CR,LF,'RUNNING TOTAL OF SALES: '
ASCII_RUNNING_TOTAL DB 15D DUP(' '),'.',?,?,'$'

PRICE_REQUEST       DB CR,LF,CR,LF,'Unit price? ','$'

QUANTITY_REQUEST    DB CR,LF,CR,LF,'Quantity? ','$'

FINAL_TOTAL         DB CR,LF,CR,LF,'**************** GRAND TOTAL OF SALES'
                    DB ' *****************',CR,LF,' '
TOTAL               DB 18D DUP(?),CR,LF,CR,LF,'$'
```

where the

```
DB 18D DUP(?)
```

in the definition of TOTAL allows for 17 digits and a decimal point.

The cash arising from the sales of a given quantity of a certain part type will be calculated by multiplying the six digits of the PRICE by the four digits of the QUANTITY in turn and then adding, as in:

```
   234.56
     2731
---------
246912000
086419200
003703680
000123456
---------
337158336
```

To record the four intermediate steps of this calculation and the total the data segment contains:

```
STEPS_IN_MULT DB 17D DUP(0)
              DB 17D DUP(0)
              DB 17D DUP(0)
              DB 17D DUP(0)

SUBTOTAL      DB 17D DUP(0)
```

The total sales accrued from all items entered into the program so far are held in locations defined by

```
RUNNING_TOTAL DB 18D DUP(0)
```

Finally, to complete the data segment, for the purposes of calculation the constant values 10D and 17D are held in locations TEN and SEVENTEEN respectively, defined by:

```
TEN          DW 10D
SEVENTEEN    DW 17D
```

In pseudo-Pascal, an outline of the main program is as follows:

```
establish data segment addressability;
ES := DS ready for string manipulation instructions;
request number of items in list of parts;

(* convert user's character stream into a number *)
set top of stack to 0;
read a character into AL;
while AL <> CR
  do begin
  copy AL into BL to free AX for arithmetic;
  convert ASCII character in BL to a digit;
  convert value in BL to a 16-bit value in BX;
  POP AX (* retrieve current total from top of stack *);
  AX := AX * 10D;
  AX := AX + BX;
  PUSH AX (* preserve new total on top of stack *);
  read a character into AL
  end;
POP CX (* so CX contains number of items in list *);

(* for each part obtain the number sold, calculate *)
(* the value of the sales and update running total of sales *)
while CX <> 0
  do begin
  PUSH CX (* to allow subsequent routines to use it *);
  request price;
  request quantity;
  calculate sales and update running total;
  copy running total across to display format;
  convert digits to ASCII;
  display running total;
  POP CX;
  CX := CX - 1
  end;

(* display the total value of sales *)
move final total into place;
display final total;
return to DOS
```

By passing the details over to subroutine calls, the implementation of this outline is made completely straightforward up to and including calculating the sales for the current part and updating the running total:

```
CODE SEGMENT
ASSUME CS:CODE,DS:DATA,SS:STACK
```

```
;establish data segment addressability
START:  MOV AX,DATA
        MOV DS,AX
;ES:=DS ready for string manipulation instructions
        MOV ES,AX
;request number of items in list of parts
        MOV DX,OFFSET INITIAL_DISPLAY
        MOV AH,9H
        INT 21H
;set top of stack to 0
        MOV CX,0
        PUSH CX
;read a character into AL
        CALL READCHAR
;while char <> CR
EXAMINE:CMP AL,CR
        JZ GOT_ITEM_COUNT
        ;do begin
        ;copy AL into BL to free AX for arithmetic
                MOV BL,AL
        ;convert ASCII character to a digit
                SUB BL,30H
        ;convert value in BL to a 16-bit value in BX
                MOV BH,0
        ;retrieve current total from top of stack
                POP AX
        ;AX := AX * 10D
                MUL TEN
        ;AX := AX + BX
                ADD AX,BX
        ;preserve new total on top of stack
                PUSH AX
        ;read a character into AL
                CALL READCHAR
        ;end
                JMP EXAMINE
;CX := number of items in list
GOT_ITEM_COUNT:POP CX
;while CX<>0
NEXT_ITEM:CMP CX,0
          JZ DISPLAY_TOTAL
          ;do begin
          ;free CX for use by subsequent routines
                PUSH CX
          ;request price
                MOV DX,OFFSET PRICE_REQUEST
                MOV AH,9
                INT 21H
                CALL GET_PRICE
          ;request quantity
                MOV DX,OFFSET QUANTITY_REQUEST
                MOV AH,9
                INT 21H
                CALL GET_QUANTITY
          ;calculate sales and update running total
                CALL CALCULATE_SALES
```

Throughout the program, we shall follow the convention established earlier: that BCD numbers are stored least significant digit in the lowest address, next least significant digit in the next lowest address, and so on. Thus, if RUNNING_TOTAL corresponds to offset n relative to the DS register and the very first entry made is for a part which costs 0123.50 dollars, 4058 of which have been sold this week, then after the call to CALCULATE_SALES the contents of locations n, $n + 1$,. . ., $n + 17$ will be as follows:

Location $n+$	0	1	2	3	4	5	6	7	8	9	10	11	12	13	14	15	16	17
Contents	0	3	6	1	1	0	5	0	0	0	0	0	0	0	0	0	0	0

since 0123.50 * 4058 = 50116.30.

Before the number referred to by RUNNING_TOTAL can be displayed, the order of its digits must be reversed, the digits must be converted to ASCII codes and preceding zeros replaced by spaces. This is all carried out in the course of moving the number from RUNNING_TOTAL to ASCII_RUNNING_TOTAL within the display framework for NORMAL_DISPLAY defined in the data segment (as described above):

```
;copy running total across to display format
;(use BH to indicate if there has been a non-zero
;digit to print yet)
       MOV BH,0
       MOV SI,OFFSET RUNNING_TOTAL+16D
       MOV DI,OFFSET ASCII_RUNNING_TOTAL
;for CX := 17D to 1 do
       MOV CX,17D
       ;begin
      MOVE_NEXT:  MOV AL,[SI]
        ;convert to ASCII
                  OR AL,30H
        ;if a non-zero digit already encountered just move this one
        ;across
                  CMP BH,1
                  JZ INSERT
        ;otherwise, if this is a zero digit
                  CMP AL,'0'
                  JNZ NON_ZERO_FOUND
        ;then replace it by a space
                  MOV AL,' '
                  JMP INSERT
        ;else record that we have a non-zero digit
    NON_ZERO_FOUND:MOV BH,1
        ;move digit across
            INSERT:MOV [DI],AL
                  DEC SI
                  INC DI
                  CMP CX,3D
                  JNZ NOT_DEC_POINT
                  INC DI
     NOT_DEC_POINT:LOOP MOVE_NEXT
        ;display running total
                  MOV DX,OFFSET NORMAL_DISPLAY
```

```
                MOV AH,9
                INT 21H
;end
;CX := CX-1
                POP CX
                DEC CX
                JMP NEXT_ITEM
```

When the sales figure for the very last item has been worked out, added to RUNNING_TOTAL and moved across to ASCII_RUNNING_TOTAL, the grand total of sales is obtained simply by copying the ASCII string referred to by ASCII_RUNNING_TOTAL to the TOTAL field in the FINAL_TOTAL display format given in the data segment. Having done so, all that remains is to display it and to return to DOS:

```
;move final total into place
DISPLAY_TOTAL:CLD
        MOV SI,OFFSET ASCII_RUNNING_TOTAL
        MOV DI,OFFSET TOTAL
        MOV CX,18D
        REP MOVSB
;display final total
        MOV DX,OFFSET FINAL_TOTAL
        MOV AH,9
        INT 21H
;return to DOS
        MOV AX,4C00H
        INT 21H
```

15.6 Implementing the subroutines for the sales program

15.6.1 READCHAR

This is our old favourite from earlier chapters:

```
READCHAR PROC NEAR
        MOV AH,1
        INT 21H
        RET
READCHAR ENDP
```

15.6.2 GET_PRICE and GET_QUANTITY

If the user types 1234.56 for the unit price, we must store the digit 6 in the location referred to by PRICE, the digit 5 in the next highest address, the digit 4 in the next, and so on. Consequently, we read a character at a time and use STOSB working backwards to store the digits in the correct format. The only other problem to be taken care of is to ignore the period (.) representing the decimal point. Since we know where it comes there is no need to store it.

```
GET_PRICE PROC NEAR
;reverse direction string manipulation
        STD
;point DI to destination for digits typed
        MOV DI,OFFSET PRICE + 5
;7 characters expected including the decimal point
        MOV CX,7
;repeat
NEXT_PRICE_DIGIT:CALL READCHAR
        ;if character typed is a period (.)
               CMP AL,'.'
        ;ignore it
               JZ   GET_REST
        ;else convert it to a digit
               SUB AL,30H
               STOSB
;until CX = 0
GET_REST:LOOP NEXT_PRICE_DIGIT
        RET
GET_PRICE ENDP
```

Dealing with QUANTITY is similar but we do not have the extra complication of the decimal point this time:

```
GET_QUANTITY PROC NEAR
;reverse direction string manipulation
          STD
;point DI to destination for digits typed
          MOV DI,OFFSET QUANTITY + 3
;four digits expected
          MOV CX,4
;repeat
NEXT_QUANTITY_DIGIT:CALL READCHAR
          ;convert from ASCII to numeric
             SUB AL,30H
             STOSB
          ;until CX = 0
             LOOP NEXT_QUANTITY_DIGIT
             RET
          GET_QUANTITY ENDP
```

15.6.3 CALCULATE_SALES

The purpose of this subroutine is to set things up so that we multiply each of the digits of PRICE by each of the four digits of QUANTITY, shift the results appropriately to take account of the position of each digit in QUANTITY, and then add up the four subtotals thus generated.

Thus, to calculate the income from sales of 3521 items each costing 1023.56 dollars, we first use the routine of Figure 15.2 to multiply 102 356 by 3 giving 307 068, shift this 3 digits to the left because the 3 in 3521 is 3 digits to the left of the units column (giving 307068000), make this up to a 17 digit number, 00 000 000 307 068 000, and record that as one of four subtotals starting at STEPS_IN_MULT.

That deals with the digit 3 in 3521, now for the digit 5. Since 102 356 multiplied by 5 is 511 780 and the digit 5 in 3521 is two digits to the left of the units digit, we shift this left two places giving 51 178 000, and the next subtotal is therefore 00 000 000 051 178 000. Similarly, the other subtotals are 00 000 000 002 047 120 and 00 000 000 000 102 356. To complete the multiplication of 102 356 by 3521 it remains to add up the four subtotals which is carried out in a separate subroutine ADDUP_SUBTOTALS:

```
               102 356
                 3 521
               -------
00 000 000 307 068 000
00 000 000 051 178 000
00 000 000 002 047 120
00 000 000 000 102 356
----------------------
00 000 000 360 395 476
```

Having done that, the UPDATE_RUNNING_TOTAL subroutine adds the result of this sale to the previous running total and updates RUNNING_TOTAL as required. The subroutine obtained from Figure 15.2 requires that the multi-digit unpacked BCD number is pointed to by SI, the single unpacked BCD digit by which it is to be multiplied is in DL, the place to store the answer is pointed to by DI, and the number of digits in the multi-digit number is in CX. Arranging this is complicated by the fact that the subtotal for each of our four multiplications must be stored in the correct place. Also, we must arrange for the appropriate left shift of each subproduct to take place.

```
CALCULATE_SALES PROC NEAR
;for BX :=3 to 0 do
         MOV BX,3
         ;begin
     NEXT_MULT:MOV SI,OFFSET PRICE
         ;calculate where to store the answer
         ;namely, DI:= OFFSET STEPS_IN_MULT + (3 - BX) * 17
               MOV DI,OFFSET STEPS_IN_MULT
               MOV AX,3
               SUB AX,BX
               MUL SEVENTEEN
               ADD DI,AX
       ;place BX zeros at DI to effect a shift left of BX places
               MOV CX,BX
       SHIFTS: CMP CX,0
               JZ  DIGITS
               MOV BYTE PTR [DI],0
               INC DI
               DEC CX
               JMP SHIFTS
       ;no of digits in PRICE is 6
       DIGITS: MOV CX,6
;next digit of QUANTITY into DL
               MOV DL,[BX+QUANTITY]
```

```
        ;now everything ready for subroutine based on Figure 15.2
          CALL ONE_DIGIT_MULT
          SUB BX,1
          JNB NEXT_MULT
        ;end
;add up subtotals
          CALL ADDUP_SUBTOTALS
;update running total
          CALL UPDATE_RUNNING_TOTAL
          RET
CALCULATE_SALES ENDP
```

15.6.4 ONE_DIGIT_MULT

This is just the routine of Figure 15.2 made into a subroutine.

```
ONE_DIGIT_MULT PROC NEAR
               PUSH AX
               PUSH CX
     ;last_carry := 0;
               MOV BYTE PTR [DI],0
     ;repeat move the first digit of the big number into AL
   NEXT_DIGIT: MOV AL,[SI]
               ;multiply this by the contents of DL
               MUL DL
               ;adjust the result
               AAM
               ;add last_carry
               ADD AL,[DI]
               ;adjust the result
               AAA
               ;save the sum digit as the current product digit
               MOV [DI],AL
               ;move pointers to next digits
               INC DI
               INC SI
               ;last carry := current carry
               MOV [DI],AH
     ;until no more digits of the multiplicand left
               DEC CX
               JNZ NEXT_DIGIT
               POP CX
               POP AX
               RET
ONE_DIGIT_MULT ENDP
```

15.6.5 ADDUP_SUBTOTALS

To simplify things, ADDUP_SUBTOTALS itself calls the subroutine UNPACKED_ADDITION. UNPACKED_ADDITION adds two unpacked numbers (pointed to by SI and DI respectively) having the number of digits given in CX and leaves the answer as an unpacked number pointed to by BX (possibly having one more digit than the number given in CX – because there may be a final carry). Consequently, in ADDUP_SUBTOTALS we simply arrange for SI and DI to point to the relevant entries in STEPS_IN_MULT and add up the subtotals two at a time, storing the intermediate results starting at SUBTOTAL. Given the constraints of our problem, and the fact that we are working with 17-digit numbers, the eighteenth digit of these intermediate results will never be non-zero and so we can ignore it.

```
ADDUP_SUBTOTALS PROC NEAR
        MOV SI,OFFSET STEPS_IN_MULT
        MOV DI,OFFSET STEPS_IN_MULT+17D
        MOV BX,OFFSET SUBTOTAL
        MOV CX,17D
        CALL UNPACKED_ADDITION
        MOV SI,OFFSET STEPS_IN_MULT+34D
        MOV DI,OFFSET SUBTOTAL
        MOV BX,OFFSET SUBTOTAL
        MOV CX,17D
        CALL UNPACKED_ADDITION
        MOV SI,OFFSET STEPS_IN_MULT+51D
        MOV DI,OFFSET SUBTOTAL
        MOV BX,OFFSET SUBTOTAL
        MOV CX,17D
        CALL UNPACKED_ADDITION
        RET
ADDUP_SUBTOTALS ENDP
```

15.6.6 UNPACKED_ADDITION

This is an unpacked version of the packed addition fragment of Figure 15.1 made into a subroutine:

```
UNPACKED_ADDITION PROC NEAR
;assume SI points to first number (CX digits)
;DI points to second number (CX digits)
;BX points to sum (CX+1 digits)
          CLC
;repeat
          ;add next pair of digits
 ADD_NEXT_PAIR:MOV AH,0
               MOV AL,[SI]
               ADC AL,[DI]
               AAA
               MOV [BX],AL
        ;prepare for next addition
               INC SI
               INC DI
               INC BX
;until CX =0
          LOOP ADD_NEXT_PAIR
;store carry
          MOV [BX],AH
          RET
UNPACKED_ADDITION ENDP
```

15.6.7 UPDATE_RUNNING_TOTAL

This uses the UNPACKED_ADDITION subroutine to implement what we may express informally as:

```
RUNNING_TOTAL := RUNNING_TOTAL + SUBTOTAL
```

In other words, the number referred to by RUNNING_TOTAL is replaced by the sum of that number and the number referred to by SUBTOTAL (again, there is no need to take account of any eighteenth digit, since we know it cannot be non-zero).

```
UPDATE_RUNNING_TOTAL PROC NEAR
        MOV CX,17D
        MOV SI,OFFSET RUNNING_TOTAL
        MOV DI,OFFSET SUBTOTAL
        MOV BX,OFFSET RUNNING_TOTAL
        CALL UNPACKED_ADDITION
        RET
UPDATE_RUNNING_TOTAL ENDP
```

15.7 Conversion between binary and BCD numbers

For some purposes, it is more convenient to perform arithmetic on BCD numbers by first converting them to binary, carrying out the arithmetic in binary, and then converting back to BCD. This section describes subroutines for converting in either direction. Since it is usually the case that digits are received from the user in ASCII format and then converted into BCD, we shall consider conversions here direct from a sequence of digits represented in ASCII to binary, and vice versa.

15.7.1 Conversion of an ASCII digit sequence to binary

We first consider a subroutine which assumes that a sequence of ASCII digit codes is stored in the order in which they were typed at a group of locations pointed to by SI. It further assumes that the number of digits typed is in BX. After execution of the subroutine, CX will contain the binary number equivalent to the sequence of digit codes interpreted as a decimal number. Thus, if SI contains 235H, BX contains 5, and locations 235H, 236H,. . .,239H (relative to DS) contain 30H, 30H, 32H, 31H, 39H, and 38H respectively, then, after execution of the subroutine, CX will contain 0896H since 0896H = 0000100010010110B which is the binary equivalent of 002198D.

The method by which the conversion is effected within the subroutine is a simple one, and we have seen all its separate ingredients at work before. Consequently, we need only give the pseudo-Pascal outline:

BP := 10*D to use as a multiplying factor*;
CX := 0;
DI := *first power of 10 to consider*;
repeat
  AL := *next digit to be considered*;
  retrieve decimal digit from the ASCII code;
  AX := *this digit* * *current power of ten*;
  CX := *CX* + *AX*;
  DI := *next power of 10*;
  BX := *BX* − 1
until *BX* = 0

and its implementation:

```
ASCII_TO_BINARY PROC NEAR
;BP := 10D to use as a multiplying factor
          MOV BP,10D
;initialize result to zero
          MOV CX,0
;DI := first power of 10 to consider
          MOV DI,1
;repeat
          ;AL := next digit to be considered
NEXT_DIGIT:            MOV AL,[SI+BX-1]
          ;retrieve decimal digit from the ASCII code
                       AND AX,000FH
          ;AX = this digit * current power of 10
                       MUL DI
          ;add to result of conversion so far
                       ADD CX,AX
          ;DI := next power of ten
                       MOV AX,DI
                       MUL BP
                       MOV DI,AX
          ;BX := BX - 1
                       DEC BX
;until BX = 0
          JNZ NEXT_DIGIT
          RET
ASCII_TO_BINARY ENDP
```

15.7.2 Conversion of a binary number to an ASCII digit sequence

Here we assume that AX contains the binary number to be converted to a stream of ASCII codes representing the digits of the corresponding decimal number. SI is assumed to point to the group of locations in which the digit codes are to be stored (most significant decimal digit in the lowest address, and so on) and that the total number of decimal digits to be produced is given in BX. Preceding zeros are replaced with ASCII blank characters.

While the method is related to that for the conversion the other way round, we have not used this particular approach before and so it is worth a slightly more detailed consideration. Suppose, just before entry to our subroutine, that AX contains 3ADH and that BX contains 4. To find the ASCII codes representing the digits of an equivalent decimal number we successively divide 3ADH by 10D until the quotient obtained is less than 10D:

	Quotient	*Remainder*
3ADH divided by 10D gives	5EH	1H
5E divided by 10D gives	9H	4H

and since 9H is less than 10D we finish. The decimal equivalent of 3ABH is therefore 941D since:

$$\begin{aligned} 3ADH &= (5EH * 10D) \qquad\qquad + 1 \\ &= (\overbrace{((9H * 10D) + 4H)}^{5EH} * 10D) + 1 \\ &= 941D \end{aligned}$$

and our desired stream of ASCII codes is 20H (replacing any preceding zeros by spaces), 39H, 34H, and 31H which, if SI contained 3DFH on entry to the subroutine, would be stored as follows:

Location	3DFH	3E0H	3E1H	3E2H
Contents	20H	39H	34H	31H

In pseudo-Pascal the outline of our subroutine is therefore:

BP := 10*D*;
DI := *address where most significant digit is to be stored*;
while *AX* >= 10*D* **do**
  begin
  clear DX ready for 16-bit DIVision;
  divide AX by BP;
  convert remainder to an ASCII digit code;
  store this digit at address in DI;
  DI := *DI* − 1
  end
store most significant digit at address in DI;
if *there are any more significant digits which are zero*
  then *set them all to ASCII space characters*
  else *we are done*

and a corresponding implementation is as follows:

```
BINARY_TO_ASCII PROC NEAR
;BP := 10D as a dividing factor
        MOV BP,10D
;DI := address where most significant digit is to be stored
        MOV DI,SI
        ADD DI,BX
        DEC DI
```

```
            ;while AX >= 10D do
         NEXT_POWER: CMP AX,10D
                     JB  MOST_SIG_DIGIT
                     ;begin
                     ;clear DX ready for 16-bit DIVision
                              MOV DX,0
                     ;divide AX by BP
                              DIV BP
                     ;convert remainder to an ASCII digit code
                              OR DL,30H
                     ;store this digit
                              MOV [DI],DL
                     ;DI := DI-1
                              DEC DI
                     ;end
                              JMP NEXT_POWER
            ;store most significant digit
     MOST_SIG_DIGIT:OR AL,30H
                  MOV [DI],AL
            ;if there are any more significant digits which are zero
                  SUB SI,DI
                  NEG SI
                  JZ DONE
            ;then set them all to ASCII space characters
                  DEC DI
                  STD
                  MOV AL,20H
                  MOV CX,SI
                  REP STOSB
            ;else we are done
            DONE: RET
            BINARY_TO_ASCII ENDP
```

EXERCISES

15.14 Carefully list the constraints on the input values for which the subroutines in Section 15.7 will give accurate conversions.

15.15 Often, answers in decimal arithmetic have to be rounded to a certain number of decimal places. In order to round a decimal number such as 429.867 having three digits after the decimal point to two decimal places we can add 5 at the unwanted decimal position, giving 429.872, and then ignore the last digit, giving 429.87. Similarly, to round 36.874 to two decimal places we add 5 to the unwanted decimal position, giving 36.879, and then ignore the last digit, giving 36.87. Write and test an assembly language subroutine which will round a given BCD number to two decimal places and print out the result. The original BCD number is pointed to by SI and stored according to our convention for unpacked BCD numbers. It contains the total number of BCD digits specified in

BX and the number of decimal digits after the decimal point as specified in CX.

15.16 Produce a subroutine which is a generalization of the one you produced for Exercise 15.15 above, in that an additional parameter may be specified in BP which determines the number of decimal places to which an answer is rounded.

SUMMARY

As we have seen, BCD representations and the associated 8086-family instructions allow us to handle arithmetic with numbers containing decimal points quite easily. For that reason, this chapter was almost given the title 'decimal arithmetic'. However, the advantages of using a BCD representation stem from more than just the consequent arithmetic ease: BCD representation *itself* has advantages when you want to represent very large numbers or when the decimal-to-binary conversion time overhead must be avoided in a program.

The 8086-family instructions for BCD arithmetic work in conjunction with the ordinary arithmetic instructions. Thus, to add or subtract two packed two-BCD-digit numbers, the numbers are first added or subtracted using ADD or SUB in the normal way (but so that the result is left in AL), and then DAA or DAS is used to adjust the result so that the contents of AL is then the correct result of adding or subtracting the two BCD numbers. (AAA and AAS similarly modify the contents of AL after addition or subtraction, respectively, of unpacked BCD digits).

A similar technique for multiplication and division can only work with unpacked BCD numbers. For multiplication, the two unpacked BCD digits are first multiplied in the normal way so that the result is in AX. The AAM instruction is then used to convert this to the correct BCD equivalent. For division, the dividend (the number to be divided into) must first be put into AX and AAD executed to adjust the contents of AX so that a DIV instruction will give the correct BCD outcome.

For reference purposes, Table 15.2 contains a summary of the 8086-family BCD instructions. The next three chapters will turn away from learning new 8086-family instructions and instead will center on a more detailed study of the pseudo-ops available with MASM.

Table 15.2 Summary of the 8086-family BCD arithmetic instructions.

Operation	*Mnemonic*	*Effect*
Addition	`AAA`	ASCII Adjust for Addition: contents of AL are modified so that it contains a valid unpacked BCD number.
	`DAA`	Decimal Adjust for Addition: contents of AL are modified so that it contains a valid packed BCD number.
Subtraction	`AAS`	ASCII Adjust for Subtraction: if AL contains the result of subtracting two packed operands, executing `DAS` modifies AL so that it contains a valid packed BCD number.
Multiplication	`AAM`	ASCII Adjust for Multiplication: if AX contains the result of multiplying two unpacked operands, executing `AAM` modifies AX so that AH and AL each contain a valid BCD digit.
Division	`AAD`	ASCII Adjust for Division: executing `AAD` prior to dividing two unpacked BCD operands modifies the contents of AL so that the quotient in AL after division is a valid unpacked BCD digit.

SELF-CHECK QUIZ

1. Write the following as unpacked BCD numbers conforming to the format given in Section 15.1:

   (a) 279981052 (b) −761 (c) −99999999

2. Repeat question 1 for packed BCD numbers.

3. Write a sequence of instructions which will perform the following operations on two-digit packed BCD numbers held in memory:

   (a) $a := b + (c - 12)$

   (b) $a := (b + c) - (d + e)$

4. Repeat question 3 for unpacked two-digit BCD numbers.

5. Write a sequence of instructions which will perform the following operations on two-digit packed BCD numbers held in memory:

   (a) $a := b * c / d$ (b) $a := (b * c) - (d / e)$

6. Repeat question 5 for unpacked two-digit BCD numbers.

7. If AL and BL contain BCD digits, then show that if:

   ```
   MUL BL
   AAM
   ```

   is to leave AH containing the most significant BCD digit of their product and AL the least significant BCD digit, then `AAM` must divide AX by 10D and leave the quotient in AH and the remainder in AL.

8. If AX contains two BCD digits and BL contains one BCD digit, then show that if:

   ```
   AAD
   DIV BL
   ```

   is to divide the digits in AX by the digit in BL, and leave AL containing the quotient and AH the remainder, then `AAM` must multiply the digit in AH by 10D and add the digit in AL.

9. How are the carry, overflow and zero conditions indicated after BCD arithmetic operations?

10. Describe the exact operation of `AAA` and `AAS`.

16 Assembly Language Features

Contents

This far, treatment of the syntactic requirements of assembly language has been informal, to say the least. And it is not the purpose of the next three chapters to redress the balance by offering a precis of large chunks of the MASM manual. Rather, the main aim in these chapters is a presentation of some of the more advanced MASM program development tools: nearly all of them aimed at saving programmer effort. Thus, some features save the programmer the bother of working out the length of a declared data structure, others allow us to specify a formula to be used in an instruction and leave MASM to work out the actual corresponding value. Further, there are features which allow us to redefine data items in different ways to suit different purposes – so that, for example, two 1-byte data items could also be regarded a one word data item. Finally, there are features similar to OFFSET (which is very familiar to us by now) which allow assembly language programs to refer to different parts of addresses given in segment:offset form.

As a means of achieving this aim, this chapter will be more precise about certain of MASM's syntactic structures, and will reveal more fully the power of certain of the MASM pseudo-ops which have hitherto been demonstrated only under very restricted circumstances.

16.1 Statements

MASM allows two kinds of assembly language **statement** which have the general forms:

label instruction mnemonic *argument,. . .,argument* ; *comment*

or

name *MASM pseudo-op* *argument,. . .,argument* ; *comment*

where both the **label** and the **name** are optional. Names and labels can be up to 31 characters in length, consist of alphabetic characters (upper and lower case, though the assembler converts lower case to upper), digits and the characters ?, –, and $, but must not begin with a digit. In order to avoid confusion, names and labels must be different from the MASM reserved words which include standard 8086-family instruction mnemonics (such as MOV, REP and ADD), register names (such as AH, DL and BP), assembler pseudo-op names (such as EQU and DB) and assembler operators (such as PTR).

A label represents a location which can be used in, for example, a JMP or CALL instruction. If a colon (:) is appended when the label is defined, MASM assumes that this label is to be referenced only from within the same segment (that is, the NEAR form of JMP or CALL is assumed for any such instruction referring to that label).

A name can be just a symbol, for example CR in

```
CR EQU ODH ;ASCII carriage return character
```

or a variable, for example RUN_ERROR in

```
RUN_ERROR DB 'COMMAND NOT UNDERSTOOD',CR,LF,'$'
```

16.1.1 SEG, OFFSET and TYPE

Labels and variables have three attributes: segment, offset and type. MASM provides operators which can be used in assembly language programs to access the values of these attributes, namely SEG, OFFSET and TYPE. We have often used OFFSET in preceding chapters and SEG is similar but returns the segment part of an address in segment:offset form rather than the offset. Thus:

```
MOV BX,SEG RUN_ERROR
```

would be assembled by MASM into an instruction equivalent to

```
MOV BX,n
```

where n is the segment address of the variable RUN_ERROR.

For a variable, TYPE returns the number of bytes occupied by the individual data items referred to by that variable. Thus, given

```
NEW_CENTURY DW 2000D
```

then

```
MOV AX,TYPE NEW_CENTURY
```

would be assembled into an instruction equivalent to

```
MOV AX,2
```

When used with labels, the TYPE operator returns −1 if the label is NEAR and −2 if it is FAR.

16.1.2 LENGTH and SIZE

MASM's LENGTH and SIZE operators allow the programmer to avoid calculating the exact number of bytes occupied by a long or complex data structure. Consequently, these operators are of particular benefit when using the MASM RECORD and STRUC pseudo-ops to be described in Chapter 17. But LENGTH and SIZE also reduce the dependence of the instructions in a program on particular numbers (rather like EQU allows a symbol such as TAXRATE to be used throughout a program rather than a number such as 25, and with similar benefits when it comes to program maintenance).

For example, LENGTH and SIZE can be used in conjunction with statements which use the DUP operator as in

```
SALES_ARRAY DB 80H DUP(0)
DATES_ARRAY DW 100H DUP(1924D)
```

(used to initialize the contents of SALES_ARRAY to zero and DATES_ARRAY to 1924) to return the total number of units allocated for the variable on which it operates. Thus

```
MOV AX,LENGTH SALES_ARRAY
MOV BX,LENGTH DATES_ARRAY
```

would be assembled into instructions equivalent to

```
MOV AX,80H
MOV BX,100H
```

If a larger SALES_ARRAY were needed for any reason, the data segment definition of SALES_ARRAY would have to be changed but MOV AX,LENGTH SALES_ARRAY would need no amendment.

As another example, the following program fragment shows a simple utility which copies the string ASTRING into the string BSTRING, assuming suitable definitions of ASTRING and BSTRING.

```
MOV SI,OFFSET ASTRING
MOV DI,OFFSET BSTRING
MOV CX,LENGTH ASTRING
CLD
REP MOVSB
```

The SIZE operator returns the product of LENGTH and TYPE. Thus

```
MOV AX,SIZE SALES_ARRAY
MOV BX,SIZE DATES_ARRAY
```

would be assembled into instructions equivalent to

```
MOV AX,80H
MOV BX,200H
```

Beware, however, when using TYPE, LENGTH and SIZE in relation to a pseudo-op such as:

```
TEST_VALUES DB 2,4,6,8,0AH,0CH,0EH
```

for in this case the name TEST_VALUES is taken to refer only to the first defined byte and so

```
MOV AX,LENGTH TEST_VALUES
MOV BX,TYPE TEST_VALUES
MOV CX,SIZE TEST_VALUES
```

will be assembled as

```
MOV AX,1
MOV BX,1
MOV CX,1
```

16.2 Expressions

In the course of writing an assembly language program, it may be that a calculation is necessary to work out just how many bytes should be the object of some group of instructions. This might be the case when designing a screen layout in six columns, for example, when it may be that we want a block move of (40 * 32 * 15) / 6 bytes. Rather than have the programmer do this calculation, MASM allows the programmer to give it in an **expression** as part of an assembly language instruction:

```
MOV CX,(40D * 32D * 15D)/6D
       └──────────────────┘
                |
          an expression
```

This will then be assembled as

```
MOV CX,0C80H
```

since the nearest whole number to

```
(40D * 32D6 * 15D)/6D
```

is 3200D = 0C80H.

When evaluating expressions, MASM does 16-bit arithmetic unless it has been explicitly told to work in 80386 mode (see Chapter 23). Otherwise, all values of expressions are truncated to a 16-bit equivalent.

By definition, a MASM expression consists of a collection of operators which act on operands to produce a value at assembly time. The operators include the four basic arithmetic operators (+, −, *, and /), the relational operators `EQ`, `NE`, `LT`, `LE`, `GT`, and `GE`, the logical operators `NOT` and `AND`, value-returning operators such as `LENGTH` and `SIZE` and operators which set or override attribute values such as `PTR`. The operands can be numbers or symbols as in

```
    .
    .
    .
TAXRATE EQU 25D
    .
    .
    .
MOV AX,(731D * TAXRATE)/100D
```

which would be assembled as

```
MOV AX,0B6H
```

since

```
(731D * 25D )/100D
```

when truncated to a 16-bit equivalent gives 182D = 0B6H.

16.2.1 MASM operators

Table 16.1 summarizes the MASM operators which can be used in expressions. Many of the logical and relational expression operators are most useful in the context of conditional assembly, which is dealt with in Section 18.4. The MASM manual specifies the operands permissible with each operator in detail. For our purposes, it is enough to remark that an operation is usually acceptable if its results make sense. Thus, in

```
DATE    DW 1922
TIME    DB 60
SECONDS DB DATE*TIME ;error!
```

`DATE*TIME` is erroneous because MASM cannot give a meaning to such a quantity. (What will happen to the bits which must be lost when the product is squeezed into a single byte? To which segment should it belong in general? That of the first or second operand?)

The remainder of this section illustrates some more of the MASM operators from each category in Table 16.1. Full details are, of course, given in the MASM manual.

Table 16.1 Some MASM operators (see Chapter 17 for more).

Operator	*Use*
Arithmetic	
HIGH, LOW	Produces the HIGH or LOW byte of an operand, for example, MOV AL,LOW(0ABC1H) is equivalent to MOV AL,0C1H
*, /, MOD	For example, CMP DX, (132*15)/3 MOD 4
SHL,SHR	Shift Left (SHL) or SHift Right (SHR) the operand, for example, CMP AH,14H SHR 6
+, −	For example, MOV AL,RECORD_START+2
Relational	
EQ, NE, LT LE, GT, GE	Return all 1s (true) or all 0s (false), for example, MOV AL,16 LT 17 is equivalent to MOV AL,0FFH
Logical	
NOT, AND OR, XOR	For example, MOV BH,NOT 15H MOV CL,22H AND 0ABH
Value returning	
LENGTH, SIZE	Return the number of data items and the number of bytes in a variable defined using DUP or containing multiple byte definitions.
SEG, TYPE, OFFSET	These operate on a variable or label and return the designated attribute.
Set or override attribute value	
Segment override	For example, MOV CL,ES:SCREEN_BYTE MOV CL,DISPLAY_SEG:SCREEN_BYTE
PTR, THIS	Override the type (byte or word) of a previously defined variable or label.
SHORT	Request encoding of a SHORT jump instruction.

Arithmetic operators

The MASM statements:

```
MOV AX,100H MOD 17D
MOV BX,0EFH SHL 2
```

would be assembled into machine code instructions equivalent to

```
MOV AX,1
MOV BH,0BCH
```

since 100H MOD 17D is 1 and 0EFH shifted left two bits is 0BCH.

Relational operators

Relational operators are also allowed as follows:

MASM relational operator	*Meaning*
EQ	EQual
NE	Not Equal
LT	Less Than
LE	Less than or Equal
GT	Greater Than
GE	Greater than or Equal

with TRUE represented as all 1s and FALSE as all 0s.

Thus:

```
MOV DL,5EH GE 6EH
```

would be assembled as:

```
MOV DL,0
```

since the result of `5EH GE 6EH` (is 5EH greater than or equal to 6EH?) is false.

Logical operators

MASM allows expressions to contain the logical operators `NOT`, `AND`, `OR` and `XOR` which have the same effect on their operands as do their 8086-family instruction counterparts. Thus,

```
MOV DL,3EH OR OFEH
```

would be assembled as

```
MOV DL,OFEH
```

since the result of the expression `3EH OR OFEH` is `OFEH`.

Value-returning operators

The operators in this category (`LENGTH`, `SIZE`, `SEG`, `TYPE`, and `OFFSET`) have already been discussed earlier in this chapter, but it is perhaps worth pointing out here that MASM operators can be used wherever their use makes sense (the MASM manual is more precise, but this is a good working rule). Thus, in the case of

```
CO_ORD_ADDRESS DW OFFSET MY_LOC+(22H*2)
```

the expression is `OFFSET MY_LOC+(22H*2)`, and if the label or variable `MY_LOC` corresponds to a location with offset 36H from the start of its defining segment then `CO_ORD_ADDRESS` will refer to a word with initial value 36H + 44H = 7AH.

Operators which set or override attribute values

In this category are the operators PTR (which is already well known to us), THIS, SHORT and segment overrides. PTR, THIS and SHORT must be used in the formats:

> *type* PTR *expression*
> SHORT *label*
> THIS *type*

respectively. Each of them allows the existing definitions of data items to be overridden in some way. Thus, PTR allows us to regard components of data items which were defined as words as bytes. THIS allows two data items defined by pseudo-ops and occupying contiguous bytes to be regarded as a word. SHORT requests a jump instruction to be encoded in the short, two byte, form rather than in the full, segment:offset four byte, form. Segment overrides allow data items defined in one segment (say, the data segment) to be accessed from a corresponding offset in another segment (say, the extra segment).

We have already seen the use of the PTR operator to remove ambiguity from an instruction such as

```
INC [BX] ;illegal ambiguous instruction
```

but PTR can also be used to override the type of a variable. Thus, given

```
MY_WORD DW 4142H
```

then

```
MOV AX,BYTE PTR MY_WORD
```

will be assembled so that its effect is the same as

```
MOV AX,41H
```

Another use of PTR is where a label has been defined to be of a particular type (say NEAR) but at some point in the program it becomes necessary to refer to the label as having the opposite type (FAR in this case). This is illustrated in the following program fragment, where NEAR_LOOP has type NEAR because of the appended colon:

```
NEAR_LOOP: ADD AX,BX
           MOV DX,AX
               .
               .
               .
           JMP NEAR_LOOP
               .
               .
               .
  FAR_LOOP EQU FAR PTR NEAR_LOOP
           JMP FAR_LOOP
```

The SHORT operator must be followed by a valid label name, as in

```
SHORT MY_LABEL
```

SHORT specifically requests the assembler to encode a JMP instruction in the signed 8-bit form (see Section 4.1) rather than the unsigned 16-bit form. However, instructions such as

```
JMP SHORT NEXT_BLOCK_LABEL
```

which use SHORT are only permitted if NEXT_BLOCK_LABEL is in the same segment as the JMP instruction itself.

The MASM operator THIS must be followed by a type, that is, one of BYTE, WORD, DWORD, FWORD, QWORD, TBYTE, NEAR, FAR or PROC. THIS WORD and THIS BYTE allow the redefinition to the assembler of variables already defined, rather like PTR allowed access to separate bytes of a word variable in our example above. Hence:

```
AB_WORD     EQU THIS WORD
FIRST_BYTE  DB  41H
SECOND_BYTE DB  42H
```

would allow the contents of the contiguous locations FIRST_BYTE and SECOND_BYTE to be accessed as a word.

THIS can also be used to define alternative labels for the same address, one being NEAR and the other FAR as, for example, in

```
FAR_LOOP EQU THIS FAR
NEAR_LOOP:ADD AX,2
```

Using the MASM segment override operators it is also possible to override the segment associated with a variable or label. Thus

```
MOV AL,ES:ABYTE
```

would be assembled so that AL were filled from a location in the segment addressed by ES, having the same offset from the start of the segment addressed by ES as ABYTE from the start of its segment of definition. Similarly:

```
MOV AL,MYSEGMENT:ABYTE
```

uses the segment name MYSEGMENT to achieve the same effect.

16.2.2 Operator precedence

Expressions are evaluated in the normal way: highest precedence operators first, then left to right for equal precedence operators. Round brackets (parentheses ()) can be used to alter precedence. Operators are listed in Table 16.2 in order of precedence, SHORT having lowest possible precedence and entries on the same line having equal precedence. Note that there are departures from the 'normal' Pascal operator precedence.

Table 16.2 MASM operator precedence. The operators are listed in descending order of precedence. Thus, `SHORT` has the lowest precedence.

An entry in square `[ ]` or round `( )` brackets (parentheses)
`LENGTH, SIZE`
A segment override operator (for example, `ES:`)
`PTR, OFFSET, SEG, TYPE, THIS`
`HIGH, LOW`
`*, /, MOD, SHL, SHR`
+, − (both unary and binary)
`EQ, NE, LT, LE, GT, GE`
`NOT`
`AND`
`OR, XOR`
`SHORT`

EXERCISE

16.1 Rewrite the following program fragment so that it does not use any of the MASM operators in Table 16.1. Check your answer by assembling and running both your rewritten program and the given one.

```
DATA SEGMENT
  INITIAL_VALUES EQU THIS WORD
  VALUE_COUNT    DB  LENGTH TEST_VALUES
  LETTER_COUNT   DB  LENGTH TEST_LETTERS
  TEST_VALUES    DB  2,4,6,8,0CH,0EH
  COUNT              EQU 168 MOD 16 + 2
  TEST_LETTERS   DB  20H DUP('A')
DATA ENDS

WORKING_STORAGE SEGMENT STACK
      DW 100H DUP(?)
WORKING_STORAGE ENDS

CODE SEGMENT
ASSUME CS:CODE,DS:DATA,SS:WORKING_STORAGE
```

```
    PROG_START:MOV AX,DATA
               MOV DS,AX
               MOV AL,TYPE TEST_VALUES - 1
               MOV CX,LENGTH TEST_VALUES * 10/COUNT
               MOV BX,OFFSET TEST_VALUES
    NEXT_VALUE:ADD AL,[BX]
               INC BX
               LOOP NEXT_VALUE
               MOV BX,0F0H SHL 4 AND 0ABH
               MOV CX,OFFSET INITIAL_VALUES
               MOV CL,CH
               MOV CH,137*14 MOD 9 LT 14
               MOV BP,OFFSET TEST_LETTERS
   NEXT_LETTER:MOV DL,DS:[BP]
               MOV DH,0
               ADD BX,DX
               INC BP
               LOOP NEXT_LETTER
               MOV AX,4C00H
               INT 21H
   CODE ENDS
   END PROG_START
```

16.3 Pseudo-ops for data definition, memory and program linkage

Many of MASM's data definition, memory and program-linkage pseudo-ops are summarized in Table 16.3. As can be seen from inspecting that table, we have already met a surprisingly large number of them. The object of the following sections, therefore, is both to introduce those which we have not met before and to point out some of the more unusual uses of some of those with which we are already familiar.

16.4 Data definition

The **data definition** pseudo-ops which we shall consider in this section are:

- `LABEL` (which defines a variable or label name)
- `DB`, `DW`, and so on
- `EQU`
- `=` (which defines a symbol which may be redefined)

Table 16.3 MASM pseudo-ops for data definition, memory and program linkage (see Section 16.7 for pseudo-ops to control assembler printout).

Pseudo-op	*Purpose*
Data definition	
name LABEL *type*	Defines a name.
DB,DW,DD,DQ,DT	Reserves and initializes variables.
name EQU *expression*	Defines a symbolic constant.
name = *expression*	Defines a name which can be redefined.
Memory	
name PROC NEAR. . .*name* ENDP	Procedure definition.
name PROC FAR. . .*name* ENDP	Procedure definition.
name SEGMENT *align type combine type class name* . . . *name* ENDS	Segment definition.
name GROUP *segname1,segname2,. . .,segnamet*	Collects the named segments under the given group name.
ASSUME *segment register:name,* *segment register:name,* . . . ASSUME *segment register:*NOTHING	Tells the assembler which segment register is to be used for accessing the given segments.
ORG *expression*	Defines location counter value.
EVEN	Sets location counter to next even address.
Program linkage	
NAME *module name*	Defines a module name.
END *expression*	Specifies the end of the source code. The optional expression specifies the start of the source program.
PUBLIC *symbol1,symbol2,. . .,symbolt*	Defines global names.
EXTRN *name1:type1,name2:type2,. . .*	Allows you to reference global names defined in another module.
INCLUDE *filename*	Inserts the contents of *filename* into the current program.

The LABEL pseudo-op

LABEL can be used to achieve essentially the same effects as the operator THIS. Thus in

```
AB_WORD LABEL WORD
FIRST_BYTE DB 41H
SECOND_BYTE DB 42H
```

AB_WORD can be used to access the contents of contiguous locations FIRST_BYTE and SECOND_BYTE as a word. More generally, given

```
ARRAYB LABEL BYTE
ARRAYA DW 100 DUP(?)
          .
          .
          .
ADD AL,ARRAYB[99]
ADD AX,ARRAYA[49]
```

the first ADD instruction adds the contents of the 100th byte to AL whereas the second adds the contents of the 50th word to AX. Similarly in

```
FAR_LOOP LABEL FAR
NEAR_LOOP:ADD AX,2
```

FAR_LOOP refers to the same address as NEAR_LOOP but FAR_LOOP has the attribute FAR whereas the colon (:) after NEAR_LOOP gives it the attribute NEAR.

The DB, DW, DD . . . pseudo-ops

We are, by now, very familiar with DB and DW of course. DD was used in Chapter 10 in one of its formats. Thus DD 10000000D initialized four locations to the 4-byte unsigned equivalent of 10000000D and so on. But the right-hand side of a DW, DD, DQ and DT may be any expression. In particular, labels can be used on the right-hand side of a DW, DD,. . . pseudo-op in order to access the address corresponding to that label. Thus, given:

```
TEST:MOV AX,BX
```

so that TEST corresponds to offset 320H from the start of the code segment which contains it, then

```
STORED_OFFSET_OF_TEST DW TEST
```

is equivalent to

```
STORED_OFFSET_OF_TEST DW 320H
```

The EQU pseudo-op

In its simplest form EQU allows a name or value to be defined. However, it can also be used to define your own mnemonics (though before such a tempting facility is used it should be borne in mind that this will make it harder for others to read your programs). For example, given

```
     ENTER EQU MOV
   ADDRESS EQU DS:[BP]
INITIALIZER EQU AX,DS
```

then

```
ENTER INITIALIZER
ENTER AX,ADDRESS
```

assembles as

```
MOV AX,DS
MOV AX,DS:[BP]
```

Wherever `ENTER` appears in the assembly language program containing the above `EQU` statement it will be replaced by `MOV` on assembly. Similarly every occurrence of `ADDRESS` and `INITIALIZER` will be replaced by `DS:[BP]` and `AX,DS` respectively.

The = pseudo-op

A name defined by an `EQU` pseudo-op may not be subsequently redefined in the same program. If you want to be able to redefine a name in your program, the = pseudo-op must be used instead. For example:

```
CR = 0DH  ;Carriage Return
     .
     .
     .
CR = 0H   ;Current Record
CR = CR+1 ;increase value of Current Record
```

is allowed but

```
CR EQU 0DH     ;Carriage Return
     .
     .
     .
CR EQU 0H      ;illegal redefinition
CR EQU CR + 1 ;illegal self reference
```

is not.

EXERCISES

16.2 MASM will not produce an object program from the following assembly language program because it contains a number of errors. Remove these errors by making any sensible assumptions where necessary so that the basic computation carried out is as close as possible to the original intention. Check your answer by submitting your revised program to MASM until there are neither warning nor severe errors. (If you do work through this exercise, you will soon see how redefining the names of instructions is *not* conducive to high programmer productivity!)

```
  X = 0
  COPY EQU MOV
  ACC  EQU AX
  COUNTREG EQU CX
  DATA SEGMENT
       INITIAL_VALUES EQU THIS WORD
       VALUE          DB    OFFSET TEST_VALUES
       LETTER_COUNT   DD    TEST_SCORES
       TEST_VALUES    LABEL WORD
       TEST_ARRAY     LABEL BYTE
       COUNT = 1990D
       TEST_SCORES    DW   COUNT DUP('?')
       LAST LABEL WORD
  DATA ENDS

  WORKING_STORAGE SEGMENT STACK
          DW 100H DUP(?)
  WORKING_STORAGE ENDS

  CODE SEGMENT
  ASSUME CS:CODE,DS:DATA,SS:WORKING_STORAGE
 PROG_START: COPY ACC,DATA
             COPY DS,ACC
             COPY ACC,TEST_VALUES
             COPY COUNTREG,TEST_ARRAY[COUNT+1EH]
             COPY BX,TEST_SCORES[200H]
 NEXT_VALUE: ADD  AL,[BX]
             INC  BX
             LOOP NEXT_VALUE
             COPY BX,0F0H SHL 4 AND 0ABH
             COPY COUNTREG,OFFSET TEST_SCORES
             COPY EQU ADD
             ENTER EQU MOV
             COPY CL,X
             COPY CH,X + 1
             X = X + 1
             ENTER BP,OFFSET TEST_VALUES
 NEXT_LETTER:COPY  DL,[BP]
             INITIAL_VALUES EQU TEST_SCORES + 80H
             ENTER DH, TEST_SCORES
             ADD  BX,DX
             INC  BP
             LOOP NEXT_LETTER
             COPY  ACC,4C00H
             INT 21H
 CODE ENDS
 END PROG_START
```

16.3 Rewrite your corrected version of the program in Exercise 16.2 so that it does not use =, LABEL, or EQU.

16.5 The ASSUME pseudo-op

Because of the mechanism of specifying addresses in segment:offset form, it is essential for MASM to know which segment register is to be used when addressing both instructions and data. For code segments, MASM does this by insisting that the ASSUME pseudo-op is used to inform the assembler of the association between segment registers and segments. Indeed, at the very beginning of (or before) any segment containing 8086-family instructions, we *must* tell the assembler what it should assume will be in the CS register when that segment of code is executed.

But for segments not containing instructions MASM is more liberal. We can either control things by using ASSUME or by using segment overrides. Consider the program fragment of Figure 16.1 and suppose we wish to copy the contents of the byte DATA_BYTE into the first entry of SCREEN_DISPLAY. Because of

```
ASSUME CS:CODE,DS:DATA,ES:EXTRA
```

DS addresses the segment containing DATA_BYTE and ES addresses the segment containing SCREEN_DISPLAY. The copy is correctly made by

```
MOV AL,DATA_BYTE
MOV SCREEN_DISPLAY,AL
```

even though both instructions normally automatically use DS as the segment register for the data item to be moved.

This is because, thanks to the ASSUME statement, MASM knows that SCREEN_DISPLAY in

```
MOV SCREEN_DISPLAY,AL
```

refers to a location in the segment addressed by ES and so generates a segment override so that ES is used rather than DS. Hence the two instructions are assembled as

```
MOV AL,DATA_BYTE
MOV ES:SCREEN_DISPLAY,AL
```

In fact, it is not essential (though much easier in practice to do so) to provide an ASSUME pseudo-op to tell MASM about DS, ES and SS. But if this is not done, we are forced to provide the assembler with the information on an instruction-by-instruction basis, using segment override instructions. For example, the copy of DATA_BYTE into SCREEN_DISPLAY could be made without ASSUME pseudo-ops as follows:

```
MOV AL,DS:DATA_BYTE
MOV ES:SCREEN_DISPLAY,AL
```

Sometimes it is not always possible to know what will be in the segment registers when a particular instruction is executed and this leads to complications for which MASM provides a special version of the ASSUME pseudo-op, namely the

```
DATA SEGMENT
   DATA_BYTE DB 41H
DATA ENDS

EXTRA SEGMENT
   SCREEN_DISPLAY DB 2000H DUP(?)
EXTRA ENDS

CODE SEGMENT
        ASSUME CS:CODE,DS:DATA,ES:EXTRA
               MOV AX,DATA
               MOV DS,AX
               MOV ES,AX
               MOV AL,DATA_BYTE
               MOV SCREEN_DISPLAY,AL
        ASSUME DS:DATA,ES:DATA
               .
               .
               .
 NEXT_LETTER:  INC DATA_BYTE
               .
               .
               .
               MOV AX,EXTRA
               MOV DS,AX
               JMP NEXT_LETTER
               .
               .
               .
CODE ENDS
END
```

Figure 16.1 Program fragment to illustrate the ASSUME pseudo-op.

ASSUME *<reg-name>*:NOTHING

option.

Referring again to Figure 16.1, the first time the INC instruction is executed everything works out correctly: DATA_BYTE is in the segment currently addressed by DS, which is the default segment register for the INC instruction. However, subsequent instructions reset DS to point to the EXTRA segment, so that after the JMP is executed we shall execute INC with DS incorrectly set. How can we prevent this happening? The problem comes from the association between DS and DATA caused by ASSUME DS:DATA. ASSUME NOTHING allows us to cancel this association.

Thus in:

```
            ASSUME DS:NOTHING
NEXT_LETTER:INC DATA_BYTE
```

the problem is solved. ASSUME DS:NOTHING tells the assembler that from this point on DS is not to be assumed to refer to any particular named segment. On reaching INC DATA_BYTE after the ASSUME DS:NOTHING pseudo-op, MASM looks to see which named segment contains DATA_BYTE. The answer is DATA, so MASM then looks to see if it has a current assumption (ASSUME) about a register which can be used to address that segment. In this case, one such exists thanks to ASSUME ES:DATA, so ES can be used to address the segment containing DATA_BYTE. But INC uses the DS register as default, so MASM automatically generates a segment override and in this case assembles INC DATA_BYTE as INC ES:DATA_BYTE.

16.6 The ORG, EVEN and INCLUDE pseudo-ops

Table 16.3 contains two other entries for memory-related pseudo-ops (ORG and EVEN) and the five program-linkage pseudo-ops (NAME, END, PUBLIC, EXTRN and INCLUDE) of which only INCLUDE has not been encountered before.

We have already seen (in Section 4.6) how ORG may be used to address absolute locations in memory, and a further typical use of ORG in a complete example program is shown in Figure 19.6. ORG allows the assembly language programmer access to the assembler's internal location counter (see Section 14.1) which keeps a record of the next free address where an instruction or data item may be stored. Thus,

```
ORG 200H
```

sets the location counter to 200H relative to the start of the segment containing it. MASM allows the programmer to refer to the current value of the location counter by using the dollar sign ($). Thus expressions such as

```
ORG $+2
```

are allowed.

In the following example program fragment, PROC_LENGTH will be set to the number of bytes occupied by the MY_CODE segment.

```
MY_CODE SEGMENT
START_COUNTER = $
        .
        .
        .
    MOV BX,AX
    ADD CX,[BX]
        .
        .
        .
PROC_LENGTH = $-START_COUNTER-1
CODE ENDS
```

As was pointed out in Section 14.1, because pass one of the assembler must keep track of these relative offsets as it examines each source instruction, certain references must be known on pass one. The MASM manual gives full details of these but they include expressions appearing in the following pseudo-ops:

ORG *expression*
.RADIX *expression*
expression DUP(. . .)

Hence ORG OFFSET LATER+15 in

```
  ORG OFFSET LATER+15
      MOV AL,5
       .
       .
       .
LATER:MOV AX,DX
       .
       .
       .
```

would generate the assembler error message

```
MUST BE DECLARED IN PASS 1
```

since the OFFSET of LATER cannot be known until it has been calculated after pass one has moved on from the ORG pseudo-op. However,

```
      MOV AL,5
       .
       .
       .
LATER:MOV AX,DX
ORG OFFSET LATER+15
       .
       .
       .
```

is perfectly acceptable to MASM since, in this case, pass one will know the value of OFFSET LATER when it comes to the ORG pseudo-op.

The EVEN pseudo-op causes the location counter to go to an even-numbered address. This is especially useful with 8086-family processors, where all memory access begins with an even-numbered address (Section 2.3).

The INCLUDE pseudo-op is designed to eliminate the need to repeat a sequence of statements that are common to several source files – perhaps a set of research data expressed as a data segment. If these statements were in a file called STMENTS.ABC then

```
INCLUDE STMENTS.ABC
```

would cause the assembler to copy them into the assembly language program at the point where the INCLUDE directive appears.

EXERCISES

16.4 Using INCLUDE and the $ option of the ORG pseudo-op, write and test an 8086-family assembly language program which, given a set of 8086-family instructions (no data definitions!) in the file INSTRUCT.SET, will print out in decimal the number of locations occupied by those instructions. Assume that the only explicit references to memory data locations concern the word variables MY_WORD_1, MY_WORD_2 and MY_WORD_3 and declare these in the data segment of your own program.

16.5 Rewrite the following program by adding ASSUME statements and removing segment overrides only, so that no explicit segment overrides are required in the program.

```
SEG1 SEGMENT
DATA1 DW ?
TIME1 DW ?
SEG1 ENDS

SEG2 SEGMENT
DATA2 DW ?
TIME2 DW ?
SEG2 ENDS

SEG3 SEGMENT
DATA3 DW ?
TIME3 DW ?
SEG3 ENDS

WORKING_STORAGE SEGMENT STACK
            DW 100H DUP(?)
WORKING_STORAGE ENDS
CODE SEGMENT
ASSUME CS:CODE,DS:SEG1,ES:SEG2,SS:WORKING_STORAGE
PROG_START:MOV AX,ES:DATA3
    MOV DATA1,AX
    MOV AX,DATA2
    MOV ES:DATA3,AX
    ADD AX,ES:TIME3
    MOV SEG2:TIME3,AX
    MOV AX,DS
    MOV ES,AX
    MOV DS,BX
    MOV AX,ES:DATA2
    MOV DS:TIME2,AX
CODE ENDS
END PROG_START
```

16.7 Controlling assembler printout

MASM supplies a range of facilities to assist the programmer in producing relevant, well-laid-out and fully titled printouts of programs or parts of programs. This section briefly discusses six of these: PAGE, TITLE, SUBTTL, .LIST, .XLIST, and %OUT. For the production of relatively small programs these facilities are hardly necessary. Even our larger example programs in Appendices II, III and IV do not really lack anything because they didn't make use of them. But for an industrial-scale project, careful production of documentation is important both during development (to ensure focusing on the important part of the large program which is being tested, and to avoid wasting time and paper through unnecessarily large printouts) and to ensure efficient maintenance of the program during its subsequent life.

PAGE is used to set the length and width of the page, since the former will depend upon the paper being used and the latter on the make and type of printer being used, as well as its current settings (many printers allow a choice of page width). PAGE can be used in three forms:

```
PAGE
PAGE+
PAGE <page length>,<page width>
```

The most general form takes two operands, the first of which controls the page length and can be a number in the range 10 to 255. The second operand specifies the page width, the default setting of which is 80 characters. It may be any number in the range 60 to 132.

If a page length is not explicitly stated, the default is 64 lines per page. Each page of the printout produced by the assembler contains a chapter number and a page number (for example 3–2 is Chapter 3, page 2). The page number is incremented when a page is full or when PAGE is used with no operands (which also causes the printer to go to the top of a new page). To increment the chapter number, the PAGE+ version of the pseudo-op is used, indicating also that the page number is to be reset to 1.

TITLE takes the form

```
TITLE <string of at most 60 characters>
```

and allows the programmer to specify a program title which will be reproduced on the first line of each page of the program printout.

SUBTTL takes one of two forms:

```
SUBTTL
SUBTTL <string of at most 60 characters>
```

and allows a subtitle to be printed on the line after the title in each page heading. Note that for both TITLE and SUBTTL the text displayed is limited to 60 characters as, for example, in:

```
TITLE MY PASCAL COMPILER VERSION 1.1
SUBTTL SYNTAX ANALYSIS ROUTINES
```

If no NAME pseudo-op is used and the first six characters of the program title form a valid name, then those six characters are taken as the module name. Subtitling is turned off by the use of the SUBTTL pseudo-op without a text string. A subsequent SUBTTL with a different text string could be used to give another subtitle, more relevant to the particular part of the assembly language program in which the pseudo-op occurs.

Output from the assembler to the file containing the printout can be controlled by the .LIST and .XLIST pseudo-ops. The default is .LIST. When a .XLIST is encountered, the formation of a printout by the assembler is stopped until a .LIST pseudo-op is encountered. When working on a large program this is a useful facility, for .LST files are large, as you will no doubt have discovered.

The %OUT pseudo-op allows messages to be displayed on the screen at programmer-selected points during a long assembly whenever a %OUT is encountered. Thus, when the assembler reaches the pseudo-op

```
%OUT ABOUT TO ASSEMBLE CALC PROCEDURE
```

the message ABOUT TO ASSEMBLE CALC PROCEDURE will be displayed on the computer's display screen.

EXERCISES

16.6 Type in the following program, assemble it observing the display screen during assembly and inspect the .LST file produced by the assembler. Obtain a printout of the .LST file and carefully inspect that.

```
PAGE   10,60
TITLE  PRINTOUT CONTROL ILLUSTRATION PROGRAM
SUBTTL DATA SEGMENT
%OUT   STARTING DATA ASSEMBLY
DATA SEGMENT
       FIRST_QUANTITY DB ?
       SECOND_QUANTITY DB ?
DATA ENDS

PAGE
SUBTTL WORKING_STORAGE SEGMENT
WORKING_STORAGE SEGMENT STACK
       DW 100H DUP(?)
WORKING_STORAGE ENDS
%OUT FINISHED STACK ASSEMBLY

PAGE+
SUBTTL MAIN PROGRAM
CODE SEGMENT
ASSUME CS:CODE,DS:DATA,SS:WORKING_STORAGE
.XLIST
```

```
PROG_START:MOV AL,FIRST_QUANTITY
           ADD AL,SECOND_QUANTITY
           %OUT IN MIDDLE OF CODE NOW
           MOV FIRST_QUANTITY,AL
       CODE ENDS
       END PROG_START
```

16.7 During assembly of the program in Exercise 16.6, the three %OUT messages are in fact displayed twice:

```
STARTING DATA ASSEMBLY
FINISHED STACK ASSEMBLY
IN MIDDLE OF CODE NOW
STARTING DATA ASSEMBLY
FINISHED STACK ASSEMBLY
IN MIDDLE OF CODE NOW
```

Can you explain why?

SUMMARY

In this chapter we have studied some of the more advanced features of MASM assembly language. Among these were: the ability to use expressions in statements and an associated set of operators; data definition pseudo-ops which allow the programmer to define data items in more than one way; the = pseudo-op which allows symbols to be defined in programs for which the value can change during the course of a program; and segment overrides.

The = pseudo-op will come to prominence in Chapter 18 for it is vital in the construction of macros. Segment overrides will be especially important when we come to discuss I/O programming in Chapters 20–22. Before that, however, the next chapter deals with RECORD and STRUC – two advanced data structuring features of MASM.

SELF-CHECK QUIZ

1. Explain the difference between a name and a label in an assembly language statement.

2. Given

```
MY_NUMS DW 50H DUP(42)
```

defined in a segment addressed by DS and that the contents of DS is 02ABH, what will be the contents of AX, BX, CX and DX after execution of:

```
NEXT:MOV AX,SEG MY_NUMS
```

```
MOV BX,TYPE MY_NUMS
MOV CX,TYPE NEXT
MOV DX,LENGTH MY_NUMS
JZ NEXT
```

3. Given

```
DATA SEGMENT
INTEREST EQU 15
RATES DW 30H DUP(0)
  .
  .
  .
```

what will be the contents of AX, BX, CX and DX after execution of :

```
MOV AX,INTEREST * (21 + 35 / 100)
MOV BX,OFFSET RATES + INTEREST
MOV CX,120H MOD INTEREST
MOV DX,NOT 23H
ADD DX,71H LT 32H
```

4. In how many different ways can we use pseudo-ops to redefine the first byte of storage assigned in:

```
MY_WORD DW 1234H
```

as a byte variable referred to by the name `MY_FIRST_BYTE`?

5. Given

```
COUNT = 21H
MY_WORDS DW COUNT DUP(1234H)
```

what will be the contents of AX, BX, CX and DX after execution of:

```
MOV AX,SIZE MY_WORDS + COUNT
COUNT = 14H
MOV BX,SIZE MY_WORDS - COUNT
COUNT = (COUNT * 6) OR 32H
MOV CX,COUNT
MOV DX,COUNT + COUNT
```

6. Write a short program fragment which makes essential use of the `ASSUME` pseudo-op and which illustrates how `ASSUME` and segment overrides can sometimes be used interchangeably.

7. What will be the contents of BL and CL after execution of

```
CODE SEGMENT
ASSUME CS:CODE,. . .
   MOV CX,3
   MOV DX,4
   ADD CX,DX
   MOV BL,BYTE PTR $
   ADD CL,BL
   MOV BL,BYTE PTR $
```

8. Write the shortest possible program fragment you can to illustrate all the different uses of `PTR`.

9. Why is:

```
MY_BYTE DB ?
  .
  .
  .
MOV AX,NOT (OFFSET MY_BYTE)
;illegal instruction
```

not allowed?

10. What is the difference between `INCLUDE` and `CALL`?

17

STRUC and RECORD

Contents

Pascal offers the convenience of records to programmers because these aid efficient program development. The 8086-family assembly language is also a programming language in its own right, so its designers decided to include several means of structuring data equivalent to Pascal's records and sets so that similar efficiency gains could be made. This chapter looks at two of these: **structure variables** and **record variables**. Structure variables correspond to Pascal's records and enable several groups of bytes to be considered as a single data item. Record variables correspond to Pascal's sets and allow us to refer to groups of bits as a single unit.

In Pascal the type of a record must be declared before we can define data items of that type. The same is true for structure and record variables. Before using them, we must first declare their composition using the STRUC and RECORD pseudo-ops. Then the variables themselves can be specified in a data defining segment of a program.

MASM provides various operators for working with structure and record variables and we shall discuss these below. But in order to use structure variables properly the important 8086-family instruction LEA

(Load Effective Address) will also be introduced. The chapter contains two complete program examples respectively showing structure and record variables in use.

17.1 The STRUC pseudo-op

The STRUC pseudo-op allows constructions which resemble records in a high-level language like Pascal. STRUC is used to define a family of structures and then individual **structure variables** belonging to this family can be used in the data-defining segments of a program.

The definition of a family of structure variables takes the general form:

structure name STRUC

.
.
.

structure name ENDS

A structure variable is a collection of bytes in which specific groups of bytes can be accessed symbolically. The groups of bytes can have different sizes, but each member of a family will have the same groupings and the symbolic names for the groups will be the same. In what follows, instead of talking about groups we shall use the preferred technical term and call them **fields**.

The fields and the names of the fields in a structure variable are defined by using DB, DW, and so on. Thus, in the family of structure variables called REPORT and defined as follows:

```
REPORT STRUC
       HEADER  DB 30H DUP(' ')
       DATE    DB 6D DUP(0)
       CONTENT DB 2000H DUP(' ')
REPORT ENDS
```

there are three fields labeled HEADER, DATE and CONTENT respectively. The HEADER field is 30H bytes long, the DATE field is 6 bytes long and the CONTENT field is 2000H bytes long. In our definition of the REPORT family, text fields have been initialized to ASCII space characters and the numeric field to zeros.

We shall conventionally define families of structure variables at the very beginning of an assembly language program. MASM does not demand that we do this, but it fits in with our philosophy of mirroring Pascal by defining our data items at the start of a program. In order to use structure variables belonging to a family, we must tell the assembler the name of each variable and the name of the family to which it belongs. We must also specify either one or more initial values for the fields by enclosing these values in angle brackets < and > or, if we do not want to override any initialization which was given in the definition of this family of structure variables then we can just specify < >.

Thus, a program which makes use of the REPORT structure family might begin:

```
REPORT STRUC
       HEADER  DB 30H DUP(' ')
       DATE    DB 6D DUP(0)
       CONTENT DB 2000H DUP(' ')
REPORT ENDS

DATA SEGMENT
          .
          .
          .
      SALES  REPORT < >
  MARKETING REPORT < >
          .
          .
          .
```

in which we have defined two structure variables belonging to the REPORT family, both of which have the initialized field values given in the definition of the REPORT family itself.

We can, if we wish, set other (not necessarily blank or zero) default values for the various fields in the initial definition of a family of structure variables. For example:

```
ADDRESS STRUC
        PERSON   DB 'THE OCCUPIER'
        STREET   DB 'IF UNDELIVERED PLEASE RETURN'
        CITY     DB 'TO SENDER'
        ZIP_CODE DB 'AB12 3DE'
        COUNTRY  DB 'UK'
ADDRESS ENDS
```

defines a family of ADDRESS structure variables in which PERSON labels a field which is 12D bytes long and has the default value THE OCCUPIER and STREET labels a field which is 28D bytes wide and has the default value IF UNDELIVERED PLEASE RETURN, and so on.

The name given to a field can be used to access the corresponding field in a structure variable belonging to this family. It represents the offset of the field from the beginning of the structure. Thus, the fields PERSON, STREET, CITY, ZIP_CODE and COUNTRY in structure variables belonging to the ADDRESS family have offsets 0, 12D, 40D, 49D and 57D from the beginning of the structure.

Having defined the ADDRESS family, let us define a structure variable belonging to this family:

```
ADDRESS STRUC
        PERSON   DB 'THE OCCUPIER'
        STREET   DB 'IF UNDELIVERED PLEASE RETURN'
        CITY     DB 'TO SENDER'
        ZIP_CODE DB 'AB12 3DE'
        COUNTRY  DB 'UK'
ADDRESS ENDS
```

```
DATA SEGMENT
  .
  .
  .
;Note that the following MUST be submitted to MASM as a single
;line.
;
HOME1 ADDRESS <'MR J. BLOGGS','14 RAILWAY CUTTINGS','LONDON','NW10 2AG','
  .
  .
  .
DATA ENDS
```

The definition of HOME1 as a member of the ADDRESS family causes storage to be reserved which is initialized as shown by the following extract from the screen display when a debugger was used to inspect the above data segment:

```
23E4:0120 4D 52 20 4A 2E 20 42 4C-4F 47 47 53 31 34 20 52 MR J. BLOGGS14 R
23E4:0130 41 49 4C 57 41 59 20 43-55 54 54 49 4E 47 53 20 AILWAY CUTTINGS
23E4:0140 20 20 20 20 20 20 20 20-4C 4F 4E 44 4F 4E 20 20         LONDON
23E4:0150 20 4E 57 31 30 20 32 41-47 47 42                 NW10 2AGGB
```

Notice that since 14 RAILWAY CUTTINGS occupies only 19D bytes of the STREET field (which is 28D bytes wide), MASM automatically fills the remaining bytes with the ASCII code for a space (20H). The same is true for LONDON which occupies only six bytes of a field nine bytes wide. As we shall see shortly, not all fields are overridable in this way however.

Alternatively, we could define an ADDRESS structure variable using the default values for the PERSON and COUNTRY fields:

```
DATA SEGMENT
  .
  .
  .
      HOME2 ADDRESS <,'27 BLACK STREET','BRIGHTON','BL5 3TW',>
  .
  .
  .
DATA ENDS
```

In this case, storage is allocated as shown by the following debugger screen dump:

```
23E4:0160 54 48 45 20 4F 43 43 55-50 49 45 52 32 37 20 42 THE OCCUPIER27 B
23E4:0170 4C 41 43 4B 20 53 54 52-45 45 54 20 20 20 20 20 LACK STREET
23E4:0180 20 20 20 20 20 20 20 20-42 52 49 47 48 54 4F 4E         BRIGHTON
23E4:0190 20 42 4C 35 20 33 54 57-20 55 4B                 BL5 3TW UK
```

and we see that:

(1) the default values of THE OCCUPIER and UK have been inserted in the PERSON and COUNTRY fields;

(2) the STREET field has been filled out with additional spaces because 27 BLACK STREET occupies 13D characters too few; and

(3) an extra space has been added to the CITY field because BRIGHTON is one character too few.

Likewise, if we want to use structure variables to record some of the details from student transcripts, then an appropriate structure family definition might be:

```
STUDENT STRUC
        PERSON   DB 'ABCDEFGHIJKLMN'
        COLLEGE  DB 'ABCDEFGHIJKLMN'
        AGE      DB 23
        GRADYEAR DW 1991
        SUBJECT  DB 'ABCDEFGHIJKLMN'
        MARKS    DB 10 DUP(0)
STUDENT ENDS
```

Then we could have:

```
DATA SEGMENT
  .
  .
  .
GOODPUPIL STUDENT <'JONES ', 'SUNDERLAND',, 1971,>
BADPUPIL  STUDENT <'BROWN ', 'SUNDERLAND',, 1970,>
  .
  .
  .
DATA ENDS
```

In this case, there are no sensible settings of the 'default' values for any of the fields. Rather, these were used merely to specify the field sizes. Consequently, even though MASM will fill the appropriate memory locations with the default values, these would be ignored:

```
23E4:0120 4A 4F 4E 45 53 20 20 20-20 20 20 20 20 20 53 55 JONES         SU
23E4:0130 4E 44 45 52 4C 41 4E 44-20 20 20 20 17 B3 07 41 NDERLAND    ...A
23E4:0140 42 43 44 45 46 47 48 49-4A 4B 4C 4D 4E 00 00 00 BCDEFGHIJKLMN...
23E4:0150 00 00 00 00 00 00 00 42-52 4F 57 4E 20 20 20 20 .......BROWN
23E4:0160 20 20 20 20 20 53 55 4E-44 45 52 4C 41 4E 44 20      SUNDERLAND
23E4:0170 20 20 20 20 B2 07 41 42-43 44 45 46 47 48 49 4A     .. ABCDEFGHIJ
23E4:0180 4B 4C 4D 4E 00 00 00 00-00 00 00 00 00 00 00 00 KLMN............
```

We have already observed that fields within a structure variable are of two types – **overridable** and **not overridable**. A field with only one entry (such as a number or a string) is overridable whereas a field with multiple entries is not overridable. Thus, in STUDENT, all the fields are overridable except MARKS because DUP defines a field with multiple entries. Similarly, in:

```
FORM_LAYOUT STRUC
       BUFFER DB 3200D DUP(' ')
       CRLF   DB 0DH,0AH
       PROMPT DB 'YOUR NAME'
       COUNT  DW 566D
FORM_LAYOUT ENDS
```

the PROMPT and COUNT fields can be overridden whereas the BUFFER and CRLF fields cannot.

Within a MASM program, access to the fields of a structure variable is gained via the *structure name.field name* convention similar to that used for records in Pascal. Thus, referring to our examples above, we could have:

```
MOV AL,GOODPUPIL.AGE
```

or

```
MOV AL,[BX].AGE
```

if BX was pointing to GOODPUPIL. As we shall see in the following example, some fields in a STRUC may not be named, in which case they are not accessible in this way.

17.1.1 A complete example program using STRUC

Given information about four students and their performance in mathematics, physics and chemistry exams, our program will display on the screen a summary of the grades obtained by all students and, for each subject, calculate the average grade for that subject on the basis that grade A counts 1, grade B counts 2. . .. Thus, when the program is run, the output will be:

```
        STUDENT NAME   MATH PHYSICS CHEMISTRY
1237 WILSON A.J.         A     E        D
2107 SMITH-JONES R.      B     D        D
8095 CUNNINGHAM M.R.     C     C        C
5184 FEATHERSTONE B.     A     F        C
     AVERAGE GRADES      B     D        C
```

We shall use:

```
GRADE_CARD STRUC
      NUMBER DB '1234'
             DB '$'
        NAME DB '123456789ABCDEF'
             DB '$'
        MATH DB 0
     PHYSICS DB 0
   CHEMISTRY DB 0
GRADE_CARD ENDS
```

wherein the field NUMBER will be used to store a 4-digit student number, the NAME field will contain the student's name (up to 15 characters), and the MATH, PHYSICS and CHEMISTRY fields will contain the ASCII code for the grade the student obtained in that subject (one of A, B, C, D, E or F). The two fields without names are there to make programming easier. By defining them to have $ values as default, the values of the NUMBER and NAME fields can be printed out using the PRINTSTRING subroutine (function 9 of INT 21H).

The data for the program is supplied as GRADE_CARD definitions in the data segment:

```
STUDENT  GRADE_CARD <'1237',,'WILSON A.J.         ',,'A','E','D'>
         GRADE_CARD <'2107',,'SMITH_JONES R.      ',,'B','D','D'>
         GRADE_CARD <'8095',,'CUNNINGHAM M.R.     ',,'C','C','C'>
         GRADE_CARD <'5184',,'FEATHERSTONE B.     ',,'A','F','C'>

AVERAGES GRADE_CARD <'    ',' ','AVERAGE GRADES',,,,>
```

Here, the AVERAGES structure is another programming device and saves us trouble organizing layout.

An outline of the program (see Figure 17.1) is now easy to write. We build up totals of the numerical equivalents of the grades for each subject in the array SUM which is initialized to zero in the data segment. (In the outline, *spaces* is a procedure which takes a single argument – a non-negative whole number *n* – and prints *n* spaces on the screen.)

Implementing this outline in 8086-family assembly language is fairly straightforward. We have divided it up into two modules. The first (in a file called GRADE.ASM) contains the main program. The second (in a file called PRINTRTS.ASM) contains subroutines PRINTCHAR, PRINTSTRING, PRINT_NEWLINE and

---

establish data segment addressability;
print headings;
for *i* := 1 **to** 4 **do**
  begin
  write(*grade_card of student*[*i*];
  spaces(3);
  write(*student*[*i*].*math*);
  sum[0] := *sum*[0] + *student*[*i*].*math*;
  spaces(6);
  write(*student*[*i*].*physics*);
  sum[1] := *sum*[1] + *student*[*i*].*physics*;
  spaces(9);
  writeln(*student*[*i*].*chemistry*);
  sum[2] := *sum*[2] + *student*[*i*].*chemistry*
  end;
write(*averages heading*);
for *i* := 0 **to** 2 **do** *sum* [*i*] := *round*(*sum*[*i*] / 4);
spaces(3);
print the math average;
spaces(6);
print the physics average;
spaces(9);
print the chemistry average;
print a new line;
return to DOS

Figure 17.1 Pseudo-Pascal outline of student marks program.

SPACES, most of which we have met before and which can now be tucked away in the PRINTRTS module for use when needed. These two modules are given in Figures 17.2 and 17.3.

```
EXTRN PRINTSTRING:FAR
EXTRN PRINTCHAR:FAR
EXTRN PRINT_NEWLINE:FAR
EXTRN SPACES:FAR

GRADE_CARD STRUC
      NUMBER    DB '1234'
                DB '$'
      NAME      DB '123456789ABCDEF'
                DB '$'
      MATH      DB 0
      PHYSICS   DB 0
      CHEMISTRY DB 0
GRADE_CARD ENDS

DATA SEGMENT
STUDENT  GRADE_CARD <'1237',,'WILSON A.J.      ',,'A','E','D'>
         GRADE_CARD <'2107',,'SMITH-JONES R.   ',,'B','D','D'>
         GRADE_CARD <'8095',,'CUNNINGHAM M.R.  ',,'C','C','C'>
         GRADE_CARD <'5184',,'FEATHERSTONE B.  ',,'A','F','C'>

AVERAGES GRADE_CARD <'    ',' ','AVERAGE GRADES',,,,>

HEADING DB '        STUDENT NAME    MATH PHYSICS CHEMISTRY','$'
SUM DB 3 DUP(0)
DATA ENDS

WORKING_STORAGE SEGMENT STACK
         DW 100H DUP(?)
WORKING_STORAGE ENDS

CODE SEGMENT
ASSUME CS:CODE,DS:DATA,SS:WORKING_STORAGE
       ;establish data segment addressability
        START: MOV AX,DATA
               MOV DS,AX
       ;print heading
               MOV  DX,OFFSET HEADING
               CALL PRINTSTRING
               CALL PRINT_NEWLINE
       ;for i := 1 to 4 do
               MOV CX,4
               MOV BX,OFFSET STUDENT
               ;begin
               ;write(grade_card of student[i])
       NEXT_STUDENT: LEA  DX,[BX].NUMBER
                     CALL PRINTSTRING
```

Figure 17.2
Contents of the file GRADE.ASM.

```
                MOV  AL,1
                CALL SPACES
                LEA  DX,[BX].NAME
                CALL PRINTSTRING
        ;spaces(3)
                MOV  AL,3
                CALL SPACES
        ;write(student[i].math)
                MOV  DL,[BX].MATH
                CALL PRINTCHAR
        ;sum[0] := sum[0] + student[i].math
                SUB  DL,40H
                ADD  SUM[0],DL
        ;spaces(6)
        ;write(student[i].physics)
                MOV  AL,6
                CALL SPACES
                MOV  DL,[BX].PHYSICS
                CALL PRINTCHAR
        ;sum[1] := sum[1] + student[i].physics
                SUB  DL,40H
                ADD  SUM[1],DL
        ;spaces(9)
                MOV  AL,9
                CALL SPACES
        ;writeln(student[i].chemistry)
                MOV  DL,[BX].CHEMISTRY
                CALL PRINTCHAR
                CALL PRINT_NEWLINE
        ;sum[2] := sum[2] + student[i].chemistry
                SUB  DL,40H
                ADD  SUM[2],DL
        ;end
                ADD  BX,SIZE STUDENT
                LOOP NEXT_STUDENT
    ;write(averages)
             MOV  DX,OFFSET AVERAGES
             CALL PRINTSTRING
    ;for i := 0 to 2 do sum[i] := round(sum[i]/4)
             MOV  CX,3
             MOV  SI,0
NEXT_AVERAGE:MOV  AL,SUM[SI]
             CBW
             MOV  BL,4
             DIV  BL
             CMP  AH,2
             JBE  DONT_ROUND
             INC  AL
  DONT_ROUND:MOV  SUM[SI],AL
             INC  SI
             LOOP NEXT_AVERAGE
    ;spaces(3)
             MOV  AL,3D
             CALL SPACES
    ;print(math average);
```

Figure 17.2
(*cont.*)

```
        MOV  DL,SUM[0]
        ADD  DL,40H
        CALL PRINTCHAR
;spaces(6)
        MOV  AL,6
        CALL SPACES
;print(physics average)
        MOV  DL,SUM[1]
        ADD  DL,40H
        CALL PRINTCHAR
;spaces(9)
        MOV  AL,9
        CALL SPACES
;print(chemistry average)
        MOV  DL,SUM[2]
        ADD  DL,40H
        CALL PRINTCHAR
        CALL PRINT_NEWLINE
;return to DOS
        MOV  AX,4C00H
        INT  21H

      CODE ENDS
      END START
```

Figure 17.2
(cont.)

There is just one minor (and easily solved) problem, however. PRINTSTRING requires the address of the string to be printed to be in register DX. We want to use it to print the NAME fields of the GRADE_CARDs for each student. Now if BX is set to point to STUDENT (the starting address of the first of the four GRADE_CARDs) as can easily be done via

```
MOV BX,OFFSET STUDENT
```

then the NAME component of the first GRADE_CARD is specified by [BX].NAME and so we want an instruction which is equivalent to the *illegal*:

```
MOV DX,OFFSET [BX].NAME ;illegal instruction
```

A solution is provided by the 8086-family instruction LEA (Load Effective Address):

```
LEA DX,[BX].NAME
```

LEA is more powerful than using OFFSET in an instruction such as

MOV *reg*,OFFSET *name*

because an index or base register can be used to form the effective address. Thus

```
MOV AX,OFFSET MY_VARIABLE
```

```
        CR EQU ODH
        LF EQU OAH
        SPACE EQU 20H

        CODE SEGMENT
        ASSUME CS:CODE
        PUBLIC PRINTSTRING,PRINTCHAR,PRINT_NEWLINE,SPACES

        PRINTSTRING PROC FAR
        MOV AH,9
        INT 21H
        RET
        PRINTSTRING ENDP

        PRINTCHAR PROC FAR
        MOV AH,2
        INT 21H
        RET
        PRINTCHAR ENDP

        PRINT_NEWLINE PROC FAR
        PUSH DX
        MOV  DL,CR
        CALL PRINTCHAR
        MOV  DL,LF
        CALL PRINTCHAR
        POP  DX
        RET
        PRINT_NEWLINE ENDP

        SPACES PROC FAR
                  PUSH CX
                  MOV  CH,0
                  MOV  CL,AL
      NEXT_SPACE: MOV  DL,SPACE
                  CALL PRINTCHAR
                  LOOP NEXT_SPACE
                  POP  CX
                  RET
        SPACES ENDP

  CODE ENDS
  END
```

Figure 17.3 Contents of the file PRINTRTS.ASM.

and

```
LEA AX,MY_VARIABLE
```

are exactly equivalent whereas

```
MOV AX,OFFSET SUM[SI] ;is illegal
LEA AX,SUM[SI]        ;is legal
```

Thus, in general, LEA and OFFSET can be used interchangeably, but if we want an index or base register to be used to form the effective address for an instruction then LEA *must* be used.

Nesting of structure variables is not allowed

The STRUC pseudo-op may *not* appear inside a

```
structure name STRUC
            .
            .
            .
structure name ENDS
```

definition. It follows that structure variables cannot be nested.

EXERCISES

17.1 Modify the example program so that:

(a) it will accept the grades of ten students not just four;

(b) it will also accept grades for biology and calculate the average biology grade for all students.

Test your answers on a computer.

17.2 Wonway Flights Inc. is a small airline operating four flights a day:

```
17.50 LONDON NEW YORK     11.50
13.00 LONDON MARSEILLES   17.00
15.50 LONDON ZAGREB       22.50
18.00 LONDON NEW YORK     20.00
```

Write and test a program which, given a required flight time and destination, will print out complete details of the nearest available flight to the specified time. Use MASM STRUC pseudo-ops to represent the flight timetable.

17.3 Using a modified version of the pseudo-random number generator of Section 14.2 (or otherwise), write a program to simulate the game of Snap with an ordinary pack of playing cards. (If you and I play Snap, we each start with one half of the pack and with the cards face down. I turn over my top card, you turn over yours. If the turned-over cards belong to the same suit the first person to say 'Snap' wins that hand. If they belong to different suits the two cards are added to a pile on the table.

This pile is collected by the person who wins the hand and added face down to the bottom of his or her pile. The next hand then commences by both players turning over their top cards. The first person to run out of cards is the loser.) Represent each card as a structure belonging to the family defined by:

```
CARD STRUC
   NUMBER DB 0
   SUIT   DB 0
CARD ENDS
```

17.4 Write an 8086-family assembly language program which simulates the operation of a simple library book issue system. When a book is issued to a reader, the date of issue, name and number of the book, name and address of the borrower, and date due for return are to be recorded in memory. All books are loaned for a period of 14 days. When a book is returned, a check is made that the book has been returned on or before its due date. Any late returns are charged for at $1 per book per week or per part of a week. At the end of a session, the program should print a total of all fines charged. Use structure variables wherever sensible.

17.2 The RECORD pseudo-op

While for most purposes it is convenient to handle data in units of a byte, when programming hardware devices at the assembly level it is often necessary to handle data in groups of bits. MASM provides the RECORD pseudo-op to assist the programmer when data has to be handled in this way. Using the RECORD pseudo-op we are able to declare families of **record variables** in 8086-family assembly language programs. These are similar to structure variables except that a record variable is a byte or word variable in which specific groups of bits can be accessed symbolically. The total number of bits occupied by all the different groups in a family cannot exceed 16 bits (32 bits for the 80386 microprocessor and more powerful members of the 8086 family – see Chapter 23).

Consider, then, the use of a family of record variables to assist in programming an IBM-PC color display. When displaying text in color, the foreground and background colors for each character position of the screen are determined by the settings within the relevant attribute byte: bits 0,1,2 and 3 determining the background color; bits 4,5 and 6 determining the foreground color; and bit 7 determining whether or not, when the character is displayed, it will flash on and off (we say, 'blink'). The attribute byte settings are shown in Figure 17.4.

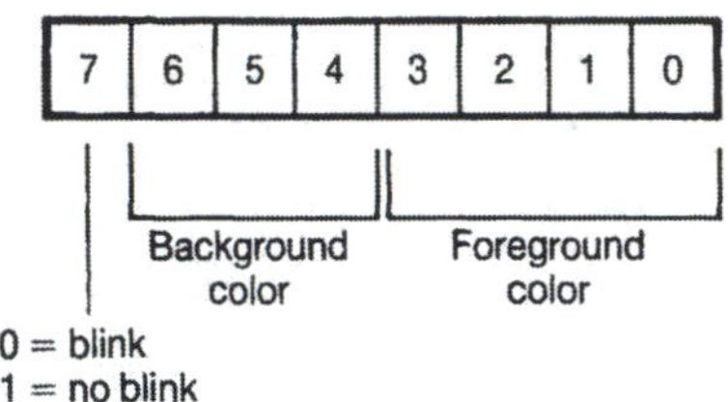

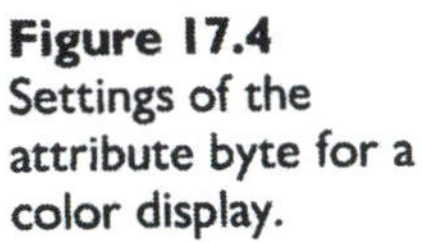
Figure 17.4
Settings of the attribute byte for a color display.

To declare a family of MASM record variables for use in this situation, we use the RECORD pseudo-op as in:

```
COLOR_SETTING RECORD BLINK:1,BACKGROUND:3,FOREGROUND:4
```

This declares the family name, COLOR_SETTING, and the names and sizes of the individual fields of bits which record variables belonging to this family will have. In this case there are three fields: BLINK which consists of a single bit; BACKGROUND which is three bits wide; and FOREGROUND which is four bits wide.

In order to use record variables belonging to this family, we must tell MASM the name of each variable and the name of the family to which it belongs. At the same time we can, if we wish, specify an initial value for any or all of the individual fields. Thus, in

```
MENU COLOR_SETTING <0,2,3>
```

we declare MENU to be a MASM record variable belonging to the COLOR_SETTING family and that the initial value for the single bit referred to by BLINK is 0, that the initial value for the three bits referred to by BACKGROUND is 010 and that the initial value for the four bits referred to by FOREGROUND is 0011.

MASM arranges that a byte or word of storage is associated with each record variable, whichever is most appropriate. In the case of record variables belonging to the COLOR_SETTING family, the total number of bytes involved in each such variable is eight and therefore a byte will be reserved in memory corresponding to MENU. As a result of

```
MENU COLOR_SETTING <0,2,3>
```

this byte will be initialized to 00100011B.

Within a program, we shall adopt the convention that declarations of families of record variables using the RECORD pseudo-op will come at the very beginning of an assembly language program. Since the declaration of a record variable actually assigns storage, record variable declarations must come within a data-defining segment of a program – which we shall normally assume is the DATA segment. Thus, the pattern of declarations for COLOR_SETTING and MENU according to our convention would be:

```
COLOR_SETTING RECORD BLINK:1,BACKGROUND:3,FOREGROUND:4
   .
   .
   .
DATA SEGMENT
   .
   .
   .
   MENU COLOR_SETTING <0,2,3>
   .
   .
   .
DATA ENDS

WORKING_STORAGE SEGMENT STACK
   .
   .
   .
WORKING_STORAGE ENDS

CODE SEGMENT
ASSUME...
     .
     .
     .
CODE ENDS
END...
```

The RECORD pseudo-op takes the following general form:

rec-name RECORD *field1*:*width1*, *field2*:*width2*,. . .

where *rec-name* gives a name to records of this type; *field1*, *field2*, and so on, give the names of the fields; and *width1*, *width2*, and so on, specify the number of bits in the field (allowed range – 1 to 16D inclusive).

In a record the first field declared goes into the most significant bits, and successively declared fields are placed in the succeeding bits to the right. The total number of bits in the different fields which make up a record variable must be at most 16, but otherwise can be any number between 1 and 16. If the total number of bits can be represented in a byte then MASM will make record variables of that type correspond to bytes, otherwise they will correspond to words. If the total number of bits is less than 8 (byte) or 16 (word), the fields are right justified into the least significant bit positions of the byte or word, respectively.

For example, given

```
TIME RECORD HOURS:6,MINUTES:6
   .
   .
   .
DATA SEGMENT
   .
   .
   .
```

```
    START_TIME TIME <10,02>
    .
    .
    .
```

the total width of the fields in START_TIME is 12 bits and so MASM reserves a word of storage corresponding to START_TIME in which the HOURS and MINUTES fields are right justified and the unused bits are indeterminate. Thus, the result of

```
START_TIME TIME <10,02>
```

is that a word is reserved in store, initially set to ????001010000010B (where a ? denotes a bit which is indeterminate).

Note that we could *not* have declared

```
TIME RECORD HOURS:6,MINUTES:6,SECONDS:6 ;illegal total field width
```

because the total width of the fields would then be 18 – more than can be accommodated in a word. (As we shall see in Chapter 23, this would, however, be possible using an 80386 processor.)

If we do not wish to give initial values to any of the fields then a value is simply omitted. Thus, given

```
DATE RECORD MONTH:4,DAY:5,YEAR:7
    .
    .
    .
DATA SEGMENT
    .
    .
    .
    START_DATE DATE <10,,91>
    .
    .
    .
```

START_DATE is initialized with MONTH as 1010 and YEAR as 1001011 and DAY indeterminate. Similarly:

```
START_DATE DATE <,1,91>
```

leaves the MONTH field uninitialized,

```
START_DATE DATE <,,91>
```

leaves both MONTH and DAY fields uninitialized,

```
START_DATE DATE <10,1,>
```

leaves YEAR uninitialized and

```
START_DATE DATE <>
```

leaves all three fields uninitialized.

More than one member of a record variable family may be declared at once by using the DUP pseudo-op, in much the same way that DUP can be used in conjunction with DB, DW, and so on. Thus:

```
MY_DATES DATE 24H DUP(<>)
```

causes MASM to reserve 24H words of storage, the first of which can be referred to by the variable MY_DATES. Each of these words will be regarded by MASM as corresponding to a record variable of DATE type.

17.2.1 Sets and RECORD operators

This section will illustrate the operators MASM provides for manipulating RECORD variables – shift count, WIDTH and MASK – in the context of describing how the RECORD pseudo-op is extremely useful when implementing sets.

Given, for example, the Pascal declarations

type *colors* = (*brown*, *yellow*, *green*, *red*, *orange*);
palette = *set of colors*;
var *davinci*, *rubens*, *renoir*: *palette*;

then some of the possible values of *davinci* are [*red*, *green*], [*orange*], [*brown*, *yellow*, *red*] and [*brown..red*]. If we use a single bit to represent the presence (bit set to 1) or absence (bit set to 0) of each possible element of a set then, in the example above, five bits – one for each color – are adequate to represent a variable of type palette:

Set	*Representation*
[*red*, *green*]	00110
[*orange*]	00001
[*brown*, *yellow*, *red*]	11010
[*brown..red*]	11110

Thus:

```
PALETTE RECORD BROWN:1, YELLOW:1, GREEN:1, RED:1, ORANGE:1
```

implements the Pascal type palette. A byte is used by the assembler for each palette record and the least significant five bits of this byte contain the data of interest. Thus,

```
DAVINCI PALETTE <1,1,0,1,0>
```

associates the MASM name DAVINCI with a byte of storage corresponding to a PALETTE record and initialized to ???11010. Given also

```
RUBENS PALETTE <0,1,0,1,1>
RENOIR PALETTE <1,1,0,0,1>
```

then the Pascal

rubens := *davinci*

is implemented by the 8086-family instructions

```
MOV AL,DAVINCI
MOV RUBENS,AL
```

(the use of the record variable name allowing access to the corresponding storage in just the same way as with any other variable name).

To isolate the individual fields of a `RECORD`, there are three operators: shift count, `WIDTH` and `MASK`. The shift count operation is brought into effect by using the field name. Thus

```
MOV CL,GREEN
```

would be assembled by MASM into an instruction equivalent to

```
MOV CL,2
```

since the `GREEN` field must be right shifted two bits to be right justified. The `WIDTH` operator brings the width operation into effect and returns the width of a field in a record. Thus

```
MOV CL,WIDTH ORANGE
```

assembles into an instruction equivalent to

```
MOV CL,1
```

Finally, `MASK` returns a bit mask for the bit positions occupied by a field. For example

```
MOV CL,MASK YELLOW
```

assembles as

```
MOV CL,00001000B
```

An 8086-family implementation of the Pascal

davinci := [*yellow*, *red*]

is then easy using these `RECORD` operations:

```
MOV AL,1
MOV CL,YELLOW
SHL AL,CL
MOV DAVINCI,AL
MOV AL,1
MOV CL,RED
SHL AL,CL
OR  AL,DAVINCI
MOV DAVINCI,AL
```

(There are many other approaches. As ever, ours is but one possible solution.)

EXERCISES

17.5 Make a trace of the execution of our implementation of the Pascal

davinci := [*yellow*, *red*]

17.6 Given

```
PALETTE RECORD BROWN:1, YELLOW:1, GREEN:1, RED:1, ORANGE:1
```

and

```
DAVINCI PALETTE <1,1,0,1,0>
RUBENS  PALETTE <0,1,0,1,1>
RENOIR  PALETTE <1,1,0,0,1>
```

make a trace of the execution of the following program fragment:

```
MOV AL,DAVINCI
MOV BL,RUBENS
OR  AL,BL
AND AL,RENOIR
MOV CL,DAVINCI
AND CL,MASK BROWN
SHL RUBENS,CL
AND RUBENS,AL
MOV CL,MASK GREEN
AND AL,CL
SHL AL,1
AND RENOIR,AL
```

17.7 Given

```
DATE RECORD MONTH:4, DAY:5, YEAR:7
 .
 .
 .
BIRTHDAY DATE <1,27,76>
```

what will be in registers AX, BX, CX, DX and in the locations referred to by `BIRTHDAY` after running the following program extract:

```
MOV AX,BIRTHDAY
MOV BX,0
MOV CL,DAY
MOV DL,YEAR
ADD DL,WIDTH MONTH
SHR AX,CL
AND AX,0FFFEH
SHL AX,CL
MOV BIRTHDAY,AX
MOV BX,NOT MASK MONTH
```

Check your answer using a computer.

17.2.2 Implementing set operations using `RECORD`

In Pascal the available set operations include the relational operators and the set operators. Typical relational operators are:

= set equality

<> set inequality
<= is contained in
>= contains

and typical set operators include:

\+ set union
* set intersection
− set difference
in set membership

Let us give examples of the implementation of some of these in our present context. The remainder will appear in the exercises!

- **Set union** for example, *renoir* := *davinci* + *rubens*

```
MOV AL,DAVINCI
OR  AL,RUBENS
MOV RENOIR,AL
```

- **Set intersection** for example, *renoir* := *davinci* * *rubens*

```
MOV AL,DAVINCI
AND AL,RUBENS
MOV RENOIR,AL
```

- **Set inclusion** for example, *davinci* <= *rubens*

  Here we observe that, given sets a and b, $a <= b$ if and only if $a * b = a$. Hence

```
MOV AL,DAVINCI
AND AL,RUBENS
XOR AL,DAVINCI
```

  leaves AL set to zero if *davinci* <= *rubens* and set to non-zero otherwise.

EXERCISES

17.8 Complete similar implementations to those given above for all the remaining Pascal set operations mentioned.

17.9 Using records with *record name* DATE where DATE is defined by:

```
DATE RECORD MONTH:4,DAY:5,YEAR:7
```

write an assembly language program which asks its user for his or her date of birth in an appropriate form and compares it with your own birthday. If the program user's birthday has the day, month or year in common with your own, print messages such as CONGRATULATIONS, YOU WIN A PRIZE BECAUSE YOUR BIRTHDAY IS ON THE SAME DAY AS THE PROGRAMMER'S.

17.10 Using records of the form:

```
TEMPERATURE RECORD MAX:6,MIN:6
```

write an assembly language program which asks its user for the maximum and minimum temperatures (in degrees Celsius) during each day in the previous week, displays a list of these daily maxima and minima on the screen, and then shows the average maximum and minimum temperatures for the week (to the nearest whole degree).

17.2.3 A complete example program using `RECORD`

To illustrate the use of record variables in MASM we shall write an assembly language program which repeatedly displays the same piece of text on the screen in various ways until the user types an X. What text is actually displayed is unimportant for our purposes, but it will in fact consist of 232D characters and be defined in the data segment of the program as follows:

```
TEXT DB 'THE GREAT BEAUTY OF THE NORTH OF ENGLAND IS THAT NOT MANY '
     DB 'PEOPLE KNOW ABOUT THE ABSOLUTELY UNSPOILT COUNTRYSIDE '
     DB 'THE MARVELLOUS EXAMPLES OF BRITISH ARCHITECTURE AND THE '
     DB 'EXTREMELY FRIENDLY AND APPROACHABLE LOCAL INHABITANTS '
```

Initially, the text will be displayed in upper case and occupy 40 columns on the display screen. The program will then pause, waiting for the user to press one of the L, U, W, N, or X keys. (We do not check for incorrect keys, and the program insists that upper-case letters are used. As usual, it is an exercise for the reader to remove this restriction.)

If the user presses the L key then the same text will be redisplayed but with lower-case letters instead of upper-case. Pressing U causes the same piece of text to be redisplayed in upper-case letters. Likewise, pressing N causes the same text to be redisplayed occupying only 20 columns of the screen, not 40 (N stands for Narrow-screen). Pressing W at any time returns to 40 columns of text (W stands for Wide-screen). Any of U, L, W and N can be used as many times as the user wishes. If the user presses X then we return to DOS.

Thus, when the program is executed, the text is first displayed in the form:

```
THE GREAT BEAUTY OF THE NORTH OF ENGLAND
 IS THAT NOT MANY PEOPLE KNOW ABOUT TH
E ABSOLUTELY UNSPOILT COUNTRYSIDE THE
 MARVELLOUS EXAMPLES OF BRITISH ARCHITE
CTURE AND THE EXTREMELY FRIENDLY AND
APPROACHABLE LOCAL INHABITANTS
```

and then the program pauses waiting for the user to press a key. If the user presses N then the text is redisplayed as follows:

```
THE GREAT BEAUTY OF
THE NORTH OF ENGLAND
 IS THAT NOT MANY PE
OPLE KNOW ABOUT TH
E ABSOLUTELY UNSPOI
LT COUNTRYSIDE THE
 MARVELLOUS EXAMPLES
 OF BRITISH ARCHITE
CTURE AND THE EXTREM
ELY FRIENDLY AND
APPROACHABLE LOCAL
INHABITANTS
```

and again the program waits for the user to press a key. If now the L key is pressed the display continues:

```
the great beauty of
the north of england
 is that not many pe
ople know about th
e absolutely unspoi
lt countryside the
 marvellous examples
 of british archite
cture and the extrem
ely friendly and
approachable local
inhabitants
```

When the program pauses this time, let us suppose that the user presses W. The text is then redisplayed in the following format:

```
the great beauty of the north of england
 is that not many people know about th
e absolutely unspoilt countryside the
 marvellous examples of british archite
cture and the extremely friendly and
approachable local inhabitants
```

Finally, let us suppose that the user now presses U. Then the text is redisplayed in the format:

```
THE GREAT BEAUTY OF THE NORTH OF ENGLAND
 IS THAT NOT MANY PEOPLE KNOW ABOUT TH
E ABSOLUTELY UNSPOILT COUNTRYSIDE THE
 MARVELLOUS EXAMPLES OF BRITISH ARCHITE
CTURE AND THE EXTREMELY FRIENDLY AND
APPROACHABLE LOCAL INHABITANTS
```

And so on.

The program uses the RECORD pseudo-op:

```
DISPLAY_SPEC RECORD CASE:6,SIZE;6
```

to declare a family of record variables each of which has two fields. CASE is a 6-bit wide field which will be used for the hexadecimal number which must be added to the ASCII code for each character of the text to convert it into the user's current choice of upper- or lower-case letters. Thus, if the user has pressed the L key (denoting lower case), then the CASE field will contain 20H because adding 20H to the ASCII codes for each of the letters defined in TEXT gives the code for the corresponding letter in lower case. On the other hand, if the user has pressed U then CASE will be set to 0. The SIZE field contains either 20D or 40D to represent the number of screen columns in which the text is to be displayed and its contents depend on whether the user has pressed N (20D) or W (40D).

In the data segment of the program, we shall declare a record variable belonging to the DISPLAY_SPEC family called STYLE:

```
STYLE DISPLAY_SPEC <0,40D>
```

in which CASE is initialized to 0 and SIZE to 40D. This is in order that, when the text is displayed initially, it is displayed in upper-case letters and occupies the first 40 columns of the screen only.

A pseudo-Pascal outline of the program is as follows:

```
establish data segment addressability;
chars_printed := 0;
repeat
  BH := current case conversion factor;
  for SI := 0 to 231D do
    begin
    if chars_printed = size then
      begin
      chars_printed := 0;
      print(new line)
      end;
    DL := next character;
    if char<>' ' then DL := DL + BH;
    display DL;
    chars_printed := chars_printed + 1
    end;
  readchar;
  chars_printed := 0;
  print a new line;
  if char = 'U' then reset case to upper
  else if char = 'L' then reset case to lower
  else if char = 'W' then reset size to wide
  else if char = 'N' then reset size to narrow
until char = 'X';
return to DOS
```

In order not to have spurious characters appearing on the screen amongst the TEXT, we shall implement *readchar* of this outline using DOS function 7 of interrupt 21H (see Section 4.3). This will cause the program to wait until a character has been typed at the keyboard. When the user presses a key, the character typed does *not* appear on the display screen but its ASCII code is returned in AL.

As usual, our method of implementation has been chosen with pedagogy in mind. A corresponding complete program is given in Figure 17.5. There are certainly easier ways of implementing this outline, but this illustrates as many as possible of the record variable handling features available from MASM in a context reflecting their normal use – but with due regard to our state of knowledge of the 8086-family and microcomputer hardware at this point.

```
CR EQU ODH
LF EQU OAH
DISPLAY_SPEC RECORD CASE:6,SIZE:6
DATA SEGMENT
TEXT DB 'THE GREAT BEAUTY OF THE NORTH OF ENGLAND IS THAT NOT MANY '
     DB 'PEOPLE KNOW ABOUT THE ABSOLUTELY UNSPOILT COUNTRYSIDE '
     DB 'THE MARVELLOUS EXAMPLES OF BRITISH ARCHITECTURE AND THE '
     DB 'EXTREMELY FRIENDLY AND APPROACHABLE LOCAL INHABITANTS '
STYLE DISPLAY_SPEC <0,40D>
DATA ENDS

WORKING_STORAGE SEGMENT STACK
         DW 100H DUP(?)
WORKING_STORAGE ENDS

CODE SEGMENT
ASSUME CS:CODE, DS:DATA, SS:WORKING_STORAGE
;establish data segment addressability
  START:MOV AX,DATA
        MOV DS,AX
;chars_printed := 0
        MOV DI,0
;repeat
    ;BH := current case conversion factor
  DISP_TEXT:MOV  DX,MASK CASE
            MOV  CX,STYLE
            AND  DX,CX
            MOV  CL,CASE
            SHR  DX,CL
            MOV  BH,DL
    ;for SI := 0 to 231D do
   NEW_TEXT:MOV SI,0
                 ;begin
                 ;if chars_printed = size then begin
                          CYCLE_BEGINS:MOV DX,MASK SIZE
                                       MOV CX,STYLE
                                       AND DX,CX
                                       CMP DI,DX
                                       JNZ DISPLAY_NEXT_CHAR
                                  ;chars_printed := 0;
                                       MOV DI,0
```

Figure 17.5
A complete example program using RECORD.

```
                                ;print(new line)
                                  CALL PRINT_NEWLINE
                                  ;end
                    ;dl := next character
DISPLAY_NEXT_CHAR:      MOV DL,[SI]
                    ;if char <> ' ' then put character in current case
                        CMP DL,' '
                        JZ  MISS_CONVERSION
                        ADD DL,BH
                    ;display it
  MISS_CONVERSION:      CALL PRINTCHAR
                    ;chars_printed := chars_printed + 1
                        INC DI
                    ;end
                        INC SI
                        CMP SI,232D
                        JNZ CYCLE_BEGINS
;readchar
        MOV AH,7
        INT 21H
;chars_printed := 0
        MOV DI,0
;print a new line
        CALL PRINT_NEWLINE
;if char = 'U'
        CMP   AL,'U'
        JNZ   TRY_L
;then reset case
        MOV   BX,MASK CASE
        NOT   BX
        AND   STYLE,BX
        JMP   TRY_X
;else if char = 'L'
  TRY_L: CMP  AL,'L'
        JNZ   TRY_W
;then reset case
        MOV   BX,MASK CASE
        NOT   BX
        AND   STYLE,BX
        OR    STYLE,0800H
        JMP   TRY_X
;else if char = 'W'
  TRY_W: CMP  AL,'W'
        JNZ   TRY_N
;then reset size
        MOV   BX,MASK SIZE
        NOT   BX
        AND   STYLE,BX
        OR    STYLE,28H
        JMP   TRY_X
;else if char = 'N'
  TRY_N: CMP  AL,'N'
        JNZ   TRY_X
;then reset size
        MOV   BX,MASK SIZE
```

Figure 17.5
(cont.)

```
                NOT   BX
                AND   STYLE,BX
                OR    STYLE,14H
;until char = 'X'
        TRY_X: CMP AL,'X'
                JZ FINISH
                JMP DISP_TEXT
;return to DOS
FINISH:MOV AX,4C00H
        INT 21H

PRINTCHAR PROC NEAR
        MOV AH,2
        INT 21H
        RET
PRINTCHAR ENDP

PRINT_NEWLINE PROC NEAR
        MOV DL,CR
        CALL PRINTCHAR
        MOV DL,LF
        CALL PRINTCHAR
        RET
PRINT_NEWLINE ENDP

CODE ENDS
END START
```

Figure 17.5
(cont.)

EXERCISES

17.11 The program in Figure 17.5 assumes that its users are well behaved. Add to it the capability of suitably informing users if they press keys to which the program does not respond.

17.12 Further extend the program of Figure 17.5 by adding another two options which are selected when the user types either S or A. If the user types an S then spaces within the text (ASCII code 20H) are displayed as spaces in the normal way. If the user types an A then spaces in the text are to be displayed as asterisks '*' (ASCII code 2AH). Do this by adding another field to record variables belonging to the DISPLAY_SPEC family.

17.13 In the program of Figure 17.5 replace

```
;until char = 'X'
 TRY_X:CMP AL,'X'
        JZ FINISH
        JMP DISP_TEXT
;return to DOS
```

```
FINISH:MOV AX,4C00H
       INT 21H
```

with the simpler

```
;until char = 'X'
 TRY_X:CMP AL,'X'
       JNZ DISP_TEXT
;return to DOS
       MOV AX,4C00H
       INT 21H
```

and try to assemble the resulting program. Why can't the simpler version be used?

17.14 Write an 8086-family assembly language program which turns your microcomputer into a set calculator. Elements of sets may be any of the digits 0,1,2,. . .,9 and up to 26 sets may be used, called A,B,C,. . .,Z respectively. To define a set called B having 3,5 and 8 as its elements, the user should type:

```
(3 5 8)->B
```

To display the current contents of a set the user simply types its name followed by pressing the ENTER key:

```
B<ENTER>
```

whereupon the contents of the set is displayed in the form:

```
(3 5 8)
```

Your calculator should allow as many of the set operations as you have time to implement, but at least union and intersection. Thus, if the set B is defined as above and the set A is defined by:

```
(0 1 2 3 4 5)->A
```

then giving your calculator the sequence of commands

```
A*B->C
C<ENTER>
```

should result in C becoming the intersection of sets A and B and the contents of C appearing on the display as:

```
(3 5)
```

Similarly:

```
A+B->D
D<ENTER>
```

defines D as the union of sets A and B and should result in the display:

```
(0 1 2 3 4 5 8)
```

Use `RECORD` pseudo-ops and record variables wherever possible.

SUMMARY

This chapter has covered very important material. Indeed, in some ways it is the counterpart of Chapter 8 which described how to structure assembly language programs for efficient program development. STRUC and RECORD make it possible to structure data similarly. The facilities MASM provides for handling structure and record variables reduce the requirement for us to count things – such as where within a complex data structure does a certain field begin. And thereby they reduce the dependence of a program on a particular set of numbers, thus improving the ease with which a program can be maintained during its working life – much as does the EQU directive.

As a measure of its importance, most large-scale 8086-family assembly language programs use the STRUC pseudo-op in one way or another. However, in what follows that will rarely be reflected. Good pedagogy says to try to teach one thing at once. No doubt we have already failed miserably in this respect. But we shall continue to try to adhere to the maxim, and consequently both STRUC and RECORD – even though they are now available to us – will be underutilized in what follows in an attempt to keep the focus on the new material.

Somewhat hidden away in the core of the chapter was a rather important 8086-family instruction, LEA. The point of introducing it here was that it can be difficult to see the need for such an instruction. But where first introduced, its use was essential to avoid very messy alternatives.

SELF-CHECK QUIZ

1. A computerized hotel reservations system is to be written, and a STRUC family definition is required so that variables belonging to the family can be used to describe individual reservations. Given that the data required for each reservation is name, address, nationality, and room number, and that the hotel has 1100 bedrooms, design an appropriate STRUC which you should call RESERVATION.

2. A large company keeps records for each of its employees containing their name, address, telephone number, date of joining the company, date of leaving (if relevant), and current salary. Design an appropriate STRUC for computerizing such a personnel records system and declare a variable belonging to this family for John Smith whose details are as follows:

   John Smith – 12 Railroad Heights
   E 24 St
   New York
   1234
   – 212 123 4567
   – 6/1/73
   – still with the company
   – $63000

3. Given:

```
 DATE  STRUC
MONTH DB ?
DAY   DB ?
YEAR  DW ?
 DATE ENDS
```

and

```
DATA SEGMENT
   BIRTHDAY_JOHN DATE <6,1,1953>
   BIRTHDAY_PETE DATE <8,23,1964>
        .
        .
        .
```

what will be the contents of AX, BL and CL after execution of:

```
MOV AX,BIRTHDAY_JOHN.YEAR
ADD AX,BIRTHDAY_PETE.YEAR
MOV BL,BIRTHDAY_PETE.MONTH
SUB BL,BIRTHDAY_JOHN.MONTH
MOV CL,BIRTHDAY_PETE.DAY
MOV DL,BIRTHDAY_JOHN.DAY
MOV BIRTHDAY_JOHN.DAY,CL
MOV BIRTHDAY_PETE.DAY,DL
```

4. Referring to `DATE` and `BIRTHDAY_JOHN` and `BIRTHDAY_PETE` in question 3, what will be the contents of AX and CX after execution of:

```
LEA BX,BIRTHDAY_JOHN
LEA SI,BIRTHDAY_PETE
LEA AX,[BX].DAY
LEA CX,[SI].MONTH
```

5. The computer control of a certain set of indicator lights requires three bits to denote the color of the light which is to be turned on, four bits to specify the length of time for which that light is to be turned on, and one bit to denote whether the light should be on constantly or blink. Define an appropriate `RECORD` family.

6. Define two members of the family you defined in question 5 corresponding to:

WARNING – orange (code 010)
– 1 minute (code 0111)
– constant (code 0)

EMERGENCY – red (code 111)
– 5 minutes (code 1111)
– blink (code 1)

7. Given

```
DRINK_SELECTION RECORD
POWDER:4,SWEETENER:2,MILK:1,TEMP:1
```

and

```
DATA SEGMENT
   TEA DRINK_SELECTION <0111B,01B,1B,1B>
   JUICE DRINK_SELECTION <1010B,00B,0B,0B>
        .
        .
        .
```

what will be the contents of AL, BL, CL and DL after execution of:

```
MOV AL,TEA
MOV DL,JUICE
MOV CL,MILK
SHL DL,CL
AND AL,JUICE
MOV BL,MASK SWEETENER
AND BL,JUICE
MOV CL,WIDTH POWDER
```

8. Is it possible to simulate `RECORD` variables using `STRUC` variables? Explain your answer.

9. Is it possible to simulate `STRUC` variables using `RECORD` variables? Explain your answer – and do not jump to hasty conclusions!

10. Write an appropriate structure variable definition, declare one or more such structures and write a subroutine to use these definitions to illustrate how structure variables could be employed in the implementation of an assembler.

18 Macros and Conditional Assembly

Contents

This chapter concerns two important MASM features which aid programmer productivity: macros and conditional assembly. A **macro** is a block of text to which you assign a name. Whenever the assembler encounters that name in an assembly language program, it is replaced by the actual block of text it represents. (It is helpful to think of the macro name being expanded into the full text of the macro.) Macros can be passed parameters and may contain local labels.

Conditional assembly allows groups of assembly language statements in a program to be included or excluded from the assembly process, depending on the values of certain parameters. In effect, a conditional assembly statement allows the programmer to say things such as: IF the value of MEMORY_EXTENSION_PRESENT is TRUE then assemble the following group of statements . . . ELSE assemble the following statements . . .. One assembly language program could therefore contain all the code for two versions: one for an IBM-PC with basic 640K memory, and one for a machine with, perhaps, a megabyte of expanded memory. All the programmer has to do is change the setting of MEMORY_EXTENSION_PRESENT and the assembler arranges that only the appropriate instructions are assembled. This is more organizationally convenient (less housekeeping) than having two distinct versions of the same program, and generally produces a smaller object program than if the production version contained code for both possibilities.

18.1 Macros

18.1.1 Writing macros

Let us consider the construction of an example macro which is a sequence of 8086-family instructions to check that, given two locations, the unsigned contents of the first location is larger than or equal to the contents of the second location and, if not, swaps these so that this is true.

Figure 18.1 Program fragment to check location contents are in numerical order.

```
          MOV  AL,FIRST_LOCATION
          CMP  AL,SECOND_LOCATION
          JNB  FINISHED
          XCHG AL,SECOND_LOCATION
          MOV  FIRST_LOCATION,AL
FINISHED:
```

The program fragment in Figure 18.1 does this for FIRST_LOCATION and SECOND_LOCATION. Making this program fragment into a macro is easy. The general form of a macro definition is

name MACRO *dummylist*

```
      .
      .
      .
      ENDM
```

where *dummylist* is a list of names for the macro's parameters – rather like *myvar* and *total* are **dummy parameters** in the Pascal procedure declaration which begins

proc *paycalcs*(**var** *myvar*:*int*;*total*:*real*);

Figure 18.2 shows the corresponding macro PUT_IN_ORDER with dummy parameters FIRST_LOCATION and SECOND_LOCATION. We must also declare the label FINISHED as a local variable by means of the pseudo-op:

```
LOCAL FINISHED
```

```
PUT_IN_ORDER    MACRO FIRST_LOCATION,SECOND_LOCATION
                LOCAL FINISHED
                MOV   AL,FIRST_LOCATION
                CMP   AL,SECOND_LOCATION
                JNB   FINISHED
                XCHG  AL,SECOND_LOCATION
                MOV   FIRST_LOCATION,AL
      FINISHED:
                ENDM
```

Figure 18.2
The PUT_IN_ORDER macro definition.

The complete program in Figure 18.3 uses this macro definition. Three characters are read from the keyboard, their ASCII codes are put into TOTAL, SUM and MILES and the contents of these locations are rearranged into non-ascending order. Then the characters corresponding to the ASCII codes stored in TOTAL, SUM and MILES respectively are displayed on the screen before the program returns control to DOS. Thus if the user types

```
579
```

then the program displays

```
975
```

and returns to DOS.

```
PUT_IN_ORDER    MACRO FIRST_LOCATION,SECOND_LOCATION
                LOCAL FINISHED
                MOV   AL,FIRST_LOCATION
                CMP   AL,SECOND_LOCATION
                JNB   FINISHED
                XCHG  AL,SECOND_LOCATION
                MOV   FIRST_LOCATION,AL
      FINISHED:
                ENDM

DATA SEGMENT
     TOTAL DB ?
     SUM   DB ?
     MILES DB ?
DATA ENDS

WORKING_STORAGE SEGMENT STACK
         DB 100H DUP(?)
WORKING_STORAGE ENDS

CODE SEGMENT
ASSUME CS:CODE,DS:DATA,SS:WORKING_STORAGE
;establish data segment addressability
```

Figure 18.3
A complete example program using a macro.

```
            MOV  AX,DATA
            MOV  DS,AX
;total := readchar
            CALL READCHAR
            MOV  TOTAL,AL
;sum := readchar
            CALL READCHAR
            MOV  SUM,AL
;miles := readchar
            CALL READCHAR
            MOV  MILES,AL
;reorder values
            PUT_IN_ORDER TOTAL,SUM
            PUT_IN_ORDER SUM,MILES
            PUT_IN_ORDER TOTAL,SUM
;print the contents of TOTAL, SUM and MILES
            MOV  DL,TOTAL
            CALL PRINTCHAR
            MOV  DL,SUM
            CALL PRINTCHAR
            MOV  DL,MILES
            CALL PRINTCHAR
;return to DOS
            MOV  AX,4C00H
            INT  21H

READCHAR:   MOV  AH,1
            INT  21H
            RET

PRINTCHAR:  MOV  AH,2
            INT  21H
            RET

CODE ENDS
END
```

Figure 18.3
(*cont.*)

When assembled, this program will produce the sequence of instructions shown in the extract from an assembler listing in Figure 18.4. Assembly language statements which are the result of expanding a macro are denoted on the listing by preceding them with the digit 1.

Figure 18.4
An extract from the assembler printout after assembly of the program in Figure 18.3.

```
PUT_IN_ORDER MACRO FIRST_LOCATION,SECOND_LOCATION
             LOCAL FINISHED
             MOV   AL,FIRST_LOCATION
             CMP   AL,SECOND_LOCATION
             JNB   FINISHED
             XCHG  AL,SECOND_LOCATION
```

```
                                 MOV    FIRST_LOCATION,AL
                       FINISHED:
                                 ENDM

0000                             DATA   SEGMENT
0000 00                                 TOTAL  DB?
0001 00                                 SUM    DB?
0002 00                                 MILES  DB?
0003                             DATA   ENDS

0000                             WORKING_STORAGE SEGMENT STACK
0000 0100[                       DB 100H DUP(?)
          ??
             ]

0100                             WORKING_STORAGE ENDS

0000                             CODE SEGMENT
                                 ASSUME CS:CODE,DS:DATA,SS:WORKING_STORAGE
                                 ;establish data segment addressability
0000 B8 ---- R                             MOV   AX,DATA
0003 8E D8                                 MOV   DS,AX
                                 ;total := readchar
0005 E8 0061 R                             CALL  READCHAR
0008 A2 0000 R                             MOV   TOTAL,AL
                                 ;sum := readchar
000B E8 0061 R                             CALL  READCHAR
000E A2 0001 R                             MOV   SUM,AL
                                 ;miles := readchar
0011 E8 0061 R                             CALL  READCHAR
0014 A2 0002 R                             MOV   MILES,AL
                                 ;reorder values
                                           PUT_IN_ORDER TOTAL,SUM
0017 A0 0000 R                             1       MOV    AL,TOTAL
001A 3A 06 0001 R                          1       CMP    AL,SUM
001E 73 07                                 1       JNB    ??0000
0020 86 06 0001 R                          1       XCHG   AL,SUM
0024 A2 0000 R                             1       MOV    TOTAL,AL
0027                                       1       ??0000:
                                           PUT_IN_ORDER SUM,MILES
0027 A0 0001 R                             1       MOV    AL,SUM
002A 3A 06 0002 R                          1       CMP    AL,MILES
002E 73 07                                 1       JNB    ??0001
0030 86 06 0002 R                          1       XCHG   AL,MILES
0034 A2 0001 R                             1       MOV    SUM,AL
0037                                       1       ??0001:
                                           PUT_IN_ORDER TOTAL,SUM
0037 A0 0000 R                             1       MOV    AL,TOTAL
003A 3A 06 0001 R                          1       CMP    AL,SUM
003E 73 07                                 1       JNB    ??0002
0040 86 06 0001 R                          1       XCHG   AL,SUM
0044 A2 0000 R                             1       MOV    TOTAL,AL
0047                                       1       ??0002:
                                 ;print the contents of TOTAL, SUM and MILES
0047 8A 16 0000 R                          MOV DL,TOTAL
```

Figure 18.4
(cont.)

```
0048 E8 0066 R                       CALL PRINTCHAR
004E 8A 16 0001 R                    MOV DL,SUM
0052 E8 0066 R                       CALL PRINTCHAR
0055 8A 16 0002 R                    MOV DL,MILES
0059 E8 0066 R                       CALL PRINTCHAR
                       ;return to DOS
005C B8 4C00                         MOV AX,4C00H
005F CD 21                           INT 21H

0061 B4 01                           READCHAR: MOV AH,1
0063 CD 21                                     INT 21H
0065 C3                                        RET

0066 B4 02                           PRINTCHAR: MOV AH,2
0068 CD 21                                      INT 21H
006A C3                                         RET

006B                   CODE ENDS
                       END
```

Figure 18.4
(cont.)

From the listing, three things should be noted in particular: the difference between a subroutine `CALL` and use of a `MACRO`; the replacement of the macro's `LOCAL` label `FINISHED` by a unique label in each of its three expansions (??0000, ??0001, and ??0002 respectively); and the replacement of the dummy parameters `FIRST_LOCATION` and `SECOND_LOCATION` by the corresponding actual parameter pairs in each expansion (`TOTAL,SUM`; `SUM,MILES`; and `TOTAL,SUM` respectively).

18.1.2 Macros vs. subroutines

Now that we know how to write a simple macro, it is convenient to return to the question, when should we use them? There are no hard and fast rules about when to use macros. Both subroutines and macros can improve a program when, if they were not used, the program would contain repeated occurrences of a group of instructions. Subroutines would normally be used when the repeated group of instructions is *exactly* the same in all its occurrences. Macros could sensibly be used when the instruction mnemonics are the same but the labels, variables, or expressions involved change from one occurrence to the next.

By way of an example of where a macro is more appropriate than a subroutine, consider the following program extract:

```
ADD AX,BX
MUL DX
CMP AX,3
JNZ TEST1
  .
  .
  .
```

```
ADD AX,BX
MUL DX
CMP AX,3
JNZ TEST2
  .
  .
  .
ADD AX,BX
MUL DX
CMP AX,3
JNZ TEST3
  .
  .
  .
```

The same basic group of instructions appears three times, but each has a different label as the object of the JNZ instruction. Because of this change we cannot easily replace all four instructions in each group by a subroutine, but we *can* usefully replace them by a macro.

We simply define a macro called OUR_TEST which takes one parameter, the name of the label to be used in the final JNZ instruction, and which during assembly will be replaced by the string of characters:

```
ADD AX,BX
MUL DX
CMP AX,3
JNZ <parameter name>
```

Thus, we could rewrite the above program extract as:

```
OUR_TEST MACRO JNZ_LABEL
          ADD AX,BX
          MUL DX
          CMP AX,3
          JNZ JNZ_LABEL
          ENDM
           .
           .
           .
         OUR_TEST TEST1
           .
           .
           .
         OUR_TEST TEST2
           .
           .
           .
         OUR_TEST TEST3
           .
           .
           .
```

The nearest equivalent approach using a subroutine would be to define the subroutine:

```
ADD_MUL_AND_COMPARE:ADD AX,BX
                    MUL DX
                    CMP AX,3
                    RET
```

and use it instead, but this omits the `JNZ` test which really belongs to the other group of four instructions.

18.1.3 Macro parameters

As we saw in the previous section, dummy parameters in macro definitions are not confined to variable names. They may also be used to represent registers, instructions, 8086-family instruction opcodes, strings or numerical values. Here are some examples of their use to represent a register, numbers and strings.

First, the use of a dummy parameter to represent a register. The statements in the macro definition in Figure 18.5 have the same effect as the `PUT_IN_ORDER` macro, but in this case the register to be used as a temporary store is supplied as a dummy parameter.

The invocations of `PUT_IN_ORDER` in the program of Figure 18.3 could thus be replaced by

```
NEW_PUT_IN_ORDER AL,TOTAL,SUM
```

and so on.

By way of illustration of the use of numbers as macro parameters, let us now write two macros – `FORDO` and `ENDFOR` – which, when used in conjunction, provide the Pascal programming structure

for *i* := *lower* **to** *upper* **do begin**

.

.

.

end

in macro form. `FORDO` will have five dummy parameters: *lower*, *upper*, two labels to control looping and the name of a register which is to be used for the loop counter *i*. `ENDFOR` has just two dummy parameters, both of them labels used to control looping. Figure 18.6 gives the definitions of `FORDO` and `ENDFOR`.

```
NEW_PUT_IN_ORDER   MACRO TEMP_REG,FIRST_LOCATION,SECOND_LOCATION
                   LOCAL FINISHED
                   MOV   TEMP_REG,FIRST_LOCATION
                   CMP   TEMP_REG,SECOND_LOCATION
                   JNB   FINISHED
                   XCHG  TEMP_REG,SECOND_LOCATION
                   MOV   FIRST_LOCATION,TEMP_REG
         FINISHED:
                   ENDM
```

Figure 18.5 The macro `NEW_PUT_IN_ORDER`.

```
      FORDO MACRO LOWER,UPPER,START_ADD,STOP_ADD,CALC_REG
            MOV CALC_REG,UPPER
            SUB CALC_REG,LOWER
            JB  STOP_ADD
            INC CALC_REG
START_ADD:  CMP CALC_REG,0
            JE  STOP_ADD
            DEC CALC_REG
            ENDM

     ENDFOR MACRO START_ADD,STOP_ADD
            JMP START_ADD
 STOP_ADD :
            ENDM
```

Figure 18.6 Definitions of FORDO and ENDFOR.

It follows that the program fragment:

```
FORDO 1,12H,BEGINADD,ENDADD,SI
   MOV AH,1
   INT 21H
ENDFOR BEGINADD,ENDADD
```

would, when expanded, become a sequence of 8086-family instructions to read 12H characters typed at the keyboard:

```
     FORDO  1,12H,BEGINADD,ENDADD,SI
1              MOV SI,12H
1              SUB SI,1
1              JB  ENDADD
1              INC SI
1 BEGINADD:    CMP SI,0
1              JE  ENDADD
1              DEC SI

               MOV AH,1
               INT 21H

    ENDFOR     BEGINADD,ENDADD
1              JMP BEGINADD
1   ENDADD:
```

Notice that, as in Pascal proper, a check is made that lower is not greater than upper.

The following program fragment illustrates the use of string parameters in a macro invocation and uses FORDO, ENDFOR and the PRINTCHAR subroutine from Figure 18.3 to print

```
AaBbCcDdEeFfGgHhIiJjKkLlMmNnOoPpQqRrSsTtUuVvWwXxYyZz
```

on the display screen:

```
FORDO 'A','Z',BEGINPRINT,ENDPRINT,CL
    MOV  DL,'Z'
    SUB  DL,CL
    ;print upper-case letter
    CALL PRINTCHAR
    ;convert to lower-case
    ADD  DL,20H
    ;print lower-case letter
    CALL PRINTCHAR
    ;convert back to upper-case
    SUB  DL,20H
ENDFOR BEGINPRINT,ENDPRINT
```

Dummy parameters in macro definitions may be instructions but cannot themselves be macros. However, macro definitions may be nested, as the following definition illustrates:

```
DOLOTS MACRO NUMBER,COUNTREG,INSTRUCTION,OPERAND
       FORDO 1,NUMBER,BEGINDOLOTS,ENDDOLOTS,COUNTREG
       INSTRUCTION OPERAND
       ENDFOR BEGINDOLOTS,ENDDOLOTS
       ENDM
```

The invocation

```
DOLOTS 27D,AH,INC,BX
```

would, on assembly, be expanded into 8086-family instructions which will perform `INC BX` a total of 27D times.

Because macros are really a string replacement facility, the order of definition does not matter. Thus, MASM does not mind whether `DOLOTS` is defined before or after `FORDO` and `ENDFOR` in an assembly language program. However, as a programmer, one's greatest concern is always to produce programs that someone else will find easy to follow, so this should not be taken as a license for obscurity!

EXERCISES

18.1 Using the `FORDO` and `ENDFOR` macros, write and test assembly language programs to carry out the following tasks. In each program use at least one other macro.

(a) Calculate the sum of the squares of the first 30D whole numbers.

(b) Given the day of the week on which the first of the month falls and the number of days in the month, print out a calendar for the month in the form:

```
 M Tu  W Th  F Sa Su
    1  2  3  4  5  6
 7  8  9 10 11 12 13
14 15 16 17 18 19 20
21 22 23 24 25 26 27
28 29 30 31
```

18.2 Write macro equivalents of the **while** and **repeat** loop constructs of Pascal. Use them as appropriate in programs to carry out the following tasks:

(a) Input a sequence of parentheses, '(' and ')', and determine whether the sequence is well formed, that is, if there are equal numbers of (and), and the number of) read never exceeds the number of (read.

(b) Find all three-digit decimal whole numbers equal to the sum of the cubes of their digits. For example

$$153 = 1^3 + 5^3 + 3^3$$

18.2 Using macros to define tables

This section considers facilities for using macros to define data items, and in particular, for defining tables. Using a macro can save a lot of repetitive work in setting up tables.

Suppose, then, that we want to use macros to define a set of double words containing increasing powers of two which can be individually addressed as TWO1 (containing 2D), TWO2 (containing 4D) and so on up to TWO10 (containing 1024D). This will in fact require two macros. The first of these, TWO_POWER, is defined as follows:

```
TWO_POWER MACRO LABEL_COUNT,VALUE
          TWO&LABEL_COUNT DD VALUE
          ENDM
```

The invocation TWO_POWER 1,2 would produce the assembly language statement

```
TWO1 DD 2
```

and the invocation TWO_POWER 8,256 would produce

```
TWO8 DD 256
```

since the special macro symbol & in the definition of TWO_POWER indicates that the string TWO is to be concatenated with the actual parameter corresponding to the dummy parameter LABEL_COUNT.

It is also possible to use symbols defined in an EQU or = MASM pseudo-op as parameters in macro invocations. Thus, given:

```
THIS_POWER = 4
EXPONENT   = 2
```

the invocation TWO_POWER %EXPONENT %THIS_POWER would result in

```
TWO2 DD 4
```

because the macro % symbol indicates that EXPONENT and THIS_POWER are expressions which must be evaluated to a number before string substitution takes place.

To complete our definition of a macro which will define a table of powers of two using TWO_POWER we need to use one of three pseudo-ops MASM provides for repeating blocks of statements (which do not have to be macros). The simplest of these has the general form

REPT *expression*

  .
  . *block of statements to be repeated*
  .

ENDM

Thus, the first 10 powers of two could be defined via the macro TWO_POWERS_TABLE which has the following definition:

```
TWO_POWERS_TABLE MACRO
                 REPT 10D
                 EXPONENT=EXPONENT+1
                 THIS_POWER=THIS_POWER*2
                 TWO_POWER %EXPONENT,%THIS_POWER
                 ENDM
                 ENDM
```

Here the REPT. . .ENDM pseudo-op directs MASM to repeat the enclosed statements 10 times so that the sequence

```
THIS_POWER = 1
EXPONENT   = 0
TWO_POWERS_TABLE
```

will be expanded to yield the set of statements

```
THIS POWER= 1
EXPONENT  = 0
TWO1   DD 2
TWO2   DD 4
TWO3   DD 8
          .
          .
          .
TWO10 DD 1024
```

Often, tables do not contain a sequence of values so easily related by formulae. Consider, for example, the problem of setting up a table of unsigned 8-bit equivalents of the first 10 prime numbers by using a macro. Once again this will require two macros. The first is defined very similarly to TWO_POWER above:

```
PRIME MACRO COUNT,APRIME
      PRIME&COUNT DB APRIME
ENDM
```

The second uses the IRP pseudo-op, which has the general form

IRP *dummy*,<*arg1*,*arg2*,. . .,*argN*>

.

. *block of statements to be repeated*

.

ENDM

and which directs the assembler to repeat the statements within the IRP. . .ENDM block *N* times. Starting with *arg1*, on each repetition MASM replaces the dummy parameter with an actual parameter from the parameter list.

Using IRP our FIRST_10_PRIMES macro can thus be defined:

```
FIRST_10_PRIMES MACRO
        IRP APRIME,<2,3,5,7,11,13,17,19,23,29>
        COUNT=COUNT+1
        PRIME %COUNT,APRIME
        ENDM
        ENDM
```

so that the statements

```
COUNT=0
FIRST_10_PRIMES
```

would be expanded on assembly to

```
COUNT=0
PRIME1  DB 2
PRIME2  DB 3
PRIME3  DB 5
        .
        .
        .
PRIME10 DB 29
```

Similarly

```
SAVE_REGS MACRO
          IRP REGISTER,<AX,BX,CX,DX,SI,DI,BP>
          PUSH REGISTER
          ENDM
          ENDM
```

would enable a copy of the registers AX, BX, CX, DX, SI, DI and BP to be saved on the stack via the single invocation

```
SAVE_REGS
```

since MASM actually views each argument as a character string and produces:

```
PUSH AX
PUSH BX
PUSH CX
  .
  .
  .
PUSH BP
```

The IRPC pseudo-op is a variation of IRP and takes the general form

IRPC *dummy,string*

```
  .
  .   block of statements to be repeated
  .
ENDM
```

In this case the statements within an IRPC. . .ENDM block are repeated once for each character in the string with the dummy parameter taking successive character values from the string, starting with the left-most character.

Note that use of REPT, IRP and IRPC is not confined to within the body of a macro. They are pseudo-ops in their own right and consequently our use of IRPC to define a table of codes would be perfectly acceptable as it stands in the data segment of a program. Thus

```
DATA SEGMENT
  .
  .
  .
IRPC CODE,CXPRLMNYZTUABVDIJKEFGHOQSW
DB '&CODE&'
ENDM
  .
  .
  .
```

would be expanded into

```
DATA SEGMENT
  .
  .
  .
DB 'C'
DB 'X'
  .
  .
  .
DB 'S'
DB 'W'
  .
  .
  .
```

representing, perhaps, a secret code in which the letter A is coded as a letter C, a B as an X and so on.

EXERCISES

18.3 Use `REPT`, `IRP` or `IRPC` as appropriate to initialize variables as follows:

(a) The squares of the first ten non-zero whole numbers in unsigned 8-bit form labeled `SQUARE1`, `SQUARE2`, and so on.

(b) The number of days in each month labeled `MONTH1`, `MONTH2`, and so on, starting with January and in unsigned 8-bit form.

(c) Twenty-six variables labeled *A*,*B*,*C*,. . .,*Z* and initialized to an indeterminate byte value.

(d) The first 10 powers of 3, labeled `THREE1`, `THREE2`, and so on, in unsigned 64-bit form.

18.4 Write and test a macro `SPACES` which takes one parameter – a non-negative whole number – and produces instructions for printing that number of spaces.

18.5 Examine the `FORDO` macro of Section 18.1. Is it possible to rewrite the definition, omitting the parameters `START_ADD` and `STOP_ADD`? If not, explain why in detail. If so, verify your new definition on a computer.

18.3 More macro pseudo-ops

Table 18.1 gives a summary of the MASM macro pseudo-ops. Of the special symbols only ;; and ! remain to be discussed. The symbol ;; suppresses comments in macros, and ! indicates that the next character in a list of arguments is to be interpreted literally. Let us consider each of these in turn.

Most macro definitions will require comments (following our pseudo-Pascal convention, of course) but, more often than not in practice, one does not require these comments to be reproduced at every macro expansion in the main body of the program. Indeed, the whole purpose behind the use of a macro is often to free oneself from one level of complexity (for example, manipulating the statements to control a `FOR` loop as in `FORDO`). Those comments in a macro definition prefaced with ;; will therefore not be reproduced. This is illustrated in Figure 18.7.

Table 18.1 Macro pseudo-ops.

Pseudo-op	*Purpose*
name MACRO *dummylist* . . . ENDM	Defines a macro.
REPT *expression* . *block of statements* . *to be repeated* . ENDM	Statements are repeated the number of times determined by the expression.
IRP *dummy*,<*arg1*,*arg2*,. . .,*argN*> . *block of statements* . *to be repeated* . ENDM	Statements are repeated *N* times with dummy being substituted by *arg1*,*arg2*,. . .,*argN*.
IRPC *dummy*,*string* . *block of statements* . *to be repeated* . ENDM	Statements are repeated once for each character in the string, with each repetition substituting the next string character for dummy.
LOCAL *dummy1*,*dummy2*,. . .,*dummyN*	The assembler creates a unique identifier for each of *dummy1*,. . .,*dummyN* and substitutes this for each occurrence in the containing macro. If LOCAL statements are used, they must be the first statements in the macro body.
PURGE *macro name1*,. . .,*macro nameN*	Removes the definition of the named macros from the assembler's list of macros.
EXITM	Used in conjunction with conditional pseudo-ops to terminate macro expansion (see Section 18.4).
.LALL	Expands all source statements in a macro during a listing, except macro comments preceded by a double semicolon.
.XALL	Expands only those source statements in a macro during a listing which generate code or data.
.SALL	Suppresses listing of any macro expansions.
Special symbols	
string1&*string2*	Concatenates two strings.
%*expression*	Causes the expression to be evaluated to a number.
!*character*	Indicates that the character is to be treated literally as an argument.
;;*string*	Comments following ;; are not reproduced on each macro invocation expansion.

```
QUIETMAC  MACRO DUMMY
          ;;save working register
          PUSH AX
          ;;PC-DOS function
          MOV   AH,DUMMY
          INT   21H
          ;;restore working register
          POP   AX
          ENDM
 LOUDMAC  MACRO
          ;double AX
          ADD   AX,AX
          ;add BX
          ADD AX,BX
          ENDM
            .
            .
            .
        CODE SEGMENT
              .
              .
              .
        QUIETMAC 2
1         PUSH AX
1         MOV   AH,2
1         INT   21H
1         POP   AX
            .
            .
            .
        LOUDMAC
1         ;double AX
1         ADD   AX,AX
1         ;add BX
1         ADD   AX,BX
            .
            .
            .
```

Figure 18.7 Extract from an assembler listing showing use of the ;; special symbol.

As a special macro character, the ! character indicates that the character following it in a list of arguments is to be taken literally. Thus

```
IRP DUMMY, <!,,a,B>
    DB '&DUMMY&'
ENDM
```

produces

```
DB ','
DB 'a'
DB 'B'
```

because the ! symbol informs MASM that the comma following it is not to be taken as a parameter separator in the normal way as with an IRP pseudo-op, but is to be taken literally.

Returning to macro pseudo-ops in Table 18.1 which have yet to be discussed, the .LALL, .SALL and .XALL pseudo-ops control the levels of printout of macro expansions. Thus .LALL lists the complete macro text for all expansions – though comments prefaced by ;; still do not appear. .SALL suppresses listing of all text and object code produced by the macros and .XALL is the default condition – a source line is listed only if it generates object code. (This will appear a more sensible choice of default after you have read Section 18.4.)

Generally, macros can be redefined in the course of an assembly language program and the most recently defined version is used for a given invocation. The PURGE pseudo-op of Table 18.1 deletes a macro definition entirely so that subsequent references to a PURGEd macro will cause an error. (In fact, PURGE sets the definition of the PURGEd macro to the empty string.)

PURGE has the general format:

PURGE *macro-name1,macro-name2,. . .*

Normally it is not necessary to use the PURGE pseudo-op when redefining a macro since redefining a macro will automatically purge the old definition. (Care is needed when redefining the names of 8086-family instructions because macro definitions may be recursive (see Section 18.5), but this can be a useful thing to do on occasion.)

The next section discusses conditional pseudo-ops which permit statements and macros to be included or excluded from the assembly process, depending on the settings of certain variables. It is therefore possible that a macro invocation must be terminated prior to reaching the ENDM pseudo-op. EXITM (see Table 18.1) allows this premature termination and will be discussed more fully in the next section.

EXERCISES

18.6 Give two distinct reasons why COMMENT (see Section 4.4) cannot be redefined as a macro. (Try doing it and assemble your attempt if necessary.)

18.7 Try to use PURGE in a short program which redefines the 8086-family ADD instruction by using the fact that $A + B = A - (-B)$.

18.8 Examine the calculator simulator program in Appendix II and decide where – if at all – macros could be used to advantage. Rewrite the program and assemble and test the new version.

18.9 Repeat Exercise 18.8 for the text editor program of Appendix III.

18.4 Conditional assembly

Conditional assembly allows the production of one large assembly language program covering various possibilities – for example, presence or absence of the 80*n*87 family of numeric data processors (which extend the arithmetic capabilities of the related 8086-family member to floating-point arithmetic) or available memory size, or whether the host computer is based on an 8086, 80286, 80386 or 80486 processor – which at assembly time can be tailored to just one of these possibilities. In this way, the actual machine code supplied to a given microcomputer user with given facilities is not cluttered up with memory-consuming unnecessary alternatives, and the programmer does not have the bother of maintaining multiple versions of a piece of software (not to mention the increased risk of errors owing to one version being updated and another not).

Suppose, for example, that we wish to keep just one assembly language program on disk from which we can assemble one of two versions of the same program: one of which talks to the user in English, the other in Italian. Because the length of the Italian text is greater than that of the corresponding English, we wish to set BX to 0CF00H in the English version and to 0D8E0H in the Italian version. We can do this with a macro which uses conditional assembly:

```
SET_TEXT_SIZE MACRO
     IF ENGLISH
         MOV BX,0CF00H
     ELSE
         MOV BX,0D8E0H
     ENDIF
         ENDM
```

To include the instruction which establishes the relevant text length the value of `ENGLISH` is set to 1 (denotes TRUE) or 0 (denotes FALSE) as appropriate. The `IF` statement checks the value of `ENGLISH` and, if it is 1, includes the statement

```
MOV BX,0CF00H
```

in the assembly, and otherwise includes the statement

```
MOV BX,0D8E0H
```

By incorporating both possibilities in a macro, the greater part of the program can be written without reference to either language. Figure 18.8 shows an extract from an assembly listing in which the macro `SET_TEXT_SIZE` is used.

To emphasize the advantage of conditional assembly here, note that once the assembly language program, from which the extract in Figure 18.8 is taken, has been assembled, the resulting object program will contain only the

```
ENGLISH=0
SET_TEXT_SIZE MACRO
    IF ENGLISH
        MOV BX,0CF00H
    ELSE
        MOV BX,0D8E0H
    ENDIF
        ENDM
      .
      .
      .
CODE SEGMENT
      .
      .
      .
SET_TEXT_SIZE
1   MOV BX,0D8E0H
MOV AL,[BX]
      .
      .
      .
```

Figure 18.8 Extract from an assembly listing showing conditional assembly.

instruction `MOV BX,0D8E0H` – the other possibility will have been eliminated by the inclusion of:

```
ENGLISH = 0
```

Thus, while the assembly language program itself contains the necessary code to deal with the two different possibilities, the resulting executable program contains code for only one of them. The programmer makes all necessary choices before the assembly language program is submitted to the assembler, but the programmer's job is made easier because only one assembly language program – covering all the possibilities – has to be maintained.

18.4.1 General format of conditional pseudo-ops

MASM conditional pseudo-ops are summarized in Table 18.2. They may all take one of two forms, either:

IF*xxx expression*
 .
 . *block of statements* (1)
 .
ELSE
 .
 . *block of statements* (2)
 .
ENDIF

or the simpler:

```
IFxxx expression
  .
  . block of statements (3)
  .
ENDIF
```

where the *xxx* represents some condition which the expression is to satisfy and, if it does, statements (1) (first format) or statements (3) (second format) are assembled. If the expression does not satisfy the condition then, in the first format, statements (2) are assembled whereas in the second format no statements are assembled as a result of this pseudo-op.

Table 18.2 MASM conditional pseudo-ops.

IF*xxx*	*Condition under which statements (1) or (3) are assembled (see text)*
IF *expression*	If *expression* evaluates to a non-zero number.
IFE *expression*	If *expression* evaluates to zero.
IF1	If encountered on assembly pass one.
IF2	If encountered on assembly pass two.
IFDEF *symbol*	If *symbol* is defined or has been declared external via EXTRN.
IFNDEF *symbol*	If *symbol* is undefined or not declared external via EXTRN.
IFB <*argument*>	If *argument* is blank.
IFNB <*argument*>	If *argument* is not blank.
IFIDN <*arg1*>,<*arg2*>	If the string *arg1* is identical to the string *arg2*.
IFDIF <*arg1*>,<*arg2*>	If the string *arg1* is different from the string *arg2*.

18.4.2 Some examples

The remainder of this section illustrates the various conditional pseudo-ops in Table 18.2 beginning with IFB.

Suppose we require two macros which can save (and restore) some or all of the registers AX, BX, CX, DX, SI, DI, BP, DS and ES on (or from) the stack. Let us call these macros PUSH_REGS and POP_REGS. We can use IFB to define PUSH_REGS since:

```
IFB <argument>. . .ELSE. . .ENDIF
```

includes the statements before the ELSE in the assembly IF *argument* is Blank, but otherwise includes the statements after the ELSE:

```
PUSH_REGS MACRO   R1,R2,R3,R4,R5,R6,R7,R8,R9
        IRP  REGISTER,<R9,R8,R7,R6,R5,R4,R3,R2,R1>
        IFB <REGISTER>
     ;;if REGISTER is blank do nothing
        ELSE
          PUSH REGISTER
     ENDIF
     ENDM
ENDM
```

On the invocation

```
PUSH_REGS BX,CX,DX
```

dummy parameters `R4`, `R5`,. . .,`R9` are set to blank so that the following expansion will result:

```
PUSH DX
PUSH CX
PUSH BX
```

It is an exercise for the reader to write the corresponding macro `POP_REGS`.

Using the

`IFDEF` *symbol*. . .`ELSE`. . .`ENDIF`

pseudo-op we can illustrate how one might allow for different memory sizes on users' machines. `IFDEF` *symbol*. . . is TRUE if symbol is either defined in the program containing the `IFDEF` statement or is declared as external via the `EXTRN` pseudo-op. Hence in

```
MINMEMORY EQU 640
   .
   .
   .
IFDEF MINMEMORY
     USER_WORK_SPACE DB 2000H DUP(?)
ELSE
     USER_WORK_SPACE DB 0A000H DUP(?)
ENDIF
   .
   .
   .
```

the statement

```
USER_WORK_SPACE DB 2000H DUP(?)
```

would be assembled. Notice that, as with all the conditional pseudo-ops, use of `IFDEF` is not limited to within a macro. However, any argument to a conditional must be known on pass one to avoid errors and incorrect evaluation, since macro definitions are recorded by MASM on pass one.

The pseudo-ops `IF1`. . . and `IF2`. . . are similar in format and use to `IFB` except that neither takes an argument. In

```
IF1
%OUT NOW DOING PASS 1
ENDIF
IF2
%OUT AND NOW DOING PASS 2
ENDIF
```

one message is sent to the display on each assembler pass, since the statements between IF1 and ENDIF are assembled only IF it is assembler pass 1, and the statements between IF2 and ENDIF only IF it is assembler pass 2.

It is possible to keep a library of macros in a separate file called, for instance, MACRO.LIB, which can then be incorporated into the main program via an INCLUDE pseudo-op. One often wants to do this for macros which would clearly be of use in contexts other than the problem in hand. If the INCLUDE is executed only on pass one, both operations and print time will be accelerated. This can be done as follows:

```
IF1
    INCLUDE MACRO.LIB
ENDIF
```

IF1 and IF2 are dangerously special tools, really beyond the scope of this book. The power which they seem to offer the programmer is tempered by the difficulty of avoiding phase errors during assembly, wherein values calculated by the assembler on pass one do not agree with corresponding values calculated on pass two.

18.4.3 A generalized MOVE instruction

The final forms of MASM conditional pseudo-op to be discussed from Table 18.2 are the IFIDN (IF IDeNtical) and IFDIF (IF DIFferent) pseudo-ops. IFIDN takes the general form

```
IFIDN <arg1>,<arg2>
   .
   . block of statements (1)
   .
ELSE
   .
   . block of statements (2)
   .
ENDIF
```

in which statements (1) are assembled if the string *arg1* is identical to the string *arg2*, and statements (2) otherwise. IFDIF is similar, except that statements (1) are assembled if the string *arg1* is different from the string *arg2*, and statements (2) otherwise.

We shall use IFIDN to write a macro MOVE16, a generalized form of the 8086-family 16-bit MOV instruction which, additionally, will allow the exchange of data between two memory locations. Register AX will be used as a temporary store for these transfers but will be saved beforehand and restored afterwards. The definition of MOVE16 uses another macro, ISREG, which decides if its single argument is one of the 8086-family's 16-bit registers and sets IS_A_REGISTER to 1 if so and to 0 if not:

```
ISREG MACRO REGISTER
IS_A_REGISTER=0
IRP REG,<AX,BX,CX,DX,BP,SP,DI,SI,CS,DS,ES,SS>
IFIDN <REG>,<REGISTER>
    IS_A_REGISTER=1
ENDIF
ENDM
ENDM
```

Because of the IRP pseudo-op, REG takes the successive values AX, BX, CX, and so on. IFIDN then compares the value of REGISTER to see if it is identical with REG and sets IS_A_REGISTER to 1 if this is the case. Otherwise IS_A_REGISTER is left set to 0.

Once a correspondence between the value of REGISTER and one of the instances of REG has been found, there is no point in checking through the remainder of the list of possible values for REG since we know a match will be impossible. It would be an improvement, therefore, to rewrite ISREG using the EXITM pseudo-op discussed briefly at the end of Section 18.3. EXITM is used when you want to terminate a REPT, IRP, IRPC or MACRO invocation once some test proves that the remainder of that expansion is not required. When an EXITM is executed, the expansion or repetition is terminated immediately at that level, but expansion in any containing pseudo-ops is allowed to continue. Here, then, is our thus improved version of ISREG:

```
ISREG MACRO REGISTER
  IS_A_REGISTER=0
  IRP REG,<AX,BX,CX,DX,BP,SP,DI,SI,CS,DS,ES,SS>
  IFIDN <REG>,<REGISTER>
    IS_A_REGISTER=1
    EXITM
  ENDIF
  ENDM
  ENDM
```

MOVE16 is now easy to complete (see Figure 18.9) using the IFE. . . conditional pseudo-op:

IFE *expression*

.

. *block of statements* (1)

.

ELSE

.

.*block of statements* (2)

.

ENDIF

```
MOVE16 MACRO TO,FROM
       ISREG TO
       IFE IS_A_REGISTER
               ISREG FROM
               IFE IS_A_REGISTER
                       PUSH AX
                       MOV  AX,FROM
                       XCHG AX,TO
                       MOV  FROM,AX
                       POP  AX
                  ELSE
                       MOV TO,FROM
                  ENDIF
       ELSE
            MOV TO,FROM
       ENDIF
ENDM
```

Figure 18.9
MOVE16: a generalization of the 8086-family MOV instruction.

in which statements (1) are assembled IF, when evaluated, the expression is Equal to zero (and statements (2) are assembled otherwise).

Figure 18.10 contains an extract from an assembly listing of a program in which MOVE16 was used.

```
                        MOVE16 AX,BX
0076 8B C3          1       MOV AX,BX
                        MOVE16 AX,[BX]
0078 8B 07          1       MOV AX,[BX]
                        MOVE16 AX,MY
007A A1 0000 R      1       MOV AX,MY
                        MOVE16 [BX],AX
007D 89 07          1       MOV [BX],AX
                        MOVE16 MY,AX
007F A3 0000 R      1       MOV MY,AX
                        MOVE16 [BX],[BP]
0082 50             1       PUSH AX
0083 8B 46 00       1       MOV  AX,[BP]
0086 87 07          1       XCHG AX,[BX]
0088 89 46 00       1       MOV  [BP],AX
008B 58             1       POP  AX
                        MOVE16 [BX],MY
008C 50             1       PUSH AX
008D A1 0000 R      1       MOV  AX,MY
0090 87 07          1       XCHG AX,[BX]
0092 A3 0000 R      1       MOV  MY,AX
0095 58             1       POP  AX
                        MOVE16 MY,[BX]
0096 50             1       PUSH AX
0097 8B 07          1       MOV  AX,[BX]
0099 87 06 0000 R   1       XCHG AX,MY
009D 89 07          1       MOV  [BX],AX
009F 58             1       POP  AX
```

Figure 18.10
Expansion of MOVE16 invocations in an assembly listing.

Debugging complicated macros such as MOVE16 is facilitated by using the non-default .LALL macro expansion printout control. Since the existence of MOVE16 slows down the assembly process considerably, judicious use of %OUT can reassure the anxious programmer that assembly has not gone into an infinite loop thanks to a typing error.

EXERCISES

18.10 Write and test MASM macros which perform the following tasks:

(a) A macro MADD which generalizes the ADD instruction to allow multiple operands. Thus

```
MADD AX,BX,CX,[BX]
```

would generate

```
ADD AX,BX
ADD AX,CX
ADD AX,[BX]
```

(b) A macro MSHL which generalizes the SHL instruction so that, for example:

```
MSHL AH,4
```

would generate

```
PUSH CX
MOV  CL,4
SHL  AH,CL
POP  CX
```

(c) A macro MEM which allows register-to-register and memory-to-memory unsigned 8-bit addition, subtraction, multiplication and division. Thus, an invocation

```
MEM ADD,[BX],[BP]
```

should be expanded to 8086-family instructions which add [BX] and [BP]. Similarly:

```
MEM SUB,[BX],[BP]
MEM MUL,[BX],MY_LOC
MEM DIV,TOTAL,MY_LOC
```

should each produce corresponding expansions.

Make sensible simplifying assumptions and use auxiliary macro definitions to structure and simplify the task.

18.11 In order to better understand the problems of assembly phase error, incorporate the macro MYORG, defined below, into a program which reads two characters from the keyboard and prints them out using subroutines

READCHAR and PRINTCHAR and has the structure given below. Invoke MYORG immediately after the first character is read:

```
        .LALL
          .
          .
          .
        CODE SEGMENT
                    .
                    .
                    .
              CALL READCHAR
              MYORG PRINTCHAR
                    .
                    .
                    .
READCHAR: . . .
                    .
                    .
                    .
PRINTCHAR: . . .
                    .
                    .
                    .
        CODE ENDS
```

The definition of MYORG is as follows:

```
MYORG MACRO MYLABEL
IF1
IFNDEF MYLABEL
    ORG $+30H
ENDIF
ENDIF
ENDM
```

Try to assemble the resulting program and study the contents of the .LST file in order to explain what has gone wrong.

18.12 Write and test a set of macros which mimic the string manipulation facilities available in Pascal. Assume that all string arguments for these macros are terminated by a $ character. Your macros should include, for example, one called LENGTH so that the invocation

```
LENGTH BX
```

would expand to 8086-family instructions which left the length of the string pointed to by BX in register AX; a string insertion macro INSERT; a substring deletion macro DELETE; and a string concatenation macro CONCAT.

18.5 Recursive macros

Macro definitions can be **recursive**. The following examples illustrate the format of recursive macro definitions and the resulting expansion of a typical invocation.

18.5.1 Factorials

The first example defines the macro FACT which expands to code which calculates the factorial of the unsigned number in AX and leaves the result in AX.

Definition

```
FACT MACRO N
     IF N-1
          MOV BX,N-1
          MUL BX
          FACT N-1
     ENDIF
     ENDM
```

Typical invocation

```
NUM EQU 5
MOV AX,NUM
FACT %NUM
```

Resulting expansion

```
BB 0004 1 MOV BX,5-1
F7 E3   1 MUL BX
BB 0003 2 MOV BX,5-1-1
F7 E3   2 MUL BX
BB 0002 3 MOV BX,5-1-1-1
F7 E3   3 MUL BX
BB 0001 4 MOV BX,5-1-1-1-1
F7 E3   4 MUL BX
```

Notice here the way in which the numbers which precede the instructions resulting from each recursive macro invocation indicate the level of recursion (1,2,3 and 4) at each stage.

18.5.2 Sum of the whole numbers 1 to *N*

The second example is a macro SUM which expands to code that calculates $1 + 2 + 3 + \ldots + N$ and leaves the result in AX assuming N is in AX before an invocation.

Definition

```
SUM MACRO N
    IF N-1
         ADD AX,N-1
         SUM N-1
    ENDIF
    ENDM
```

Typical invocation

```
NUM EQU 4
MOV AX,NUM
SUM %NUM
```

Resulting expansion

```
05 0003 1 ADD AX,4-1
05 0002 2 ADD AX,4-1-1
05 0001 3 ADD AX,4-1-1-1
```

18.5.3 Raising *M* to the power *N*

The third and final example is a macro POWER which expands to code that raises the positive whole number *M* to the positive whole number power *N*, assuming that *M* is in AX before an invocation.

Definition

```
POWER MACRO M,N
         IF   N-1
         MOV BX,M
         MUL BX
         POWER M,N-1
      ENDIF
      ENDM
```

Typical invocation

```
NUM EQU 2
MOV AX,NUM
POWER %NUM,3
```

Resulting expansion

```
BB 0002 1 MOV BX,2
F7 E3   1 MUL BX
BB 0002 2 MOV BX,2
F7 E3   2 MUL BX
```

It should be clear from these examples that the programmer needs to control the use of recursively defined macros very carefully. The use of any of them to calculate with just medium-sized numbers (10! for example) will consume vast quantities of program memory space and, in general, will cause the program to run very much more slowly than non-recursively produced coding for a given task.

EXERCISES

18.13 Find out how much memory the machine code generated by macro `FACT` will occupy for calls of the form

```
FACT N
```

where *n* is 5, 10, 15, 20 and 100.

18.14 Write and test a recursively defined macro `FIB` for which the invocation

FIB N

will generate code to leave the *N*th Fibonacci number in AX. (The first two Fibonacci numbers are 1 and 2. After that, each Fibonacci number is the sum of the previous two. Thus, the first five Fibonacci numbers are 1, 2, 3, 5, and 8.)

SUMMARY

In this chapter we have studied macro definitions and conditional assembly. Macro invocations differ from subroutine calls in that macro invocations are replaced by the strings of symbols they represent before assembly takes place; subroutine calls have a direct machine code equivalent. Thus, macros are used in preference to subroutine calls when the same sequence of instructions is needed in several places in a program but with different text (for example, different labels) attached to them at each occurrence. Macros can also be used to help define data items within an assembly language program.

Conditional assembly pseudo-ops allow the programmer to avoid the problems which arise when multiple versions of a program are maintained over a long period of time. They are also useful when constructing macro definitions.

The next chapter raises a very important topic which will release a limit which has hitherto constrained the kinds of program we could write: namely, how to handle disk files.

SELF-CHECK QUIZ

1. Write a macro which, when invoked, will cause statements to be inserted in an assembly language program to carry out an `OR` operation between two double words stored in memory and specified by the macro's dummy parameters. The result is to be left in DX,AX.

2. Repeat question 1 for the `AND` operation.

3. Write a macro which embraces both the examples in questions 1 and 2. That is, one of the dummy parameters of the macro should specify whether the operation to be performed between the two double words in memory is `AND` or `OR`.

4. Write a macro to leave in AX the absolute difference between the signed numbers in the registers given in its dummy parameters. Thus, if the two registers named in these dummy parameters contain a and b respectively, then AX should contain:

   $a - b$, if $a - b > 0$, and
   $b - a$, otherwise

5. Using the `REPT` pseudo-op show how it is possible to define a sequence of reserved bytes containing the numbers 5, 11, 23, 47, 95.

6. A certain company manufactures 100D different products. Each product is known within the company by an identification code which is 2 bytes long and 15 bytes of descriptive information. 50D products have the codes 0100H 0131H and the others have the codes 0200H to 0231H. Use one of the repeat pseudo-ops to initialize storage in memory for this information for all 100 products.

7. Can one macro be used to define a sequence of macros? If your answer is yes then give an example. If the answer is no, then explain why not.

8. A programmer had a 'brilliant' idea. To make the same program cover a certain set of arithmetic operations on both signed and unsigned numbers, he would use the macro `APPROPRIATE_MUL` which, according to the setting of a single dummy parameter, would either cause `MUL` or `IMUL` to be assembled in the appropriate place. Do you agree that this was a brilliant idea?

9. Write a program fragment such that

   ```
   MOV PRINTER,0
   ```

   is assembled if the dummy parameter `PRINTER_TYPE` has the value 'parallel' and

   ```
   MOV PRINTER,1
   ```

   is assembled otherwise.

10. Write a program fragment that causes

    ```
    ADD AX,2
    ```

    to be assembled nine times if the length of `MY_STRING` is greater than 10.

Disk Files

19

Contents

DOS allows the programmer to handle disk storage via operating system function calls much like those we first met in Chapter 4 for keyboard input and printing to the screen. This chapter studies the use of DOS disk-handling facilities in detail, and constructs four complete example programs: for dumping the contents of a file on to the display screen; storing keyboard input in a disk file; a file copy utility; and a random access read utility. We shall also see how DOS functions allow us to regard the standard input and output devices such as the keyboard, display and printer as files. Finally, a new form of executable file will be introduced. These are files which have the second name (file extension) COM and contain programs which are severely restricted in many ways, but which do have certain advantages over EXE files.

19.1 Programming disk file operations with INT 21H

If we make use of the facilities provided by INT 21H in DOS, programming **disk file** operations at the assembly language level follows a similar pattern to that for file handling in high-level languages like Pascal. To **read** the contents of a file, the file must first be **opened** ready for reading, and then, during sequential file access, successive reads automatically work through the contents of the file until the end of the file is reached. To **write** to an existing file, the file must first be opened for writing, the new data written in the file, and then the file must be **closed** for the changes made to be permanently recorded. Writing to a new file is similar except that instead of opening a file, the new file must first be **created**.

Within the facilities afforded by INT 21H, DOS offers two types of function call for carrying out the operations of opening, closing, reading from and writing to files. We shall only consider the so-called **extended** DOS function calls which allow our file operations to use path names, are much simpler to use, and also offer other additional facilities beyond the scope of this book.

19.1.1 ASCIIZ strings

When using the extended DOS function calls to open or create a file, the name of the file must be specified in an **ASCIIZ string**. An ASCIIZ string is a string which specifies the name of a file in any legal DOS way, followed by a single byte set to zero. Thus, apart from the file name itself, an ASCIIZ string may also contain either or both of a disk drive specification and a directory path. Thus, examples of the definition of ASCIIZ strings are:

```
FILE1 DB 'C:\COMPILERS\TURBO.EXE',0

FILE2 DB 'MYFILE.ASM',0

FILE3 DB 'A:DATA.FIL',0
```

19.1.2 File handles

A **file handle** is a 16-bit numerical code for the specification of a file. When a file is first opened or created using one of the extended DOS function calls, a corresponding handle is assigned to that file. The programmer does not need to know the details of the code used in the handle, but it is necessary to pass the handle to other extended DOS functions – such as those for reading from, writing to, and closing files – in order for them to operate successfully.

19.1.3 Extended DOS function calls

Data transfers involving a disk file must take place via a **buffer** in memory. The offset address of this buffer is passed to each appropriate DOS function together with the number of bytes to be read or written. We shall conventionally adopt 512D bytes as the size of the data transfer buffer though the maximum permitted size is 64K bytes. Even though DOS does not regard files as being made up of records at the device level, for the purposes of this chapter we can think of files as being made up of 512D byte records. Thus, a record is just the collection of 512D bytes (or less) which is read from or written to a disk file.

Following this convention, and thanks to the extended DOS function calls of `INT 21H`, having opened or created a disk file, all the programmer has to do to read from or write to that file is:

(1) Provide an ASCIIZ string which specifies the name of the file to be acted on;

(2) Nominate a buffer in main memory (512D bytes according to our convention) which will either contain the data to be written to the disk file of the given name or will be used to store the next group of bytes read from the named file;

(3) Specify the number of bytes to be read or to be written (512D according to our convention) in register CX; and

(4) If necessary, specify which record in the file is to be the object of the transfer.

(Note that it is not necessary to open the file before every read or write operation. This needs to be done just once, before any read or write operation is attempted.)

The first examples will all work with sequential files. That is, we shall only access the data bytes in a file in the order in which they are stored in the file, and one after another. Using the extended DOS functions, movement through the data bytes in sequential files is handled totally automatically.

When we first try to read from or write to a sequential file, DOS organizes things so that the number of bytes specified in CX is read from or written to the very beginning of the file *by default*. Then the internal DOS file pointer, which is used to remember which byte in the file is next to be read in sequence, is incremented by the contents of CX so that the next read or write operation will affect the next group of CX bytes in sequence.

After a read or write operation, the extended DOS functions leave AX containing the actual number of bytes read or the actual number of bytes written. If there has not been an error, the Carry Flag (CF) will be set to 0 after a read or write operation. The contents of AX will then specify exactly how many bytes were read from, or written to, the file. If the contents of AX is 0, then the end of the file has been reached. If the contents of AX is less than the contents of CX then a partial record at the end of the file was read. If an error does occur, then CF will be set to 1 and AX will then contain a code indicating the cause of the error.

The actions of the most important extended DOS function calls for file handling are summarized in Table 19.1. As with previous operating system function calls, they are brought into action by loading register AH with the function number and executing an `INT 21H`.

Table 19.1 A summary of `INT 21H` extended disk file-handling functions.

Function number	*Purpose*	*Input parameters required*	*Output parameters*
3CH	create a file	Given that DS:DX points to an ASCIIZ string representing an unopened file and CX is a valid attribute setting, a corresponding new file is created. If the file specified in the ASCIIZ string already exists, then that file will be destroyed.	
		AH = 3CH CX = file attribute DX = offset of ASCIIZ string (relative) to DS	If CF = 0 then AX = allocated handle If CF = 1 then AX = 3,4, or 5 specifying an error condition. AX = 3 indicates that the given path has not been found. AX = 4 indicates that no handle is spare. AX = 5 indicates that access was denied – perhaps because the directory is full.
3DH	open a file	Opens the file specified by the ASCIIZ string pointed to bv DS:DX.	
		AH = 3DH DX = offset of ASCIIZ string (relative) to DS AL = 0 to open for reading AL = 1 to open for writing AL = 2 to open for reading and writing	If CF = 0 then AX = allocated handle If CF = 1 then AX = 2,4,5 or 12 specifying an error condition. AX = 2 indicates that the file has not been found. AX = 4 indicates that there is no spare handle. AX = 5 indicates that access was denied – perhaps because

Table 19.1 (*cont.*)

Function number	*Purpose*	*Input parameters required*	*Output parameters*
			the directory is full. AX = 12 indicates that AL has not been set to one of the three permitted values.
3EH	close a file	This function must be called after writing to a file to ensure that all directory information is updated. BX must contain the handle of the file to be closed.	
		AH = 3EH BX = handle of file to be closed	AX = file handle If CF = 0 then no error. If CF = 1 and AX = 6 then either the handle is invalid or the file with this handle is not open.
3FH	read from a file or device	This function works only if the file with the file handle in BX has either been opened by function 3DH or newly created by the create function, 3CH. Provided that this has been done, the number of bytes specified in CX are read into memory starting at the address having the offset (relative to DS) given in DX. Data is read from the file starting at the position indicated by the current value of the internal file pointer. After a successful read the file pointer is updated to point to the byte in the file following the last byte read.	
		AH = 3FH BX = file handle CX = number of bytes to be read DX = offset of buffer (relative to DS) in which to store the bytes read	If CF = 0 then AX = numbern of bytes read (If CF = 0 and AX < CX then a partial record at the end of the file was read. If CF = 0 and AX = 0 then the end of the file has been reached.) If CF = 1 then AX = 5 or 6 specifying an error condition. AX = 5 indicates that access has been denied. AX = 6 indicates that the file is invalid.

Table 19.1 *(cont.)*

Function number	*Purpose*	*Input parameters required*	*Output parameters*
40H	write to a file or device	This function works only if the file with the file handle in BX has either been opened by function 3DH or newly created by the create function, 3CH. Provided that this has been done, the number of bytes specified in CX is written into the file from the group of memory locations starting at the address having the offset (relative to DS) given in DX. Data is written into the file starting at the position indicated by the current value of the internal file pointer. After a successful write the file pointer is updated to point to the byte in the file following the last byte written.	
		AH = 40H BX = file handle CX = number of bytes to be written (if CX = 0 then the file is truncated or extended to the current file pointer). DX = offset of buffer (relative to DS is which to store the bytes read	If CF = 0 then AX = number of bytes written (If CF = 0 and AX < CX then the destination disk is full.) If CF = 1 then AX = 5 or 6 specifying an error condition. AX = 5 indicates that access has been denied. AX = 6 indicates that the file is invalid.
41H	delete a file	Given that DS:DX points to an ASCIIZ string representing a valid file name, the corresponding file is deleted.	
		AH = 41H DX = offset of ASCIIZ string (relative) to DS	If CF = 0 then deletion is successful. If CF = 1 then AX = 2,3 or 5 specifying an error condition. AX = 2 indicates that the given file has not been found. AX = 3 indicates that the given path has not been found. AX = 5 indicates that access was denied.

Table 19.1 (*cont.*)

Function number	*Purpose*	*Input parameters required*	*Output parameters*
42H	move read/ write pointer	Sets the position of the file pointer for the next read or write operation. The value in CX,DX is interpreted as a 32-bit number (CX containing the most significant bits) which specifies an offset according to one of three methods. Which method is to be used is given by the value in AL. With AL set to 0, the value in CX,DX is interpreted as a 32-bit *positive* integer – so the file pointer is always set relative to the beginning of the file. With AL set to 1 or 2, CX,DX is interpreted as a 32-bit signed integer, and so the file pointer can be moved either forwards or backwards. If AL is set to 1, this forward or backward movement takes place from the current position of the file pointer. If AL is set to 2, the forward or backward movement takes place from the end of the file. With method 0, specifying an offset of 0 positions the file pointer at the beginning of the file. Similarly, with method 2, specifying an offset of 0 positions the file pointer at the end of the file.	
		AH = 42H AL = method code: 00H byte offset from beginning of file. 01H byte offset from current location of file pointer. 02H byte offset from end of file BX = file handle CD,DX = number of bytes by which to move file pointer.	If CF = 0 then DX,AX = new file pointer position as a byte offset from the beginning of the file. If CF = 1 then AX = 1 or 6 specifying an error condition. AX = 1 indicates that AL is neither 0,1 nor 2. AX = 6 indicates that the handle is invalid.

19.2 Accessing the records of a file sequentially – writing a file dump utility

19.2.1 Specification

The aim in this section is to give a complete program example showing the use of the extended DOS function calls to read successive records from a disk file in the order they occur in the file. To be specific, we shall write a program which will take as input the name of any existing file (including a pathname) and display the contents of that file on the screen in hexadecimal format, 512D bytes at a time.

Once the program is started up, the first 512D bytes of the file will be displayed. To have the second group of 512D bytes displayed the user must press any key other than X or keys such as SHIFT and CTRL. If the user presses the X key then the program stops and exits to the operating system. After the second group of 512D bytes has been displayed, pressing any key different from X and keys such as SHIFT and CTRL displays the next record (X causes an exit). And so on. When eventually the end of the file has been reached the program pauses, and pressing any sensible key causes an automatic exit to the operating system.

As usual, the assembly language program to carry out this task must be put into a file having the second name (file extension) `ASM`. Since the object of the program is to dump the contents of any chosen file on the screen, we shall put the program to do this in a file called `DUMP.ASM`.

19.2.2 The method

A pseudo-Pascal outline of our program is as follows:

establish data segment addressability;
prompt user for filename;
read filename;
print a new line;
prepare ASCIIZ string representing user's filename;
AL := *code for open file for reading only*;
DX := *address of ASCIIZ string giving filename*;
call DOS open file function;
if *carry flag clear* **then**
  begin
  store handle;
  repeat
    DX := *address of data buffer*;
    CX := *number of bytes to read*;

```
        BX := file handle;
        read into buffer;
        chars_read := AX;
        if carry flag is clear and AX <> 0 then
          begin
          print out bytes just read (of length chars_read) in hexadecimal;
          read(char); print(new line);
          clear carry to indicate a char was read
          end
      until carry set or char = 'X' or AX = 0
      end;
  return to DOS
```

We obtain the filename from the user by first issuing a prompt via DOS function 9H, and then using DOS function 0AH (see Table 4.1) to accept up to a predetermined maximum number of characters typed by the user until the ENTER key is pressed. This maximum number must be given in the first byte of a buffer pointed to by DS:DX. The second byte of the buffer is set to the number of characters actually typed, not including the terminating CR character. The remaining bytes of the buffer contain the string itself. This latter string is then converted to an ASCIIZ string.

To open the file corresponding to this ASCIIZ string, we shall then call DOS function 3DH (see Table 19.1). Before doing so, the program must set AL to a code (0,1 or 2) indicating the mode of access that will be required. If AL is 0 when function 3DH is executed, the file will be opened for reading only; if AL is 1 then the file will be opened for writing only; and if AL is 2 then the file will be opened for reading and writing. Our `DUMP` program requires read access only so AL will be set to 0.

Attempting to open the file causes the operating system to scan the disk in the specified disk drive. If the file cannot be found, CF is set to 1, otherwise it is set to zero. If the file has been opened successfully, DOS assigns a handle number to the file and this is returned in AX.

Having successfully opened the file, we store the file handle in memory and read the next 512D bytes from the file using function 3FH of `INT 21H` (see Table 19.1) which requires that the relevant file has already been opened. Having made the transfer, DOS automatically increments the internal file pointer so that any future read operation will act on the next 512D bytes in sequence. If the read was successful, CF is set to 0, otherwise CF is set to 1. However, we must also check that AX is not zero. For, if it is, then we have reached the end of the file. Displaying the bytes read from the disk on the screen in hexadecimal format now boils down to printing the contents of each of the locations in the buffer in hexadecimal.

If we have not reached the end of the file to be dumped, we wait for a key to be pressed and then repeat the read. . .print cycle, unless it was the X key. If it was, we stop and return control to the operating system.

19.2.3 The program

The complete program is given in Figure 19.1. Each 512D byte buffer-full is printed by using the LODS string primitive to bring bytes from the buffer one by one into AL. The subroutine PRINT_AL_IN_HEX is then employed to print the contents of AL in hexadecimal. To see how it works, suppose AL contains 0101011B = 57H. After executing the

```
MOV CL,4
ROR AL,CL
```

instructions, the contents of AL will be 01110101B (75H); the digits in the hexadecimal representation of the initial contents of AL (57H) have been swapped round. The PRINT_AL_IN_HEX subroutine now calls the subroutine PRINT_ONE_HEX_DIGIT, which first masks out the second digit of the current contents of AL via the AND AL,0FH instruction, leaving 00000101B in AL. Then we add 30H or 37H as necessary to convert the digit into ASCII ready for printing, print the digit (5) and return from this subroutine call. We now POP the saved initial value of AL off the stack, which in our example leaves 01010111B in AL. After AND AL,0FH, register AL contains 00000111B and we add 30H or 37H as necessary to convert this to ASCII and print the result (7).

```
CR EQU 0DH
LF EQU 0AH
DATA SEGMENT
PROMPT      DB 'PLEASE TYPE THE NAME OF THE FILE TO BE DUMPED '
            DB 'AND THEN PRESS THE ENTER KEY',CR,LF,'$'

USER_STRING LABEL BYTE
MAX_LENGTH   DB 30H
NAME_LENGTH  DB ?
FILENAME     DB 31H DUP(' ')

HANDLE     DW ?
BUFFER     DB 512D DUP(?)
CHARS_READ DW ?
DATA ENDS

WORKING_STORAGE SEGMENT STACK
       DW 100H DUP(?)
WORKING_STORAGE ENDS

CODE SEGMENT
ASSUME CS:CODE,DS:DATA,SS:WORKING_STORAGE
;establish data segment addressability
   START:MOV AX,DATA
         MOV DS,AX
;prompt user for filename
         MOV AH,9H
```

Figure 19.1
The complete DUMP program.

```
        LEA DX,PROMPT
        INT 21H
;read filename
        MOV AH,0AH
        LEA DX,USER_STRING
        INT 21H
;print a new line
        CALL PRINT_NEWLINE
;prepare ASCIIZ string representing user's filename
        MOV BL,NAME_LENGTH
        MOV BH,0
        ADD BX,OFFSET FILENAME
        MOV [BX],BYTE PTR 0
;DOS open file function
        MOV  AH,3DH
;open for reading only
        MOV  AL,0
;DX := address of ASCIIZ string
        LEA  DX,FILENAME
        INT  21H
;if carry flag clear then
        JC   DONE
       ;begin
       ;store handle
             MOV HANDLE,AX
       ;repeat
           NEXT_RECORD:MOV AH,3FH ;DOS read file function
                 ;DX := address of data buffer
                       LEA DX,BUFFER
                 ;CX := number of bytes to read
                       MOV CX,512D
                 ;BX := file handle
                       MOV BX,HANDLE
                 ;read next group of bytes into buffer
                       INT 21H
                 ;chars_read := AX
                       MOV CHARS_READ,AX
                 ;if carry flag is clear
                       JC  UNTILCHECK
                 ;and AX <> 0
                       CMP AX,0
                       JZ  UNTILCHECK
                    ;then begin
                    ;print out record just read in hex
                              CALL HEX_RECORD_PRINT
                    ;read(char); print(new line)
                              MOV  AH,1
                              INT  21H
                              CALL PRINT_NEWLINE
                    ;clear carry to indicate a char was read
                              CLC
                    ;end
      ;until carry set or char = 'X' or AX=0
  UNTILCHECK:JC   DONE
```

Figure 19.1
(*cont.*)

```
                        CMP AL,'X'
                        JZ   DONE
                        CMP AX,0
                        JZ   DONE
                        JMP NEXT_RECORD
                ;end
        ;return to DOS
DONE:MOV AX,4C00H
     INT 21H

     HEX_RECORD_PRINT PROC NEAR
                      LEA  SI,BUFFER
                      MOV  CX,CHARS_READ
             PRINTING:LODSB
                      PUSH CX      ;preserve CX so we do not lose count
                      CALL PRINT_AL_IN_HEX
                      POP  CX
                      LOOP PRINTING
                      CALL PRINT_NEWLINE
                      RET
     HEX_RECORD_PRINT ENDP

     PRINT_AL_IN_HEX PROC  NEAR
                           PUSH AX
                           MOV  CL,4
                           ROR  AL,CL
                           CALL PRINT_ONE_HEX_DIGIT
                           POP  AX
     PRINT_ONE_HEX_DIGIT:  AND  AL,0FH
                           ADD  AL,30H
                           CMP  AL,3AH
                           JB   DISPLAY_IT
                           ADD  AL,7H
              DISPLAY_IT:  MOV  DL,AL
                           MOV  AH,2H
                           INT  21H
                           RET
   PRINT_AL_IN_HEX ENDP

     PRINT_NEWLINE  PROC NEAR
                    PUSH AX
                    MOV  AH,2H
                    MOV  DL,CR
                    INT  21H
                    MOV  DL,LF
                    INT  21H
                    POP  AX
                    RET
     PRINT_NEWLINE  ENDP

     CODE ENDS
     END START
```

Figure 19.1
(cont.)

EXERCISES

19.1 Improve the user-friendliness of the DUMP utility just written. If the file for which a DUMP has been requested cannot be opened because the file does not exist then print out the message FILE DOESN'T EXIST – TYPING ERROR IN FILENAME? When all the records of a particular file have been DUMPed, display the message ALL RECORDS NOW DUMPED before exiting to the operating system.

19.2 Write an 8086-family assembly language program which performs in exactly the same way as our DUMP program but which prints out each record in ASCII format whenever possible. In other words, for each byte read from disk, if that byte is the ASCII code for a printable character, then display that character else display a period (.). Store the program in a file call ASCIDUMP.ASM.

19.3 Putting data into files

Before gaining access to a file it is necessary to open it if the file already exists, or to create it if the file is new. Creating a file is in fact the operation of making an entry for that file in the **file directory** held on the appropriate disk. This is done by a call to function number 3CH (the 'create file' function). Given the offset (relative to DS) of an ASCIIZ string representing a filename in register DX, the create-file function amends the appropriate disk directory and initializes a file handle in the same manner as a call to the open-file function. For this reason, a file need not be opened after it has been created. If an error occurs during a call to the create-file function (because there is no room left in the directory, for example) then CF is set to 1. If all is well, CF is set to 0.

DOS function number 40H will write the number of bytes specified in CX from the group of memory locations pointed to by DX (relative to DS) to the file with handle in BX, starting at the current position of the internal DOS file pointer. After writing, the file pointer is adjusted to point to the byte after the last one written in the file. If the write was successful, CF is set to 0, otherwise CF is set to 1 and AX contains an error code (see Table 19.1).

Closing the file is carried out by operating system function number 3EH. This function must be called after writing to a file has finished, or the data written to the file will not be permanently recorded on disk. Function 3EH requires that the handle for the file to be closed is in BX. If the close operation is successful, the carry flag is set to 0 and the data held on the disk concerning the relevant file is updated and the new file made permanent. Otherwise CF is set to 1 and AX contains an error code.

19.3.1 DATAGRAB A complete program example showing file input

By way of illustration of the process involved in writing data into a file, we shall now construct a program which will accept an arbitrary number of characters typed at the keyboard and store the ASCII codes for those characters in a disk file. Input is accepted until the user types a CTRL-Z character which we shall interpret as the user signalling the end of the data to be written to the file. We shall assume that the program itself is in a file called DATAGRAB.ASM.

Once again the method consists of a few simple steps:

```
establish data segment addressability;
ES := DS; (* ready for string manipulation instructions *)
prompt user for filename;
read filename;
print a new line;
prepare ASCIIZ string representing user's filename;
set AH ready for DOS create file function;
set CX to 'normal file' attribute;
DX := address of ASCIIZ string;
create the file;
if CF = 0 then
  begin
  store handle;
  repeat
    count := 512D;
    DI := buffer address;
    repeat read(ch);
           next available buffer location := ch;
           count := count - 1
    until ch = 1AH or count = 0;
    if ch = 1AH then chars_read := 512D - count;
    write chars_read bytes from BUFFER to file
  until CF <> 0 or chars_read <> 512D;
  close file;
  end;
return to DOS
```

Figure 19.2 shows the complete DATAGRAB program, in which register CX has been used for the variable *count* in the above outline. The reader is invited to type in the program and verify that it works, using the DUMP program of Section 19.2 to check the contents of files created using DATAGRAB.

```
CR EQU 0DH
LF EQU 0AH

DATA SEGMENT
PROMPT     DB 'PLEASE TYPE THE NAME OF THE FILE TO BE CREATED '
           DB 'AND THEN PRESS THE ENTER KEY',CR,LF,'$'

USER_STRING LABEL BYTE
MAX_LENGTH    DB 30H
NAME_LENGTH   DB ?
FILENAME      DB 31H DUP(' ')

HANDLE        DW ?
BUFFER        DB 512D DUP(?)

CHARS_READ    DW 512D
DATA ENDS

WORKING_STORAGE SEGMENT STACK
       DW 100H DUP(?)
WORKING_STORAGE ENDS

CODE SEGMENT
ASSUME CS:CODE,DS:DATA,SS:WORKING_STORAGE
;establish data segment addressability
   START: MOV AX,DATA
          MOV DS,AX
;ES := DS
          MOV ES,AX
;prompt user for filename
          MOV AH,9H
          LEA DX,PROMPT
          INT 21H
;read filename
          MOV AH,0AH
          LEA DX,USER_STRING
          INT 21H
;print a new line
          CALL PRINT_NEWLINE
;prepare ASCIIZ string representing user's filename
          MOV BL,NAME_LENGTH
          MOV BH,0
          ADD BX,OFFSET FILENAME
          MOV [BX],BYTE PTR 0
;set DOS create file function
          MOV AH,3CH
;set 'normal file' attribute
          MOV CX,0
;DX := address of ASCIIZ string
          LEA DX,FILENAME
;create the file
          INT 21H
;if carry flag clear then
          JC   DONE
```

Figure 19.2 The complete DATAGRAB program.

```
                ;begin
                ;store handle
                            MOV HANDLE,AX
                ;repeat
               READ_RECORD: CLD
                            ;count := 512D
                            MOV CX,512D
                            ;DI := buffer address
                            LEA DI,BUFFER
                            ;repeat read(ch)
            NEXT_DATA_BYTE:   CALL READ_A_CHARACTER
                              ;next available buffer location := ch
                              STOSB
                              ;count := count - 1
                            ;until ch = 1AH or count = 0
                            CMP AL,1AH
                            JZ   SET_CHAR_COUNT
                            LOOPNZ NEXT_DATA_BYTE ;LOOP does count := count - 1
                            ;if ch = 1AH then chars_read := 512D - count
            SET_CHAR_COUNT: CMP AL,1AH
                            JNZ WRITE_RECORD
                            MOV AX,512D
                            SUB AX,CX
                            MOV CHARS_READ,AX
                            ;write chars_read bytes from BUFFER to file
              WRITE_RECORD: MOV AH,40H
                            MOV BX,HANDLE
                            MOV CX,CHARS_READ
                            LEA DX,BUFFER
                            INT 21H
                ;until CF <> 0 or chars_read <> 512D
                       JC   CLOSE
                       CMP CHARS_READ,512D
                       JZ   READ_RECORD
                ;close file
                CLOSE: MOV AH,3EH
                       MOV BX,HANDLE
                       INT 21H
                ;end
;return to DOS
DONE: MOV AX,4C00H
      INT 21H

READ_A_CHARACTER PROC NEAR
                 MOV  AH,1
                 INT  21H
                 RET
READ_A_CHARACTER ENDP

PRINT_NEWLINE PROC NEAR
              PUSH AX
              MOV  AH,2H
              MOV  DL,CR
              INT  21H
              MOV  DL,LF
```

Figure 19.2
(cont.)

```
                INT  21H
                POP  AX
                RET
PRINT_NEWLINE ENDP

CODE ENDS
END START
```

Figure 19.2 (*cont.*)

EXERCISES

19.3 If you have tried to inspect the contents of files created using DATAGRAB with the DOS TYPE instruction, some very strange results will have been obtained if the ENTER key was pressed during data input to the file. The ENTER key has code 0DH (carriage return) which is dutifully entered into the file by DATAGRAB. However, when printing out the contents of your file, TYPE displays exactly what is in the file and therefore prints just a carriage return and no line feed. As a result the subsequent line overprints the previous one. Alter DATAGRAB so that TYPE prints out the contents of a text file correctly. One way of doing this would be to insert two code bytes, 0AH (line feed) and 0DH, in the file for every ENTER typed by the user.

19.4 Add more informative error messages to the DATAGRAB program. If a new file cannot be created because there would then be too many open files, display the error message TOO MANY FILES ALREADY OPEN. If an error occurs whilst a group of bytes is being written then display WRITE ERROR – EXECUTION STOPPED.

19.5 Write an 8086-family assembly language program which will allow its user to store as many decimal numbers as he or she wants in the range 0–100 (inclusive) in a disk file. Any number which is out of range should be rejected and a suitable error message printed. Input should be terminated when the user presses CTRL-Z. Store the program in a file called NUMGRAB.ASM.

19.4 Copying files

The aim in this section is to write a program, the assembly language version of which will be held in a file called FILECOPY.ASM. This program will request two filenames from the user and will make a copy of the first named file in the second. (Of course, just such a copy facility is already available from DOS, but the point here is to give another illustration of the DOS file-handling functions.)

The method is more or less straightforward:

establish data segment addressability;
ES := *DS*;
prompt for source filename;
read source filename;
print a new line;
prepare ASCIIZ string representing source filename;
prompt for name of file in which copy is to be made;
read source filename;
print a new line;
prepare ASCIIZ string representing file in which copy is to be made;
error := *false*;
try to open source file for reading only;
save handle for source file;
if *CF* <> 0 **then** *error* := *true*;
DX := *address of 'open' error message*;
if not *error* **then**
  begin
  create new object file;
  save object file handle;
  if *CF* <> 0 **then** *error* := *true*;
  DX := *address of 'create' error message*
  end;
if not *error* **then**
  repeat
    fill buffer from source file;
    DI := *AX* (* *no. of bytes read* *);
    write contents of buffer to the object file;
    if *CF* <> 0 **then** *error* := *true*;
    DX := *address of 'write' error message*
  until *DI* < 512*D* **or** *error*;
if not *error* **then**
  begin
  close object file;
  DX := *address of 'close' error message*;
  if *CF* = 0 **then** *DX* := *address of 'normal end' message*
  end;
print message addressed by DX;
return to DOS

A complete program which implements this pseudo-Pascal outline is given in Figure 19.3.

```
CR EQU ODH
LF EQU OAH

DATA SEGMENT
PROMPT1  DB 'PLEASE TYPE THE NAME OF THE SOURCE FILE '
         DB 'AND THEN PRESS THE ENTER KEY',CR,LF,'$'
PROMPT2  DB 'PLEASE TYPE THE NAME OF THE FILE IN WHICH '
         DB 'THE COPY IS TO BE MADE AND THEN PRESS THE '
         DB 'ENTER KEY',CR,LF,'$'

USER_STRING1 LABEL BYTE
MAX_LENGTH1   DB 30H
NAME_LENGTH1  DB ?
FILENAME1     DB 31H DUP(' ')
HANDLE1       DW ?

USER_STRING2 LABEL BYTE
MAX_LENGTH2   DB 30H
NAME_LENGTH2  DB ?
FILENAME2     DB 31H DUP(' ')
HANDLE2       DW ?

BUFFER        DB 511D DUP(?)
LAST_OF_DATA  DB ?

;error messages
NO_SUCH_FILE         DB 'NO SUCH FILE EXISTS',CR,LF,'$'
DIRECTORY_FULL       DB 'CANNOT CREATE A NEW FILE — TOO MANY '
                     DB 'FILES ON THE DISK',CR,LF,'$'
DISK_FULL            DB 'NO ROOM LEFT ON THE DISK',CR,LF,'$'
DISK_WRITE_PROTECTED DB 'DISK WRITE PROTECTED',CR,LF,'$'
NORMAL_END           DB 'COPY COMPLETED',CR,LF,'$'

DATA ENDS

WORKING_STORAGE SEGMENT STACK
     DW 100H DUP(?)
WORKING_STORAGE ENDS

CODE SEGMENT
ASSUME CS:CODE,DS:DATA,SS:WORKING_STORAGE
;establish data segment addressability
  START: MOV AX,DATA
         MOV DS,AX
;ES := DS
         MOV ES,AX
;prompt for source filename
         MOV AH,9H
         LEA DX,PROMPT1
         INT 21H
;read source filename
         MOV AH,OAH
         LEA DX,USER_STRING1
         INT 21H
```

Figure 19.3
The FILECOPY program.

```
;print a   new line
           CALL PRINT_NEWLINE
;prepare   ASCIIZ string representing source filename
           MOV BL,NAME_LENGTH1
           MOV BH,0
           ADD BX,OFFSET FILENAME1
           MOV [BX],BYTE PTR 0
;prompt for name of file in which copy is to be made
           MOV AH,9H
           LEA DX,PROMPT2
           INT 21H
;read source filename
           MOV AH,0AH
           LEA DX,USER_STRING2
           INT 21H
;print a new line
           CALL PRINT_NEWLINE
;prepare ASCIIZ string representing file in which copy is to be made
           MOV BL,NAME_LENGTH2
           MOV BH,0
           ADD BX,OFFSET FILENAME2
           MOV [BX],BYTE PTR 0
;error := false;
           MOV BH,0
;try to open source file for reading only
           MOV AH,3DH
           MOV AL,0
           LEA DX,FILENAME1
           INT 21H
;save handle for source file
           MOV HANDLE1,AX
;if CF <> 0 then error := true;
           JNC OPEN_OK
           MOV BH,1
;DX := address of 'open' error message
 OPEN_OK:LEA DX,NO_SUCH_FILE
;if not error then
           CMP BH,0
           JNZ READ_BLOCK
           ;begin
           ;create new object file;
                   MOV   AH,3CH
                   MOV   CX,0
                   LEA   DX,FILENAME2
                   INT   21H
           ;save object file handle
                   MOV   HANDLE2,AX
           ;if CF <> 0 then error := true
                   JNC   CREATE_OK
                   MOV   BH,1
           ;DX := address of 'create' error message
        CREATE_OK: LEA DX, DIRECTORY_FULL
           ;end
;if not error then
           READ_BLOCK: CMP BH,0
```

Figure 19.3
(cont.)

```
          JNZ END_OF_FILE_BLOCK
       ;repeat
           ;fill buffer from source file
              MOV   AH,3FH
              LEA   DX,BUFFER
              MOV   CX,512D
              MOV   BX,HANDLE1
              INT   21H
           ;DI := AX (* no of bytes read *)
              MOV   DI,AX
           ;write contents of buffer
           ;to the object file;
              MOV AH,40H
              MOV BX,HANDLE2
              MOV CX,DI
              LEA DX,BUFFER
              INT 21H
           ;if CF <> 0 then error := true
              JNC   WRITE_OK
              MOV   BH,1
           ;DX := address of 'write' error message
    WRITE_OK:LEA DX, DISK_FULL
      ;until DI < 512D or error;
             CMP   DI,512D
             JB    END_OF_FILE_BLOCK
             CMP   BH,0
             JNZ   END_OF_FILE_BLOCK
             JMP   READ_BLOCK
;if not error then
END_OF_FILE_BLOCK:CMP BH,0
                  JNZ DONE
      ;begin
      ;close object file
       END_OF_FILE: MOV AH,3EH
                    MOV BX,HANDLE2
                    INT 21H
      ;DX := address of 'close' error message
                    LEA DX,DISK_WRITE_PROTECTED
      ;if CF = 0 then DX := address of 'normal end' mess
                    JC   DONE
                    MOV DX,OFFSET NORMAL_END
      ;end
;print message addressed by DX
DONE:   MOV   AH,09H
        INT   21H
;return to DOS
        MOV   AX,4C00H
        INT   21H

PRINT_NEWLINE PROC NEAR
            PUSH AX
            MOV   AH,2H
            MOV   DL,CR
            INT   21H
            MOV   DL,LF
```

Figure 19.3
(cont.)

```
                INT   21H
                POP   AX
                RET
PRINT_NEWLINE ENDP

CODE ENDS
END START
```

Figure 19.3 (*cont.*)

EXERCISES

19.6 Amend the FILECOPY program so that if the file which is to contain the copy already exists, the user is asked if he or she really does wish to have the existing file deleted. If not, return control to the operating system. Otherwise delete the file (using DOS function 41H of INT 21H – see Table 19.1) and then make the desired copy.

19.7 Write an 8086-family assembly language program which is to be called up from DOS by typing the command

```
CHANGE
```

and which requests two filenames. If the user responds by typing first the filename PRIVATE.OLD and then the filename PUBLIC.NEW, then the program should copy the contents of PRIVATE.OLD into PUBLIC.NEW but replacing every occurrence of the string LTD by the string PLC.

19.8 Write a utility program COUNT which counts the number of occurrences in a file of an alphabetic string of between one and eight characters. This number is then printed on the screen and control is returned to the operating system.

19.5 Random access files

The example programs so far have accessed files sequentially. That is, they started at the beginning of a file and stepped through the files on which they operated byte by byte. But often access needs to be on a **random** basis. For example, when dealing with incoming purchase orders we may need to access customer details at random from a file stored alphabetically: first the details for J.BLOGGS, and then for R.SMITH, and finally for T.THOMAS. In this case, instead of using the automatic (sequential) positioning of the file pointer, programs must make use of the extended DOS function 42H (see Table 19.1) to move the file pointer arbitrarily.

Extended DOS function 42H sets the position of the file pointer for the next read or write operation according to the value in CX,DX interpreted as a 32-bit number (CX containing the most significant bits) which is used as an offset in one of three ways. BX must contain the file handle for the file to be affected, and AL contains a code indicating which kind of interpretation of CX,DX is to be used.

If AL is set to 0, the value in CX,DX is interpreted as a 32-bit *positive* integer – so the file pointer is always set relative to the beginning of the file. With AL set to 1 or 2, CX,DX is interpreted as a 32-bit signed integer, and so the file pointer can be moved either forwards or backwards. If AL is set to 1, this forward or backward movement takes place from the current position of the file pointer. If AL is set to 2, the forward or backward movement takes place from the end of the file. With AL set to 0, specifying an offset of 0 positions the file pointer at the beginning of the file. Similarly, with method 2, specifying an offset of 0 positions the file pointer at the end of the file.

After execution of extended DOS function 42H, if CF = 0 then DX,AX represents the new file pointer position as a byte offset from the beginning of the file. If CF = 1 then AX = 1 or 6 specifying an error condition. If AX = 1 then AL was not set to one of 0,1 or 2. If AX = 6 then the file handle given is not valid.

19.5.1 A random access read utility

We shall now write a program which will allow its users to look at any of the first 10 groups of 512D bytes of a (text) file in any order. The assembly language version of the program will be stored in a file called `RANDREAD.ASM`. The program will ask the user to type, first a file name and then a digit *n* (one of 0,1,2,3,. . .,9). It will then cause the *n*th group of 512D bytes in the file to be printed on the display screen. If there is no *n*th group of 512D bytes in the file then a question mark (`?`) will be displayed and the program will wait for another *n* to be typed in. The question mark error symbol is likewise displayed if any character other than a digit is typed, except that typing X terminates the execution of the program.

The method involves gluing together the necessary function calls:

establish data segment addressability;
prompt user for filename;
read filename;
print a new line;
prepare ASCIIZ string representing user's filename;
DOS open file function;
open for reading only;
DX := address of ASCIIZ string;
if *carry flag clear* **then**
  begin
  store handle;

read(*ch*); *print*(*new line*);
while *ch* <> '*X*' **do**
begin
if *ch* **in** ['0'..'9'] **then**
begin
DX,*AX* := 512*D* ∗ *digit read*;
CX,*DX* := *DX*,*AX*;
set file pointer to ch*th group of 512 bytes*;
read the ch*th group of 512D bytes into buffer*;
if *AX* <> 0 **and** *CF* = 0 **then** *display buffer contents*
end
else *print error message*;
read(*ch*); *print*(*new line*)
end
end;
return to DOS

An implementation of this pseudo-Pascal outline is given in Figure 19.4.

```
CR EQU 0DH
LF EQU 0AH
DATA SEGMENT
PROMPT   DB 'PLEASE TYPE THE NAME OF THE FILE TO BE READ '
         DB 'AND THEN PRESS THE ENTER KEY',CR,LF,'$'

USER_STRING LABEL BYTE
MAX_LENGTH    DB 30H
NAME_LENGTH   DB ?
FILENAME      DB 31H DUP(' ')

HANDLE   DW ?
BUFFER   DB 512D DUP(?)
DATA ENDS

WORKING_STORAGE SEGMENT STACK
     DW 100H DUP(?)
WORKING_STORAGE ENDS

CODE SEGMENT
ASSUME CS:CODE,DS:DATA,SS:WORKING_STORAGE
;establish data segment addressability
  START: MOV AX,DATA
         MOV DS,AX
;prompt user for filename
         MOV AH,9H
         LEA DX,PROMPT
         INT 21H
;read filename
```

Figure 19.4
The RANDREAD program.

```
          MOV AH,0AH
          LEA DX,USER_STRING
          INT 21H
   ;print a new line
          CALL PRINT_NEWLINE
   ;prepare ASCIIZ string representing user's filename
          MOV BL,NAME_LENGTH
          MOV BH,0
          ADD BX,OFFSET FILENAME
          MOV [BX],BYTE PTR 0
   ;DOS open file function
          MOV AH,3DH
   ;open for reading only
          MOV AL,0
   ;DX := address of ASCIIZ string
          LEA DX,FILENAME
          INT 21H
   ;if carry flag clear then
          JC    DONE
     ;begin
     ;store handle
      MOV HANDLE,AX
     ;read(ch); print(new line);
      MOV  AH,1
      INT  21H
      CALL PRINT_NEWLINE
     ;while ch <> 'X' do
A_RECORD: CMP  AL,'X'
        JZ    DONE
             ;begin
             ;if ch in ['0'..'9'] then
                           SUB  AL,30H
                           JAE  CHECK_UPPER_LIMIT
                           JMP  KEY_IN
        CHECK_UPPER_LIMIT: CMP  AL,10D
                           JNB  KEY_IN
                 ;begin
                 ;DX,AX := 512D * digit read
                           MOV  AH,0
                           MOV  BX,512D
                           MUL  BX
                 ;CX,DX := DX,AX
                           MOV  CX,DX
                           MOV  DX,AX
                 ;set file pointer to ch-th group of 512 bytes
                           MOV  AH,42H
                           MOV  AL,0
                           MOV  BX,HANDLE
                           INT  21H
                 ;read the ch-th group of 512D bytes into buffer
                           MOV  AH,3FH
                           LEA  DX,BUFFER
                           MOV  CX,512D
                           MOV  BX,HANDLE
                           INT  21H
```

Figure 19.4
(cont.)

```
                  ;if AX <> 0   and CF = 0
                              CMP   AX,0
                              JZ    READ_NEXT_INS
                              JC    KEY_IN
                     ;then display buffer contents
                              CLD
                              MOV   CX,AX
                              LEA   SI,BUFFER
                              LODSB
                              MOV   DL,AL
                              CALL  PRINT_A_CHARACTER
                              LOOP  NEXT_CHARACTER
                        ;end
                              JMP   READ_NEXT_INS
                  ;else print error message
              KEY_IN: CALL ERROR_MESSAGE
                  ;read(ch); print(new line)
       READ_NEXT_INS: CALL PRINT_NEWLINE
                      MOV  AH,1
                      INT  21H
                      CALL PRINT_NEWLINE
                 ;end
                NEXT: JMP  A_RECORD
         ;end
;return to DOS
DONE: MOV AX,4C00H
      INT 21H

PRINT_A_CHARACTER PROC NEAR
      MOV AH,2
      INT 21H
      RET
PRINT_A_CHARACTER ENDP

PRINT_NEWLINE PROC NEAR
      PUSH AX
      MOV  AH,2
      MOV  DL,CR
      INT  21H
      MOV  DL,LF
      INT  21H
      POP  AX
      RET
PRINT_NEWLINE ENDP

ERROR_MESSAGE PROC NEAR
      MOV  AH,2
      MOV  DL,'?'
      INT  21H
      RET
ERROR_MESSAGE ENDP

CODE ENDS
END START
```

Figure 19.4
(cont.)

EXERCISES

19.9 The error messages in `RANDREAD` are primitive, to say the least. Add more informative error messages to it as well as the ability to display 512D groups of bytes from group 0 to group 99 inclusive.

19.10 Construct the counterpart, `RANDWRIT`, to `RANDREAD` which operates in much the same way, except that, when a digit *n* is typed, the program then waits for the user to type in 512D characters which are to be stored as the *n*th group of 512D bytes in the file named when `RANDWRIT` was called up. Use `RANDREAD` to check that `RANDWRIT` works!

19.6 Devices as files

Extended DOS functions allow us to regard certain hardware devices such as the keyboard, display and printer as files which are permanently open and have standard handles associated with them as follows:

Device	*Standard handle*
Input, normally keyboard	0
Output, normally display	1
Error output, normally display	2
Auxiliary device	3
Printer	4

Thus, extended DOS functions 3FH and 40FH (see Table 19.1) allow us to accept input from the keyboard and send output to the display or printer, respectively. As usual with these functions, CX must be set to the number of bytes to be read or displayed, DX must point to the input or output area and BX must contain the appropriate handle. Thereafter, the operation of functions 3FH and 40H is exactly the same as for disk files, except that we do not need to open the device 'files', and input from the keyboard via function 3FH is terminated when the user presses the ENTER key.

The complete example program in Figure 19.5 asks the user to type a seven-letter name followed by the ENTER key and then displays a greeting based on that name. Thus, if the user types

```
ALFONSO<ENTER>
```

the program responds

```
HOWDY ALFONSO
```

```
CR EQU 0DH
LF EQU 0AH

DATA SEGMENT
PROMPT    DB 'PLEASE TYPE A SEVEN LETTER NAME',CR,LF
REPLY     DB CR,LF,'HOWDY '
PERSON    DB 7 DUP(' '),CR,LF
DATA ENDS

WORKING_STORAGE SEGMENT STACK
     DW 100H DUP(?)
WORKING_STORAGE ENDS

CODE SEGMENT
ASSUME CS:CODE,DS:DATA,SS:WORKING_STORAGE
;establish data segment addressability
    START:MOV AX,DATA
          MOV DS,AX
;prompt user for name
          MOV AH,40H
          MOV BX,1
          LEA DX,PROMPT
          MOV CX,33D
          INT 21H
;read filename
          MOV AH,3FH
          LEA DX,PERSON
          MOV BX,0
          MOV CX,7
          INT 21H
;display greeting
          MOV AH,40H
          MOV BX,1
          LEA DX,REPLY
          MOV CX,17D
          INT 21H
;return to DOS
     DONE:MOV AX,4C00H
          INT 21H

CODE ENDS
END START
```

Figure 19.5
A complete example program showing how certain hardware devices may be regarded as files thanks to extended DOS functions.

If you try running the program in Figure 19.5 (which we assume is in a file called `GREETING.ASM`) and give it the name

```
ALFONSO ALBERTI<ENTER>
```

then the program appears to work correctly because the message `HOWDY ALFONSO` is displayed on the screen. However, if the program is run again immediately afterwards, so that the dialog sequence is:

```
C>GREETING
PLEASE TYPE A SEVEN LETTER NAME
ALFONSO ALBERTI<ENTER>
HOWDY ALFONSO
C>GREETING
```

then running the program for the second time goes ahead without any further user intervention:

```
PLEASE TYPE A SEVEN LETTER NAME
 ALBERT
HOWDY ALBERT
C>
```

The extra characters typed when the program was run the first time were held in the keyboard buffer. So the second time the program was run, function 3FH – which gets its input from that buffer – already had characters available. To avoid this, we could use DOS function 0CH which flushes the standard input (that is, the keyboard) buffer (see Table 4.1) if we set register AH to 0CH, register AL to 0 and execute an `INT 21H`.

EXERCISES

19.11 Amend the example program of Figure 19.5 in two different ways so that if the user types extra characters they are ignored completely. In particular, subsequent runs of `GREETING` should not be affected by any additional characters the user types. Use DOS function 0CH as the basis of one of the amendments.

19.12 As we have observed, when extended DOS function 3FH is employed to read from the keyboard it normally obtains its input from the keyboard buffer. Use this fact to produce versions of the example programs in the preceding sections which allow the user to type the names of files to be affected at the same time as the name of the program. For example, to dump the contents of the file `MYFILE.ABC` using the program in `DUMP.ASM` of Section 19.1, the user should type:

```
DUMP MYFILE.ABC
```

straight after the operating system prompt.

19.7 COM and EXE files

You may have noticed that, while our executable programs have been stored in disk files with second name EXE (for example, RANDREAD.EXE), DOS can actually execute programs which have the second name COM. Many of these come with DOS. Thus, the COMMAND, PRINT and FORMAT programs are all stored in files with second name (file extension) COM. COM files occupy less disk space and can generally be read into memory faster than their EXE equivalents, so this section will describe how to produce COM program files.

However, they are not a panacea because COM files are limited to 64K bytes and the program contained in a COM file may not address more than a single segment.

The restriction to a single segment has several consequences. Most important, perhaps, is that this makes it particularly difficult to use modules constructed by other programmers who may have given their segments different names from your own. Also, a single segment necessarily leads us away from the careful separation of data and instructions possible when multiple segments can be employed. Consequently, EXE files are preferred for all but the very smallest of programs.

Another disadvantage of COM files is that the programs contained in them cannot be debugged symbolically using Code View. However, the COM format is a good choice for stand-alone assembly language programs of less than a few thousand bytes. (This is true of all of our program examples so far but, as usual, the absolute best way of doing something has been sacrificed to approaches which we thought explained things better. Only you the reader can tell if that has been a success or not!)

The remainder of this section describes how to construct COM files containing executable programs. Actually, we first create EXE files (as normal) from programs structured in a certain way, and then use a DOS utility program EXE2BIN to convert the EXE file to a COM file.

19.7.1 Rules for creating programs which are to be used in COM files

Detailed rules for the creation of programs for COM files are given in the MASM manual, but the essence of them is as follows:

(1) Only a single segment is allowed which must therefore be the code segment. (A COM program automatically generates a stack. The data for a COM program must be given in the code segment).

(2) All segment registers must be initialized to point to this single segment.

(3) Since the first 100H bytes in a COM program are occupied by the Program Segment Prefix (PSP), the program entry point must be preceded by the pseudo-op

```
ORG 100H
```

so that the program is loaded into memory 100H bytes after the beginning of the code segment, and thus does not override the PSP.

(4) In order to contain the program within a single segment, all procedures must be NEAR.

(5) The data should be given in a block at either the beginning or end of the program. (We shall follow the pattern adopted for EXE programs and give the data at the beginning of the code segment. It will therefore be necessary to start a COM program with a JMP instruction to pass over the data.

(6) If the program is to be a used as a secondary module, then rules 1 through 5 apply equally, but also the segment name for the secondary module must be the same as that for the main module.

Figure 19.6 contains a complete example program which follows these rules for constructing COM programs. It simply asks the user to guess a digit stored in memory. If the guess is correct the message GENIUS is displayed, otherwise the message NOPE is displayed.

To complete the production of a COM file containing the program in Figure 19.6, the file containing it, which we shall assume is GUESSING.ASM, must first be submitted to the assembler and linker in the normal way:

```
MASM GUESSING,,,,
LINK GUESSING,,,;
```

(LINK will generate a warning that our program has no stack segment. Since one will be generated automatically by DOS this is not a problem for us).

We then call up the DOS utility EXE2BIN – which actually does the final conversion from EXE format to the BINary format demanded of COM files:

```
EXE2BIN GUESSING GUESSING.COM
```

(Notice that because EXE2BIN requires an EXE file as the source file, we do not have to specify a second name for GUESSING when giving the first parameter. EXE2BIN will assume the second name of the source file to be EXE. However, the second parameter is the name of file in which the BINary version of the EXE is to be created. By default, that will be called GUESSING.BIN, so it is essential to give the second name in this case.)

We can then delete GUESSING.EXE (as it is no longer needed) and run the executable program in GUESSING.COM in the normal way – by typing its name after the operating system prompt:

```
C>GUESSING
GUESS MY NUMBER
2
NOPE
C>
```

Before deleting GUESSING.EXE however, it is interesting to compare the sizes of

```
CR EQU ODH
LF EQU OAH

CODE SEGMENT
ASSUME CS:CODE
ORG 100H
   ENTRY:JMP START
;------------------------ data --------------
  PROMPT DB 'GUESS MY NUMBER',CR,LF,'$'
  REPLY1 DB CR,LF,'GENIUS',CR,LF,'$'
  REPLY2 DB CR,LF,'NOPE',CR,LF,'$'
  NUMBER DB '3'
;---------------------------------------------
;display the user prompt
  START: LEA DX,PROMPT
         MOV AH,9H
         INT 21H
;read a digit
         MOV AH,1
         INT 21H
;if guess is correct then DX points to GENIUS message
         CMP AL,NUMBER
         JNZ BAD_GUESS
         LEA DX,REPLY1
         JMP GIVE_MESSAGE
    ;else DX   points to NOPE message
 BAD_GUESS:  LEA DX,REPLY2
    ;display   message
GIVE_MESSAGE:  MOV AH,9H
               INT 21H
   ;return to dos
               MOV AX,4C00H
               INT 21H

CODE ENDS
END ENTRY
```

Figure 19.6 Contents of GUESSING.ASM – a complete COM format program.

the files GUESSING.EXE and GUESSING.COM. From a directory listing, these are respectively 846 bytes and 78 bytes. The COM file is less than one tenth of the size of the EXE file, partly because an EXE file always begins with a 512-byte header block.

The COM stack

For a COM program DOS automatically sets all four segment registers to the same value and defines a stack. If there is enough room within the 64K limit, the stack is defined within the single segment containing the program and SP is initialized to 0FFFEH. If the single 64K segment does not contain enough space for a stack, DOS sets the stack at the end of memory.

Debugging

If, for any reason, EXE2BIN cannot convert your EXE file to a COM file, then the simple error message

```
File cannot be converted
```

will be displayed, with no further explanation. It can therefore sometimes be difficult to discover why the conversion cannot be done. But remember, omission of just one of the requirements for a COM file will cause the conversion to fail.

Note also that symbolic debuggers such as CodeView cannot display the source code when debugging a COM file – yet another reason why we prefer to work with EXE files for the purposes of this book.

SUMMARY

By explaining how to handle disk storage via operating system function calls, this chapter has removed a major constraint on the kinds of assembly language program we could write. We also saw how to store suitable programs as COM files and how the extended DOS file-handling functions could be used to program certain standard I/O devices. The next three chapters will take up the theme of I/O programming in more detail.

SELF-CHECK QUIZ

1. Explain the difference between an ASCIIZ string and a file handle.
2. How does DOS inform the programmer that the end of a file has been reached?
3. When is it necessary to open a file?
4. When is it necessary to close a file?
5. What is the difference between a file accessed sequentially and one accessed randomly?
6. Write a program fragment to show how to print out the contents of a DOS file by regarding the printer as a file.
7. Write a COM program to perform single-digit decimal addition. The user should type two digits and the sum of these digits should then be displayed on the next line.
8. Write two macros, one for opening files called OPENFILE and one for closing files called CLOSEFILE.
9. Write a pseudo-Pascal program fragment to show how you would design a utility program called COMPARE which will check if the contents of two DOS files are the same.
10. Why do you think DOS allows the programmer control of the size of the unit which is read from or written to a disk during each read or write operation?

20

Device Drivers I: Programmed I/O and Printers

Contents

The theme of the next three chapters is how to use assembly language programs to drive some of the I/O devices connected to a microcomputer, namely: a printer, the keyboard, and the display. There will be a chapter which discusses driving each of these three devices. But also, each chapter will have as an equally important theme one of the three main ways in which it is possible to drive hardware devices: **programmed I/O** through I/O ports; **interrupt I/O** using (hardware) interrupts; and **direct memory access**.

To begin, then, programmed I/O, which involves driving hardware devices through I/O ports, will be considered.

20.1 I/O ports and instructions

Some devices which are external to the main microcomputer are capable of both receiving and sending data. Thus a disk drive is, by design, external to the main computer's circuits, but may receive data to write on to a disk and may also send data read from a disk to an area of memory. If the external device is a printer, communication is one way only as far as our data is concerned. But if we are to be able to take 'intelligent' actions (such as stopping the computer from sending out data to be printed when the printer has run out of paper), some primitive form of two-way communication is essential.

External devices are almost always connected not directly to the system bus but to an **interface**. Most interfaces are designed so that a range of such possibilities can be catered for, leaving the programmer to specify his or her requirements. This is done by setting certain registers in the peripheral **interface chip** used by the interface. Because of the possible confusion with the main registers of the 8086 family, peripheral interface chip registers are usually referred to as **ports**.

A typical interface may have three or more ports associated with it:

- A **control port**, the setting of which will determine if the interface is to send or receive.
- A **data port** for the data element to be transmitted or to hold a data element received.
- A **status port** which can be used to obtain information such as 'printer out of paper, don't send any more data' or, for a serial transmission, 'all the bits of the data element haven't yet been received'.

Any interface will have a least a data port, but the functions of status port and control port may be combined into one port for a simple interface. On the other hand, sophisticated interfaces may have several control and status ports. Interfaces usually come on a circuit board which plugs into the main computer circuit board (the **motherboard**) and, while the actual port numbers and port settings may differ from machine to machine, the techniques involved will always be similar.

To illustrate how to use I/O ports to drive printers, it will be assumed that your computer has a parallel printer interface compatible with the IBM Parallel Printer Adapter and a serial interface compatible with the IBM Serial Adapter. If it does not, it may be that you have to modify the example programs given slightly, in order for them to run exactly as specified on your computer. The necessary changes may range from specifying different addresses from those given for the I/O ports to different arrangements for the control and status ports.

20.1.1 Input and output instructions

Just as locations in memory are referred to by their numeric addresses, so the various ports attached to an 8086-family based microcomputer are numbered. There is provision for ports numbered 0 to 0FFFFH. Which port is given which number is more or less determined by the designer of a particular microcomputer.

Setting a port is accomplished by the 8086-family `OUT` instruction. It has the general formats:

(1) `OUT DX`, *accumulator*

(2) `OUT` *port number, accumulator*

where *accumulator* denotes AL or AX depending on whether an 8-bit or 16-bit port is involved. If the port number is between 0 and 0FFH inclusive then format (2) can be used and the contents of the named register are copied thereby into the specified port. In all other cases format (1) must be used, in which case the contents of the named register are copied into the port whose number is given in register DX.

The contents of a port are obtained by using the 8086-family `IN` instruction, which has two general formats corresponding to those for the `OUT` instruction:

`IN` *accumulator*, `DX`
`IN` *accumulator, port number*

20.2 Programming parallel printers

Parallel printers require data to be transmitted to them in parallel. The parallel transmission of the letter A (ASCII code 01000001) to a printer is illustrated in Figure 20.1.

This section will describe how to program the transmission of data in parallel through a parallel printer interface. In our case, the parallel printer interface has three 8-bit I/O ports:

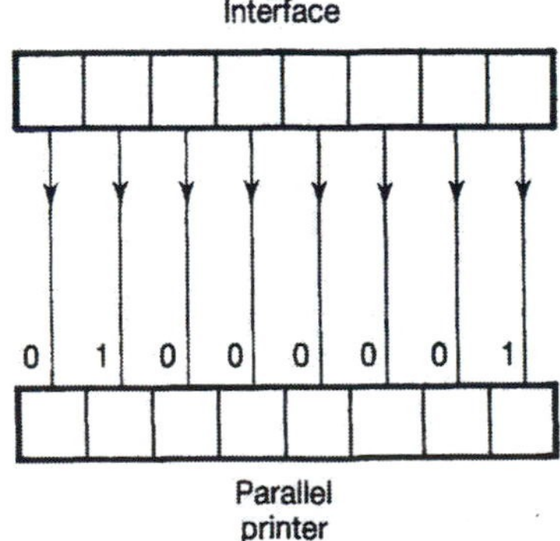

Figure 20.1 Parallel transmission of the ASCII code for 'A' – eight bits are transmitted at a time, so eight data lines are necessary.

Port function	*Port number*
data	3BCH
output control	3BEH
printer status	3BDH

Port number 3BCH is the data port. If this port is set to the ASCII code for a character, and the output control and printer status registers are set correctly, then that character will be printed wherever printing last left off. Thus, the sequence

```
MOV AL,42H
MOV DX,3BCH
OUT DX,AL
```

would set the data port of the parallel printer interface to the ASCII code for the letter B.

Having set up the data port we must next check the printer status before telling the printer to print the data. The sequence

```
MOV DX,3BDH
IN  AL,DX
```

copies the contents of the printer status port into AL and the setting of the eight bits in the resulting value signifies various printer conditions, as shown in Figure 20.2 for both the output control and the printer status ports.

To test if the printer is busy we can use the TEST instruction. Remembering that 80H = 10000000B:

```
TEST AL,80H
```

sets the Z-flag if the printer is busy but does not change the contents of AL. If the printer is busy we simply have to wait until it is ready:

```
              MOV  DX,3BDH
TEST_IF_BUSY: IN   AL,DX
              TEST AL,80H
              JZ   TEST_IF_BUSY
```

Repeatedly checking to see if the printer is ready like this is known as **polling** the printer. (Generally, polling is the programmed testing of one or more bits which indicate whether or not a device is ready to undertake some action or has completed some action.)

Each character is sent to the printer following a timing pulse. Once we know that the printer is ready, we use the output control port to send signals which we can therefore regard as being to start and stop the printing of the character in the data port. Since the printer can capture the character from the data port very quickly, the stop and start instructions can come one after another. To start printing, the right-most bit of the contents of the output control port must be set to 1; to stop printing it is set back to 0. This must be

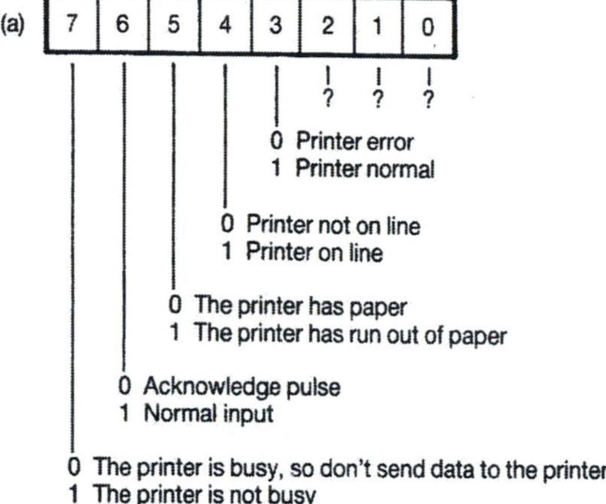

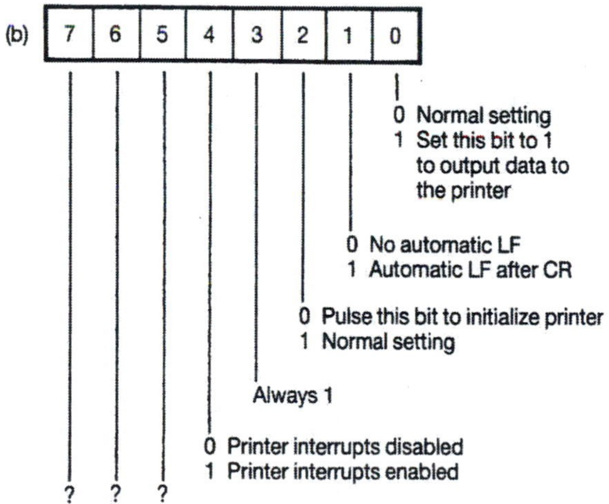

Figure 20.2 Configurations of (a) printer status port and (b) output control port.

done for each and every character printed. Lastly, bits 2 and 3 must always be set to 1 during printing.

Thus, given that 0DH = 00001101B and that 0CH = 00001100B, the following instruction sequence prints the character whose ASCII code is in the data port, provided the printer is not busy:

```
MOV DX,3BEH
MOV AL,0DH
OUT DX,AL    ;start printing
MOV AL,0CH
OUT DX,AL    ;stop printing
```

Before beginning a session, the printer must be initialized by setting bit 2 of the output control register to 0 for at least 50 microseconds (0.000 050 seconds) and then setting it back to 1. This wait can be timed by executing 50D NOP instructions (NOP – No Operation – is an 8086-family instruction provided for just such timing purposes. It has no effect on the state of either memory or registers, but since its execution nevertheless takes a certain amount of time, repeated execution of NOP can be used to synchronize operations.)

Putting all this together we can easily construct (Figure 20.3) a program which turns the computer into a typewriter. Those printable characters typed at the keyboard are sent to a printer connected via the parallel interface until the letter X is typed, when a return is made to DOS.

```
CR EQU 0DH
LF EQU 0AH

DATA SEGMENT
DATA ENDS

WORKING_STORAGE SEGMENT STACK
          DW 100H DUP(?)
WORKING_STORAGE ENDS

CODE SEGMENT
ASSUME CS:CODE,DS:DATA,SS:WORKING_STORAGE
;set up data segment addressability
 START:MOV   AX,DATA
       MOV   DS,AX
;initialize the printer
       MOV   DX,3BEH
;set bit 6 of output control port to 0
       MOV   AL,08H
       OUT   DX,AL
       MOV   AL,0CH
       MOV   CX,50D
;wait at least 50 microseconds
 WAIT: NOP
       LOOP WAIT
;repeat read a character from the keyboard
        READ: CALL READCHAR
     ;print it
              CALL SEND_TO_PRINTER
     ;if char = CR
              CMP AL,CR
              JNZ XCHECK
     ;then begin
             ;print a LF
              MOV AL,LF
              CALL SEND_TO_PRINTER
             ;LF to display
              CALL DISPLAY_NEWLINE
             ;end
```

Figure 20.3 Parallel printer control program.

```
  ;until char=X
XCHECK: CMP AL,'X'
        JZ  DONE
        JMP READ
  ;return to DOS
 DONE: MOV AX,4C00H
       INT 21H

  SEND_TO_PRINTER PROC NEAR
       ;save char on stack
              PUSH AX
       ;transfer character to data port
              MOV   DX,3BCH
              OUT   DX,AL
       ;check if the printer is busy
              MOV   DX,3BDH
TEST_IF_BUSY: IN    AL,DX
              TEST  AL,80H
              JZ    TEST_IF_BUSY
       ;now print  the character
              MOV   DX,3BEH
              MOV   AL,0DH
       ;start printing
              OUT   DX,AL
              MOV   AL,0CH
       ;stop printing
              OUT   DX,AL
       ;restore character from stack
              POP   AX
              RET
  SEND_TO_PRINTER ENDP

  READCHAR PROC NEAR
          MOV AH,1
          INT 21H
          RET
  READCHAR ENDP

  DISPLAY_NEWLINE PROC NEAR
          MOV AH,2
          MOV DL,LF
          INT 21H
  DISPLAY_NEWLINE ENDP

  CODE ENDS
  END START
```

Figure 20.3 (*cont.*)

EXERCISES

20.1 Enhance the program in Figure 20.3 so that if the printer runs out of paper a suitable message is displayed on the screen and the program waits until more paper has been inserted. Once this has been done the program should return to normal execution.

20.2 The bit in position 4 of the printer status port is set to 1 if the printer is on-line (that is, it is switched on and capable of receiving data from the computer and not left in some printer test mode). If the printer is not on-line this bit is set to 0. Amend the program in Figure 20.3 so that a suitable message is displayed on the screen if the printer is not on-line and the program waits until it is.

20.3 Asynchronous serial communications

Dealing with parallel printers is, in many respects, easier than dealing with printers which expect data to arrive from a serial interface. This is because although most serial transmission of data conforms to one of a family of electrical standards usually referred to informally as *the* RS232 standard, considerable choice is available in the format in which data is transmitted, in the speed at which it is to be transmitted, and in the electrical connections used to join the two communicating devices together. This section examines some of these various possibilities from the point of view of **asynchronous** serial communications: that is, serial communications in which the characters transferred are separated by special bit patterns, so that the transmitter and receiver need not work at precisely the same speed. Section 20.4 will then discuss how to write 8086-family assembly language software to carry out the serial transmission of data.

20.3.1 Serial data transmission

To transmit the letter A serially, the ASCII code 01000001 has to be transmitted. Electronically, a 1 is represented by a high voltage and a 0 by a low voltage. (From the point of view of our current discussion, the exact voltages do not matter.) Thus to transmit a letter A the pulse train shown in Figure 20.4 must pass along the transmit wire.

While no transmission is taking place, the signal on the wire between a computer and a serial printer is kept at a high voltage. On its own, therefore,

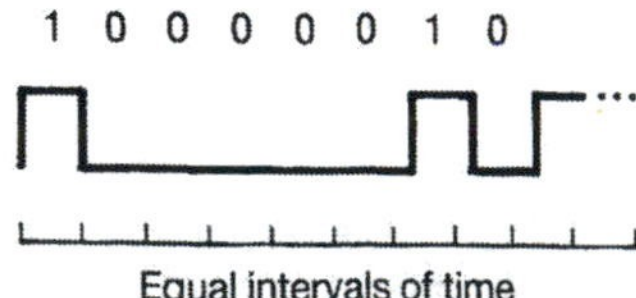

Figure 20.4 Serial transmission of the ASCII code for the letter A.

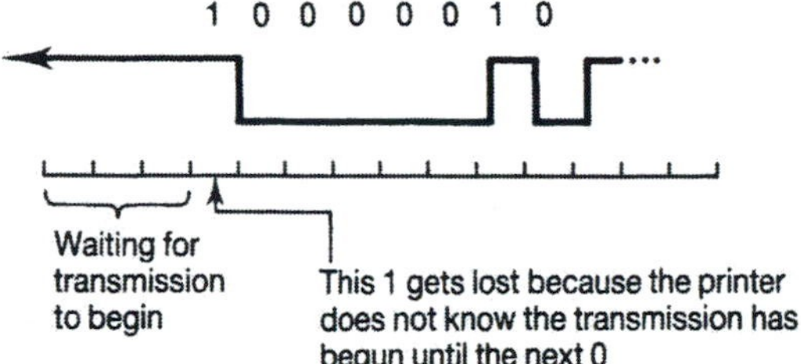

Figure 20.5 Why the pulse train for the bits in the ASCII code for the letter A is not adequate on its own.

this pulse train is inadequate because it does not allow for the possibility that the letter A might begin a transmission, as shown in Figure 20.5.

To solve the problem a convention is adopted. In order to begin transmission without missing any data a **start bit** is added to the front of each data character. Thus A is transmitted as 01000001 (see Figure 20.6).

Parity bits

Any scheme adopted for serially transmitted data must, if it is not to be severely limited in its scope, allow for sending data along telephone lines and between machines in environments which can corrupt electrical signals flowing along a wire. To give protection against the corruption of a '0' into a '1' (or vice versa) by outside electrical interference and to assist in synchronization of the transmission and reception of signals, one or two bits are added to the actual data bits for each character. These extra bits are known as **parity bits**.

One or more parity bits are added at the end of the data bits to guard against interference accidentally changing one letter into another. For example, the ASCII code for B is 01000010 and the ASCII code for C is 01000011. Thus, if electrical interference corrupted the right-most 0 bit of the code for B into a 1 bit, the receiver would think that C had been transmitted, not B.

At the heart of the problem is how very 'close' the code for B is to the code for C. One solution then would be to change the code, but there are several objections to this. In particular, changing the code might mean that B and C no longer have similar codes, but that L and X do. Theory shows that the only way you can represent all the upper- and lower-case letters and digits and punctuation marks without any two codes being very similar is to have a longer code. This is, in effect, what we do with parity bits. However, there are two systems for adding parity bits to create a longer code: the **odd parity** system and the **even parity** system.

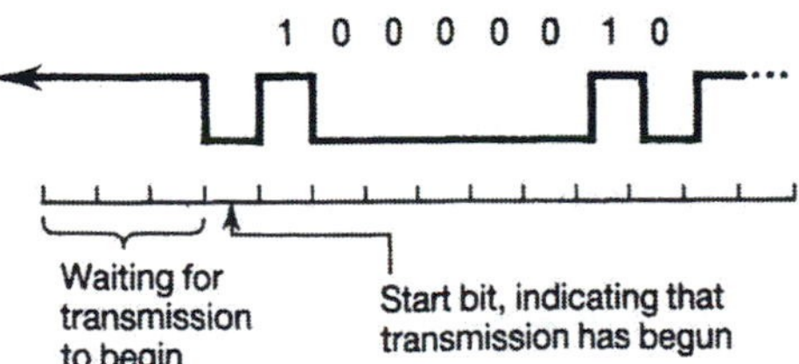

Figure 20.6 The use of a start bit.

Let us first consider odd parity. In this system, since the ASCII for B – 01000010 – contains two 1-bits and two is even we put a 1 after the last data bit to be transmitted to make the total number of 1s odd. Thus we transmit B as 101000010. The ASCII for C on the other hand (01000011) contains three 1-bits; three is odd so we put a 0 after the last bit (001000011) to keep the total number of 1s transmitted odd.

Now, if B (101000010) gets corrupted to C (001000011), two bits will have been corrupted. Since this is much less likely to happen, we have achieved a degree of protection. And the hardware or software can be designed to check for oddities so that if

101000010

was corrupted to

101000011

then an error would be signaled because 101000011 cannot be the code of any real data item under our odd parity system.

The system we have described is called odd parity because we have arranged always to transmit an odd number of 1s. Here are a few more examples:

Character	*ASCII code*	*With odd parity*
H	01001000	101001000
Z	01011011	001011011
;	00111011	000111011

Under the alternative, even parity, system a 0 or 1 bit is added to the code to ensure that the number of 1s transmitted is always even. These days it is more likely that a system uses even parity than odd parity if it uses parity bits at all.

Stop bits

Stop bits are added to the data bits (and parity bit if there is one) quite simply to assist in the synchronization of transmitter and receiver. Just one stop bit is added usually. Thus the letter A, ASCII code 01000001, with even parity and one stop bit is actually transmitted as 00010000010 (Figure 20.7). Eleven bits for a single character! On slower printers, particularly the heavier old-fashioned models like teletypes, it was found that it was a good idea, practically speaking, to have a couple of stop bits and dispense with parity. The two stop bits aided electrical synchronization and gave the printer's mechanism a chance to keep up with the speed of the electrical signals. (When the print head gets to the end of a line, for example, there will be an appreciable delay whilst the print head returns to the start of the next line.)

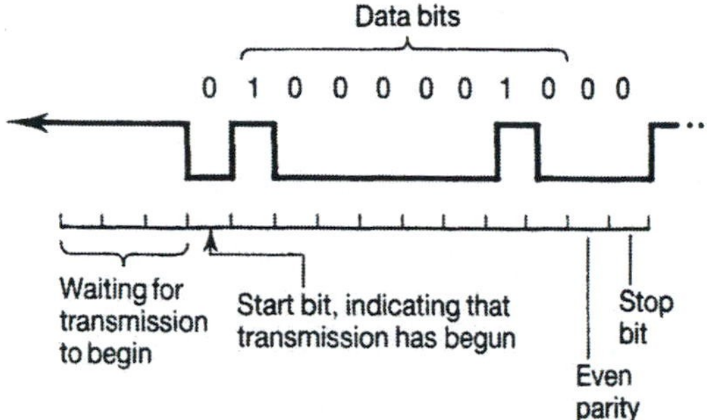

Figure 20.7
The use of a single stop bit and even parity.

With two stop bits and no parity the letter F (ASCII code 01000110) will be transmitted in the form shown in Figure 20.8.

All serially connected devices require one start bit and at least one stop bit. That is for sure. Thereafter, more or less any combination is to be found on some device or other. It is rare, in fact, for the full 8-bit ASCII codes to be used. A 7-bit ASCII code allows 128 characters, which is often as many as less sophisticated peripherals and software will handle. (128 characters will include a,b,. . .,z,A,B,. . .,Z,0,1,. . .,9, and punctuation marks for example.) However, if there were such a thing as an average device with an RS232 interface, my guess is that it would as likely as not transmit data in the format:

1 start bit: 1 stop bit: 7 data bits: even parity (7-bit ASCII)

(Of course, you may go through the whole of your life and never meet such a device; that is the nature of the business. But if one had to guess because of inadequate, missing or lost documentation, the above format would be a sensible first try.)

20.3.2 Speed of transmission

For the speed of transmission in serial communications, the basic unit is not a mile per hour but a **baud**, which in our context is a bit per second. (Baudot was an early pioneer in data communications.) Since the earliest computer terminals were made by US-based Teletype Corporation, and they used the data format 1 start bit, 7 data bits, even parity and 2 stop bits (that is, 11 bits in all), and printed 10 characters per second, this meant that the actual

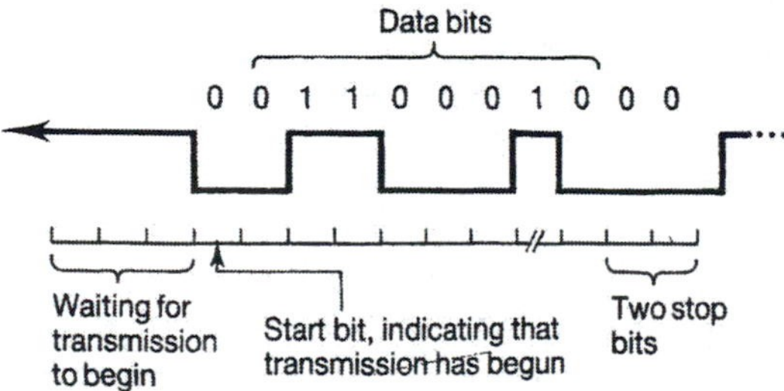

Figure 20.8
The use of two stop bits and no parity.

transmission speed between computer and terminal was 110 baud (110 bits per second). No-one would want a printer slower than a teletype, so 110 baud has become the slowest transmission rate used in the microcomputer environment by historical accident.

Close on the heels of the Teletype Corporation, General Electric produced a 300 baud terminal. This used 1 start bit, 1 stop bit, 7 data bits and even parity, so that in this case 300 baud was exactly equivalent to 30 characters per second. As speeds of printers and the like increased, other manufacturers tended to produce devices operating at speeds which were multiples of 300 baud. Speeds of 1200, 2400 and 9600 baud are particularly common, 9600 baud being mostly used for transmission between a computer and its display.

Notice then, that the operating speed of a printer which the manufacturer says can be fed at, say, 300 baud will effectively depend on the data transmission format. If 11 bits are used to transmit one character, such a printer will operate at 300 / 11 = 27 characters per second whereas if only 9 bits are used, the effective rate is 300 / 9 = 33 characters per second.

20.3.3 Serial and parallel data transmission compared

For communication over lines with a given maximum bit rate, parallel data communication is quicker than serial because of the use of several lines. The disadvantage of parallel communication is the cost of the extra lines. These costs increase with the distance over which data has to be transmitted or received, and consequently parallel communication is used over long distances only if very high data transfer rates are required.

20.4 Programming an asynchronous serial interface

In this section it will be assumed that a correct electrical connection has been made between the serial interface of the computer and that of the printer. Serial interfaces can be constructed in many different ways, but perhaps the most popular of them is based on a support chip called the **8250 asynchronous communications element**. This section will illustrate how to program serial interfaces using assembly language with reference to such an interface.

From the programmer's point of view, a serial interface for an 8086-family microprocessor based on the 8250 chip will have two data ports (one for data to be transmitted and one for data received), two status ports, and six control ports, as shown in Table 20.1.

Five of these ports must be programmed to initialize the interface before any communication begins, but thereafter can be ignored. These are:

Table 20.1 8250 registers.

I/O port address	*Register selected*	*Input or output*
3F8H	Bit 7 of line control register = 0: Transmitter holding register	Output
	Bit 7 of line control register = 0: Receiver data register	Input
	Bit 7 of line control register = 1: Baud rate divisor (LSB)	Output
3F9H	Bit 7 of line control register = 1: Baud rate divisor (MSB)	Output
	Bit 7 of line control register = 0: Interrupt-enable register	Output
3FAH	Interrupt-identification register	Input
3FBH	Line control register	Output
3FCH	Modem control register	Output
3FDH	Line status register	Input
3FEH	Modem status register	Input

- Baud rate divisor (LSB)
- Baud rate divisor (MSB)
- Line control register
- Modem control register
- Interrupt enable register

In the complete program example it will be assumed that the printer in use has an interface which expects to receive data transmitted from the computer at 1200 baud in the format 7 data bits, 1 stop bit and odd parity. To initialize the computer's interface to 1200 baud the **baud rate divisor registers** must be set to an appropriate value as given in Table 20.2.

Table 20.2 Baud rate divisor values.

Desired baud rate	*Value for baud rate divisor registers* *MSB*	*LSB*
110	04H	17H
300	01H	80H
600	00H	C0H
1200	00H	60H
2400	00H	30H
4800	00H	18H
9600	00H	0CH

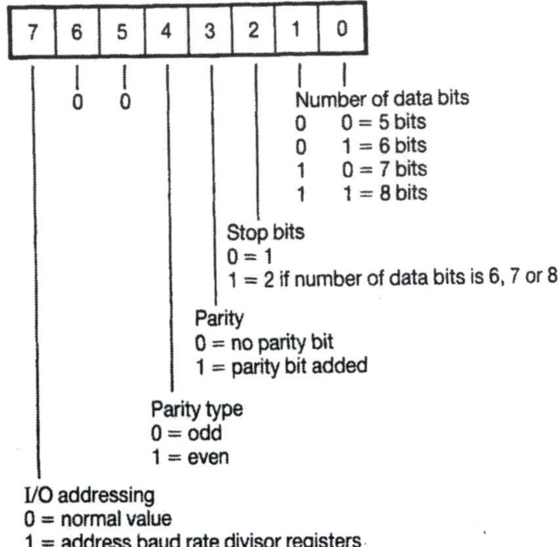

Figure 20.9 The line control register.

Having initialized the baud rate divisor registers, the next step is to initialize the **line control register**. This determines the character length, number of stop bits and the type of parity to be used in a serial communication (see Figure 20.9).

Normally, bits 5,6, and 7 of the line control register should be set to 0. Bit 7 is set to 1 to enable access to the baud rate divisor registers but is otherwise set to 0, while non-zero settings of bits 5 and 6 have a special purpose beyond the scope of this book.

After the line control register, the next register to be initialized is the **modem control register** (see Figure 20.10). It has only two settings of interest to us here, determined respectively by bits 0 and 1.

Interrupts will be discussed in detail in Chapter 21. However, while the **interrupt enable register** allows the programmer selectively to enable or disable four different types of interrupts, for our present purposes we do not wish to confuse the issue by allowing interrupts of any kind during our serial transmissions, and so the interrupt enable register must be initialized to zero. This completes all the necessary initializations.

Before a character can be transmitted we must first check the **line status register** (Figure 20.11) to see if the transmitter holding register is empty. (Many of the status indications provided are beyond our current terms of reference and will not be discussed further here.) This involves waiting until all

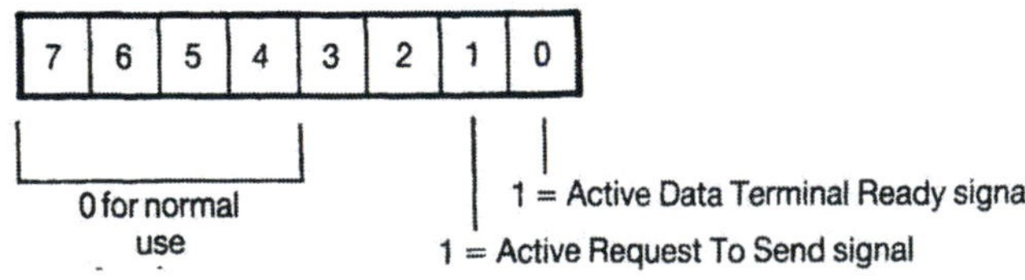

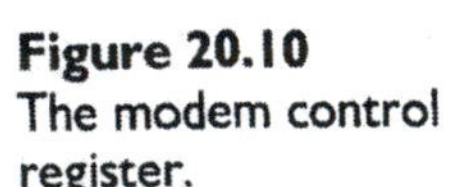
Figure 20.10 The modem control register.

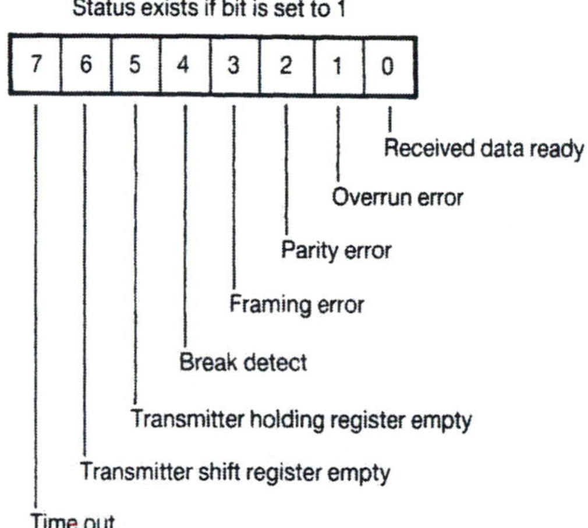

Figure 20.11 The line status register.

the bits in the line status register are zero except for bit 5. Once this is the case, then the ASCII code for a character can be placed in the transmitter holding register, and the character will then be transmitted in the form determined by the initializations of the five control registers.

A complete example program constructed along these lines and showing serial transmission of characters typed at the keyboard to a printer is given in Figure 20.12. When the letter X is typed at the keyboard, control returns to DOS.

SUMMARY

Programmed I/O relies on the IN and OUT instructions. These allow us to write device drivers which depend entirely upon the construction of an interface which is plugged into the main computer. We saw this in the context of both a parallel printer interface and an asynchronous serial printer interface.

In order to give illustrative programs we had to be specific as far as certain details of the underlying hardware are concerned. However, it is the principles involved which are important here, not a particular set of port addresses or the individual control, status and data register configuration of a given chip around which a specific interface has been designed. Indeed, the basic ideas in this chapter will also permeate the next two chapters, which deal with different aspects of writing device drivers in 8086-family assembly language.

```
CR EQU 0DH
LF EQU 0AH

DATA SEGMENT
DATA ENDS

WORKING_STORAGE SEGMENT STACK
        DW 100H DUP(?)
WORKING_STORAGE ENDS

CODE SEGMENT
ASSUME CS:CODE,DS:DATA,SS:WORKING_STORAGE
;set up data segment addressability
 START:MOV AX,DATA
       MOV DS,AX
;access 8250 baud rate divisor registers
       MOV DX,3FBH
       MOV AL,80H
       OUT DX,AL
;set the baud rate to 1200 baud
       MOV DX,3F8H
       MOV AL,60H
       OUT DX,AL
       MOV DX,3F9H
       MOV AL,0
       OUT DX,AL
;initialize the line control register to give data
;format of 7 data bits, 1 stop bit, odd parity
       MOV DX,3FBH
       MOV AL,0AH
       OUT DX,AL
;initialize the modem control register
;to give RTS and DTR signals
       MOV DX,3FCH
       MOV AL,3H
       OUT DX,AL
;disable all interrupts during transmission of data
       MOV DX,3F9H
       MOV AL,0
       OUT DX,AL
;repeat read a character from the keyboard
      READ:CALL READCHAR
    ;print it
           CALL SEND_TO_PRINTER
    ;if char = CR
           CMP AL,CR
JNZ XCHECK
    ;then begin
           ;print a LF
           MOV AL,LF
           CALL SEND_TO_PRINTER
           ;LF to display
           CALL DISPLAY_NEWLINE
           ;end
```

Figure 20.12
Serial printer control program.

```
;until char = X
 XCHECK: CMP AL,'X'
         JZ DONE
         JMP READ
;return to DOS
   DONE: MOV AX,4C00H
         INT 21H
      SEND_TO_PRINTER PROC NEAR
      ;save char on stack
              PUSH AX
      ;repeat
           ;get status register contents
READY_CHECK:  MOV DX,3FDH
              IN  AL,DX
      ;until transmitter holding register empty
              TEST AL,20H
              JZ  READY_CHECK
      ;put char in transmitter holding register
              MOV DX,3F8H
              OUT DX,AL
      ;restore character from stack
              POP AX
              RET
SEND_TO_PRINTER ENDP

READCHAR PROC NEAR
        MOV AH,1
        INT 21H
        RET
READCHAR ENDP

DISPLAY_NEWLINE PROC NEAR
        MOV AH,2
        MOV DL,LF
        INT 21H
DISPLAY_NEWLINE ENDP

CODE ENDS
END START
```

Figure 20.12
(cont.)

SELF-CHECK QUIZ

1. Why do you think 8086-family microprocessors make provision for so many I/O ports (numbered from 0 to 0FFFFH inclusive)?

2. What is wrong with:

```
MOV AL,01100101B
OUT 38ABH,AL
```

3. If the printer has run out of paper and is not on-line, what will be the contents of the printer status port in Figure 20.2? How would you test this with an 8086-family assembly language program fragment?

4. Draw a diagram showing the serial

transmission of the letter X bit by bit, given that it is to be transmitted with 1 start bit, 2 stop bits and even parity.

5. In a certain serial data transmission, each normal ASCII 7-bit code is transmitted with 1 start bit, 2 stop bits and no parity bit, and the baud rate is 1200 baud. What is the effective transmission rate for text?

6. Write a program sequence to transmit serially at 4800 baud with 7 data bits, 2 stop bits and even parity using the 8250 chip.

7. **Handshaking** is the name given to the idea that a certain device tells another it is ready for a communication by sending the other device a signal. On receipt of this signal, if the other device is ready to communicate, it in turn sends a signal to (and thus 'handshakes') the original device. Can you find any examples of the use of handshaking in the text?

8. Summarize the differences between transmission of data to a printer serially and in parallel.

9. Design a code for the serial transmission of all the characters on your microcomputer's numerical keypad (effectively, the digits 0,1,. . .,9, eight arrow keys, INS, DEL, +, −, *, and /, ENTER and Num Lock). The code should be as short as possible for each character to be transmitted.

10. In an alternative form of serial communications (not described in the main text since it is not normally used for communicating with printers in the microcomputer context), instead of characters being sent asynchronously between the sender and receiver, characters are sent synchronously. In other words, one of the devices involved in the communication decides the intervals of time at which each *character* is transmitted. Can a start bit still be used to indicate the start of a transmission? If not, what alternative scheme could be used?

21

Device Drivers II: Interrupt I/O and the Keyboard

Contents

As we saw in the last chapter, in programmed I/O a considerable amount of time is spent waiting for devices to become ready to receive or to transmit. If communication between the keyboard and the microprocessor were organized by programmed I/O, and we assume that inputting a character takes just 10 millionths of a second while a user can only type 10 characters a second, then an astonishing 99.99% of the microprocessor time would not be spent on useful work! Consequently, **interrupt I/O** is used between the keyboard and the microprocessor so that the keyboard can leave the microprocessor to get on with useful work until another character has been typed. When a character is ready the keyboard's interface can then issue an **interrupt** to the microprocessor to gain attention.

During normal program execution, an interrupt causes an automatic transfer of execution to a location where an **interrupt service routine** is stored. The interrupt service routine is executed and then sequential execution resumes from where it left off before the interrupt. There are two types of interrupt depending on whether the transfer is initiated by an instruction in a program (software interrupts) or by a hardware device (hardware interrupts).

We are already familiar with software interrupts thanks to our frequent (and, by now, routine) use of `INT 21H`. But the microcomputer's Basic Input and Output System (BIOS) gives us another supply of software interrupts which afford the programmer more detailed control over hardware devices than those provided through DOS by `INT 21H`. The first part of this chapter examines the 8086-family interrupt mechanism in detail and briefly studies some of the many available BIOS software interrupts. The rest of the chapter is devoted to the construction of a keyboard driver program which interprets the signal sent from the keyboard when an interrupt is caused by the user pressing a key, and displays a corresponding character via a BIOS software interrupt.

21.1 Interrupts

21.1.1 Software interrupts

Chapter 19 demonstrated the labor-saving advantages of software interrupts such as `INT 21H`, which allows programmers access to file-handling routines within DOS. Interrupts are used to access these and other system software resources because they avoid dependence on particular addresses. Thus, if a new version of DOS is issued, programs which we write and which access routines within DOS will still work without alteration if access is through **interrupts**, whereas if subroutine calls or jump instructions were used (both of which require actual addresses), our program would require modification to run under the updated DOS.

The reason for this is that whereas a `CALL` causes a direct transfer of execution to a location in memory where the body of the corresponding subroutine is stored, transfer to the 8086-family instructions corresponding to a **software interrupt** is indirect. Thus, executing a software interrupt first causes DOS to look at a predetermined address in memory where the *address* of the routine which executes the interrupt – the **interrupt service routine** – is stored. This address is loaded into CS:IP (the previous contents of CS, IP and the flags register having been saved on the stack) so that execution then continues from the beginning of the interrupt service routine. The last instruction in the interrupt service routine will be an `IRET` (Interrupt RETurn) instruction. When executed, `IRET` pops off the stack the contents of CS, IP and the flags register prior to the execution of the interrupt service routine so that normal execution of the main program can continue where it left off.

To make the connection between an interrupt and its interrupt service routine, each interrupt is assigned an **interrupt type**. Thus, software interrupts are caused by executing an `INT` instruction which has the general format

`INT` *interrupt type*

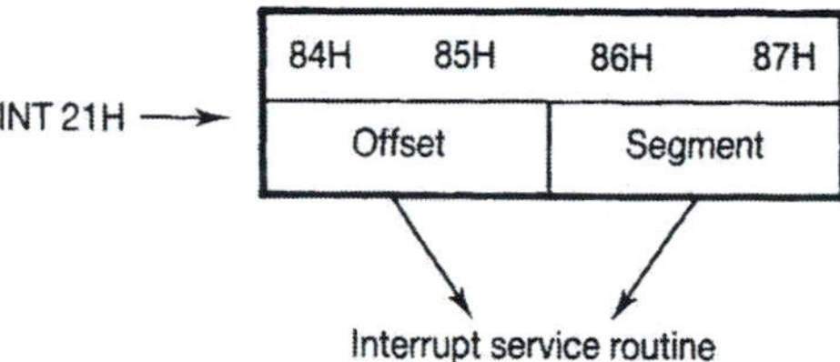

Figure 21.1 The software interrupt mechanism.

where *interrupt type* is a whole number between 0 and 0FFH. For an interrupt of a given type, the 4-byte address of the interrupt service routine – the **interrupt vector** – is stored at an address calculated by multiplying the interrupt type by 4. Hence, the interrupt vector for INT 21H will be found at location (21 * 4)H, that is, 84H. Figure 21.1 illustrates this mechanism.

All the first 100H * 4 = 400H absolute locations in memory are thus taken up with interrupt vectors, most of which are reserved for DOS or BASIC use. For example, execution of INT 5 will cause a transfer of control to the address given in the interrupt vector at absolute locations 14H–17H inclusive, where there is code to send the screen contents to the printer. However, the programmer can employ the interrupt vectors at addresses 100H–1FFH (absolute) for his or her own purposes (these correspond to interrupt types 40H–7FH). Table 21.1 summarizes DOS interrupt types and their functions.

21.1.2 Hardware interrupts

Software interrupts aid programmer productivity in a way which does not increase program maintenance costs as a computer manufacturer upgrades its operating system. But the principal reason for having interrupts is to provide an efficient way for external devices to get the attention of the 8086 family. Rather than us having to check at regular intervals whether a key on the keyboard has been pressed, the keyboard hardware itself can send a pulse along the interrupt line of the 8086-family microprocessor to demand attention.

The mechanism is the same as for a software interrupt, except that the hardware arranges that the 8086-family microprocessor knows the type of interrupt the electrical pulse has signaled. Thus, pressing or releasing a key causes a **hardware interrupt** equivalent to executing the INT 9 instruction. When such an interrupt is received, the 8086-family microprocessor can break off from its current task – though note that, with all interrupts, the current instruction being executed is first completed – service the keyboard, and return to the original task. Since an interrupt service routine is nothing other than an 8086-family machine code program, it is itself interruptable. Indeed, there may be several devices all claiming attention one after another. Consequently, there has to be a **priority order** in which interrupts are dealt with, the keyboard coming higher in priority than other external devices so that, for example, CTRL-BREAK and CTRL-ALT-DELETE can always be used to return control to the operating system or reboot whilst a user program is running.

Table 21.1 Summary of DOS interrupt types and their functions.

Type	*Vector address*	*Interrupt class*	*Interrupt purpose*
0	0–3	8086-family	Division by zero
1	4–7	interrupts	Single step
2	8–B		Non-maskable interrupt (NMI)
3	C–F		Breakpoint
4	10–13		Overflow
5	14–17		Print screen
6,7	18–1B		Reserved
8	20–23	8259	Timer
9	24–27	hardware	Keyboard
A,B,C,D	28–37	interrupts	Reserved
E	38–3B		Disk
F	3C–3F		Reserved
10	40–43	Software	Display I/O
11	44–47	interrupts	Equipment check
12	48–4B	to BIOS	Memory size check
13	4C–4F		Disk I/O
14	40–53		Communication I/O
15	54–57		Cassette I/O
16	58–5B		Keyboard input
17	5C–5F		Printer I/O
18	60–63	Software	ROM BASIC
19	64–67	interrupts	Bootstrap from disk
1A	68–6B		Time of day
1B	6C–6F		Keyboard break
1C	70–73		Timer strobe
1D	74–77	Table pointers	Video table pointer
1E	78–7B		Disk table pointer
1F	7C–7F		Graphics character table pointer
20	80–83	Interrupts	Terminate program
21	84–87	to DOS	Function calls
22	88–8B		Program termination address
23	8C–8F		CTRL-BREAK exit address
24	90–93		Fatal error
25	94–97		Absolute disk read
26	98–9B		Absolute disk write
27	9C–9F		End program, remain resident
28,3F	A0–FF		Reserved: used by DOS
40–7F	100–1FF	User interrupts	
80,F0	200–3C3	BASIC interrupts	

By default, both hardware interrupts and INT disable all but any unstoppable further interrupts within an interrupt service routine, so that the interrupt service routine is executed without further interruption unless we so wish. Some interrupts cannot be stopped, however, and these are called **non-maskable interrupts**. Non-maskable interrupts use a special line into the 8086-family microprocessor to signal an interrupt which takes overriding priority, even when interrupts have otherwise been disabled. For example, the type 2 interrupt is non-maskable for it signals a memory parity error indicating a hardware misfunction.

21.1.3 The trap flag and the interrupt enable flag

Two flags in the flags register assist in controlling interrupts and it is therefore necessary to study them before we examine the detailed mechanism by which execution is transferred to the interrupt service routine. These are the **trap flag** (T-flag) and the **interrupt enable flag** (I-flag) – see Figure 1.7.

The trap flag is primarily provided to assist in debugging programs. If the trap flag is set to 1, the 8086-family microprocessor causes a type 1 interrupt to occur after each and every instruction has been executed. By making the interrupt vector point to an interrupt service routine which prints out the contents of pertinent registers and memory locations, this enables a facility similar to the single-stepping T facility of DEBUG and CodeView.

No instructions are provided for setting and clearing the trap flag directly, but it can be set by modifying the flags register as in

```
PUSHF
POP  AX
OR   AX,0100H
PUSH AX
POPF
```

which sets the trap flag to 1.

The interrupt enable flag allows us to control whether an interrupt service routine can itself be interrupted (though we cannot prevent non-maskable interrupts under any circumstances). It must be set to 1 if further interrupts *are* to be allowed, and to 0 if further interrupts *are not* allowed. Within an 8086-family assembly language program this is carried out via the STI (SeT Interrupt enable flag) and CLI (CLear Interrupt enable flag) instructions, respectively. Thus, to emphasize, STI enables all maskable interrupts, CLI disables them. (Table 21.2 contains a summary of all the 8086-family flag setting instructions.)

21.1.4 The interrupt mechanism

On executing an INT instruction, the flags register and current offset and segment addresses of the interrupted program are saved on the stack, the trap and interrupt enable flags are cleared (thus prohibiting further interrupts), and CS and IP are loaded with the address of the interrupt service routine. In detail, the action is:

Table 21.2 Summary of the 8086-family flag setting instructions.

Instruction	*Purpose*	*Effect*
CLC	CLear Carry flag	(CF := 0)
STC	SeT Carry flag	(CF := 1)
CLI	CLear Interrupt flag – disable interrupts	(IF := 0)
STI	SeT Interrupt flag – allow interrupts	(IF := 1)
CLD	CLear Direction flag – LODS, STOS. . .work forwards	(DF := 1)
STD	SeT Direction flag – LODS, STOS. . .work backwards	(DF := 1)
CMC	CoMplement Carry flag	(if CF = 0 then CF := 1 else CF := 0)

(1) Decrement SP by 2.

(2) Push flags register on to stack.

(3) Clear trap and interrupt enable flags, thus disabling further interrupts.

(4) Decrement SP by 2.

(5) Push current CS on to stack.

(6) Load CS with segment address from interrupt vector.

(7) Decrement SP by 2.

(8) Push current IP on to stack.

(9) Load IP with offset address from interrupt vector.

Following execution of an interrupt service routine, a return to the program which was interrupted is effected by the IRET (Interrupt RETurn) instruction, which pops the top two stack bytes into IP, the next two stack bytes into CS and the succeeding two stack bytes into the flags register.

21.1.5 A complete example program using interrupts

Figure 21.2 contains a complete program example using hardware interrupts. If, during execution, the 8086-family microprocessor finds it has a DIV or IDIV instruction to execute in which the divisor is zero, then a type 0 hardware interrupt occurs. DOS provides its own interrupt service routine for a type 0 interrupt, but we shall reset the type 0 interrupt vector so that instead of pointing to the DOS routine for a division-by-zero error the vector points to our own interrupt service routine.

This simply displays an abusive message to the user (it calls the perpetrator of the division by zero a JERK) and returns control to DOS, thus terminating any user program which contains a zero division. (It is usually a better idea to be helpful to users, but for once we have given way to a naughty desire.)

For illustration, we have embedded the new zero divisor interrupt service routine in a program which reads two digits from the keyboard (having

```
PRINT_LETTER MACRO
             MOV AH,2
             INT 21H
             ENDM

CR EQU ODH
LF EQU OAH
DATA SEGMENT
ZERO_DIVISOR DW ?
DATA ENDS

WORKING_STORAGE SEGMENT STACK
     DW 100H DUP(?)
WORKING_STORAGE ENDS

CODE SEGMENT
ASSUME CS:CODE,DS:DATA,SS:WORKING_STORAGE
;change interrupt vector
      START:MOV  AX,0
            MOV  ES,AX
;disable interrupts while resetting the interrupt vector
            CLI
            MOV  ES:ZERO_DIVISOR,OFFSET OUR_ZERO_DIVISOR_ROUTINE
            MOV  ES:ZERO_DIVISOR+2,SEG OUR_ZERO_DIVISOR_ROUTINE
;enable interrupts again
            STI
;read a character from the keyboard
            MOV  AH,1
            INT  21H
;convert it to numeric form: a
            SUB  AL,30H
            MOV  BL,AL
;read another character
            MOV  AH,1
            INT  21H
;convert it to numeric form: b
            SUB  AL,30H
;calculate a/b
            MOV  AH,0
            XCHG AL,BL
            DIV  BL
;result now in AL
            ADD  AL,30H
            MOV  DL,AL
            MOV  AH,2
            INT  21H
;return to DOS
            MOV  AX,4C00H
            INT  21H

OUR_ZERO_DIVISOR_ROUTINE:MOV DL,'J'
                         PRINT_LETTER
                         MOV DL,'E'
                         PRINT_LETTER
```

Figure 21.2
Program to change the divide-by-zero interrupt.

```
                    MOV DL,'R'
                    PRINT_LETTER
                    MOV DL,'K'
                    PRINT_LETTER
                    MOV DL,CR
                    PRINT_LETTER
                    MOV DL,LF
                    PRINT_LETTER
                    ;return to DOS
                    MOV AX,4C00H
                    INT 21H
                    IRET

CODE ENDS
END START
```

Figure 21.2
(cont.)

numeric equivalent, say, *a* and *b*), prints out the result of *a* **div** *b*, and then returns to DOS. If the user gives *b* a zero value, nothing in the main program detects this so it will be passed as an operand to DIV. The hardware will then detect a division by zero and a type 0 interrupt will occur. Since the program begins by resetting the zero divisor interrupt service routine, the type 0 interrupt will have the effect we have programmed, rather than the effect of a DOS type 0 interrupt.

In the program itself, notice that we disable interrupts while the divide-by-zero error interrupt vector is reset. Were interrupts allowed during this process, a divide-by-zero error occurring somewhere deep in the operating system's code would crash the system trying to access an interrupt service routine at a garbled address. Note also the use of a segment override to ensure that the new interrupt vector is written at absolute location $4 * 0 = 0$.

Once the new zero divisor interrupt service routine is in place, it will remain there until DOS is reloaded or our interrupt service routine is overwritten (as it well may be since, unlike DOS, we have not stored our zero divisor interrupt service routine away in a place where other programs will not interfere with it). Consequently, any subsequent programs which attempt a division by zero may either be successfully intercepted by our new zero divisor interrupt service routine, or may exhibit strange behaviour (quite possibly the machine will hang) because the interrupt has occurred but the service routine has been overwritten.

To check this out, first assemble and link the program in Figure 21.3 (which contains a deliberate division by zero). Execute the program in Figure 21.2 to reset the divide-by-zero interrupt, and then execute the program in Figure 21.3 and note what happens (you will be called a JERK). Then reboot DOS, so that the divide-by-zero interrupt service routine is restored to the DOS original, and now execute the program in Figure 21.3 again. This time you will receive the more polite message

```
Division by zero
```

```
DATA SEGMENT
DATA ENDS

WORKING_STORAGE SEGMENT STACK
    DW 100H DUP(?)
WORKING_STORAGE ENDS

CODE SEGMENT
ASSUME CS:CODE,DS:DATA,SS:WORKING_STORAGE
 START: MOV AX,1234H
        MOV BX,0
        DIV BX
CODE ENDS
END START
```

Figure 21.3 Program to verify permanent change of the division-by-zero interrupt.

21.1.6 WAIT, ESC, HLT, LOCK and INTO

HLT and WAIT suspend the execution of instructions pending electronic (that is, not software) interruptions of some kind. Thus the HLT instruction HaLTs the processor until a hardware interrupt is received by the 8086-family microprocessor, after which normal execution resumes. Consequently there is no practical use for the HLT instruction in programs which, like all of those in this book, are not involved with the direct control of hardware beyond our limited considerations of the keyboard and display screen.

The WAIT instruction halts pending either a hardware interrupt or the arrival of the appropriate electronic signal on the TEST input line of the 8086-family microprocessor chip, after which the wait state resumes.

The ESC (ESCape) instruction has the format

ESC *<6-bit external opcode>*,*<source>*

and causes no action to be taken as far as the 8086-family microprocessor is concerned. Rather it is used to initiate action by another attached processor (for example, one of the 80*n*87 family of numeric data processors – which can perform floating-point arithmetic). The 6-bit opcode specified as a part of the instruction is placed on the system bus for examination by another processor. Once it has been fetched, the source operand (which may be in memory or a register) is also placed on the bus.

LOCK is useful in resource scheduling and synchronization, for example when several independent 8086-family processors share the same memory. To prevent one processor accessing a location in shared memory while another processor is changing the contents of that location, the LOCK instruction – used as a prefix to a main instruction – sends an electronic signal from the LOCK output of the 8086-family microprocessor.

There are two special interrupt instructions which should also be mentioned here for completeness, though they will not be explored in any detail. INTO (INTerrupt on Overflow) generates a type 4 interrupt if the overflow flag is set to 1. It is up to the programmer to provide an appropriate interrupt service routine – if required – and to set the type 4 vector to point to that routine: DOS initializes this to point to a single IRET instruction. On the other hand, a type 3 interrupt is special because it has both a normal two-byte opcode like all instructions of the form INT *n* and a single byte opcode. This is because a type 3 interrupt can be used to provide program **breakpoints**.

A breakpoint in a program allows you to control program execution for the purpose of debugging. A breakpoint is a nominated address which stops execution each time that address is encountered. To implement a breakpoint, the first byte of the instruction at the breakpoint address is replaced with the single-byte type 3 interrupt instruction. This causes an interrupt to occur when an attempt is made to execute the instruction which starts at that location, and the interrupt service routine can now display the status of registers and memory as required. Typically, the instruction byte replaced by the type 3

Table 21.3 Summary of the 8086-family synchronization and interrupt instructions.

Instruction	*Description*
HLT	HaLT – the processor halts and leaves the halt state on receipt of a non-maskable hardware interrupt or, if IF is set, on receipt of a maskable hardware interrupt.
WAIT	Causes the processor to enter the wait state until a signal is received on the TEST pin. The processor may also leave this state if an interrupt occurs. On return from the interrupt service routine the wait state is resumed.
ESC *external opcode,source*	This instruction is used to place a memory operand (specified by *source*) on the system bus. The external opcode is usually an instruction for another processor such as an 80*n*87 floating-point processor.
LOCK	This instruction is attached as a prefix to another instruction. Then, during execution of the instruction to which it is attached, there is output from the microprocessor LOCK pin.
INT *interrupt type*	Causes transfer of control to the location given in the interrupt service vector to which a pointer is stored at absolute address 4 * (*interrupt type*).
IRET	Returns control to the point where the interrupt occurred.
INTO	INTerrupt if Overflow – this interrupt only executes if OF = 1. It is executed in exactly the same way as any other interrupt except that DOS makes it point to an IRET instruction.

interrupt will have been saved so that it can be restored and executed when the debugging routine allows the program to continue.

The single-byte form is essential when replacing single-byte instructions at breakpoints, since otherwise an earlier jump to the location following the breakpoint might be corrupted.

The 8086-family interrupt and synchronization instructions are summarized in Table 21.3.

EXERCISES

21.1 Edit the program in Figure 21.2 so that everything remains the same except for the statements which reset the division-by-zero vector. Remove these and reassemble, link and run the program for the following trial pairs of operands: (6,3), (1,4), (8,0).

21.2 Write a program similar to that in Figure 21.2 but which redefines a type 4 interrupt. Thus, you should provide your own overflow error interrupt service routine (and reset the relevant interrupt vector to point to it) which prints `ARITHMETIC OVERFLOW` and returns to DOS if the overflow flag is set to 1. Embed this in a main program which accepts a digit typed in at the keyboard and adds its numeric value to 7CH via an `ADD BL,AL` instruction and then prints out the result in hexadecimal (assuming if there is no overflow), thereafter returning to the operating system.

21.3 Define a type 40H interrupt which works rather like `INT 21H` from DOS, in that it waits for the user to press a key at the keyboard. If the key pressed corresponds to a letter then, if BH is set to 0, that character is converted to upper case whereas, if BH is set to 1, then that character is converted to lower case. Embed this definition in a program which uses `INT 40H` to conduct a simulated conversation with the user. During this conversation, the user types a line of text terminated by the ENTER key and then the machine 'replies' to this text by simply repeating it, except that if the user types 'I', the machine replies 'you' and if the user types 'am' then the machine replies 'are not'. All the user's remarks are to be in lower case and the computer's replies in upper case. Thus, a typical 'conversation' might be:

```
I am happy
YOU ARE NOT HAPPY
oh yes I am
OH YES YOU ARE NOT
```

21.4 Write a mini-version, `MINDEBUG`, of an 8086-family debugger such as DEBUG or CodeView which uses type 1 and type 3 interrupts to offer its users the following facilities. Assuming a program is loaded in memory starting at CS:IP, it should accept any number of commands of two types: either the command `S` which executes one single step of the given program, or a breakpoint address in the range 0–0FFH. By repeating `S` commands the user should be able to work through the program looking at the contents of registers AX, BX, CX and DX on the way. Once a breakpoint has been set, execution resumes from the previous breakpoint (or the beginning of the program) until that breakpoint is reached. Then the contents of registers AX, BX, CX and DX are displayed.

21.2 BIOS: another source of software interrupts

The microcomputer's Basic Input Output System (BIOS) is a set of 8086-family machine code programs which are held in ROM and which initialize the entire system when the computer is turned on. In addition, these programs provide the minimum software support necessary to control the various devices that may be attached to the computer.

On power up, the 8086-family microprocessor enters 8086 mode in its reset state wherein CS is set to 0FFFFH and IP to 0. Hence, the first instruction the 8086-family microprocessor will execute is at absolute address 0FFFF0H, which is part of the memory allocated to ROM. Through this instruction the BIOS gains control, interrogates the various I/O ports to determine which devices are attached, initializes those which are, emits a beep from the speaker and then sets up the **interrupt service routine address table**. Since this table contains addresses within the BIOS itself we can access them via the `INT` instruction. Table 21.4 lists some of the BIOS routines for handling the keyboard and the display, and the corresponding `INT` types. More complete information can be obtained from the listing of the entire BIOS usually supplied with a microcomputer, from your computer's technical manual or in the MS-DOS Encyclopedia (Duncan, R. (ed.), 1988. Washington DC: Microsoft Press).

If the BIOS discovers that a disk drive is attached to the system, it will bootstrap the DOS. DOS fills in additional entries in the interrupt vector table before issuing the 'Enter Date' command. With DOS booted, the memory map of an 8086-based microcomputer is shown in Figure 21.4.

Apart from `INT 21H` (the facilities offered by which, it should be noted, are at a much higher level than those of the BIOS interrupt service routines in Table 21.1), DOS provides seven other interrupts which may be of use to the programmer. These are summarized in Table 21.5. Full details can be found in your computer's technical manual or in the MS-DOS Encyclopedia.

Table 21.4 Some BIOS routines for the keyboard and display and their interrupt types.

Interrupt	*Register settings and effect*			
INT 10H	**Display output**			
AH = 0	Sets display to the mode specified by the AL register			
				DMA at (see Chapter 22)
	AL = 00H	40 * 25	16-shade gray text EGA: 64-color	B000:8000H
	AL = 01H	40 * 25	16/8-color text EGA: 64-color	B000:8000H
	AL = 02H	80 * 25	16-shade gray text EGA: 64-color	B000:8000H
	AL = 03H	80 * 25	16/8-color text EGA: 64-color	B000:8000H
	AL = 04H	320 * 200	4-color graphics	B000:8000H
	AL = 05H	320 * 200	4-shade gray graphics	B000:8000H
	AL = 06H	640 * 200	2-shade gray graphics	B000:8000H
	AL = 07H	80 * 25	monochrome text	B000:0000H
	AL = 08H	160 * 200	16-color graphics	B000:0000H
	AL = 09H	320 * 200	16-color graphics	B000:0000H
	AL = 0AH	80 * 25	4-color graphics	B000:0000H
	AL = 0DH	320 * 200	16-color graphics	A000:0000H
	AL = 0EH	640 * 200	16-color graphics	A000:0000H
	AL = 0FH	640 * 350	monochrome graphics	A000:0000H
	AL = 10H	640 * 350	16/64-color graphics	A000:0000H
AH = 2	Set cursor on screen to position specified. Row 0, column 0 is upper-left corner. BH = display page, DH = row number, DL = column number			
AH = 0EH	Display character specified on screen at current cursor position and advance cursor. BX = 0, AL = character			
INT 16H	**Keyboard input**			
AH = 0	Read character from keyboard into AL. Afterwards, if ASCII character was read, then AH = the standard keyboard scan code for that character. Otherwise, if extended ASCII character was read, then AH = 0			
AH = 1	Set ZF = 0 if any key has been pressed, otherwise ZF = 1			
AH = 2	Return shift key status in the bits of the AL register: Bit 7 = INSERT key, Bit 3 = ALT SHIFT Bit 6 = CAPS LOCK, Bit 2 = CTRL SHIFT Bit 5 = NUM LOCK, Bit 1 = left SHIFT Bit 4 = SCROLL LOCK, Bit 0 = right SHIFT			

```
00000H    interrupt VECTOR TABLE
00400H    BIOS data
00500H    DOS data
00600H    resident part of DOS
                    .
                    .
                    .
                  free
                  memory
                    .
                    .
                    .
          transient part of DOS
                    .
                    .
                    .
F6000H    ROM BASIC
FE000H    ROM BIOS
FFFFFH
```

Figure 21.4 An 8086-based microcomputer's memory map under DOS.

Table 21.5 DOS interrupts.

Interrupt	*Function*
20H	Program termination.
21H	Function call.
22H	Terminate and transfer control to termination address.
23H	Activated when CTRL-BREAK is pressed.
24H	Fatal error.
25H	Absolute disk read – select by sectors.
26H	Absolute disk write – select by sectors.
27H	Terminate current program but keep it in memory.
28H–35H	Reserved for DOS use.

EXERCISES

21.5 Without using any software interrupts other than BIOS `INT 16H` and `INT 10H`, write a program which simply copies what is typed at the keyboard on to the display screen. Be sure that upper and lower case are faithfully displayed. For control keys, display an exclamation mark (!).

21.6 Under the same constraints as in Exercise 21.5, write a program which allows its users to type in the abbreviations on the left of the following list and displays their full equivalent shown on the right-hand side:

Abbreviation	*Full equivalent*
E	ERASE
D	DIRECTORY
R	RENAME
T	TYPE

21.3 A simple keyboard driver

The ultimate aim in this section is to produce keyboard support software so that when a key is pressed and the microcomputer hardware therefore signals that a type 9 interrupt has occurred, the corresponding interrupt service routine will be one that we shall now construct. Although we shall use the BIOS `INT 10H` interrupt to display characters typed in, all the handling of keyboard input will be performed by our own software – not that provided by BIOS or DOS. We shall embed this keyboard interrupt service routine in a program which turns your microcomputer into a sort of typewriter! (As always, it is the principles involved which are important here, not the real-world usefulness of our example program.)

The keyboard is interfaced to the rest of the microcomputer system through the interrupt mechanism and various system support chips, two of which we need to know about in order to write our own keyboard driver. System support chips undertake a variety of tasks which enable the computing power derivable from the 8086-family microprocessor to be maximized. Among the most important of these are the two we need to know about: the **8259 interrupt controller chip** and the **8255 programmable peripheral interface chip**. Both of these chips are programmable, each of them containing two or more internal registers which can be accessed via the `IN` and `OUT` instructions using an appropriate port address as given in Table 21.6.

Table 21.6 I/O addresses for the 8259 and 8255 chips.

8259 interrupt controller	
20H	Interrupt command register
21H	Interrupt mask register
8255 programmable peripheral interface	
60H	Input port, PA
61H	Input/Output port, PB
62H	Input port, PC
63H	Command register

Table 21.7 Type codes associated with 8259 interrupt sources (lower codes have higher priority).

Interrupt source	*Type code*	*Corresponding interrupt mask register bit*
8253 timer chip	08H	0
Keyboard	09H	1
Color/graphics adapter*	0AH	2
Unused	0BH	3
RS232 serial interface	0CH	4
Unused	0DH	5
Disk interface	0EH	6
Printer	0FH	7

* Denotes 'if present in system as configured'.

On power-up, the BIOS configures the 8259 chip internally to correspond to its physical connections on the microcomputer main system board. Because the 8086-family microprocessor has just one input line on which to receive a normal (that is, not a non-maskable) interrupt, the task of the 8259 chip is to queue up interrupts from all the eight possible sources – keyboard, disk drive, and so on – and present them one by one to the 8086-family microprocessor along with a unique interrupt type as shown in Table 21.7.

Thanks to BIOS initialization, programming the 8259 involves sending values to one of its two registers. To enable or disable a given interrupt source, a value must be output to the interrupt mask register. This is a 1-byte register accessed through I/O port 21H. Setting a given bit to 1 disables (or masks) interrupts from the corresponding source, and setting that bit to 0 enables interrupts from that source. Table 21.7 shows the correspondence. Thus, the fragment

```
MOV AL,7FH
OUT 21H,AL
```

disables interrupts from all devices except the printer.

So that the next queued interrupt in priority order can be passed on to the 8086-family microprocessor, the end of an interrupt service routine must be signaled by sending 20H to the interrupt command register within the 8259 chip. The interrupt command register is at I/O port 21H. Thus

```
MOV AL,20H
OUT 20H,AL
```

signals the end of an interrupt service routine.

The 8255 programmable peripheral interface chip contains two registers of interest to us at present – PA and PB – located at I/O ports 60H and 61H respectively. (There is also a 1-byte command register on the chip which the

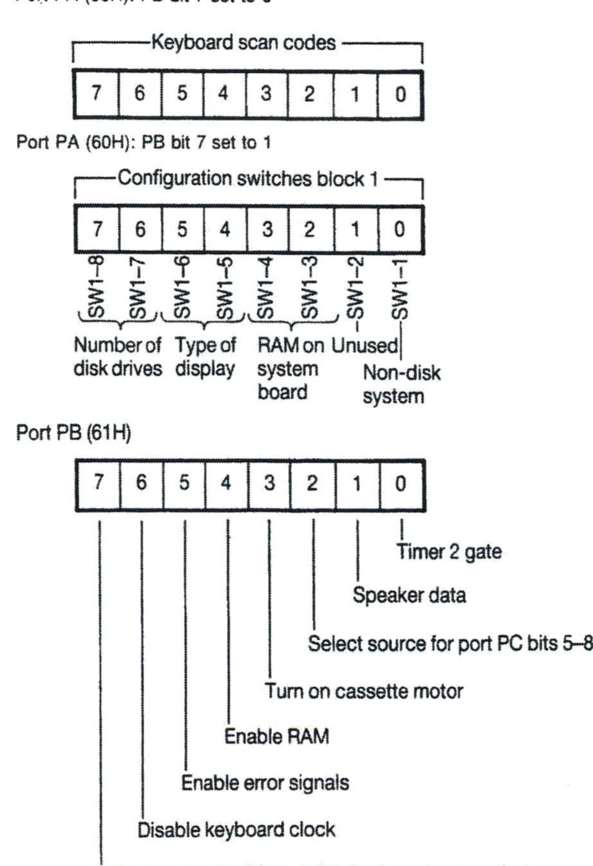

Figure 21.5
8255 registers PA and PB.

BIOS initializes so that PA is configured for input and PB for output.) Figure 21.5 shows the significance of the bits in these registers, the situation being slightly complicated by the ability to select two sources of input to PA by setting certain bits in PB. Note that we can read back the last value which was written to PB by inputting from PB.

Within the keyboard itself is hardware which receives its basic power and clock signals from the main microcomputer system board, and which scans for and detects any change in the state of the keys. It must be enabled by setting bits 6 and 7 of port PB of the 8255 chip to 0 and 1 respectively. If this is done, the keyboard will send an interrupt to the 8259 chip whenever any key is pressed or released.

Once a key has been pressed, a 1-byte keyboard **scan code** is sent to the system board and the keyboard waits for an 'acknowledge' signal. This is provided by setting bit 1 of port PB to 1 momentarily. The keyboard driver software must now deal with the keyboard interrupt.

The scan code transmitted to the system board is obtained by reading port PA of the 8255 chip. It will be a number between 1 and 83 because there

Function keys

F1	59	F5	63	F9	67
F2	60	F6	64	F10	68
F3	61	F7	.65		
F4	62	F8	66		

Alphanumeric and punctuation keys

1	2	Y	21	'	40
2	3	U	22	#	41
3	4	I	23	\	43
4	5	O	24	Z	44
5	6	P	25	X	45
6	7	{	26	C	46
7	8	}	27	V	47
8	9	A	30	B	48
9	10	S	31	N	49
0	11	D	32	M	50
.	12	F	33	,	51
=	13	G	34	.	52
Q	16	H	35	/	53
W	17	J	36	PrtSc	55
E	18	K	37	SPACE BAR	57
R	19	L	38		
T	20	;	39		

Numeric keypad area

7	71	5	76	3	81
8	72	6	77	0	82
9	73	+	78		83
–	74	1	79		
4	75	2	80		

Control keys

ESC	1	TAB	15	Right SHIFT	54
BACKSPACE	14	ENTER	28	ALT	56
NUM LOCK	69	CTRL	29	CAPS LOCK	58
SCROLL LOCK	70	Left SHIFT	42		

Figure 21.6 Keyboard scan codes (in decimal).

are effectively 83 different keys on the PC keyboard (some, such as all of those in the numeric keypad to the right of the keyboard except Num Lock, are effectively the same key provided in two different places). Each of these 83 scan codes identifies which key changed state and whether the key was pressed or released. Figure 21.6 shows the decimal scan codes associated with each keyboard key. In 8-bit binary form the highest order bit is set to 0 to indicate that the key was pressed and to 1 to indicate that the key was released.

Since the scan code can be interpreted in any way we please, the meaning of each key will be decided by our keyboard driver. Of course, the usual meaning of a given key depends on whether one of the SHIFT, ALT or CTRL keys is also being pressed and on whether the CAPS LOCK or NUM LOCK key has been pressed. To focus better on the essential processes involved, our simple keyboard driver will ignore such factors and give a single response (if any) to each key depression. If a key normally corresponds to a letter, then pressing that key will cause the letter to be displayed on the screen in upper case. If a key normally has more than one printable character corresponding to it, then the lower of the two characters printed on the key will be displayed when that key is pressed. Pressing any other keys will have no effect – they are just ignored.

Taking special action on the 'simultaneous' depression of two keys such as CTRL and A requires the software to store sequences of scan codes and react accordingly. Indeed, a buffer of the order of 100 bytes in length is normally employed to give users a 'type-ahead' facility. Once again we shall simplify the programming task by employing a 1-byte buffer, and the reader will be invited to expand our simple example into a more realistic keyboard driver in Exercises 21.7–21.11. In this 1-byte buffer, we shall store the rogue value 0FFH whenever we are waiting for a keyboard interrupt to arrive.

21.3.1 The specification of the program containing a simple keyboard driver

The program will:

(1) define a new Keyboard Interrupt Service Routine (KISR) and put this in place of the KISR from the BIOS; and then

(2) accept characters typed at the keyboard and display these on the screen as they are typed until the computer is turned off. Keys such as SHIFT and CTRL will not work.

Here is a pseudo-Pascal outline of the program:

establish data segment addressability;

(* *set up our own keyboard interrupt service routine KISR* *)
disable all interrupts;
set ES register to segment address of our KISR;

set AX to offset address of our own KISR;
set DI to offset of vector for INT 09H;
place address of our KISR in the interrupt vector table using ES, AX, DI;
program the 8259 chip to allow timer and keyboard interrupts only;
enable interrupts;

(* *main program* *)
repeat
  CALL GET_A_CHARACTER;
  display the corresponding character;
  if *key was ENTER* **then** *display a LF as well*
forever

The pseudo-Pascal outline of our KISR follows the steps we described earlier. The 1-byte buffer for characters typed will be maintained through a MASM variable called KEYBOARD_CHARACTER. At the outset, this will contain a rogue value (a value which is not the ASCII code of any printable character which appears on the actual keys) to indicate that a key has not been pressed. When a key is pressed, our KISR will leave a corresponding ASCII code in KEYBOARD_CHARACTER:

save registers which will be altered;
AL := the scan code for the key pressed from 8255 port PA;
PUSH AX; (* *save the scan code* *)
read 8255 port PB;
set keyboard acknowledge signal;
send keyboard acknowledge signal via PB;
reset keyboard acknowledge signal;
restore original 8255 port PB;
POP AX; (* *restore the scan code* *)
if *the key is not being released* **then**
  begin
  convert scan code to ASCII;
  if *it is printable ASCII*
    then *put it into KEYBOARD_CHARACTER*
  end;
indicate the end of interrupt to the 8259 chip;
restore altered registers

The subroutine GET_A_CHARACTER waits for the ASCII code for a printable character to arrive in KEYBOARD_CHARACTER, copies it into AL, and restores the rogue value 0FFH to KEYBOARD_CHARACTER. While looking to see if a character has arrived we must be careful to disallow any further maskable interrupts or we may miss characters:

repeat
  disallow all maskable interrupts;
  if *KEYBOARD_CHARACTER = 0FFH*

then *found* := *FALSE*
else begin
AL := *ASCII code for key pressed*;
reset rogue value;
found := *TRUE*
end
allow maskable interrupts
until *found*

Figure 21.7 shows an expansion of these pseudo-Pascal outlines into a complete program containing our KISR. As usual, the reader is invited to type it in and to try it out. Because of our 1-byte buffer and response to scan codes, the important control key combinations CTRL-BREAK and CTRL-ALT-DEL are ignored by our keyboard driver program. Consequently, running it will lock up the machine and the only way to exit is to turn the machine off.

```
LF EQU 0AH
CR EQU 0DH

DATA SEGMENT
KEYBOARD_CHARACTER DB 0FFH
SCAN_TABLE DB 0,0,'1234567890-=',8,0
           DB 'QWERTYUIOP{}',CR,0
           DB 'ASDFGHJKL;',0,0,0,0
           DB 'ZXCVBNM,./',0,0,0
           DB ' ',0,0,0,0,0,0,0,0,0,0,0,0,0
           DB '789-456+1230'
DATA ENDS

WORKING_STORAGE SEGMENT STACK
    DW 100H DUP(?)
WORKING_STORAGE ENDS

CODE SEGMENT
ASSUME CS:CODE,DS:DATA,SS:WORKING_STORAGE
;establish data segment addressability
  START: MOV AX,DATA
         MOV DS,AX
;(* set up our own keyboard interrupt service routine KISR *)
;disable all interrupts
         CLI
;set ES register to segment address of our KISR
         MOV AX,0
         MOV ES,AX
;set AX to offset address of our own KISR
         MOV AX,OFFSET KISR
;set DI to offset of vector for INT 09H
         MOV DI,09H*4
;place address of our KISR in the interrupt vector table using ES, AX,
;DI
```

Figure 21.7 The keyboard driver program.

```
        CLD
        STOSW
        MOV AX,CS
        STOSW
;program the 8259 chip to allow timer and keyboard interrupts only
        MOV AL,0FCH
        OUT 21H,AL
;enable interrupts
        STI
;(* main program *)
;repeat
    FOR_EVER: CALL GET_CHAR
              PUSH AX
              ;display the corresponding character
              CALL DISPLAY_CHAR
              POP  AX
              ;if character read was a CR
              CMP  AL,CR
              JNZ  REPEAT_LOOP
              ;then print an LF as well
              MOV  AL,LF
              CALL DISPLAY_CHAR
;forever
REPEAT_LOOP: JMP FOR_EVER

;***********************************************************
     GET_CHAR:;repeat
                 ;disallow all maskable interrupts
                      CLI
                 ;if KEYBOARD_CHARACTER = 0FFH
                      CMP KEYBOARD_CHARACTER,0FFH
                      JNZ ACCEPT_CODE
                 ;then found := FALSE
                      MOV CL,0
                      JMP RE_ENABLE_INTERRUPTS
                 ;else begin
                      ;AL := ASCII code for key pressed
          ACCEPT_CODE:MOV AL,KEYBOARD_CHARACTER
                      ;reset rogue value;
                       MOV KEYBOARD_CHARACTER,0FFH
                      ;found := TRUE
                       MOV CL,1
                      ;end
                 ;allow maskable interrupts
 RE_ENABLE_INTERRUPTS:STI
              ;until found
                  CMP CL,1
                  JNZ GET_CHAR
                  RET

;*************************************************************
      KISR:;save registers which will be altered
           PUSH BX
           PUSH AX
           ;AL := the scan code for the key pressed from 8255 port PA
```

Figure 21.7
(*cont.*)

```
          IN   AL,60H
          ;(* save the scan code *)
          PUSH AX
          ;read 8255 port PB
          IN   AL,61H
          ;set keyboard acknowledge signal
          OR   AL,80H
          ;send keyboard acknowledge signal via PB
          OUT  61H,AL
          ;reset keyboard acknowledge signal
          AND  AL,7FH
          ;restore original 8255 port PB
          OUT  61H,AL
          ;(* restore the scan code *)
          POP  AX
          ;if the key is not being released then
          TEST AL,80H
          JNZ  SEND_EOI
               ;begin
               ;convert scan code to ASCII
               MOV BX,OFFSET SCAN_TABLE
               XLAT
               ;if it is printable ASCII then
               CMP AL,0
               JZ   SEND_EOI
               ;then put it into KEYBOARD_CHARACTER
               MOV KEYBOARD_CHARACTER,AL
               ;end;
          ;indicate the end of interrupt to the 8259 chip
SEND_EOI: MOV  AL,20H
          OUT  20H,AL
          ;restore altered registers
          POP  AX
          POP  BX
          IRET

;************************************************************
DISPLAY_CHAR: PUSH BX
              MOV  BX,0
              MOV  AH,0EH
              INT  10H
              POP  BX
              RET

CODE ENDS
END START
```

Figure 21.7
(cont.)

EXERCISES

21.7 Augment the buffer in our keyboard driver to a (circular) queue of length 50H.

21.8 Using the version with larger buffer from Exercise 21.7, alter the interpretation of scan codes so that upper and lower case are correctly displayed.

21.9 Add to the version prepared in Exercise 21.8 the facility to recognize CTRL codes. If, for example, CTRL-Z is pressed then `^Z` should be printed on the screen.

21.10 Add to the version prepared in Exercise 21.9 the ability to return to DOS if CTRL-BREAK is pressed.

21.11 The following program fragment leaves in AL the number of disk drives attached to the system:

```
IN  AL,61H
OR  AL,80H ;set bit 7 of PB
OUT 61H,AL
IN  AL,60H ;examine PA
NOT AL
MOV CL,6
SHR AL,CL ;isolate the relevant bits of PA
```

Using this and similar fragments, write a program which prints on the display screen the number of disk drives attached to the system and the amount of RAM on the system board. (Codings for switch settings can be found in your microcomputer's technical manual.)

SUMMARY

This chapter has focused on the second of the three main ways of communicating with hardware devices: interrupts. The next chapter turns to the last of them, direct memory access – which is how communication takes place with the microcomputer display. Linking the keyboard driver in this chapter with one of the display drivers in the next will therefore effectively form a sort of mini-BIOS of our own, capable of accepting users' keyboard input and displaying it on the screen.

SELF-CHECK QUIZ

1. Where will the interrupt service routine address be stored for `INT 11H`?

2. Draw a picture showing the precise contents of the stack when an `INT 14H` is executed, given that it is called from address CS:0234H, and that, before execution, the contents of CS is 10ABH and the contents of SP is 300H.

3. If the interrupt service routine corresponding to `INT 14H` in question 2 were:

```
MOV AX,0FFFFH
IRET
```

draw a picture showing the precise contents of the stack during the execution of this routine.

4. Write a program sequence which sets both the trap flag and the interrupt enable flag to 0. What will be the consequences of so doing?

5. Given that the sequence

```
WAIT
ESC
```

can be used to prevent an instruction being sent to an attached processor (such as the 80*n*87) until it is ready, what do you think will be the effect of the sequences:

(a)
```
ESC
WAIT
```

(b)
```
WAIT
ESC
WAIT
```

6. Explain in detail, with the aid of a diagram showing memory, how to organize a breakpoint using a type 3 interrupt.

7. Write a program fragment to switch the display to 16-color graphics with 640 * 200 points.

8. Write a program fragment to disable interrupts from all devices except the disk interface.

9. Write a program fragment to illustrate the difference between an interrupt and a subroutine.

10. Write a program fragment which will display the keyboard scan code for that key when a key in the numeric pad on your computer is pressed.

22

Device Drivers III: Direct Memory Access I/O and the Display Screen

Contents

Direct memory access I/O is used to drive devices for which neither programmed I/O nor interrupt I/O can provide the required data transfer rate. Thus, communication with the computer's display screen is organized through direct memory access because of the very high data transfer rate demanded by the display screen's circuitry, which, like a normal TV, has to arrange for an electron beam to traverse the screen so fast that the image appears constant to the human eye.

If there is direct memory access to a hardware device, then that device is wired into the microcomputer in such a way that communicating with it simply involves communicating with a group of locations in memory. Since the display screen for 8086-family computers is driven via direct memory access, to display a text character on the screen at a certain position, one has simply to arrange that the ASCII code for that character is stored in a certain location and the character will appear on the screen. (Another coded byte is also stored to specify the attributes with which that character is to be displayed – which color, or should it blink, or . . ..)

It will be assumed throughout this chapter that the computer on which you are running your 8086-family assembly language programs has a color display. This display will be capable of several modes of operation, enabling programs to communicate with their users through text and graphics in both black and white and color. To illustrate the basic principle behind the direct memory access method of programming hardware devices, we shall first consider black and white text displays. Initially, the display driver that is provided as part of the BIOS will be used, but then we shall construct our own as a complement to the keyboard driver written in the last chapter. Subsequent sections then examine how to arrange for the display of text and graphics in color.

In fact, it is assumed that your computer has a display circuit board compatible with the IBM color/graphics adapter. If it does not, because there are so many types of color display (which are usually provided by means of a circuit board that plugs into the computer's motherboard), it may be that you have to modify the given example programs slightly in order for them to run exactly as specified on your computer. The necessary changes may range from specifying the colors to be used in different ways, to using different addresses from those given for one or both of the direct memory access of the display and the I/O ports used to control it.

22.1 Text display

Using BIOS `INT 10H` (Table 21.4), we can select the display to work in black and white text mode, in which the screen image has 80 columns and 25 lines, thus allowing 80 * 25 = 2000 characters to be displayed at the same time. In this mode, thanks to the hardware configuration allowing **direct memory access**, our programs can regard such a display as being 16K bytes of memory, addressable at absolute locations 0B8000H and following (the so-called **DMA address**).

Starting at 0B8000H, each location having an even-numbered address contains a character representation for a character to be displayed in the corresponding screen position, and each odd-numbered location contains an attribute byte, specifying the manner in which the associated character is to be displayed (normal video, reverse video, blinking, and so on). Figure 22.1 shows the possible settings for the attribute byte.

The precise correspondence between display memory location and screen position is as follows. On the display, rows are numbered 0–24, with row 0 at the top of the screen, and columns 0–79, with column 0 at the left of the screen. From the 8086-family microprocessor's point of view, the offset addresses from the start of the display DMA area for a character in row x, column y are therefore given by:

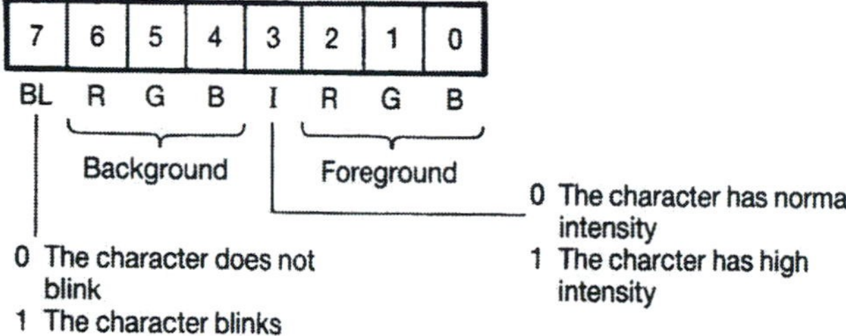

Background			Foreground			Display attribute
R	G	B	R	G	B	
0	0	0	0	0	0	Nothing appears in the corresponding position
1	1	1	1	1	1	A white box appears in the corresponding character position
0	0	0	1	1	1	White character on black background (normal video)
1	1	1	0	0	0	Black character on white background (reverse video)

Figure 22.1 Display attribute byte settings for color display in black and white 80 ∗ 25 text mode.

$$(160 * y) + (2 * x)$$

the attribute byte occupying the next location in each case.

Thus, if we wish to place a character at the top left-hand corner of the screen, then the (ASCII) code for that character must be placed in location 0B8000H + (0 ∗ 160D) + (0 ∗ 2) = 0B8000H and the attribute byte in 0B8000H + 1. Likewise, to display a character in the bottom right-hand corner (row 24, column 79), the two corresponding bytes should be stored in locations 0B8000H + (24 ∗ 160D) + (79 ∗ 2) = 0B8F9EH and 0B8F9EH + 1.

Figure 22.2 contains a complete program which displays all possible character images. There are 256 such images, since in this mode the display uses an extended ASCII code, the extra characters being obtained by using an 8-bit code in which the most significant bit is set to 1. Thus, whilst the second table in Appendix I shows the images of characters with codes 20H to 7EH, higher (non-control) codes give fancier characters such as Greek letters, French and German accents, and teletext-like block graphics.

There are also seven possible (non-blank) display attributes, so the user is expected to enter a digit in the range 1–7, in which case all the character images are displayed with a corresponding attribute. Pressing any other key (except keys such as SHIFT and CTRL) clears the screen and returns control to DOS. If a digit in the given range was entered and all the character images have been displayed, then entering another digit causes the cycle to be repeated, but for the new attribute value.

```
DATA SEGMENT
ATTRIBUTES EQU THIS BYTE
NORMAL                DB 07H
REVERSE               DB 70H
INTENSE               DB 0FH
BLINK                 DB 87H
INTENSE_AND_BLINK     DB 8FH
REVERSE_AND_BLINK     DB 0F0H
REV_AND_INT_AND_BLINK DB 0F8H
DATA ENDS

WORKING_STORAGE SEGMENT STACK
        DW 100H DUP(?)
WORKING_STORAGE ENDS

CODE SEGMENT
ASSUME CS:CODE,DS:DATA,SS:WORKING_STORAGE
;establish data segment addressability
      START:MOV   AX,DATA
            MOV   DS,AX
;set ES to point to display memory
            MOV   AX,0B800H
            MOV   ES,AX
;clear the screen
            CLD
            MOV   DI,0
            MOV   AL,' '
            MOV   AH,NORMAL
            MOV   CX,2000D
            REP   STOSW
;read(ch) through the BIOS so no screen echo
            MOV   AH,0
            INT   16H
;while ch in ['1' .. '7'] do
IN_RANGE:   CMP   AL,31H
            JC    DONE
            CMP   AL,38H
            JNC   DONE
            ;begin
            ;set the attribute value in AH
                   SUB   AL,31H
                   MOV   BL,AL
                   MOV   BH,0H
                   MOV   AH,ATTRIBUTES[BX]
            ;DI := start of row 1
            ;display character code (AL) := 0
                   MOV   DI,(1*160D)+(0*2)
                   MOV   AL,0
            ;column count(DH) := 0
                   MOV   DH,0
            ;repeat display char with code in AL, attribute in AH
          NEXT_CHARACTER: MOV   ES:[DI]+1,AH
                          MOV   ES:[DI],AL
                   ;miss a column before next character
```

Figure 22.2
A program to display all possible character images.

```
                          ADD   DI,4
                          ADD   DH,2
                    ;if we are now beyond column 79
                          CMP   DH,79D
                          JB    NEXT_CODE
                    ;then begin
                    ;skip a line
                          ADD   DI,160
                    ;reset column counter
                          MOV   DH,0
                    ;end
                    ;next character code
                 NEXT_CODE: INC AL
           ;until code in AL is 0H
                      CMP   AL,0H
                      JZ    NEXT_ATTRIBUTE
                      JMP   NEXT_CHARACTER
;read(ch) through BIOS so no screen echo
NEXT_ATTRIBUTE:       MOV   AH,0
                      INT   16H
                      JMP   IN_RANGE
;blank out screen
DONE: MOV   DI,0
      MOV   AL,' '
      MOV   AH,NORMAL
      MOV   CX,2000D
      REP   STOSW
;return to DOS
      MOV   AX,4C00H
      INT   21H

CODE ENDS
END START
```

Figure 22.2 (*cont.*)

22.2 A display driver for black and white text

In this section a display driver will be written for the color/graphics adapter which will be the counterpart of our simple keyboard driver in Chapter 21. In fact, the program will accept characters typed in at the keyboard via BIOS INT 16H and then – thanks to the display driver – display them at the current cursor position, afterwards moving the cursor to a new position. A backspace character will move the cursor back one column on the same line unless the cursor is already in column zero, in which case no action will be taken. If the display driver receives a carriage return character it will move the cursor to the beginning of the same line, whereas a line feed causes a move down one line to the same column position. Once the cursor is on the bottom line, the display is scrolled up instead of the cursor being moved down. In other words, the contents of the top line of the display is replaced with the contents of the second line, those of the second by the contents of the third, and so on. Then the last line of the display is blanked out, so that the cursor is now in the correct column of a blank line.

In order to write this driver program, a rudimentary understanding of the role of the **6845 Cathode Ray Tube** (CRT) **controller** chip in the design of the color/graphics adapter is required.

22.2.1 The 6845 CRT controller

The 6845 CRT controller (or one of its more modern descendants), is often used to control what actually appears on the display screen in 8086-family based microcomputers. It is then the main component responsible for selecting each character code to be displayed, for selecting which of the several rows of miniature dots that make up a character on the screen should be displayed next, for synchronizing operations between the other components in the display circuitry, for generating the cursor image, and for positioning the cursor.

Table 22.1 shows a list of the 6845 ports and their functions. In fact a total of 16 registers within the 6845 chip have to be accessed through two ports. Thus, if we want to access the cursor start register of the 6845 chip, we must first place its register number (10D) in port 3D4H; outputting to port 3D5H will then, in fact, be setting the cursor start register.

The horizontal registers determine the number of characters per line and the width of each character, and the vertical registers the number of characters

Table 22.1 The 6845 ports and corresponding registers.

PC port address	*6845 register*	*Register number*	*Description*
3D4H	Address register		
3D5H	Horizontal registers	0–3	Control horizontal characteristics of the display.
	Vertical registers	4–9	Control vertical display characteristics.
	Cursor start and end registers	10–11	Define cursor image.
	Start address high	12	Determine which part of the adapter memory is used.
	Start address low	13	
	Cursor address high	14	Determine the display position of the cursor.
	Cursor address low	15	

per column and the number of lines of miniature dots which are to make up the display of each character on the screen. These are initialized by the BIOS and it is beyond the scope of this book to discuss their use. The contents of the cursor-start and cursor-end registers determine where the cursor is displayed in relation to ordinary text characters and the height and position of the cursor.

The start address registers in the 6845 chip (12D and 13D) choose where, in the 16K of memory it can address, the code for the first character to be displayed is located. (We shall return to a fuller discussion of the start address registers in Section 22.3).

If we place the monochrome adapter memory address of the appropriate character code into the cursor-address registers, the cursor can be positioned over a specific character display position. The only slight complication is that the 6845 chip views the direct memory access area as being in two distinct blocks. In fact, a 0 bit is appended to a character code address generated by the 6845 chip (thus giving the 'correct' even 8086-family address) and a 1 bit is appended to attribute code addresses (giving, similarly, the 'correct' odd 8086-family address). From the programming point of view, this simply means that if we want to position the cursor on row x, column y using 6845 cursor-address registers, then the corresponding offset from the start of the 2K character code memory is given by

$$(x * 80D) + y$$

Assuming definitions

```
COLUMN DW ?
ROW DB ?
```

then the following subroutine will position the cursor on the screen at the column specified by the (unsigned) contents of COLUMN and at the row specified by the (unsigned) contents of ROW – we assume both numbers are within the appropriate ranges.

```
POSITION_CURSOR PROC NEAR
;BX := the 6845 cursor address
        MOV AL,80D
        MUL ROW
        ADD AX,COLUMN
        MOV BX,AX
;set the 6845 address register to access register 14D
        MOV DX,3B4H
        MOV AL,14D
        OUT DX,AL
;set cursor address (high)
        MOV DX,3B5H
        MOV AL,BH
        OUT DX,AL
;set 6845 address register to access register 15D
        MOV DX,3B4H
        MOV AL,15D
        OUT DX,AL
;set cursor address (low)
```

```
        MOV DX,3B5H
        MOV AL,BL
        OUT DX,AL
        RET
POSITION_CURSOR ENDP
```

The complete program containing our display driver (and using the POSITION_CURSOR subroutine) is given in Figure 22.3. By way of illustration, the program uses the LES instruction which, together with its counterpart LDS, can be useful when either of the registers DS or ES is to be loaded with a segment address and another register loaded with an offset. The format of these instructions is

LDS *reg,double-word pointer*
LES *reg,double-word pointer*

and on execution, for example,

```
LES BX,ROW
```

is equivalent to the three instructions

```
MOV BX,OFFSET ROW
MOV AX,SEG ROW
MOV ES,AX
```

In conjunction with LES and LDS it is often helpful to employ the fact that if the DD pseudo-op is used to redefine a variable as in

```
MY_ADDRESS DD ROW
ROW     DB 0
```

then locations MY_ADDRESS and MY_ADDRESS+1 contain the offset of ROW and the next two locations the segment base value of ROW. In the program we have taken a slightly different, but entirely compatible, approach.

```
NORMAL_ATTRIBUTE EQU 07H
BS EQU 08H
LF EQU 0AH
CR EQU 0DH

DATA SEGMENT
MDA EQU THIS DWORD
START_OF_DISPLAY DW 0
MDA_SEGMENT      DW 0B800H

COLUMN DW 0
ROW    DB 0
TWO    DW 2
DATA ENDS

WORKING_STORAGE SEGMENT STACK
         DW 100H DUP(?)
```

Figure 22.3 Program containing a monochrome display driver.

```
WORKING_STORAGE ENDS

CODE SEGMENT
ASSUME CS:CODE,DS:DATA,SS:WORKING_STORAGE
;establish data segment addressability
                MOV AX,DATA
                MOV DS,AX
;point ES to monochrome display adapter memory and DI to
;offset of start of display
                LES DI,MDA
;clear the display
                MOV AL,' '
                MOV AH,NORMAL_ATTRIBUTE
                MOV CX,2000D
                CLD
                REP STOSW
;position cursor at top left of screen (column = 0, row = 0)
                CALL POSITION_CURSOR
;repeat read(ch)
         NEXT_CHAR:        MOV   AH,0
                           INT   16H
                           PUSH AX
         ;display(ch)
                           CALL DISPLAY_DRIVER
                           POP   AX
         ;if ch = CR then display an LF also
                           CMP   AL,CR
                           JNZ   SKIP_LF
                           MOV   AL,LF
                           CALL DISPLAY_DRIVER
;forever
         SKIP_LF: JMP NEXT_CHAR

POSITION_CURSOR PROC NEAR
;BX := the 6845 cursor address
                MOV  AL,80D
                MUL  ROW
                ADD  AX,COLUMN
                MOV  BX,AX
;set the 6845 address register to access register 14D
                MOV  DX,3D4H
                MOV  AL,14D
                OUT  DX,AL
;set cursor address (high)
                MOV  DX,3D5H
                MOV  AL,BH
                OUT  DX,AL
;set 6845 address register to access register 15D
                MOV  DX,3D4H
                MOV  AL,15D
                OUT  DX,AL
;set cursor address (low)
                MOV  DX,3D5H
                MOV  AL,BL
```

Figure 22.3
(cont.)

```
                OUT  DX,AL
                RET
POSITION_CURSOR ENDP

DISPLAY_DRIVER PROC NEAR
;case AL of ...
                CMP  AL,BS
                JZ   DO_BS
                CMP  AL,LF
                JZ   DO_LF
                CMP  AL,CR
                JZ   DO_CR
                CALL DISPLAY_CHAR
                JMP  END_CASE
         DO_BS: CALL BACKSPACE
                JMP  END_CASE
         DO_LF: CALL LINE_FEED
                JMP  END_CASE
         DO_CR: MOV  COLUMN,0
;reposition cursor
      END_CASE: CALL POSITION_CURSOR
                RET
DISPLAY_DRIVER ENDP

BACKSPACE PROC NEAR
;if column <> 0 then column := column-1
                CMP  COLUMN,0
                JZ   DO_NOTHING
                DEC  COLUMN
    DO_NOTHING: RET
BACKSPACE ENDP

LINE_FEED PROC NEAR
;if row <> 24 then row := row-1
                CMP  ROW,24
                JZ   SCROLL
                INC  ROW
                JMP  DONE_LF
;else begin
        SCROLL: PUSH DS
        ;set ES and DS to adapter memory
                        MOV  AX,MDA_SEGMENT
                        MOV  DS,AX
        ;start the block move with the 2nd display line
                        MOV  SI,(160D*1)+(2*0)
        ;relocate the block starting at the first display line
                        MOV  DI,0
        ;move 24D rows of 80D characters
                        MOV  CX,24D*80D
        ;do the move
                        REP  MOVSW
        ;now blank out the bottom line of the screen
                        MOV  AL,' '
                        MOV  AH,NORMAL_ATTRIBUTE
                        MOV  CX,80D
```

Figure 22.3
(*cont.*)

```
                        REP   STOSW
                        POP   DS
         DONE_LF:   RET
LINE_FEED ENDP

DISPLAY_CHAR PROC NEAR
;save AL in BL
                   MOV   BL,AL
;AX := offset of current cursor position from 6845 point of view
                   MOV   AL,80D
                   MUL   ROW
                   ADD   AX,COLUMN
;double this to get address from 8086-family
;microprocessor point of view
                   MUL   TWO
;display the character in BL
                   MOV   DI,AX
                   MOV   ES:[DI],BL
;column := column + 1
                   INC    COLUMN
;if column = 80D then
                   CMP    COLUMN,80D
                   JNZ    DONE_DISPLAY
                   ;begin
                          MOV   COLUMN,0
                          CALL  LINE_FEED
                   ;end
DONE_DISPLAY: RET
DISPLAY_CHAR ENDP

CODE ENDS
END
```

Figure 22.3
(*cont.*)

EXERCISES

22.1 Amend the program in Figure 22.3 so that a backspace character not only moves the cursor back but also erases the character the cursor was on before the backspace was received.

22.2 Write a display driver and main program to use the driver similar to that in Figure 22.3, but which uses only rows 0 to 12 and columns 0 to 39 of the display, thus producing a windowing effect.

22.3 Displaying text in color

With the color/graphics adapter installed in your microcomputer, several different display modes can be selected using BIOS INT 10H – as can be seen from Table 21.1. If one of the alphanumeric modes is selected (25 rows of 40 columns of text in black and white or color, or 25 rows of 80 columns of text in black and white or color) then several complete displays, or pages, of text can be kept in the DMA area: four pages of 80 * 25 display; eight pages of 40 * 25. Pages are placed sequentially in memory so that, for an 80 * 25 display, each page is 2K long.

Which page is displayed is determined by the value in the 6845 chip's start-address registers, and thus advancing the beginning of the displayed page by one line of character images (40 * 2 = 80 bytes for the 40 * 25 display and 160 bytes for the 80 * 25 display), the display image can be scrolled faster than by moving characters around in memory. This is **hardware scrolling**.

For displaying color text images there are 16 possible foreground colors (for the text characters themselves) and 8 possible background colors (for the screen surrounding each text character) as shown in Table 22.2. Background colors may be selected from either the first eight or the last eight colors, but colors from the two different groups of eight cannot be displayed as backgrounds simultaneously.

After the display mode has been set to color text display, the **color-select register** in the 6845 chip (port 3D9H) must be initialized to set the screen

Table 22.2 Colors available in alphanumeric mode.

I	*R*	*G*	*B*	*Color*
0	0	0	0	Black
0	0	0	1	Blue
0	0	1	0	Green
0	0	1	1	Cyan
0	1	0	0	Red
0	1	0	1	Magenta
0	1	1	0	Brown
0	1	1	1	Light Gray
1	0	0	0	Dark Gray
1	0	0	1	Light Blue
1	0	1	0	Light Green
1	0	1	1	Light Cyan
1	1	0	0	Light Red
1	1	0	1	Light Magenta
1	1	1	0	Yellow
1	1	1	1	White

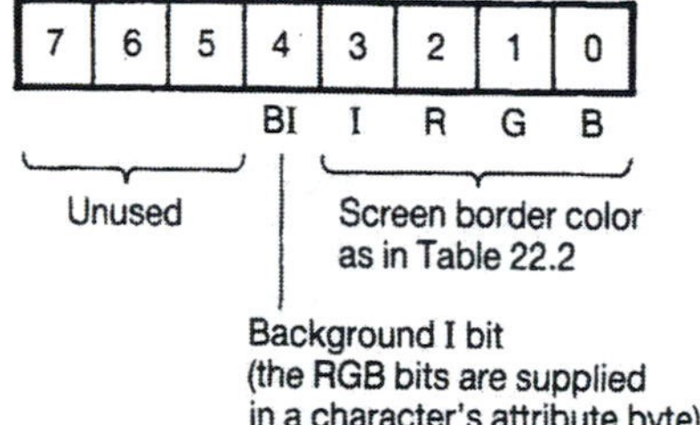

Figure 22.4 Color-select register configuration in alphanumeric mode.

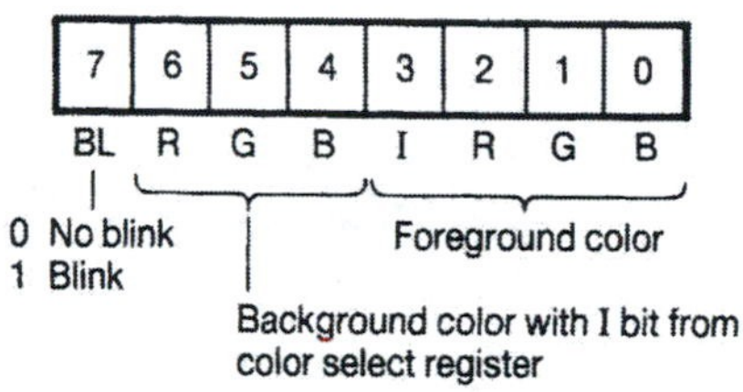

Figure 22.5 Display attribute byte for color/graphics monitor adapter.

border color and to determine whether the first eight or last eight colors in Table 22.2 are to be used for backgrounds. Its configuration is shown in Figure 22.4. The configuration of an attribute byte is shown in Figure 22.5.

The program in Figure 22.6 displays the letter A in every possible foreground color and with every possible background color in the first eight of the list in Table 22.2. The program then pauses. A hardware scroll is then performed each time a key (not SHIFT, CTRL,. . .) is pressed until the image has scrolled off the screen, when the program returns control to DOS.

```
        DATA SEGMENT
        FOREGROUND DB 0
        BACKGROUND DB 0
        DATA ENDS

        WORKING_STORAGE SEGMENT STACK
                DW 100H DUP(?)
        WORKING_STORAGE ENDS

        CODE SEGMENT
        ASSUME CS:CODE,DS:DATA,SS:WORKING_STORAGE
        ;establish data segment addressability
START:  MOV   AX,DATA
           MOV   DS,AX
        ;initialize the color adapter to 40 * 25 color mode
           MOV   AH,0
           MOV   AL,1
           INT   10H
        ;select blue screen border via color-select register
```

Figure 22.6 Program to display 'A' in every color combination and then to illustrate hardware scrolling.

```
        MOV  AL,1
        MOV  DX,3D9H
        OUT  DX,AL
      ;set ES to address color adapter memory
        MOV  AX,0B800H
        MOV  ES,AX
      ;blank out screen and the whole memory with blue on blue
        MOV  DI,0
        MOV  AL,' '
        MOV  AH,1*16D+0
        MOV  CX,8000D
        CLD
        REP  STOSW
      ;DI := column 0, row 20D
        MOV  DI,(80D * 20D) + (2 * 0)
      ;for foreground := 0 to 15 do
      ;for background := 0 to 7 do begin
        MOV  FOREGROUND,0
        MOV  BACKGROUND,0
      ;display a letter A in those foreground and background colors
DO_NEXT:        MOV  BYTE PTR ES:[DI],'A'
                MOV  AL,16D
                MUL  BACKGROUND
                ADD  AL,FOREGROUND
                MOV  ES:[DI]+1,AL
                ADD  DI,2
                INC  BACKGROUND
                CMP  BACKGROUND,8
                JNZ  DO_NEXT
                MOV  BACKGROUND,0
                INC  FOREGROUND
                CMP  FOREGROUND,15
                JNZ  DO_NEXT
              ;end
      ;(* now prepare for scrolling *)
      ;set cursor address to the first character
        MOV  BX,0
      ;set 6845 address register to access register 14D
        MOV  DX,3D4H
        MOV  AL,14D
        OUT  DX,AL
      ;set cursor address (high)
        MOV  DX,3D5H
        MOV  AL,BH
        OUT  DX,AL
      ;set 6845 address register to access register 15D
        MOV  DX,3D4H
        MOV  AL,15D
        OUT  DX,AL
      ;set cursor address (low)
        MOV  DX,3D5H
        MOV  AL,BL
        OUT  DX,AL
      ;repeat read(ch)
      NEXT_CH: MOV  AH,0
```

Figure 22.6
(cont.)

```
          INT   16H
     ;scroll down one line
          ADD   BX,40D
     ;set 6845 address register to access register 12D
          MOV   DX,3D4H
          MOV   AL,12D
          OUT   DX,AL
     ;set start address(high)
          MOV   DX,3D5H
          MOV   AL,BH
          OUT   DX,AL
     ;set 6845 address register to access register 13D
          MOV   DX,3D4H
          MOV   AL,13D
          OUT   DX,AL
     ;set start address (low)
          MOV   DX,3D5H
          MOV   AL,BL
          OUT   DX,AL
  ;until BX = 40 * 20
     CMP  BX,40D * 20D
     JNZ  NEXT_CH
  ;reset the color adapter to 80 * 25 black and white mode
    MOV   AH,0
    MOV   AL,2
    INT   10H
  ;return to DOS
    MOV   AX,4C00H
    INT   21H
  CODE ENDS
  END START
```

Figure 22.6
(cont.)

EXERCISE

22.3 Write a program to display the poem:

The egg and the duck
Didn't have much luck
When the river flooded
Both were stuck
In the water
Which was cold

in eight different color presentations using the color adapter memory. The user is to select a presentation by keying a digit 1–8, at which point the display scrolls backwards or forwards to the next screen. When the program is started up, presentation 1 automatically appears.

22.4 Color graphics mode

In **graphics mode**, two resolutions are possible: 320 * 200 plottable points in black and white or color; and 640 * 200 plottable points in black and white only. Using color, each point or dot in a given display can be one of four colors. Having chosen the first (background) color from Table 22.2, the other three colors may either be red, green and yellow, or cyan, magenta and white. To emphasize: a given graphics display can contain only four colors; and the combinations of colors are restricted.

Once again we shall use the BIOS `INT 10H` to set up a (color) graphics display. When we have done so, the color-select register is used to select the working color-set. Figure 22.7 shows the configuration of this register in graphics mode.

Addressing an actual point is complicated by the desire to restrict the amount of memory used to control each point. In fact, two bits are used to represent each point on the color graphics screen, the setting of these two bits determining the color displayed at that point as follows:

00	background color
01	green or cyan
10	red or magenta
11	brown or white

depending on the choice of color set. Since a dot displayed in the 00 form will be in the background color it will not be distinguishable from the background.

Mapping every point in the 200 row, 320 column display down to two bits in the DMA area is carried out as follows. Even row numbers (0,2,4,. . .,198) map to the memory starting at offset address 0 from the start of the DMA area; odd row numbers map to memory starting at offset address 2000H. Each row of 320 dots needs 320 * 2 bits = 80 bytes of display memory. Hence to place a dot at row x, column y, the group of 80 bytes representing row y has offset

$$(x \text{ div } 2) * 80$$

from the appropriate start address. Similarly the expression

$$(y * 2) \text{ div } 8 = y \text{ div } 4$$

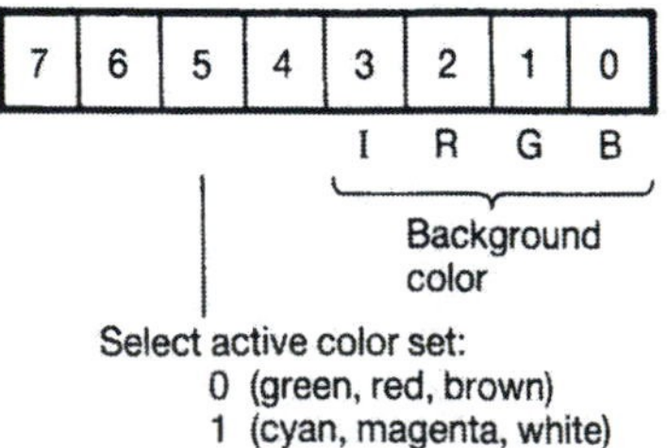

Figure 22.7 Color-select register configuration for graphics mode.

will give the number of the byte containing the appropriate two bits for a given dot and

$y \bmod 4$

specifies which of the four groups of two bits in a byte (numbering most significant two bits as pair 0, next most significant two bits as pair 1, and so on) represent that column. Most of this calculation can be accomplished by shift operations as is done in the example program, Figure 22.8.

This program allows its user to doodle on the screen. When it is run, a white dot appears on a blue background. The user can then move the white dot around using the U (UP), D (DOWN), L (LEFT) and R (RIGHT) keys and thus doodle on the screen (note that only upper-case letters are accepted). The program can be exited at any time by pressing the X (eXit) key. When reading through the program, note that, when a dot within a byte is changed, the other dots represented by that byte must be preserved.

```
DATA SEGMENT
ROW      DW 100D
COLUMN   DW 160D
MASKS    DB 11000000B
         DB 00110000B
         DB 00001100B
         DB 00000011B
WHITE    DB 11111111B
EIGHTY   DB 80D
DATA ENDS

WORKING_STORAGE SEGMENT STACK
          DW 100H DUP(?)
WORKING_STORAGE ENDS

CODE SEGMENT
ASSUME CS:CODE,DS:DATA,SS:WORKING_STORAGE
;set up data segment addressability
  START:MOV   AX,DATA
        MOV   DS,AX
;set mode using BIOS for 320*200 color image
        MOV   AH,0
        MOV   AL,4
        INT   10H
;use color-select register for white on blue
        MOV   DX,3D9H
        MOV   AL,00100001B
        OUT   DX,AL
;set ES to address adapter memory
        MOV   AX,0B800H
        MOV   ES,AX
;fill screen with background color
        CLD
```

Figure 22.8
A color graphics doodle drawing program.

```
        MOV   AL,0
        MOV   CX,3FFFH
        MOV   DI,0
        REP   STOSB
;place dot in centre of screen (row 100, column 160)
        CALL DRAW_DOT
;repeat read(ch)
    NEXT_CH: MOV  AH,0
             INT  16H
      ;case ch of ...
             CMP  AL,'U'
             JZ   DO_U
             CMP  AL,'D'
             JZ   DO_D
             CMP   AL,'L'
             JZ   DO_L
             CMP  AL,'R'
             JZ   DO_R
             JMP  DONE_COMMAND
       DO_U: CMP  ROW,0
             JZ   SKIP_U
             DEC  ROW
             CALL DRAW_DOT
     SKIP_U: JMP  DONE_COMMAND
       DO_D: CMP  ROW,199D
             JZ   SKIP_D
             INC  ROW
             CALL DRAW_DOT
     SKIP_D: JMP  DONE_COMMAND
       DO_L: CMP  COLUMN,0
             JZ   SKIP_L
             DEC  COLUMN
             CALL DRAW_DOT
     SKIP_L: JMP  DONE_COMMAND
       DO_R: CMP  COLUMN,319D
             JZ   DONE_COMMAND
             INC  COLUMN
             CALL DRAW_DOT
;until ch = 'X'
DONE_COMMAND:CMP  AL,'X'
             JNZ NEXT_CH
;reset the color adapter to 80 * 25 black and white mode
         MOV  AH,0
         MOV  AL,2
         INT  10H
;return to DOS
         MOV  AX,4C00H
         INT  21H

DRAW_DOT PROC NEAR
;preserve value of ROW
         PUSH ROW
;if least significant bit of ROW is 1
         SHR  ROW,1
         JNC   EVEN
```

Figure 22.8
(cont.)

```
;then DI := 2000H
         MOV  DI,2000H
         JMP  ROW_OFFSET
;else DI := 0;
  EVEN: MOV  DI,0
;calculate the row offset
ROW_OFFSET:  MOV  AX,ROW
             MUL  EIGHTY
             ADD  DI,AX
;DX := within row offset
             MOV  DX,COLUMN
             SHR  DX,1
             SHR  DX,1
             ADD  DI,DX
;SI := within byte offset
             MOV  SI,COLUMN
             AND  SI,03H
;get color mask for this portion
             MOV  AL,MASKS[SI]
             MOV  BL,WHITE
             AND  BL,AL
             NOT  AL
;get byte containing dot to be changed
             MOV  AH,ES:[DI]
;select the dot
             AND  AH,AL
;turn the yellow dot on
             OR   AH,BL
;store it in the adapter memory
             MOV  ES:[DI],AH
;restore original value of ROW
             POP  ROW
             RET
DRAW_DOT ENDP

CODE ENDS
END START
```

Figure 22.8
(cont.)

EXERCISES

22.4 Modify the program in Figure 22.8 so that pressing one of the letters G (Green), B (Blue), Y (Yellow), R (Red) means that the movable dot becomes the corresponding color. Change the control keys so that the arrow keys on the numeric keypad are used to move the dot around the screen.

22.5 High-level language interfaces to graphical displays often allow users to specify two points and then have a straight line drawn between them.

Write an 8086-family assembly language program to provide such a facility, assuming the two given points are specified in variables COLUMN1, ROW1 and COLUMN2, ROW2.

SUMMARY

In this chapter we have considered the third and final of the means of communicating with hardware devices to be considered in this book: direct memory access. While we illustrated the relevant techniques with specific reference to the microcomputer's display, it should be borne in mind that DMA is not limited in its application to providing display facilities, nor to output. Many other devices can be connected to a microcomputer in this way, both for input and output. (A DMA input device leaves its input in specific memory locations.)

In the course of this chapter we also met the last two instructions which are found on all the lower members of the 8086-family of microprocessors: LDS and LES. These enable us to load a segment register and an offset at the same time. In the next (and final) chapter we shall examine some of the instructions which are only available from higher members of the 8086-family of microprocessors. Since many of these are provided to assist in the construction of sophisticated operating systems our consideration of them will be necessarily brief; we shall simply hope to impart enough of their flavor to encourage the reader to pursue them independently.

SELF-CHECK QUIZ

1. What will be the relevant attribute byte setting for a color display in black and white 80 * 25 text mode if a character is to appear in reverse video?

2. For such a display, in which location must we place a character if we want it to appear in the center of the screen (or as near to that as possible)?

3. Draw a diagram showing the correspondence between the position on the screen of a character displayed in black and white text mode and the settings of the 6845 cursor address registers. Give two examples to show how it works out for characters positioned in different parts of the screen display.

4. Is it possible to arrange a display using the color/graphics adapter which has a red border, a blue background and green text?

5. When displaying color graphics, in which bytes in memory will the bits for the dot in each of the four corners of the screen and for the central line down the middle of the screen be stored?

6. List the differences:

(a) between driving a text display and a graphics display; and

(b) between driving a color display and a black and white display.

7. Write a subroutine to draw a square box on the color graphics screen, the size of the box being passed to your subroutine as a parameter in AX.

8. Repeat question 7 for the black and white text screen, but the size of the box should be given as a number of characters and the box should be drawn from asterisks as in:

```
********
*      *
*      *
*      *
*      *
********
```

9. Repeat question 8 for the color text screen.

10. Is it possible to scroll the text on the display screen from top to bottom instead of from bottom to top? Write a program sequence to illustrate your answer.

23

Advanced Instructions for the 80386 and Higher Members of the 8086 Family

Contents

The final chapter introduces some of the instructions available only with the more advanced members of the 8086 family of microprocessors. Our main purpose is to survey the general-purpose (32-bit) instructions which only the higher members of the 8086 family can execute. From the applications programmer's point of view, these may be viewed as extensions of the instructions with which we are already familiar.

To illustrate these advanced instructions this chapter begins with an examination of the extended general-purpose register set (including the extended 32-bit flags register) which the more advanced of the 8086 family (such as the 80386 and 80486 microprocessors) possess, and which may be used in the development of 32-bit applications programs. Then follows a description of the 32-bit instructions which make use of these registers and other general-purpose instructions, the changes which must be made to our assembly language when using the higher members of the 8086 family, and the main part of the chapter concludes by employing many of these in a complete example program.

Section 23.5 is an overview of the instructions possessed by the 80286 and higher members of the 8086-family, which were provided by their designers to facilitate the development of sophisticated operating systems, such as those which allow multi-tasking (see Section 2.2 and Figure 2.4) and the use of virtual memory. The treatment will be very brief, since a full understanding of the use and implications of these instructions requires a background in operating system theory beyond the scope of this book.

23.1 Registers, flags and memory for 32-bit applications development

The 32-bit registers which the programmer may use for data storage and computation in the development of applications programs are shown in Figure 23.1. Each of the eight 8086-family general-purpose 16-bit registers (AX, BX, CX, DX, SP, BP, SI and DI) has a 32-bit counterpart (EAX, EBX, ECX, EDX, ESP, EBP, ESI, and EDI respectively), the least significant 16 bits of which can be regarded as the corresponding 16-bit register. Also, in the case of EAX, EBX, ECX and EDX, the least significant 16 bits can be regarded as comprising of the two corresponding 8-bit registers. Apart from this change, there are two new 16-bit segment registers, FS and GS, and the flags register is extended to a 32-bit register called EFLAGS and the IP register is extended to a 32-bit register called EIP.

The only values in the 32-bit EFLAGS register (Figure 23.2) which are used and not mentioned in the description (see Figure 1.7) of the 16-bit flags register employed by lower members of the 8086 family than the 80386 microprocessor are the **Virtual Mode** (VM) and **Resume Flag** (RF) flags.

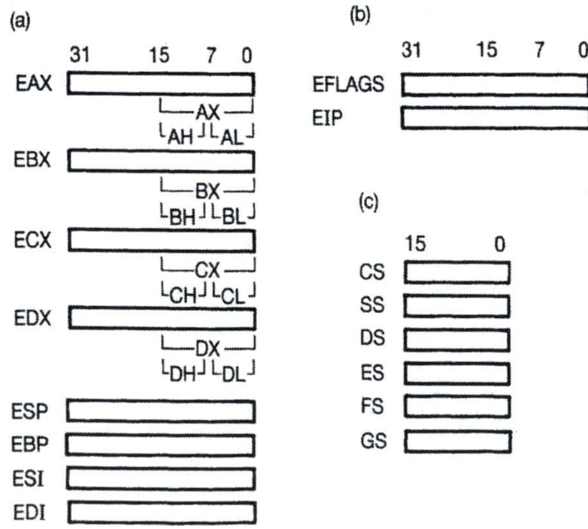

Figure 23.1 32-bit registers for applications development: (a) general-purpose registers; (b) status registers; (c) segment registers.

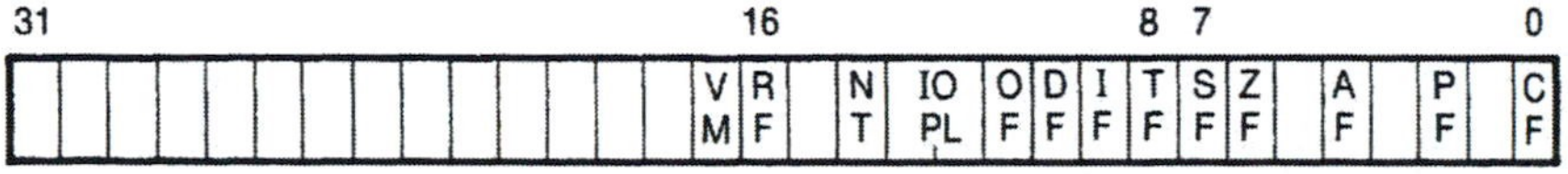

31 16 8 7 0

VM	RF	NT	IOPL	OF	DF	IF	TF	SF	ZF	AF	PF	CF

Figure 23.2 The EFLAGS register.

If the VM flag is set to 1, the 80386 and more powerful microprocessors will operate in virtual 8086 mode so that, to the programmer, they look exactly the same as a very fast 8086 microprocessor with 32-bit arithmetic capabilities and a larger and more orthogonal instruction set. Apart from a brief survey of the other features of these more powerful microprocessors at the very end of this chapter, the remainder of the material in this chapter will be concerned with programming the 80386 for use in this mode.

When set to 1, RF indicates that an operation has only been partially completed and needs to be resumed when the containing task is restarted.

23.1.1 Memory and addresses

Because the 80386 microprocessor has a 32-bit external data bus, it has a physical address space of 4 294 967 296 bytes (4 gigabytes). With such a large address space, some logical or symbolic addressing scheme is essential, but the needs of the applications programmer and the systems engineer are different. In this book, we are more interested in the requirements of applications programming. Consequently, we shall concern ourselves most with the management of addresses based on the segmented memory concept with which we are already familiar, rather than with the more sophisticated capabilities provided for systems engineers (and operating systems designers in particular).

Notice from Figure 23.1 that the 80386 microprocessor has six 16-bit segment registers. As well as uses similar to those for the ES register which we have already discussed in earlier chapters, FS and GS can be used to point to auxiliary data to which a program needs less frequent access.

From the application programmer's point of view, as throughout this book, an address is, in effect, calculated by combining a segment address and an offset address. But because the 80386 equivalent of a segment address can be a much more general object, the preferred term is **selector**. Thus, all addresses for the 80386 microprocessor are determined by a selector and an offset.

One of the other differences between the 80386 chip and earlier members of the 8086 family is that 80386 segments are not limited to 64K bytes and may be any size up to 4 gigabytes. It is possible to work with 64K segments in the normal way, but enabling the larger segments allows use of an enriched range of addressing modes. If larger segments are enabled, the corresponding offsets are 32-bit quantities. A physical address is then calculated by somehow converting the contents of the corresponding 16-bit segment register (the selector) to a 32-bit physical address and then the 32-bit offset is added to that.

Because of the two choices of working segment size (limited to 64K or any size) and the length of the corresponding offset pointers (16 bits or 32 bits respectively), the assembler must be told which to use when it converts assembly language instructions into their machine code equivalents. Briefly, this is done via the USE pseudo-op which is described in Section 23.3. Effectively, USE16 selects 16-bit offsets and USE32 selects 32-bit offsets.

If 16-bit offsets are in use then 80386 addressing modes correspond exactly to those for the 8086 microprocessor. However, if 32-bit offsets are in use then the addressing modes available from the 80386 chip are a superset of those available with less powerful members of the 8086 family. All of those addressing modes described in Chapter 13 are available, the main difference being that 80386 32-bit addressing modes do not rely on the use of certain registers in certain roles. Instead, a perfectly general pattern is attached to each of them.

Thus, in register indirect addressing mode *any* of the eight general-purpose 32-bit registers (not just EBX) can be used to specify the indirect address. Also, for any of the addressing modes involving an index (for example, direct indexed addressing), any of the general-purpose registers except ESP can be used as an index – not just EDI or ESI. The same register can even be used twice: both as the base and as an index, as can be seen from the following examples:

```
CMP EDX,[EAX]
MOV CL,[ESP+234H]
INC BYTE PTR [ECX][EAX]
SUB DX,SALES[EAX][EAX]
```

In an addressing mode involving indexing, the register used for the index could be DI or SI, but may – in the 80386 context – be any register other than SP. Also, this index register can have a **scaling factor** of 1, 2, 4 or 8 associated with it. The scaling factor is specified by appending a * to the register name followed by the required scaling factor. Valid examples are:

```
MOV EAX,DOUBLE_ARRAY [EDX*4]
MOV EBX,[ESI*8] [EDI]
ADD MY_WORD_LIST [ECX+2] [EDX*2], AX
```

The contents of the index register are then multiplied by this scaling factor before being used in the relevant instruction.

If two registers are used in one operand, only one of them may have a scaling factor and that register is then defined to be the index register. The other register will be the base register. If scaling is not used, the assembler takes the first register to be the base register. If only one register is used, it is taken to be the base register, regardless of scaling.

Which is the base register is important in determining the segment register that will be used for accessing that particular data item. If the base register is EBP or ESP then the default segment register is SS. For all other base registers, the default segment register is DS. Thus, in:

```
ADD EDX,[EAX] [EBP*2]
```

EAX is the base since it is not scaled and so the default segment register used is DS. In:

```
ADD EDX,[EAX*2][EBP]
```

EBP is the base register since it is not scaled, and so the default segment register used is SS. However, in:

```
ADD EDX,[EAX] [EBP]
```

EDX is the base register since it appears first and so the default segment register is taken to be DS. Finally, in:

```
ADD EDX,[EBP*8]
```

EBP is the base since it is the only register used and hence the default segment register will be SS.

Instructions can mix 16-bit and 32-bit registers for it is perfectly allowable for a 16-bit register to point into a 32-bit segment. However, CX may *not* be used as a 16-bit pointer (though ECX *can* be used as a 32-bit pointer). The effect of such mixed instructions depends on whether 16-bit offsets or 32-bit offsets are being used. Thus:

```
MOV EAX,[BX]
```

makes sense in either case, the 32-bit value pointed to by BX being moved into EAX. However:

```
MOV BX,[EAX]
```

is fine if we are using 32-bit offsets, in which case the 16-bit value pointed to by EAX will be moved into BX. But if we are using 16-bit offsets, then a 32-bit pointer into a 16-bit segment can only be meaningful if the most significant 16 bits of the pointer are zero. Otherwise the processor will generate an error condition.

23.2 General-purpose instructions

The general-purpose (32-bit) instruction set of the 8086 family is a superset of that available with the 8086 microprocessor. Some 8086 instructions run on 32-bit processors unchanged, others have special 32-bit versions but their 16-bit versions will execute unchanged, others require slight changes before they will execute in a 32-bit environment, and others exist only with a 32-bit microprocessor. This section examines each of these possibilities in turn.

23.2.1 No special 32-bit version

Many instructions can simply be used on the new 32-bit register set without change. These include:

```
AAA AAD AAM AAS ADC ADD AND
CBW CLC CLD CLI CMC CMP CWD
DAA DAS DEC
HLT
```

```
IN INC
LEA LOCK
MOV
NEG NOP NOT
OR OUT
REP, REPZ,. . .
STC STD STI SUB
TEST
WAIT
XCHG XOR
```

23.2.2 No change to instruction mnemonic or effect but the detail of execution differs

Another large group of instructions can be used unchanged in programs and with any of the appropriate 32-bit registers, but the details of their execution may be slightly different from their use in, say, an 8086 context. These include:

```
CALL
DIV
IDIV IMUL INT INTO IRET
Jcc JMP
LOOP
MUL
POP POPF PUSH PUSHF
RCL RCR RET ROL ROR
SAHF SAL SAR SBB SHL SHR
XLAT
```

For the most part, the changes are simple extensions to the 32-bit environment. For example, CALL saves the 32-bit contents of EIP on the stack, and IMUL and MUL can multiply a 32-bit number by a 32-bit number with a 64-bit result. However, there is an extended version of IMUL which allows extra operands. The possibilities may be summarized as follows:

```
IMUL reg/mem              ;acc := acc * reg    or
                          ;acc := acc * mem
IMUL reg,reg/mem/num      ;operand1 := operand1 * operand2
IMUL reg,reg/mem,num      ;operand1 := operand2 * operand3
```

where *acc* is one of AL, AX or EAX as appropriate and *num* is an 8-, 16- or 32-bit number as appropriate. Note also, that in the single operand form the result is stored in AX, DX:AX or EDX:EAX according to the size of the operand. With two or three operands, IMUL must have all three operands the same size.

Another exception concerns the execution of PUSH SP on an 80386 or more powerful member of the 8086 family. In this case, the value saved on the stack is the pre-incremented value, whereas for less powerful members of the 8086 family the value is the post-incremented value. Consequently, if, in a program originally written to run on one of the less powerful members of the 8086 family, the exact value pushed on to the stack is important, then changes will have to be made to it before it can be run with the same effect on an 80386 or more powerful microprocessor.

Also, `IRET` is always taken to mean that a 16-bit value should be popped into IP while a new version of `IRET` – to be described in the next section – is used to pop a 32-bit value for EIP.

23.2.3 Instructions which have new versions in advanced processors

The 32-bit equivalents of some of the 16-bit instructions described in earlier chapters have the letter D (for Doubleword) attached to the end of their mnemonic:

`MOVSD` copy a group of 32-bit data items
`LODSD` examine a group of 32-bit data items
`STOSD` initialize a group of 32-bit data items
`CMPSD` 32-bit comparison
`SCASD` scan a group of 32-bit data items
`IRETD` return from an interrupt, but pop 32-bit EIP

Both `SHLD` (SHift Left Double) and `SHRD` (SHift Right Double) which take the formats:

`SHLD` *mem/reg,reg,num* `SHRD` *mem/reg,reg,num*
`SHLD` *mem/reg,reg,*CL `SHRD` *mem/reg,reg,*CL

work in the same way. The first operand is concatenated with the second operand and the resulting value is shifted (respectively) left or right. After execution, the lower order bits of the result of this shift will be in the first operand, the higher order bits in the second operand. Either CL or a 32-bit unsigned number may be used to specify the number of bits to be shifted in the third operand. In any case, the maximum size of a shift is 31 bits and the third operand is masked with 1FH before execution to ensure this.

Others simply have their range extended to include all the 32-bit registers:

`LDS` *reg,mem*
`LES` *reg,mem*
`LFS` *reg,mem*
`LGS` *reg,mem*
`LSS` *reg,mem*

Thus, `LDS` and `LES` are extended (but defined more or less as before) and the 32-bit instructions `LFS`, `LGS` and `LSS` have similar effects. *mem* specifies a pointer consisting of an offset and a selector. The offset is moved into *reg* and the selector is copied into the segment register specified in the instruction mnemonic.

23.2.4 General-purpose 32-bit instructions

These instructions are described in summary form below. An even briefer treatment is given in Table 23.1 which is provided for reference purposes.

BSF ***reg,reg/mem***
BSR ***reg,reg/mem***

BSF (Bit Scan Forward) finds the first bit (working from the lowest order bit to the highest order bit) set to 1 in the word or double word specified by the second operand. BSR (Bit Scan Reverse) finds the last bit set. If the word is all zero, then ZF is set to 1, otherwise ZF is set to 0. In the latter case, the position of the bit found is left in the first operand.

BT ***reg/mem, reg/num_less_than_32***
BTC ***reg/mem, reg/num_less_than_32***

BT (Bit Test) copies the bit of the first operand specified by the second operand into CF. If the second operand is a number it must be in the range 0 to 31 inclusive. If it is held in a register then all possible unsigned values are allowed (even if these are not meaningful). BTC (Bit Test with Complement) is similar except that the complement of the designated bit is copied into CF.

BTR ***reg/mem, reg/num_less_than_32***
BTS ***reg/mem, reg/num_less_than_32***

BTR (Bit Test and Reset) copies the bit of the first operand specified by the second operand into CF and then resets the original bit in the first operand to 0. BTS (Bit Test and Set) copies the bit of the first operand specified by the second operand into CF and then sets the original bit in the first operand to 1.

BOUND ***reg,mem***

This instruction causes a type 5 interrupt if an array index exceeds the bounds on the relevant array. *reg* contains the index and the array's lower bound is pointed to by *mem*, the following location containing the upper bound.

CDQ

CDQ (Convert Doubleword to Quadword) converts the 32-bit signed number in EAX to a 64-bit signed equivalent in EDX,EAX.

CWDE

CWDE (Convert Word to Doubleword Extended) converts the 16-bit signed number in AX to a 32-bit signed equivalent in EAX.

`ENTER` ***number,number***

This instruction is used to `ENTER` a new stack frame. It automatically sets up the stack frame used by high-level languages like Pascal for procedure entry. In the form

```
ENTER n,0
```

it is equivalent to the instructions:

```
PUSH EBP
MOV EBP,ESP
SUB ESP,n
```

which saves the previous frame pointer (EBP), sets the frame to the current top of stack (ESP), and allocates space for local variables. Parameters passed to the corresponding procedure are therefore addressed as positive offsets from EBP while local variables are addressed as negative offsets from EBP (as in Sections 8.7 and 13.1).

Use of this instruction with a second operand greater than 0 will only be possible when the relevant high-level language allows nesting of procedure definitions. Then, the second operand specifies the number of pointers to previous stack frames which are to be pushed on to the stack to allow addressing of stack-resident variables whose scopes are outside the current stack frame.

`LEAVE`

This instruction is used to `LEAVE` the current stack frame. Thus, `ENTER` is executed immediately after a procedure call to set up a new stack frame, whereas `LEAVE` is executed prior to the final `RET` in order to release the returning procedure's stack frame.

`LEAVE` is equivalent to

```
MOV ESP,EBP
POP EBP
```

`INSB,INSW,INSD` **string input from 32-bit I/O port**
`OUTSB,INSW,INSD` **output to a 32-bit I/O port**

`INS` (INput String from an I/O port) and `OUTS` (OUTput String to an I/O port) are I/O counterparts of `LODS`, `STOS`, and so on. For `INS`, the location specified by EDI (relative to ES) receives data from the I/O port specified in DX. After that, EDI is adjusted by one (`INSB`), two (`INSW`), or four (`INSD`). If DF is 0 the adjustment is an increment, if DF is 1 the adjustment is a decrement. `OUTS` is similar but the string pointed to by ESI is sent to the I/O port specified in DX.

`MOVSX` ***reg,reg/mem***
`MOVZX` ***reg,reg/mem***

`MOVSX` (MOVe with Sign eXtension) and `MOVZX` (MOVe with Zero eXtension) copy the second operand into the first operand and, respectively, either sign extend or zero extend the second operand to do so. An 8-bit operand may be extended to 16-bit or 32-bit form, and a 16-bit operand may be extended to a 32-bit form. Sign extension is performed by duplicating the highest order bit of the second operand throughout the upper bits of the first. Zero extension is performed by filling the upper bits of the first operand with zeros.

PUSHA
PUSHAD

PUSHA stores a copy of all eight 16-bit registers (AX, CX, DX, BX, SP, BP, SI and DI) on the stack. The value of SP which is saved is the one it had before execution of this instruction began. In detail, the effect of PUSHA is therefore:

```
temp := SP
PUSH AX
PUSH CX
PUSH DX
PUSH BX
PUSH temp
PUSH BP
PUSH SI
PUSH DI
```

PUSHAD is similar except that the eight 32-bit general registers (EAX, ECX, EDX, EBX, ESP, EBP, ESI and EDI) are saved on the stack.

POPA
POPAD

POPA retrieves the values of the 16-bit general-purpose registers from the stack assuming they were put there by PUSHA. However, the value of SP retrieved from the stack is ignored. Thus, the effect of POPA is:

```
POP DI
POP SI
POP BP
ADD ESP,2
POP BX
POP DX
POP CX
POP AX
```

POPAD is similar except that (1) the values retrieved are for the 32-bit general registers which POPAD assumes were stored on the stack by use of PUSHAD, and, (2) in order to ignore the retrieved value for ESP, 4 is added to ESP after popping BP.

Table 23.1 8086-family 32-bit instructions for applications development.

Instruction	*Purpose*
`BSF` *reg,reg/mem* `BSR` *reg,reg/mem*	Bit Scan Forward finds the first bit set to 1 in the word or double word specified by the second operand. Bit Scan Reverse finds the last bit set. The position of the bit found is left in the first operand.
`BT` *reg/mem, reg/num* `BTC` *reg/mem, reg/num*	Bit Test copies the bit of the first operand specified by the second operand into CF. Bit Test with Complement is similar except that the complement of the designated bit is copied into CF.
`BTR` *reg/mem, reg/num* `BTS` *reg/mem, reg/num*	Bit Test and Reset copies the bit of the first operand specified by the second operand into CF and then resets the original bit in the first operand to 0. Bit Test and Set copies the bit of the first operand specified by the second operand into CF and then sets the original bit in the first operand to 1.
`BOUND` *reg,mem*	Causes a type 5 interrupt if an array index exceeds the bounds of the array with lower bound pointed to by *mem*, the following location containing the upper bound and *reg* indexing the array element.
`CDQ`	Convert Doubleword to Quadword converts the 32-bit signed number in EAX to a 64-bit signed equivalent in EDX,EAX.
`CWDE`	Convert Word to Doubleword Extended converts the 16-bit signed number in AX to a 32-bit signed equivalent in EAX.
`ENTER` *num,num*	ENTER a new stack frame.
`LEAVE`	LEAVE the current stack frame.
`INSB, INSW, INSD` `OUTSB, INSW, INSD`	INput String from a 32-bit I/O port. OUTput String to a 32-bit I/O port. These are I/O counterparts of `LODS`, `STOS`, and so on.
`MOVSX` *reg,reg/mem* `MOVZX` *reg,reg/mem*	MOVe with Sign eXtension and MOVe with Zero eXtension: copy the second operand into the first operand and, respectively, either sign extend or zero extend the second operand to do so.
`PUSHA POPA` `PUSHAD POPAD`	Store and retrieve a copy of all eight 16-bit (PUSHA, POPA) and 32-bit (PUSHAD, POPAD) registers on the stack.
`PUSHFD` `POPFD`	Store and retrieve the 32-bit EFLAGS register.
`SET`*cc reg/mem*	Operand set to 1 if the condition *cc* is true, or to 0 if it is not.

```
PUSHFD
POPFD
```

PUSHFD and POPFD respectively push the 32-bit EFLAGS register on to and pop it from the stack.

SET ***cc reg/mem***

This instruction sets its operand to 1 if the condition denoted by *cc* is true, or to 0 if it is not. The same range of conditions is provided as for the J*cc* instruction. Thus, we can have SETZ, SETNZ, SETC, SETNC, SETA, SETNA, SETG, SETNG, and so on.

23.3 Assembly language for 32-bit operation

When the target machine is a 32-bit member of the 8086 family such as the 80386 microprocessor, the types of change necessary for working in assembly language resemble those which have to be made within the instruction set. Thus, some assembly language facilities have extended ranges or capabilities to match the 32-bit microprocessor's capabilities, while there are new pseudo-ops to enable programmers to use the newly available instructions at the assembly language level. In this section we shall consider just a handful of the most important new pseudo-ops, and one important pseudo-op extension. These are summarized in Table 23.2.

.386

This enables assembly of the non-privileged instructions of the 80386 microprocessor (that is, the instructions provided for applications development). It also enables 80387 coprocessor instructions. This pseudo-op must be given outside of a SEGMENT. . .ENDS definition.

.386P

This is equivalent to the .386 pseudo-op except that it also enables assembly of the privileged instructions of the 80386 microprocessor (that is, the instructions provided for operating systems development). This pseudo-op must be given outside of a SEGMENT. . .ENDS definition.

USE

Available for the 80386 microprocessor and higher members of the 8086 family only, the USE type is another category of qualifier given in the SEGMENT. . .ENDS pseudo-op. Thus, in the 80386 environment, its most general form extends that given in Section 14.2 as follows:

```
<seg_name> SEGMENT <align_type><combine_type><use_type><class_name>
                .
                .
                .
           ENDS
```

The *<use_type>* can only be employed in the .386 context and must be either USE16 or USE32. USE16 selects 16-bit segments whereas USE32 selects 32-bit segments and allows the assembler to accept the full range of 80386 addressing modes. Since USE32 allows access to the full addressing space of the 80386 microprocessor and higher members of the 8086 family, it is really only of interest to operating systems programmers. Applications development can be completely undertaken via USE16 and 16-bit segments.

DF

DF (Define Farword) is normally only used with the 80386 microprocessor or higher members of the 8086 family and allows a name to be associated with storage for a 6-byte quantity. This is very useful when storing far pointers to subroutines since, if USE32 has been selected, such a far pointer to a routine will consist of 48 bits: 16 bits for the segment and 32 bits for the offset. In that case,

Table 23.2 Some pseudo-ops for 32-bit 8086-family assembly language programming.

Pseudo-op	*Purpose*
.386	Enables assembly of the non-privileged instructions of the 80386 microprocessor and for the 80387 coprocessor instructions. Must be given outside of a SEGMENT. . .ENDS definition.
.386P	Equivalent to the .386 pseudo-op but also enables assembly of the privileged instructions of the 80386 microprocessor. Must be given outside of a SEGMENT. . .ENDS definition.
USE*n*	Can only be employed in the .386 context: must be either USE16 or USE32. USE16 selects 16-bit segments. USE32 selects 32-bit segments and allows the assembler to accept the full range of 80386 addressing modes.
DF	Define Farword allows a name to be associated with storage for a 6-byte quantity.
RECORD	As described in Chapter 17, but with the 80386 chip and higher members of the 8086 family, RECORDs can consist of up to 32-bits provided .386 has been used to set the assembler into 80386 mode.

its format will be as follows:

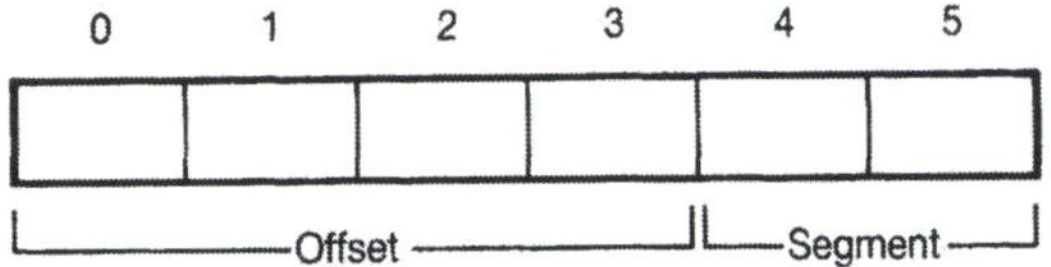

RECORD

With the 80386 microprocessor and higher members of the 8086 family, RECORDs can be doubleword variables (that is, consist of up to 32 bits) provided .386 has been used to set the assembler into 80386 mode. If the total field width is 8 bits or less the assembler uses 1 byte; if the total field width is 9 to 16 bits, the assembler uses two bytes, and if the total width is larger than 16 bits the assembler uses 4 bytes.

23.4 Running 32-bit programs under DOS

At the time of writing, DOS does not allow the use of the operating system construction instructions provided with the 80386 microprocessor and higher members of the 8086 family. Consequently, running 32-bit 8086-family programs under DOS is very similar to running the other 8086-family programs in this book. From our point of view DOS does not operate any differently with the more powerful processors like the 80386 microprocessor, than for the (relatively) humble 8086 microprocessor. We have simply to use the new applications development instruction repertoire, and everything else works more or less the same.

We are limited to 16-bit segments (it was pointed out earlier that this is not a major restriction for the applications programmer), so these must always be defined via the USE16 directive. 32-bit registers can be used for calculations and can be used as pointers into 16-bit segments; it is the programmer's responsibility to ensure that a 32-bit register so used actually contains a valid 16-bit offset address.

Let us now consider a complete example program which runs under DOS on computers with an 8086-family microprocessor which can execute 32-bit instructions (for example, the 80386 microprocessor). As usual, our method in the program has been chosen to illustrate certain features of the 32-bit instruction set. You should easily spot better ways of achieving the same end. It is an exercise to re-implement the example once you have tried it out.

23.4.1 A complete example program using 32-bit instructions

To illustrate 8086-family assembly language programming in a 32-bit environment, Figure 23.3 contains a complete program which displays textual data in neatly arranged rows and columns on the display screen. The program first asks its user for three parameters: the number of rows to be displayed (which should be in the range 1–20), the number of columns of data to be displayed (which should be in the range 1–80) and the width of each column of data (the number of characters in the range 1–39).

Three typical dialogs with the program might therefore be:

(1) Number of rows: 3
Number of columns: 4
Width of columns: 5

12345 27834 67910 10203
27839 01947 28019 55738
75028 50275 46705 10293

(2) Number of rows: 6
Number of columns: 10
Width of columns: 2

12 34 52 78 34 67 91 01 02 03
27 83 90 19 47 28 01 95 57 38
75 02 85 02 75 46 70 51 02 93
45 93 48 03 90 78 20 49 30 32
73 29 96 37 13 43 90 86 92 49
10 56 85 49 30 47 59 37 49 54

(3) Number of rows: 2
Number of columns: 2
Width of columns: 20

12345278346791010203 27839019472801955738
75028502754670510293 45934803907820493032

```
.386

CR EQU ODH
LF EQU OAH
SPACE EQU 20H

DATA SEGMENT USE16
        ROWS_MESSAGE      DB 'Number of rows: ','$'
        COLS_MESSAGE      DB 'Number of columns: ','$'
        COL_WIDTH_MESSAGE DB 'Width of columns: ','$'

        ROWS         DW 0
        COLUMNS      DW 0
        COL_WIDTH    DW 0
        DISPLAY_DATA DB '12345278346791010203'
                     DB '27839019472801955738'
```

Figure 23.3 Program to display data in columns.

```
                     DB '75028502754670510293'
                     DB '45934803907820493032'
                     DB '73299637134390869249'
                     DB '10568549304759374954'
       ERROR_MESSAGE DB 'LINE WIDTH TOO BIG TO FIT ON SCREEN',CR,LF,'$
DATA ENDS

WORKING_STORAGE SEGMENT STACK USE16
        DW 100H DUP(?)
WORKING_STORAGE ENDS

CODE SEGMENT USE16
ASSUME CS:CODE,DS:DATA,SS:WORKING_STORAGE
;set up data segment addressability
 START: MOV   AX,DATA
        MOV   DS,AX
;read rows
        MOV   EDX,OFFSET ROWS_MESSAGE
        CALL  NUM_READ
        MOV   BYTE PTR ROWS,BL
;read columns
        MOV   EDX,OFFSET COLS_MESSAGE
        CALL  NUM_READ
        MOV   BYTE PTR COLUMNS,BL
;read col_width
        MOV   EDX,OFFSET COL_WIDTH_MESSAGE
        CALL  NUM_READ
        MOV   BYTE PTR COL_WIDTH,BL
;if (columns - 1) * (col_width - 1) + col_width <= 80 then
        MOV   AX,COLUMNS
        MOV   BX,COL_WIDTH
        DEC   AX
        DEC   BX
        IMUL  AX,BX
        MOV   BX,COL_WIDTH
        ADD   AX,BX
        CMP   AX,80D
        JA    TOO_BIG
        ;for AX := 1 to rows do
        MOV   AX,1
           ;begin
           ;for BX := 1 to columns do
  NEXT_ROW: MOV BX,1
               ;begin
               ;for CX := 1 to col_width do
   NEXT_COLUMN: MOV CX,1
                    ;begin
         NEXT_CHAR: PUSH AX
                    PUSH BX
                    PUSH CX
                    ;EAX := (AX - 1) * (columns * col_width) +
                    ;(BX - 1) * col_width + (CX - 1)
                    DEC   AX
                    DEC   BX
                    DEC   CX
```

Figure 23.3
(cont.)

```
                        IMUL AX,COLUMNS
                        IMUL AX,COL_WIDTH
                        IMUL BX,COL_WIDTH
                        MOVSX EAX,AX
                        MOVSX EBX,BX
                        MOVSX ECX,CX
                        ADD EAX,EBX
                        ADD EAX,ECX
                        ;display character at DISPLAY_DATA[EAX]
                        MOV DL,DISPLAY_DATA[EAX]
                        CALL PRINTCHAR
                        POP CX
                        POP BX
                        POP AX
                        ;end;
                        CMP CX,COL_WIDTH
                        JZ CHECK_SPACE
                        INC CX
                        JMP NEXT_CHAR
                   ;if  BX < 80 then display a space
      CHECK_SPACE: CMP  BX,80D
                   JE   NO_SPACE
                   MOV  DL,SPACE
                   CALL PRINTCHAR
                   ;end;
         NO_SPACE: CMP  BX,COLUMNS
                   JZ   NEW_LINE
                   INC  BX
                   JMP  NEXT_COLUMN
              ;display a new line
     NEW_LINE: CALL PRINTNEWLINE
              ;end;
              CMP AX,ROWS
              JZ  FINISH
              INC AX
              JMP NEXT_ROW
              ;else display an error message
      TOO_BIG: MOV EDX,OFFSET ERROR_MESSAGE
              MOV AH,9
              INT 21H
        ;display a new line;
FINISH: CALL PRINTNEWLINE
;return to DOS
        MOV AX,4C00H
        INT 21H

NUM_READ PROC NEAR
        ;display message
        MOV AH,9
        INT 21H
        ;read an ASCII digit code
        CALL READCHAR
        ;convert to numeric
        SUB AL,30H
        CBW
```

Figure 23.3
(*cont.*)

```
            ;prepare for two-digit number
            IMUL BX,AX,10D
            ;read next character
            CALL READCHAR
            ;if it is an ASCII digit code
            CMP  AL,CR
            JZ   NOT_DIGIT
            ;then begin
                 ;convert it to a number
                     SUB AL,30H
                 ;and add it to BL
                     ADD BL,AL
                 ;read the next character which must be a CR
                     CALL READCHAR
                 ;end;
                     JMP DONE
            ;else restore BL to correct single digit value
NOT_DIGIT:MOVSX AX,BL
            MOV CL,10D
            IDIV CL
            MOV BL,AL
     DONE: CALL PRINTNEWLINE
            RET
 NUM_READ  ENDP

READCHAR  PROC NEAR
            MOV AH,1
            INT 21H
            RET
READCHAR  ENDP

PRINTCHAR PROC NEAR
            MOV AH,2
            INT 21H
            RET
PRINTCHAR ENDP

PRINTNEWLINE PROC NEAR
            MOV DL,CR
            CALL PRINTCHAR
            MOV DL,LF
            CALL PRINTCHAR
            RET
PRINTNEWLINE ENDP

CODE ENDS
END START
```

Figure 23.3 (*cont.*)

(As shown, the program is very inefficient. Can you see why? A good exercise at this stage would be to re-write the program so that it still works in exactly the same way but without the ineffiicient programming.)

23.5 Brief overview of instructions for operating system construction

In order that a given applications program cannot interfere with another during multi-tasking, or with the operating system itself, each program is assigned a **privilege level**. Briefly, a group of memory locations can only be accessed if the program that wishes to access them has the necessary privilege level. Instructions are provided to control this mechanism which can only be used if the microprocessor is running in **privileged mode**. Thus, `ARPL` (Adjust Requested Privilege Level) can be used when running in privileged mode to ensure that a request for access to a memory location is not exceeding the privilege level assigned to a given application program. Similarly, `VERR` (Verify Read Access) and `VERW` (Verify Write Access) can be used to verify that a program can, respectively, read from or write to a memory location without violating its privilege level.

A generalized form of the `MOV` instruction can be used to enter and leave privileged mode on 80386 microprocessors and higher members of the 8086 family, but two special instructions are provided for this with the 80286, namely `LMSW` (Load Machine Status Word) and `SMSW` (Save Machine Status Word).

Many of the privileged mode instructions concern **descriptor tables**. Put simply, in virtual mode, the values in segment registers are regarded as pointers to these descriptor tables which are then used to effect the translation of a virtual address into a physical address. During execution, the operating system needs access to the **global descriptor table** and a **local descriptor table** for the currently executing task. Each task has its own local descriptor table whereas the global descriptor table is shared between all the programs running on the machine. The global descriptor table refers to space occupied by the operating system and shared data and library routines. There is also an **interrupt descriptor table** which is used to implement the interrupt mechanism in the virtual memory context. The relevant privileged mode instructions for accessing these descriptor tables are as follows:

`LGDT` Load Global Descriptor Table
`SGDT` Store Global Descriptor Table

`LIDT` Load Interrupt Descriptor Table
`SIDT` Save Interrupt Descriptor Table

`LLDT` Load Local Descriptor Table
`SLDT` Save Local Descriptor Table

Tasks are identified by a value which is held in the **task register**. It also has a significant role to play in the reduction of virtual addresses to physical addresses. The relevant privileged mode instructions are `LTR` (Load Task Register) and `STR` (Store Task Register).

`LAR` (Load Access Rights) allows a program to determine whether a virtual memory segment is accessible to it without causing a memory protection fault. If this is the case, then LSL (Load Segment Limit) enables the offset of the last addressable byte in that virtual segment to be loaded into a register. Finally, CLTS (Clear Task Switched Flag) is used to control interaction with the 80*n*87 family of numeric coprocessors.

SUMMARY

This chapter began by demonstrating how easy it is to extend our knowledge of the 8086 family into the 32-bit world of microprocessors such as the 80386 microprocessor: generally speaking, for applications program development fairly minor modifications and extensions to our previous way of working are all that is required.

On the other hand, the very last part of the chapter was nothing more than a launch pad for those interested in the use of 8086-family assembly language for operating systems development. The best next step is a detailed study of operating system design and construction followed by a detailed study of the Intel literature on the privileged mode instructions. There is no apology for this cyclic structure of the text, however, which has many parallels, even in the world of classical music. Indeed, the title of one such composition – '*Mon fin est mon commencement*' (My end is my beginning) – written nearly half a century ago, could hardly be more apposite. I say this, not necessarily to warn my family as to what may next tempt me to neglect them, but rather to reassure the reader that one journey usually stimulates consideration of another. *A bientôt, mes amis*!

SELF-CHECK QUIZ

1. Write a program fragment which uses EAX, EBX, ECX and EDX to evaluate the expression:

   (84000000H + 26000000H) – (7234A5H * 2)

   and show the contents of the EFLAGS register after execution of your program fragment.

2. Write a program fragment to verify that the 16 bits of AX form the least significant 16 bits of EAX.

3. Write a program fragment which would be illegal for the 8086 microprocessor (because in certain addressing modes it uses registers which are not allowed) but which is legal for the 80386 microprocessor and higher members of the 8086-family.

4. Write a program fragment to store in memory the values of $2^n - 1$ for $n = 1,2,\ldots,30$.

5. Write a program fragment to store in memory a

table of values I, P, T, R where

$$I = (D * T * R) / 100$$

and $D = 5000$, $T = 1,2,3,\ldots,25$ and $R = 15$. (If D is an amount of money in dollars, T is time in years and R is the interest rate as a percentage, then I is the simple interest payable on \$$D$ invested for T years at R% rate of annual interest.)

6. Do you think an assembly language program written using 80386 instructions would be easier for an experienced programmer to read and understand than one which uses 8086 instructions? Explain your answer.

7. Assuming the serial port addresses given in Chapter 20 are the same, write a program fragment to show how you could take advantage of the `INSB` and `OUTSB` instructions in writing a serial I/O driver.

8. The hardware has been arranged so that a set of indicator lights can be controlled by setting bits in EAX. The most significant two bits denote the color of the light which is to be turned on

00 green
01 yellow
10 orange
11 red

the next significant 8 bits specify the length of time for which that light is to be turned on in seconds, the next significant bit denotes whether the light should be on constantly (1) or blink (0), the next bit whether a car is approaching the lights (1) or is not (0), and the next 8 bits specifying the speed of the approaching car in miles per hour as an unsigned number.

Write program fragments:

(a) to turn on a blinking green light for 60 seconds; and

(b) to turn on a constant green light for 30 seconds if a car is approaching at more than 50 mph.

9. Write as many different program fragments in 80386 assembly language as you can think of which could be used to evaluate the expression:

$$(8 * n) + 1$$

10. List some of the instructions you would have liked to have seen in the 80386 instruction set but which the designers did not provide. Explain the advantages of those you propose.

The ASCII Character Set

APPENDIX I

Control codes

Character		*Binary*	*Hex*	*Decimal*
NUL	Null	00000000	00	0
SOH	Start of heading	00000001	01	1
STX	Start of text	00000010	02	2
ETC	End of text	00000011	03	3
EOT	End of transmission	00000100	04	4
ENQ	Enquiry	00000101	05	5
ACK	Acknowledge	00000110	06	6
BEL	Bell	00000111	07	7
BS	Backspace	00001000	08	8
HT	Horizontal tabulation	00001001	09	9
LF	Line feed	00001010	0A	10
VT	Vertical tabulation	00001011	0B	11
FF	Form feed	00001100	0C	12
CR	Carriage return	00001101	0D	13
SO	Shift out	00001110	0E	14
SI	Shift in	00001111	0F	15
DLE	Data link escape	00010000	10	16
DC1	Device control 1	00010001	11	17
DC2	2	00010010	12	18
DC3	3	00010011	13	19
DC4	4	00010100	14	20
NAK	Negative acknowledge	00010101	15	21
SYN	Synchronous idle	00010110	16	22
ETB	End of transmission block	00010111	17	23
CAN	Cancel	00011000	18	24
EM	End of medium	00011001	19	25
SUB	Substitute	00011010	1A	26
ESC	Escape	00011011	1B	27
FS	File separator	00011100	1C	28
GS	Group separator	00011101	1D	29
RS	Record separator	00011110	1E	30
US	Unit separator	00011111	1F	31
DEL	Delete	01111111	7F	127

The printable character codes

Character	*Binary*	*Hex*	*Dec*	*Character*	*Binary*	*Hex*	*Dec*
SPACE	00100000	20	32	P	01010000	50	80
!	00100001	21	33	Q	01010001	51	81
″	00100010	22	34	R	01010010	52	82
#	00100011	23	35	S	01010011	53	83
$	00100100	24	36	T	01010100	54	84
%	00100101	25	37	U	01010101	55	85
&	00100110	26	38	V	01010110	56	86
′	00100111	27	39	W	01010111	57	87
(	00101000	28	40	X	01011000	58	88
)	00101001	29	41	Y	01011001	59	89
*	00101010	2A	42	Z	01011010	5A	90
+	00101011	2B	43	[	01011011	5B	91
,	00101100	2C	44	\	01011100	5C	92
–	00101101	2D	45	]	01011101	5D	93
.	00101110	2E	46	^	01011110	5E	94
/	00101111	2F	47	_	01011111	5F	95
0	00110000	30	48	$	01100000	60	96
1	00110001	31	49	a	01100001	61	97
2	00110010	32	50	b	01100010	62	98
3	00110011	33	51	c	01100011	63	99
4	00110100	34	52	d	01100100	64	100
5	00110101	35	53	e	01100101	65	101
6	00110110	36	54	f	01100110	66	102
7	00110111	37	55	g	01100111	67	103
8	00111000	38	56	h	01101000	68	104
9	00111001	39	57	i	01101001	69	105
:	00111010	3A	58	j	01101010	6A	106
;	00111011	3B	59	k	01101011	6B	107
<	00111100	3C	60	l	01101100	6C	108
=	00111101	3D	61	m	01101101	6D	109
>	00111110	3E	62	n	01101110	6E	110
?	00111111	3F	63	o	01101111	6F	111
@	01000000	40	64	p	01110000	70	112
A	01000001	41	65	q	01110001	71	113
B	01000010	42	66	r	01110010	72	114
C	01000011	43	67	s	01110011	73	115
D	01000100	44	68	t	01110100	74	116
E	01000101	45	69	u	01110101	75	117
F	01000110	46	70	v	01110110	76	118
G	01000111	47	71	w	01110111	77	119
H	01001000	48	72	x	01111000	78	120
I	01001001	49	73	y	01111001	79	121
J	01001010	4A	74	z	01111010	7A	122
K	01001011	4B	75	{	01111011	7B	123
L	01001100	4C	76	|	01111100	7C	124
M	01001101	4D	77	}	01111101	7D	125
N	01001110	4E	78	~	01111110	7E	126
O	01001111	4F	79				

The Calculator Simulator

APPENDIX II

```
CR EQU ODH
LF EQU OAH
DOLLAR EQU '$'

DATA SEGMENT
POWERS_TABLE DD 10000000
             DD 1000000
             DD 100000
             DD 10000
             DD 1000
             DD 100
             DD 10
             DD 1

TOO_BIG_MESS  DB 'NUMBER TOO BIG — RESTART CALCULATION',CR,LF,DOLLAR
ILLEGAL_MESS  DB 'ILLEGAL CHARACTER — RESTART CALCULATION',CR,LF,DOLLAR
ZERO_DIV_MESS DB 'DIVISION BY ZERO NOT ALLOWED',CR,LF,DOLLAR
DATA ENDS

WORKING_STORAGE SEGMENT STACK
       DW 100H DUP(?)
WORKING_STORAGE ENDS

CODE SEGMENT
ASSUME DS:DATA, SS:WORKING_STORAGE, CS:CODE
 MAIN PROC NEAR
 ;establish data segment addressability
       MOV AX,DATA
       MOV DS,AX
 ;repeat
     ;digits_read := 5;
         START: MOV CH,5
     ;while digits_read = 5 or code <> 1 do
          TEST: CMP CH,5
                JZ  READ_1ST_DECIMAL
                CMP CL,1
```

```
                        JNZ READ_1ST_DECIMAL
                        JMP READ_2ND_DECIMAL
                  ;begin
                  ;print(newline);
            READ_1ST_DECIMAL: CALL PRINT_NEWLINE
                              CALL GET_OK_NUM_AND_TERM_NON_SPACE_CHAR
                  ;if digits_read = 5 then print(too long)
                              CMP  CH,5
                              JNZ  TRY_CODE
                              CALL TOO_LONG
                  ;if code <> 1 then print(illegal character)
                    TRY_CODE: CMP CL,1
                              JZ   NO_NUM_BEFORE_OPERATOR
                              CALL ILLEGAL_CHAR
                  ;if digits_read = 0 and code = 1 then
      NO_NUM_BEFORE_OPERATOR: CMP  CL,1
                              JNZ  END_FIRST_WHILE
                              CMP  CH,0
                              JNZ  END_FIRST_WHILE
                              ;begin
                              ;print(illegal character)
                                    CALL ILLEGAL_CHAR
                              ;code := 0
                                    MOV  CL,0
                        ;end;
             END_FIRST_WHILE: JMP    TEST
            ;preserve operator and operand on the stack
            ;call GET_OK_NUM_AND_TERM_NON_SPACE_CHAR
      READ_2ND_DECIMAL: PUSH AX
                        PUSH BX
                        CALL GET_OK_NUM_AND_TERM_NON_SPACE_CHAR
            ;if digits_read = 5 then begin clear stack;print(too long) end
                        CMP  CH,5
                        JNZ  TRY_DO_SUM
                        POP  BX
                        POP  AX
                        CALL TOO_LONG
                        JMP  REPEAT_LOOP
            ;else if digits_read <> 0 and code = 2 then begin
             TRY_DO_SUM: CMP  CH,0
                        JZ   NO_DIGITS
                        CMP  CL,2
                        JNZ  NO_DIGITS
            ;pop operand and operator
                        POP  AX
                        POP  DX          ;operand into DL
            ;case operator of . . .
                        CMP  DL,'+'
                        JZ   PLUS
                        CMP  DL,'-'
                        JZ   MINUS
                        CMP  DL,'*'
                        JZ   STAR
                        CMP  DL,'/'
                        JZ   SLASH
```

```
             JMP   REPEAT_LOOP
       PLUS: CALL DOPLUS
             JMP   REPEAT_LOOP
      MINUS: CALL DOSUB
             JMP   REPEAT_LOOP
       STAR: CALL DOMULT
             JMP   REPEAT_LOOP
      SLASH: CALL DODIVISION
             JMP   REPEAT_LOOP
    ;else begin clear stack; print(illegal character) end
    NO_DIGITS: POP  AX
             POP  BX
             CALL ILLEGAL_CHAR
;forever
   REPEAT_LOOP: JMP  START
MAIN ENDP

;****************************************************************************

        GET_OK_NUM_AND_TERM_NON_SPACE_CHAR: MOV BX,OH
        ;code:=3
               MOV CL,3
        ;digits_read :=0;
               MOV CH,0
        ;repeat read(char) until char <> ' ';
      SKIP_SPACES: CALL READCHAR
                  CMP  AL, ' '
                  JZ   SKIP_SPACES
        ;while char in ['0' .. '9'] and digits_read <> 4 do
      CHECK_NUMERIC: CMP AL,'0'
                    JB  MISS_TRAIL_SPACES
                    CMP AL,'9'
                    JA  MISS_TRAIL_SPACES
                    CMP CH,4
                    JZ  MISS_TRAIL_SPACES
                    ;begin
                    ;digits_read := digits_read + 1
                    INC CH
                    ;BX :=BX * 10D + binary_value_of(char)
                    MOV CL,AL  ;copy the contents of AL for safe
                               ;keeping
                    MOV AX,10D
                    MUL BX
                    MOV BX,AX  ;BX now contains 10D times its
                               ;previous contents
                    MOV AL,CL  ;restore AL
                    SUB AL,30H ;retrieve numeric value from character
                    MOV AH,0H  ;prepare AX for 16-bit addition
                    ADD BX,AX
                    ;read(char)
                    CALL READCHAR
                    ;end
                    JMP CHECK_NUMERIC
         ;while char = ' ' do read(char)
      MISS_TRAIL_SPACES: CMP  AL,' '
```

```
                        JNZ   IS_THIS_FIFTH_DIGIT
                        CALL  READCHAR
                        JMP   MISS_TRAIL_SPACES
        ;if char in ['0' .. '9'] then digits_read := digits_read +1
      IS_THIS_FIFTH_DIGIT: CMP AL,'0'
                         JB  TRY_OPERATOR
                         CMP AL,'9'
                         JA  TRY_EQUALS
                         INC CH
                         JMP DONE_THIS
        ;else if char in ['+','-','*','/'] then CL := 1
      TRY_OPERATOR: CMP AL,'+'
                    JZ   GOT_OPERATOR
                    CMP  AL,'-'
                    JZ   GOT_OPERATOR
                    CMP  AL,'*'
                    JZ   GOT_OPERATOR
                    CMP  AL,'/'
                    JZ   GOT_OPERATOR
        ;else if char = '=' then CL := 2
        TRY_EQUALS: CMP AL,'='
                    JNZ DONE_THIS
                    MOV  CL,2
                    JMP DONE_THIS
      GOT_OPERATOR: MOV CL,1
         DONE_THIS: RET

;**************************************************************************
        DOPLUS: CALL ADDITION
                CALL PRINTOUT
                RET

;**************************************************************************
           DOSUB: CALL SUBTRACTION
                  ;check if result was negative
                  JNB   RESULT_NOT_NEG
                  ;if so print minus sign
                  PUSH DX
                  MOV   DL,'-'
                  CALL PRINTCHAR
                  POP   DX
                  ;then negate DX,CX
                  MOV   BX,DX
                  MOV   AX,CX
                  MOV   DX,0
                  MOV   CX,0
                  CALL BIG_SUB
                  ;now convert to decimal and print
RESULT_NOT_NEG:   CALL PRINTOUT
                  RET

;**************************************************************************

     DOMULT: CALL MULTIPLICATION
             CALL PRINTOUT
             RET
```

```
;***************************************************************************

    DODIVISION:CMP  BX,0                  ;check for division by zero
               JZ   DIVISION_ERROR
           ;otherwise do the division
               CALL DIVISION
            ;print the quotient
               PUSH AX                    ;preserve remainder
               PUSH BX                    ;on stack
               CALL PRINTOUT
               MOV  DL,'R'
               CALL PRINTCHAR             ;print R for Remainder
               POP  DX
               POP  CX                    ;now restore and print
               CALL PRINTOUT              ;remainder
               JMP  DONE_DIV
DIVISION_ERROR: CALL DIVISION_BY_ZERO     ;prints error message
      DONE_DIV: RET

;***************************************************************************

         ;power := 7;
        PRINTOUT:MOV BP,7
                 MOV SI,OFFSET POWERS_TABLE
         ;digit_printed_yet := false
                 MOV BH,0
         ;repeat count := 0
       NEXT_POWER:MOV BL,0
         ;while DX,CX >= 0 do
REMOVE_POWER:      MOV    AX,DX
                          RCL    AX,1
                          JB     ADD_BACK
                ;begin
                ;DX,CX := DX,CX_10^power
                              PUSH BX
                              MOV   AX,[SI]
                              MOV   BX,2[SI]
                              CALL  BIG_SUB
                ;count := count + 1
                              POP   BX
                              INC   BL
                ;end;
                 JMP    REMOVE_POWER
            ;DX,CX := DX,CX + 10^power
            ADD_BACK:  PUSH BX
                       MOV   AX,[SI]
                       MOV   BX,2[SI]
                       CALL  BIG_ADD
            ;count := count-1;
                       POP   BX
                       DEC   BL
            ;if count <> 0 then
                       CMP   BL,0
                       JZ    TRY_COUNT_ZERO
                  ;begin
```

```
                              ;digit_printed_yet := true
                                   MOV   BH,1
                              ;print(count)
                                   ADD   BL,30H
                                   PUSH  DX
                                   MOV   DL,BL
                                   CALL  PRINTCHAR
                                   POP   DX
                              ;end;
                    ;if count = 0 and (digit_printed_yet or power = 0)
 TRY_COUNT_ZERO: CMP   BL,0
                 JNZ   DONE_THIS_POWER
                 CMP   BH,1
                 JZ    PRINT_THIS_ZERO
 TRY_POWER_ZERO: CMP   BP,0
                 JZ    PRINT_THIS_ZERO
                 JMP   DONE_THIS_POWER
                    ;then print(count);
PRINT_THIS_ZERO: PUSH  DX
                 MOV   DL,BL
                 ADD   DL,30H
                 CALL  PRINTCHAR
                 POP   DX
                    ;power := power-1
DONE_THIS_POWER: ADD   SI,4
                 SUB   BP,1
                    ;until power = 0
                 JAE   NEXT_POWER
DONE_ALL_DIGITS: RET

;***************************************************************************

       ADDITION: ADD AX,BX
                 CWD
                 MOV CX,AX
                 RET

;***************************************************************************

    SUBTRACTION: SUB AX,BX
                 CWD
                 MOV CX,AX
                 RET

;***************************************************************************

 MULTIPLICATION: MUL BX
                 MOV CX,AX
                 RET

;***************************************************************************

       DIVISION: MOV DX,0
                 DIV BX
                 MOV CX,AX
```

```
                MOV AX,DX
                MOV DX,0
                MOV BX,0
                RET

;***************************************************************************

       BIG_ADD: ADD CX,AX
                ADC DX,BX
                RET

;***************************************************************************

       BIG_SUB: SUB CX,AX
                SBB DX,BX
                RET

;***************************************************************************

  ILLEGAL_CHAR: CALL  PRINT_NEWLINE
                MOV   AH,09H
                MOV   DX,OFFSET ILLEGAL_MESS
                INT   21H
                RET

;***************************************************************************

      TOO_LONG: CALL  PRINT_NEWLINE
                MOV   AH,09H
                MOV   DX,OFFSET TOO_BIG_MESS
                INT   21H
                RET

;***************************************************************************

DIVISION_BY_ZERO:CALL  PRINT_NEWLINE
                MOV   AH,09H
                MOV   DX,OFFSET ZERO_DIV_MESS
                INT   21H
                RET

;***************************************************************************

      READCHAR: MOV AH,1H
                INT 21H
                RET

;***************************************************************************

     PRINTCHAR: MOV AH,2H
                INT 21H
                RET
;***************************************************************************
 PRINT_NEWLINE: MOV DL,CR
                CALL PRINTCHAR
```

```
                MOV DL,LF
                CALL PRINTCHAR
                RET

;**************************************************************************

CODE ENDS
END MAIN
```

The Text Editor

APPENDIX III

```
LF     EQU 0AH
CR     EQU 0DH
STAR   EQU '*'
COLON  EQU ':'
DOLLAR EQU '$'

DATA SEGMENT
START_OF_TEXT    DB 675D DUP(?)
READ_LINE_BUFFER DB 80D DUP(?)
LINE_LENGTHS     DB 0,0,0,0,0,0,0,0,0

ILLEGAL_MESS DB 'ILLEGAL CHARACTER IN INPUT',CR,LF,DOLLAR
FORMAT_ERROR DB 'SPACE MISSING AFTER COMMAND',CR,LF,DOLLAR
NO_SUCH_LINE DB 'NO SUCH LINE EXISTS.'
             DB 'ILLEGAL CHARACTER IN LINE NUMBER?',CR,LF,DOLLAR
ENTER_ERROR  DB 'A COMMAND MUST BE TERMINATED BY '
             DB 'PRESSING THE ENTER KEY',CR,LF,DOLLAR
TOO_LONG     DB 'STRING TOO LONG',CR,LF,DOLLAR
DELETE_OK    DB 'DELETION COMPLETED',CR,LF,DOLLAR
SWAP_OK      DB 'SWAP COMPLETED',CR,LF,DOLLAR
SEARCH_ERROR DB '%SIGN(S) MISSING IN FIND COMMAND',CR,LF,DOLLAR
FIND_OK      DB 'SEARCH COMPLETED',CR,LF,DOLLAR
DATA ENDS

WORKING_STORAGE SEGMENT STACK
      DW 100H DUP(?)
WORKING_STORAGE ENDS

CODE SEGMENT
       ASSUME DS:DATA,SS:WORKING_STORAGE,CS:CODE

MAIN PROC FAR
;address our program's data segment
       MOV   AX,DATA
       MOV   DS,AX
       MOV   ES,AX ;for string manipulation instructions
```

```
 ;call initialize
       CALL  INITIALIZE
 ;print(prompt)
       MOV   DL,STAR
       CALL  PRINTCHAR
 ;read(char1, char2);
       CALL  READCHAR
       MOV   CL,AL
       CALL  READCHAR ;CL = char1, AL = char2
 ;while not (char1 = E and char2 = CR) do
PROCESS:CMP   CL,'E'
       JNZ   NOT_END
       CMP   AL,CR
       JNZ   NOT_END
       JMP   DONE
    ;begin
    ;if char1 = P and char2 = CR
        NOT_END: CMP   CL,'P'
                 JNZ   TRY_LINE
                 CMP   AL,CR
                 JNZ   TRY_LINE
    ;then print all the text
                 CALL  PRINT_ALL OTEXT
                 JMP   GET_COMMAND
    ;else if char1 = P then print a line
    TRY_LINE:  CMP   CL,'P'
               JNZ   TRY_S
               CALL  PRINT_A_LINE
               JMP   GET_COMMAND
    ;else if char1 = S then call swap
       TRY_S:  CMP   CL,'S'
               JNZ   TRY_N
               CALL  SWAP
               JMP   GET_COMMAND
    ;else if char1 = N then call new_text
       TRY_N:  CMP   CL,'N'
               JNZ   TRY_D
               CALL  NEW_TEXT
               JMP   GET_COMMAND
    ;else if char1 = D then call delete
       TRY_D:  CMP   CL,'D'
               JNZ   TRY_F
               CALL  DELETE
               JMP   GET_COMMAND
    ;else if char1 = F then call find
       TRY_F:  CMP   CL,'F'
               JNZ   ILLEGAL
               CALL  FIND
               JMP   GET_COMMAND
    ;else print(illegal character);
      ILLEGAL:CALL  ILLEGAL_CHARACTER
    ;print(newline);
  GET_COMMAND:  CALL  PRINT_NEWLINE
    ;print(prompt);
               MOV   DL,'*'
```

```
                CALL PRINTCHAR
    ;read(char1, char2);
                CALL READCHAR
                MOV  CL,AL
                CALL READCHAR
    ;end;
                JMP  PROCESS
;return to DOS
    DONE:  MOV AX,4C00H
           INT 21H
MAIN ENDP

;**********************************************************************

ILLEGAL_CHARACTER PROC NEAR
    CALL PRINT_NEWLINE
    MOV  DX,OFFSET ILLEGAL_MESS
    CALL PRINT_STRING
    RET
ILLEGAL_CHARACTER ENDP

;*****************************************************************************

        INITIALIZE PROC NEAR
        ;for i := 1 to 9 do line[i] := (CR,LF,DOLLAR);
                   MOV  CX,9
                   MOV  SI,OFFSET START_OF_TEXT
        INIT_NEXT: MOV  [SI],BYTE PTR CR
                   MOV  1[SI],BYTE PTR LF
                   MOV  2[SI],BYTE PTR DOLLAR
                   ADD  SI,75D
                   LOOP INIT_NEXT
                   RET
        INITIALIZE ENDP

;*****************************************************************************

       PRINT_ALL_TEXT PROC NEAR
       ;for i := 1 to 9 do print(line[i]);
          CALL PRINT_NEWLINE
          MOV  CX,9
          MOV  DX,OFFSET START_OF_TEXT
NEXT_LINE: CALL PRINT_STRING
          ADD  DX,75D  ;set address pointer to next line
          LOOP NEXT_LINE
          RET
       PRINT_ALL_TEXT ENDP

;*****************************************************************************

    VERIFY_RANGE_AND_FORMAT PROC NEAR
    ;if char2 not in ['1' .. '9'] then
        CMP  AL,'1'
        JB   OUT_OF_RANGE
        CMP  AL,'9'
```

```
        JBE   IN_RANGE
            ;begin
            ;set DX to address of error message
OUT_OF_RANGE: MOV DX,OFFSET NO_SUCH_LINE
            ;set AH to indicate error
              MOV   AH,0FFH
            ;end
              JMP   RF_ERROR
    ;else begin
            ;read(char3)
     IN_RANGE:MOV   BL,AL          ;char2 now in BL
              CALL READCHAR
            ;if char3 <> CR then
              CMP   AL,CR
              JZ   RF_OK
              ;begin
              ;set DX to address of error message
                       MOV   DX,OFFSET ENTER_ERROR
              ;set AH to indicate error
                       MOV   AH,0FFH
              ;end
                       JMP   RF_ERROR
            ;else set AH to indicate OK
       RF_OK: MOV AH,0
    RF_ERROR: RET
     VERIFY_RANGE_AND_FORMAT ENDP

;*****************************************************************************

        PRINT_A_LINE PROC NEAR
              CALL VERIFY_RANGE_AND_FORMAT
              CALL PRINT_NEWLINE
        ;if AH <> 0FFH
              CMP   AH,0FFH
              JZ    PRINT_DONE
              ;then begin
                     ;DX:= (BL-31H) * 75D + (OFFSET START_OF_TEXT)
                        SUB BL,31H
                        MOV AL,75D
                        MUL BL
                        MOV DX,AX
                        ADD DX,OFFSET START_OF_TEXT
                     ;call PRINT_STRING
           PRINT_DONE:  CALL PRINT_STRING
                        RET
        PRINT_A_LINE ENDP

;*****************************************************************************

        NEW_TEXT PROC NEAR
                CALL VERIFY_RANGE_AND_FORMAT
                CALL PRINT_NEWLINE
        ;if AH = 0FFH then print error message
                CMP   AH,0FFH
                JNZ   OBEY_NEW
                CALL PRINT_STRING
```

```
        JMP   NEW_DONE
      ;else begin
        ;print (colon prompt)
      OBEY_NEW: CLD
                MOV DL,COLON
                CALL PRINTCHAR
        ;DI := address of READ_LINE_BUFFER
                MOV DI,OFFSET READ_LINE_BUFFER
        ;CX := 73D
                MOV CX,73D
        ;repeat read(char)
    READ_MORE: CALL READCHAR
                ;store char in buffer
                STOSB
        ;until CX = 0 or char = CR
                CMP   AL,CR
                LOOPNZ READ_MORE
                JZ    END_OF_LINE
        ;if char <> CR then print(TOO_LONG)
                MOV   DX,OFFSET TOO_LONG
                CALL  PRINT_STRING
                CALL  PRINT_NEWLINE
                JMP   NEW_DONE
        ;append LF and $ to text in READ_LINE_BUFFER;
   END_OF_LINE: MOV BYTE PTR [DI],LF
                INC DI
                MOV BYTE PTR [DI],DOLLAR
        ;set DI to starting address of buffered text's destination
        ;step 1 - work out number of 75D blocks from START_OF_TEXT
                SUB BL,31H
        ;step 2 - use this to work out start address relative
        ;to START_OF_TEXT
                MOV AL,75D
                MUL BL              ;start address relative to
                                    ;START_OF_TEXT now in AX
        ;set DI to the actual offset address
                MOV DI,AX
                ADD DI,OFFSET START_OF_TEXT
        ;calculate the length of the text in READ_LINE_BUFFER
                MOV DX,75D
                SUB DX,CX           ;length now in DX
                MOV CX,DX           ;save length ready for text move
        ;store the text length in appropriate place
                SUB DL,3            ;remove CR,LF,$ from count
                MOV BH,0            ;BX now contains the line no.-1
                ADD BX,OFFSET LINE_LENGTHS
                MOV [BX],DL         ;save the line length
        ;set SI to point to the buffer
                MOV SI,OFFSET READ_LINE_BUFFER
        ;move the text into place
                REP MOVSB
        ;end
;end
 NEW_DONE: RET
NEW_TEXT ENDP
```

```
;******************************************************************************

        DELETE PROC NEAR
                CALL VERIFY_RANGE_AND_FORMAT
                CALL PRINT_NEWLINE
        ;if AH = 0FFH then print error message
                CMP  AH,0FFH
                JNZ  DO_DELETE
                CALL PRINT_STRING
                JMP  DELETE_DONE
        ;else begin
                ;find start address of line to be deleted
          DO_DELETE: SUB  BL,31H ;our line is this many 75D blocks
                                 ;from start
                     MOV  AL,75D
                     MUL  BL
                     ADD  AX,OFFSET START_OF_TEXT
                ;start address now in AX
                ;insert CR, LF, DOLLAR at beginning of line with this address
                     MOV  SI,AX
                     MOV  BYTE PTR [SI],CR
                     MOV  BYTE PTR 1[SI],LF
                     MOV  BYTE PTR 2[SI],DOLLAR
                ;reset line length to zero
                     MOV  SI,OFFSET LINE_LENGTHS
                     MOV  BH,0H ;BX now contains the line no.-1
                     ADD  SI,BX
                     MOV  [SI],BH
                ;print deletion OK message
                     MOV  DX,OFFSET DELETE_OK
                     CALL PRINT_STRING
                ;end
        DELETE_DONE: RET
        DELETE ENDP

;******************************************************************************

    SWAP PROC NEAR
    ;if AL not in ['1' .. '9'] then print(no such line)
               CMP  al,'1'
               JB   TOO_LOW
               CMP  AL,'9'
               JBE  LINE_NO_OK
    TOO_LOW:   CALL PRINT_NEWLINE
               MOV  DX,OFFSET NO_SUCH_LINE
               CALL PRINT_STRING
               JMP  SWAP_DONE
    ;else begin
    LINE_NO_OK:MOV  CL,AL
           ;read(char)
               CALL READCHAR
               CALL VERIFY_RANGE_AND_FORMAT
           ;print(newline)
               CALL PRINT_NEWLINE
           ;if AH = 0FFH then print error message
               CMP  AH,0FFH
```

```
        JNZ   DO_THE_SWAP
        CALL  PRINT_STRING
        JMP   SWAP_DONE
     ;else begin
             ;swap the recorded line lengths
   DO_THE_SWAP: SUB CL,31H
                SUB BL,31H
                CALL LENGTH_SWAP
             ;DX := address of first text line
                MOV AL,75D
                MUL BL
                ADD AX,OFFSET START_OF_TEXT
                MOV DX,AX
             ;AX := address of second text line
                MOV AL,75D
                MUL CL
                ADD AX,OFFSET START_OF_TEXT
             ;move string pointed to by AX into READ_LINE_BUFFER
                MOV SI,AX
                MOV DI,OFFSET READ_LINE_BUFFER
                MOV CX,75D
                REP MOVSB
             ;move string pointed to by DX to locations
             ;pointed to by AX
                MOV SI,DX
                MOV DI,AX
                MOV CX,75D
                REP MOVSB
             ;copy string in READ_LINE_BUFFER to locations
             ;pointed to by DX
                MOV SI,OFFSET READ_LINE_BUFFER
                MOV DI,DX
                MOV CX,75D
                REP MOVSB
             ;print(swap complete)
                MOV DX,OFFSET SWAP_OK
                CALL PRINT_NEWLINE
                CALL PRINT_STRING
             ;end
     ;end
SWAP_DONE: RET
SWAP ENDP

;***************************************************************************

        LENGTH_SWAP PROC NEAR
        ;preserve BL on the stack
                PUSH BX
                MOV   SI,OFFSET LINE_LENGTHS
        ;set BX to point to offset of the location where
        ;the length of the line referred to by BL is kept
                MOV   BH,0
                ADD   BX,SI
        ;set SI to point to offset of the location where
        ;the length of the line referred to by CL is kept
```

```
                MOV   CH,0
                ADD   SI,CX
        ;swap the lengths
                MOV   AL,[SI]
                XCHG  AL,[BX]
                MOV   [SI],AL
        ;restore the value of BL
                POP   BX
RET
        LENGTH_SWAP ENDP

;*****************************************************************************

        FIND PROC NEAR
        ;if AL <> '%' then DX := address of SEARCH_ERROR message
                  CMP AL,'%'
                  JZ  GET_FIND_STRING
                  MOV DX,OFFSET SEARCH_ERROR
                  JMP FIND_DONE
             ;else begin
                  ;count := 73D;
        GET_FIND_STRING:MOV CX,73D
                  ;point DI to start of READ_LINE_BUFFER
                       MOV DI,OFFSET READ_LINE_BUFFER
                  ;repeat
                       ;call readchar
             MORE_STRING: CALL READCHAR
                       ;store char
                          STOSB
                  ;until char = % or count = 0;
                   CMP    AL,'%'
                   LOOPNZ MORE_STRING
                  ;if count = 0 then DX := address of TOO_LONG message
                   JZ     END_OF_STRING
                   MOV    DX,OFFSET TOO_LONG
                   JMP    FIND_DONE
                  ;else begin
                      ;read(char);
                  END_OF_STRING: CALL READCHAR
                       ;if char <> CR then DX := address of ENTER_ERROR
                                                          ;message
                               CMP   AL,CR
                               JZ    START_SEARCH
                               MOV   DX,OFFSET ENTER_ERROR
                               JMP   FIND_DONE
                           ;else begin
                                  ;BX := length of search text
                         START_SEARCH:MOV BX,73D
                                  SUB BX,CX
                                  DEC BX         ;ignore final % sign
                              ;if BX <> 0 then
                                  CMP BX,0
                                  JZ   FIND_DONE
                                       ;begin
                                        MOV   BP,BX
```

```
                                        CALL PRINT_NEWLINE
                                        CALL LOCATE
                                       ;DX := address of FIND_OK message
                                        MOV  DX,OFFSET FIND_OK
                                       ;end
                                ;end
                    ;end
               ;end
FIND_DONE: CALL PRINT_NEWLINE
           CALL PRINT_STRING
           RET
          FIND ENDP

;*****************************************************************************

  LOCATE PROC NEAR
   ;for DL := 8 downto 0 do
             MOV DL,8
             ;begin
             ;AX := length of line DL + 1
    SEARCH_NEXT_LINE: MOV  BX,OFFSET LINE_LENGTHS
                      MOV  AL,DL
                      XLAT BX
                      MOV  AH,0
              if AX < BP then AX := 0
                      CMP  AX,BP
                      JAE  SET_SCANS
                      MOV  AX,0
                      JMP  SET_ADDRESS
            ;else AX := max necessary scans of this line
           SET_SCANS: SUB  AX,BP
                      INC  AX
             ;BX := offset address of the (DL + 1)th line
         SET_ADDRESS: PUSH AX
                      MOV  BL,DL
                      MOV  AL,75D
                      MUL  BL
                      ADD  AX,OFFSET START_OF_TEXT
                      MOV  BX,AX
                      POP  AX
             ;found := false
                      MOV  CL,0FFH
             ;while not found and AX <> 0 do
     CHECK_THIS_LINE: CMP  AX,0
                      JZ   END_FOR
                      CMP  CL,0FFH
                      JNZ  END_FOR
                  ;begin
                           PUSH AX
                           PUSH CX
                  ;CX := length of search string
                           MOV  CX,BP
                  ;set DI to start of text being searched
                  ;DI := AX + BX - 1
                           DEC  AX
                           ADD  AX,BX
```

```
                        MOV   DI,AX
                    ;set SI to start of search text
                        MOV   SI,OFFSET READ_LINE_BUFFER
                    ;compare the strings
                        REPZ CMPSB
                    ;if strings equal then
                        JNZ   TRY_FURTHER_ALONG
                        ;begin
                        ;print line number DL + 1
                                    ADD   DL,31H
                                    CALL  PRINTCHAR
                                    CALL  PRINT_NEWLINE
                                    SUB   DL,31H
                        ;found := true
                                    POP   CX
                                    MOV   CL,0
                                    POP   AX
                                    DEC   AX
                        ;end
                                    JMP   END_WHILE
                        ;else begin
                    TRY_FURTHER_ALONG: POP CX
                                    POP AX
                                    DEC AX
                                ;end
              ;end (*of while*)
              END_WHILE: JMP CHECK_THIS_LINE
     ;end (*of for loop*)
     END_FOR: SUB DL,1
              JB   LOCATE_DONE
              JMP SEARCH_NEXT_LINE
     ;set DX to address of completion message
LOCATE_DONE: MOV DX,OFFSET FIND_OK
RET
    LOCATE ENDP

;*******************************************************************************

        READCHAR PROC NEAR
                 MOV AH,1
                 INT 21H
                 RET
        READCHAR ENDP

;*******************************************************************************

        PRINTCHAR PROC NEAR
                  PUSH AX
                  MOV  AH,2
                  INT  21H
                  POP  AX
                  RET
        PRINTCHAR ENDP

;*******************************************************************************
```

```
PRINT_STRING PROC NEAR
        PUSH AX
        MOV  AH,9
        INT  21H
        POP  AX
        RET
PRINT_STRING ENDP

;***************************************************************************

  PRINT_NEWLINE PROC NEAR
        PUSH DX
        MOV  DL,CR
        CALL PRINTCHAR
        MOV  DL,LF
        CALL PRINTCHAR
        POP  DX
        RET
  PRINT_NEWLINE ENDP

;***************************************************************************

CODE ENDS
END MAIN
```

Calculating Sales

APPENDIX IV

```
CR EQU ODH
LF EQU OAH

DATA SEGMENT
INITIAL_DISPLAY     DB CR,LF,'No of items in list?  ','$'

NORMAL_DISPLAY      DB CR,LF,CR,LF,'RUNNING TOTAL OF SALES:   '
ASCII_RUNNING_TOTAL DB 15D DUP(' '),'.',?,?,'$'

PRICE_REQUEST       DB CR,LF,CR,LF,'Unit price? ','$'

QUANTITY_REQUEST    DB CR,LF,CR,LF,'Quantity? ','$'

FINAL_TOTAL         DB CR,LF,CR,LF,'**************** GRAND TOTAL OF SALES'
                    DB ' ****************',CR,LF,'                    '

TOTAL               DB 18D DUP(?),CR,LF,CR,LF,'$'

TEN           DW 10D
SEVENTEEN     DW 17D

PRICE         DB 6D DUP(?)
QUANTITY      DB 4D DUP(?)

STEPS_IN_MULT DB 17D DUP(O)
              DB 17D DUP(O)
              DB 17D DUP(O)
              DB 17D DUP(O)

SUBTOTAL      DB 17D DUP(O)

RUNNING_TOTAL DB 18D DUP(O)

DATA ENDS
```

```
WORKING_STORAGE SEGMENT STACK
       DW 100H DUP(?)
WORKING_STORAGE ENDS

CODE SEGMENT
ASSUME CS:CODE,DS:DATA,SS:WORKING_STORAGE
;establish data segment addressability
 START: MOV   AX,DATA
        MOV   DS,AX
;set up ES for string manipulation instructions
        MOV   ES,AX
;request number of items in list
        MOV   DX,OFFSET INITIAL_DISPLAY
        MOV   AH,9H
        INT   21H
;set top of stack to 0
        MOV   CX,0
        PUSH  CX
        CALL  READCHAR
;while char<> CR
EXAMINE:CMP   AL,CR
        JZ    GOT_ITEM_COUNT
       ;do begin
       ;copy AL into BL to free AX for arithmetic
                MOV BL,AL
        ;convert ASCII character to a digit
                SUB BL,30H
        ;prepare for addition to AX
                MOV BH,0
        ;multiply running total by 10D
                POP AX
                MUL TEN
        ;add in new value
                ADD AX,BX
        ;preserve total
                PUSH AX
        ;read a character
                CALL READCHAR
        ;end
                JMP EXAMINE
;CX := number of items in list
GOT_ITEM_COUNT:POP CX
;while CX <> 0
NEXT_ITEM:CMP CX,0
          JZ DISPLAY_TOTAL
;do begin
                 PUSH CX
         ;request price
                 MOV DX,OFFSET PRICE_REQUEST
                 MOV AH,9
                 INT 21H
                 CALL GET_PRICE
         ;request quantity
                 MOV DX,OFFSET QUANTITY_REQUEST
                 MOV AH,9
```

```
                INT 21H
                CALL GET_QUANTITY
        ;calulate sales and update running total
                CALL CALCULATE_SALES
        ;copy running total across to display format
        ;(use BH to indicate if there has been a non_zero
        ;digit to print yet)
                MOV BH,0
                MOV SI,OFFSET RUNNING_TOTAL+16D
                MOV DI,OFFSET ASCII_RUNNING_TOTAL
                MOV CX,17D
       MOVE_NEXT:MOV AL,[SI]
        ;convert to ASCII
                OR  AL,30H
                CMP BH,1
                JZ  INSERT
                CMP AL,'0'
                JNZ NON_ZERO_FOUND
                MOV AL,' '
                JMP INSERT
  NON_ZERO_FOUND:MOV BH,1
          INSERT:MOV [DI],AL
                DEC SI
                INC DI
                CMP CX,3D
                JNZ NOT_DEC_POINT
                INC DI
   NOT_DEC_POINT:LOOP MOVE_NEXT
        ;display running total
                MOV DX,OFFSET NORMAL_DISPLAY
                MOV AH,9
                INT 21H
        ;CX := CX - 1
                POP CX
                DEC CX
        ;end
                JMP NEXT_ITEM
;move final total into place
DISPLAY_TOTAL:CLD
       MOV SI,OFFSET ASCII_RUNNING_TOTAL
       MOV DI,OFFSET TOTAL
       MOV CX,18D
       REP MOVSB
;display final total
       MOV DX,OFFSET FINAL_TOTAL
       MOV AH,9
       INT 21H
;return to DOS
       MOV AX,4C00H
       INT 21H

;**********************************************************************

READCHAR PROC NEAR
       MOV AH,1
```

```
        INT 21H
        RET
READCHAR ENDP

;*******************************************************************************

CALCULATE_SALES PROC NEAR
;for BX:=3 to 0 do
        MOV BX,3
        ;begin
       NEXT_MULT:MOV SI,OFFSET PRICE
        ;calculate where to store answer
        ;namely, DI := OFFSET STEPS_IN_MULT + (3 - BX) * 17
                MOV DI,OFFSET STEPS_IN_MULT
                MOV AX,3
                SUB AX,BX
                MUL SEVENTEEN
                ADD DI,AX
        ;place BX zeros at DI
                MOV CX,BX
        SHIFTS: CMP CX,0
                JZ  DIGITS
                MOV BYTE PTR [DI],0
                INC DI
                DEC CX
                JMP SHIFTS
        ;no of digits in PRICE is 6
        DIGITS: MOV CX,6
        ;next digit of QUANTITY into DL
                MOV DL,[BX+QUANTITY]
        ;now everything ready for subroutine
                CALL ONE_DIGIT_MULT
                SUB BX,1
                JNB NEXT_MULT
        ;end
;add up subtotals
        CALL ADDUP_SUBTOTALS
;update running total
        CALL UPDATE_RUNNING_TOTAL
        RET
CALCULATE_SALES ENDP

;*******************************************************************************

ADDUP_SUBTOTALS PROC NEAR
        MOV SI,OFFSET STEPS_IN_MULT
        MOV DI,OFFSET STEPS_IN_MULT+17D
        MOV BX,OFFSET SUBTOTAL
        MOV CX,17D
        CALL UNPACKED_ADDITION
        MOV SI,OFFSET STEPS_IN_MULT+34D
        MOV DI,OFFSET SUBTOTAL
        MOV BX,OFFSET SUBTOTAL
        MOV CX,17D
        CALL UNPACKED_ADDITION
```

```
       MOV SI,OFFSET STEPS_IN_MULT+51D
       MOV DI,OFFSET SUBTOTAL
       MOV BX,OFFSET SUBTOTAL
       MOV CX,17D
       CALL UNPACKED_ADDITION
       RET
ADDUP_SUBTOTALS ENDP

;*********************************************************************

UPDATE_RUNNING_TOTAL PROC NEAR
       MOV CX,17D
       MOV SI,OFFSET RUNNING_TOTAL
       MOV DI,OFFSET SUBTOTAL
       MOV BX,OFFSET RUNNING_TOTAL
       CALL UNPACKED_ADDITION
       RET
UPDATE_RUNNING_TOTAL ENDP

;*********************************************************************

GET_PRICE PROC NEAR
       STD
       MOV DI,OFFSET PRICE + 5
       MOV CX,7
;repeat
NEXT_PRICE_DIGIT:CALL READCHAR
                 CMP AL,'.'
                 JZ GET_REST
                 SUB AL,30H
                 STOSB
;until CX = 0
        GET_REST: LOOP NEXT_PRICE_DIGIT
                 RET
GET_PRICE ENDP

;*********************************************************************

GET_QUANTITY PROC NEAR
       STD
       MOV DI,OFFSET QUANTITY + 3
       MOV CX,4
;repeat
NEXT_QUANTITY_DIGIT:CALL READCHAR
                    SUB AL,30H
                    STOSB
;until CX = 0
       LOOP NEXT_QUANTITY_DIGIT
       RET
GET_QUANTITY ENDP

;*********************************************************************

ONE_DIGIT_MULT PROC NEAR
              PUSH AX
```

```
                PUSH CX
            ;last_carry := 0;
                MOV BYTE PTR [DI],0
            ;repeat move the first digit of the big number into AL
  NEXT_DIGIT:  MOV AL,[SI]
                ;multiply this by the contents of DL
                MUL DL
                ;adjust the result
                AAM
                ;add last_carry
                ADD AL,[DI]
                ;adjust the result
                AAA
                ;save the sum digit as the current product digit
                MOV [DI],AL
                ;move pointers to next digits
                INC DI
                INC SI
                ;last carry := current carry
                MOV [DI],AH
            ;until no more digits of the multiplicand left
                DEC CX
                JNZ NEXT_DIGIT
                POP CX
                POP AX
                RET
ONE_DIGIT_MULT ENDP

;***************************************************************************

UNPACKED_ADDITION PROC NEAR
;assume SI points to first number (CX digits)
;DI points to second number (CX digits)
;BX points to sum (CX+1 digits)
          CLC
;repeat
          ;add next pair of digits
 ADD_NEXT_PAIR: MOV AH,0
                MOV AL,[SI]
                ADC AL,[DI]
                AAA
                MOV [BX],AL
          ;prepare for next addition
                INC SI
                INC DI
                INC BX
;until CX =0
          LOOP ADD_NEXT_PAIR
;store carry
          MOV [BX],AH
          RET
UNPACKED_ADDITION ENDP

;***************************************************************************

CODE ENDS
END START
```

Instruction Set Summary and Instruction Encoding

APPENDIX V

V.A Instruction set summary†

Flag registers

AF = Auxiliary carry	PF = Parity
CF = Carry	SF = Sign
DF = Direction	TF = Trap
IF = Interrupt	ZF = Zero
OF = Overflow	

Legend for flag conditions

A = Altered to reflect results of operation
R = Replaced from storage
U = Undefined
0 = Unconditionally cleared to 0
1 = Unconditionally set to 1
None = No flags affected

Processors

The notation 80386+ denotes that the specified instruction is available only for the 80386 or compatible processors, or for more powerful members of the 8086 family. 80186+ and 80286+ are used similarly. Where there is no indication of this kind, the given instruction is available for all members of the 8086 family but note that instruction length may be increased by 2-bytes for a 32-bit processor.

† The material in this section has been taken from *Macro Assembler/2*, IBM Reference Number 95×3068, by kind permission of International Business Machines Corporation and has been adapted as discussed under the heading *Processors*.

AAA (no operands) – ASCII adjust for addition			
Operands	**Bytes**	**Example**	**Flags**
none	1	AAA	AF=A PF=U CF=A SF=U OF=U ZF=U

AAD (no operands) – ASCII adjust for division			
Operands	**Bytes**	**Example**	**Flags**
none	2	AAD	AF=U PF=A CF=U SF=A OF=U ZF=A

AAM (no operands) – ASCII adjust for multiply			
Operands	**Bytes**	**Example**	**Flags**
none	1	AAM	AF=U PF=A CF=U SF=A OF=U ZF=A

AAS (no operands) – ASCII adjust for subtraction			
Operands	**Bytes**	**Example**	**Flags**
none	1	AAS	AF=A PF=U CF=A SF=U OF=U ZF=U

ADC destination,source – Add with carry			
Operands	**Bytes**	**Example**	**Flags**
register,register	2	ADC AX,SI	AF=A
register,memory	2-4	ADC DX,BETA [SI]	PF=U
memory,register	2-4	ADC ALPHA [BX] [SI],DI	CF=A
register,immediate	3-4	ADC BX,256	SF=U
memory,immediate	3-6	ADC GAMMA,30H	OF=U
accumulator,immediate	2-3	ADC AL,5	ZF=U

ADD destination,source – Addition			
Operands	**Bytes**	**Example**	**Flags**
register,register	2-4	ADD CX,DX	AF=A
register,memory	2-4	ADD DI,[BX].ALPHA	PF=U
memory,register	3-4	ADD TEMP,CL	CF=A
register,immediate	3-6	ADD CL,2	SF=U
memory,immediate	2-3	ADD ALPHA,2	OF=U
accumulator,immediate		ADD AX,200	ZF=U

AND destination,source – Logical AND			
Operands	**Bytes**	**Example**	**Flags**
register,register	2	AND AL,BL	AF=U
register,memory	2-4	AND CX,FLAG WORD	PF=A
memory,register	2-4	AND ASCII [DI],AL	CF=0
register,immediate	3-4	AND CX,0F0H	SF=A
memory,immediate	3-6	AND BETA,01H	OF=0
accumulator,immediate	2-3	AND AL,01010000B	ZF=A

ARPL destination,source – Adjust RPL field of selector				80286+
Operands	**Bytes**	**Example**	**Flags**	
register,register memory,register	2 2–6	ARPL AX,BX ARPL AX,[EBP+2]	AF=U PF=U CF=U SF=U DF=U ZF=X	

BOUND destination,source – Check array boundaries				80186+
Operands	**Bytes**	**Example**	**Flags**	
register,memory	2–6	BOUND EAX,A_LIMIT	none	

BSF destination,source – Bit scan forward				80386+
Operands	**Bytes**	**Example**	**Flags**	
register,register register,memory	3 3–7	BSF EBX,ECX BSF EAX,MY_LOC	AF=U OF=U PF=U ZF=A CF=U SF=U	

BSR destination,source – Bit scan forward				80386+
Operands	**Bytes**	**Example**	**Flags**	
register,register register,memory	3 3–7	BSR AX,BX BSR EAX,MY_LOC	AF=U OF=U PF=U ZF=A CF=U SF=U	

BT destination,index – Bit test				80386+
Operands	**Bytes**	**Example**	**Flags**	
register,immediate register,register memory,immediate memory,register	4 3 4–8 4–8	BT EAX,1AH BT BX,CX BT A_LOC,11H BT SEMAPHORE,EAX	AF=U OF=U PF=U ZF=U CF=A SF=U	

BTC destination,index – Bit test and complement				80386+
Operands	**Bytes**	**Example**	**Flags**	
register,immediate register,register memory,immediate memory,register	4 3 4–8 4–8	BTC EAX,1AH BTC BX,CX BTC A_LOC,11H BTC SEMAPHORE,EAX	AF=U OF=U PF=U ZF=U CF=A SF=U	

BTR destination,index – Bit test and reset				80386+
Operands	**Bytes**	**Example**	**Flags**	
register,immediate register,register memory,immediate memory, register	4 3 4–8 4–8	BTC EAX,1AH BTC BX,CX BTC A_LOC,11H BTC SEMAPHORE, EAX	AF=U OF=U PF=U ZF=U CF=A SF=U	

BTS destination,index – Bit test and reset				80386+
Operands	**Bytes**	**Example**	**Flags**	
register,immediate register,register memory,immediate memory, register	4 3 4–8 4–8	BTC EAX,14H BTC BX,CX BTC A_LOC,11H BTC SEMAPHORE, EAX	AF=U OF=U PF=U ZF=U CF=A SF=U	

CALL target – Call a procedure			
Operands	**Bytes**	**Example**	**Flags**
near-proc far-proc memptr 16 regptr 16 memptr 32	3 5 2-4 2 2-4	CALL NEAR_PROC CALL FAR_PROC CALL PROC_TABLE [SI] CALL AX CALL [BX],TASK [SI]	none

CBW (no operands) – Convert byte to word			
Operands	**Bytes**	**Example**	**Flags**
none	1	CBW	none

CDQ (no operands) – Convert doubleword to quadword				80386+
Operands	**Bytes**	**Example**	**Flags**	
none	1	CDQ	none	

CLC (no operands) – Clear carry flag			
Operands	**Bytes**	**Example**	**Flags**
none	1	CLC	CF=0

CLD (no operands) – Clear direction flag			
Operands	**Bytes**	**Example**	**Flags**
none	1	CLD	DF=0

CLI (no operands) – Clear interrupt flag			
Operands	**Bytes**	**Example**	**Flags**
none	1	CLI	DF=0

CLTS (no operands) – Clear task switched bit				80286+
Operands	**Bytes**	**Example**	**Flags**	
none	2	CLTS	none	

CMC (no operands) – Complement Carry Flag			
Operands	**Bytes**	**Example**	**Flags**
none	1	CMC	CF=A

CMP destination,source – Compare destination to source			
Operands	**Bytes**	**Example**	**Flags**

register,register
register,memory
memory,register
register,immediate
memory,immediate
accumulator,immediate
	2
	2-4
	2-4
	3-4
	3-6
	2-3
		CMP BX,CX
		CMP DH,ALPHA
		CMP [BP + 2],SI
		CMP BL,02H
		CMP [BX] RADAR [DI],3420H
		CMP AL,00010000B
			AF=A
			PF=A
			CF=A
			SF=A
			OF=A
			ZF=A

CMPSB/CMPSW (no operands) – Compare string (byte/word)			
Operands	**Bytes**	**Example**	**Flags**
none (repeat)	1 1	CMPS REPE CMPS	AF=A PF=A CF=A SF=A OF=A ZF=A

CWD (no operand) – Convert word to doubleword			
Operands	**Bytes**	**Example**	**Flags**
none	1	CWD	none

CWDE (no operand) – Convert word to doubleword extended				80386+
Operands	**Bytes**	**Example**	**Flags**	
none	1	CWDE	none	

DAA (no operand) – Decimal adjust for addition			
Operands	**Bytes**	**Example**	**Flags**
none	1	DAA	AF=A PF=U CF=A SF=U OF=U ZF=U

DAS (no operand) – Decimal adjust for subtraction			
Operands	**Bytes**	**Example**	**Flags**
none	1	DAS	AF=A PF=A CF=A SF=A OF=A ZF=A

DEC destination – Decrement by 1			
Operands	**Bytes**	**Example**	**Flags**
reg16 reg8 memory	1 2 2-4	DEC AX DEC AL DEC ARRAY [SI]	AF=A SF=A OF=A ZF=A PF=A

DIV source – Division, unsigned			
Operands	**Bytes**	**Example**	**Flags**
reg8 reg16 mem8 mem16	2 2 2-4 2-4	DIV CL DIV BX DIV ALPHA DIV TABLE [SI]	AF=U PF=U CF=U SF=U OF=U ZF=U

ENTER locals,nesting – Enter new stack frame				80186+
Operands	**Bytes**	**Example**	**Flags**	
ENTER immediate,immediate	4	ENTER 4,0	none	

ESC external-op code,source – Escape			
Operands	**Bytes**	**Example**	**Flags**
immediate,memory immediate,register	2-4 2	ESC 6,ARRAY [SI] ESC 20,AL	none

HLT (no operands) – Halt			
Operands	**Bytes**	**Example**	**Flags**
none	1	HLT	none

IDIV source – Integer division			
Operands	**Bytes**	**Example**	**Flags**
reg8 reg16 mem8 mem16	2 2 2-4 2-4	IDIV BL IDIV CX IDIV DIVISOR_BYTE [SI] IDIV [BX],DIVISOR_WORD	AF=U PF=U CF=U SF=U OF=U ZF=U

IMUL op1,op2,op3 – Integer multiplication				
Operands	**Bytes**	**Example**	**Flags**	
reg mem	2 2–4	IMUL BX IMUL MY_NUM	AF=U PF=U CF=A SF=U OF=A ZF=U	
reg,reg reg,mem reg,imm reg,reg,imm reg,mem,imm	3 3 2–6 4 4–8	IMUL CX,DX IMUL BX,MY_NUM IMUL CX,35H IMUL CX,DX,24H IMUL CX,[BX],37H		**80386+**

IN accumulator,port – Input byte or word			
Operands	**Bytes**	**Example**	**Flags**
accumulator,immed8 accumulator,DX	2 1	IN AL,0FAH IN AX,DX	none

INC destination – Increment by 1			
Operands	**Bytes**	**Example**	**Flags**
reg19 reg8 memory	1 2 2-4	INC CX INC BL INC ALPHA [DI] [BX]	AF=A SF=A OF=A ZF=A PA=A

INSB/INSW (no operands) – Input string from I/O port (byte/word)				**80186+**
Operands	**Bytes**	**Example**	**Flags**	
byte word doubleword	1 1 1	INSB INSW INSD	none	

INT interrupt-type – Interrupt			
Operands	**Bytes**	**Example**	**Flags**
immed8(type=3) immed8(type≠3)	1 2	INT 3 INT 67	IF=0 TF=0

INTO (no operands) – Interrupt if overflow			
Operands	**Bytes**	**Example**	**Flags**
none	1	INTO	IF=0 TF=0

IRET (no operands) – Interrupt return			
Operands	**Bytes**	**Example**	**Flags**
none	1	IRET	AF=R PF=R CF=R SF=R DF=R TF=R IF=R ZF=R

JA/JNBE short-label – Jump if above/Jump if not below or equal			
Operands	**Bytes**	**Example**	**Flags**
short-label	2	JA ABOVE	none

JAE/JNB short-label – Jump if above or equal/Jump if not below			
Operands	**Bytes**	**Example**	**Flags**
short-label	2	JAE ABOVE_EQUAL	none

JB/JNAE short-label – Jump if below/Jump if not above nor equal			
Operands	**Bytes**	**Example**	**Flags**
short-label	2	JB BELOW	none

JBE/JNA short-label – Jump if below or equal/Jump if not above			
Operands	**Bytes**	**Example**	**Flags**
short-label	2	JNA NOT_ABOVE	none

JC short-label – Jump if carry			
Operands	**Bytes**	**Example**	**Flags**
short-label	2	JC CARRY_SET	none

JCXZ short-label – Jump if CX is zero			
Operands	**Bytes**	**Example**	**Flags**
short-label	2	JCXZ COUNT_DONE	none

JE/JZ short-label – Jump if equal/Jump if zero			
Operands	**Bytes**	**Example**	**Flags**
short-label	2	JZ ZERO	none

JG/JNLE short-label – Jump if greater/Jump if not less than			
Operands	**Bytes**	**Example**	**Flags**
short-label	2	JG GREATER	none

JGE/JNL short-label – Jump if greater or equal/Jump if not less			
Operands	**Bytes**	**Example**	**Flags**
short-label	2	JGE GREATER_EQUAL	none

JL/JNGE short-label – Jump if less/Jump if not greater nor equal			
Operands	**Bytes**	**Example**	**Flags**
short-label	2	JL LESS	none

JLE/JNG short-label – Jump if less or equal/Jump if not greater			
Operands	**Bytes**	**Example**	**Flags**
short-label	2	JNG NOT_GREATER	none

JMP target – Jump			
Operands	**Bytes**	**Example**	**Flags**
short-label	2	JMP SHORT	none
near-label	3	JMP WITHIN_SEGMENT	
far-label	5	JMP FAR LABEL	
memptr16	2-4	JMP [BX],TARGET	
regptr16	2	JMP CX	
memptr32	2-4	JMP OTHER_SEG [SI]	

JNC short-label – Jump if not carry			
Operands	**Bytes**	**Example**	**Flags**
short-label	2	JNC NOT_CARRY	none

JNE/JNZ short-label – Jump if not equal/Jump if not zero			
Operands	**Bytes**	**Example**	**Flags**
short-label	2	JNE NOT_EQUAL	none

JNO short-label – Jump if not overflow			
Operands	**Bytes**	**Example**	**Flags**
short-label	2	JNO NO_OVERFLOW	none

JNP/JPO short-label – Jump if not parity/Jump if parity ODD			
Operands	**Bytes**	**Example**	**Flags**
short-label	2	JPO ODD_PARITY	none

JNS short-label – Jump if not sign			
Operands	**Bytes**	**Example**	**Flags**
short-label	2	JNS POSITIVE	none

JO short-label – Jump if overflow			
Operands	**Bytes**	**Example**	**Flags**
short-label	2	JO SIGNED OVRFLW	none

JP/JPE short-label – Jump if parity/Jump if parity even			
Operands	**Bytes**	**Example**	**Flags**
short-label	2	JPE EVEN PARITY	none

JS short-label – Jump if sign			
Operands	**Bytes**	**Example**	**Flags**
short-label	2	JS NEGATIVE	none

LAHF (no operands) – Load AH from flags			
Operands	**Bytes**	**Example**	**Flags**
none	1	LAHF	none

LAR destination,select – Load access rights				80286+
Operands	**Bytes**	**Example**	**Flags**	
register,register register,memory	3 3–7	LAR CX,BX LAR DX,A_LOC	AF=U PF=U CF=U SF=U OF=U ZF=A	

LDS destination,source – Load pointer using DS			
Operands	**Bytes**	**Example**	**Flags**
reg16,mem32	2-4	LDS SI,DATA.SEG[DI]	none

LEA destination,source – Load effective address			
Operands	**Bytes**	**Example**	**Flags**
register,memory	2–4	LEA BX,[BP][DI]	none

LEAVE (no operands) – Leave current stack frame				80186+
Operands	**Bytes**	**Example**	**Flags**	
none	1	LEAVE	none	

LES destination,source – Load pointer using ES			
Operands	**Bytes**	**Example**	**Flags**
reg16,mem32	2-4	LES DI,[BX].TEXT_BUFF	none

LGDT op – Load GDT register				80286+
Operands	**Bytes**	**Example**	**Flags**	
memory	3–7	LGDT MY_TABLE	none	

LIDT op – Load IDT register				80286+
Operands	**Bytes**	**Example**	**Flags**	
memory	3–7	LIDT MY_TABLE	none	

LLDT op – Load LDT register				80286+
Operands	**Bytes**	**Example**	**Flags**	
register memory	3 3–7	LLDT AX LLDT MY_TABLE	none	

LMSW op – Load machine status word				80386+
Operands	**Bytes**	**Example**	**Flags**	
register memory	3 3–7	LMSW CX LMSW MY_LOC	none	

LOCK (no operands) – Lock bus			
Operands	**Bytes**	**Example**	**Flags**
none	1	LOCK XCHG FLAG,AL	none

LODSB/LODSW (no operands) – Load string (byte/word)			
Operands	**Bytes**	**Example**	**Flags**
none (repeat)	1 1	LODSW REP LODSB	none

LOOP short-label – Loop			
Operands	**Bytes**	**Example**	**Flags**
short-label	2	LOOP AGAIN	none

LOOPE/LOOPZ short-label – Loop if equal/Loop if zero			
Operands	**Bytes**	**Example**	**Flags**
short-label	2	LOOPE AGAIN	none

LOOPNE/LOOPNZ short-label – Loop if not equal/Loop if not zero			
Operands	**Bytes**	**Example**	**Flags**
short-label	2	LOOPNE AGAIN	none

Lseg destination,source – Load segment register				
Operands	**Bytes**	**Example**	**Flags**	
LDS reg,mem LES reg,mem	2–6 2–6	LDS ESI,BIG_PTR LES ESI,BIG_PTR	none	
LSS reg,mem LFS reg,mem LGS reg,mem	3–7 3–7 3–7	LSS ESI,BIG_PTR LFS ESI,BIG_PTR LGS ESI,BIG_PTR		80386+

LSL destination,select – Load segment limit — **80286+**

Operands	Bytes	Example	Flags
register,register	3	LSL EAX,EBX	AF=U PF=U CF=U SF=U
register,memory	3–7	LSL EAX,[BP+12]	OF=U ZF=A

LTR selector – Load task register — **80286+**

Operands	Bytes	Example	Flags
register	3	LTR AX	none
memory	3–7	LTR A_LOC	

MOV destination,source – MOVE

Operands	Bytes	Example	Flags
memory,accumulator	3	MOV ARRAY [SI],AL	none
accumulator,memory	3	MOV AX,TEMP RESULT	
register,register	2	MOV AX,CX	
register,memory	2-4	MOV BP,STACK_TOP	
memory,register	2-4	MOV COUNT [DI],CX	
register,immediate	2-3	MOV CL,2	
memory,immediate	3-6	MOV MASK [BX][SI],2CH	
seg-reg,reg16	2	MOV ES,CX	
seg-reg,mem16	2-4	MOV DS,SEGMENT_BASE	
reg16,seg-reg	2	MOV BP,SS	
memory,seg-reg	2-4	MOV [BX].SEG_SAVE,CS	

MOVSB/MOVSW (no operands) – Move string (byte/word)

Operands	Bytes	Example	Flags
none	1	MOVSB	none
(repeat) none	1	REP MOVSW	

MOVSX destination, source – Move with sign extension — **80386+**

Operands	Bytes	Example	Flags
register,register	3	MOVSX EAX,AL	none
register,memory	3–7	MOVSX EDI,MY_WORD	

MOVZX destination,source – Move with zero extension				80386+
Operands	**Bytes**	**Example**	**Flags**	
register,register register,memory	3 3–7	MOVZX EAX,AL MOVZX EDI,MY_WORD	none	

MUL source – Multiplication, unsigned			
Operands	**Bytes**	**Example**	**Flags**
reg8 reg16 mem8 mem16	2 2 2-4 2-4	MUL BL MUL CX MUL MONTH [SI] MUL BAUD_RATE	AF=U PF=U CF=A SF=U OF=A ZF=U

NEG destination – Negate			
Operands	**Bytes**	**Example**	**Flags**
register memory	2 2-4	NEG AL NEG MULTIPLIER	AF=A PF=A CF=1* SF=A OF=A ZF=A

NOP no operands – No operation			
Operands	**Bytes**	**Example**	**Flags**
none	1	NOP	none

NOT destination – Logical not			
Operands	**Bytes**	**Example**	**Flags**
register memory	2 2-4	NOT AX NOT CHARACTER	none

OR destination,source – Logical inclusive OR			
Operands	**Bytes**	**Example**	**Flags**
register,register register,memory memory,register accumulator,immediate register,immediate memory,immediate	2 2-4 2-4 2-3 3-4 3-6	OR AL_BI OR DX,PORT_ID [DI] OR FLAG_BYTE_CI OR AL_0110110B OR CL,01FH OR [BX] CMD_WORD 0CFH	AF=U PF=A CF=0 SF=A OF=0 ZF=A

OUT port,accumulator – Output byte or word			
Operands	**Bytes**	**Example**	**Flags**
immed8.accumulator DX.accumulator	2 1	OUT 44.AX OUT DX.AL	none

OUTSB/OUTSW (no operands) – Output string to I/O port (byte/word)				80186+
Operands	**Bytes**	**Example**	**Flags**	
byte word doubleword	1 1 1	OUTSB OUTSW INSD	none	

POP destination – Pop word off stack			
Operands	**Bytes**	**Example**	**Flags**
register seg-reg (CS illegal) memory	1 1 2-4	POP DX POP DS POP PARAMETER	none

POPA (no operands) – POP all general registers (16-bit)				80186+
Operands	**Bytes**	**Example**	**Flags**	
none	1	POPA	none	

POPAD (no operands) – POP all general registers (32-bit)				80386+
Operands	**Bytes**	**Example**	**Flags**	
none	1	POPAD	none	

POPF (no operands) – POP stack into flags			
Operands	**Bytes**	**Example**	**Flags**
none	1	POPF	all

POPFD (no operands) – POP stack into E flags			
Operands	**Bytes**	**Example**	**Flags**
none	1	POPFD	AF=A PF=A CF=A SF=A OF=A ZF=A

PUSH op – PUSH value on to stack				
Operands	**Bytes**	**Example**	**Flags**	
reg seg reg memory	1 1 2–6	PUSH AX PUSH CS PUSH [BX]	none	
immediate	2–5	PUSH 57H		80386+

PUSHA (no operands) – PUSH all general registers (16-bit)			
Operands	**Bytes**	**Example**	**Flags**
none	1	PUSHA	none

PUSHAD (no operators) – PUSH all general registers (32-bit)				80386+
Operands	**Bytes**	**Example**	**Flags**	
none	1	PUSHAD	none	

PUSHF (no operands) – PUSH flags register			
Operands	**Bytes**	**Example**	**Flags**
none	1	PUSHF	none

PUSHFD (no operands) – PUSH E-flags register				80386+
Operands	**Bytes**	**Example**	**Flags**	
none	1	PUSHFD	none	

RCL destination,count – Rotate left through carry			
Operands	**Bytes**	**Example**	**Flags**
register,1	2	RCL CX,1	CF=A
register,CL	2	RCL AL,CL	OF=A
memory,1	2-4	RCL ALPHA,1	
memory,CL	2-4	RCL [BP].PARM,CL	

RCR destination,count – Rotate right through carry			
Operands	**Bytes**	**Example**	**Flags**
register,1	2	RCR BX,1	CF=A
register,CL	2	RCR BL,CL	OF=A
memory,1	2-4	RCR [BX].STATUS,1	
memory,CL	2-4	RCR ARRAY [DI],CL	

REP (no operands) – Repeat string operation			
Operands	**Bytes**	**Example**	**Flags**
none	1	REP MOVS DEST.SRCE	none

REPE/REPZ (no operands) – Repeat string operation equal/while zero			
Operands	**Bytes**	**Example**	**Flags**
none	1	REPE CMPS DATA.KEY	none

REPNE/REPNZ (no operands) – Repeat string operation not equal/not zero			
Operands	**Bytes**	**Example**	**Flags**
none	1	REPNE SCAS INPUT_LINE	none

RET optional-pop-value – Return from procedure			
Operands	**Bytes**	**Example**	**Flags**
(intra-segment,no pop)	1	RET	none
(intra-segment,pop)	3	RET 4	
(inter-segment,no pop)	1	RET	
(inter-segment,pop)	3	RET 2	

ROL destination,count – Rotate left			
Operands	**Bytes**	**Example**	**Flags**
register,1	2	ROL BX,1	CF=A
register,CL	2	ROL DI,CL	OF=A
memory,1	2-4	ROL FLAG_BYTE[DI],1	
memory,CL	2-4	ROL ALPHA,CL	

ROR destination,count			
Operands	**Bytes**	**Example**	**Flags**
register,1	2	ROR AL,1	CF=A
register,CL	2	ROR BX,CL	OF=A
memory,1	2-4	ROR PORT_STATUS,1	
memory,CL	2-4	ROR CMD WORD,CL	

SAHF (no operands) – Store AH into flags			
Operands	**Bytes**	**Example**	**Flags**
none	1	SAHF	AF=A SF=R CF=R ZF=R PF=R

SAL/SHL destination,count – Shift arithmetic left/Shift logical left			
Operands	**Bytes**	**Example**	**Flags**
register,1	2	SAL AL,1	CF=A
register,CL	2	SHL DI,CL	OF=A
memory,1	2-4	SHL [BX] OVERDRAW,1	
memory,CL	2-4	SAL STORE_COUNT,CL	

SAR destination,source – Shift arithmetic right			
Operands	**Bytes**	**Example**	**Flags**
register,1	2	SAR DX,1	AF=U PF=A
register,CL	2	SAR DI,CL	CF=A SF=A
memory,1	2-4	SAR N_BLOCKS,1	OF=A ZF=A
memory,CL	2-4	SAR N_BLOCKS,CL	

SBB destination,source – Subtract with borrow			
Operands	**Bytes**	**Example**	**Flags**
register,register	2	SBB BX,CX	AF=A
register,memory	2-4	SBB DI,[BX].PAYMENT	PF=A
memory,register	2-4	SBB BALANCE,AX	CF=A
accumulator,immediate	2-3	SBB AX,2	SF=A
register,immediate	3-4	SBB CL,1	OF=A
memory,immediate	3-6	SBB COUNT[SI],10	ZF=A

SCASB/SCASW (no operands) – Scan string (byte/word)			
Operands	**Bytes**	**Example**	**Flags**
dest-string (repeat string)	1 1	SCAS INPUT_LINE REPNE SCAS BUFFER	AF=A PF=A CF=A SF=A OF=A ZF=A

seg – Segment override pre-fix				
Legal forms	**Bytes**	**Example**	**Flags**	

CS:
DS:
SS:
ES:
	1
	1
	1
	1
		JMP CS:[BX]
		ADD DS:[BP],7
		ADD SS:[BX],7
		ADD ES:[BX],7
			none	

FS: GS:	1 1	ADD FS:[EBX],7 ADD GS:[EBX],7		**80386+**

SETcc destination – Set byte on condition				**80386+**
Operands	**Bytes**	**Example**	**Flags**	
register memory	2 2	SETcc AL SETcc [EBX]	none	
cc = same range of conditions as for Jcc				

SGDT destination – Store GDT register				**80286+**
Operands	**Bytes**	**Example**	**Flags**	
mem	2–6	SGDT [EBX]	none	

SHL destination,count – Shift left logical			
Operands	**Bytes**	**Example**	**Flags**
register,immediate memory,immediate register,CL memory,CL	2–6 9–8 2 2–6	SHL AX,1 SHL [BX],1 SHL DX,CL SHL [BX[,CL	AF=U PF=A CF=A SF=A OF=A ZF=A
NB: for 8086, 80186, 80286, immediate operand can only be 1			

SHLD destination,source,count – Shift left double				**80386+**
Operands	**Bytes**	**Example**	**Flags**	
reg,reg,imm mem,reg,imm reg,reg,CL mem,reg,CL	3–7 3–7 3–7 3–7	SHLD AX,BX,6 SHLD [BX],CX,5 SHLD EBX,DL,CL SHLD [ESI+4],EAX,7	AF=R PF=A CF=A SF=A OF=R ZF=A	

SHR destination,count – Shift logical right			
Operands	**Bytes**	**Example**	**Flags**
register.1 register.CL memory.1 memory.CL	2 2 2-4 2-4	SHR SI,1 SHR SI,CL SHR ID_BYTE [SI] [BX].1 SHR INPUT_WORD.CL	CF=A OF=A

SHRD destination,source,count – Shift right double				80386+
Operands	**Bytes**	**Example**	**Flags**	
reg,reg,imm mem,reg,imm reg,reg,CL mem,reg,CL	3–7 3–7 3–7 3–7	SHRD AX,BX,6 SHRD [BX],CX,5 SHRD EBX,EDX,CL SHRD [ESI+4],EAX,7	AF=R PF=A CF=A SF=A OF=R ZF=A	

SIDT destination – Store IDT register				80286+
Operands	**Bytes**	**Example**	**Flags**	
mem	3–7	SIDT MY_TABLE	none	

SLDT destination – Store LDT register				80286+
Operands	**Bytes**	**Example**	**Flags**	
reg mem	3 3–7	SLDT DX SLDT MY_TABLE	none	

SMSW destination – Store machine status word				80286+
Operands	**Bytes**	**Example**	**Flags**	
reg mem	3 3–7	SMSW CX SMSW [DI]	none	

STC (no operands) – Set carry flag			
Operands	**Bytes**	**Example**	**Flags**
none	1	STC	CF=1

STD (no operand) – Set direction flag			
Operands	**Bytes**	**Example**	**Flags**
none	1	STD	DF=1

STI (no operands) – Set interrupt enable flag			
Operands	**Bytes**	**Example**	**Flags**
none	1	STI	IF=1

STOS dest-string – Store byte or word string			
Operands	**Bytes**	**Example**	**Flags**
dest-string (repeat) dest-string	1 1	STOS PRINT_LINE REP STOS	none

STR destination – Store task register			
Operands	**Bytes**	**Example**	**Flags**
register memory	3 3–7	STR CX STR MY_TABLE	none

SUB destination,source – Subtraction			
Operands	**Bytes**	**Example**	**Flags**

register,register
register,memory
memory,register
accumulator,immediate
register,immediate
memory,immediate
	2
	2-4
	2-4
	2-3
	3-4
	3-6
		SUB AX,BX
		SUB DX,MATH_TOTAL[SI]
		SUB [BP+2],CL
		SUB AL,10
		SUB SI,5280
		SUB [BP].BALANCE,1000
			AF=U
			PF=A
			CF=A
			SF=A
			OF=A
			ZF=A

TEST destination,source – Test or non-destructive logical AND			
Operands	**Bytes**	**Example**	**Flags**
register,register register,memory accumulator,immediate register,immediate memory,immediate	2 2-4 2-3 3-4 3-6	TEST SI,DI TEST SI,END_COUNT TEST AL,00100000B TEST BX,0CC4H TEST RETURN_CODE,01H	AF=U PF=A CF=0 SF=A 0F=0 ZF=A

VERR select – Verify read access				80286+
Operands	**Bytes**	**Example**	**Flags**	
register memory	3 3–7	VERR CX VERR WORD PTR [EBP]	ZF=A	

VERW select – Verify write access				80286+
Operands	**Bytes**	**Example**	**Flags**	
register memory	3 3–7	VERW CX VERW WORD PTR [EBP]	ZF=A	

WAIT (no operands) – Wait while TEST pin not asserted			
Operands	**Bytes**	**Example**	**Flags**
none	1	WAIT	none

XCHG destination,source – Exchange			
Operands	**Bytes**	**Example**	**Flags**
accumulator,reg16 memory,register register,register	1 2-4 2	XCHNG AX,BX XCHG SEMAPHORE,AX XCHG AL,BL	none

XLAT source-table – Translate			
Operands	**Bytes**	**Example**	**Flags**
source-table	1	XLAT ASCII_TAB	none

XOR destination,source – Logical exclusive OR			
Operands	**Bytes**	**Example**	**Flags**
register,register	2	XOR CX,BX	AF=U
register,memory	2-4	XOR CL,MASK_BYTE	PF=A
memory,register	2-4	XOR ALPHA [SI].DX	CF=0
accumulator,immediate	2-3	XOR AL.01000010B	SF=A
register,immediate	3-4	XOR SI.00C2H	OF=0
memory,immediate	3-6	NOR RETURN_CODE,0D2H	ZF=A

V.B Instruction encoding†

Introduction to the 80386 instruction set

The 80386 instruction set is an extended version of the 8086 and 80286 instruction sets. The instruction sets have been extended in two ways:

- The instructions have extensions that allow operations on 32-bit operands, registers, and memory.
- A 32-bit addressing mode allows flexible selection of registers for base and index as well as index scaling capabilities (×2, ×4, ×8) for computing a 32-bit effective address. The 32-bit effective address yields a 4 GB address range.
  Note The effective address size must be less than 64 KB in the real-address or virtual-address modes to avoid an exception.

Code and data segment descriptors

Although the 80386 microprocessor supports all 80286 code and data segment descriptors, there are some differences in the format. The 80286 segment descriptors contain a 24-bit base address and a 16-bit limit field, while the 80386 segment descriptors have a 32-bit base address, a 20-bit limit field, a default bit and a granularity bit (see Figure V.1).

† Reproduced from *PS/2 Hardware Interface Technical Reference,* IBM Reference Number S01F–0 242, by kind permission of International Business Machines Corporation.

<table>
<tr><td>31 24</td><td colspan="5">23 16</td><td>15 08</td><td>07 00</td><td></td></tr>
<tr><td colspan="6">Segment Base (SB) Bits 15–0</td><td colspan="2">Segment Limit (SL) Bits 15–0</td><td>0</td></tr>
<tr><td>SB Bits 31–24</td><td>G</td><td>D</td><td>0</td><td>0</td><td>SL 19–16</td><td>Access Rights Byte</td><td>SB Bits 23–16</td><td>4</td></tr>
</table>

Offset

Figure V.1 80386 code and data segment descriptor format.

Note Bits 31 through 16 shown at offset 4 are set to 0 for all 80286 segment descriptors.

The default (D) bit of the code segment register is used to determine whether the instruction is carried out as a 16-bit or 32-bit instruction. Code segment descriptors are not used in either the real-address mode or the virtual-8086 mode. When the system microprocessor is operating in either of these modes, a D-bit value of 0 is assumed and operations default to a 16-bit length compatible with 8086 and 80286 programs.

The granularity (G) bit is used to determine the granularity of the segment length (1 = page granular, 0 = byte granular). If the value of the 20 segment-limit bits is defined as N, a G-bit value of 1 defines the segment size as follows:

$$\text{Segment size} = (N + 1) \times 4 \text{ KB}$$

4 KB represents the size of a page.

Prefixes

Two prefixes have been added to the instruction set. The **operand size** prefix overrides the default selection of the operand size; the **effective address size** prefix overrides the effective address size. The presence of either prefix toggles the default setting to its opposite condition. For example:

- If the operand size defaults to 32-bit data operations, the presence of the operand size prefix sets it for 16-bit data operations.
- If the effective address size is 16 bits, the presence of the effective address size prefix toggles the instruction to use 32-bit effective address computations.

The prefixes are available in all 80386 modes, including the real-address mode and the virtual-8086 mode. Since the default of these modes is always 16 bits, the prefixes are used to specify 32-bit operations. If needed, either or both of the prefixes may precede any opcode bytes and affect only the instruction they precede.

Instruction format

The instructions are presented in the format shown in Figure V.2. The instructions use a variety of fields to indicate register selection, the addressing mode, and so on. Table V.1 is a summary of these fields.

Opcode	Mode specifier	Address displacement	Immediate data

Term	Description
Opcode	The opcode may be one or two bytes in length. Within each byte, smaller encoding fields may be defined.
Mode specifier	Consists of the 'mod r/m' byte and the 'scale-index-base' (s-i-b) byte. The mod r/m byte specifies the address mode to be used. Format: mod T T T r/m The 's-i-b' byte is optional and can be used only in 32-bit address modes. It follows the mod r/m byte to specify fully the manner in which the effective address is computed. Format: ss index base
Address displacement	Follows the 'mod r/m' byte or 's-i-b' byte. It may be 8, 16, or 32 bits.
Immediate data	If specified, follows any displacement bytes and becomes the last field of the instruction. It may be 8, 16, or 32 bits. The term '8-bit data' indicates a fixed data length of 8 bits. The term '8-, 16-, or 32-bit data' indicates a variable data length. The length is determined by the w field and the current operand size. If w = 0, the data is always 8 bits. If w = 1, the size is determined by the operand size of the instruction.

Figure V.2 Instruction format.

Table V.1 80386 instruction set encoding field summary.

Field name	*Description*	*Bit information*
w	Specifies if data is byte or full size. (Full size is either 16 or 32 bits.)	1
d	Specifies the direction of data operation.	1
s	Specifies if an immediate data field must be sign-extended.	1
reg	General address specifier.	3
mod r/m	Address mode specifier (effective address can be a general register).	2 for mod; 3 for r/m
ss	Scale factor for scaled index address mode.	2
index	General register to be used as an index register.	3
base	General register to be used as base register.	3
sreg2	Segment register specifier for CS, SS, DS, and ES.	2
sreg3	Segment register specifier for CS, SS, DS, ES, FS, and GS.	3
tttn	For conditional instructions; specifies a condition asserted or a condition negated.	4

Encoding

This section defines the encoding of the fields used in the instruction sets.

Address mode

The first addressing byte is the mod r/m byte. The Effective Address (EA) of the memory operand is computed according to the mod and r/m fields. The mod r/m byte can be interpreted as either a 16-bit or 32-bit addressing mode specifier. Interpretation of the byte depends on the address components used to calculate the EA. Table V.2 defines the encoding of 16-bit and 32-bit addressing modes with the mod r/m byte.

The displacement follows the second byte of the instruction (before data, if required).

The scale-index-base (s-i-b) byte can be specified as a second byte of addressing information. The s-i-b byte is specified when using a 32-bit addressing mode and the mod r/m byte has the following values:

- r/m = 100
- mod = 00, 01, or 10

When the s-i-b byte is present, the 32-bit effective address is a function of the mod, ss, index, and base fields. Tables V.3–V.5 show the scale factor, index register selected, and base register selected when the s-i-b byte is present.

Table V.2 Effective address (16-bit and 32-bit address modes).

mod r/m	*16-bit mode*	*32-bit mode (no s-i-b byte)*
00 000	DS:[BX + SI]	DS:[EAX]
00 001	DS:[BX + DI]	DS:[ECX]
00 010	SS:[BP + SI]	DS:[EDX]
00 011	SS:[BP + DI]	DS:[EBX]
00 100	DS:[SI]	s-i-b present (see Table V.6)
00 101	DS:[DI]	DS:d32
00 110	d16	DS:[ESI]
00 111	DS:[BX]	DS:[EDI]
01 000	DS:[BX + SI + d8]	DS:[EAX + d8]
01 001	DS:[BX + DI + d8]	DS:[ECX + d8]
01 010	SS:[BP + SI + d8]	DS:[EDX + d8]
01 011	SS:[BP + DI + d8]	DS:[EBX + d8]
01 100	DS:[SI + d8]	s-i-b present (see Table V.6)
01 101	DS:[DI + d8]	SS:[EBP + d8]
01 110	SS:[BP + d8]	DS:[ESI + d8]
01 111	DS:[BX + d8]	DS:[EDI + d8]
10 000	DS:[BX + SI + d16]	DS:[EAX + d32]
10 001	DS:[BX + DI + d16]	DS:[ECX + d32]
10 010	SS:[BP + SI + d16]	SS:[EDX + d32]
10 011	SS:[BP + DI + d16]	DS:[EBX + d32]
10 100	DS:[SI + d16]	s-i-b present (see Table V.6)
10 101	DS:[DI + d16]	SS:[EBP + D32]
10 110	SS:[BP + d16]	DS:[ESI + d32]
10 111	DS:[BX + d16]	DS:[EDI + d32]

Table V.3 Scale factor (s-i-b byte present).

ss	*Scale factor*
00	1
01	2
10	4
11	8

Table V.4 Index registers (s-i-b byte present.)

Index	*Index register*
000	EAX
001	ECX
010	EDX
011	EBX
100	No index register The ss field must equal 00 when the index field is 100; if not, the effective address is undefined.
101	EBP
110	ESI
111	EDI

Table V.5 Base registers (s-i-b byte present).

Base	*Base register*	
000	EAX	
001	ECX	
010	EDX	
011	EBX	
100	ESP	
101	EBP	If mod = 00, then EBP is not used to form the EA; immediate 32-bit address displacement follows the mode specifier byte.
110	ESI	
111	EDI	

The scaled-index information is determined by multiplying the contents of the index register by the scale factor. The following example shows the use of the 32-bit addressing mode with scaling where:

- EAX is the base of ARRAY_A;
- ECX is the index of the desired element;
- 2 is the scale factor.

```
; ARRAY_A is an array of words
MOV EAX, offset ARRAY_A
MOV ECX, element_number
MOV BX, [EAX][ECX*2]
```

Table V.6 defines the encoding of the 32-bit addressing mode when the s-i-b byte is present. (**Note:** The mod field is from the mod r/m byte. The base field and scaled-index information are from the s-i-b byte.)

Table V.6 Effective address (32-bit address mode, s-i-b byte present).

Mod base	*32-bit address mode*
00 000	DS:[EAX + (scaled index)]
00 001	DS:[ECX + (scaled index)]
00 010	DS:[EDX + (scaled index)]
00 011	DS:[EBX + (scaled index)]
00 100	SS:[ESP + (scaled index)]
00 101	DS:[d32 + (scaled index)]
00 110	DS:[ESI + (scaled index)]
00 111	DS:[EDI + (scaled index)]
01 000	DS:[EAX + (scaled index) + d8]
01 001	DS:[ECX + (scaled index) + d8]
01 010	DS:[EDX + (scaled index) + d8]
01 011	DS:[EBX + (scaled index) + d8]
01 100	SS:[ESP + (scaled index) + d8]
01 101	SS:[EBP + (scaled index) + d8]
01 110	DS:[ESI + (scaled index) + d8]
01 111	DS:[EDI + (scaled index) + d8]
10 000	DS:[EAX + (scaled index) + d32]
10 001	DS:[ECX + (scaled index) + d32]
10 010	DS:[EDX + (scaled index) + d32]
10 011	DS:[EBX + (scaled index) + d32]
10 100	SS:[ESP + (scaled index) + d32]
10 101	SS:[EBP + (scaled index) + d32]
10 110	DS:[ESI + (scaled index) + d32]
10 111	DS:[EDI + (scaled index) + d32]

Operand length (w) field

For an instruction performing a data operation, the instruction is executed as either a 32-bit or 16-bit operation. Within the constraints of the operation size, the w field encodes the operand size as either one byte or full operation (see Table V.7).

Table V.7 Operand field length encoding.

w	*16-bit data operation*	*32-bit data operation*
0	8 bits	8 bits
1	16 bits	32 bits

Segment register (sreg) field

The 2-bit segment register field (sreg2) allows one of the four 80286 segment registers to be specified. The 3-bit segment register (sreg3) allows the 80386 FS and GS segment registers to be specified (see Table V.8).

Table V.8 Segment register field encoding.

sreg2	*sreg3*	*Segment register*
00	000	ES
01	001	CS
10	010	SS
11	011	DS
–	100	FS
–	101	GS
–	110	Reserved
–	111	Reserved

General register (reg) field

The general register is specified by the reg field, which may appear in the primary opcode bytes as the reg field of the mod reg r/m byte, or as the r/m field of the mod reg r/m byte when mode = 11 (see Table V.9).

Table V.9 General register field encoding.

reg	*16 bit (without w)*	*16 bit (w = 0)*	*16 bit (w = 1)*	*32 bit (without w)*	*32 bit (w = 0)*	*32 bit (w = 1)*
000	AX	AL	AX	EAX	AL	EAX
001	CX	CL	CX	ECX	CL	ECX
010	DX	DL	DX	EDX	DL	EDX
011	BX	BL	BX	EBX	BL	EBX
100	SP	AH	SP	ESP	AH	ESP
101	BP	CH	BP	EBP	CH	EBP
110	SI	DH	SI	ESI	DH	ESI
111	DI	BH	DI	EDI	BH	EDI

The physical addresses of all operands addressed by the BP register are computed using the SS segment register. For string primitive operations (those addressed by the DI register), addresses of the destination operands are computed using the ES segment, which may not be overridden.

Operation direction (d) field

The operation direction (d) field is used in many two-operand instructions to indicate which operand is the source and which is the destination (see Table V.10).

Table V.10 Operand direction field encoding.

d	*Direction of operation*
0	Register/Memory <– Register The 'reg' field indicates the source operand; 'mod r/m' or 'mod ss index base' indicates the destination operand.
1	Register <– Register/Memory The 'reg' field indicates the destination operand; 'mod r/m' or 'mod ss index base' indicates the source operand.

Sign-extend (s) field

The sign-extend (s) field appears primarily in instructions having immediate data fields. The s field affects only 8-bit immediate data being placed in a 16-bit or 32-bit destination (see Table V.11).

Table V.11 Sign-extend field encoding.

s	*8-bit immediate data*	*16/32-bit immediate data*
0	No effect on data	No effect on data
1	Sign-extend 8-bit data to fill 16-bit or 32-bit destination	No effect on data

Conditional test (tttn) field

For conditional instructions (conditional jumps and set-on condition), the conditional test (tttn) field is encoded, with n indicating whether to use the condition (n = 0) or its negation (n = 1), and ttt defining the condition to test (see Table V.12).

Table V.12 Conditional test field encoding.

tttn	*Condition*	*Mnemonic*
0000	Overflow	O
0001	No Overflow	NO
0010	Below/Not Above or Equal	B/NAE
0011	Not Below/Above or Equal	NB/AE
0100	Equal/Zero	E/Z
0101	Not Equal/Not Zero	NE/NZ
0110	Below or Equal/Not Above	BE/NA
0111	Not Below or Equal/Above	NBE/A
1000	Sign	S
1001	Not Sign	NS
1010	Parity/Parity Even	P/PE
1011	Not Parity/Parity Odd	NP/PO
1100	Less than/Not Greater or Equal	L/NGE
1101	Not Less than/Greater or Equal	NL/GE
1110	Less than or Equal/Not Greater than	LE/NG
1111	Not less or Equal/Greater than	NLE/G

Control, debug, or test register (eee) field

Table V.13 shows the encoding for loading and storing the control, debug, and test registers (eee).

Table V.13 Control, debug, and test register field encoding.

eee Code	*Interpreted as control register*	*Interpreted as debug register*	*Interpreted as test register*
000	CR0	DR0	–
001	–	DR1	–
010	CR2	DR2	–
011	CR3	DR3	–
100	–	–	–
101	–	–	–
110	–	DR6	TR6
111	–	DR7	TR7

80386 micro-processor instruction set encoding

Data transfer

MOV = Move

Register to Register/Memory

1 0 0 0 1 0 0 w	mod reg r/m

Register/Memory to Register

1 0 0 0 1 0 1 w	mod reg r/m

Immediate to Register/Memory

1 1 0 0 0 1 1 w	mod 0 0 0 r/m	8-, 16-, or 32-bit data

Immediate to Register (Short Form)

1 0 1 1 w reg	8-, 16-, or 32-bit data

Memory to Accumulator (Short Form)

1 0 1 0 0 0 0 w	full 16- or 32-bit displacement

Accumulator to Memory (Short Form)

1 0 1 0 0 0 1 w	full 16- or 32-bit displacement

Register/Memory to Segment Register

1 0 0 0 1 1 1 0	mod sreg3 r/m

Segment Register to Register/Memory

1 0 0 0 1 1 0 0	mod sreg3 r/m

MOVSX = Move with Sign Extension

Register from Register/Memory

0 0 0 0 1 1 1 1	1 0 1 1 1 1 1 w	mod reg r/m

MOVZX = Move with Zero Extension

Register from Register/Memory

0 0 0 0 1 1 1 1	1 0 1 1 0 1 1 w	mod reg r/m

PUSH = Push

Register/Memory

1 1 1 1 1 1 1 1	mod 1 1 0 r/m

Register (Short Form)

0 1 0 1 0 reg

Segment Register (ES, CS, SS, or DS) Short Form

0 0 0 sreg2 1 1 0

Segment Register (FS or GS)

0 0 0 0 1 1 1 1	1 0 sreg3 0 0 0

Immediate

0 1 1 0 1 0 s 0	8-, 16-, or 32-bit data

PUSHA = Push All

0 1 1 0 0 0 0 0

POP = Pop

Register/Memory

1 0 0 0 1 1 1 1	mod 0 0 0 r/m

Register (Short Form)

0 1 0 1 1 reg

Segment Register (ES, SS, or DS) Short Form

0 0 0 sreg2 1 1 1

Segment Register (FS or GS)

0 0 0 0 1 1 1 1	1 0 sreg3 0 0 1

POPA = Pop All

0 1 1 0 0 0 0 1

XCHG = Exchange

Register/Memory with Register

1 0 0 0 0 1 1 w	mod reg r/m

Register with Accumulator (Short Form)

1 0 0 1 0 reg

IN = Input From:

Fixed Port

1 1 1 0 0 1 0 w	port number

Variable Port

1 1 1 0 1 1 0 w

OUT = Output To:

Fixed Port

1110011w	port number

Variable Port

1110111w

LEA = Load EA to Register

10001101	mod reg r/m

Segment control

LDS = Load Pointer to DS

11000101	mod reg r/m

LES = Load Pointer to ES

11000100	mod reg r/m

LFS = Load Pointer to FS

00001111	10110100	mod reg r/m

LGS = Load Pointer to GS

00001111	10110101	mod reg r/m

LSS = Load Pointer to SS

00001111	10110010	mod reg r/m

Flag control

CLC = Clear Carry Flag

11111000

CLD = Clear Direction Flag

11111100

CLI = Clear Interrupt Enable Flag

11111010

CLTS = Clear Task Switched Flag

00001111	00000110

CMC = Complement Carry Flag

11110101

LAHF = Load AH Into Flag

10011111

POPF = Pop Flags

10011101

PUSHF = Push Flags

10011100

SAHF = Store AH Into Flags

10011110

STC = Set Carry Flag

11111001

STD = Set Direction Flag

11111101

STI = Set Interrupt Enable Flag

11111011

Arithmetic

ADD = Add

Register to Register

000000dw	mod reg r/m

Register to Memory

0000000w	mod reg r/m

Memory to Register

0000001w	mod reg r/m

Immediate to Register/Memory

100000sw	mod 000 r/m	8-, 16-, or 32-bit data

Immediate to Accumulator (Short Form)

0000010w	8-, 16-, or 32-bit data

ADC = Add with Carry

Register to Register

000100dw	mod reg r/m

Register to Memory

0001000w	mod reg r/m

Memory to Register

0001001w	mod reg r/m

Immediate to Register/Memory

100000sw	mod 010 r/m	8-, 16-, or 32-bit data

Immediate to Accumulator (Short Form)

0001010w	8-, 16-, or 32-bit data

INC = Increment

Register/Memory

1111111w	mod 000 r/m

Register (Short Form)

01000 reg

SUB = Subtract

Register from Register

001010dw	mod reg r/m

Register from Memory

0010100w	mod reg r/m

Memory from Register

0010101w	mod reg r/m

Immediate from Register/Memory

100000sw	mod 101 r/m	8-, 16-, or 32-bit data

Immediate from Accumulator (Short Form)

0010110w	8-, 16-, or 32-bit data

SBB = Subtract with Borrow

Register from Register

0 0 0 1 1 0 d w	mod reg r/m

Register from Memory

0 0 0 1 1 0 0 w	mod reg r/m

Memory from Register

0 0 0 1 1 0 1 w	mod reg r/m

Immediate from Register/Memory

1 0 0 0 0 0 s w	mod 0 1 1 r/m	8-, 16-, or 32-bit data

Immediate from Accumulator (Short Form)

0 0 0 1 1 1 0 w	8-, 16-, or 32-bit data

DEC = Decrement

Register/Memory

1 1 1 1 1 1 1 w	mod 0 0 1 r/m

Register (Short Form)

0 1 0 0 1 reg

CMP = Compare

Register with Register

0 0 1 1 1 0 d w	mod reg r/m

Memory with Register

0 0 1 1 1 0 0 w	mod reg r/m

Register with Memory

0 0 1 1 1 0 1 w	mod reg r/m

Immediate with Register/Memory

1 0 0 0 0 0 s w	mod 1 1 1 r/m	8-, 16-, or 32-bit data

Immediate with Accumulator (Short Form)

0 0 1 1 1 1 0 w	8-, 16-, or 32-bit data

NEG = Change Sign

1 1 1 1 0 1 1 w	mod 0 1 1 r/m

AAA = ASCII Adjust for Add

0 0 1 1 0 1 1 1

AAS = ASCII Adjust for Subtract

00111111

DAA = Decimal Adjust for Add

00100111

DAS = Decimal Adjust for Subtract

00101111

MUL = Multiply (Unsigned)

Accumulator with Register/Memory

1111011w	mod 100 r/m

IMUL = Integer Multiply (Signed)

Accumulator with Register/Memory

1111011w	mod 101 r/m

Register with Register/Memory

00001111	10101111	mod reg r/m

Register/Memory with Immediate to Register

011010s1	mod reg r/m	8-, 16-, or 32-bit data

DIV = Divide (Unsigned)

Accumulator by Register/Memory

1111011w	mod 110 r/m

IDIV = Integer Divide (Signed)

Accumulator by Register/Memory

1111011w	mod 111 r/m

AAD = ASCII Adjust for Divide

11010101	00001010

AAM = ASCII Adjust for Multiply

11010100	00001010

CBW = Convert Byte to Word

10011000

CWD = Convert Word to Doubleword

10011001

Logic

Shift/Rotate Instructions
Not Through Carry (ROL, ROR, SAL, SAR, SHL, and SHR)

Register/Memory by 1

1101000w	mod T T T r/m

Register/Memory by CL

1101001w	mod T T T r/m

Register/Memory by Immediate Count

1100000w	mod T T T r/m	8-bit data

Shift/Rotate Instructions
Through Carry (RCL and RCR)

Register/Memory by 1

1101000w	mod T T T r/m

Register/Memory by CL

1101001w	mod T T T r/m

Register/Memory by Immediate Count

1100000w	mod T T T r/m	8-bit data

T T T	Instruction
0 0 0	ROL
0 0 1	ROR
0 1 0	RCL
0 1 1	RCR
1 0 0	SHL/SAL
1 0 1	SHR
1 1 1	SAR

SHLD = Shift Left Double

Register/Memory by Immediate

00001111	10100100	mod reg r/m	8-bit data

Register/Memory by CL

00001111	10100101	mod reg r/m

SHRD = Shift Right Double

Register/Memory by Immediate

00001111	10101100	mod reg r/m	8-bit data

Register/Memory by CL

00001111	10101101	mod reg r/m

AND = And

Register to Register

001000dw	mod reg r/m

Register to Memory

0010000w	mod reg r/m

Memory to Register

0010001w	mod reg r/m

Immediate to Register/Memory

100000sw	mod 100 r/m	8-, 16-, or 32-bit data

Immediate to Accumulator (Short Form)

0010010w	8-, 16-, or 32-bit data

TEST = AND Function to Flags; No Result

Register/Memory and Register

1000010w	mod reg r/m

Immediate Data and Register/Memory

1111011w	mod 000 r/m	8-, 16-, or 32-bit data

Immediate Data and Accumulator (Short Form)

1010100w	8-, 16-, or 32-bit data

OR = Or

Register to Register

000010dw	mod reg r/m

Register to Memory

0000100w	mod reg r/m

Memory to Register

0000101w	mod reg r/m

Immediate to Register/Memory

100000sw	mod 001 r/m	8-, 16-, or 32-bit data

Immediate to Accumulator (Short Form)

0C00110w	8-, 16-, or 32-bit data

XOR = Exclusive OR

Register to Register

001100dw	mod reg r/m

Register to Memory

0011000w	mod reg r/m

Memory to Register

0011001w	mod reg r/m

Immediate to Register/Memory

100000sw	mod 110 r/m	8-, 16-, or 32-bit data

Immediate to Accumulator (Short Form)

0011010w	8-, 16-, or 32-bit data

NOT = Invert Register/Memory

1111011w	mod 010 r/m

String manipulation

CMPS = Compare Byte/Word

1010011w

INS = Input Byte/Word from DX Port

0110110w

LODS = Load Byte/Word to AL/AX/EAX

1010110w

MOVS = Move Byte/Word

1010010w

OUTS = Output Byte/Word to DX Port

0110111w

SCAS = Scan Byte/Word

1010111w

STOS = Store Byte/Word from AL/AX/EX

1010101w

XLAT = Translate String

11010111

Repeated string manipulation

Repeated by Count in CX or ECX

REPE CMPS = Compare String (Find Non-Match)

11110011	1010011w

REPNE CMPS = Compare String (Find Match)

11110010	1010011w

REP INS = Input String

11110010	0110110w

REP LODS = Load String

11110010	1010110w

REP MOVS = Move String

11110010	1010010w

REP OUTS = Output String

11110010	0110111w

REPE SCAS = Scan String (Find Non-AL/AX/EAX)

11110011	1010111w

REPNE SCAS = Scan String (Find AL/AX/EAX)

11110010	1010111w

REP STOS = Store String

11110010	1010101w

Bit manipulation

BSF = Scan Bit Forward

00001111	10111100	mod reg r/m

BSR = Scan Bit Reverse

00001111	10111101	mod reg r/m

BT = Test Bit

Register/Memory, Immediate

00001111	10111010	mod 1 0 0 r/m	8-bit data

Register/Memory, Register

00001111	10100011	mod reg r/m

BTC = Test Bit and Complement

Register/Memory, Immediate

00001111	10111010	mod 1 1 1 r/m	8-bit data

Register/Memory, Register

00001111	10111011	mod reg r/m

BTR = Test Bit and Reset

Register/Memory, Immediate

00001111	10111010	mod 1 1 0 r/m	8-bit data

Register/Memory, Register

00001111	10110011	mod reg r/m

BTS = Test Bit and Set

Register/Memory, Immediate

00001111	10111010	mod 1 0 1 r/m	8-bit data

Register/Memory, Register

00001111	10101011	mod reg r/m

Control transfer

CALL = Call

Direct within Segment

11101000	full 16- or 32-bit displacement

Register/Memory Indirect within Segment

11111111	mod 010 r/m

Direct Intersegment

10011010	offset, selector

Indirect Intersegment

11111111	mod 011 r/m

JMP = Unconditional Jump

Short

11101011	8-bit disp.

Direct within Segment

11101001	full 16- or 32-bit displacement

Register/Memory Indirect within Segment

11111111	mod 100 r/m

Direct Intersegment

11101010	offset, selector

Indirect Intersegment

11111111	mod 101 r/m

RET = Return from Call

Within Segment

11000011

Within Segment Adding Immediate to SP

11000010	16-bit displacement

Intersegment

11001011

Intersegment Adding Immediate to SP

11001010	16-bit displacement

Conditional jumps

JO = Jump on Overflow

8-Bit Displacement

01110000	8-bit disp.

Full Displacement

00001111	10000000	full 16- or 32-bit displacement

JNO = Jump on Not Overflow

8-Bit Displacement

01110001	8-bit disp.

Full Displacement

00001111	10000001	full 16- or 32-bit displacement

JB/JNAE = Jump on Below/Not Above or Equal

8-Bit Displacement

01110010	8-bit disp.

Full Displacement

00001111	10000010	full 16- or 32-bit displacement

JNB/JAE = Jump on Not Below/Above or Equal

8-Bit Displacement

01110011	8-bit disp.

Full Displacement

00001111	10000011	full 16- or 32-bit displacement

JE/JZ = Jump on Equal/Zero

8-Bit Displacement

01110100	8-bit disp.

Full Displacement

00001111	10000100	full 16- or 32-bit displacement

JNE/JNZ = Jump on Not Equal/Not Zero

8-Bit Displacement

01110101	8-bit disp.

Full Displacement

00001111	10000101	full 16- or 32-bit displacement

JBE/JNA = Jump on Below or Equal/Not Above

8-Bit Displacement

0 1 1 1 0 1 1 0	8-bit disp.

Full Displacement

0 0 0 0 1 1 1 1	1 0 0 0 0 1 1 0	full 16- or 32-bit displacement

JNBE/JA = Jump on Not Below or Equal/Above

8-Bit Displacement

0 1 1 1 0 1 1 1	8-bit disp.

Full Displacement

0 0 0 0 1 1 1 1	1 0 0 0 0 1 1 1	full 16- or 32-bit displacement

JS = Jump on Sign

8-Bit Displacement

0 1 1 1 1 0 0 0	8-bit disp.

Full Displacement

0 0 0 0 1 1 1 1	1 0 0 0 1 0 0 0	full 16- or 32-bit displacement

JNS = Jump on Not Sign

8-Bit Displacement

0 1 1 1 1 0 0 1	8-bit disp.

Full Displacement

0 0 0 0 1 1 1 1	1 0 0 0 1 0 0 1	full 16- or 32-bit displacement

JP/JPE = Jump on Parity/Parity Even

8-Bit Displacement

0 1 1 1 1 0 1 0	8-bit disp.

Full Displacement

0 0 0 0 1 1 1 1	1 0 0 0 1 0 1 0	full 16- or 32-bit displacement

JNP/JPO = Jump on Not Parity/Parity Odd

8-Bit Displacement

0 1 1 1 1 0 1 1	8-bit disp.

Full Displacement

0 0 0 0 1 1 1 1	1 0 0 0 1 0 1 1	full 16- or 32-bit displacement

JL/JNGE = Jump on Less/Not Greater or Equal

8-Bit Displacement

01111100	8-bit disp.

Full Displacement

00001111	10001100	full 16- or 32-bit displacement

JNL/JGE = Jump on Not Less/Greater or Equal

8-Bit Displacement

01111101	8-bit disp.

Full Displacement

00001111	10001101	full 16- or 32-bit displacement

JLE/JNG = Jump on Less or Equal/Not Greater

8-Bit Displacement

01111110	8-bit disp.

Full Displacement

00001111	10001110	full 16- or 32-bit displacement

JNLE/JG = Jump on Not Less or Equal/Greater

8-Bit Displacement

01111111	8-bit disp.

Full Displacement

00001111	10001111	full 16- or 32-bit displacement

JCXZ = Jump on CX Zero

11100011	8-bit disp.

JECXZ = Jump on ECX Zero

11100011	8-bit disp.

Note: The operand size prefix differentiates JCXZ from JECXZ.

LOOP = Loop CX Times

11100010	8-bit disp.

LOOPZ/LOOPE = Loop with Zero/Equal

11100001	8-bit disp.

LOOPNZ/LOOPNE = Loop while Not Zero

11100000	8-bit disp.

Conditional byte set

SETO = Set Byte on Overflow

To Register/Memory

00001111	10010000	mod 000 r/m

SETNO = Set Byte on Not Overflow

To Register/Memory

00001111	10010001	mod 000 r/m

SETB/SETNAE = Set Byte on Below/Not Above or Equal

To Register/Memory

00001111	10010010	mod 000 r/m

SETNB = Set Byte on Not Below/Above or Equal

To Register/Memory

00001111	10010011	mod 000 r/m

SETE/SETZ = Set Byte on Equal/Zero

To Register/Memory

00001111	10010100	mod 000 r/m

SETNE/SETNZ = Set Byte on Not Equal/Not Zero

To Register/Memory

00001111	10010101	mod 000 r/m

SETBE/SETNA = Set Byte on Below or Equal/Not Above

To Register/Memory

00001111	10010110	mod 000 r/m

SETNBE/SETA = Set Byte on Not Below or Equal/Above

To Register/Memory

00001111	10010111	mod 000 r/m

SETS = Set Byte on Sign

To Register/Memory

00001111	10011000	mod 000 r/m

SETNS = Set Byte on Not Sign

To Register/Memory

00001111	10011001	mod 000 r/m

SETP/SETPE = Set Byte on Parity/Parity Even

To Register/Memory

00001111	10011010	mod 000 r/m

SETNP/SETPO = Set Byte on Not Parity/Parity Odd

To Register/Memory

00001111	10011011	mod 000 r/m

SETL/SETNGE = Set Byte on Less/Not Greater or Equal

To Register/Memory

00001111	10011100	mod 000 r/m

SETNL/SETGE = Set Byte on Not Less/Greater or Equal

To Register/Memory

00001111	01111101	mod 000 r/m

SETLE/SETNG = Set Byte on Less or Equal/Not Greater

To Register/Memory

00001111	10011110	mod 000 r/m

SETNLE/SETG = Set Byte on Not Less or Equal/Greater

To Register/Memory

00001111	10011111	mod 000 r/m

ENTER = Enter Procedure

11001000	16-bit displacement	8-bit level

LEAVE = Leave Procedure

11001001

Interrupt instructions

INT = Interrupt

Type Specified

11001101	type

Type 3

11001100

INTO = Interrupt 4 if Overflow Flag Set

11001110

BOUND = Interrupt 5 if Detect Value Out of Range

01100010	mod reg r/m

IRET = Interrupt Return

11001111

Processor control

HLT = Halt

11110100

MOV = Move to and from Control/Debug/Test Registers

CR0/CR2/CR3 from Register

00001111	00100010	11 eee reg

Register from CR0-3

00001111	00100000	11 eee reg

DR0-3, DR6-7 from Register

00001111	00100011	11 eee reg

Register from DR0-3, DR6-7

00001111	00100001	11 eee reg

TR6-7 from Register

00001111	00100110	11 eee reg

Register from TR6-7

00001111	00100100	11 eee reg

NOP = No Operation

10010000

WAIT = Wait until BUSY Pin is Negated

10011011

Processor extension

ESC = Processor Extension Escape

11011TTT	mod LLL r/m

Note: TTT and LLL bits are opcode information for the coprocessor.

Prefix bytes

Address Size Prefix

01100111

Operand Size Prefix

01100110

LOCK = Bus Lock Prefix

11110000

Note: The use of LOCK is restricted to an exchange with memory, or bit test and reset type of instruction.

Segment Override Prefix

CS:

00101110

DS:

00111110

ES:

00100110

FS:

01100100

GS:

01100101

SS:

00110110

Protection control

ARPL = Adjust Requested Privilege Level from Register/Memory

01100011	mod reg r/m

LAR = Load Access Rights from Register/Memory

00001111	00000010	mod reg r/m

LGDT = Load Global Descriptor Table Register

00001111	00000001	mod 0 1 0 r/m

LIDT = Load Interrupt Descriptor Table Register

00001111	00000001	mod 0 1 1 r/m

LLDT = Load Local Descriptor Table Register to Register/Memory

00001111	00000000	mod 0 1 0 r/m

LMSW = Load Machine Status Word from Register/Memory

00001111	00000001	mod 1 1 0 r/m

LSL = Load Segment Limit from Register/Memory

00001111	00000011	mod reg r/m

LTR = Load Task Register from Register/Memory

00001111	00000000	mod 0 0 1 r/m

SGDT = Store Global Descriptor Table Register

00001111	00000001	mod 0 0 0 r/m

SIDT = Store Interrupt Descriptor Table Register

00001111	00000001	mod 0 0 1 r/m

SLDT = Store Local Descriptor Table Register to Register/Memory

00001111	00000000	mod 0 0 0 r/m

SMSW = Store Machine Status Word

00001111	00000001	mod 1 0 0 r/m

STR = Store Task Register to Register/Memory

00001111	00000000	mod 0 0 1 r/m

VERR = Verify Read Access; Register/Memory

00001111	00000000	mod 100 r/m

VERW = Verify Write Access

00001111	00000000	mod 101 r/m

Index